Croatia

Peter Dragicevich,
Anthony Ham, Jessica Lee

PLAN YOUR TRIP

IASCIC/SHUTTERSTOCK ©
KOPAČKI RIT NATURE PARK P120

JUSTIN FOULKES/LONELY PLANET ©
VELIKI TABOR CASTLE P107

ON THE ROAD

Contents

COVID-19

We have re-checked every business in this book before publication to ensure that it is still open after the COVID-19 outbreak. However, the economic and social impacts of COVID-19 will continue to be felt long after the outbreak has been contained, and many businesses, services and events referenced in this guide may experience ongoing restrictions. Some businesses may be temporarily closed, have changed their opening hours and services, or require bookings; some unfortunately could have closed permanently. We suggest you check with venues before visiting for the latest information.

SPECIAL FEATURES

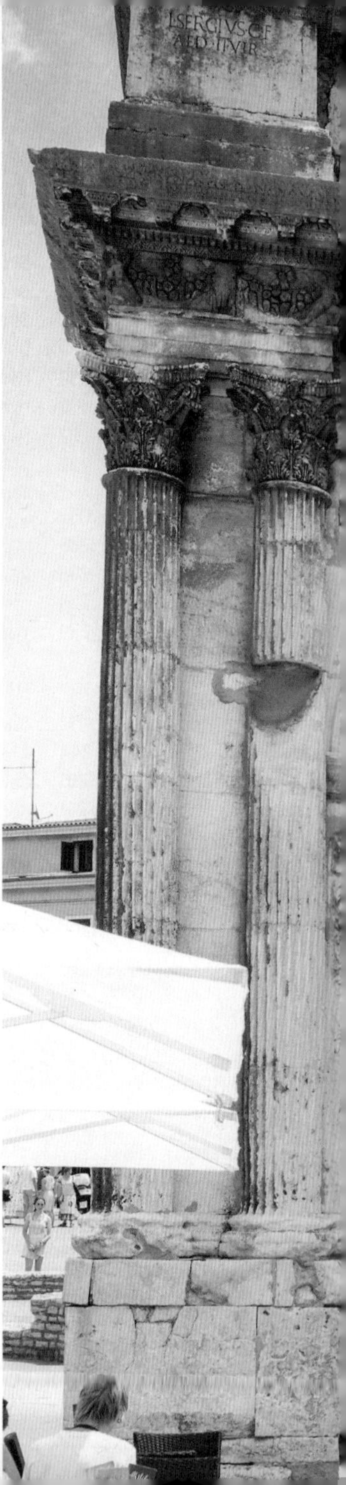

JUSTIN FOULKES/LONELY PLANET ©

Right: Arch of the Sergii (p132), Pula

WELCOME TO

Croatia

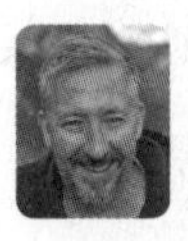

I'll admit: as my grandparents hail from here, I'm more than a little biased, but Croatia is quite simply my favourite country to visit. It offers a unique combination of all the things I love: breathtaking natural beauty, great swimming, summertime sun, oodles of history, interesting architecture, incredible wine, delicious seafood...I could go on. True, Croats don't always present the sunniest face to complete strangers, but break through that initial reserve and you'll discover the friendliest, most hospitable people you could hope to meet.

By Peter Dragicevich, Writer
@PeterDragNZ peterdragnz
For more about our writers, see p384

RESTAURANT

Croatia

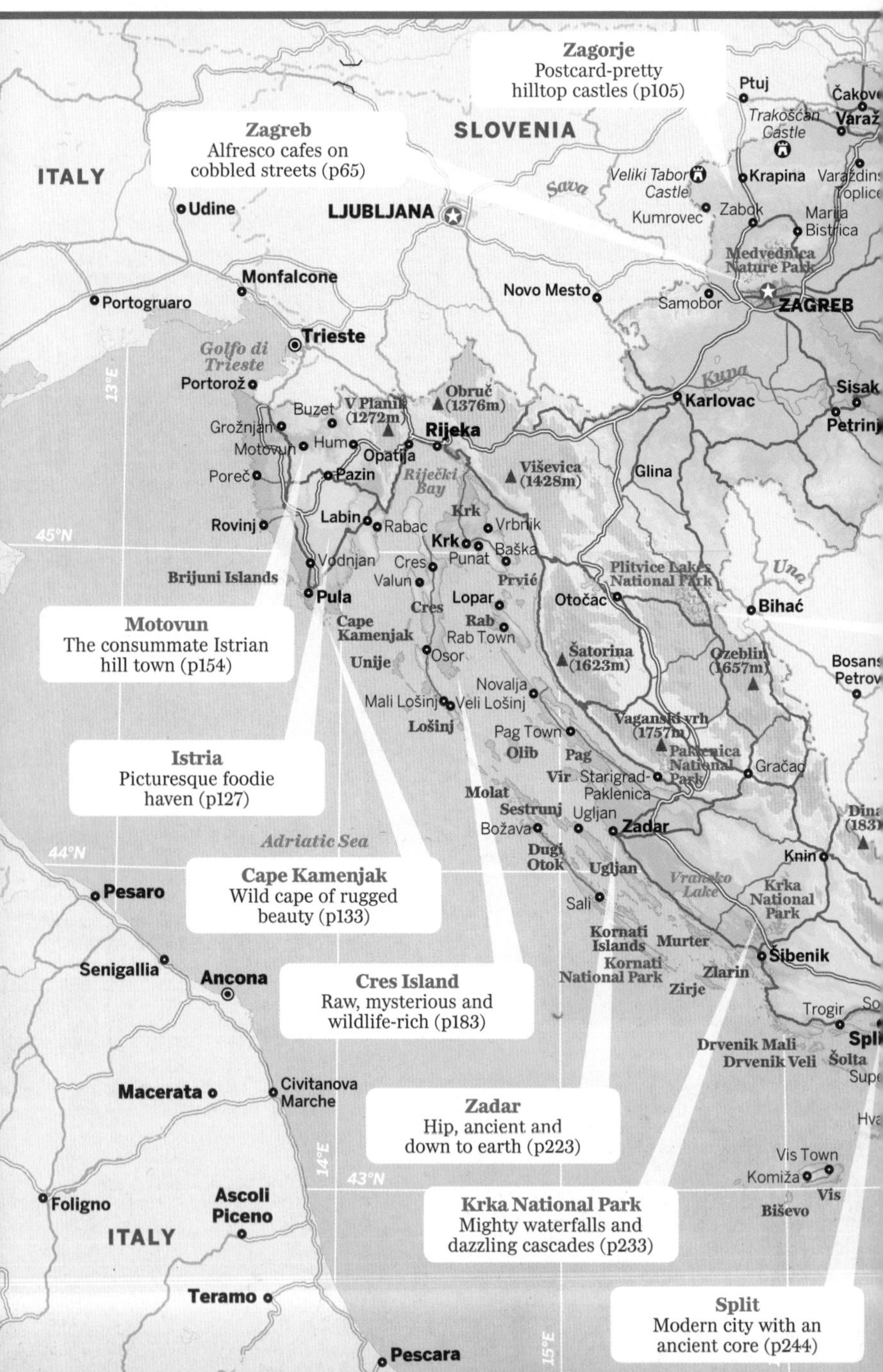

Zagorje
Postcard-pretty hilltop castles (p105)
Zagreb
Alfresco cafes on cobbled streets (p65)
Motovun
The consummate Istrian hill town (p154)
Istria
Picturesque foodie haven (p127)
Cape Kamenjak
Wild cape of rugged beauty (p133)
Cres Island
Raw, mysterious and wildlife-rich (p183)
Zadar
Hip, ancient and down to earth (p223)
Krka National Park
Mighty waterfalls and dazzling cascades (p233)
Split
Modern city with an ancient core (p244)
ITALY
SLOVENIA
LJUBLJANA
ZAGREB
Udine
Monfalcone
Portogruaro
Trieste
Golfo di Trieste
Portorož
Buzet
Grožnjan
Motovun
Hum
Poreč
Pazin
Rovinj
Labin
Rabac
Vodnjan
Brijuni Islands
Pula
V Planik (1272m)
Obruč (1376m)
Rijeka
Opatija
Riječki Bay
Višcevica (1428m)
Krk
Vrbnik
Punat
Baška
Cres
Valun
Prvić
Lopar
Rab
Rab Town
Cape Kamenjak
Unije
Osor
Novalja
Mali Lošinj
Veli Lošinj
Lošinj
Pag Town
Olib
Pag
Vir
Molat
Sestrunj
Božava
Ugljan
Zadar
Dugi Otok
Sali
Starigrad-Paklenica
Paklenica National Park
Vaganski vrh (1757m)
Šatorina (1623m)
Ozeblin (1657m)
Otočac
Plitvice Lakes National Park
Bihać
Una
Gračac
Glina
Karlovac
Kupa
Sisak
Petrinj
Novo Mesto
Samobor
Sava
Veliki Tabor Castle
Kumrovec
Zabok
Krapina
Ptuj
Trakošćan Castle
Marija Bistrica
Medvednica Nature Park
Knin
Krka National Park
Vransko Lake
Kornati Islands
Murter
Kornati National Park
Zlarin
Zirje
Šibenik
Trogir
Drvenik Mali
Drvenik Veli
Šolta
Vis Town
Komiža
Vis
Biševo
Adriatic Sea
45°N
44°N
43°N
13°E
14°E
15°E
Pesaro
Senigallia
Ancona
Macerata
Civitanova Marche
Foligno
Ascoli Piceno
Teramo
Pescara

0 100 km
0 50 miles
Lake Balaton
Mura
Nagykanizsa
Kaposvár
HUNGARY
Koprivnica
Pécs
Subotica
Mohács
Drava
Bjelovar
Virovitica
Drava
Kopački Rit
Wetland heaven for birdwatchers (p120)
Kopački Rit Nature Park
Danube
Osijek
Duna v
Tisa
Kapovac (790m)
Kutina
Našice
Slavonska Požega
Lonjsko Polje National Park
Sava
Vukovar
Bačka Palanka
Novi Sad
Đakovo
Vinkovci
Nova Gradiška
Ilok
Slavonski Brod
Danube
Dunav
Sremska Mitrovica
Bosut
Prijedor
Bosna
Brčko
Sava
Šabac
BELGRADE
Banja Luka
Plitvice Lakes National Park
Lush paradise laced with waterfalls (p211)
Drina
Sava
SERBIA
Vrbas
BOSNIA & HERCEGOVINA
Bol
Glorious beach and wind-surfers' playground (p274)
Jajce
Travnik
Čačak
Livno
SARAJEVO
Mljet Island
Heavenly isle with cobalt-coloured lakes (p320)
Goražde
Sinj
Konjić
Neretva
Pljevlja
Brela
Sv Jure (1762m)
Mostar
Brač
Bol
Makarska
Biokovo Nature Park
Dubrovnik
Dazzlingly beautiful walled old town (p293)
Stari Grad
Jelsa
Hvar
Piva
Tara
Metković
Korčula Town
Pelješac Peninsula
Korčula
Neum
ELEVATION
1500m
1000m
700m
500m
300m
200m
100m
0
Vela Luka
Lumbarda
MONTENEGRO
Ston
Trsteno Gardens
Nikšić
Mljet National Park
Mljet
Elafiti Islands
Lastovo
Trebinje
Dubrovnik
Hvar Town
Island hot spot for beach parties (p278)
Cavtat
PODGORICA
18°E
Kotor
Herceg Novi

Croatia's Top Experiences

1 ISLAND HOPPING

Croatia's crystalline waters are speckled with a multitude of islands and – whether you're travelling by luxury yacht or public ferry – exploring them is the consummate Croatian experience. Some are tiny and unpopulated while others are large and buzzing with bars and restaurants. Some are arid and rocky while others have sandy beaches backed with verdant forest. With 1244 to choose between, there truly is a place to suit everyone's taste.

Above: Pakleni Islands (p284)

NINOPAVISIC/SHUTTERSTOCK ©

AJAN ALEN/SHUTTERSTOCK ©

Vis

The most remote of Croatia's main islands, Vis is also one of its most captivating. A duo of attractive towns adds historic interest to its northern and western coasts, while hidden to the south and east are some of the nation's most idyllic coves. p286

Right: Stiniva cove (p286)

MICHIEL TON/GETTY IMAGES ©

MARCUTTI/GETTY IMAGESTT ©

Hvar

People come to party on Croatia's sunniest isle thanks to its glam hub Hvar Town (pictured above). In high summer, there's no better place to dress up and get your groove on. Pack beach gear and shoes suitable for dancing on tables. p277

Mljet

Cloaked in dense pine forests, Mljet (pictured above) is long, slender and beguiling. The entire western section is a national park, where you'll find two cobalt-coloured lakes, an island monastery and a little port. Eastern Mljet has tranquil bays and a couple of excellent restaurants. p320

2 TIME-DEFYING WALLED TOWNS

Built for defence but breathtakingly picturesque, Croatia's walled towns are among the nation's greatest treasures. Most famous of all are the dazzling settlements spread along the coast, their honey-coloured stone fortifications contrasting magnificently with the azure waters of the Adriatic, while the fairy-tale hilltop towns of central Istria rise mysteriously from a verdant landscape where time stands still.

IHOR PASTERNAK/SHUTTERSTOCK ©

Korčula Town

Like Dubrovnik in miniature, the sparkling seaside town of Korčula has its own set of imposing walls and towers but only a fraction of the tourists of its more famous sibling. The highlight is an extraordinary Gothic-Renaissance cathedral adorned with kooky carvings. p327

Below: Detail, St Mark's Cathedral (p327)

ZVONIMIR ATLETIC/SHUTTERSTOCK ©

LUCERTOLONE/SHUTTERSTOCK ©

CGE2010/SHUTTERSTOCK ©

Dubrovnik

The extraordinary walled city of Dubrovnik (pictured above and left) is a Unesco World Heritage Site and Croatia's most popular attraction. Despite being shelled relentlessly during the 1990s war, its towers, medieval monasteries, baroque churches, graceful squares and fascinating residential quarters all look magnificent once more. p293

Motovun

This picture-perfect hilltop town (pictured above) rises from a forested valley that appears untouched by the 21st century. The lush, expansive views from its fortifications are virtually the same as when they were built. p154

3 SUMPTUOUS NATURAL BEAUTY

MARCOS MESA SAM WORDLEY/SHUTTERSTOCK ©

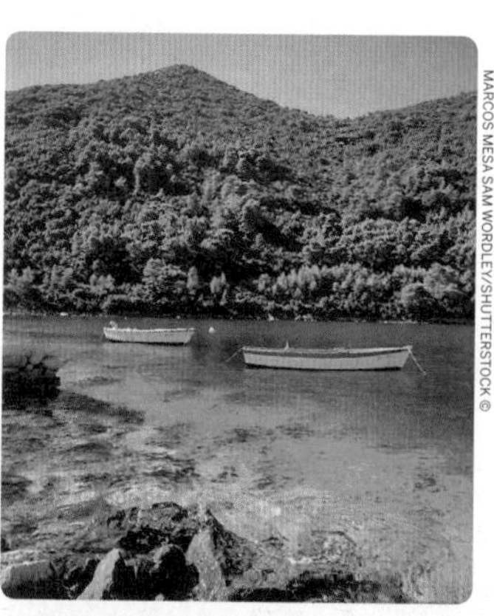

Croatia's appeal is grounded in nature – its waterfalls, lakes, forests, mountains and, of course, its dazzling Adriatic coast. There are 444 protected areas in total, encompassing 9% of the country, including 12 nature parks and eight national parks. The national parks can roughly be divided into islands (Brijuni, Kornati, Mljet), lakes (Plitvice, Krka) and mountains (Risnjak, Northern Velebit, Paklenica), all of which are well worth exploring.

Left: Mljet Island (p320);
Below: Brijuni Islands (p136)

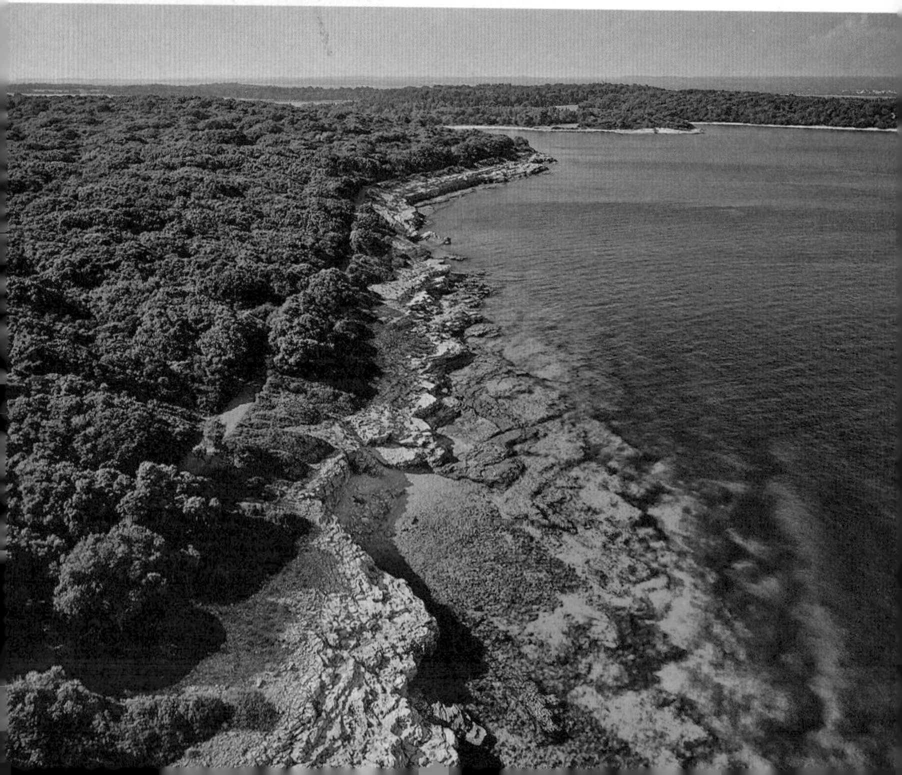

KELLY CHENG TRAVEL PHOTOGRAPHY/GETTY IMAGES ©

GORAN AFAREK/ALAMY ©

ANNA GORIN/GETTY IMAGES ©

NICHOLAS FARRUGGIO/SHUTTERSTOCK ©

Kopački Rit Nature Park

A flood plain of the Danube and Drava Rivers, Kopački Rit is part of a Unesco biosphere reserve and offers some of Europe's best birdwatching opportunities. Join a boat trip and keep your eyes peeled for eagles, storks (pictured top), herons and woodpeckers. p120

Krka National Park

The star of this highly scenic national park is the Krka River itself, rushing through canyons, broadening into lakes and splashing over numerous falls and cascades (pictured above left). Stroll along the boardwalks and marvel at the multitude of fish darting through the emerald waters. p233

Plitvice Lakes National Park

This turquoise ribbon of lakes, linked by gushing waterfalls (pictured above right) in the forested heart of continental Croatia, is an awe-inspiring sight. Travertine expanses covered with mossy plants divide the multi-coloured lakes in this exquisite watery world. p211

4 LAZING ON BEACHES

From its highly indented coastline to its multitudinous islands, Croatia has literally hundreds of beaches to choose between – so, whether you like to laze around in an old pair of trunks, show off the latest designer swimsuit, or get your kit off altogether, you'll find a place to do it here. Beaches can be sandy, pebbly, shingly or rocky but what unites them all is the astonishingly clear water.

FEDERICO ZOVADELLI/SHUTTERSTOCK ©

WIRESTOCK CREATORS/SHUTTERSTOCK ©

Cape Kamenjak

Just south of Pula, this rugged peninsula (pictured top left) is fringed by a string of pebble bays and secluded rocky beaches, surrounded by a crystalline blue-green sea. p133

Lubenice

Leafy, sparsely populated and never overwhelmed by tourists, Cres (pictured above left) is unique for its small, secluded beach. Nestled below a remote hilltop village, it is sensational but difficult to reach. p188

Zlatni Rat

The town of Bol, on the southern coast of Brač Island, is home to the highly photogenic Zlatni Rat beach (pictured above), with its unusual hornlike shape, golden pebbles and buzzy bars. p274

5 EXPLORING ANCIENT RUINS

CAROL ANNE/SHUTTERSTOCK ©

ALEXANDRU STAIU/SHUTTERSTOCK ©

GEVISION/SHUTTERSTOCK ©

Once positioned near the very heart of the Empire, Croatia has some of the most impressive Roman structures still standing today. What's even more remarkable is the effortless way in which they've been incorporated into contemporary life, with people sleeping, dining, drinking, worshipping and being entertained in structures erected thousands of years before. The country's museums are jam-packed with Roman artefacts, too.

Split

Diocletian's 4th-century palace (pictured left), complete with an intact temple and mausoleum, remains the city's living heart. On Split's outskirts are the ruins of an entire major Roman city, Salona. p244

Zadar

Roman ruins protrude from the most unlikely places in this ancient city. Set on its own peninsula, the old town of Zadar is still centred on its Roman forum. p223

Pula

Along with its magnificent 1st-century amphitheatre, Pula has a complete Roman temple and a triumphal arch. There's even a floor mosaic hidden at the edge of an unremarkable car park. p129

Bottom: Temple of Augustus (p131), Pula

6 WINING & DINING

For a real taste of Croatia, hunt down the nation's best home-grown ingredients and traditional dishes. While you're at it, take a chance on a wine varietal you've never heard of. You'll notice a distinct difference between the food of the Austrian- and Hungarian-influenced interior and that of the coast, which was long dominated by Venice. A growing number of boutique food and wine producers now welcome visitors.

Inland edibles

Order a schnitzel stuffed with ham and cheese *(zagrebački odrezak)* in Zagreb, a traditional custard pie (*kremšnite;* pictured below) in Samobor, and a paprika-spiced meaty stew *(čobanac)* in Slavonia. p56

MOODYBLUES/SHUTTERSTOCK ©

Istrian specialties

La dolce vita reigns supreme in Istria, Croatia's top foodie destination. The local seafood, truffles, wild asparagus, award-winning olive oils and boutique wines all stand out. p56

Above: Grilled sardines, Split (p244)

Dalmatian delights

Seafood dominates in Venetian-influenced coastal Dalmatia, paired with the timeless Mediterranean flavours of parsley, bay leaves, garlic and olive oil. Dalmatian wine is wonderful, too. p57

Right: Dalmatian flavours

7 CONTINENTAL CULTURE

While the coast grabs most of the attention, the Croatian interior has its own distinct charms and unique culture. Here you'll find a lifestyle oriented towards Central Europe, with architecture and an arts scene to match. The capital's concert halls and theatres stage a busy programme of opera, ballet and drama, while punk and the blues find a home in grungy bars scattered around town.

Zagreb's coffee buzz

Elevated to the status of ritual, lingering in one of Zagreb's outdoor cafes (pictured above) is a seminal experience, involving hours of people-watching, gossiping and soul-searching, unhurried by waiters. p76

Go baroque in Varaždin

Soak up the genteel ambience of this northern town's historic heart, lined with grand mansions and churches. Try to catch a classical music performance while you're there. p108

Zagorje's castles

The postcard-perfect medieval castles of Zagorje are prime for time travel. Journey back to 1334 at Trakošćan Castle and enter the 16th century via hilltop Veliki Tabor. p107

Need to Know

For more information, see Survival Guide (p361)

Currency
Kuna (KN)

Language
Croatian

Visas
Generally not required for stays of up to 90 days. Some nationalities (such as Chinese, Indian, Russian, South African, Turkish) do need them.

Money
ATMs are widely available. Credit cards are accepted in most hotels and restaurants. Smaller restaurants, shops and private-accommodation owners only take cash.

Mobile Phones
Users with unlocked phones can buy a local SIM card, which are easy to find. Otherwise, you may be charged roaming rates.

Time
Central European Time (GMT/UTC plus one hour)

When to Go

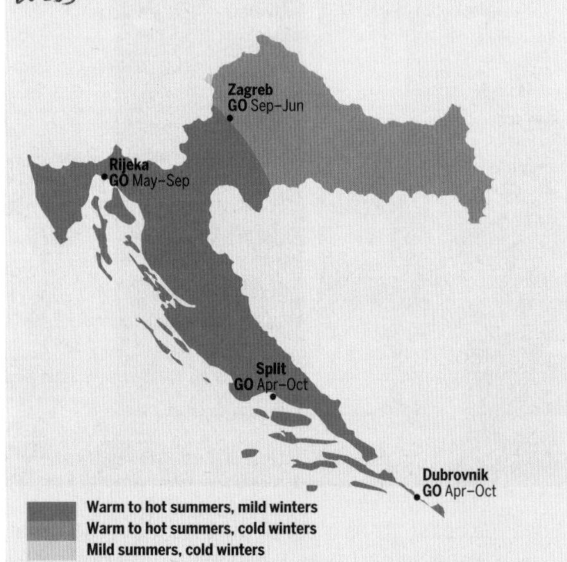

High Season
(Jul & Aug)

- Peak season brings the best weather. Hvar Island gets the most sun, followed by Split, Korčula Island and Dubrovnik.
- Prices are at their highest and coastal destinations at their busiest.

Shoulder
(May–Jun & Sep)

- A great time to visit the coast: the Adriatic is warm enough for swimming, the crowds are sparser and prices are lower.
- In spring and early summer, the *maestral* (strong, steady westerly wind) makes for great sailing.

Low Season
(Oct–Apr)

- Winters are cold, prices are low and ferry schedules are reduced.
- Christmas brings a buzz to Zagreb's streets, even with the snow, plus there's skiing.

Useful Websites

Croatian Tourism (www.croatia.hr) Official tourism site; the best starting point for planning.

Croatia Times (www.croatia-times.com) Click the Like Croatia tab for an online guide.

Taste of Croatia (www.tasteofcroatia.org) Excellent and informative culinary website.

Parks of Croatia (www.parkovihrvatske.hr) Covers Croatia's national parks and nature parks.

Chasing the Donkey (www.chasingthedonkey.com) Travel blog by an Aussie family of Croatian extraction living in Dalmatia.

Lonely Planet (www.lonelyplanet.com/croatia) Destination information, hotel reviews, traveller forum and more.

Important Numbers

To call from outside Croatia, dial your international access code, then the Croatian country code, the area code (without the initial 0) and the local number.

Country code	385
International access code	00
General emergency	112
Ambulance	194
Roadside assistance	1987

Exchange Rates

Australia	A$1	4.82KN
Canada	C$1	4.84KN
Europe	€1	7.42KN
Japan	¥100	5.49KN
New Zealand	NZ$1	4.39KN
UK	UK£1	8.46KN
US	US$1	5.97KN

For current exchange rates, see www.xe.com.

Daily Costs

Budget: Less than 600KN

- Dorm bed: 100–360KN
- Tent site for two people: 100–430KN
- Meal in a local tavern: 60KN
- Bus, tram or train ticket: 10–150KN

Midrange: 600–1400KN

- Double room in a hotel: 450–900KN
- Meal in a decent restaurant: 120KN
- City tour by bike: 175KN
- Short taxi trip: 30KN

Top end: More than 1400KN

- Double room in a luxury hotel: from 900KN
- Meal in a top eatery: 300KN
- Private sailing trip: 1000KN
- Car rental per day: 450KN

Opening Hours

We've provided high-season opening hours; hours generally decrease in the shoulder and low seasons.

Banks 8am or 9am–8pm weekdays and 7am–1pm or 8am–2pm Saturday

Cafes and bars 8am or 9am–midnight

Offices 8am–4pm or 8.30am–4.30pm weekdays

Post offices 7am–8pm weekdays and 7am–1pm Saturday; longer hours in coastal towns in summer.

Restaurants Noon–11pm or midnight; often closed Sundays outside peak season.

Shops 8am–8pm weekdays, to 2pm or 3pm Saturday; some take a 2pm–5pm break. Shopping malls have longer hours.

Arriving in Croatia

Zagreb Airport Croatia Airlines buses (30KN) leaves from the airport every half-hour or hour from about 7am to 10.30pm. Taxis to the centre cost between 150KN and 200KN.

Split Airport An airport shuttle bus heads to the main bus station at least 14 times a day (30KN, 30 minutes). Local buses 37 and 38 stop near the airport every 20 minutes, heading to Split (17KN) or Trogir (13KN). Taxis to Split cost between 250KN and 300KN.

Dubrovnik Airport Atlas runs the airport bus service (40KN, 30 minutes), timed around flights. Buses to Dubrovnik stop at the Pile Gate and the bus station. A taxi costs up to 280KN.

Getting Around

Transport in Croatia is reasonably priced, quick and generally efficient.

Car Useful for travelling at your own pace, or for visiting regions with minimal public transport. Cars can be hired in every city or larger town. Drive on the right.

Bus Reasonably priced, with comprehensive coverage of the country and frequent departures.

Boat Sizeable network of car ferries and faster catamarans all along the coast and the islands.

Air A surprisingly extensive schedule of domestic flights, especially in summer.

Train Less frequent and much slower than buses, with a limited network.

For much more on **getting around**, see p368

What's New

Between Zagreb's major earthquake of March 2020 and the global Covid-19 pandemic, Croatia has had it tough in recent years. Tourism is still at a fraction of pre-Covid levels, making for a pleasantly uncrowded experience for those fortunate enough to be able to travel.

Best in Travel

The Kvarner Gulf was awarded 9th place in Lonely Planet's list of Top 10 regions to travel to in 2020... but then along came Covid-19. Part of the reason for its selection was that its principal city, Rijeka, was designated a European Capital of Culture for that year. Due to the pandemic that title was extended into 2021, so it's only fair that we extend our ranking as well.

Sandwiched between the tourist hotspots of Dalmatia and Istria, this less-heralded part of the Croatian coast has been quietly building up its credentials in the culinary and environmental-protection spheres over the last decade. Shiny new spaces in Rijeka, created to support its Capital-of-Culture role, include older buildings repurposed by local architects into museums and arts centres. Then there are the gulf islands (Cres, Lošinj, Krk and Rab being the main ones), with their ageless beauty, varied beaches and historic walled towns replete with Venetian-era architecture.

Earthquake Damage in Zagreb

The 5.5 magnitude earthquake that hit Zagreb on 22 March 2020 caused extensive damage to most of the old town's churches and museums. The Cathedral of the Assumption (p69) lost one of its spires and the other had to be removed when it developed a lean; this icon of the city remains closed. The Jesuit Church of St Catherine in the Upper Town was also badly damaged, as was Mirogoj Cemetery, although St Mark's Church, with its distinctive tiled roof, fared much better.

LOCAL KNOWLEDGE

WHAT'S HAPPENING IN CROATIA

Peter Dragicevich, Lonely Planet author

In March 2020 – the same month that its capital, Zagreb, experienced its worst earthquake in 140 years – Croatia reported its first death due to Covid-19. While the earthquake caused substantial damage to the historic city centre, the city got off lightly, with only one fatality. Sadly, the same cannot be said with regards to the pandemic. At the time of writing, Croatia was sitting in the top 20 in the world for death rates as a percentage of its population, with over 2000 deaths per million people.

Pre pandemic, tourism directly accounted for around 10% of Croatia's GDP and up to 25% in terms of total contribution. In May 2020 the national tourist board reported that international visitor numbers had dropped to 1% of pre-pandemic numbers. By summer 2021, that number had increased to around 30%.

The government's response has been to lure tourists by focussing on vaccinating front-line tourism workers. Visitors are welcome as long as they can prove they're fully vaccinated or have tested negative before arrival.

The Archaeological Museum, Croatian Natural History Museum and Art Pavilion suffered considerable damage to both their buildings and their collections, and are closed until reconstruction is completed (possibly 2023 for the Natural History Museum). However the Galerija Klovićevi Dvori, the Gallery of Modern Art, the Ethnographic Museum, the Museum of Contemporary Art and the City Museum were largely unaffected, and have been able to remain open.

Dinara Nature Park

In February 2021 Croatia got its 12th official 'nature park', with 630 sq km of the Dinaric Alps on the border with Bosnia protected by legislation. The area includes the highest peak in Croatia (Dinara, 1831m), karst fields and the upper reaches of the Cetina River. It is home to brown bears, lynx, wild boars, wolves and over 1000 plant species.

New Air Connections

Bucking the pandemic, both Delta and United airlines launched direct seasonal flights from the USA to Dubrovnik Airport (p367) in summer 2021, the former flying from JFK (New York) and the latter from Newark (New Jersey). A new Croatian charter airline, ETF Airways (standing for 'enjoy the flight'), was also launched.

Boutique Beverages

Proving that it's not immune to global trends, craft beer has taken off in Croatia. The craze is most pronounced in Zagreb, but you'll now find boutique beers being touted everywhere from Osijek to Dubrovnik. Also riding the zeitgeist, Castrum gin was launched in mid-2021, flavoured with the unique botanicals of its Slavonian home.

Drive-in Movies and Concerts

One surprising by-product of the Covid-19 era has been the coming of the very American tradition of the drive-in to Zagreb, Pula and Osijek. Check www.driveinkultura.com for details of movie screenings and live music performances.

LISTEN, WATCH AND FOLLOW

For inspiration and up-to-date news visit www.lonelyplanet.com/Croatia/articles.

Croatia Times (www.croatia-times.com) Fascinating features on Croatia, in English, including travel tips and recommendations.

Coronavirus in Croatia (www.croatiacovid19.info) Up-to-date tourist-focussed information on Covid-19 outbreaks from the Croatian Institute of Public Health, sorted by area.

Koronavirus (www.koronavirus.hr) Official government website listing the latest regulations for entering the country, case numbers by region and locations of testing centres.

Croatian Tourism (www.croatia.hr) The official tourism site, with trip ideas and information about upcoming events.

FAST FACTS

Food trend Plant-based food (although still in its infancy)

Number of islands and islets 1244

Total length of coastline (including islands) 6278 km

Population 4.3 million

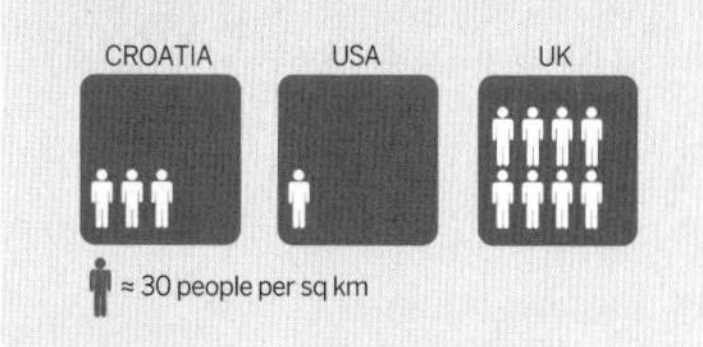

Rapid Antigen Testing

Zagreb, Split and Dubrovnik airports (p367) now offer rapid antigen testing for Covid-19, should you need a test before you can fly home.

Love Stories Museum

This quirky Dubrovnik museum (p304) provides a sunny Dalmatian counterpoint to Zagreb's Museum of Broken Relationships.

Month by Month

TOP EVENTS

Rijeka Carnival, February

INmusic Festival, June

Cest is D'Best, June

Motovun Film Festival, July

Ultra Europe, July

January

As the country goes back to work after the holidays, snow makes inland roads difficult to tackle, while strong winds on the coast and islands limit the ferry schedule.

Skiing on Sljeme

Hit the downhill slopes right outside Zagreb at Sljeme, the main peak of Mt Medvednica, complete with ski runs and lifts. Skiing is a popular pastime for many sporty Croats. (p103)

Night of Museums

Dozens of museums and galleries around the country throw open their doors to the public on the last Friday in January for a free slice of culture.

February

Enjoy scenic snowy hikes in continental Croatia but still be mindful on the roads. *Bura* (cold northeasterly) winds blow along the Adriatic, ferries run infrequently and many hotels in coastal towns shut down.

Feast of St Blaise

On 3 February each year, the streets of Dubrovnik perk up with folk dancing, concerts, food, processions and lots of street action, all happening in honour of St Blaise, the city's patron saint.

Carnival

To fully experience the colourful costumes and revelry associated with this pre-Lent celebration, head to Rijeka, where Carnival is the pinnacle of the year's calendar. Zadar, Split, Dubrovnik and Samobor host colourful celebrations, too. (p175)

March

Days start to get longer and temperatures begin to rise, especially at the seaside. As winter ice melts, it's a great time to catch the waterfalls in Plitvice and Krka. Most action is still indoors.

Zagrebdox

Catch documentary films from around the globe during this annual international festival in Zagreb. Zagrebdox starts in late February and continues into March, drawing a small crowd of avid doco lovers. (p82)

April

Soak up some sunshine and enjoy the solitude on southern islands and the coastline. Continental Croatia is still chilly, but trees start to blossom and, as rivers swell with water, rafting and kayaking are tops.

Music Biennale Zagreb

Held in the capital city each April during odd-numbered years since the 1960s, this is Croatia's most high-profile contemporary music event. By 'contemporary', do not read 'pop' – this prestigious fest celebrates modern-day classical music. (p82)

Wild Asparagus Harvest, Istria

During early spring, the fields and meadows of inland Istria become dotted with wild asparagus. Do like the locals do and head out to pick some, and then cook up a mean asparagus *fritaja* (omelette).

Holy Week

Holy Week celebrations are particularly elaborate on the islands of Hvar and Korčula. Hvar's 500-year-old, all-night-long Following the Cross procession, starting after Mass on Holy Thursday, is inscribed on the Unesco Cultural Heritage of Humanity list. (p286)

May

It's sunny and warm on the coast, and you can take a dip in the sea. Hotels are cheaper, too, and crowds have yet to come. Cafe life in Zagreb and Split kicks into full gear.

Sudamja

The 7 May feast of St Domnius, Split's patron saint, is stretched out into a weeklong extravaganza starting at the beginning of the month. Expect concerts, rowing races, religious rituals and fireworks. (p249)

Subversive Festival

Mingle with Europe's activists and revolutionaries, who storm Zagreb for this two-week festival each May. The first week has a series of film screenings, while the second week's program includes lectures and panels by left-leaning movers and shakers. (p82)

Ljeto na Štrosu, Zagreb

Kicking off in late May, this ultrafun summer-long event features free outdoor film screenings, concerts by local bands, artsy workshops, best-in-show mongrel dog competitions and other quirky happenings, all along the leafy Strossmayer promenade. (p83)

Open Wine Cellar Day

On the last Sunday in May each year, renowned winemakers and winegrowers of Istria open the doors to their wine cellars for free tastings and wine-fuelled merrymaking.

June

Swim in the Adriatic, take in festivals across the country and enjoy outdoor activities galore. Ferries start their summer schedule, peak-season prices haven't quite kicked in and hotels are still not packed.

Cest is d'Best

For several days in late May through early June, Zagreb's streets come alive with music, dance, theatre, art, sports and other fun events. This street festival is a much-loved affair, with several stages around the city centre and around 200 international performers. (p82)

INmusic Festival

Get your groove on during this three-day music extravaganza, which takes over leafy Jarun Lake with multiple stages and spots for camping. This is Zagreb's highest-profile music festival. (p83)

July

Tourist season is in full swing: hotels along the coast get booked out and beaches are full. Ferries run on their maximum schedule and there are festivals aplenty. Head inland to escape the coastal crowds.

Hideout

The festival that put Zrće on the electronic-dance-music map takes over the beach bars and clubs in late June/early July. Expect big-name DJs and multiple nights of mayhem. (p218)

Dubrovnik Summer Festival

Kicking off in the middle of July and lasting into late August, this festival has been taking place in Dubrovnik since the 1950s. It features classical music, theatre and dance at different venues around town, including Fort Lawrence. (p306)

Split Summer Festival

Open-air stages are set up for plays, ballet, opera and concerts all over the harbourside city. The festival runs from 15 July through until 15 August. (p251)

✩ Ultra Europe

One of the world's largest electronic music festivals takes over Split's Poljud stadium for three days in July, before heading to Bol, Hvar and Vis for the rest of the week. (p251)

✩ Motovun Film Festival

This film festival, Croatia's most fun and glamorous, presents a roster of independent and avant-garde films in late July each year. Nonstop outdoor and indoor screenings, concerts and parties take over the medieval streets of the hilltop town of Motovun. (p155)

✩ Dance & Nonverbal Theatre Festival, Svetvinčenat

The otherwise sleepy Istrian town of Svetvinčenat comes alive during this late-July festival, which showcases contemporary dance pieces, street theatre, circus and mime acts, and other nonverbal forms of expression. (p161)

Full Moon Festival

During this three-day festival spanning the high-summer full moon (either late July or early August), Zadar's quays are lit with torches and candles, stalls sell local delicacies, and boats lining the quays become floating fish markets. (p226)

Top: Rijeka Carnival (p175)

Bottom: Chris Blaze performs at Cest is d'Best (p82)

August

Tourist season peaks in the Adriatic, with the hottest days and sea temperatures, swarming beaches and highest prices. Zagreb is hot but empty, as people escape to the coast.

Krk Fair

Held in the main town of the island of Krk, this three-day, Venetian-inspired event includes concerts, medieval costumes and stalls selling traditional food and handicrafts. (p196)

Sonus

Big names in electronic music head to Zrće Beach on Pag Island for five days and nights, entertaining the up-for-it young crowds. In previous years the festival has featured the likes of John Digweed and Laurent Garnier. (p218)

Špancirfest

In late August this eclectic festival enlivens the parks and squares of Varaždin with a rich repertoire of events that range from world music (Afro-Cuban, gypsy, tango and more) to acrobats, theatre, traditional crafts and illusionists. (p110)

September

The summer rush is over, but sunshine is still plentiful, the sea is warm and the crowds have largely gone – it's a great time to visit Croatia. Zagreb comes alive again after the summer exodus to the coast.

Festival of Subotina, Buzet

The white-truffle season kicks off with this one-day festival on the second Saturday in September. Stick around to help consume the giant truffle omelette. (p157)

Varaždin Baroque Evenings

Baroque music takes over the baroque city of Varaždin for two weeks each September. Local and international orchestras play in the cathedral, churches and theatres around town. (p110)

World Theatre Festival

High-quality contemporary theatre comes to Zagreb for a couple of weeks each year, often extending into early October and delighting the country's die-hard theatre buffs. (p83)

October

Children are back in school, parents are at work and the country sways to its regular rhythms. Ferries change to their winter schedule but the weather is still pretty mild.

Zagreb Film Festival

Don't miss this major cultural event that takes place in mid-October each year, with film screenings, accompanying parties and international film directors competing for the coveted Golden Pram award. (p83)

November

The continent chills but the seaside can still be sunny, albeit not warm. Many hotels along the coast shut their doors for the season, as do many restaurants.

Feast of St Martin

Martinje (St Martin's Day) is celebrated in all the wine-producing regions across Croatia on 11 November. There are wine celebrations and lots of feasting and sampling of new wines.

December

It's freezing everywhere, but marginally less so on the coast. In this deeply Catholic country the churches are fill to bursting for midnight Mass on Christmas morning.

Fuliranje

Zagrebians brave the freezing temperatures for the mulled wine and street food at this site-shifting Advent market. (p83)

Human Rights Film Festival, Zagreb

This film festival sheds light on human-rights issues around the world. It takes place for a week each December at Zagreb's Kino Europa. (p83)

ANDREY OMELYANCHUK/500PX ©

Plan Your Trip
Itineraries

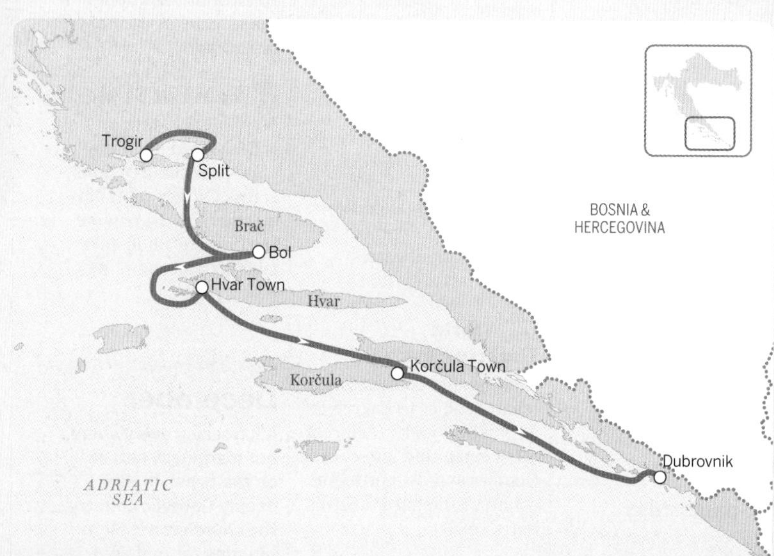

Essential Croatia

This itinerary focuses on the essential Croatian experience – a sunny island-hopping trip along the Dalmatian coast stopping at three World Heritage Sites along the way. Conveniently, it has an international airport at each end. We've envisaged it as a journey that can be made predominantly by ferry.

Start with a stroll through the marbled streets of the postcard-perfect walled town of **Trogir**. Either relax here for a night or continue on to Croatia's exuberant second city **Split**. Diocletian's Palace is a living part of this seafront city, a throbbing ancient quarter that's home to 220 historic buildings and about 3000 people. Base yourself here for a day or two of sightseeing and nightlife.

Hop on a fast catamaran to **Bol** on the island of Brač (or alternatively a car ferry to Supetar and then a bus). This pretty little port is most famous for Zlatni Rat beach – a glorious spur of pebbles that extends 500m into the Adriatic.

Peristil (p244), Diocletian's Palace, Split

Next, catch the catamaran to historic **Hvar Town**, the vibrant capital of the island of the same name. This picturesque place offers an intriguing mix of European glamour and a raucous bar scene.

From Hvar Town there are year-round connections to **Korčula Town** – a highly photogenic walled town jutting out into the Adriatic on its own little peninsula. From May to mid-October, there are catamarans from here to Dubrovnik, otherwise you'll need to catch the car ferry to Orebić on the Pelješac Peninsula and continue by bus.

Your first sight of the magnificent old town of **Dubrovnik**, ringed by mighty defensive walls and the sparkling blue Adriatic, is bound to blow you away. Spend the next two days taking in its sights.

SLOVENIA
HUNGARY
ZAGREB
SERBIA
Plitvice Lakes National Park
Pag Island
Zadar
Krka National Park
Šibenik
BOSNIA & HERCEGOVINA
Split
Trogir
ADRIATIC SEA
Hvar Town
ITALY
MONTENEGRO
Mljet
Dubrovnik

NOVAK ELCIC/SHUTTERSTOCK ©

JUSTIN FOULKES/LONELY PLANET ©

Top: Mljet Island (p320)
Bottom: Restaurants in Zagreb (p85)

2 WEEKS Capital to Coast

Take in the heavyweights of Croatia in this two-week journey, including the capital city, three national parks and the gems of the Dalmatian coast.

Start in the capital, **Zagreb**, and set aside two days to delve into its booming cafe culture, cutting-edge art scene, simmering nightlife and interesting museums. En route south, spend the day at the World Heritage–listed **Plitvice Lakes National Park**, exploring its verdant maze of turquoise lakes and cascading waterfalls.

Cut down through the Velebit mountains to the coast and cross onto **Pag Island** to try some of its famously pungent cheese and indulge in its summertime beach-club scene. Continue on to **Zadar**, one of Croatia's most underrated cities. It's simultaneously ancient and modern and packed with attractions.

The next day, stop en route at **Krka National Park** and do the hour-long loop along the boardwalks connecting the little islands in the emerald-green river. End the outing with a swim at the lake below Skradinski Buk, the park's largest waterfall. Continue on to **Šibenik**, another gem of an old town with a truly magnificent cathedral.

Next day, stop at **Trogir** to admire the World Heritage–listed walled town sitting on its own little island, then travel south to the buzzing Dalmatian city of **Split** for a two-day fling focused on Diocletian's Palace.

If you hired a car, return it here and hop over to chic **Hvar Town** by ferry for a taste of its happening nightlife and for some clothing-optional sunbathing on the Pakleni Islands, immediately offshore.

Catch another ferry to Pomena on the gorgeous island of **Mljet**, gateway to Mljet National Park – you'll get a great view of Korčula Town from the boat. Walk through the forest and around the salt lakes before hiring a car to drive to the eastern end of the island to spend the night. The following morning, return the car to Pomena and catch the ferry on to **Dubrovnik**. Spend the next two days exploring the old town's gleaming marble lanes, vibrant street life and fine architecture.

Note that the Hvar–Pomena–Dubrovnik ferries only operate from May to mid-October. At other times it's easiest to omit Mljet, ferry back to Split and catch the bus to Dubrovnik.

1 WEEK Highlights of Istria

Explore the Istrian peninsula for its coastal resorts, pretty beaches, hilltop medieval towns, top-rated food, award-winning wines and lovely rural hotels.

Start your trip in **Pula**, the peninsula's coastal capital, home to a remarkably well-preserved Roman amphitheatre that overlooks the city's harbour. The Arena, as it's known locally, once hosted gladiatorial contests with up to 20,000 spectators; today you can tour its remains and take in the small museum in the chambers downstairs. Base yourself in Pula for two days to see the smattering of other Roman ruins and take at least an afternoon to explore nearby **Cape Kamenjak** by bike or on foot. This entirely uninhabited cape, Istria's southernmost point, features rolling hills, wildflowers (including 30 species of orchid), medicinal herbs and around 30km of virgin beaches and coves.

Stop to check out the captivating town of **Bale**, an offbeat place and one of Istria's best-kept secrets. Push on to **Rovinj** and set aside at least two days for the coast's showpiece resort town. Its steep cobbled streets and piazzas lead up to St Euphemia's Church, an imposing construction with a 60m-high tower that punctuates the peninsula. Take time to explore the verdant beaches and some of the 14 green islands that make up the Rovinj archipelago just offshore.

Zip up the coast to **Poreč** to gape at its World Heritage–listed Euphrasian Basilica, one of Europe's finest intact examples of Byzantine architecture, with magnificent 6th-century frescos.

Spend the rest of your trip exploring the peninsula's wooded interior. Drop into music-filled **Grožnjan** before continuing on through to **Motovun**, a similarly artsy hilltop settlement known for its summer film festival. The hilltop town of **Buzet**, known as Istria's truffle epicentre, makes for a good base for exploring the villages of Croatia's foodie heartland.

Stop to wander around the 'world's smallest town', the adorable **Hum**. Head southwest towards **Pazin** to walk through the famous chasm which once inspired Jules Verne. On your way back to Pula, make a final stop to stroll through scenic **Svetvinčenat**, with its Renaissance-era square and castle.

SIARHEI KELNIK/EYEEM/GETTY IMAGES ©

ZVONIMIR ATLETIC/SHUTTERSTOCK ©

Top: Roman Amphitheatre (p131), Pula
Bottom: Detail from the altarpiece in the Euphrasian Basilica (p146), Poreč

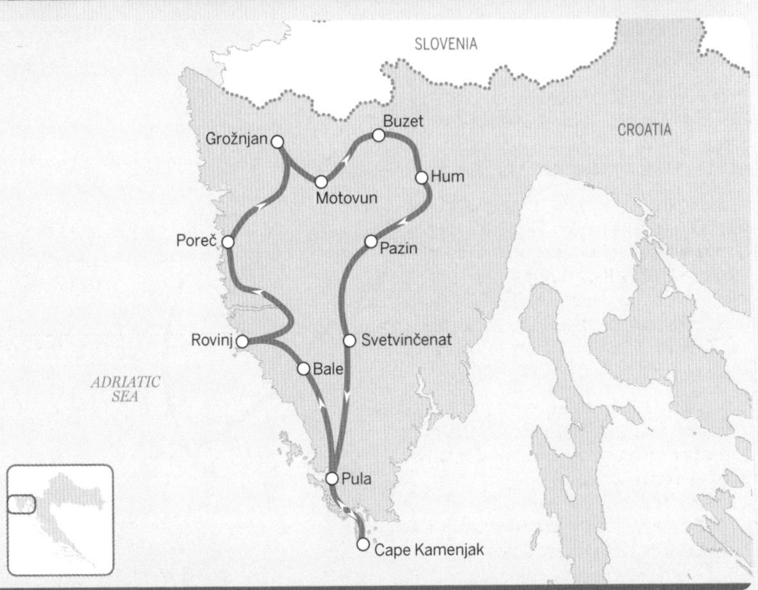
SLOVENIA
CROATIA
Buzet
Grožnjan
Hum
Motovun
Poreč
Pazin
Rovinj
Svetvinčenat
Bale
ADRIATIC SEA
Pula
Cape Kamenjak

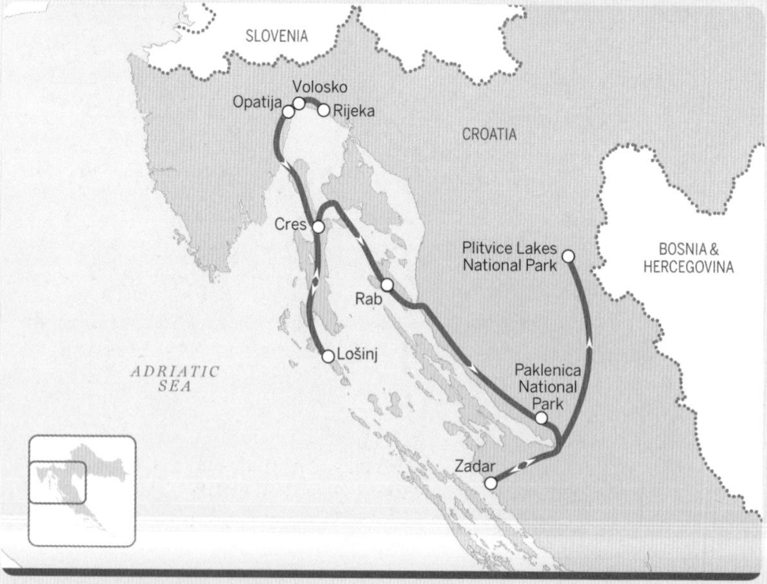

SLOVENIA
Volosko
Opatija
Rijeka
CROATIA
Cres
Plitvice Lakes National Park
BOSNIA & HERCEGOVINA
Rab
Lošinj
ADRIATIC SEA
Paklenica National Park
Zadar

XBRCHX/SHUTTERSTOCK ©

PETR NOVACEK/SHUTTERSTOCK ©

Top: Rijeka (p173)
Bottom: Paklenica National Park (p215)

Kvarner & Northern Dalmatia

Take in the delights of Croatia's northern coastal stretches and their wild hinterland, starting with the Kvarner Gulf and moving south to northern Dalmatia with its wide spectrum of appealing sights.

Start in the capital of the Kvarner, **Rijeka**, Croatia's third-largest city and a thriving port with a laid-back vibe and a lively cafe scene. Take a day to explore this undervisited city and another to visit the elegant seaside resort town of **Opatija**. Its beautiful belle époque villas date from the dying days of the Austro-Hungarian Empire, when the town was the stomping ground of the Viennese elite. While you're at it, take time to stroll Lungomare, a picturesque path that winds along the coast through exotic bushes and thickets of bamboo to **Volosko**, a pretty fishing village that's become one of Croatia's gastronomic destinations; make sure you have lunch or dinner in one of its acclaimed restaurants.

Next, hop over to one of the Kvarner islands for two days – the interconnected **Cres** and **Lošinj** are the most offbeat. Wilder, greener Cres has remote campgrounds, pristine beaches, a handful of medieval villages and an off-the-radar feel. More populated and touristy Lošinj sports a pair of pretty port towns, a string of beautiful bays, and lush and varied vegetation throughout, with 1100 plant species and 230 medicinal herbs, many brought from faraway lands by sea captains. Spend another two days chilling on **Rab**, lounging on the sandy beaches of Lopar Peninsula and exploring the postcard-pretty Rab Town with its ancient stone alleys and the four bell towers that rise from them.

Back on the mainland, if you're feeling adventurous, don't miss a hike through the alpine trails and canyons of **Paklenica National Park**. Next head down to **Zadar** for an amble through this vibrant coastal city with its medley of Roman ruins, Habsburg architecture and a lovely seafront; stick around for two days to take it all in. Head back inland to spend a day exploring the dazzling natural wonderland of **Plitvice Lakes National Park**, with its gorgeous turquoise lakes linked by a series of waterfalls and cascades.

Off the Beaten Track

HUM

Istria has many gorgeous walled hilltop towns, but what's particularly charming about Hum is its tiny size (basically one street) and tucked-away location. (p158)

PLEŠIVICA WINE ROAD

Tour past wee red-roofed villages, stopping at family-run wineries along the way. This route is located in the countryside west of Zagreb, 20km south of the town of Samobor. (p103)

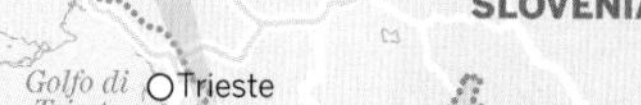

STARA BAŠKA

It's nice to know that even the busy island of Krk has quieter coves, such as this pebble-and-sand stretch accessed from a minor road heading south from Punat. (p197)

OLIVE GARDENS OF LUN

With a name worthy of a fantasy novel, this area near the northern tip of the island of Pag has marked walking trails through the groves and signs pointing out significantly venerable trees. (p219)

SILBA ISLAND

An obscure choice among the multitude of Adriatic islands, Silba nonetheless has ferry services, beaches and a legendary tower. (p227)

VRANSKO LAKE NATURE PARK

Although it's Croatia's largest natural lake, Vransko Jezero doesn't register on many travellers' radars – unless they happen to be birdwatchers, then it's a must-visit attraction. (p231)

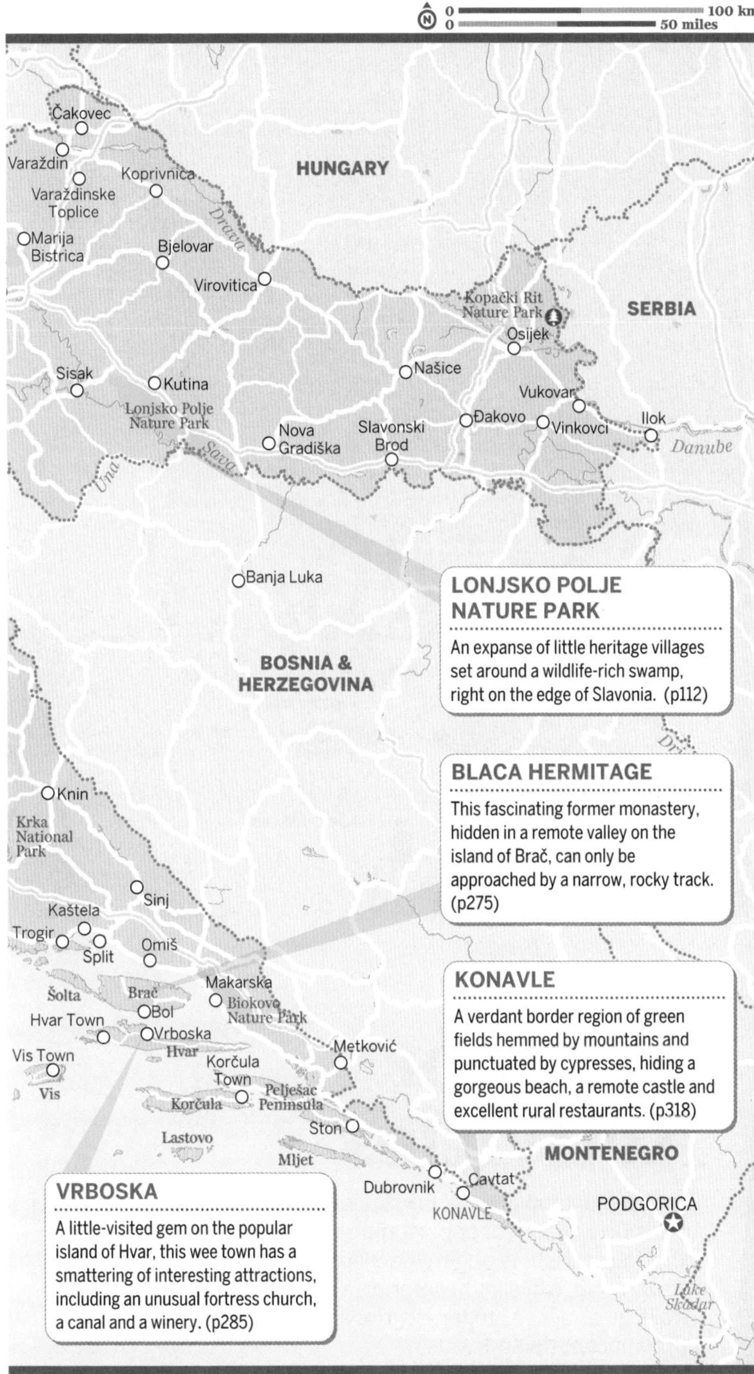

LONJSKO POLJE NATURE PARK

An expanse of little heritage villages set around a wildlife-rich swamp, right on the edge of Slavonia. (p112)

BLACA HERMITAGE

This fascinating former monastery, hidden in a remote valley on the island of Brač, can only be approached by a narrow, rocky track. (p275)

KONAVLE

A verdant border region of green fields hemmed by mountains and punctuated by cypresses, hiding a gorgeous beach, a remote castle and excellent rural restaurants. (p318)

VRBOSKA

A little-visited gem on the popular island of Hvar, this wee town has a smattering of interesting attractions, including an unusual fortress church, a canal and a winery. (p285)

Stiniva (p286)

Plan Your Trip

Outdoor Activities

Croatia's juxtaposition of crystalline waters and rugged mountains opens up a wealth of opportunities for the active traveller. The gorgeous coastline and myriad islands are a renowned boaties' playground, while in the interior, a network of hiking and biking trails gives access to forest-fringed lakes, verdant valleys and magnificent uplands.

NINOPAVISIC/SHUTTERSTOCK ©

Best Experiences

Vis

Swimming in the secluded bays.

Plitvice Lakes National Park

Strolling the lakeside paths – preferably when it's not too busy.

Parenzana Bike Trail

Cycling the 78km Croatian section of this off-road trail in Istria.

Crveni Otok

Snorkelling around the rocky coast of this island near Rovinj.

Split

Shooting the breeze on a day's sailing.

Dubrovnik

Watching the sunset over the old town from atop a kayak.

Bol

Trying your hand at windsurfing on the island of Brač.

Paklenica National Park

Tackling the park's rock-climbing routes.

Cetina River

Rafting along the river near Omiš.

Swimming

If there's just one activity you're planning to partake in during a Croatian holiday, we'd put money on it being this one. Croatia's clear waters are nigh on irresistible on a hot day, and the European Environment Agency rates 98% of Croatia's bathing sites as having excellent water quality. In summer the water temperature can reach over 25°C, and it's usually over 20°C from June right through to October.

There are good swimming spots along the entire coast and throughout the islands. Beaches come in a variety of textures: sandy, shingly, rocky. Some of the best – like blissful little Stiniva (p286), on Vis, and Dubovica (p280), on Hvar – have large smooth white pebbles. Locals tend to favour the pebbly beaches, partly because many of the sandy beaches are extremely shallow. This is especially true of those around Lopar (p207) on Rab, although less so for the sandy beaches at the eastern end of Vis (p286) and places like Prapratno (p323) on the Pelješac Peninsula.

In summer the Adriatic can more closely resemble a millpond than the sea, but the waves pick up when the wild wind known as the *bora* arrives in winter. During the peak season, however, conditions are generally safe and the main hazards are the sea urchins that reside in the rocky shallows. Many people wear plastic swimming shoes as a precaution.

Away from the coast, popular swimming spots include the lakes at Krka National Park (p233), Zagreb's Jarun Lake (p79), and the island of Ada, on the Danube, near Vukovar.

Hiking

Hiking in Croatia can be as untaxing as a slow stroll around the boardwalks and well-maintained lakeside trails of Plitvice (p211) or as challenging as an assault on the high reaches of Paklenica (p215). Local tourist and national-park offices are well equipped to recommend a walk to suit your time constraints and level of ability. Many produce their own free walking maps or sell detailed maps for more remote areas. If you're contemplating a serious expedition, consider contacting the **Croatian Mountaineering Association** (Hrvatski planinarski savez; ☎01-48 23 624; www.hps.hr; Kozarčeva 22, Zagreb; ⏰8am-4pm Mon-Fri), which can provide information and access to a network of mountain huts, or joining a guided walk organised by one of the many agencies specialising in adventure tourism.

Spring, early summer and autumn are prime hiking times, beating the worst of both the crowds and the summer sun. The karstic coastal mountains roast in July and August, offering very little shade or water, while the leafy trails of Plitvice and Krka get clogged with people. In these months, try less-visited Risnjak National Park (p178) or head even further inland.

Žumberak Samoborsko Gorje Nature Park (p102), near Samobor, offers the best hiking in Croatia's interior, featuring forests, caves, river canyons, waterfalls and nine mountain huts. Medvednica Nature Park (p104), north of Zagreb, is also good.

In Istria (p127), there are trails around Buzet (p155) and Poreč (p145), and a well-marked 11.5km circular hiking track leading from Gračišće (p164). The Kvarner region offers off-the-beaten-track hiking in both Učka Nature Park (p182) and Risnjak National Park (p178). Risnjak's Leska Path is a recommended, easy 4.2km trail through the forest where you might even spot wildlife. The islands of Cres and Lošinj (p183) and Rab (p202) also have a wealth of good trails.

Dalmatia is spoilt for choice, but the most obvious hiking highlights are the national parks Plitvice (p211), Krka (p233) and Paklenica (p215), and Biokovo Nature Park (p271). The first two offer plenty of easy lakeside strolls, although they do get insanely busy in summer. Paklenica and Biokovo are both mountainous terrains, offering superb views over the coast and islands. There are also brilliant walks on the islands of Brač (p272), Hvar (p277), Vis (p286), Lastovo (p332) and Mljet (p320), and in the mountains above Omiš (p268) and Orebić (p324).

Plitvice Lakes National Park (p211)

Cycling

Bicycle touring is increasingly popular in Croatia, both independently or with organised groups. Bike hire is easy to arrange and there are plenty of relatively quiet roads to explore, especially on the islands. Try to avoid the main Adriatic highway – there are no bike lanes, few passing spaces and it's extremely busy. Thankfully much of it can be bypassed by catching ferries; bikes can be taken on car ferries for an additional charge but not on catamarans.

March, April, September and October are the best cycling months, with mild, mostly dry weather. The traffic is much busier from June to August, and it can get extremely hot.

Slavonia has a couple of excellent long-distance trails: the 80km Pannonian Peace Route (p115) between Osijek and Sombor in Serbia, and the 138km Danube Route (p115), tracing the Hungarian and Serbian border.

The best route, however, is the Parenzana Bike Trail (p149), which follows a former railway line between the Italian city of Trieste and Poreč in Istria (the Croatian section is 78km long). Also in Istria, there are bike trails around Buzet, Pazin, Poreč and Rovinj, and an unchallenging 60km cycling trail winding around the coast from Pula to Medulin.

Kvarner is another great region for cyclists, with 19 routes around Opatija, Učka Nature Park and the islands of

SKIING

Only 20 minutes from Zagreb, the Sljeme Ski Resort (p104) has lifts heading up to five downhill runs on the side of Mt Medvednica. The best snow cover is in February, but the season can stretch for three to four months with the use of snowmaking equipment. Night skiing is also possible.

Mountain biking in Grožnjan (p153)

Cres, Lošinj, Krk and Rab detailed in the *Kvarner by Bicycle* brochure, available from local tourist offices.

In Dalmatia, there are scenic cycling trails on the islands of Mljet and Lastovo. The *Central Dalmatia Bike* brochure details six routes on the Makarska Riviera, ranging from an easy 15km ride around Makarska to a gruelling 61km climb up Biokovo to a height of 1749m. Biokovo is also good for mountain bikers, as are the islands of Korčula and Brač, where trails lead to the island's highest point, Vidova Gora (778m).

Useful websites with information for cyclists include www.pedala.hr (in Croatian) and www.istria-bike.com.

Diving & Snorkelling

The most striking thing about the Adriatic coast is the clarity of the water. Snorkelling is worthwhile pretty much everywhere, although there are some extraspecial spots, such as Crveni Otok (p142) near Rovinj.

The area's turbulent history has also bequeathed it with numerous interesting underwater sights, from wrecks dating to antiquity through to a downed WWII plane. The latter is off the coast of Vis (p288), where there's also an amphorae field and shipwrecks to explore – although the most interesting sites here are at depths that require technical diving skills.

Other famous wrecks include the *Taranto,* an 1899 Italian merchant ship sunk by a WWII mine off Dubrovnik; a 3rd-century Roman ship and a German WWII torpedo boat off the island of Mljet; the *Rosa,* off Rab; the *Peltastis,* a 60m Greek cargo ship, off Krk; and the *Baron Gautsch,* an Austrian passenger steamer sunk by a mine near Rovinj during WWI.

On top of that there are plenty of reefs, drop-offs and caves to investigate. Marine life includes scorpionfish, conger eels, sea snails, sea slugs, octopuses, lobsters, the rare giant mussel, red coral, red gorgonian fans and colourful sponges.

There are diving centres all along the coast, with particular hot spots be-

XBRCHX/SHUTTERSTOCK ©

Sailing in Zadar (p223)

ing Poreč, Rovinj, Pula and the Brijuni Islands in Istria; the islands of Krk, Cres, Lošinj and Rab in the Kvarner area; the Dalmatian islands of Dugi Otok, Brač, Hvar, Vis and Mljet; and Dubrovnik.

For further information, refer to the Croatian-only website of the **Croatian Diving Association** (www.diving-hrs.hr).

BEST TIMES TO GO

Spring The best season for rock climbing, rafting, and spotting birds in Kopački Rit Nature Park. Great weather for hiking, cycling and windsurfing.

Summer The best for swimming, diving, kayaking, sailing and more sedate rafting.

Autumn Excellent for hiking, cycling, windsurfing, and birdwatching at Kopački Rit, and still good for swimming, rafting, diving and kayaking.

Winter Skiing, obviously, but also birdwatching in Krka National Park.

Sailing

Could there be a more blissful holiday than gliding between remote islets and otherwise-hard-to-access beaches all day, before finding a pretty spot to moor for the night?

Sailing was once the exclusive preserve of the rich, but Croatia now offers plenty of more affordable opportunities for both day sails and organised multiday tours. Operators such as Sail Croatia (p370) even target cruises to young backpacker types.

If you'd prefer to go it alone, it's an easy matter to charter a boat, either with a skipper or, if you're suitably experienced, on a 'bareboat' basis. Useful contacts include the **Adriatic Croatia International Club** (www.aci-marinas.com), which manages 22 marinas, and the following charter companies:

Cosmos Yachting (www.cosmosyachting.com).

Nautika Centar Nava (Map p246; ☎021-407 700; www.navaboats.com; Uvala baluni 1)

Sunsail (www.sunsail.com; ACI Marina Dubrovnik, Na skali bb, Mokošica; ⏲8am-4pm Mon-Fri, 9am-7pm Sat & Sun)

Ultra Sailing (Map p246; ☎021-398 578; www.ultra-sailing.hr; ACI Marina Split, Uvala Baluni 6a; ⏲8am-4pm Mon-Sat).

Yacht Rent (☎098 726 065; www.yacht-rent.com; Braće Stipčić 41, Rijeka)

Yacht Charter Croatia (www.croatiacharter.com).

Kayaking

Kayaking, of both the sea and the river varieties, is a popular activity in Croatia. Kayaks can be hired from numerous locations, and there are many specialist operators offering both short paddles and multiday island-hopping expeditions.

It's particularly popular in Dubrovnik, where you'll see great shoals of kayakers heading out on guided trips – with sunset paddles being especially well subscribed. There are also good crews operating out of Split, Cape Kamenjak, Rovinj, Poreč and the islands of Korčula, Vis, Hvar and Rab.

Inland, don't miss the opportunity to kayak on the Danube at Vukovar and on Zagreb's Jarun Lake (p79).

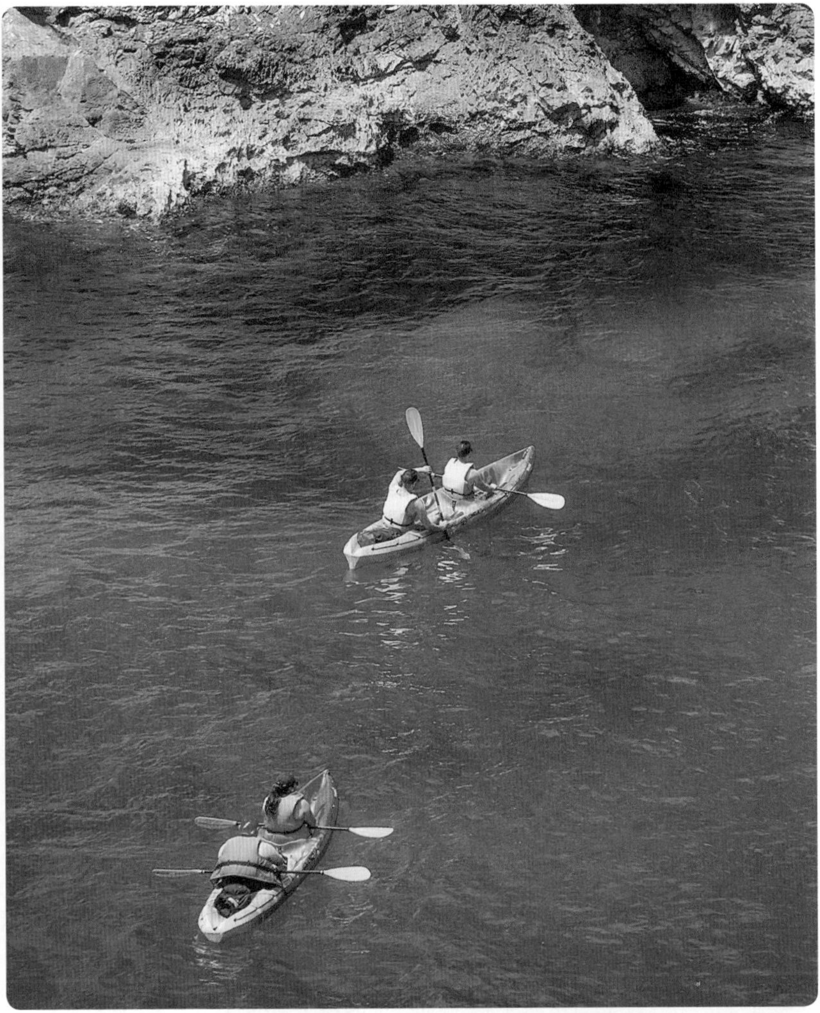

AQUAPIX/SHUTTERSTOCK ©

Top: Kayaking off the coast of Dubrovnik (p304)

Bottom: Diving the *Baron Gautsch* shipwreck near Rovinj (p141)

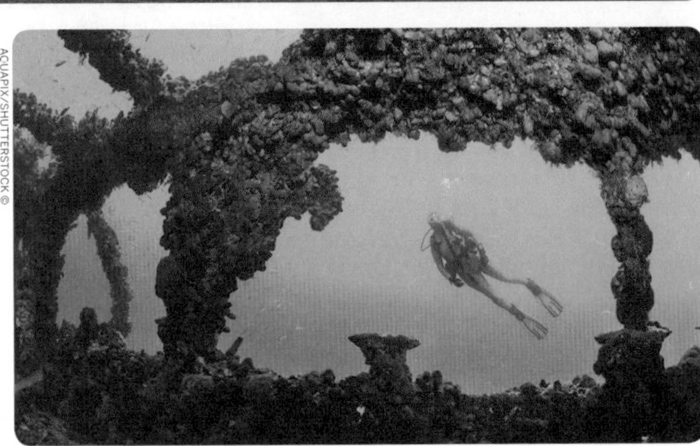

Adrenalin-Inducing Activities

Visiting daredevils will find activities scattered throughout the country to satisfy their adrenalin needs.

Starting at the gentler end of things, Dubrovnik's cable car (p304) heads up to a height of 405m, offering an unbeatable eagle's-eye view of the famous old town. Another one suitable for the whole family are the ziplines at Zlatna Greda (p120) in Kopački Rit Nature Park. On a similar theme, but more hair-raising, are the eight ziplines (p268) over the Cetina canyon near Omiš; the highest is 150m up, while the longest stretches for 700m. Europe's longest zipline (1700m) is the intriguingly named Beware of the Bear (p214), in the Lika region. There's also a zipline (p160) over the 100m-deep Pazin Chasm in Istria.

Paragliding Kvarner (p200), based in Crikvenica near Rijeka, offers tandem flights taking off from 770m above the Adriatic. In Slavonia, Parafreek (www.parafreek.hr) offers jumps from a launch site near Japetić (879m), the highest peak of the Žumberak Samoborsko Gorje range.

On the island of Krk, the Cable Krk Wakeboard Center (p196) offers both wakeboarding and waterskiing. If you fancy trying skydiving, contact the **Croatian Aeronautical Federation** (www.caf.hr).

WINDSURFING

Croatia's two prime windsurfing locations are Bol (p274) on the island of Brač, and Viganj, near Orebić (p324) on the Pelješac Peninsula. Both are exposed to the *maestral*, a strong constant westerly that generally blows from morning to early afternoon from April to October. The optimum conditions tend to be at the end of May/early June and the end of July/early August.

Other good spots include Makarska, Mali Lošinj, Cape Kamenjak and Poreč, and you can even windsurf inland on Zagreb's Jarun Lake (p79). At all of these locales you can hire boards and take lessons.

Another worthwhile contact is the local extreme-sports association **Cro Challenge** (www.crochallenge.com).

As with all activities in Croatia, it's often easiest to arrange them though a specialist adventure agency. Here are some worthwhile operators:

Alter Natura (p289) Vis-based adventure specialists, offering paragliding, caving, kayaking and abseiling.

CroActive & Adventure (p249) Kayaking, rafting, hiking, rock climbing, cycling, canyoning, sailing, zip-lining and stand-up paddleboarding trips, out of Split.

Huck Finn (www.huckfinncroatia.com) Specialises in adventure travel and runs the gamut of adrenalin-lifting tours around Croatia: river and sea kayaking, rafting, canoeing, cycling, hiking and sailing.

Hvar Adventure (p280) Sailing, kayaking, cycling, climbing, hiking, skydiving, 4WD safaris and triathlon training.

Outdoor (www.outdoor.hr) Adventure and team-building travel.

Portal Trogir (☎021-885 016; www.portal-trogir.com; Bana Berislavića 3, Trogir; ⏰8am-8pm May-Sep, 9am-1pm Mon-Fri Oct-Mar, 9am-4pm Mon-Sat Apr) Quad-bike safaris, rafting, diving and canyoning.

Red Adventures (p249) Based in Split and offering sea kayaking, rock climbing, hiking and bike tours.

Rock Climbing

Croatia's best rock climbing is in Paklenica National Park (p215), with graded climbs for all levels of ability including 72 short sports routes and 250 longer routes. A rescue service is also available. Sticking in Dalmatia, there are climbing crags on Marjan Hill, right in the centre of Split.

Heading up the coast, there are a couple of sites near Baška (p198) on Krk Island. The best climbing in Istria is in a defunct Venetian stone quarry near Rovinj, which has 80 climbing routes. Free climbing is also possible near Buzet and Pazin.

There's also a famous rock-climbing area in the Plešivica section of the Žumberak Samoborsko Gorje range, west of Zagreb.

March, April and May are the best months for climbing, before the summer heat kicks in. The wind tends to pick up in autumn and winter.

The easiest way to get started is to enquire at local tourist offices or to contact one of the local agencies specialising in adventure tourism. The Croatian Mountaineering Association (p37) also has some information on its website (in Croatian).

DIAMIRSTUDIO/GETTY IMAGES ©

Rock climbing in Paklenica National Park (p215)

Rafting

Croatia's prime rafting locale is the Cetina River (p268), which spills through a steep gorge and into the Adriatic at Omiš. It's an easy matter to join a trip in the pretty little town, as operators tout for business by the riverside. Otherwise, specialist adventure agencies in Split and Makarska organise transfers and expeditions with reputable rafting companies.

Trips are possible from around April to October, with the fastest flows in April and after heavy rains. In summer it's a more gentle experience, of more interest to first-timers.

Wildlife-Watching

Croatia's premier wildlife-watching spot is Kopački Rit Nature Park (p120) in Slavonia, a significant wetlands on the flood plain of the rivers Danube and Drava. Nearly 300 species of bird have been spotted here, including white-tailed and imperial eagles, black storks, great crested grebes, purple herons, spoonbills, wild geese and woodpeckers. They're joined by 44 species of fish and 21 different kinds of mosquito (bring repellent). If you're extremely lucky, you might spot some of its mammalian inhabitants, such as red deer, wild boar, beavers, pine martens and foxes. The best time for spotting birdlife is during the spring (March to May) and autumn (September to November) migrations.

The Kvarner region is also rich in wildlife. The mighty griffon vulture roosts on the islands of Cres, Krk and Prvić, while Lošinj has centres devoted to the preservation of sea turtles and dolphins. Risnjak National Park (p178) is named after the lynx, which lives in the virgin forest here alongside brown bears, wolves, chamois and wild boar. You're unlikely to see these superstars of the forest, but you might spot deer at feeding stations along the tracks and you're bound to see some of the 500 species of butterfly. The Učka Nature Park (p182) also has brown bears, wild boar, roe deer and golden eagles.

Despite the summertime hordes, Plitvice Lakes National Park (p211) hides bears, wolves, deer and boar, alongside rabbits, foxes and badgers. If you can divert your gaze from the waterfalls, you might spot hawks, owls, cuckoos, kingfishers, wild ducks, herons, black storks and ospreys.

In Dalmatia, Paklenica National Park (p215) is home to various birds of prey, while Krka National Park (p233) has eagles and migratory marsh birds.

Hvar Town (p278)

Plan Your Trip

Croatia's Islands

Croatia is often promoted as the 'Land of 1000 Islands', and while tourism marketing usually leans towards hyperbole, in this case they're rounding down. In fact Croatia has a total of 1244 islands and islets. If at all possible, aim to add at least a couple to your itinerary.

When to Go

May, Jun, Sep & Oct

The best time to visit is the less crowded shoulder season, although June and September are increasingly busy. The water should have warmed up enough to swim in May, and most places will have opened their doors.

Jul & Aug

The peak season offers the best weather, the most frequent ferry services and the most to do. On the downside, prices are at their highest and many places enforce minimum stays. The popular destinations get packed and the queues for the car ferries can be long.

Nov–Apr

The appeal of few tourists and cheap accommodation has to be weighed up against reduced ferry services and nearly everything being closed. The bigger towns have at least one *konoba* (tavern) and a cafe-bar that stays open, but most of the rest shut up shop, including hotels and museums. And it does get cold and windy.

Island-Hopping

Croatia's ferry network (p368) is efficient and extensive, making an island-hopping holiday a breeze. It's a relaxing way to travel – much less stressful than contending with traffic on the busy coastal highway – and the views on every route are impossibly scenic.

It makes sense to start your trip from either Dubrovnik or Split, as these vibrant Dalmatian cities have the busiest international airports, are major ferry hubs and are brilliant destinations in their own right. The easiest option is to fly into one and out of the other, limiting your trip to the islands in between; you could easily fill three blissful weeks this way, stopping on the Elafiti Islands, Mljet, Korčula, Vis, Hvar and Brač en route. Boats also link Split and Trogir, so you can easily add the World Heritage town, set on its own little island, to a water-based itinerary of essential Dalmatian sights.

Zadar and Rijeka are also possible starting points for an island-hopping holiday, and you could spend a week travelling in a large loop starting from either. From Zadar boats head north to the island of Lošinj, which is joined by a bridge to the island of Cres. From Cres ferries head to the island of Krk, which is joined by another bridge to the mainland, near Rijeka. From Rijeka you can hop south to the island of Rab and then on to the island of Pag, which is also joined by bridge to the mainland, near Zadar.

Be aware that there are no boats between Northern and Central Dalmatia. To link up the two halves of the coast, you'll need to factor in a three-hour bus trip between Split and Zadar.

Ferries fall into two categories: car ferries, operated by state-owned Jadrolinijia, and the much faster, passenger-only catamarans, operated by Jadrolinijia and a handful of private companies (p369). Boats are generally comfortable and well maintained. Most have cafe-bars and some, on the longer routes, have restaurants. The larger boats offer a combination of indoor and outdoor seating, with tables and power points for those wanting to work. Free wi-fi is the norm.

The frequency of services increases from May to September, peaking in July and August. An island-hopping holiday can still be undertaken in winter, but not all of the fast catamaran services operate, and those that do are prone to cancellations in bad weather. The slower car ferries are more dependable and these operate year-round, albeit with fewer sailings in winter.

Find Your Perfect Island

So how do you choose when faced with such a multitude of options? Whether you want to hunker down on just one island or you're aiming to slot several into a broader itinerary, here's a guide to get you started.

Best for Beaches

There are good swimming spots to be found on almost all of Croatia's major islands, so making a decision based on beaches isn't going to eliminate many contenders (Lastovo is one of the few islands that's disappointing on this front). That said, if we had to narrow it down to just the three best, we'd pick Vis, for its range of idyllic pebbly and sandy coves; Brač, for famous Zlatni Rat (p274) beach and further good options around Supetar; and Hvar, for pretty white-pebble coves like Dubovica and easy access to the pristine waters off the Pakleni Islands.

Best for Families

Families will find little to complain about on any Croatian island, but our favourites for all-age holidays are all in the Kvarner Gulf. The extremely shallow, sandy beaches near Lopar, at the northern end of the island of Rab (p202), are perfect for toddlers but less so for older kids. Krk (p194) is a better bet for the next age bracket up; there are waterslides at busy Baška beach and ziplines nearby. Lošinj (p183) is also a good option, offering beaches, family-friendly accommodation, a sea-turtle rescue centre and a marine education centre.

Best for Escaping the Crowds

Far-flung Lastovo (p332) doesn't get anywhere near the number of visitors of Croatia's other inhabited islands. Cres (p183) is also good on this front, especially if you stay in one of its tiny seaside or hilltop villages. Another great option is Mljet (p320). Most travellers head to the national park at its western end on day trips, leaving the equally verdant eastern end of the island much less explored. Then there are the 140 uninhabited islets of the Kornati (p233) archipelago, although you'll need a yacht to get there.

Best for History & Culture

Korčula Town (p327) stands out for its historic walled core and extraordinary cathedral. Mljet (p320) has ancient Roman ruins and legendary connections to both Odysseus and St Paul. Hvar (p277) has two historic walled towns and fields that still follow their ancient Greek boundaries. There are also gorgeous walled towns on Krk, Cres, Rab and Pag, and historic churches and monasteries almost everywhere.

Fishing on Rab Island (p202)

Best for Foodies

The obvious first choice is Pag (p216), famous across Croatia for its strongly flavoured sheep cheese and fragrant herb-fed lamb.

The age-old fishing traditions and relative isolation of Vis (p286) have made it one of the best places to try customary Dalmatian fare – particularly meals roasted under hot coals beneath the metal dome called a peka. Vis Town also has an exceptional contemporary restaurant.

Korčula (p326), too, has some excellent konobe (taverns) around the interior of the island. It's also famous for producing Croatia's best white wine, which can be sampled at cellar doors in Čara, Smokvica and Lumbarda, and in restaurants all over Croatia.

Best for Nightlife

Hardcore clubbers should look no further than Zrće on the island of Pag (p216), dubbed the 'Ibiza of Croatia' for its strip of highly rated beach clubs. The vibe is quite different at the other party hot spot: the eponymous capital of the island of Hvar (p278). Here backpackers and yachties merge at beach bars at sunset before con-

Zlatni Rat (p274), Bol

tinuing on to drink and dance at tiny bars in the old town. The seriously up-for-it can then catch a shuttle boat to the island of Marinkovac, in the Pakleni group, for all-night clubbing at Carpe Diem Beach (p284).

Best for Water Sports

As you might imagine, there's no shortage of watery activities to indulge in on any of the main islands. Worthy of a special mention is Brač (p272), which offers excellent windsurfing at Bol, along with parasailing, stand-up paddleboarding, sea kayaking, boating and diving. At Supetar, on the other side of the island, there's also wakeboarding, waterskiing and jet skiing.

Vis (p286) is great for sea kayaking, with many sea caves and coves, and even a hidden Yugoslav-era submarine base to explore. Thrill-seekers and show-offs should head to Krk (p194), where there's a centre offering mechanical cable-drawn wakeboarding and waterskiing. Both Vis and Krk also have experienced diving operators.

Best for Sailing

Yachties could spend many blissful days exploring the many rocky islets spread over 300 sq km of sea that forms Kornati National Park (p233). There are few signs of human activity here except for a convenient selection of seafood restaurants catering to the passing boats.

Lastovo (p332) is also exceptional, surrounded by the protected Lastovo Archipelago Nature Park, home to dolphins, sea turtles and shearwaters. The main island has safe bays to shelter in, most with at least one yacht-friendly restaurant with its own moorings.

Continuing the archipelago theme, don't miss the Pakleni Islands (p284) off Hvar. The clear, sheltered waters between the islands offer lagoon-like swimming, and here too there are excellent restaurants with marinas for customers.

Best for Hiking & Biking

There are brilliant trails on the island of Brač (p272), particularly those heading to the remarkable and remote Blaca Hermitage (p275) and to the extraordinary Vidova Gora (p275) lookout, at the island's highest point.

Little green Lastovo (p332) is wonderful for cycle touring; there aren't many cars or

LITTLEAOM/SHUTTERSTOCK ©

Top: Veliki Revelin Tower (p329), Korčula Town

Bottom: Stara Baška (p197), Krk

other tourists on this isolated island. It is hilly, however.

At the other end of the Adriatic, Rab (p202) has 100km of hiking trails and 80km of biking trails detailed on maps available from its tourist office. It's a great way to explore the diverse environment that has earned the island Geopark status.

Further excellent options can be found on Cres, Lošinj, Krk, Hvar, Vis and Mljet.

Best for Nature

An obvious contender is Mljet (p320), the greenest of the islands. Half of it is a national park but even the other half is densely forested and sparsely populated. The conjoined islands of Cres and Lošinj (p183) are home to a diverse array of wildlife, including griffon vultures and, in the surrounding waters, the Adriatic's only known resident dolphin population. The eastern end of Lošinj is now a protected dolphin reserve. Lastovo (p332) also has a marine reserve, aiming to preserve its dolphins, sea turtles, corals and rare sea snails.

TROFIMENKO NICKOLAI/SHUTTERSTOCK ©

Dolphin swimming in the Adriatic Sea

Best for Camping

The islands of the Kvarner Gulf are particularly well served by campgrounds. Cres (p183) has the best selection, with excellent sites in Cres Town, Valun, Lubenice, Martinšcica and Osor. Krk (p194) is also good on this front, with notable options for families and for naturists.

Way down south, the happiest campers can be found on Korčula (p326), where there's a selection of small, family-run plots; our favourite is hidden away at the northwestern tip, past Vela Luka.

Best for Backpackers

Unusually, the most glamorous of all of Croatia's island locations also has its best selection of hostels. Backpackers in Hvar Town (p278) are truly spoilt for choice, although the prices in the hostels are substantially higher here than elsewhere. Not at all coincidentally, Hvar also has the best bars – but be warned: hefty fines have been instituted for drunken behaviour and public nudity.

The next-best option is the island of Brač (p272), which has a great hostel in Bol and a sociable but rough-around-the-edges one in Supetar.

Best for Luxury

Rubbing shoulders with the backpackers in Hvar (p277) are the well-heeled travellers who keep the town's pricey restaurants and plush resorts afloat. Nearby Brač (p272) is also well served by luxury accommodation and restaurants. But for the best selection of high-end hotels, the island of Krk (p194) takes the prize, with terrific options in Malinska, Krk Town, Vrbnik and Baška.

Best for Day Trippers

Lokrum (p296), just out of Dubrovnik, is easily Croatia's favourite day-trip island, its rocky beaches, gardens and forested paths offering some relief from the tourism overload of the old town. Also near Dubrovnik, the three main Elafiti Islands – Koločep (p318), Lopud (p319) and Šipan (p319) – are packaged together on various 'three islands and a fish picnic' tours.

Equally brilliant is Veli Brijun, the largest of Istria's Brijuni archipelago, easily visited from Pula or Rovinj. Once an exclusive retreat for Tito and visiting dignitaries, it's now the most accessible part of the Brijuni Islands National Park.

Croatia's Islands

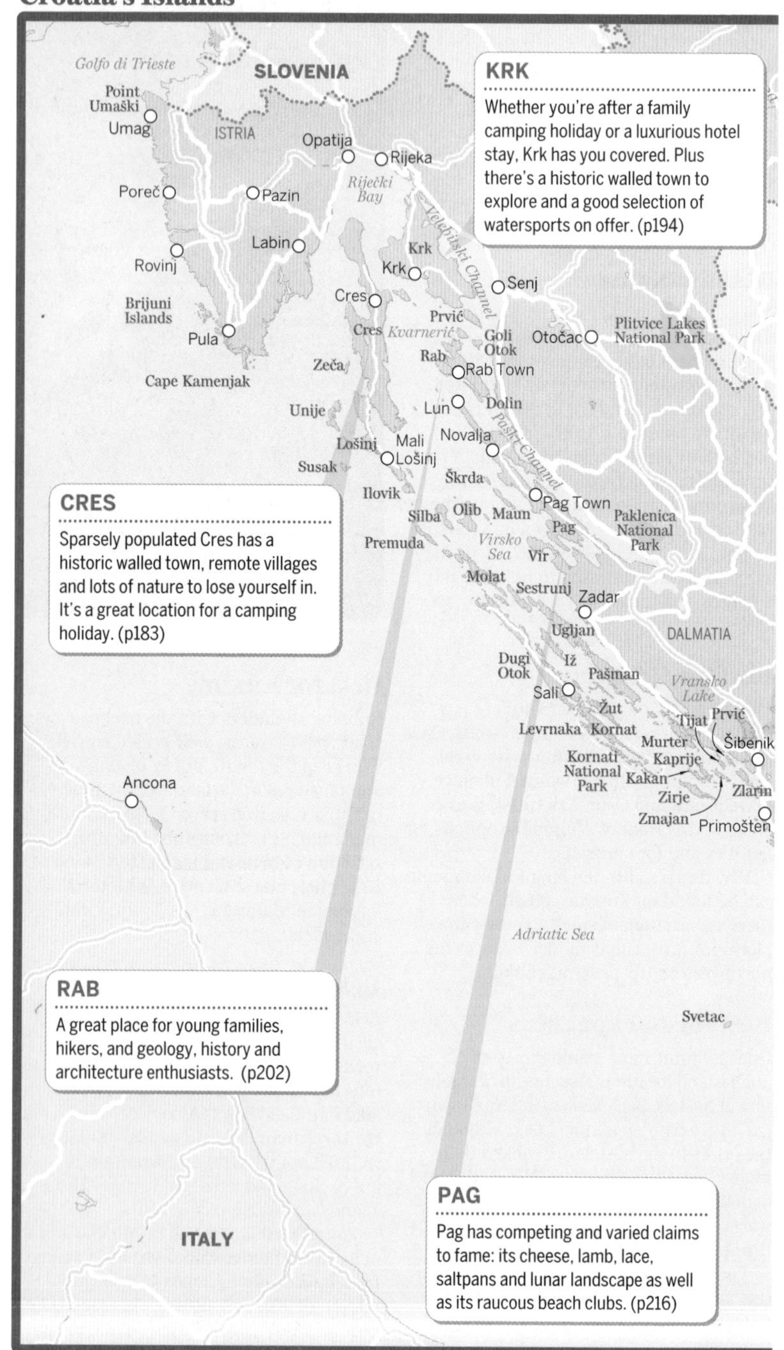

KRK

Whether you're after a family camping holiday or a luxurious hotel stay, Krk has you covered. Plus there's a historic walled town to explore and a good selection of watersports on offer. (p194)

CRES

Sparsely populated Cres has a historic walled town, remote villages and lots of nature to lose yourself in. It's a great location for a camping holiday. (p183)

RAB

A great place for young families, hikers, and geology, history and architecture enthusiasts. (p202)

PAG

Pag has competing and varied claims to fame: its cheese, lamb, lace, saltpans and lunar landscape as well as its raucous beach clubs. (p216)

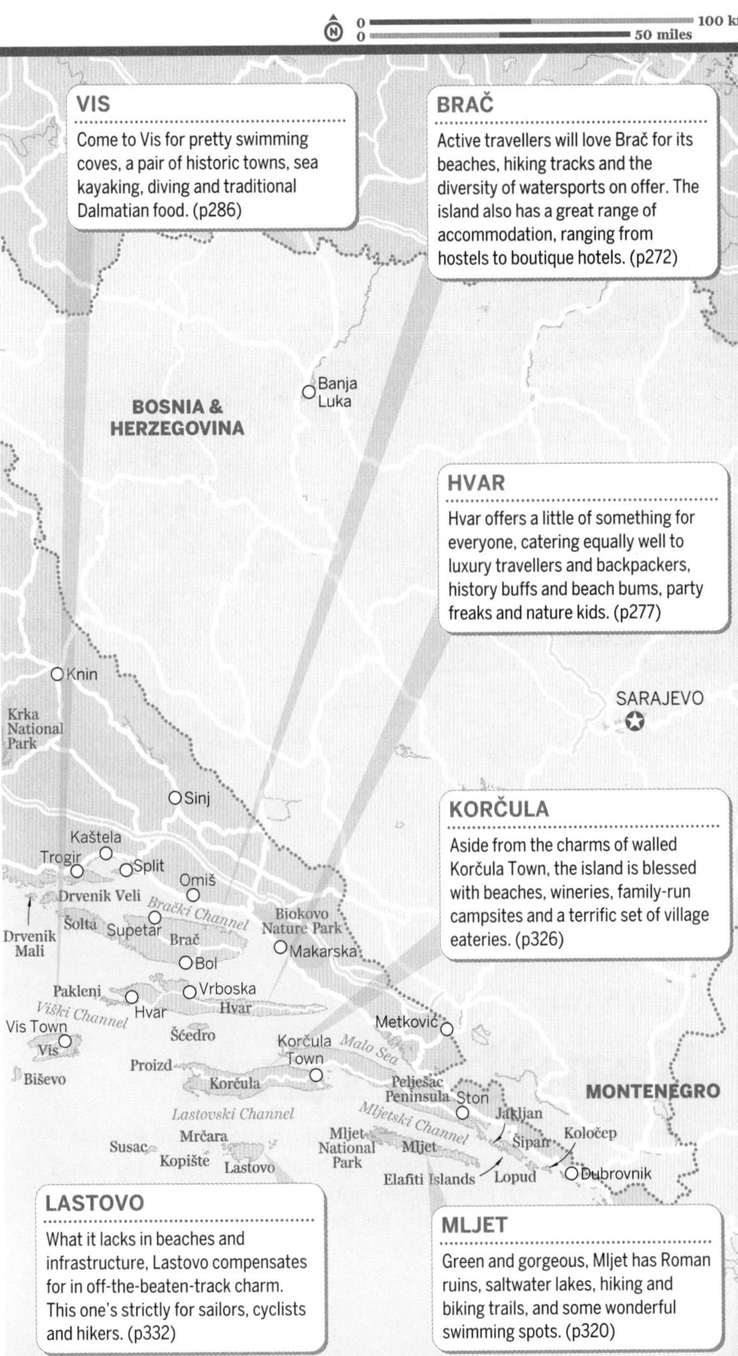
0 100 km
0 50 miles
VIS
Come to Vis for pretty swimming coves, a pair of historic towns, sea kayaking, diving and traditional Dalmatian food. (p286)
BRAČ
Active travellers will love Brač for its beaches, hiking tracks and the diversity of watersports on offer. The island also has a great range of accommodation, ranging from hostels to boutique hotels. (p272)
HVAR
Hvar offers a little of something for everyone, catering equally well to luxury travellers and backpackers, history buffs and beach bums, party freaks and nature kids. (p277)
KORČULA
Aside from the charms of walled Korčula Town, the island is blessed with beaches, wineries, family-run campsites and a terrific set of village eateries. (p326)
LASTOVO
What it lacks in beaches and infrastructure, Lastovo compensates for in off-the-beaten-track charm. This one's strictly for sailors, cyclists and hikers. (p332)
MLJET
Green and gorgeous, Mljet has Roman ruins, saltwater lakes, hiking and biking trails, and some wonderful swimming spots. (p320)
BOSNIA & HERZEGOVINA
Banja Luka
SARAJEVO
MONTENEGRO
Knin
Krka National Park
Sinj
Kaštela
Trogir
Split
Omiš
Drvenik Veli
Drvenik Mali
Šolta
Supetar
Brački Channel
Brač
Bol
Biokovo Nature Park
Makarska
Pakleni
Vrboska
Hvar
Viški Channel
Vis Town
Vis
Šćedro
Biševo
Proizd
Korčula Town
Korčula
Malo Sea
Metković
Pelješac Peninsula
Ston
Lastovski Channel
Mljetski Channel
Jakljan
Šipan
Koločep
Mrčara
Susac
Kopište
Lastovo
Mljet National Park
Mljet
Elafiti Islands
Lopud
Dubrovnik

Sea Organ (p223), Zadar

Plan Your Trip

Family Travel

With safe beaches, hiking and biking tracks to suit all abilities, a clutch of interactive museums, and lots of ancient towns and fortresses for would-be knights and princesses to explore, Croatia offers entertainment aplenty for those with children in tow.

Best Regions for Kids

Northern Dalmatia

Kids are fascinated by Zadar's nature-powered *Sun Salutation* and *Sea Organ*. Šibenik hosts an excellent children's festival.

Dubrovnik & Southern Dalmatia

Offers lots of beach action and unique experiences; let the little ones off the leash in the car-free old towns of Dubrovnik and Korčula.

Split & Central Dalmatia

Wander Diocletian's Palace and then head to the beaches of the Makarska Riviera.

Istria

Poreč and Rovinj are great bases for exploring nearby caves, dinosaur parks and beaches.

Kvarner

Toddler-friendly beaches on Rab Island, and beaches for all the family on Krk, Cres and Lošinj.

Zagreb

Ride the funicular, check out the many museums, get active at Jarun and Bundek, and hike up to the mountain peak of Sljeme.

Inland Croatia

Savour Croatian country life at Vuglec Breg and Grešna Gorica, tour the interactive Neanderthal museum in Krapina and visit medieval castles.

Croatia for Kids

Croatia has a lot of open spaces, playgrounds aplenty and pedestrian zones where there's no danger of traffic. Most seaside towns have a *riva* (seafront promenade) away from the water's edge that's perfect for strolling and letting the toddlers run around.

There are beaches galore, although some of what are referred to as 'beaches' are rocky indentations with steep drop-offs. Many of the sandy beaches are extremely shallow: perfect for toddlers but not so great for the teens. The numerous pebbly beaches tend to offer better swimming.

Keep in mind that some of Croatia's smaller seaside towns can be too quiet for fun-seeking teenagers. They (and you in turn) will be a lot happier in the more happening coastal destinations where there are buzzy cafes and seasonal funfair rides.

Children's discounts are widely available for everything from museum admissions to hotel accommodation. The cut-off age is often nine, when student discounts kick in. Many attractions offer free entry for the little ones.

Children's Highlights

Beaches

Baška, Krk Island (p198) A 2km-long crescent of beach with a little water park at one end.

Cres & Lošinj Islands (p183) Lots of family-friendly campsites set right by the beach.

Crveni Otok, Rovinj (p142) Two connected islets awash with pebble beaches.

Lopar, Rab Island (p207) Shallow, sandy beaches that are perfect for toddlers.

Mljet National Park, Mljet Island (p321) The smaller of the saltwater lakes is warm and perfect for babies.

Day Trips

Krka National Park (p233) Have a dip in a cool lake underneath cascading waterfalls.

Plitvice Lakes National Park (p211) Stroll along the paths and take in the turquoise lakes, towering waterfalls and dense forests.

Lokrum (p296) Escape to this forested island and take the little ones for a swim in the saltwater lake.

Mt Medvednica (p103) Tire the tweens out on the verdant tracks of Zagreb's favourite mountain.

Sights

Museum of the Krapina Neanderthal, Krapina (p107) Get up close and personal with our ancestors' neighbours.

Sun Salutation, Zadar (p223) Come sunset, tots have a ball racing around this marvellous light display.

Kumrovec Staro Selo Museum, Zagorje (p102) An entertaining slice of traditional village life.

Istralandia (p153) Shoot down the slides and ride the waves in this big water park northeast of Novigrad.

Museum of Illusion, Zagreb (p78) Full of optical illusions, mirrors and holograms.

Planning

When to Go

➡ The coastal city of Šibenik hosts a renowned **International Children's Festival** (www.mdf-sibenik.com) in late June/early July, with craft workshops, music, dance, children's film and theatre, puppets and parades.

➡ July and August coincide with the European school holidays, so they tend to have the most laid on for kids.

➡ If you'd prefer fewer people and lower prices, June and September are the best times, as the sea is warm enough for swimming and the days are sunny.

Lotrščak Tower and funicular railway (p69), Zagreb

Accommodation

➡ Consider renting a private apartment – they're usually cheaper than a hotel room and give you more flexibility. Make sure you ask for specifics about the facilities – whether there's air-conditioning, a full kitchen and laundry facilities, and how far away the beach is, for example.

➡ Hotels may have cots, but numbers are usually limited and sometimes there's a surcharge. Kids under three often stay for free, while those under nine get a considerable discount.

➡ Most properties in Croatia are family friendly but few are family specialists. Of those, the best are Rovinj's Amarin Family Hotel (p142), Zadar's **Club Funimation Borik** (☎023-555 600; www.borik.falkensteiner.com; Majstora Radovana 7; r incl full board from 1400KN; P ❄ @ 🛜 ≋) and Mali Lošinj's **Hotel Vespera** (☎051-667 300; www.losinj-hotels.com; Sunčana Uvala bb; s/d from 1050/1400KN; P ❄ 🛜 ≋).

What to Pack

Don't stress too much about the packing as anything you forget can almost always be purchased after you arrive. Beach gear is a must, including sunhats and plastic water shoes to prevent sea-urchin injuries.

Before You Go

➡ Children under five years old are required to travel in a suitable child seat, so make sure you're very clear with your hire-car company about your needs before you turn up.

➡ No vaccinations are required for Croatia.

Plan Your Trip

Eat & Drink Like a Local

Croatian food echoes the varied cultures that have influenced the country over its history. There's a sharp divide between the Italian-style cuisine along the coast and the flavours of Hungary, Austria and Turkey in the continental parts. Regardless of the region you'll find tasty food made from fresh, seasonal ingredients.

Food Experiences

Although Croats are not overly experimental when it comes to food, they're particularly passionate about it. They'll spend hours discussing the quality of the lamb or the first-grade fish, and why it overshadows all food elsewhere. Foodie culture is on the rise here, inspired by the slow-food movement, which places emphasis on fresh, local and seasonal ingredients and the joy of slow-paced dining. The Istria and Kvarner regions have quickly shot to the top of the gourmet ladder, but other places aren't lagging far behind. Wine and olive-oil production have been revived, and there's now a network of signposted routes around the country celebrating these precious commodities.

A new breed of restaurants offers the opportunity to spend hours feasting on slow-food delicacies or savouring the innovative concoctions of up-and-coming chefs. There is a limit to what the local crowd can afford to pay, so restaurants still cluster in the middle of the price spectrum – few are unbelievably cheap, and few are exorbitantly expensive. Whatever your budget, you're unlikely to get a truly bad meal anywhere in Croatia. Another plus is that, in the warmer months, alfresco dining is the norm.

The Year in Food

While local food and wine festivals go into full swing come autumn, there's never a bad time to chow down in Croatia.

Spring (March–May)

Asparagus comes into season in Istria and gets its own festival. Korčula restaurants show off signature dishes in April and Istrian winemakers throw open their cellar doors in late May.

Summer (June–August)

Dine on freshly caught seafood by the sea, and beat the heat with gelato and cocktails.

Autumn (September–November)

Food festivals showcase truffles (in Istria), homemade *rakija* (grappa; also in Istria), chestnuts (in Kvarner) and wine (just about everywhere). Don't miss Dubrovnik's Good Food Festival in October.

Winter (December–February)

Time for hearty Christmas and Carnival treats.

Meals of a Lifetime

Pelegrini (p238) A celebration of Mediterranean cuisine on the old streets of Šibenik.

Restaurant 360° (p310) Dubrovnik's finest offers contemporary dining perched right on the famous city walls.

Meneghetti (p138) Istria is Croatia's premier foodie region, and this winery restaurant is Istria's best.

Konoba Marjan (p255) This unassuming Split tavern is arguably the best place in Dalmatia for traditional seafood dishes.

Cheap Treats

For a taste of local fast food, you can snack on *ćevapčići* (small spicy meatballs of minced beef, lamb or pork), *pljeskavica* (an ex-Yugo version of a hamburger patty), *ražnjići* (small chunks of pork grilled on a skewer) or *burek* (pastry stuffed with ground meat, spinach or cheese). These are available at fast-food outlets.

Regional Specialities

Zagreb & Zagorje

Zagreb and northwestern Croatia favour the kind of hearty meat dishes you might find in Vienna. Juicy *pečenje* (spit-roasted and baked meat) showcases *janjetina* (lamb), *svinjetina* (pork) and *patka* (duck), often accompanied by *mlinci* (baked noodles) or *pečeni krumpir* (roast potatoes). Meat slow-cooked under a *peka* (domed baking lid) is especially delicious, but needs to be ordered in advance at many restaurants.

COOKING COURSES

Cooking courses in Croatia are becoming increasingly popular. **Culinary Croatia** (www.culinary-croatia.com) is a great source of information, and offers a variety of cooking classes and culinary and wine tours, mainly in Dalmatia. Other good options include Kuhaona (p81) in Zagreb and Eat Istria (p133), based near Pula.

Purica (turkey) with *mlinci* is an institution on Zagreb and Zagorje menus, along with *zagrebački odrezak* (veal schnitzel stuffed with ham and cheese, then crumbed and fried) – another calorie-laden speciality. *Štrukli* (a type of cheese-filled dumpling) is a particular favourite of the Zagorje region. Another mainstay is *sir i vrhnje* (fresh cottage cheese and cream), bought at local markets and paired with bread.

For those with a sweet tooth, *palačinke* (thin pancakes) with various fillings and toppings are a common dessert.

Slavonia

Spicier than the food of other regions, Slavonian cuisine uses liberal amounts of paprika and garlic. The Hungarian influence is most prevalent here in the northeast: many typical dishes, such as *čobanac* (a meat stew), are in fact versions of *gulaš* (goulash). The nearby Drava River provides fresh fish, such as carp, pike and perch, which is stewed in a paprika sauce and served with noodles in a dish known as *fiš paprikaš*. Another speciality is *šaran u rašljama* (carp on a forked branch), roasted in its own oils over an open fire. The region's sausages are particularly renowned, especially *kulen*, a paprika-flavoured sausage cured over a period of nine months and usually served with cottage cheese, peppers, tomatoes and often *turšija* (pickled vegetables).

Istria

Istrian cuisine has been attracting international foodies in recent years for its long gastronomic tradition, fresh ingredients and unique specialities. Typical dishes include *maneštra* (thick vegetable-and-bean soup similar to minestrone), *fuži* (hand-rolled pasta often served with *tartufi*, truffles, or *divljač*, game meat) and *fritaja* (omelette often served with seasonal veggies, such as wild asparagus). Truffles find their way into most dishes including, in more adventurous establishments, ice cream and chocolate cake.

Look for dishes featuring *boškarin*, an indigenous species of ox. Thin slices of dry-cured Istrian *pršut* (prosciutto) – also excellent in Dalmatia – are often on the appetiser list; it's expensive because of the long hours and personal attention involved in smoking the meat. Istrian olive oil is highly rated and has won international awards. The tourist board has marked an olive-oil route along which you can visit local growers, tasting oils at the source. The best seasonal ingredients include white truffles, picked in autumn, and wild asparagus, harvested in spring.

Kvarner & Dalmatia

Coastal cuisine in Kvarner and Dalmatia is typically Mediterranean, using a lot of olive oil, garlic, flat-leaf parsley, bay leaves and all manner of seafood. Favourites include baked whole fish, fried *lignje* (squid, sometimes stuffed with cheese and prosciutto) and *hobotnica* (octopus, either carpaccio, in a salad or cooked under a *peka*).

Meals often begin with a first course of pasta or *rižot* (risotto) topped with seafood. For a special appetiser, try *paški sir,* a pungent hard sheep cheese from the island of Pag. Lamb from Cres and Pag is deemed Croatia's best; they feed on fresh herbs, which gives the meat a distinct flavour.

Other Dalmatian favourites include *brodet* (a slightly spicy seafood stew served with polenta; also known as *brodetto, brudet* or *brujet,* depending on which part of the coast you're from) and *pašticada* (beef stewed in wine, prunes and spices and served with gnocchi). The most typical side dish is *blitva* (silverbeet served with slightly mushy potatoes and drenched in olive oil and garlic).

When & Where to Eat

When to Eat

Throughout the former Yugoslavia, the *doručak* (breakfast) of the people was *burek* (pastry stuffed with meat, spinach or cheese). Modern Croats have opted for a lighter start to their day, usually just coffee and a pastry with some yoghurt and fresh fruit. If you're staying in hostels or private accommodation, the easiest thing to do is to get coffee at a cafe and pastries from a bakery; an English-style cooked breakfast is hard to come by. If you're staying in a hotel you'll be served a cold buffet breakfast that includes cornflakes, bread, yoghurt, a selection of cold meat and cheese, and powdered 'juice'. More upmarket

OLGA ILINICH/SHUTTERSTOCK ©

Burek

hotels offer extensive hot and cold buffets, sometimes with a cooked-to-order omelette or bacon and eggs.

Restaurants open for *ručak* (lunch) around noon and usually serve continuously until midnight, which can be a major convenience if you're arriving in town at an odd hour or just feel like spending more time at the beach. Croats tend to eat either an earlier *marenda* or *gablec* (cheap, filling lunch) or a large, late lunch. Fruit and vegetables from the market and a selection of cheese, bread and ham from a grocery store can make a healthy picnic lunch. If you ask nicely, the person behind the deli counter at supermarkets or grocery stores will usually make a *sir* (cheese) or *pršut* (prosciutto) sandwich (*sendvič,* in Croatian) and you only pay the regular price of the ingredients.

Večera (dinner) is typically a light affair, but most restaurants have adapted their schedules to the needs of tourists, who tend to load up at night. Few Croats can afford to eat out regularly; when they do, it's likely to be a large family outing on Saturday night or Sunday afternoon.

Seafood risotto

Where to Eat

When eating out in Croatia, it pays to book ahead at the very top places, especially during the peak summer season and on weekends. Otherwise, it's almost always fine just to turn up.

Restoran Restaurants are at top of the food chain, generally presenting a more formal dining experience and a decent wine list.

Konoba or gostionica Usually a traditional family-run tavern – the produce may come from the family garden.

Kavana A cafe-bar where you can nurse your coffee for hours and, if you're lucky, have cakes and ice cream.

Slastičarna A pastry shop that serves cakes, strudels and sometimes ice cream or coffee.

Vegetarians & Vegans

A useful phrase is *'Ja ne jedem meso'* ('I don't eat meat'), but even then you may be served soup with bits of bacon swimming in it. That is slowly changing and vegetarians are making inroads in Croatia, but changes are mostly happening in the larger cities. Osijek, Zagreb, Poreč and Split now have dedicated vegetarian restaurants, while Dubrovnik has a vegan one. Some restaurants in the big cities are beginning to offer vegetarian menus – although many seem to view salt as the most vital ingredient of their dishes.

Vegetarians may have a harder time in the north (Zagorje) and the east (Slavonia), where traditional fare has meat as its main focus. Specialities that don't use meat include *maneštra od bobića* (bean and fresh maize soup), *juha od krumpira na zagorski način* (Zagorje potato soup) and *štrukli* (cheesy dumplings). Along the coast you'll find plenty of meat-free pizza, pasta and risotto dishes.

Wine

Wine from Croatia may be a novelty to international consumers but *vino* has been an embedded part of the region's lifestyle for more than 25 centuries. Today the tradition is undergoing a renaissance in the hands of a new generation of winemakers with a focus on preserving indigenous varietals and revitalising ancestral estates.

Quality is rising, exports are increasing and the wines are garnering global awards and winning the affections of worldly wine lovers thirsty for authentic stories and unique terroirs.

Croatia is roughly divided into four winemaking regions: Slavonia and the Croatian Uplands in the continental zone, with a cooler climate; and Istria/Kvarner and Dalmatia along the Adriatic, with a Mediterranean climate. Within each lie multiple subregions *(vinogorje)*, with 16 distinct areas recognised as Protected Designations of Origin *(Zaštićena oznaka izvornosti)* under EU regulations; wines produced using the specific grape varieties permitted in these geographically defined appellations are marked ZOI on the label.

Continental Zone

White varieties such as *graševina, traminac,* pinot blanc, chardonnay and sauvignon blanc dominate the continental zone. Styles range from fruity, mildly aromatic, refreshing wines from cool northern areas to rich, savoury, age-worthy whites from warmer Slavonia, as well as luscious dessert *(predikatno)* wines. Kutjevo is a particular sweet spot for vine growing; many wineries are located in the hamlet.

Ensconced in the pastoral hills of Međimurje, Plešivica and Zagorje, the Croatian Uplands is a land of crisp, food-friendly whites (although pinot noir does well in spots). Beside *graševina* and native *škrlet,* international varieties like chardonnay, pinot blanc, pinot gris and sauvignon blanc thrive. For ice wine *(ledeno vino)*, a coveted bottle of Bodren makes a delicious souvenir.

Coastal Zone

Crowning the northern Adriatic coast is Istria, home of *malvazija istarska,* a variety capable of award-winning wines with diverse profiles: lean and light to unctuous and sweet; crisp and unoaked to acacia-wood-aged and orange wines. Istria also boasts a fiery signature red: *teran.*

Just below Istria is Kvarner, home of *žlahtina,* a seafood-friendly white found in abundance on Krk.

Going south, the rugged beauty of Dalmatia, with its island vineyards (Hvar, Vis, Brač, Korčula), fosters a fascinating array of indigenous grape varieties that prosper in the Mediterranean climate, yielding full-bodied wines of rich character. Here *plavac mali,* scion of zinfandel *(crljenik kašteljanski)* and the obscure *dobričić,* is king of reds. Wines labelled 'Dingač' are *plavac mali* from a specific mountainside high above the sea on the Pelješac Peninsula that's widely regarded as producing Croatia's best reds. Production is tiny and good examples command premium prices.

Other indigenous varieties worth seeking are *babić* (red), *pošip* (an elegant white, the best of which is from the island of Korčula), *grk* (a fruit-driven white, exclusively produced in Lumbarda on Korčula) and *malvasija* (a white from the Kvarner region, near Dubrovnik, not to be confused with *malvazija* with a 'z'). For easy-chair quaffing, the lovely rosés of Dalmatia are perfect for lazy Mediterranean days.

WINE QUALITY

Croatian wines are classified and labelled according to three levels of quality: *stolno vino* (table wine), *kvalitetno vino* (quality wine) and *vrhunsko vino* (premium quality wine). Varietals from a protected appellation are marked ZOI *(Zaštićena oznaka izvornosti)*.

Regions at a Glance

Zagreb

Cafes
Architecture
Food

Cafe Culture

There's more than a dash of Vienna to Zagreb's cafe vibe, with a pinch of Venice and Turkey added to the mix. For many, the peak of the social week is the coffee-sipping and people-watching ritual known as *špica*, which happens on warm-weather Saturday mornings.

Architectural Diversity

Zagreb is an architectural onion, with a medieval centre ringed by a Habsburg and then a Socialist layer. A short stroll can reveal Gothic churches, grand 19th-century administrative buildings, secessionist town houses, art deco hotels and brutalist apartment blocks. Colourful street art brightens up the greyest corners.

Modern Croatian Cuisine

On the food front, there is plenty to explore in Croatia's capital, where the culinary scene has diversified in recent years. A handful of destination restaurants showcase Croatia's unique style of cooking, prepared with high-quality ingredients from around the country.

p65

Inland Croatia

Architecture
Wildlife
Scenery

Castles

Fairy-tale castles dot the wooded hills of this bucolic region. Neo-Gothic Trakošćan offers insight into the life of former Croatian nobility, while the formidable Veliki Tabor comes complete with towers, turrets and other castle trimmings. There are further examples in Varaždin, Varaždinske Toplice, Vukovar and Ilok.

Birdwatching

One of Europe's most important wetlands, Kopački Rit Nature Park occupies the floodplain where the Danube meets the Drava. Famed for its diverse birdlife, the park is best visited during the spring or autumn migrations.

Rural Vistas

The pretty pastoral panoramas of Zagorje's vineyard-covered hills and dense forests, and Slavonia's verdant fields and gingerbread cottages are the stuff of storybooks. Savour traditional Croatian farm life as it unfolds away from the tourist hullabaloo down south.

p99

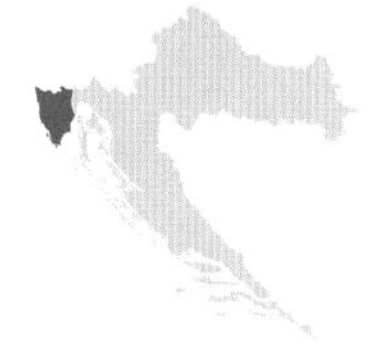

Istria

Food
Architecture
Coast

Istrian Cuisine

Indulge in *la dolce vita* Istrian-style, feasting on meals prepared in creative ways using top-quality local ingredients. From white truffles and wild asparagus to award-winning olive oils and wines, dining and wining is a highlight of any stay in Istria, Croatia's most foodie-friendly place.

Historic Buildings

Istria's hotchpotch of architecture includes a world-famous Roman amphitheatre and a Byzantine basilica, along with Venetian-style town houses and medieval hilltop towns, all packed tightly and prettily into one small peninsula.

Beaches

From pine-fringed, activity-packed pebbly beaches a hop and a skip from Pula, Rovinj and Poreč, to the wild landscapes of Cape Kamenjak and its string of secluded coves, Istria has some wonderful beaches – just no sandy ones.

p127

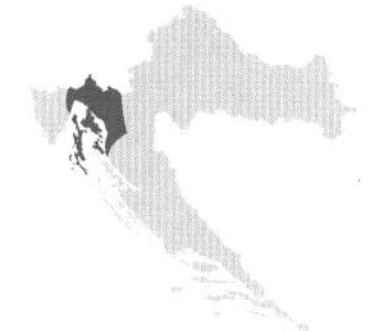

Kvarner

Architecture
Nature
Food

Medieval Towns

Krk Town has a beautifully preserved medieval core, while the small but perfectly formed Rab Town features a string of historic churches and bell towers. The town houses in Cres Town, Veli Lošinj and Mali Lošinj all show strong Venetian influences.

Wildlife

The island of Lošinj boasts worthy wildlife projects: in Veli Lošinj you'll find a fascinating Adriatic dolphin research centre, while up in Mali Lošinj there's a centre devoted to rescuing sea turtles. Brown bears roam freely in Risnjak National Park and Učka Nature Park.

Gourmet Villages

The tiny villages of Volosko and Kastav, between Opatija and Rijeka, are gastronomic hotbeds of Croatian cooking – both traditional and modern – with a clutch of high-quality, atmospheric *konobe* (taverns) and restaurants.

p171

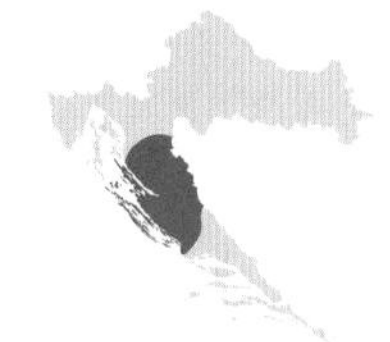

Northern Dalmatia

Nature
Cities
Sailing

Mountains & Lakes

Most visitors come to Dalmatia for the coast, but this region also has a highly appealing hinterland. Krka and Plitvice National Parks showcase lovely lakes and exquisite waterfalls. Head to Paklenica for soaring mountains and great hiking.

Living Historic Cities

Northern Dalmatia's two cities both offer culture and history while being far from touristy. Šibenik arguably has Croatia's most elegant cathedral and a remarkable old quarter, while the walled town of Zadar offers up Roman ruins, intriguing sights, hip bars and restaurants.

Island-Dotted Waters

See the Mediterranean as it looked to the ancients, sailing between the isles of Kornati National Park, the largest and densest archipelago in the Adriatic, with 140 uninhabited islands.

p209

Split & Central Dalmatia

Coast
Architecture
Activities

Beaches

From fun-filled Bačvice, Split's adored city beach, to horn-shaped Zlatni Rat on Brač Island, to the adorable pebbly and sandy coves of Vis Island, Central Dalmatia has some of Croatia's best beaches – both popular and off the well-worn trail.

Ancient Town Centres

Two Unesco World Heritage Sites sit a quick drive from one another in Central Dalmatia: the buzzing Roman-era quarter that is Diocletian's Palace in Split, and the architectural medley of Trogir's compact old walled town, set on its own tiny island.

Outdoor Pursuits

Be it sailing, mountain biking, sea kayaking, diving, hiking, rafting, rock climbing, zip-lining or windsurfing, active travellers will find plenty of distraction in Central Dalmatia's varied environment.

p241

Dubrovnik & Southern Dalmatia

History
Nature
Wine

Old Walled Towns

One of the world's most evocatively situated and historic cities, Dubrovnik is a dream to look at, a delight to explore and a wrench to leave. Much smaller but almost as gorgeous, Korčula Town and Ston offer similarly affecting experiences.

Islands

The thinly populated, pine-forested islands of Mljet and Korčula are rightfully acclaimed for their natural beauty and beaches. But don't neglect little Lokrum and the lovely Elafitis.

Dalmatian Varietals

The Pelješac Peninsula is Croatia's premier wine region. Try the rich, vibrant, local red *plavac mali* while visiting vineyards in the prestigious appellations of Postup and Dingač. Neighbouring Korčula is renowned for its white wines from the *pošip* and *grk* grapes, while the Konavle region, south of Dubrovnik, has its own white, *malvasija*.

p291

On the Road

AT A GLANCE

POPULATION
803,700

ELEVATION
158m

BEST COFFEE CULTURE
Quahwa (p89)

BEST CROATIAN RESTAURANT
Heritage (p87)

BEST FUNICULAR RAILWAY
Opposite Lotrščak Tower (p69)

WHEN TO GO

Apr
Great for hotel deals and the warmer weather has locals flocking back to pavement cafes.

Jul
Join the crowds soaking up the buzzing summer energy and street festivals.

Dec
One of Europe's best Christmas markets adds winter-wonderland sparkle to the city centre.

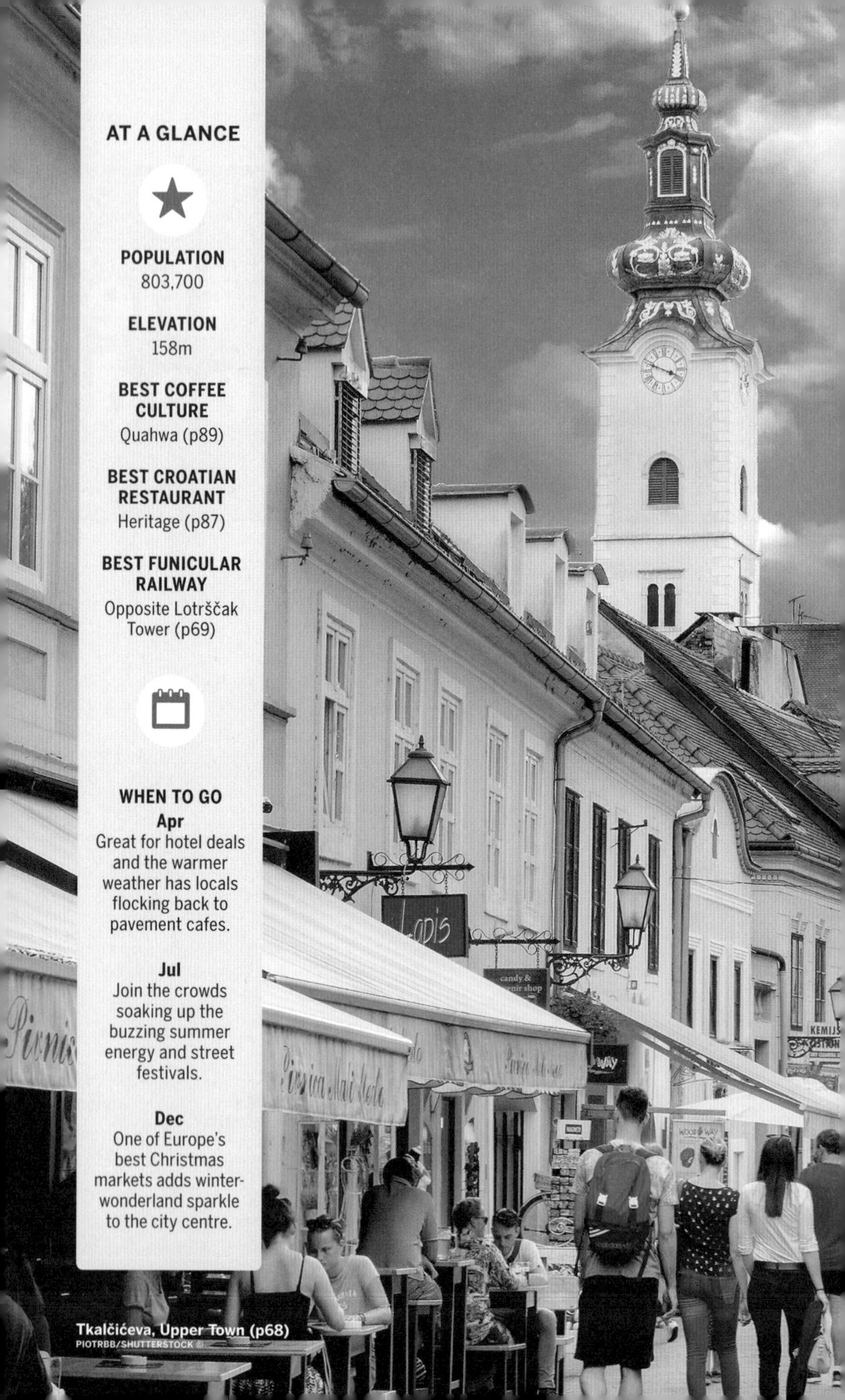

Tkalčićeva, Upper Town (p68)

Zagreb

This city is made for strolling. Wander through the Upper Town's red-roof and cobblestone glory, peppered with church spires. Crane your neck to see the domes and ornate upper-floor frippery of the Lower Town's mash-up of secessionist, neobaroque and art deco buildings. Search out the grittier pockets of town where ugly-bland concrete walls have been transformed into colourful murals by local street artists. This city rewards those on foot. Afterwards, do as the locals do and head to a cafe. The cafe culture here is just one facet of this city's vibrant street life, egged on by a year-round swag of events that bring music, pop-up markets and food stalls to the plazas and parks. Even when there's nothing on, the centre thrums with youthful energy so it's no surprise that Croatia's capital is now bringing in the city-break crowd. Zagreb is the little city that could.

INCLUDES

Zagreb Highlights

1 Katarinin Trg (p69) Soaking up the red-roof views from this plaza before strolling the Upper Town lanes to explore Zagreb's most ancient section.

2 Mirogoj (p68) Marvelling at this cemetery's grand architecture and highly idiosyncratic tombs and crypts.

3 Tkalčićeva (p88) Putting your feet up with a coffee or cocktail along this cafe-bar pedestrian strip while watching the world promenade by.

4 Dolac Market (p69) Diving into the bustle and buzz of Zagreb's central produce market.

5 Croatian Museum of Naïve Art (p68) Discovering the major works of Croatia's homegrown art genre.

6 Museum of Broken Relationships (p68) Tapping into the weird, wonderful and painful depths of the human condition amid the exhibits.

7 Craft beer (p76) Bar-hopping along Opatovina to delve into the city's craft-beer scene.

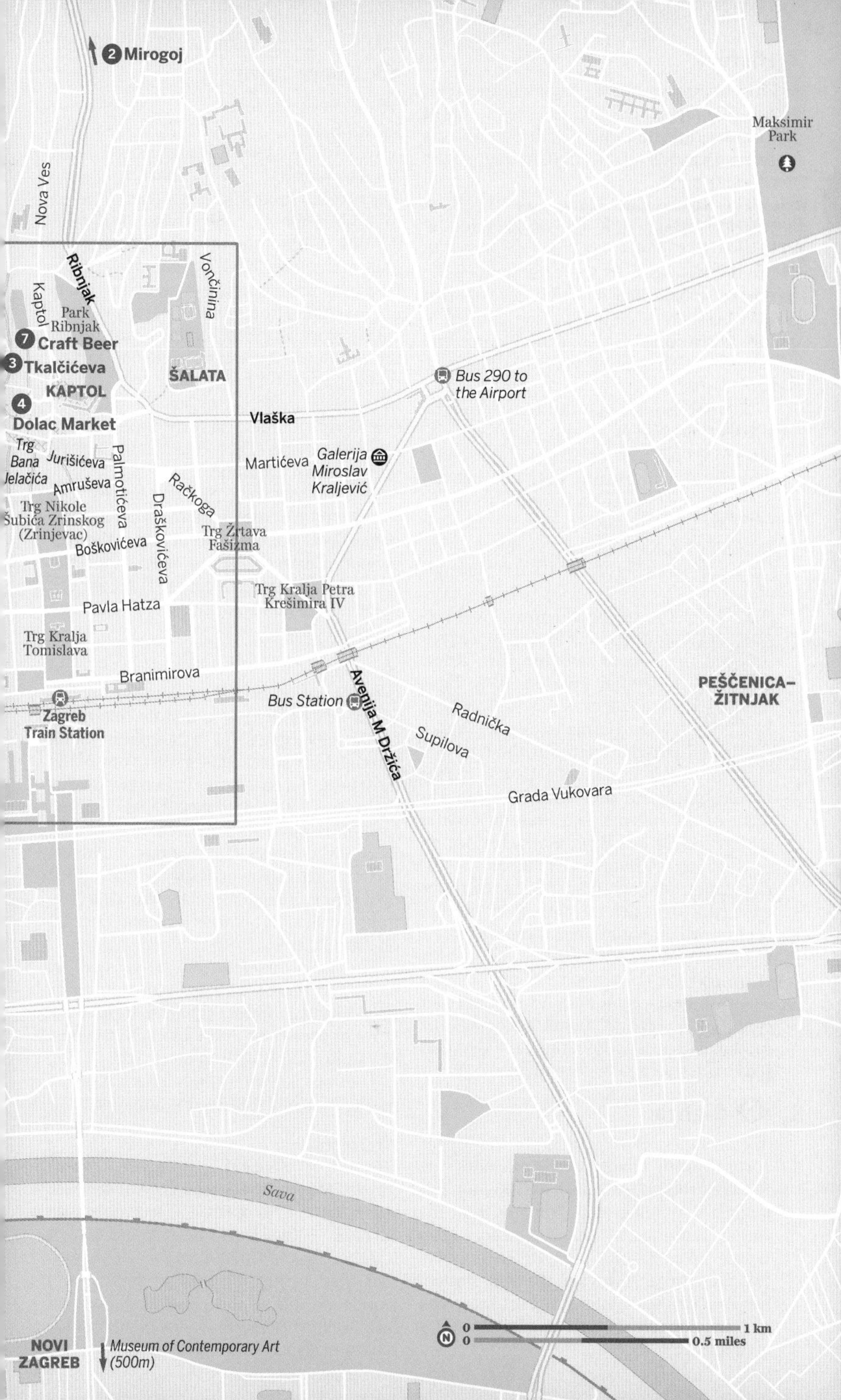

2 Mirogoj
Nova Ves
Maksimir Park
Ribnjak
Vončinina
Kaptol
Park Ribnjak
7 Craft Beer
3 Tkalčićeva
ŠALATA
KAPTOL
4 Dolac Market
Bus 290 to the Airport
Vlaška
Trg Bana Jelačića
Jurišićeva
Palmotićeva
Martićeva
Galerija Miroslav Kraljević
Amruševa
Račkoga
Trg Nikole Šubića Zrinskog (Zrinjevac)
Draškovićeva
Trg Žrtava Fašizma
Boškovićeva
Trg Kralja Petra Krešimira IV
Pavla Hatza
Trg Kralja Tomislava
Branimirova
Avenija M Držića
PEŠČENICA–ŽITNJAK
Bus Station
Zagreb Train Station
Radnička
Supilova
Grada Vukovara
Sava
0 1 km
0 0.5 miles
NOVI ZAGREB
Museum of Contemporary Art (500m)

History

Zagreb's known history begins in medieval times with two hills: Kaptol, now the site of Zagreb's cathedral, and Gradec. When the two settlements merged in 1850, Zagreb was officially born.

The space now known as Trg Bana Jelačića became the site of Zagreb's lucrative trade fairs, spurring construction around its edges. In the 19th century the economy expanded with the development of a prosperous clothing trade and a rail link connecting Zagreb with Vienna and Budapest. The city's cultural life blossomed, too.

Zagreb also became the centre for the Illyrian movement. Count Janko Drašković, lord of Trakošćan Castle, published a manifesto in Illyrian in 1832 and his call for a national revival resounded throughout Croatia. Drašković's dream came to fruition when Croatia and its capital joined the Kingdom of Serbs, Croats and Slovenes after WWI.

Between the two world wars, working-class neighbourhoods emerged in Zagreb between the railway and the Sava River, and new residential quarters were built on the southern slopes of Mt Medvednica. In April 1941 the Germans invaded Yugoslavia and entered Zagreb without resistance. Ante Pavelić and the Ustaše (p342) moved quickly to proclaim the establishment of the Independent State of Croatia (Nezavisna Država Hrvatska), with Zagreb as its capital. Although Pavelić ran his fascist state from Zagreb until 1944, he never enjoyed a great deal of support within the capital, which maintained support for Tito's Partisans.

In postwar Yugoslavia, Zagreb (to its chagrin) took second place to Belgrade but continued to expand. Zagreb was made the capital of Croatia in 1991, the same year that the country became independent.

Sights

As the oldest part of Zagreb, the Upper Town (Gornji Grad), which includes the neighbourhoods of Gradec and Kaptol, has landmark buildings and churches from the earlier centuries of Zagreb's history. The Lower Town (Donji Grad), which runs between the Upper Town and the train station, has the city's most interesting art museums and fine examples of 19th- and 20th-century architecture.

Upper Town

★Museum of Broken Relationships MUSEUM

(www.brokenships.com; Ćirilometodska 2; adult/student 40/30KN; 9am-10.30pm Jun-Sep, to 9pm Oct-May) From romances that withered to broken family connections, this wonderfully quirky museum explores the mementoes leftover after a relationship ends. Displayed amid a string of all-white rooms are donations from around the globe, each with a story attached. Exhibits range from the hilarious (the toaster someone nicked so their ex could never make toast again) to the heartbreaking (the suicide note from somebody's mother). In turns funny, poignant and moving, it's a perfect summing up of the human condition.

The innovative collection toured the world until it settled here in its permanent home. Check out the adjacent store – the 'bad memories eraser' is a best seller – and the cosy cafe with pavement tables. There are jazz nights on Thursdays during summer and autumn.

★Mirogoj CEMETERY

(Aleja Hermanna Bollea 27; 6am-8pm Apr-Oct, 7.30am-6pm Nov-Mar) A 10-minute ride north of the city centre (or a 30-minute walk through leafy streets) takes you to one of the most beautiful cemeteries in Europe, sited at the base of Mt Medvednica. It was designed in 1876 by Austrian-born architect Herman Bollé, who created numerous buildings around Zagreb. The majestic arcade, topped by a string of cupolas, looks like a fortress from the outside, but feels calm and graceful on the inside.

The lush cemetery is criss-crossed by paths and dotted with sculptures and artfully designed tombs. Highlights include the grave of poet Petar Preradović and the bust of Vladimir Becić by Ivan Meštrović.

Take bus 106 from the Cathedral of the Assumption of the Blessed Virgin Mary.

★Croatian Museum of Naïve Art MUSEUM

(Hrvatski Muzej Naivne Umjetnosti; 01-48 51 911; www.hmnu.hr; Ćirilometodska 3; adult/concession 25/15KN; 10am-6pm Mon-Sat, to 1pm Sun) A feast for fans of Croatia's naive art (a form that was highly fashionable locally and worldwide during the 1960s and '70s and has declined somewhat since), this small museum displays 80 artworks (a smidgen of the museum's total 1900 holdings) that illustrate the full range of colourful, and often dreamlike, styles within the genre. The discipline's most important artists, such as Generalić, Mraz, Rabuzin and Smajić, are all displayed here.

Dolac Market MARKET

(off Trg Bana Jelačića; ⏲open-air market 6.30am-3pm Mon-Sat, to 1pm Sun, covered market 7am-2pm Mon-Fri, to 3pm Sat, to 1pm Sun) Right in the heart of the city, Zagreb's bustling fruit and vegetable market has been trader-central since the 1930s when the city authorities set up a market space on the 'border' between the Upper and Lower Towns. Sellers from all over Croatia descend here daily to hawk fresh produce.

The main part is on an elevated square; the street level has indoor stalls selling meat and dairy products and (a little further towards the square) flowers. The stalls at the northern end of the market are packed with locally produced honey, oil, handicrafts and cheap food.

Trg Bana Jelačića SQUARE

Zagreb's main orientation point and its geographic heart is Trg Bana Jelačića – it's where most people arrange to meet up. If you enjoy people-watching, sit in one of the cafes and watch the tramloads of people getting out, greeting each other and dispersing among the newspaper- and flower-sellers.

The square's name comes from Ban Jelačić, the 19th-century *ban* (viceroy or governor) who led Croatian troops into an unsuccessful battle with Hungary in the hope of winning more autonomy for his people. The **equestrian statue** of Jelačić stood in the square from 1866 until 1947, when Tito ordered its removal because it was too closely linked with Croatian nationalism. Franjo Tuđman's government dug it up out of storage in 1990 and returned it to the square.

Katarinin Trg VIEWPOINT

(Katarinin trg) One of the best views in town – across red-tile roofs towards the cathedral – is from this square behind the Jesuit Church of St Catherine. It's the perfect spot to begin or end an Upper Town wander. The square is also home to Zagreb's most famous street art; the **Whale**, gracing the facade of the abandoned Galerija Gradec building, is a 3D work by French artist Etien.

Cathedral of the Assumption of the Blessed Virgin Mary CHURCH

(Katedrala Marijina Uznešenja; Kaptol 31; ⏲10am-5pm Mon-Sat, 1-5pm Sun) This cathedral's twin spires – seemingly permanently under repair – soar over the city. Formerly known as St Stephen's, the cathedral's original Gothic structure has been transformed many times over, but the sacristy still contains a cycle of frescos dating from the 13th century. An earthquake in 1880 badly damaged the building and reconstruction in a neo-Gothic style began around the turn of the 20th century. It was closed at the time of research for repairs after the 2020 earthquake.

If it's open when you visit, don't miss the baroque marble altars, statues and pulpit, or the tomb of Cardinal Alojzije Stepinac by Ivan Meštrović.

Galerija Klovićevi Dvori GALLERY

(☎01-48 51 926; www.gkd.hr; Jezuitski trg 4; admission varies, up to 40KN; ⏲11am-7pm Tue-Sun) Hosting a swath of temporary exhibitions throughout the year, this gallery, housed in a former Jesuit monastery, is among the city's most prestigious art spaces. Check if anything's on while you're in town. Past exhibits have included Picasso and Chagall, as well as collections by prominent Croatian fine artists. The gallery's atrium hosts concerts in July as part of the Evenings on Grič (p83) festival. There's a nice cafe here also.

Lotrščak Tower HISTORIC BUILDING

(Kula Lotrščak; Strossmayerovo Šetalište 9; adult/child 20/10KN; ⏲9am-9pm Mon-Fri, 10am-5pm Sat & Sun) Lotrščak Tower was built in the middle of the 13th century to protect the south city gate. Normally you can enter and climb up to the top for a sweeping 360-degree view of the city, but it was temporarily closed at the time of research, with no date set for reopening. Directly across the street is the **funicular railway** (Tomiceva; 1 way 4KN; ⏲6.30am-10pm), constructed in 1888, which connects the Lower and Upper Towns.

For the last 100 years a cannon has been fired from the tower every day at noon, allegedly to commemorate one day in the mid-15th century when the cannon was fired at the Turks at noon, who were camped across the Sava River. On its way down, the cannonball happened to hit a rooster, which was blown to bits – according to legend, this was so demoralising for the Turks that they decided not to attack the city. (A less fanciful explanation is that the

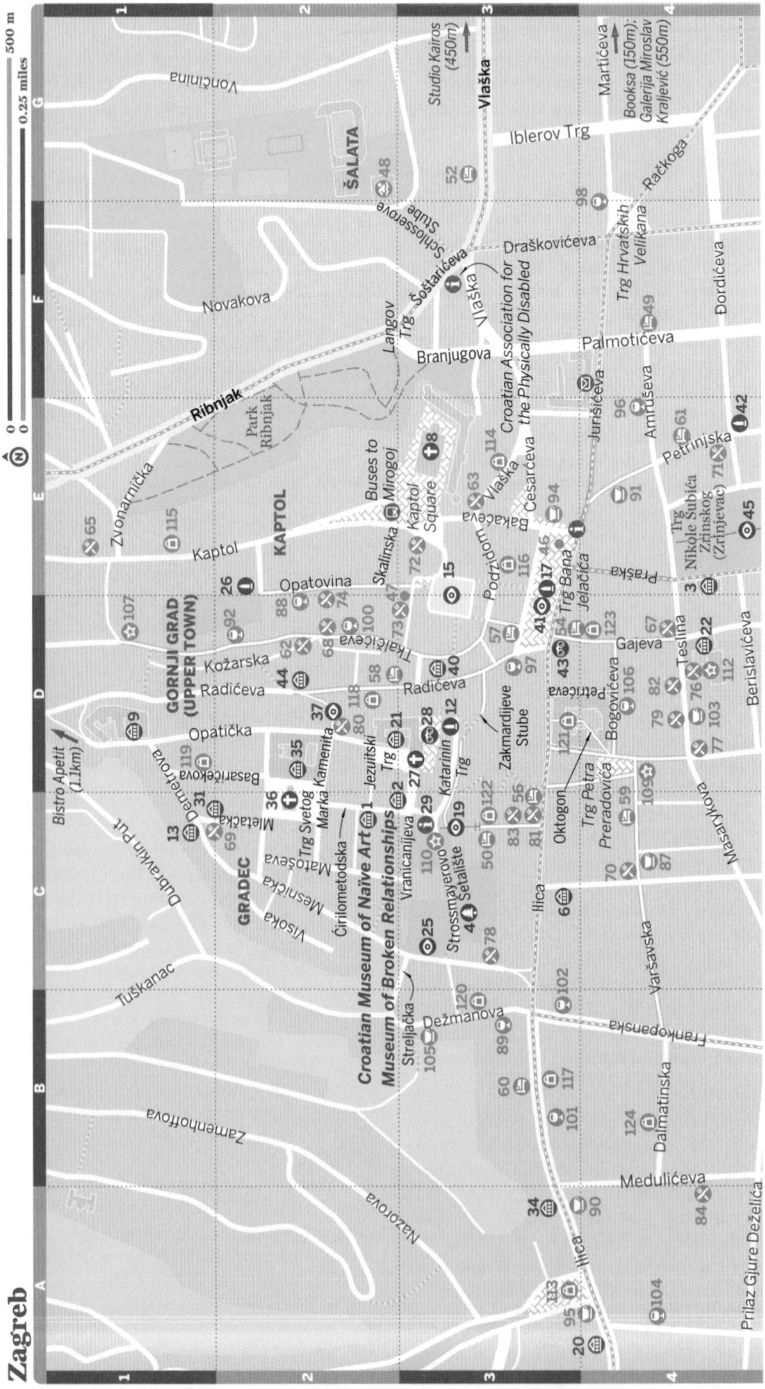

Zagreb

0 — 500 m
0 — 0.25 miles

A B C D E F G
1 2 3 4

Bistro Apetit (1.1km)
Zamenhoffova
Tuškanac
Dubravkin Put
Nazorova
13 Demetrova
119
31
9
GORNJI GRAD (UPPER TOWN)
107
65
Zvonarnička
115
Ribnjak
Park Ribnjak
Novakova
Vončinina
GRADEC
69 Mletačka
Basaričekova
Opatička
Radićeva
Kožarska
92
26
Kaptol
KAPTOL
Visoka
Mesnička
Matoševa
36
35
Trg Svetog Marka
Kamenita
37
44
62
88
Opatovina
Ćirilometodska
68
74
80
118
100
Tkalčićeva
ŠALATA
48
Croatian Museum of Naïve Art 1
Museum of Broken Relationships 2
Jezuitski Trg
21
58
73
47
Skalinska
Buses to Mirogoj
Langov Trg
Šoštarićeva
Schlosserove Stube
Streljačka
Vranicanijeva
27
28
Radićeva
72
Kaptol Square
8
105
Dežmanova
25
110
29
Strossmayerovo Šetalište
4
19
Katarinin Trg
12
40
15
Branjugova
Studio Kairos (450m)
52
Vlaška
120
78
50
122
Zakmardijeve Stube
57
Podzidom
Bakačeva
63
Vlaška
114
Croatian Association for the Physically Disabled
Draškovićeva
Iblerov Trg
60
89
83
56
81
97
116
Cesarčeva
34
Ilica
41
17
46
94
113
95
20
Ilica
101
117
102
6
Oktogon
121
Petrićeva
43
54
Trg Bana Jelačića
90
Trg Petra Preradovića
123
Jurišićeva
98
Martićeva
70
59
Bogovićeva
106
Gajeva
Praška
91
96
Trg Hrvatskih Velikana
124
Varšavska
109
79
82
67
Amruševa
Palmotićeva
49
Booksa (150m); Galerija Miroslav Kraljević (550m)
104
Dalmatinska
87
Teslina
Trg Nikole Šubića Zrinskog (Zrinjevac)
Petrinjska
61
Račkoga
84
Medulićeva
Frankopanska
Masarykova
77
103
76
112
22
3
71
Đorđićeva
42
45
Prilaz Gjure Deželića
Berislavićeva

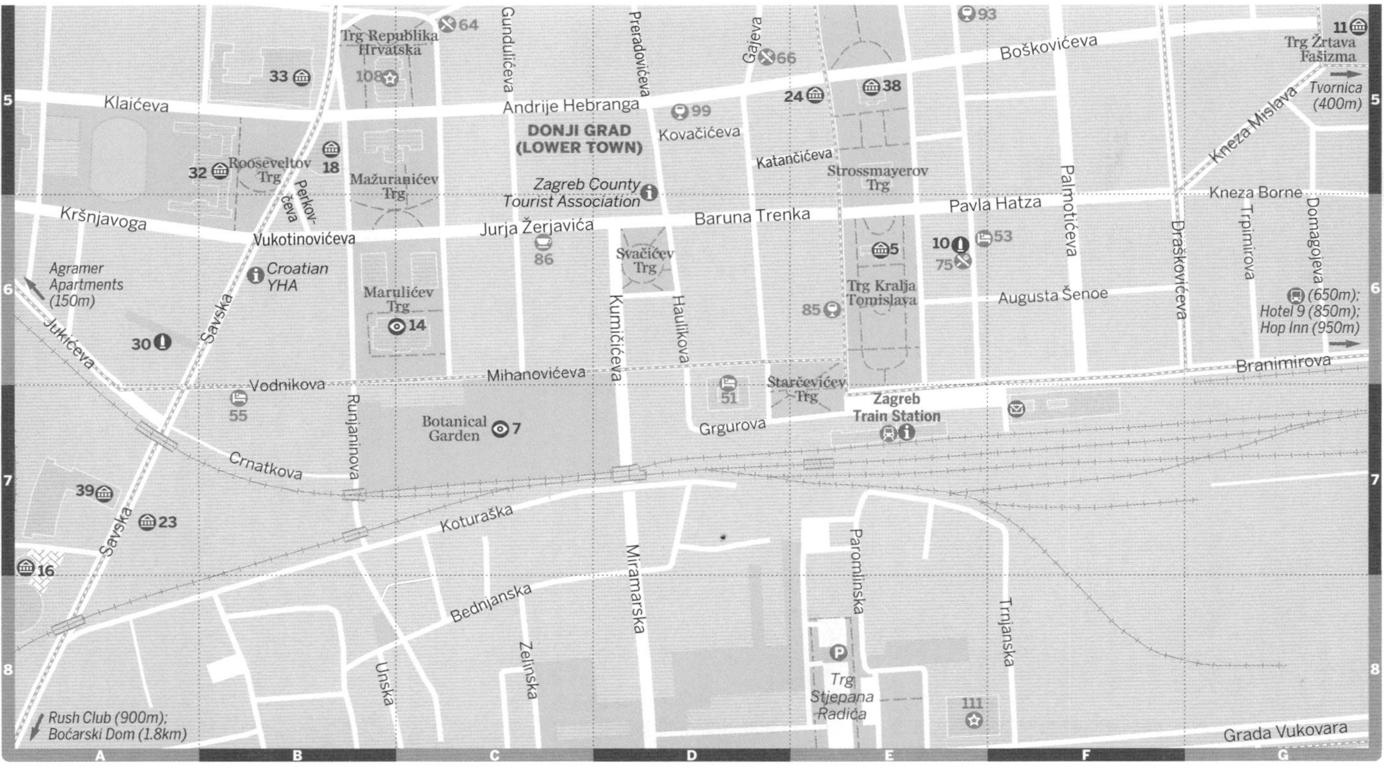
Boškovićeva
Trg Žrtava Fašizma
Tvornica (400m)
Kneza Mislava
Kneza Borne
Trpimirova
Domagojeva
(650m); Hotel 9 (850m); Hop Inn (950m)
Draškovićeva
Palmotićeva
Augusta Šenoe
Branimirova
Pavla Hatza
Baruna Trenka
Jurja Žerjavića
Vukotinovićeva
Kršnjavoga
Klaićeva
Andrije Hebranga
Gundulićeva
Preradovićeva
Gajeva
Kovačićeva
Katančićeva
Strossmayerov Trg
Trg Kralja Tomislava
Starčevićev Trg
Zagreb Train Station
Trg Republika Hrvatska
Mažuranićev Trg
Marulićev Trg
Rooseveltov Trg
Perkov-čeva
DONJI GRAD (LOWER TOWN)
Zagreb County Tourist Association
Svačićev Trg
Croatian YHA
Agramer Apartments (150m)
Savska
Jukićeva
Vodnikova
Mihanovićeva
Kumičićeva
Haulikova
Grgurova
Runjaninova
Botanical Garden
Crnatkova
Koturaška
Miramarska
Bednjanska
Unska
Zelinska
Paromlinska
Trnjanska
Trg Stjepana Radića
Grada Vukovara
Rush Club (900m); Boćarski Dom (1.8km)
5
6
7
8
A
B
C
D
E
F
G
93
11
38
24
66
64
33
108
99
32
18
86
10
53
75
5
85
14
30
55
51
7
39
23
16
111

Zagreb

cannon shot allows churches to synchronise their clocks.)

Tortureum MUSEUM
(Museum of Torture; ☎01-64 59 803; www.tortureum.com; Tkalčićeva 13, 1st fl; adult/child/family 40/30/100KN; ⏰11am-7pm) Horror buffs will love the display of 70-plus full-scale historic instruments of torture. But seeing, touching and trying out the 1792 guillotine replica, pendulum, rack or iron maiden gives more than a sensationalist take on violence. Experiencing the museum's multisensory rooms, such as the semidark Cabinet of Wonders or the Dungeon, allows an idea of the terror these instruments once wielded.

The museum is signposted from Tkalčićeva but can also be entered from Radićeva.

Zagreb 80's Museum MUSEUM
(www.zagreb80.com; Radićeva 34, 1st fl; adult/child 40/25KN; ⏰10am-10pm) Take a trip back in time within this four-room museum devoted to Zagreb in the 1980s. There are reconstructions of typical lounge and kitchen interiors in the decade, a room devoted to iconic games with both Commodore 64 and Atari in the display, and plenty of memorabilia. Visitors are encouraged to interact with the exhibits, so kids can have great fun here playing dress up in '80s fashion and trying to figure out how all those low-tech gadgets work.

Stone Gate GATE
(Kamenita Vrata; Kamenita) Make sure you take a peek at the Stone Gate, the eastern gate to medieval Gradec Town, which is

63 Amelie E3
64 b041 C5
65 Baltazar E1
66 Bistro Fotić D5
67 Boban D4
68 Curry Bowl D2
69 Didov San C1
70 Green Point C4
71 Heritage E4
72 Kaptolska Klet E3
73 La Štruk D3
74 Lanterna na Dolcu D2
75 Lari & Penati E6
Le Bistro (see 51)
Mali Bar (see 52)
76 Pingvin D4
77 Ribice i Tri Točkice D4
78 Stari Fijaker 900 C3
79 Time Pastry Shop D4
80 Trilogija D2
81 Vincek C3
82 Vinodol D4
83 Vis à Vis C3
Zinfandel's (see 51)
84 Zrno A4

Drinking & Nightlife

85 Bacchus E6
86 Cafe u Dvorištu C6
87 Cogito Coffee Shop C4
88 Craft Room D2
89 Dežman Bar B3
90 Eliscaffe A3
91 Express E4
92 Funk D2
93 Hotpot E5
94 Johann Franck E3
95 Kava Tava A4
Kino Europa (see 109)
96 Kolaž E4
97 MK Krolo D3
98 Mojo F4
99 Old Pharmacy Pub D5
100 Pivnica Mali Medo D2
101 Pivnica Medvedgrad B3
102 Pupitres B3
103 Quahwa D4
104 Sedmica A4
105 Velvet B3
106 Vinyl D4

Entertainment

107 Booze & Blues D1
Cibona Tower (see 16)
108 Croatian National Theatre B5
109 Kino Europa D4
110 Strossmarte C3
111 Vatroslav Lisinski Concert Hall E8
112 Zagrebačko Kazalište Mladih D4

Shopping

113 Antiques Market A3
114 Aromatica E3
115 Bornstein E1
Boudoir (see 59)
116 Cahun E3
117 Cerovečki Umbrellas B3
118 Galerija Link D2
I-GLE (see 120)
119 Koza D1
120 Love, Ana B3
121 Salon Croata D3
122 Take Me Home C3
Vintesa (see 52)
123 Znanje D4
124 Zvonimir B4

now a shrine. According to legend, a great fire in 1731 destroyed every part of the wooden gate except for the painting of the Virgin and Child (by an unknown 17th-century artist). People believe that the painting possesses miraculous powers and come regularly to pray, light candles and leave flowers. Square stone slabs are engraved with thanks and praise to the Virgin.

On the western facade of the Stone Gate you'll see a statue of Dora, the hero of an 18th-century historical novel, who lived with her father next to the Stone Gate.

Jesuit Church of St Catherine CHURCH
(Crkva Svete Katarine; Katarinin trg bb; Mass 6pm Mon-Fri, 11am Sun) This fine baroque church was built between 1620 and 1632. Although battered by fire and earthquake, the facade still gleams and the interior (only open during Mass) contains a fine altar dating from 1762. The interior stucco work dates from 1720. Look for the 18th-century medallions depicting the life of St Catherine on the ceiling of the nave.

Art Park PARK
(off Tomićeva) FREE This small park hosts numerous activities from June to October, including live-music sessions, film screenings and family-friendly mural-painting sessions. There's basic playground equipment, too. Access the park through the Grič Tunnel or from the alleyway off Tomićeva.

Grič Tunnel TUNNEL
(9am-9pm) FREE The mystery-laden Grič Tunnel that connects Mesnička and

Radićeva streets opened to the public in the summer of 2016. Built in 1943 for use as a WWII air-raid shelter and rarely used since (except for the legendary rave party that took place here in 1993), this 350m-long tunnel is now yours to cross.

There's nothing to see inside but walking under the Upper Town is a great way to beat the heat. Enter from Mesnička or by the Art Park below Stross and get out in a passageway just off Ilica, next door to NAMA department store. There are ambitious plans to turn the tunnel into an interactive Museum of the Senses.

St Mark's Church CHURCH

(Crkva Svetog Marka; Trg Svetog Marka 5; ⌚Mass 7.30am & 6pm Mon-Fri, 7.30am Sat, 10am, 11am & 6pm Sun) The 13th-century St Mark's Church is one of Zagreb's most emblematic buildings. Its colourful tiled roof, constructed in 1880, has the medieval coat of arms of Croatia, Dalmatia and Slavonia on the left side, and the emblem of Zagreb on the right. The Gothic portal, composed of 15 figures in shallow niches, was sculpted in the 14th century. The interior contains sculptures by Ivan Meštrović, though the church is open only at Mass times.

From late April to October there's a guard-changing ceremony outside the church every Saturday and Sunday at noon.

Sabor HISTORIC BUILDING

(Trg Svetog Marka 6) The eastern side of Trg Svetog Marka is taken up by the Croatian *sabor* (parliament), built in 1910 on the site of baroque 17th- and 18th-century town houses. Its neoclassical style is quite incongruous on the square, but the historical importance of this building is undeniable – Croatia's secession from the Austro-Hungarian Empire was proclaimed from its balcony in 1918.

Meštrović Atelier GALLERY

(☎01-48 51 123; www.mestrovic.hr; Mletačka 8; adult/child 30/15KN; ⌚10am-6pm Tue-Fri, to 2pm Sat & Sun) Croatia's most recognised artist is Ivan Meštrović. This 17th-century building is his former home, where he worked and lived from 1922 to 1942; it houses an excellent collection of some 100 sculptures, drawings, lithographs and pieces of furniture from the first four decades of his artistic life. Meštrović, who also worked as an architect, designed many parts of the house himself.

Croatian Natural History Museum MUSEUM

(Hrvatski Prirodoslovni Muzej; ☎01-48 51 700; www.hpm.hr; Demetrova 1; adult/child 30/20KN; ⌚10am-5pm Tue, Wed & Fri, to 8pm Thu, to 7pm Sat, to 1pm Sun) This museum houses a collection of prehistoric tools and bones excavated from the Krapina cave, inhabited by neanderthals, as well as exhibits showing the evolution of animal and plant life in Croatia. Temporary exhibits often focus on specific regions.

City Museum MUSEUM

(Muzej Grada Zagreba; ☎01-48 51 926; www.mgz.hr; Opatička 20; adult/child/family 30/20/50KN; ⌚10am-7pm Tue-Sat, to 2pm Sun) Since 1907 the 17th-century Convent of St Claire has housed this museum which presents the history of Zagreb through a hodgepodge of exhibits. The displays include archaeological finds unearthed during the building's restoration in the 1990s; old city plans, lithographs and documents; altars and stone masonry from the Cathedral and St Mark's; and socialist-era paraphernalia. Summaries of the exhibits are in English.

⊙ Lower Town

Croatian Association of Artists GALLERY

(Hrvatsko Društvo Likovnih Umjetnika; ☎01-46 11 818; www.hdlu.hr; Meštrović Pavilion, Trg Žrtava Fašizma 16; admission varies, up to 65KN; ⌚hours vary according to exhibit) East of the centre, this gallery is housed in one of the few architectural works by Ivan Meštrović and has a busy and diverse rolling program of exhibitions and events throughout the year. It's a must on the art circuit of Zagreb; check out what's on while you're in town. The building itself has also had several fascinating incarnations, reflecting the region's history in a nutshell.

Originally designed by Meštrović in 1938 as an exhibition pavilion, the structure honoured King Petar Karađorđević, the ruler of the Kingdom of Serbs, Croats and Slovenes – which grated against the sensibilities of Croatia's nationalists. With the onset of a fascist government, the building was renamed the Zagreb Artists' Centre in May 1941; several months later Ante Pavelić, Croatia's fascist leader, gave orders for the building to be evacuated of all artwork and turned into a mosque (claiming it was to make the local Muslim population feel at home). There were murmurs of disapproval from the

DON'T MISS

HUNTING DOWN ZAGREB'S STREET ART

Keep your eyes peeled as you're strolling around Zagreb and you'll discover that the city's art scene doesn't end in its galleries. Hunt down the murals that have covered – and drastically cheered up – drab concrete and brick walls and brought a shot of vibrant, fun colour to the streets. Some of our favourite street art pieces:

Xenophora (Đorđićeva) These mammoth photo-realistic shells, by Lonac, decorate the brick wall of the building on the corner of Đorđićeva and Petrinjska.

City Waterfall (Petrinjska) Keep walking down Petrinjska to find this highly detailed B&W waterfall. It's the work of Miron Milić.

Gulliver (Opatovina) In the park at the top of Opatovina you'll see this 30m-long mural of a sleeping Gulliver being tied up by the Lilliputians. It's a collaborative work by Boris Bare and Dominik Vuković.

Croatian Inventors (Katarinin trg) Boris Bare and Dominik Vuković are also the artists behind these two murals celebrating the work of electricity pioneer Nikola Tesla and the inventor of the mechanical pencil, Slavoljub Penkala. They're painted across the walls of the staircase terrace which provides a short cut from Strossmayerovo to Katarinin trg (p69).

Fakin (Tkalčićeva) FREE These rockabilly chickens, commissioned by the Medvedgrad Brewery for the northern wall of their Pivnica Mali Medo (p88), are a collaborative project by Bare and Modul (Boris Bare and Miroslav Petković Modul).

Open My Eyes That I May See (Većeslava Holjevca) If you head out to the Museum of Contemporary Art (p79), don't miss this 90m-long montage-style mural by OKO which is painted along the west wall.

Medika Diving & Technicolour Dream (off Savska) To hunt down two of Zagreb's best pieces of street art, head south on Savska from Rooseveltov Trg, past the Westin Hotel and the DM department store directly to its south. Straight after DM, turn right into the small garden. Here you'll find Lonac's *Medika Diving* portraying a diver in vibrant yellow and green tones and incorporating the wall's chimney pipe as the snorkel for a 3D effect. On the opposite wall is *Technicolour Dream*, a collaboration between Lonac and Chez 186 that depicts a sleeping blue-hued girl.

artists, but the building was significantly restructured and eventually surrounded by three minarets.

With the establishment of socialist Yugoslavia, however, the mosque was promptly closed and the building's original purpose restored – though it was renamed the Museum of the People's Liberation. A permanent exhibition was set up and in 1949 the government had the minarets knocked down. In 1951 an architect called V Richter set about returning the building to its original state according to Meštrović's design.

The building has remained an exhibition space ever since, with a nonprofit association of Croatian artists making use of it. Despite being renamed the Croatian Association of Artists in 1991 by the country's new government, everyone in Zagreb still knows it as 'the old mosque'.

Art Pavilion GALLERY

(Umjetnički Paviljon; ☎01-48 41 070; www.umjetnicki-paviljon.hr; Trg Kralja Tomislava 22; adult/child/family 50/30/130KN; ⏲11am-8pm Tue-Thu, Sat & Sun, to 9pm Fri) This stunning, yellow art nouveau–style pavilion presents changing exhibitions of contemporary art. In the past it's hosted major works by Rodin and Miró. Check the website to find out if anything is on during your time in Zagreb.

Gallery of Modern Art GALLERY

(Moderna Galerija; ☎01-60 41 040; www.moderna-galerija.hr; Andrije Hebranga 1; adult/child/family 40/30/70KN; ⏲11am-7pm Tue-Fri, to 2pm Sat & Sun) Take in this glorious display of work by Croatian artists from the last 200 years, including such 19th- and 20th-century masters as Bukovac, Mihanović and Račić. It's a fine overview of the nation's vibrant arts scene.

LAZY DAYS IN ZAGREB

When you've had enough of churches, museums and shopping, Zagreb offers myriad options for sitting about and simply soaking up the vibe. The fact that many of them can be enjoyed with a beverage in hand is purely coincidental.

COFFEE BREAK

If a Zagreb local has time on their hands, chances are you'll find them at a cafe. To experience the zenith of this quintessential Zagreb pastime, head into the town centre for the *špica*, the very local tradition of sipping coffee between 11am and 2pm on Saturday, before or after a run at the Dolac Market. This showdown of latest fashions, mobile phones and gossip has people competing for prime pavement tables along Bogovićeva, Preradovićeva and Tkalčićeva.

CRAFT-BEER QUAFFING

Zagreb's craft-beer scene is heating up, with various places now devoted to both local and global craft brews. For an easy bar-hop, head to Opatovina. This street is home to a whole clutch of bars that serve a fine range of craft beer brands. Some of our favourite places for sampling the scene are Craft Room (p88), Garden Brewery (p92), Hop Inn (p92), Pivnica Medvedgrad (p89) and, its sister pub, Pivnica Mali Medo (p88)

1. Tkalčićeva cafes
2. Craft beer from the Garden Brewery (p92)
3. Bogovićeva cafes

POSZTOS/SHUTTERSTOCK ©

VIGO-S/SHUTTERSTOCK ©

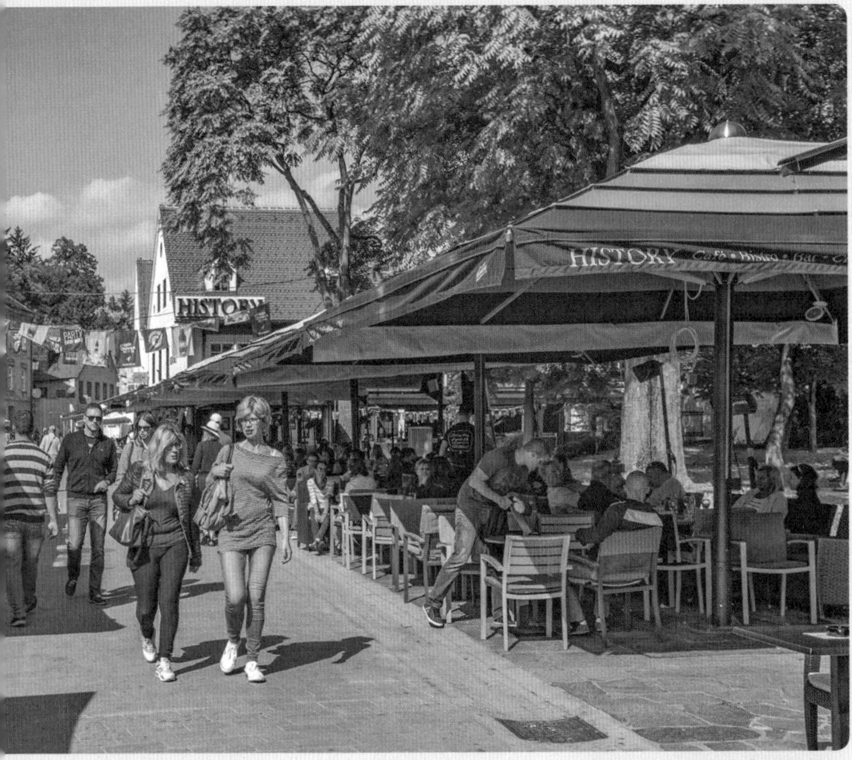

3

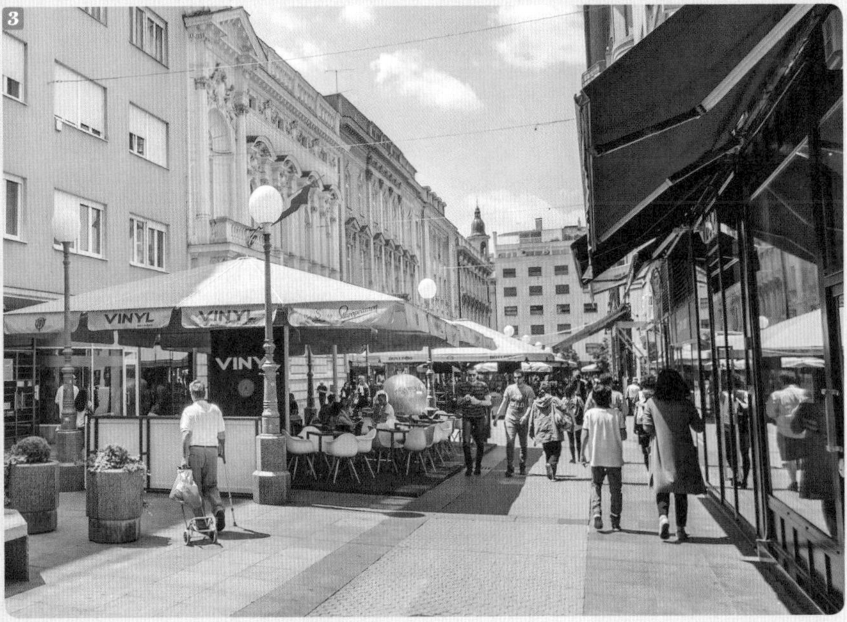

Zrinjevac SQUARE

(Trg Nikole Šubića Zrinskog) Officially called Trg Nikole Šubića Zrinskog but lovingly known as Zrinjevac, this verdant square is a major hang-out during sunshiny weekends and hosts pop-up cafe stalls during the summer months. It's also a venue for many festivals and events, most centred on the ornate music pavilion that dates from 1891.

Zrinjevac is part of the Green Horseshoe, also known as Lenuci Horseshoe, a U-shaped series of seven city squares with parks.

Archaeological Museum MUSEUM

(Arheološki Muzej; ☎01-48 73 101; www.amz.hr; Trg Nikole Šubića Zrinskog 19; adult/child/family 30/15/50KN; ⏰10am-6pm Tue, Wed, Fri & Sat, to 8pm Thu, to 1pm Sun) Spread over three floors, the artefacts housed here stretch from the prehistoric era to the medieval age. The 2nd floor holds the most interesting – and well-curated – exhibits. Here, displays of intricate Roman minor arts, such as decorative combs and oil lamps, and metal curse tablets are given as much prominence as the more usual show-stopping marble statuary. An exhibit devoted to Croatia's early medieval Bijelo Brdo culture displays a wealth of grave finds unearthed in the 1920s.

The 3rd floor is home to Bronze and Iron Age finds as well as the museum's Egyptology collection, which includes a delicately beautiful Ptolemaic funeral mask, while the numismatic exhibit on the ground floor holds some 260,000 coins, medals and medallions and is one of the most important in Europe.

Museum of Illusion MUSEUM

(www.muzejiluzija.com; Ilica 72; adult/concession/family 40/25/100KN; ⏰9am-10pm) This quirky museum delivers a fantastic sensory adventure to visitors of all ages. Children in particular are in for a great time. The Slanted Room or the Mirror of Truth are among 70-plus intriguing exhibits, hologram pictures, puzzles and educational games that offer up a fun mental workout. The museum shop has fabulous 3D puzzles and Dilemma Games – didactic toys that make a perfect souvenir.

Museum Mimara MUSEUM

(Muzej Mimara; ☎01-48 28 100; www.mimara.hr; Rooseveltov trg 5; adult/child 40/30KN; ⏰10am-7pm Tue-Fri, to 5pm Sat, to 2pm Sun Jul-Sep, 10am-5pm Tue, Wed, Fri & Sat, to 7pm Thu, to 2pm Sun Oct-Jun) Housed in an imposing neo-Renaissance former school is the eclectic, globe-trotting private art collection of Ante Topić Mimara, who donated over 3750 priceless objects to his native Zagreb (even though he spent much of his life in Salzburg, Austria). Inside you'll find Ptolemaic glassware from Alexandria, delicate jade and ivory Qing-dynasty ornaments, ornate 14th-century wooden crosses encrusted with semiprecious stones and a vast European painting collection with works by Caravaggio, Rembrandt, Bosch, Velázquez, Goya, Renoir and Degas.

Botanical Garden GARDENS

(Botanički Vrt; ☎01-48 98 060; Marulićev trg 9a; ⏰9am-2.30pm Mon & Tue, to 7pm Wed-Sun Apr-Oct) FREE If you need a change from museums and galleries, take a break in this lovely, verdant retreat. Laid out in 1890, the garden has 10,000 species of plants and plenty of restful corners and paths.

Croatian State Archives ARCHITECTURE

(www.arhiv.hr; Marulićev trg 21; adult/child 20/10KN; ⏰entry by tour only 1pm & 2pm Mon-Fri) Zagreb's most majestic art deco building, with massive owls of wisdom staring out from the corners of the roof, was built in 1913 to house the royal library and land archives. Today it's home to the state archives, and two daily tours allow you a peek inside its grand interiors. The tour highlight is the Great Reading Room, decked out with huge chandeliers and Vlaho Bukovac's *Development of Croatian Culture* painting portraying major figures from Croatian history.

Strossmayer Gallery of Old Masters GALLERY

(Strossmayerova Galerija Starih Majstora; Trg Nikole Šubića Zrinskog 11; adult/child/family 30/10/50KN; ⏰10am-7pm Tue, to 4pm Wed-Fri, to 1pm Sat & Sun) The 2nd floor of the stately 19th-century neo-Renaissance Croatian Academy of Arts and Sciences building showcases the impressive fine-art collection donated to the city by Bishop Strossmayer in 1884. It includes Italian masters from the 14th to 19th centuries, such as Tintoretto, Veronese and Tiepolo; Dutch and Flemish painters such as Brueghel the Younger; and the classic Croatian artists Medulić and Benković.

The building's interior courtyard also contains the Baška Tablet (Bašćanska Ploča), a stone panel from the island of Krk, which features the oldest example of Glagolitic script, dating from 1102, as well as a statue of Bishop Strossmayer by Ivan Meštrović.

Zagreb 360° Observation Deck VIEWPOINT
(☎01-48 76 587; www.zagreb360.hr; Ilica 1a, 16th fl; adult/child/family 60/30/150KN; ⏲10am-5pm Mon, 2-10pm Tue, 10am-11pm Wed-Sun) Don't expect the dizzying heights of observation decks elsewhere: Zagreb's tallest central high-rise is a minnow in the skyscraper category. However, this outdoor deck that rims the 16th-floor cafe-bar is high enough for panoramic vistas of the entire city and great views down onto Trg Bana Jelačića below. Admission gets you unlimited access to the deck and cafe, if you want to come back for sunset or night-time views.

Museum of Art & Crafts MUSEUM
(Muzej za Umjetnost i Obrt; ☎01-48 82 123; www.muo.hr; Trg Republike Hrvatske 10; adult/child/family 40/20/70KN; ⏲10am-7pm Tue-Sat, to 2pm Sun) From ornate walnut furniture and garish rococo ornaments to liturgical vestments and votive images, this museum explores artisanship from the Middle Ages to today. The highlight is the collection of B&W photography, showcasing Croatia up until the 1950s, on the 2nd floor. English information sheets are hung on hooks near every room entrance. The museum also hosts frequent temporary exhibitions.

Ethnographic Museum MUSEUM
(Etnografski Muzej; ☎01-48 26 220; www.emz.hr; Mažuranićev trg 14; adult/child/family 20/15/50KN; ⏲10am-6pm Tue-Fri, to 1pm Sat & Sun) The ethnographic heritage of Croatia is catalogued in this museum housed in a domed 1903 building. Out of 70,000 items, about 2750 are on display, including ceramics, jewellery, musical instruments, tools, weapons and folk costumes, such as gold-embroidered scarves from Slavonia and lace from the island of Pag. Thanks to donations from the Croatian explorers Mirko and Stevo Seljan, there are also artefacts from South America, Ethiopia, China, Japan and Australia.

Other Neighbourhoods

Lauba GALLERY
(☎01-63 02 115; www.lauba.hr; Baruna Filipovića 23a; adult/child 25/10KN; ⏲2-10pm Mon-Fri & Sun, 11am-10pm Sat) This private art collection, housed in a former textile-weaving mill in an industrial area of western Zagreb, provides an insight into Croatian contemporary art from the 1950s to today. Works on display change frequently. There's a dynamic roster of events, including free creative workshops for kids (no reservations needed) on Saturday, and the cool Lauba Bistro (p88) is located on-site.

Jarun Lake LAKE
(Jarunska) Jarun Lake in south Zagreb is a popular getaway for residents at any time of the year, but especially in summer, when the clear waters are ideal for swimming. Although part of the lake is marked off for boating competitions (rowing, kayaking and canoeing), there is plenty of space to enjoy a leisurely swim. Other recreational options include biking, rollerblading and kids' parks. On arrival, head left to Malo Jezero for swimming and canoe or pedal-boat rental, or right to Veliko Jezero, where there's a pebble beach and windsurfing.

Take tram 5 or 17 to Jarun and follow signs to the *jezero* (lake).

Museum of Contemporary Art MUSEUM
(Muzej Suvremene Umjetnosti; ☎01-60 52 700; www.msu.hr; Avenija Dubrovnik 17; adult/concession 30/15KN; ⏲11am-6pm Tue-Fri & Sun, to 8pm Sat) Housed in a city icon designed by local star architect Igor Franić, this museum displays both solo and thematic group shows by Croatian and international artists in its 17,000 sq

ZAGREB'S CONTEMPORARY ART SCENE

Zagreb's palpable creative energy is driven by a host of young ambitious artists and curators. The city has a variety of places where you can catch home-grown art. If you want to discover new art trends in Croatia, check out:

Galerija Greta (www.greta.hr; Ilica 92; ⏲5-8pm Mon-Sat) FREE

Galerija SC (Galerija Studentski Centar; ☎01-45 93 602; www.sczg.unizg.hr/kultura; Savska 25; ⏲noon-8pm Mon-Fri, 10am-1pm Sat)

Galerija Nova (☎01-48 72 582; www.whw.hr/galerija-nova; Teslina 7; ⏲noon-8pm Tue-Fri, 11am-2pm Sat) FREE

Lauba (p78)

Galerija Miroslav Kraljević (www.g-mk.hr; Šubićeva 29; ⏲noon-7pm Tue-Fri, 11am-1pm Sat) FREE

Croatian Association of Artists (p74)

Note that many of these shut their doors in August so check before you head there.

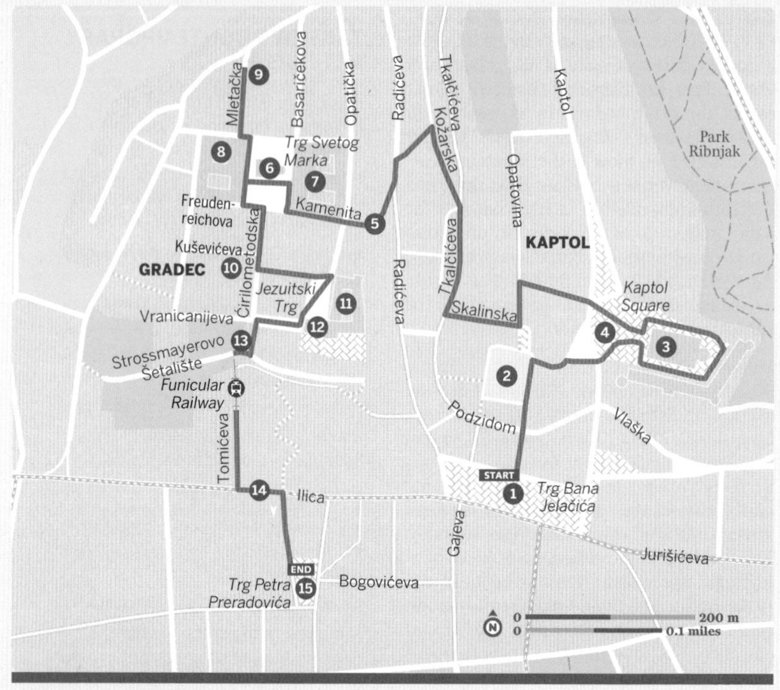

City Walk
Architecture, Art & Street Life

START TRG BANA JELAČIĆA
END TRG PETRA PRERADOVIĆA
LENGTH 1KM; 1½ HOURS

The natural starting point of any walk in Zagreb is buzzing 1 **Trg Bana Jelačića** (p69), the city's main meeting point and its heart. Climb the steps up to 2 **Dolac Market** (p69) and pick up some fruit or a quick snack before heading for the neo-Gothic 3 **Cathedral of the Assumption of the Blessed Virgin Mary** (p69). Cross 4 **Kaptol Square** (lined with 17th-century buildings), walk down Skalinska and come out at Tkalčićeva. Wander up the street, then climb the stairs that will take you up to 5 **Stone Gate** (p72), a fascinating shrine and the eastern gate to medieval Gradec Town. Next, go up Kamenita and you'll come out at Trg Svetog Marka, the site of the 13th-century 6 **St Mark's Church** (p74), one of Zagreb's most emblematic buildings, with a colourful tiled roof; the 7 **Sabor** (p74), the country's parliament; and 8 **Banski Dvori**, the presidential palace.

Wander through the winding streets of the Upper Town, and find out more about Ivan Meštrović, Croatia's most renowned artist, in 9 **Meštrović Atelier** (p74). Walk back across Trg Svetog Marka and down Ćirilometodska, stepping into one of the country's most singular museums, the 10 **Croatian Museum of Naïve Art** (p68). Cross Jezuitski trg and enter 11 **Galerija Klovićevi Dvori** (p69), where local and international contemporary-art exhibitions await. When you're finished with art, gaze up at the gorgeous 12 **Jesuit Church of St Catherine** (p73), before finally emerging at 13 **Lotrščak Tower** (p69), built in the middle of the 13th century and today offering dazzling 360-degree vistas of the city. Near the tower is a historic funicular railway, constructed in 1888, which connects the Lower and Upper Towns. Take in the cityscape then go down in the funicular, or take the verdant stairway – either will leave you on the side of 14 **Ilica**, Zagreb's commercial artery.

Cross Ilica and walk to 15 **Trg Petra Preradovića**, known to locals as Cvjetni trg, and take a break at one of the many outdoor cafes.

metres. The permanent display, *Collection in Motion,* showcases 620 edgy works by 240 artists, roughly half of whom are Croatian. There's a packed year-round schedule of film, theatre, concerts and performance art.

Inside is a fun interactive *Double Slide* piece by Belgian artist Carsten Holler, and the stirring *Ženska Kuća* installation by Croatia's foremost artist, Sanja Iveković, dealing with the theme of violence against women.

Admission is free on the first Wednesday of each month. On summer Saturdays catch concerts on the rooftop.

Maksimir Park PARK

(01-23 20 460; www.park-maksimir.hr; Maksimirski perivoj bb; info centre 10am-4pm Tue-Fri, to 6pm Sat & Sun) Maksimir Park is a peaceful wooded enclave covering 18 hectares, easily accessible by trams 11 and 12 from Trg Bana Jelačića. Opened to the public in 1794, it was the first public promenade in southeastern Europe. It's landscaped like an English garden, with alleys, lawns and artificial lakes. The most photographed structure in the park is the exquisite Bellevue Pavilion, constructed in 1843. Also here is the Echo Pavilion, as well as a house built to resemble a rustic Swiss cottage.

Technical Museum Nikola Tesla MUSEUM

(Tehnički Muzej Nikola Tesla; www.tehnicki-muzej.hr; Savska 18; adult/child 20KN/free; 9am-5pm Tue-Fri, to 1pm Sat & Sun) Science fans and kids will enjoy the motley collection here, which segues from steam-engine locomotives to scale models of satellites with a replica of a mine and exhibits on agriculture, geology, energy and transport along the way. The **planetarium** (additional entry 15KN) is great for older kids.

Dražen Petrović Memorial Museum MUSEUM

(01-48 43 146; www.drazenpetrovic.net; Trg Dražena Petrovića 3; adult/child 30/10KN; 10am-5pm Mon-Fri, to 2pm Sat) Basketball is popular in Zagreb, which is home to the Cibona basketball team. Pay homage to the team's most famous player at the Dražen Petrović Memorial Museum, which holds a swag of basketball memorabilia. Games take place frequently at the **Cibona Tower** (01-48 43 333; www.cibona.com; Savska 30; tickets 10-150KN) nearby.

Zoo Zagreb ZOO

(www.zoo.hr; Maksimir Park; adult/child/under 7yr 30/20KN/free; 9am-8pm, ticket booth to 6.30pm) The Zagreb Zoo has a modest collection of the world's fauna and daily feeding times for seals, sea lions, otters and piranhas. Renovations have seen many of the animal habitats upgraded and enlarged. Admission is reduced on Monday.

Tours

Secret Zagreb WALKING

(097 67 38 738; www.secret-zagreb.com; per person 75KN; 7pm Tue & Fri Nov-Mar, 9pm Fri Apr, & Wed & Sun May-Oct) An ethnographer and inspiring storyteller, Iva Silla is the guide who reveals the Zagreb of curious myths and legends and peculiar historical personalities. Take her hit walking tour Zagreb Ghosts and Dragons to peek into the city's hidden corners or forgotten graveyards, all set in the city centre.

Old Zagreb Tour TOURS

(95 65 46 544; www.oldzagreb.com; ride from 200KN) Turn up the style factor and explore Zagreb in a 1908 Ford Model T. Route 1 does a loop through Gornji Grad between Katarinin trg to Kaptol, or choose a circular cruise past the grand parks of the Lower Town.

Zagrebee Tours WALKING

(091 40 00 306; www.zagrebee.com; 120KN; 5pm Tue, Wed & Fri Apr-Sep, 10am Oct-Mar) Zagrebee's Street Art tour introduces you to the city's thriving outdoor-art scene on a tour of some of the best murals, including plenty of background information on Zagreb's street-art scene.

Kuhaona FOOD & DRINK

(01-41 04 841; www.kuhaona.com; Opatovina 13; food tour per person €75; food tour 10am Mon-Sat) Kuhaona's Zagreb food tours are a Croatian cuisine 101 and a favourite with foodies, taking you on a four-hour gastro-journey through the country. Pack your appetite. Cooking workshops at its studio, steps from Dolac Market, are also offered, with a range of different Croatian regional menus to choose from.

Funky Zagreb Tours TOURS

(091 16 02 222; www.funky-zagreb.com; walk & wine tour per person 1-4/over 4 people €64/60) Private tours that range in theme from a city walking tour with wine tasting (450KN for 2½ to three hours) to a gourmet tour with and cooking class (€140 per person for two people).

Blue Bike Tours CYCLING

(098 18 83 344; www.zagrebbybike.com; Trg Bana Jelačića 15; tour adult/child €29/14.50) The popular Zagreb Highlights bike tour

ZAGREB FOR CHILDREN

Zagreb is a child-friendly city with both some wonderful attractions directly catering for kids plus a bundle of free social events taking place in the city centre during the May to September high season. All in all the city's infrastructure is good for strollers, with pavement curbs sloping at all pedestrian crossings, though hopping on trams is problematic due to high entry stairs.

Children up to the age of seven travel free on public transport and some sights have free entry for under-fives, half-price entry for older kids and a discounted family-ticket option. If ordering a taxi, Ekotaxi (p97) has car seats for babies and toddlers but you must book at least two hours before and specify the age of your little one. If you want to do some family cycling, Bike.com (p96) has children's bicycles and helmets to hire. In Zagreb, cyclists use pavements, not the road, and some wider main pavements have designated cycle lanes.

Museum of Illusion (p78) Budding scientists will be fascinated while exploring the rooms of optical illusions, mirrors and holograms here.

Backo Mini Express (☎01-48 33 226; www.backo.hr; Gundulićeva 4; adult/child/family 22/20/70KN; ⊙10am-6pm Thu-Sat) Little ones will be mesmerised by the trains chugging across the landscape of this massive model railway.

Tortureum (p72) Most young teens will be engrossed by the macabre exhibits here.

Zagreb 80's Museum (p72) Let the kids' minds boggle at the 'ye olde' pre-internet era, plus little ones will enjoy the dress-up opportunities.

Boćarski Dom (Prisavlje 2) This park is the best place for tots to work off some steam with excellent playground equipment, playing fields and a rollerblading ramp as well as a relaxing path along the Sava River. To get there, take tram 17 west to the Prisavlje stop.

Maksimir Park (p81) Has two playgrounds and a zoo (p81).

Sports & Recreational Centre Šalata (☎01-46 17 255; www.sportskiobjekti.hr; Schlosserove Stube 2; day ticket adult/child/family weekend 30/20/60KN, weekday 20/15/40KN; ⊙public swimming 1.30-6pm Mon-Fri, 11am-7pm Sat & Sun Jun-Sep) Beat the heat and take a break from pounding the city streets at the pools here.

Jarun Lake (p79) On summer weekends join local families here for swimming and pedal-boating.

is a great introduction to the central city's sights. The Back to Socialism tour explores the socialist architecture of Novi Zagreb. Tours last around 2½ hours and run year-round (at 10am or 2pm except for during the hot summer months when start times move to 5pm).

Festivals & Events

For a complete listing of Zagreb events, see www.infozagreb.hr. Croatia's largest international fairs are the Zagreb spring (mid-April) and autumn (mid-September) grand trade fairs.

Night of Museums CULTURAL
(⊙last day Jan) More than 40 cultural institutions in Zagreb, from museums and galleries to private collections, open their doors for free and stay open till 1am. It's the one night everyone in Zagreb hits the museums.

Zagrebdox FILM
(http://zagrebdox.net; ⊙late Feb-early Mar) This annual Zagreb festival celebrates documentary film.

Music Biennale Zagreb MUSIC
(www.mbz.hr; ⊙Apr) Croatia's most important contemporary-music event. By 'contemporary', do not read 'pop' – this prestigious fest celebrates modern-day classical music. Held in odd numbered years.

Subversive Festival CULTURAL
(www.subversivefestival.com; ⊙May) Europe's activists and philosophers descend on Zagreb in droves for film screenings and lectures over two weeks in May.

Cest is d'Best CULTURAL
(www.cestisdbest.com; ⊙May-Jun) This street festival delights Zagreb citizens for a few days in late May through early June each

year, with six stages around the city centre, around 200 international performers, and acts that include music, dance, theatre, art and sports.

Ljeto na Štrosu CULTURAL
(www.ljetonastrosu.com; ⌚late May–mid-Sep) This quirky annual event stages free outdoor film screenings, concerts, art workshops and best-in-show mongrel dog competitions, all along the leafy Strossmayerovo Šetalište.

INmusic Festival MUSIC
(www.inmusicfestival.com; Jarun Lake; ⌚Jun) A three-day extravaganza every June, this is Zagreb's highest-profile music festival. Previous years have seen Alice in Chains, PJ Harvey, Nick Cave and the Bad Seeds, and St Vincent take to the Jarun Lake main stage.

Animafest Zagreb FILM
(World Festival of Animated Film; www.animafest.hr; ⌚Jun) This prestigious festival has taken place in Zagreb since 1972 – odd-numbered years are devoted to feature films, even-numbered ones to short films.

International Folklore Festival CULTURAL
(www.msf.hr; ⌚Jul) Taking place in Zagreb since 1966, this festival highlights folk culture and traditions with performances from both Croatian and international folk musicians and dancers. Performances take place at two main stages, on Trg Bana Jelačića and in the Upper Town, as well as various events held throughout the city centre.

Evenings on Grič MUSIC
(⌚Jul) This festival presents a cycle of concerts in the Upper Town each July. The atrium of Galerija Klovićevi Dvori (p69) and the Gradec stage are used for performances of classical music, jazz, blues and world tunes.

Courtyards CULTURAL
(Dvorišta; www.dvorista.in; ⌚Jul) For 10 days each July, Zagreb's historic Upper Town courtyards, many of which are normally off limits, open their doors for a string of concerts and performances, combined with food, booze and merrymaking.

Puppet International Festival PERFORMING ARTS
(www.pif.hr; ⌚Sep) Typically taking place during the month of September, this prominent puppetry festival, around since 1968, showcases star ensembles, workshops on puppet making and puppetry exhibits.

World Theatre Festival THEATRE
(www.zagrebtheatrefestival.hr; ⌚Sep-Oct) High-quality contemporary theatre comes to Zagreb for a couple of weeks each September, sometimes extending into early October.

25 FPS Festival FILM
(www.25fps.hr; ⌚late Sep/early Oct) This offbeat festival presents alternative visual expressions during a week of screenings, typically in late September or early October.

Zagreb Film Festival FILM
(www.zff.hr; ⌚Oct-Nov) This major cultural event covers nine days with more than 100 film screenings taking place at various locations in the city centre. The main competition section sees directors vie for the Golden Pram award.

Fuliranje CHRISTMAS MARKET
(www.adventzagreb.com; ⌚Dec) Zagreb's award-winning Christmas market, which uses various locations around the city centre including Trg Bana Jelačića and Zrinjevac. It's held throughout December, as part of a bustling and packed Advent program in Zagreb, despite the subzero temperatures. The focus is on street food, mulled wine, craft stores, live music and plenty of activities to keep the wee ones busy.

Human Rights Film Festival FILM
(www.humanrightsfestival.org; ⌚Dec) Screenings of films that shed light on human-rights issues around the world, taking place for a week each December at Kino Europa.

Sleeping

Zagreb's accommodation scene has plenty of variety, with most of the best options located in, or within easy walking distance to, the central city. Note that room rates fluctuate wildly throughout the year in all price categories. Outside the busy May to mid-September period most budget places slash rates by up to half.

Upper Town

★**Swanky Mint Hostel** HOSTEL €
(☎01-40 04 248; www.swanky-hostel.com/mint; Ilica 50; dm 170-200KN, s/d 400/600KN; ❄@🛜🏊) This backpacker vortex, converted from a 19th-century textile-dye factory, has a very happening bar at its heart. Dorms are small but thoughtfully kitted out with lockers, privacy curtains and reading lamps, while private rooms are bright and large.

The hostel's popularity, however, lies in its supersocial, friendly vibe, with welcome shots of *rakija* (grappa), organised pub crawls and an on-site travel agency.

Hostel 63 HOSTEL €
(☎01-55 20 557; www.hostel63.eu; Vlaška 63/7; dm/d/apt €22/65/75;) Everything is kept shipshape and squeaky clean at this grey-yellow-and-white themed hostel, run by helpful staff. Four-bed dorms are thoughtfully equipped with lockers, privacy curtains and private bathrooms; there's even two dorms with two double-bed bunks for couples. Breakfast is €4. Its quiet location, in a courtyard off the main road, means you should get a good night's sleep.

Chillout Hostel Zagreb Downtown HOSTEL €
(☎01-48 49 605; www.chillout-hostel-zagreb.com; Tomićeva 5a; dm 130-145KN, d 400KN; P@) Located down a squiggle of an alley, just off Tomićeva, Chillout has a great bar and a swag of dorms and private rooms. Good-sized dorms are well kitted-out, with lockers and individual power points, reading lights and shelf for each bunk. The vibe is friendly and very social with pub crawls, day trips and free walking tours on offer.

Rooms Zagreb 17 BOUTIQUE HOTEL €€
(☎091 17 00 000; www.sobezagreb17.com; Radićeva 22; r €60-80, apt €120;) In the heart of the city, these spacious rooms overlooking the cafe-buzz of Tkalčićeva have swags of style thanks to owner Irena's eye for detail. Lashings of white are offset by fun, vibrant art, minifridges and perspex chairs, and all come well equipped with satellite TV (plentiful international channels) and kettles. Grab Room 2 for the nautical theme.

★**Hotel Jägerhorn** HISTORIC HOTEL €€€
(☎01-48 33 877; www.hotel-jagerhorn.hr; Ilica 14; s/d/ste 950/1050/1500KN; P@) The oldest hotel in Zagreb (around since 1827) is a peaceful oasis, brimming with character. The 18 rooms are elegantly outfitted, with soft neutral decor offset by blue accents, king-sized beds, kettles, and swish, contemporary bathrooms. Top-floor rooms have views over leafy Gradec. Staff are charming and the downstairs terrace cafe is the perfect hang-out after your sightseeing is done.

Lower Town

Shappy Hostel HOSTEL €
(☎01-48 30 483; www.hostel-shappy.com; Varšavska 8; dm 170KN, d from 550KN; P) This small hostel is a peaceful oasis tucked away in a courtyard. Private rooms are decked out with lashings of grey and white. Four-bed dorms (all sharing spotless bathrooms) are some of the most spacious in town. The sun-dappled terrace here is a relaxing hideaway for when you want to chill out.

★**Studio Kairos** B&B €€
(☎01-46 40 690; Vlaška 92; s/d/tr/q from €36/50/65/70;) This adorable B&B in a street-level apartment has four well-appointed rooms decked out by theme – Writers', Crafts, Music and Granny's. The cosy common space, where a delicious breakfast is served, and the enthusiastic hosts, who are a fount of knowledge on all things Zagreb, adds to this place's intimate and homely appeal. Bikes are also available for rent.

4 City Windows B&B €€
(☎01-88 97 999; www.4citywindows.com; Palmotićeva 13; s/d €55/90; P) Tanja and Ivo provide personalised service at this intimate B&B slap in the centre, making it feel more

SHORT-TERM APARTMENTS

If you want to experience the city like a local, Zagreb has a dizzying choice of short-term apartment-rental options.

Local, well-regarded agencies **Irundo** (☎01-88 95 433; https://irundo.com; reception Petrinjska 9; apt €57-100; P) and **InZagreb** (☎091 65 23 201; www.inzagreb.com; apt €65-95;) both have a list of apartments scattered throughout the central city, which suit couples through to large family groups.

For booking directly through apartment owners, award-winning **Main Square Apartment** (☎091 15 11 967; www.accrommodation.com; Trg Bana Jelačića 3; 1-2/3/4 people €80/90/100;) is slap-bang on the main square, while the bijou, well-equipped studio of **Agramer Apartments** (☎091 60 90 764; https://agramerzagreb.wordpress.com; Jukićeva 34; per night/week €40/250; P) is better value for solo travellers and couples than most of the city's hotel rooms.

like staying with two cool Zagreb-insiders rather than in a hotel. Spacious rooms are filled with fun arty flair, and thanks to thick walls, you're guaranteed a good sleep. Breakfast is a feast including *štrukli* (baked cheese dumplings), pancakes and homemade jams.

Hotel Astoria BUSINESS HOTEL €€
(01-48 08 900; www.hotelastoria.hr; Petrinjska 71; s/d from €80/90;) Hotel Astoria is a solid choice just a short stroll from the train station. Part of the Best Western Premier hotel family, the hotel has bright, business-brisk rooms all comfortably fitted out with kettles, TVs and good-sized bathrooms. Staff are superfriendly and keen to help.

Hotel Garden HOTEL €€
(01-48 43 720; www.gardenhotel.hr; Vodnikova 13; d/tr €95/105;) Right by the Botanical Garden (hence the name), the Garden is all clean lines and lashings of white. We like the soothing neutral decor topped off by B&W prints above the bed. Corner rooms (billed as 'economy doubles') are much smaller than standards and €10 cheaper. If you're worried about tram-line noise, ask for a room at the back.

Hotel Dubrovnik BUSINESS HOTEL €€
(01-48 63 555; www.hotel-dubrovnik.hr; Gajeva 1; d from €110;) Smack on Zagreb's main square, this city landmark has friendly staff and freshly renovated spacious rooms, comfortably outfitted with big TVs (with plentiful English channels), bigger beds and modern bathrooms. Try to get a view of Trg Bana Jelačića and watch Zagreb pass by under your window.

Esplanade Zagreb Hotel HISTORIC HOTEL €€€
(01-45 66 666; www.esplanade.hr; Mihanovićeva 1; r from €130;) This art deco masterpiece was purpose-built to welcome the Orient Express crowd in 1925 and still holds onto many original features, from its grand marble staircase and intricate stained-glass windows to the glorious Emerald Ballroom. Rooms exude timeless elegance – as you'd expect for a place that has a roll call of kings and politicians on its past guest list.

Other Neighbourhoods

Hotel 9 BOUTIQUE HOTEL €€
(01-56 25 040; www.hotel9.hr; Avenija Marina Držića 9; r from €90;) This slick contemporary outfit is straight across the road from the bus station. Large rooms, most with balconies, have funky mirror-stripe walls and either white, silver or gold accents. Even front-facing rooms are wonderfully quiet thanks to double glazing. Breakfast with all the trimmings is served on the rooftop terrace.

Eating

Zagreb's restaurants are big on traditional Croatian and Italian cuisine but you'll also find plenty of bistro cookery utilising the fresh produce from Dolac Market. For cheap eats, bakeries, snack bars and fast-food joints cluster in the city centre. Many restaurants close in August for their summer holiday, which lasts anywhere from two weeks to a month.

Upper Town

La Štruk CROATIAN €
(www.facebook.com/La-Struk; Skalinska 5; mains 29-40KN; 11am-10pm;) Serving one thing only, La Štruk devotes itself to *štrukli* (baked cheese dumplings). Keep traditional with a salty or sweet cheese *kuhani* (boiled) version or veer completely off-piste with the roasted-pepper or truffle *zapečeni* (baked) options – more like an ultracheesy lasagna. If inside is full, there's seating in the hidden garden accessed through an alley to the side.

Amelie CAFE €
(www.slasticeamelie.com; Vlaška 6; cakes 17-19KN; 8am-11pm;) Many locals regard this cafe as one of Zagreb's best cake-and-coffee stops. Seasonal specialities such as plum cake in summer are particularly good. On fine days, sit on the terrace, directly across the street.

Curry Bowl SRI LANKAN €
(01-55 79 175; www.srilankancurrybowl.com; Tkalčićeva 44; mains 39-55KN; 11am-11pm Sun-Thu, to midnight Fri & Sat;) Pining for some spice? Head here for Sri Lankan sunshiny flavours. Order the *kotthu* (spicy mix of roti bread, vegetables and egg), add in a serving of pineapple chutney or *pol sambol* (coconut condiment) to chuck on the top and don't forget a bottle of the island's favourite brew, Lion beer, to wash it all down.

★ **Mali Bar** TAPAS €€
(01-55 31 014; www.facebook.com/MaliBarZagreb; Vlaška 63; dishes 45-150KN; 12.30pm-midnight Mon-Sat;) This earthy-toned spot by star chef Ana Ugarković is all about small plates, with influences cherry-picked from across the Mediterranean, Middle East and Asia. Dig into *labneh* (strained yoghurt cheese)

balls on a bed of chard and roasted beetroot, smoked tuna dressed in saffron and Chinese pork dumplings all in the same sitting.

Lanterna na Dolcu CROATIAN €€

(☎01-48 19 009; www.lanterna-zagreb.com; Opatovina 31; mains 55-95KN; ⏰11am-11pm Tue-Sat, 4-11pm Sun & Mon; 📶) Modern tweaks on traditional Croatian classics and fabulous service make Lanterna stand out amid the central city's glut of restaurants. In the cosy basement with brick-vaulted ceiling, dig into mains of plum-stuffed pork loin doused in a brandy and plum jus or steak in a pickled pepper sauce. There's an excellent wine list here, too.

Trilogija MEDITERRANEAN €€

(☎01-48 51 394; www.trilogija.com; Kamenita 5; mains 88-140KN; ⏰11am-midnight Mon-Thu, to 10am Fri & Sat, to 4pm Sun; ❄) Right by the Stone Gate, in a location that has seen many a restaurant open and close, Trilogija seems to be here to stay. The secret lies in its friendly staff and Mediterranean-fusion menu with dishes like tuna steak with beetroot and a risotto of shrimp and mango.

Didov San DALMATIAN €€

(☎01-48 51 154; www.konoba-didovsan.com; Mletačka 11; mains 95-140KN; ⏰10am-midnight; ❄) Delve into the traditional cuisine of the Neretva River delta in Dalmatia's hinterland at this rustic Upper Town tavern. Grilled eel, snails on polenta and frogs wrapped in prosciutto are three of its specialities not to be missed.

ZAGREBIAN VEGETARIAN

Traditionally a carnivore-pleasing place, Zagreb has never been the greatest destination for vegetarians and vegans. In recent years, though, quite a number of the city restaurants have expanded their vegetarian menu options, so you shouldn't struggle to find a meal. There's also a handful of dining options catering specifically for a vegetarian and vegan clientele – though be prepared for salt as your sole seasoning as the spice rack is sorely missing.

For vegetarian meals our prime pick is Curry Bowl (p85), which has a vegetarian option for all of its flavoursome curries. Mali Bar (p85) has a good range of nonmeat options. For pure vegetarian and vegan food head to **Zrno** (www.zrnobiobistro.hr; Medulićeva 20; mains 59-75KN; ⏰noon-9.30pm Mon-Sat; ❄🖊) or **Green Point** (www.green-point.hr; Varšavska 10; dishes 24-39KN; ⏰9am-10pm Mon-Sat; ❄📶🖊).

Kaptolska Klet CROATIAN €€

(☎01-48 76 502; www.kaptolska-klet.eu; Kaptol 5; mains 80-170KN; ⏰11am-midnight) Dig into traditional central European flavours in the slightly staid beer-hall-style interior or on the huge outdoor terrace. It also serves regular seasonal specialities such as deep-fried balls of duck meat served on a bed of stewed red cabbage.

Stari Fijaker 900 CROATIAN €€

(☎01-48 33 829; www.starifijaker.hr; Mesnička 6; mains 66-150KN; ⏰11am-11pm Mon-Sat, to 10pm Sun; ❄) Once the height of dining out in Zagreb, this grand dame is a great place to sample Croatian and central European staples while soaking up the atmosphere of yesteryear. Hearty shepherd stews from the Slavonia region, Zagreb-style schnitzel and *mlinci* (baked noodles) with turkey all feature on the traditional menu.

★ **Bistro Apetit** EUROPEAN €€€

(☎01-46 77 335; www.bistroapetit.com; Jurjevska 65a; mains 132-202KN; ⏰10am-midnight Tue-Sun; ❄) High up on villa-lined Jurjevska steet, this restaurant run by chef Marin Rendić, who previously worked at Copenhagen's Noma, serves up Zagreb's suavest contemporary dishes. Start with tuna tartare with pear and sesame seeds then move on to beef cheeks on bean spread, laced by carrot and pistachio. Opt for a degustation menu (five/seven courses 420/620KN) for flavour-packed feasting.

Agava INTERNATIONAL €€€

(☎01-48 29 826; www.restaurant-agava.hr; Tkalčićeva 39; mains 77-200KN; ⏰9am-11pm; ❄📶) The front terrace is perfect for a lazy long lunch while soaking up the sun and gazing down onto the pedestrian promenade below. The menu cherry-picks influences from across the globe, including tuna steak in a sesame sauce served on couscous, and risotto with sheep cheese and pear, as well as some classic Croatian dishes.

Baltazar CROATIAN €€€

(www.facebook.com/restoranbaltazar; Nova Ves 4; mains 90-200KN; ⏰noon-midnight Mon-Sat, to 5pm Sun; ❄) Meaty grills prepared the Zagorje and Slavonian way and steak dishes are the name of the game at this upmarket old-timer. The summer terrace is a great place for dining under the stars.

Lower Town

Heritage CROATIAN €

(Petrinjska 14; mains 18-39KN; 11am-8pm Mon-sat;) Tapas dishes, Croatian-style. This teensy place, with just one counter and a few bar stools, serves cheese and meat platters using all locally sourced ingredients. Try the flatbreads with prosciutto from Zagora, black-truffle spread and cheese from Ika, or the *kulen* (spicy paprika-flavoured sausage) with grilled peppers and cream cheese. Service is warm and friendly.

Time Pastry Shop DESSERTS €

(www.facebook.com/timepastry; Teslina 14; cakes 30-40KN; 10am-11pm Mon-Sat) It's almost a crime to eat the miniature works of art at this high-end Parisian-style patisserie, but if someone's got to do it, we'll take one for the team.

b041 ICE CREAM €

(www.facebook.com/nacestib041; Masarykova 25; scoops 11KN; 9am-midnight;) Zagreb's most decadently rich ice cream with plenty to keep the chocoholics happy as well as more quirky, fun flavours like orange cheesecake and almond amaretto.

Vincek DESSERTS €

(www.vincek.com.hr; Ilica 18; cakes & pastries 10-24KN; 8.30am-11pm Mon-Sat) A Zagreb institution, this *slastičarna* (pastry shop) has been keeping the city's dentists in business since 1978. Come here to reward yourself with a fluffy cherry parfait, a slice of walnut cake or a scoop of ice cream after pounding the cobblestones.

Vis à Vis DESSERTS €

(www.vincek.com.hr; Tomićeva 2; cakes & pastries 12-24KN; 9am-10pm Mon-Sat;) Little-sister cafe to Vincek, Vis à Vis dishes up scrummy treats, but with no white sugar used and all gluten-free. Many of the cakes on offer are also vegan, with the carrot, almond and ginger cake getting the thumbs up from us.

Pingvin SANDWICHES €

(Teslina 7; sandwiches 18-30KN; 10am-4am Mon-Sat, 6pm-2am Sun) You ain't been to Zagreb if you haven't had a Pingvin sandwich. This fast-food joint has been churning out chicken fillets and burgers, stuffed in pita bread and topped off with a mountain of pickles and salads, since 1987.

Vinodol CROATIAN €€

(01-48 11 427; www.vinodol-zg.hr; Teslina 10; mains 85-160KN; 11.30am-midnight;) Giving central European fare a modern tweak, Vinodol is much loved by locals. On warm days, eat on the covered patio (entered through an ivy-clad passageway off Teslina). Menu highlights include succulent lamb or veal and potatoes cooked under *peka* (a domed baking lid), and almond-crusted trout.

Boban ITALIAN €€

(01-48 11 549; www.boban.hr; Gajeva 9; mains 65-148KN; 11am-11pm Mon-Thu, to midnight Fri & Sat, noon-11pm Sun;) Italian is the name of the game in this cellar restaurant owned by Croatian football star Zvonimir Boban. Tuck into hearty portions of homemade pasta and gnocchi. There are good children's menu options (48KN–62KN) as well.

Bistro Fotić BISTRO €€

(01-48 10 476; www.bistrofotic.com; Gajeva 25; mains 55-90KN; 8am-11pm Mon-Sat;) Chow down on *tiramola* pizza (Margherita pizza with prosciutto slices pegged on a rope above the plate) or, for something lighter, a slice of quiche at this cosy bistro eclectically decorated with old cameras and radios cluttered together on shelves and B&W photos on the walls.

Ribice i Tri Točkice SEAFOOD €€

(01-56 35 479; www.ribiceitritockice.hr; Preradovićeva 7/1; mains 70-110KN; 9am-11pm;) Head upstairs to this fun seafood spot to dine on fish while surrounded by colourful aquatic murals. Simple but good Dalmatian mainstays are served up, with specialities such as cuttlefish and squid stew and tuna and gnocchi.

Lari & Penati CROATIAN €€

(01-46 55 776; www.laripenati.hr; Petrinjska 42a; mains 40-90KN; noon-11pm Mon-Sat) This small, stylish bistro is good for a light lunch, with quiche, salads and open sandwiches on the menu along with tapas-style dishes made for sharing.

Zinfandel's INTERNATIONAL €€€

(01-45 66 644; www.zinfandels.hr; Mihanovićeva 1; mains 165-230KN; 6am-11pm Mon-Sat, 6.30am-11pm Sun;) One of the top tables in town, Zinfandel's is headed by chef Ana Grgić, whose menu of creative flair is served in the grand dining room of the Esplanade Zagreb

Hotel (p85). Don't miss the confit pigeon with beetroot and cherries with a rhubarb sauce. After dinner move onto the Oleander Terrace for a drink and prime people-watching across Starčevićev Trg.

Le Bistro FRENCH €€€
(www.lebistro.hr; Mihanovićeva 1; mains 95-270KN; 9am-11pm;) Executive chef Ana Grgić leads the team at the casual-chic restaurant of the Esplanade Zagreb Hotel (p85), much favoured by local business folk for its lunchtime three-course daily menu (160KN). It's known for its *štrukli* (cottage-cheese-filled dumplings), and its classic French-style menu.

Other Neighbourhoods

Lauba Bistro BISTRO €€
(01-63 02 140; www.lauba.hr; Baruna Filipovića 23a; mains 50-150KN; 2-10pm Mon-Fri, 11am-10pm Sat) This chic bistro is in the lobby of one of Zagreb's coolest art spaces. If you're after a small bite, it serves delicious miniloaves of bread as its signature – think quinoa and beer bread – with tasty spreads. More substantial dishes include lovely stews and daily changing mains.

Drinking & Nightlife

In the Upper Town, Tkalčićeva is throbbing with bars and cafes. With half a dozen bars and sidewalk cafes between Trg Petra Preradovića (known locally as Cvjetni trg) and Bogovićeva in the Lower Town, the scene on summer nights resembles a vast outdoor party. Things wind down by midnight, though, and get quieter from mid-July through late August.

Upper Town

Craft Room CRAFT BEER
(www.facebook.com/craftroombeer; Opatovina 35; 10am-2am;) In the city centre, this is the number-one stop for anyone interested in Croatia's craft-beer scene. Plenty of local beers are on tap and there's a huge menu of bottled international brands.

Pivnica Mali Medo CRAFT BEER
(www.pivovara-medvedgrad; Tkalčićeva 36; 10am-midnight Mon-Wed, to 1am Thu-Sat, noon-11pm Sun;) Sister pub to Pivnica Medvedgrad, Mali Medo has snaffled prime position along this pedestrian strip and gets crammed with people enjoying house-brewed beers late into the night. For those who only stopped in for a sundowner but are now too comfortable to move on, there's a decent menu of pub grub as well.

MK Krolo BAR
(Radićeva 7; 9am-1am Mon-Sat, to 11pm Sun) This darling of Zagreb's dive bars is the gathering spot for the city's artists, bohos, media types and local drunks. Socialist chic at its best.

Funk CLUB
(www.facebook.com/funkklub; Tkalčićeva 52; 11am-2am) A rather-blah cafe during the day but at night Funk comes into its own. Head down the spiral staircase and you'll see why this cult spot has locals at its beck and call. In a small basement with stone vaulted ceilings, DJs spin house, jazz, funk and broken beats for a boogie-happy crowd on Thursday, Friday and Saturday nights.

Velvet COFFEE
(Dežmanova 9; 8am-10pm Mon-Fri, to 3pm Sat, to 2pm Sun) Stylish spot for a good (but pricey) cup of java and a quick bite amid the minimalist-chic interior decked out by owner Saša Šekoranja, Zagreb's hippest florist. The Velvet Gallery bar next door, known as 'Black Velvet', stays open till 11pm (except on Sunday).

Dežman Bar BAR
(www.dezman.hr; Dežmanova 3; 8am-midnight Mon-Thu, to 1am Fri & Sat) Shielded from traffic inside the cosy passage leading to the semi-wild Tuškanac forest, this cafe-cum-bar is a chic but casual spot to sink a few cocktails on the narrow terrace outside. There are organic teas by Les Jardins de Gaia and craft beer from the UK's Brewdog.

Johann Franck CAFE
(www.johannfranck.hr; Trg Bana Jelačića 9; 8am-2am Mon-Thu & Sun, to 4am Fri & Sat) Location, location, location. Everyone from fashionable young things to gossiping grandmas and museumed-out tourists pack out the front terrace and slick couch-filled ground floor of this cafe (named after Croatia's pioneer coffee roaster and the namesake coffee brand) for coffee, cocktails and beer.

Lower Town

Pupitres WINE BAR
(098 165 80 73; http://pupitres.hr; Frankopanska 1; 9am-11pm Mon-Thu, to 1am Fri & Sat;) When a wine bar is run by a top sommelier, you know you're in good hands. Jelene Šimić

LOCAL KNOWLEDGE

LGBTIQ+ ZAGREB

The LGBTIQ+ scene in Zagreb is finally becoming more open than it has previously been – although free-wheeling, it isn't. There are a handful of major gay and lesbian city hang-outs. Also look out for performances by Le Zbor (www.lezbor.com), Croatia's lesbian and feminist choir with an activist edge. The only big event of the year is Zagreb Pride (www.zagreb-pride.net). Major city hang-outs are:

Hotpot (Petrinjska 31; ⏲11pm-5am Fri & Sat) Friendly gay bar-club with good-value drinks.

Kolaž (Amruševa 11; ⏲8am-2am Mon-Fri, 10am-2am Sat, 6pm-2am Sun) This rollicking bar, festooned with sparkly glitter-balls, attracts an arty, mixed gay/straight crowd in the evenings.

Rush (www.facebook.com/rushzg; Savska Cesta 120; ⏲midnight-5am Sat) A younger LGBTIQ+ crowd head out of the city centre to party on Saturday nights.

Valentić's casual-chic place is the best spot in town to get acquainted with Croatia's plethora of wines. Service is charming and genuinely helpful and the wine list is (unsurprisingly) a roll-call of the country's best cellars plus some international names.

Pivnica Medvedgrad CRAFT BEER
(Medvedgrad Brewery; www.pivnica-medvedgrad.hr; Ilica 49; ⏲10am-midnight Mon-Sat, noon-midnight Sun; 📶) Sip on one of five house-brewed beers (14KN–17KN), from a hoppy lager to a classic weizenbier, at this fun and bustling bar with a large, chestnut-tree-shaded courtyard. It also offers up reliably cheap and tasty grub. Access is through a shopping passageway off Ilica.

Quahwa COFFEE
(Teslina 9; ⏲9am-9pm Mon-Thu, to 10pm Fri & Sat, 10am-5pm Sun; 📶) Living up to its tagline ('for coffee lovers only'), Quahwa serves up some of the finest arabica in Zagreb, from superstrong lattes to traditional Turkish coffee. Caffeine heaven.

Cogito Coffee Shop CAFE
(www.cogitocoffee.com; Varšavska 11; ⏲8am-8pm Mon-Fri, 9am-7pm Sat; 📶) Down a passageway, this tiny ultracool Berlin-style cafe serves up coffee roasted by the local Cogito Coffee Roasters at Cafe u Dvorištu. There's delicious Medenko ice cream on offer as well. Shorter hours in August.

Old Pharmacy Pub PUB
(www.pub.pondi.hr; Andrije Hebranga 11; ⏲8am-midnight Sun-Thu, to 1am Fri & Sat) This traditional English pub hides inside an Austro-Hungarian town house, but once you walk in, all the elements are there: a mirror behind the bar, pharmacy-related paraphernalia and washed-out photos, all set up among the wood and leather decor.

Vinyl BAR
(www.vinylzagreb.com; Bogovićeva 3; ⏲8am-midnight Sun-Tue, to 2am Wed & Thu, to 4am Fri & Sat) Much beloved by the locals, this all-day lounge on a popular stretch is split into cafe and club areas. It delivers fun both day and night, including live-music events, readings and exhibitions of books and vinyl, such as Masters of Memories on Monday evening. Don't miss the vinyl-only DJ sets on weekends and the superb range of whiskey.

Kava Tava CAFE
(www.kavatava.com; Britanski trg bb; ⏲7am-midnight) This chic black-and-red cafe is a popular hang-out for families and big groups of friends. For top-notch people-watching, you really want to snag a table on the outside terrace, across the road amid the bustle of the market stalls. Sit back and drink a beer (17KN–28KN) or sip a grappa (16KN) while soaking up all the market action.

Express CAFE
(Petrinjska 4; ⏲7am-9pm Mon-Thu, to 11pm Fri & Sat, 11am-7pm Sun) A tiny little cafe with tables outside, serving some of Zagreb's best coffee and tea. It closes on Sunday in August.

Mojo BAR
(www.facebook.com/MojoBarZG; Martićeva 5; ⏲7am-2am Mon-Sat, 8am-midnight Sun) Smoky basement hang-out where live music and DJ-spun tunes happen every night. On warm nights, take your pick from 70 different types of *rakija* (grappa) and liqueurs and sample them on the pavement tables out front.

1

ZM_PHOTO/SHUTTERSTOCK ©

2

4

DARIOZG/SHUTTERSTOCK ©

1. Jesuit Church of St Catherine (p73)
Built between 1620 and 1632, the Jesuit Church of St Catherine is a fine example of the baroque style.

2. Mirogoj (p68)
One of the most beautiful cemeteries in Europe, Mirogoj is criss-crossed by paths and dotted with sculptures and artfully designed tombs.

3. Museum of Broken Relationships (p68)
This wonderfully quirky museum explores the mementoes leftover after a relationship ends.

4. Dolac Market (p69)
Sellers from all over Croatia descend on Zagreb's central produce market to hawk their goods.

HIDEAKI TSUDA/SOOPX ©

Sedmica BAR

(http://caffebar-sedmica.com; Kačićeva 7a; 8am-1am Mon-Thu, to 2am Fri & Sat, 5pm-1am Sun) This low-key bar is hidden in an alleyway off Kačićeva, with a big Guinness sign marking the entrance. A gathering point for Zagreb's boho-intellectual crowd, it has a poky interior with a mezzanine and an outside patio that buzzes in warmer months.

Cafe u Dvorištu CAFE

(Jurja Žerjavića 7/2; 9am-midnight Mon-Sat, 11am-7pm Sun;) Tucked away inside a courtyard, this sweet cafe serves excellent organic and fair-trade coffee – roasted on-site by Cogito – and tea. There are occasional readings and art exhibitions. Closed Sunday from late July to August.

Kino Europa CAFE

(www.kinoeuropa.hr/cafe; Varšavska 3; 8.30am-midnight Mon-Fri, to 2am Sat & Sun;) The front of Zagreb's oldest cinema (p93), dating from the 1920s, houses a fun cafe-wine bar-*grapperia* that attracts a diverse crowd in the evening. The coffee is decent, beers are 17KN to 24KN and there's over 30 types of grappa for you to try. Service can be on the gruff side.

Eliscaffe COFFEE

(www.eliscaffe.com; Ilica 63; 8am-7pm Mon-Sat, 9am-2pm Sun;) The award-winning coffee made from 100% arabica beans is tops. If you're a caffeine-addict don't leave town until you've tried the *triestino* (a Trieste-style large macchiato, always served in a glass).

Booksa CAFE

(www.booksa.hr; Martićeva 14d; 10am-9pm Tue-Sun;) Bookworms and poets, writers and performers, oddballs and artists...basically anyone creative in Zagreb comes here to chat and drink coffee, browse the library, surf with free wi-fi and hear readings at this lovely, book-themed cafe. There are English-language readings here, too. Closes for a month from mid-July. Note that you'll need to pay a one-time membership fee of 10KN.

Bacchus BAR

(www.facebook.com/bacchusjazzbar; Trg Kralja Tomislava 16; 11am-midnight Mon-Fri, noon-midnight Sat) You'll be lucky if you score a table at Zagreb's most bohemian courtyard garden – lush and hidden down a passageway behind an ornate door. In the evenings you can often catch live jazz here.

Other Neighbourhoods

Garden Brewery CRAFT BEER

(www.thegarden.hr/the-garden-brewery; Slavonska avenija 22f; noon-8pm Mon-Thu & Sun, to 2am Fri & Sat;) This boutique craft brewery and bar is worth the shlep out to the industrial east of Zagreb. Inside an old red-brick factory, it offers craft beer made on-site (try the Session Ale with floral overtones or the Kettle Sour full of fruity flavours), live music on Saturday and family-friendly Sunday sessions.

Hop Inn CRAFT BEER

(Dubravkin trg 3; 4pm-midnight;) Craft-beer fanatics may well want to take a break from the central nightlife hub to head to this small, laid-back bar where local craft beer (15KN–34KN for a large beer) is front and centre of everything they do. This is the place to get stuck into local labels like Nova Runda, Zmajsko and the Garden Brewery. It's a two-minute stroll from the bus station.

Entertainment

Zagreb's theatres and concert halls present a lively variety of programs throughout the year. Many are listed in the monthly brochure *Zagreb Events & Performances*, available from the main tourist office. Also check out the free *Zagreb 4 You* monthly, which lists cool Zagreb events.

Booze & Blues LIVE MUSIC

(www.booze-and-blues.com; Tkalčićeva 84; 8am-midnight Sun-Tue, to 2am Wed-Sat;) It does what it says on the tin. Perched at the top of the buzzy Tkalča strip, this haven of jazz, blues and soul rhythms stands out with its weekend live-music line-up. The interior is designed in the tradition of American blues and jazz clubs, with music-history memorabilia, and Heineken on tap flowing from a functioning saxophone.

Tvornica LIVE MUSIC

(www.tvornicakulture.com; Šubićeva 2; cafe 7am-11pm Mon-Fri, 4-11pm Sat & Sun, club 8pm-2am Sun-Thu, to 4am Fri & Sat) Excellent multimedia venue showcasing a variety of live-music performances, from Bosnian *sevdah* to alternative punk rock. Check out the website to see what's on.

Strossmarte LIVE MUSIC

(www.ljetonastrosu.com; Strossmayerovo Šetalište; May-Sep) During the summer months, the Strossmayer promenade in the Upper Town hosts live music most nights in the evening with makeshift bars. The mixed-bag crowd, great city views and leafy ambience make it a great spot to while away your evenings.

Kino Europa CINEMA
(www.kinoeuropa.hr; Varšavska 3) Zagreb's oldest cinema's 'Subtitled Tuesdays' program shows (usually art house) movies with subtitles in English as well as Croatian.

Zagrebačko Kazalište Mladih THEATRE
(ZKM; ☎01-48 72 554; www.zekaem.hr; Teslina 7; ⊙box office 10am-8pm Mon-Fri, to 2pm Sat, plus 1hr before the show) The Zagreb Youth Theatre, better known as ZKM, is considered the cradle of Croatia's contemporary theatre. It hosts several festivals and many visiting troupes from around the world.

Croatian National Theatre THEATRE
(☎01-48 88 415; www.hnk.hr; Trg Republika Hrvatska 15; ⊙box office 10am-7pm Mon-Fri, to 1pm Sat, plus 1hr before performances) This neobaroque theatre, established in 1895, stages a regular program of opera and ballet performances and plays. Check out Ivan Meštrović's sculpture *The Well of Life* (1905) standing out front.

Vatroslav Lisinski Concert Hall CONCERT VENUE
(☎01-61 21 166; www.lisinski.hr; Trg Stjepa-na Radića 4; ⊙box office 10am-8pm Mon-Fri, 10am-2pm & 6-8pm Sat & Sun) This is the city's most prestigious venue in which to hear symphony concerts, jazz and world-music performances; it also stages theatrical productions.

Shopping

Ilica is Zagreb's main shopping street, with fashionable international brands peeking out from the staid buildings. Design boutiques are scattered throughout the city including local fashion shops, shoemakers and craft stores. Zagreb doesn't have many markets but those it does have are stellar.

Upper Town

Galerija Link DESIGN
(www.facebook.com/GalerijaLink; Radićeva 27; ⊙10am-8pm) Ceramics, linens, clothes and home decor all made by Croatian designers.

Love, Ana DESIGN
(www.loveanadesign.com; Dežmanova 4; ⊙2-8pm Mon-Fri, noon-2pm Sat) Internationally acclaimed product designer Ana Tevšić sells her signature wares at her all-white studio-store, including portable lamps, bucket bags and beach towels.

Boudoir FASHION & ACCESSORIES
(www.boudoirzagreb.com; Radićeva 22; ⊙11am-7pm Mon-Fri, 10am-2pm Sat) When you walk up cobbled Radićeva street, stop by the buzzer that says 'press for champagne' and let yourself into an other-worldly designer shop where silk, satin and lace dresses are handmade on-site. The owners, sisters Morana and Martina, create outfits that are a unique mixture of elegance and funkiness with an added spice of Moulin Rouge.

Koza FASHION & ACCESSORIES
(Basaričekova 18; ⊙11am-7pm Mon-Sat) This tiny studio-shop on a quiet Upper Town street turns out gorgeous handmade leather bags and accessories like wallets, belts and even flip-flops. The elegant, chic yet quirky bags are crafted with all-Croatian materials, including high-quality leather.

I-GLE FASHION & ACCESSORIES
(www.i-gle.com; Dežmanova 4; ⊙10am-8pm Mon-Fri, to 3pm Sat) Get one of the almost sculptural yet wearable creations by Nataša Mihaljčišin and Martina Vrdoljak-Ranilović, the movers and shakers of Croatia's fashion industry since the 1990s.

Cahun HATS
(www.cahun.hr; Podzidom 8; ⊙9am-7pm Mon-Fri, to 2pm Sat) This 80-year-old family-run hat shop oozes old Zagreb charms. The headgear is meticulously handcrafted following a traditional approach, but infused with modern designer touches. Take your pick from hats galore, for both women and men, and for all seasons: cloche, fedora, panama and trilby hats; beret, newsboy and flat caps, and many more. Discounts available for cash payments.

Take Me Home GIFTS & SOUVENIRS
(www.takemehome.hr; Tomićeva 4; ⊙9.30am-8pm Mon-Fri, 10am-3pm Sat) An eclectic choice of cool souvenirs, all by Croatian designers.

Aromatica COSMETICS
(www.aromatica.hr; Vlaška 7; ⊙8am-8pm Mon-Fri, to 3pm Sat) Flagship store of a small chain showcasing all-natural skincare products, from handcrafted soaps to fragrant oils, with a focus on local herbs. Great gift baskets, too.

Bornstein WINE
(www.bornstein.hr; Kaptol 19; ⊙9am-8pm Mon-Fri, to 4.30pm Sat) If Croatia's wine and spirits have gone to your head, get your fix here. Stocks an astonishing collection of brandy, wine and gourmet products. There's also a wine bar on-site.

LOCAL KNOWLEDGE

MARKETS

Antiques Market (Britanski trg; ⏲7am-2pm Sat, 7.30am-2.30pm Sun) The weekend antiques market on Britanski trg is one of central Zagreb's joys. Browse tables stuffed with oddities and knick-knacks before grabbing a coffee at the cafe seating around the edge of the square.

Hrelić (⏲7am-3pm Wed, Sat & Sun) Croatia's largest and most colourful flea market, a huge space packed with everything from car parts and antique furniture to clothes, records and kitchenware. All goods are secondhand, of course, and bargaining is the norm. It's a great experience in itself and is a side of Zagreb you probably won't see anywhere else – expect lots of Roma people, music, general liveliness and grilled meat smoking in the food section. If you're going in the summer months, bring a hat and wear sunscreen, as there's no shade. Take bus 295 (15KN, 20 minutes, Sunday only) to Sajam Jakuševac from behind the railway station. By tram, take number 6 in the direction of Sopot, get off near the bridge and walk 15 minutes along the Sava to get to Hrelić; or take tram 14, get off at the last stop (Zapruđe) and begin the 15-minute walk from there.

Vintesa WINE

(www.vintesa.hr; Vlaška 63; ⏲9am-9pm Mon-Fri, to 8pm Sat) Hidden inside a courtyard, this pioneer wine shop is a treasure trove of local wines charmingly lined up on brick and wood shelves. The extrafriendly staff will not only suggest a bottle that suits everyone's taste but also unravel a story behind each grape variety, batch and bottle. The shop boasts more than 180 types of Croatian wine from all regions, among them some exclusive limited editions.

Lower Town

Znanje BOOKS

(www.znanje.hr; Gajeva 1; ⏲8am-9pm Mon-Fri, to 4pm Sat) Zagreb's best bookshop for foreign-language titles. Downstairs there's a vast range of English novels and nonfiction as well as travel guidebooks and a small range of German books.

Cerovečki Umbrellas FASHION & ACCESSORIES

(www.kisobrani-cerovecki.hr; Ilica 49; ⏲8.30am-8pm Mon-Fri, to 2.30pm Sat) Quality, design and a brand story safeguard this umbrella artisan from the onslaught of global products. The shop is a wormhole to a different era, showcasing a distinctive award-winning range of umbrellas, used by people worldwide. The red-patterned Šestine umbrella has become the epitome of Zagreb. To show off, choose one of the ladies' parasols with rich intricate lace.

Zvonimir SHOES

(www.facebook.com/balerinke; Dalmatinska 12; ⏲9am-1pm & 5-8pm Mon-Fri, 9am-3pm Sat) Nataša Trinajstić is a third-generation shoemaker from this well-known Zagreb family. Visit her small shop and studio where she craftily blends the tradition of artisanship with modern signature touches. Go for ready-made shoes (Oxfords, ballerinas, pumps, Mary Janes, stilettos), sandals or boots, or get Nataša to whip up some custom-made footwear.

Salon Croata CLOTHING

(www.croata.hr; Ilica 5, Oktogon Passage; ⏲8am-8pm Mon-Fri, to 3pm Sat) Since the necktie originated in Croatia, nothing could make a more authentic gift – and this is the place to get one. The locally made silk neckties are priced from 400KN to 2000KN.

Information

DISCOUNT CARDS

If you're in Zagreb for a day or three, getting the **Zagreb Card** (www.zagrebcard.fivestars.hr; 24/72hr 98/135KN) is a pretty good way to save money. You get free entry to the Museum of Broken Relationships, Zagreb 360° Observation Deck, Museum of Contemporary Art, Zagreb City Museum, Museum of Art & Crafts, Zagreb Zoo, as well as discounts of 10% to 50% at various other museums, and discounts in some restaurants, shops and bars. It also provides free rides on the funicular.

The card is sold at the main tourist office and in some hostels, hotels and shops.

MEDICAL SERVICES

Emergency Health Clinic (☎01-63 02 911; Heinzelova 87; ⏲24hr)

KBC Rebro Hospital (☎8am-4pm 01-23 88 029; www.kbc-zagreb.hr; Kišpatićeva 12; ⏲24hr) Good public hospital with an emergency department. It's the teaching hospital of the University of Zagreb.

POST

Main Post Office (☎01-72 303 304; Branimirova 4; ⏲7am-midnight) Holds poste restante mail. Right by the train station.

Post Office (☎072 303 304; Jurišićeva 13; ⏲7am-8pm Mon-Fri, to 2pm Sat)

TOURIST INFORMATION

Main Tourist Office (☎information 0800 53 53, office 01-48 14 051; www.infozagreb.hr; Trg Bana Jelačića 11; ⏲8.30am-8pm Mon-Fri, 9am-6pm Sat, 10am-4pm Sun) Distributes free city maps and leaflets. Has several branches throughout the city.

Lotrščak Tower Tourist Office (☎01-48 51 510; Strossmayerovo Šetalište; ⏲9am-9pm Mon-Fri, 10am-9pm Sat & Sun Jun-Sep, 9am-5pm Mon-Fri, 10am-5pm Sat & Sun Oct-May)

Main Bus Station Tourist Office (☎01-61 15 507; Avenija M Držića 4; ⏲9am-9pm Mon-Fri, 10am-5pm Sat & Sun)

Main Railway Station Tourist Office (Trg Kralja Tomislava 12; ⏲9am-9pm Mon-Fri, 10am-5pm Sat & Sun)

Zagreb Airport Tourist Office (☎01-62 65 091; Zagreb Airport; ⏲9am-9pm Mon-Fri, 10am-5pm Sat & Sun)

Zagreb County Tourist Association (☎01-48 73 665; www.tzzz.hr; Preradovićeva 42; ⏲8am-4pm Mon-Fri) Has information and materials on attractions in Zagreb's surroundings, including wine roads and bike trails.

TRAVEL AGENCIES

Atlas Travel Agency (☎01-48 07 300; www.atlas-croatia.com; Zrinjevac 17; ⏲8am-8pm Mon-Fri, 9am-2pm Sat) Group day tours from Zagreb plus multiday bus tours around Croatia.

Croatia Express (☎01-49 22 224; www.croatia-express.com; Trg Kralja Tomislava 17; ⏲8am-6.30pm Mon-Fri, 9am-1pm Sat) International trains ticketing specialist, plus bookings for car rental, air and ferry tickets and hotels around the country.

Croatian YHA (☎01-48 29 294; www.hfhs.hr; Savska 5; ⏲8.30am-4.30pm Mon-Fri) The Zagreb-based head office of the Croatian Youth Hostel Association has info on all the hostels in Croatia. The on-site travel branch can help with advance bookings.

ℹ Getting There & Away

AIR

Located 17km southeast of the city, **Zagreb Airport** (☎01-45 62 170; www.zagreb-airport.hr; Rudolfa Fizira 21, Velika Gorica), with its supermodern terminal opened in 2018, is Croatia's major airport, offering a range of international and domestic services.

BUS

The **Zagreb bus station** (☎060 313 333; www.akz.hr; Avenija M Držića 4) is located 1km east of the train station. Bus travel is generally a better option than taking a train due

TRAINS FROM ZAGREB

DOMESTIC DESTINATION	COST (KN)	DURATION (HR)	DAILY SERVICES
Osijek	132-150	4½-5½	4
Rijeka	111-118	4-5	3
Šibenik	187-194	6-10	6 (nondirect)
Split	208	6-7¾	3
Varaždin	65-81	2¼-3	14
Zadar	197-203	7-16	3 (nondirect)

INTERNATIONAL DESTINATION	COST (KN)	DURATION (HR)	DAILY SERVICES
Belgrade	184	6½	1
Budapest	214	6-7	3
Celje	67	1¾	1
Ljubljana	68	2½	5
Maribor	89	2¾	1
Munich	214	8-9	1
Vienna	223	6½	1
Zurich	289	14¾	1

to a more extensive network, faster travel times and more services. If you need to store bags, there's a *garderoba* (one to four hours per hour 5KN, additional hours per hour 2.50KN).

Before buying your ticket, ask about the arrival time – some of the buses take local roads and stop in every town en route.

TRAIN

The **train station** (www.hzpp.hr; Trg Kralja Tomislava 12) is in the southern part of the city centre. As you come out of it, you'll see a series of parks and pavilions directly in front of you that lead into the town centre.

Seating is limited as trains usually only have two or three carriages so it's advisable to book train tickets in advance. The station has a *garderoba* (locker per 24 hours 15KN) if you need to store bags.

Getting Around

TO/FROM THE AIRPORT

The **Croatia Airlines bus** (www.plesoprijevoz.hr) runs from the airport to Zagreb bus station every half-hour or hour (depending on flight schedules) from 6am to 10.30pm (35KN, 40 minutes). Returning to the airport, bus services run from 4am to 8pm.

Bus line 290 (10KN, 1¼ hour) runs between Kvaternik Trg, just east of the central city, and the airport every 35 minutes between 4.20am and midnight.

Taxis cost between 150KN and 250KN from the airport to the city centre.

BICYCLE

Bike.com (☎ Mon-Fri 95 90 10 507, Sat & Sun 98 774 574; www.bike.com.hr; A Kačića Miošića 9; adult/child bike hire per day 100/50KN; ⏲ 5-10pm Mon-Fri, 8am-10pm Sat & Sun) This excellent local bike-hire company

BUSES FROM ZAGREB

Note that listed schedules are somewhat reduced outside high season.

DOMESTIC DESTINATION	COST (KN)	DURATION (HR)	DAILY SERVICES
Dubrovnik	188-231	9½-11	12
Korčula	275	11	1
Krk	141	3-4½	7-8
Makarska	168-207	6½–7	12-15
Mali Lošinj	216	6¾	2-5
Osijek	133-139	4	17
Plitvice	85-105	2-3	11-15
Poreč	141-176	4-4½	12
Pula	121-192	3½-5½	23
Rab	207-236	4-5	1-6
Rijeka	80-121	2½-3	20-35
Rovinj	126-189	4-6	16
Šibenik	136-151	4½-7	17
Split	120-176	5-8½	32-37
Varaždin	61-87	1-2	19-28
Zadar	89-126	3½-5	30

INTERNATIONAL DESTINATION	COST (KN)	DURATION (HR)	DAILY SERVICES
Belgrade	230	6-6½	6
Ljubljana	40-205	2½-3	18
Milan	435-609	9-10	2
Munich	139-228	7-8	13-19
Sarajevo	198-226	7-8	4-5
Vienna	150-179	5	10

is run by true cycling enthusiasts and has a range of city, hybrid and mountain bikes as well as children's cycles. There are good discounts for multiday hire, and panniers and other equipment are available for hire for those planning to hit the roads for a few days or more.

NextBike (www.nextbike.hr) This bike-sharing system has several stations around the city centre. You can register at the station directly, via the website or with itsapp. The standard tourist rental tariff is 79KN per day.

BUS

Although Zagreb has an excellent bus network linking the centre with the city's suburbs, travellers will find little use for it. One exception is **bus line 106** which goes from Kaptol to Mirogoj.

CAR & MOTORCYCLE

Zagreb is a fairly easy city to navigate by car (main streets are wide, and parking in the city centre, although scarce, only costs 6KN per hour). Watch out for trams buzzing around.

A number of international car-hire companies, such as **Hertz** (☎01-72 72 7277; www.hertz.hr; Grada Vukovara 274; per day from €26; ⏰7am-6pm Mon-Fri, 8am-6pm Sat, 8am-noon Sun), are represented in Zagreb. Bear in mind that local companies usually have lower rates. Local car-rental company **Oryx** (☎01-61 15 800; www.oryx-rent.hr; Grada Vukovara 74; per day from 88KN; ⏰7am-8pm Mon-Fri, 8am-2pm Sat, 8am-noon Sun) has branches at the airport and inside the Esplanade Hotel as well.

Hrvatski Autoklub (HAK, Croatian Auto Club; ☎24hr roadside assistance 01-1987, traffic information 07-27 77 777; www.hak.hr) provides the Croatia Traffic Info app (available in English, German and Italian) for up-to-date traffic and road conditions as well as roadside assistance in case of a breakdown.

TICKETS & PASSES

Buy single-use tickets at newspaper kiosks or from the driver for 4KN (for 30 minutes) or 10KN (90 minutes). You can use the same ticket when transferring trams or buses but only in one direction. Night tram single-use tickets are 15KN.

Make sure you validate your ticket when you get on the tram or bus by getting it time-stamped in the yellow ticket-validation box at the front of the vehicle – the other boxes only work for multi-use transport cards.

TAXI

Taxi Cammeo (☎1212, 01-62 88 926; https://cammeo.hr/en/cities/zagreb; basic tariff 6KN, then per km 6KN) Typically the cheapest taxi firm. Waiting time is 40KN per hour.

Ekotaxi (☎1414, 060 77 77; www.ekotaxi.hr; basic tariff 8.80KN, then per km 6KN) Waiting time is 43KN per hour.

Radio Taxi (☎1717; www.radiotaxizagreb.com; basic tariff 10KN, then per km 6KN) Radio Taxi ranks (usually at blue-marked taxi signs) can be found throughout the centre. Waiting time is 40KN per hour.

Zagreb also has Uber.

TRAM

Zagreb's public transport (www.zet.hr) is based on an efficient network of trams, although the city centre is compact enough to make them almost unnecessary except for going to and from the bus or train station. Tram maps are posted at most stations, making the system easy to navigate.

Trams 2 and 6 run from the bus station to the train station. Tram 6 goes to Trg Bana Jelačića.

AT A GLANCE

POPULATION
Osijek: 104,600

BIODIVERSITY OF KOPAČKI RIT NATURE PARK
over 2,300 species

BEST MUSEUM
Vučedol Culture Museum (p122)

BEST SLAVONIAN RESTAURANT
Josić (p122)

BEST WINE TOUR
Lovrec Vineyard (p112)

WHEN TO GO

Apr & May
Wildflowers carpet fields, adding colour to the countryside's rolling hills.

Jul & Aug
Temperatures rise, visitors go to the coast. Enjoy music and dance at Đakovo's folk festival.

Sep
Soak up baroque music culture at Varaždin's festival.

Trakošćan Castle (p107)
XBRCHX/SHUTTERSTOCK

Inland Croatia

Most tourists forget this big chunk of Croatia, but it was made for road-tripping. The bucolic northern region of Zagorje is sprinkled with itsy-bitsy villages and vineyard-speckled hills with the odd medieval castle and spa town thrown in for good measure. On its eastern edge, on the route to Hungary, Varaždin is a baroque beauty with an important history that belies its laid-back appeal. The Pannonian plains and flat farmland of Slavonia stretch out southeast towards Serbia. In this primarily agricultural region dip into culture amid the fine architecture of lively Osijek, the two museums of Vukovar and inside Đakovo's majestic cathedral. Afterwards head out into the countryside once more to drive the wine roads and for boat trips in the vast wetlands at Kopački Rit Nature Park. A journey here is as far away in character from the bustle of the coastal resorts as you can get.

INCLUDES

Inland Croatia Highlights

1. **Osijek** (p114) Soaking up fine architecture and the lively cafe scene in Slavonia's main city.
2. **Varaždin** (p108) Strolling the compact centre, rimmed by stately baroque buildings and topped with a turreted castle.
3. **Kopački Rit Nature Park** (p120) Canoeing through vast wetlands while spotting herons, storks and geese.
4. **Vukovar** (p122) Delving into times gone by at two of Croatia's best museums.
5. **Baranja** (p120) Road-tripping the region's wine roads from cellars to tiny villages.

6 **Đakovo** (p113) Craning your neck at colourful frescos inside the cathedral.

7 **Lonjsko Polje Nature Park** (p112) Discovering the traditional villages and white storks of the region.

8 **Krapina** (p106) Taking in the baroque frippery of the church before learning about Neanderthals in the museum.

9 **Samobor** (p102) Savouring this lovely town's famous *kremšnite* (custard pies) before exploring the countryside and cellars of the Plešivica Wine Road.

AROUND ZAGREB

The old Croatian heartland surrounding Zagreb is rich with quick getaway destinations for hikers, skiers and food lovers.

Samobor

01 / POP 37,600

Samobor is where stressed-out city dwellers come to wind down and get their fix of hearty food, creamy cakes and pretty scenery. After you've filled up on *kremšnite* (custard pie) there's not much to actually do except stroll beside the shallow stream of the Gradna as it curves through the town centre and admire the fine pastel-washed buildings and churches. It makes for a relaxing half-day out from Zagreb.

Sights & Activities

Žumberak Samoborsko Gorje Nature Park NATURE PARK

(www.park-zumberak.hr) FREE Samobor is a good jumping-off point for hiking into the Žumberak Samoborsko Gorje, a mountain system that links the high peaks of the Alps with the karstic caves and abysses of the Dinaric Range. Carpeted with meadows and forests, it's the region's most popular hiking destination, and has been the cradle of organised mountaineering activity in Croatia since 1875.

In 1999 the whole area, covering 333 sq km, was proclaimed a nature park because of its biodiversity, forests, karst caves, river canyons and four waterfalls. Most of the hikes here are easy and there are well-marked trails and nine mountain huts that make pleasant rest stops. Most huts open weekends only (except in the July to August high season).

The range is divided into three sections: the Oštrc group in the centre, the Japetić group to the west and the Plešivica group to the east. Both the Oštrc and Japetić groups are accessible from the Šoićeva Kuća mountain hut and restaurant, 10km west of Samobor, reachable by bus 144 (direction Lipovec). From there it's a rather-steep 30-minute climb to the medieval hill fort of Lipovec and an hour's hike to the peak of Oštrc (752m), with another mountain hut.

Another popular hike is the 1½-hour climb from Šoićeva Kuća to Japetić (879m), the highest peak of Samobor Hills and a famous paragliding spot (see www.parafreek.hr for information). You can also follow a path from Oštrc to Japetić (two hours). The Plešivica group has ruins of a medieval fort and a protected park forest area, and it's also a famous rock-climbing spot; you can access it from the village of Rude (bus 143 services Rude and Braslovje). From Rude, head east to the hunting cabin Srndać on the mountain saddle of Poljanice (12km), from where it's a 40-minute, rather steep hike to the peak of Plešivica (779m).

As well as the information on the park website, the Croatian Mountaineering Association (p37) has further hiking details.

KUMROVEC

Nestled in the Sutla River valley near the Slovenian border, the village of Kumrovec has been transformed into **Kumrovec Staro Selo Museum** (www.mss.mhz.hr; Josipa Broza 19, Kumrovec; adult/child/family 25/15/55KN; 9am-7pm Apr-Sep, to 4pm Nov-Feb, 9am-4pm Mon-Fri, to 6pm Sat & Sun Mar & Oct), an open-air ethnographic museum. A re-creation of a 19th-century village, the Staro Selo Museum features 40 restored houses and barns made of pressed earth and wood. The village was also the birthplace of Josip Broz Tito, the former president of Yugoslavia. His house is now a museum containing original furniture, letters from foreign leaders and memorabilia, with a life-sized bronze sculpture outside.

With a stream bubbling through the idyllic setting, the museum presents a vivid glimpse of peasant traditions and village life. These *hiže* (traditional Zagorje huts) are now filled with furniture, mannequins, toys, wine presses and baker's tools (all accompanied by English captions) in order to evoke the region's traditional arts, crafts and customs. On some weekends (April to September) the museum hosts demonstrations of blacksmithing, candlemaking, pottery making and flax weaving. For Tito's birthday, on 25 May, the village comes alive with devotees from all over former Yugoslavia.

It's best to visit with your own transport as there are only two daily buses running between Zagreb and Kumrovec (57KN, 1¼ hours; weekdays only).

OFF THE BEATEN TRACK

PLEŠIVICA WINE ROAD

For a taste of the countryside – and a taste of some of that countryside's quality produce – follow the winding lanes of the Plešivica Wine Road past blink-and-you-miss-them red-roofed villages, vineyard rows and green hills. There are over 20 wineries clustered in this lush corner 20km south of Samobor (and 45km north from Zagreb) so get your glass-swirling and bouquet-sniffing hat on for some wine-tasting action. Here are a few of our favourites:

Korak (☎01-62 93 088; www.vino-korak.hr; Plešivica 34; wine tasting 100KN; ⊙by appointment) Renowned as one of the best cellars in the Plešivica wine country, with 5 hectares of vineyard. The chardonnay and pinot noir here are our top tips for your tasting. Tours take in the entire wine-production facility and then finish in the cosy tasting room with lovely old B&W photos of Plešivica in times long past.

Režek (☎091 56 46 240; www.rezek.hr; Plešivica 39; ⊙10am-8pm Fri-Sun, Mon-Thu by appointment) This family has been producing wine here for the last four generations. Tours go through the cellar area before getting stuck in to their portugizac (Blauer Portugieser), pinot gris and chardonnay. They also produce a refreshing sparkling wine. Tasting costs vary.

Šember (☎01-62 82 476; www.sember.hr; Donji Pavlovčani 11b, Jastrebarsko; wine tastings 50KN; ⊙by appointment) The riesling and chardonnay at this family-run winery in the Plešivica area are well worth a stopoff to taste. Tastings include platters of local cheese to munch on.

La Gradi (☎099 62 93 315; www.lagradi.com; Vlaškovec 156, Jastrebarsko; ⊙by appointment) Best known for its bronze-award-winning muscat, but this winery also produces a fruity riesling and velvety pinot gris. Tasting tour prices vary so check when you make your booking.

Nearly all winery tasting tours need to be booked beforehand so a bit of pre-planning doesn't go amiss. The Zagreb County Tourist Association (p95) can provide the free basic *Plešivica Wine Road* map which lists all the wineries.

Eating

U Prolazu DESSERTS €
(Trg Kralja Tomislava 5; cakes 7-12KN; ⊙7am-11pm) Right on the main square, this place is renowned for having the best *kremšnite* (9KN) in town.

Gabreku 1929 CROATIAN €€
(www.gabrek.hr; Starogradska 46; mains 55-150KN; ⊙noon-midnight) This classic local restaurant, a short walk from the town centre, has been run by the same family since the 1920s. It's known for its 40 types of sweet and savoury *palačinke* (crêpes).

Information

Tourist Office (☎01-33 60 044; www.tz-samobor.hr; Trg Kralja Tomislava 5; ⊙8am-4pm Mon-Fri, 9am-5pm Sat & Sun) For plentiful brochures and maps of Samobor, as well as maps and hiking information for Samoborsko Gorje and Žumberačko Gorje (another nearby mountain range), pop by this office in the town centre.

Getting There & Away

Samobor is easy to reach by public transport. Take a Samoborček or Autoturist Samobor bus from the main bus station in Zagreb (31KN, 40 minutes, roughly every 30 minutes). **Samobor bus station** (141 Samoborske Brigade HV) is a simple 1.5km stroll to the main square.

Mt Medvednica

Looming proudly above Zagreb, Mt Medvednica offers up an easy nature escape for Zagreb locals who ski here in winter and chuck on their hiking boots to hit the verdant hillsides for the rest of the year. As well as enjoying fresh air, forest scenery and outdoor activities, day trippers can check out the mountain's medieval fort and humongous cave before joining the locals for lunch at one of the mountain huts that pepper the slopes.

Sights

Medvedgrad FORTRESS
(☎01-45 86 317; www.pp-medvednica.hr; 15KN; ⏰11am-7pm Tue-Sun Apr-Sep, 10am-6pm Tue-Sun Oct-Dec, 10am-5pm Sat & Sun Jan-Mar) This medieval fortress, just above the city on the southern side of Mt Medvednica, is Zagreb's most important medieval monument. Built from 1249 to 1254, it was erected to protect the city from Tartar invasions. Today you can see the rebuilt thick walls and towers, a small chapel with frescos and the Shrine of the Homeland, which pays homage to those who died for a free Croatia. On a clear day it offers beautiful views of Zagreb and surrounds.

To get to Medvedgrad, you can take bus 102 from Britanski trg in Zagreb, west of the centre on Ilica, to the church in Šestine, and take the easy one-hour hiking route from there.

Veternica Cave CAVE
(www.pp-medvednica.hr; adult/child/family 40/20/70KN; ⏰10am-4pm Sat & Sun Apr-Oct) Croatia's sixth-largest cave is open for visitors on weekends from mid-April through the summer months. You can explore the first 380m of the cave on an hour-long guided tour that takes in some weirdly shaped stalagmite formations and fossils. It's located in the western part of Medvednica, which is also home to Glavica Mountain Hut.

To reach the cave from Zagreb, take city bus 124 from Črnomerec to Gornji Stenjevec (about 15 minutes). Then walk by the Dubravica stream uphill to Veternica for about 20 minutes on the trail marked 3 (it's another 15 minutes to Glavica).

Activities

Medvednica Nature Park HIKING
(www.pp-medvednica.hr) Medvednica Nature Park, just to the north of Zagreb, offers excellent hiking opportunities, with several popular and well-marked routes. Allow about three hours return for any of the hikes – and remember that this is a heavily wooded mountain with ample opportunities to get lost. Maps are available at the Croatian Mountaineering Association (p37) and at the **Info Point** (☎01-45 86 317; Bliznec 70) at the Bliznec park entrance.

One of the popular routes is the easy Leustekov trail (marked 14), which ends at Sljeme, the top of Mt Medvednica. Along the way you can stop at one of Sljeme's oldest huts, **Runolist** (☎01-45 57 519; mains 35-65KN; ⏰8am-8pm), which offers beautiful views of Zagreb and traditional food and drink.

Alternatively, you can hike in the direction of the Puntijarka and Hunjka mountain huts. There is also the shorter but steeper and more intense Bikčevićeva path (marked 18), which starts at the Bliznec park entrance.

To visit the attractive eastern side of the Medvednica mountain, take bus 205 or 208 from **Dubrava bus terminal** (Avenija Dubrava) in Zagreb to Bidrovec or Vidovec villages. From there, take marked mountain trails 24 or 25/25a to the Gorščica mountain hut; the walk takes approximately two hours.

Take water and warm clothes, and make sure you return before sundown. There is also a danger of disease-carrying ticks in spring, so wear trousers and long sleeves, and examine your body after hiking.

Ski Resort Sljeme SKIING
(☎01-45 53 382; www.sljeme.hr; day lift ticket adult/child weekdays 70/40KN, weekends 100/50KN; ⏰9am-4pm, night skiing 7-10pm Tue & Thu) Zagreb is not normally associated with winter sports, but you can ski right outside town at Sljeme, the main peak of Mt Medvednica. It has five ski runs, two ski lifts and a triple chairlift. There's night skiing on the Red Slope and the White Meadow. Passes are available at the bottom of the Red Slope.

Sleeping & Eating

Hiže na Bregu COTTAGE €€
(☎098 92 90 881; www.hizenabregu.com; Hižakovec 2/1, Donja Stubica; cottages €90; P) Hiže na Bregu, in the village of Hižakovec (near Donja Stubica), is a rural hideaway in the northern foothills of Mt Medvednica. The traditional Zagorje cottage, clad in wood, sleeps up to five with two doubles in the main house and a separate single cottage without en suite. There's a minimum stay of two nights.

Puntijarka CROATIAN €
(☎01-45 80 384; mains 35-85KN; ⏰9am-9pm Mon-Fri, 7am-9pm Sat & Sun) This mountain hut is very popular on weekends for its home-cooked traditional Croatian dishes served in a rustic setting.

Getting There & Away

Mt Medvednica is on the edge of Zagreb and easily accessed from the city. Take tram 14 to the last stop and then change to tram 15 and take it to its last stop (Dolje). Walk straight through the tunnel, which takes you directly to the Bliznec park entrance.

Alternatively, if you are driving, all of the nature-park entrances have car parks.

ZAGORJE

The bucolic Zagorje region provides rural escapades right on Zagreb's doorstep. The landscape of itsy villages squirreled between verdantly forested hills, vineyards and cornfields, and medieval castles was made for easygoing road trips and presents a relaxed foil to the bustling Mediterranean south. A trip here is blissfully crowd-free, although less so on summer weekends when day-tripping families from the capital debunk en masse to storm the area.

The Zagorje region begins north of Mt Medvednica (1035m), near Zagreb, and extends west to the Slovenian border, and as far north as Varaždin, a showcase of baroque architecture. Whether you want to feast on hearty cuisine at rustic restaurants, get a taste of village life or tour ancient castles, with Zagorje you're in for an offbeat treat.

Klanjec

☎049 / POP 2740

The pleasant town of Klanjec is a nice pit stop to catch some fantastic sculpture: it's the birthplace of a notable Croat, sculptor Antun Augustinčić (1900–79), who created the *Monument to Peace* in front of the UN building in New York, and the town is home to the **Antun Augustinčić Gallery** (Trg Antuna Mihanovića 10; adult/child 25/15KN; ⏲9am-5pm Apr-Sep, to 3pm Tue-Sun Oct-Mar).

Also here is a 17th-century **baroque church** (Mihanovićev Trg 11; 10KN), built in 1630 by the noble Erdödy brothers. The adjacent Franciscan monastery has two restored sarcophagi of the Erdödy family, elaborate findings from the baroque era, hidden in the crypt.

RURAL INDULGENCE

Rural retreats that offer food, wine, accommodation and relaxation have mushroomed in the Zagorje countryside. Weekends at these hideaways are typically packed with Zagreb day trippers, but come on a weekday and you'll have them practically to yourself.

Bolfan Vinski Vrh (www.bolfanvinskivrh.hr; Gornjaki 56, Hraščina; ⏲by appointment) For tastings of award-winning wines, head to Bolfan Vinski Vrh in the village of Hraščina, near the town of Zlatar. Inside this beautiful hilltop *klet* (typical Zagorje cottage), with sloping vineyards and some of Zagorje's best views, there's also a great **restaurant** (☎099 70 31 797; mains 75-110KN; ⏲noon-8pm Wed-Sat, to 6pm Sun; ❄).

Kućica (☎099 62 92 985; www.kuchica.com; Luka; d weekdays/weekends €60/100; Ⓟ) This Hansel & Gretel–style retreat in the hills, 35km from Zagreb, is in a traditional cottage made of 120-year-old oak wood. There are orchards, vineyards, an organic garden and a hammock, while inside you'll find a wood oven and colourful rustic decor. A long wooden table outside and a barbecue make 'the little house' a hit with families and groups of friends. There are occasional yoga retreats, photography workshops and other fun events.

Majsecov Mlin (☎049-288 092; www.majsecov-mlin.com; Obrtnička 47, Donja Stubica; mains 55-90KN; ⏲9am-11pm; Ⓟ❄📶) Housed in two traditional cottages near the village of Donja Stubica, Majsecov Mlin serves local mainstays, seasonally inspired and cooked up by one of Zagorje's best chefs. Try the delicious steak with nettle chips and Zagorje-style pesto.

On-site is an old mill, which to this day grinds maize for use in corn flour. In summer months, small producers sell their edible wares at the little market here. You can also spend the night in one of five rooms (singles/doubles 200/360KN).

Klet Kozjak (☎049-228 800; www.klet-kozjak.hr; Kozjak 18a, Sveti Križ Začretje; mains 55-110KN; ⏲8am-10pm) Klet Kozjak in Sveti Križ Začretje, 11km southeast of Krapina, is an adorable little cottage that serves traditional food from the region – such as homemade nettle pasta with cheese and vegetable sauce – and pairs it with sweeping views of the hills and valleys from the terrace.

Run by a local family that has been in the goat-breeding business for generations, it is known for its excellent goat cheese and oven-baked kid goat. If you also want to stay, there are a few rooms (singles/doubles 315/475KN) here.

Make arrangements to see the church and monastery through the useful **tourist office** (☎049-550 235; www.klanjec.hr; Trg A Mihanovića 3; ⊙8am-4pm Mon-Fri, to 1pm Sat) (but be aware that it doesn't always stick to the official office hours).

Getting There & Away

Two daily buses running from Zagreb to Kumrovec stop in Klanjec on weekdays (51KN, one to 1½ hours). There are no buses on weekends.

Krapinske Toplice

☎049 / POP 5100

The spa town of Krapinske Toplice, about 17km southwest of Krapina and 54km north of Zagreb, is located amid the rolling hills of the Zagorje countryside. The showpieces are the four thermal springs, rich in magnesium and calcium and never below a temperature of 39°C. The town itself isn't particularly attractive nor is its atmosphere upbeat, mainly catering to elderly patients in various rehabilitation programs. However, the newer, swanky thermal spa centre, Aquae Vivae, has injected energy into the town, making it a good swim-stop if you need a half-day off the road.

Activities

Aquae Vivae THERMAL BATHS

(☎049-501 999; www.aquae-vivae.hr; Ulica Antuna Mihanovića 1a; adult/child weekdays 70/50KN, weekends 90/60KN; ⊙9am-9pm) This swank thermal baths centre has brought a breath of fresh air to Krapinske Toplice. The most modern complex of indoor pools in Croatia, spanning 18,000 sq metres, it has plenty to keep the kids occupied with a wave pool, water slide and dedicated children's pool, plus a big outdoor pool and even a pool dedicated to scuba diving.

Sleeping & Eating

★**Vuglec Breg** INN €€

(☎049-345 015; www.vuglec-breg.hr; Škarićevo 151, Škarićevo; r from €80; P 📶) This rural inn has a scenic location in the village of Škarićevo, 4km from Krapinske Toplice. The five traditional cottages (featuring rooms and suites) sit amid vineyards and forests. The grounds feature tennis courts, hiking trails and a wine cellar, plus there's a playground, a badminton court and pony riding to keep the little ones busy. Mountain bikes are complimentary.

The restaurant serves Zagorje specialities (mains 95KN–120KN), such as *purica s mlincima* (slow-roasted turkey with baked noodles) and *štrukli* (baked cheese dumplings), on a terrace with panoramic vistas.

Villa Magdalena SPA HOTEL €€€

(☎049-233 333; www.villa-magdalena.net; Mirna 1; d from €145; P ❄ 📶 ≋) With jacuzzis in every room and views across the lush hills, this spa hotel dishes up a relaxing treat. Most guests are here to chill out, indulge in a massage or two (from €24), and make good use of the spa and wellness facilities (free for guests) which take up the entire 3rd floor and include a pool, sauna and deck with sun-loungers.

The restaurant serves Italian- and French-influenced dishes as well as Zagorje specialities. Check the website for online specials and packages.

Getting There & Away

Day-tripping to Krapinske Toplice from Zagreb is easy with 10 buses (42KN–52KN, 1¼ hours) daily on weekdays and six daily on weekends. Check the latest bus schedule at www.akz.hr.

Krapina

☎049 / POP 12,100

This neat-as-a-pin provincial centre hides two worthwhile sights behind its bland facade. Sitting high on the hill above town, the Church of Virgin Mary of Jerusalem is home to an opulently frescoed interior, while Krapina's main claim to fame is celebrated at the Museum of the Krapina Neanderthal. In 1899 an archaeological dig in a cave on the Hušnjakovo hill here unearthed findings of human and animal bones from a Neanderthal tribe that lived here from 100,000 BC to 35,000 BC. Alongside stone tools and weapons from the Palaeolithic era, the remains of 876 humans were found, including 196 single teeth belonging to several dozen individuals. It is the largest Neanderthal fossil haul ever found in Europe.

Sights

★**Church of Virgin Mary of Jerusalem** CHURCH

(☎caretaker 095 52 86 213; M Krieže bb; ⊙8-10am Sun) This baroque church, built in 1761, is one of Zagorje's most important pilgrimage sites and is well worth the uphill walk from the centre. Outside, the surrounding arcade is festooned with painted scenes depicting miracles and granted prayers that

DON'T MISS

ZAGORJE'S GRAND CASTLES

A distinctive feature of the Zagorje region is its medieval castles, built to protect the Croatian heartland from invaders from the east and north. Both Varaždin and Varaždinske Toplice have their own castles, but it's the rural setting of Veliki Tabor and Trakošćan that makes them the region's most impressive fortresses.

As you approach the pentagonal hilltop **Veliki Tabor Castle** (www.veliki-tabor.hr; Košnički Hum 1, Desinić; adult/child/family 25/15/55KN; 9am-5pm Mon-Fri, to 7pm Sat & Sun Apr-Sep, 9am-4pm Wed-Sun Nov-Mar, 9am-4pm Mon-Fri, to 5pm Sat & Sun Oct) , 57km northwest of Zagreb, what unfolds is a pleasing panorama of hills, cornfields, vineyards and forests. The Croatian aristocracy began building fortified castles in the region – to stave off the Turkish threat – in the 16th century. Veliki Tabor Castle, built on the grounds of an earlier medieval structure, dates from this period with the four semicircular towers added later.

Strategically perched on top of a hill, the golden-yellow castle-fortress has everything a medieval master could want: towers, turrets and holes in the walls for pouring tar and hot oil on the enemy. It even houses the skull of Veronika Desinić, a poor village girl who, according to local lore, was punished for her romance with the castle owner's son and bricked up in the walls.

The rural vistas alone make a visit worthwhile, as does good traditional dining nearby. To admire the castle from a distance, grab an alfresco table at the rustic eatery **Grešna Gorica** (049-343 001; www.gresna-gorica.hr; Taborgradska Klet 3, Desinić; mains 40-80KN; 9am-9pm;).

The castle hosts the **Tabor Film Festival** (www.taborfilmfestival.com; Jun/Jul).

There are eight daily buses from Zagreb to Desinić (62KN to 70KN, 1½ to two hours) from Monday to Saturday, and four on Sunday. You will have to walk 3km northwest to Veliki Tabor.

Trakošćan Castle (042-796 281; www.trakoscan.hr; Trakošćan 1; adult/child 40/20KN; 9am-6pm Apr-Oct, to 4pm Nov-Mar), 80km northwest of Zagreb, is worth a visit for its well-presented museum and attractive grounds. The exact origin of its construction is unknown, but the first official mention dates to 1334. Not many of the castle's original Romanesque features were retained when it was restored in neo-Gothic style in the mid-19th century; the 215-acre castle grounds were landscaped into a romantic English-style park with exotic trees and an artificial lake.

Occupied by the aristocratic Drašković family until 1944, the castle features three floors of exhibits that display the family's original furniture, a plethora of portraits, an armament's collection of swords, and a period kitchen in the basement. The rooms range in style from neo-Renaissance to Gothic and baroque.

After soaking up the history, wander along the verdant paths down to the wooden jetty at the lake, where you can rent a two-person paddleboat (30KN for 30 minutes).

No buses operate between Zagreb and Trakošćan, but there are connections from Varaždin daily except for Sunday, making a day trip here possible.

local worshippers attributed to the Virgin Mary. Inside, the church is a triumphant dazzle of baroque frescos painted by Antun Lerchinger with ornate altars and its original 18th-century organ still in place.

Museum of the Krapina Neanderthal MUSEUM
(www.mkn.mhz.hr; Šetalište Vilibalda Sluge bb; adult/child/family 60/30/120KN; 9am-7pm Tue-Sun Apr-Oct, to 5pm Nov-Mar) Those with kids should make a beeline to this brilliant museum which explores the history of the universe, earth and humanity, as well as highlighting the story of Krapina's famous 1899 Neanderthal fossil-bone find through a series of fun, colourful and high-tech exhibits. Everything from the big bang to Neanderthal daily life, their demise and the rise of Homo sapiens is covered, with interesting displays on how the excavation site was found, too.

Those with more than a passing interest in the Neanderthals may be a tad disappointed as there's very little of the actual find (which encompassed over 800 fossils) on display. Although it's one of the richest Neanderthal sites in the world, and of great scientific importance, much of the find was bone fragments, making it not the most exciting of exhibits for the layperson. One room in the museum does, however, display Neanderthal skulls from every important site across the world.

Outside the museum, you can walk up the leafy hill where the remains were found, today marked by a sculpture of Neanderthals wielding clubs.

Sleeping & Eating

Hostel Barrock HOSTEL €
(☎098 18 23 863; www.hostel-barrock.com; Magistratska 36; dm adult/child 120/75KN;) Just two minutes from the main square, this small, friendly hostel has three spotless dorms – two with four beds and one that sleeps seven – as well as a kitchenette and common area, a backyard with a barbecue and a cool cafe-bar.

Pod Starim Krovovima CROATIAN €
(☎049-370 871; Trg Ljudevita Gaja 15; mains 25-80KN; ⊗6am-10pm) On weekdays, this is central Krapina's top pick for a cheap and tasty *gablec* (lunch) or a dinner of solid traditional fare. Upstairs there are eight plain but clean private rooms should you be looking for a place to stay.

Information

Tourist Office (☎049-371 330; www.tzg-krapina.hr; Magistratska 28; ⊗8am-3pm Mon-Fri, to noon Sat) Not particularly helpful but it does offer some brochures and scant information.

Getting There & Away

Several daily buses run from Monday to Saturday from Zagreb to Krapina (36KN to 42KN, one hour); on Sunday there's only an evening bus. On weekdays, there are 14 train services from Zagreb (40KN, 1½ hours), with a change at Zabok.

The train station and bus station are both on Frana Galovića, in the centre. From the train station it's a 1km walk straight up Frana Galovića to the Museum of the Krapina Neanderthal.

Varaždin

☎042 / POP 46,300

Varaždin's spruced-up historic core is a showcase of scrupulously restored baroque architecture and well-tended gardens and parks. Although Varaždin was overlooked for years in the tourism stakes, merely used as a transit point on the way to or from Hungary, travellers are now waking up to its appeal and increasingly coming here on day trips from Zagreb, 81km to the south.

Soak up the extraordinary refinement of its 18th-century buildings, bequeathed on the city when it was Croatia's capital and most prosperous centre, with a stroll in the pedestrian zone which radiates out from Trg Kralja Tomislava. Top off your wanders with a visit to the gleaming white, turreted Stari Grad which contains the city museum.

History

The town of Garestin (now Varaždin) played an important role in Croatia's history. It first became a local administrative centre in 1181 under King Bela III, and in 1209 it was raised to the status of a free royal borough by King Andrew II, receiving its own seal and coat of arms.

When Croatia was under siege by the Turks, Varaždin was the most powerful stronghold and the residence of choice for generals. Once the Ottoman threat receded, Varaždin prospered as the cultural, political and commercial centre of Croatia. Its proximity to northern Europe facilitated the boom of baroque architecture, which flourished in Europe during this period. Top artisans and builders flocked to Varaždin, designing mansions, churches and public buildings.

The town was made the capital of Croatia in 1767, a position it held until a disastrous fire in 1776, when the Croatian *ban* (viceroy) packed up and moved his administration to Zagreb. The still-thriving town was quickly rebuilt in the baroque style, which is still visible today.

Sights

Varaždin's centre offers a fine ensemble of baroque buildings, a number of which have been turned into museums. Many of its aristocratic mansions and elegant churches are being restored as part of the town's ongoing bid to be included in Unesco's list of World Heritage Sites. Conveniently, most buildings have plaques with architectural and historical explanations in English, German and Croatian.

Town Museum CASTLE
(Gradski Muzej; www.gmv.hr; Strossmayerovo Šetalište 3; adult/concession 25/15KN; ⊗9am-5pm Tue-Fri, to 1pm Sat & Sun) This whitewashed fortress, a gem of medieval defensive architecture housed inside the Stari Grad, is surrounded by a manicured park. Construction

Varaždin

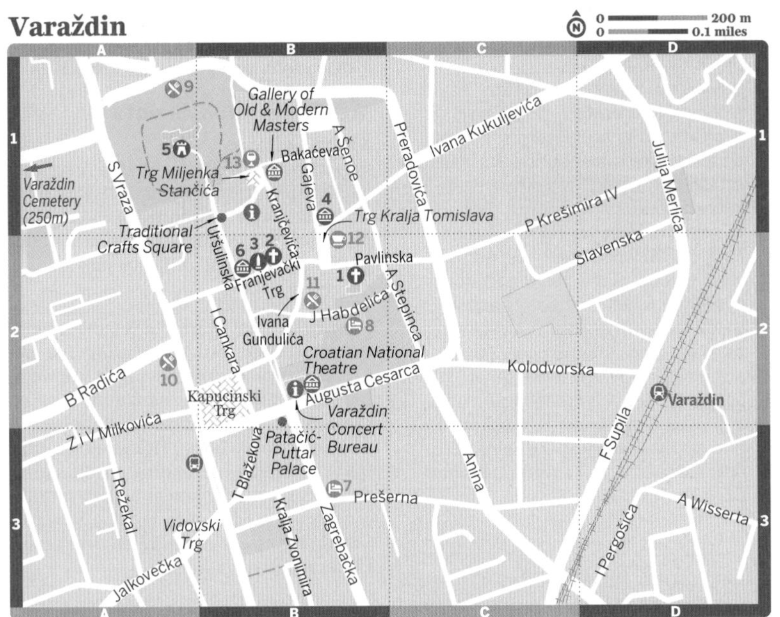

began in the 14th century, with the present Gothic-Renaissance structure dating back to the 16th century, when it was the regional fortification against the Turks.

The building was in private hands until 1925; today, as a museum, it houses a hotchpotch of furniture, paintings, watches, glassware, decorative objects, insignia and weapons, amassed over centuries and displayed throughout 30 exhibition rooms. Much more interesting than the historic collection inside, though, is the architecture: enter via a drawbridge and wander around to view the archways, courtyards and chapels of this sprawling castle-fortress.

Varaždin Cemetery CEMETERY
(Hallerova Aleja 8; 7am-9pm May-Sep, to 8pm Mar, Apr & Oct, to 5pm Jan, Feb, Nov & Dec) A 10-minute stroll west of Stari Grad takes you to this serene horticultural masterpiece, designed in 1905 by Viennese architect Hermann Helmer. Meander amid tombstones, avenues, promenades and over 7000 trees, including magnolia, beech and birch.

Cathedral of the Assumption CATHEDRAL
(Katedrala Uznesenja Marijina; Pavlinska 4; 7am-12.30pm & 3.30-7.30pm) This former Jesuit church, located southeast of Trg Kralja Tomislava, was built in 1646. The facade is distinguished by an early baroque portal bearing the coat of arms of the noble Drašković family. Occupying the central nave is the altar, which has elaborate engravings and a gilded painting of the Assumption of the Virgin Mary. Famous for its great acoustics, the cathedral is the site of concerts during the Varaždin Baroque Evenings (p110) festival.

Varaždin

Sights
1 Cathedral of the Assumption....B2
2 Franciscan Church & Monastery of St John the Baptist....B2
3 Statue of Bishop Grgur Ninski....B2
4 Town Hall....B1
5 Town Museum....A1
6 World of Insects....B2

Sleeping
7 Maltar....B3
8 Park Boutique Hotel....B2

Eating
9 Bedem....A1
10 Palatin....A2
11 Restoran Raj....B2

Drinking & Nightlife
12 Kavana Grofica Marica....B2
13 My Way....B1

WORTH A TRIP

VARAŽDINSKE TOPLICE

Sulphurous thermal springs at a steaming temperature of 58°C have been attracting weary visitors to Varaždinske Toplice since the Romans first established a health settlement here in the 1st century CE. Today it's still a relaxed and quiet spa-town, surrounded by gentle, wooded hills and with a central clutch of churches and historic buildings including the baroque castle (now the town's museum). Most people are here for the thermal pools, part of an unfortunately ugly hospital-hotel complex, but if you're passing through and interested in history, a quick stroll through the remains of the Roman Spa, built between the 1st and 4th centuries CE, is worthwhile.

Town Hall HISTORIC BUILDING
(Gradska Vijećnica; Trg Kralja Tomislava 1) This striking Romanesque-Gothic structure has been the town hall since the 16th century. Notice the town's coat of arms at the foot of the tower and the carved portal dating from 1792. There's a guard-changing ceremony every Saturday at 11am from mid-May to mid-October.

Franciscan Church & Monastery of St John the Baptist CHURCH
(Crkva Svetog Ivana Krstitelja; Franjevački Trg 8; ⌚6.30am-noon & 5.30-7.30pm) Built in 1650 in baroque style on the site of an earlier structure, this church contains the town's tallest tower (54.5m) and houses an ancient pharmacy ornamented with 18th-century ceiling frescos.

Statue of Bishop Grgur Ninski STATUE
The sculpture of medieval Croatian bishop Grgur Ninski was made by renowned Croatian sculptor Ivan Meštrović; it's a copy of the artist's original bronze statue in Split. Touch the statue's big toe and good luck will come your way (so the story goes).

World of Insects MUSEUM
(Entomološka Zbirka; Franjevački Trg 10; adult/child 35/15KN; ⌚9am-5pm Tue-Fri, to 1pm Sat & Sun) This entomological collection, housed in the classicist Hercer Palace, comprises nearly 4500 exhibits of the bug world, including 1000 different insect species. It's well set out to spark a child's interest in the natural world, with beautifully displayed examples of insect nests, habitats and reproductive habits. There's little in the way of English explanations but audioguides are available.

Festivals & Events

Špancirfest CULTURAL
(www.spancirfest.com; ⌚Aug) In late August the eclectic Špancirfest enlivens the town's parks, streets and squares with world music, street performances, theatre, creative workshops, traditional crafts and contemporary arts.

Varaždin Baroque Evenings MUSIC
(www.vbv.hr; ⌚Sep) Varaždin is famous for its baroque music festival, Varaždin Baroque Evenings, which takes place over two weeks each September. Local and international orchestras play in the cathedral, churches and theatres around town. Tickets range from 75KN to 250KN (depending on the event), and become available one hour before the concert at travel agencies or the **Varaždin Concert Bureau** (☎042-212 907; Auga Cesarca 1, Croatian National Theatre).

DOMESTIC DESTINATIONS	COST (KN)	TIME	SERVICES
Berlin (Germany)	520	15hr	1 weekly
Maribor (Slovenia)	60-65	1¾hr	2 daily
Munich (Germany)	185-215	8hr	1-3 daily
Trakošćan Castle	36	1-1¼hr	9 daily
Varaždinske Toplice	21	30min	hourly
Vienna (Austria)	135	5hr	1 daily
Zagreb	61-81	1½hr	hourly

Sleeping

★**Park Boutique Hotel** BOUTIQUE HOTEL €€
(☎042-420 300; www.park-boutique-hotel.eu; Jurja Habdelića 6; s/d/tr/q from 550/610/830/930KN; P❄📶) Varaždin doesn't get more swish than this. The 19 rooms at this boutique hotel are all Scandi-style blonde wood, smooth lines, floor-to-ceiling windows and bright pops of colour. They come in three styles – contemporary (called Park), retro and gallery (split-level rooms which can easily fit a family of four). To wake up to leafy views, request a room facing the park.

Maltar PENSION €€

(042-311 100; www.maltar.hr; Prešerna 1; s/d/tr 250/500/600KN, apt from €70; P ❄) This homey family-run guesthouse has well-kept, old fashioned rooms with wood walls and narrow bathrooms. There's also a studio with a kitchenette (which will sleep two or three people) and apartments in another building down the road.

Eating

Restoran Raj CROATIAN €

(042-213 146; Ivana Gundulića 11; mains 25-65KN; 9am-10pm Mon-Fri & Sun, to 2am Sat;) This cavernous restaurant, with lots of wood accents, serves great weekly lunches (till 1.30pm), and features a meat-heavy menu (particularly pork). The drinks menu has lots of beers and *rakija* (grappa) varieties. During warm weather, sit on the wisteria-covered back terrace.

Bedem CROATIAN €€

(042-557 545; www.bedem-varazdin.com; Vladimira Nazora 9; mains 43-140KN; 10am-10pm Mon-Thu & Sun, to 11pm Fri & Sat;) This venture by two local chefs experiments with regional cuisine using local ingredients – think foie-gras-filled puff pastry and pork belly rolled in pumpkin seeds. The downstairs covered terrace, overlooking grassy expanses and the Old Town ramparts, is lovely on warm days. The weekday *gableci* (traditional lunches; served till 3pm) are excellent value.

Palatin CROATIAN €€

(042-398 300; www.palatin.hr; Braće Radića 1; mains 55-140KN; 7.30am-11pm Mon-Sat, to 10pm Sun; ❄) A notch above everywhere else in town for the quality of its menu, with dishes like Istrian steak with truffles and perch in horseradish sauce among the house specialities. There's a large wine list of over 50 wines and great lunch specials daily, plus home-made ice cream. Sit in the vaulted basement or on the covered terrace outside.

Drinking & Nightlife

Kavana Grofica Marica CAFE

(Trg Kralja Tomislava 1; 7am-10pm;) The best place in town for a coffee. Do as the locals do and pull up a seat on the pavement out front to watch the world go by.

My Way BAR

(Trg Miljenka Stančića 1; 6.30am-11.30pm Mon-Thu, to 4am Fri & Sat, 7.30am-11.30pm Sun) This cafe-bar does a roaring trade with its seating taking over the square on sunny days. Service is on the ball and there's a huge variety of drinks to choose from, including well-priced beer (9.50KN–22KN).

Information

Tourist Office (042-210 987; www.tourism-varazdin.hr; Ivana Padovca 3; 8am-6pm Mon-Fri, 10am-5pm Sat May-Oct, 8am-4pm Mon-Fri, 10am-1pm Sat Nov-Apr) A wealth of information and plenty of colourful brochures are available here. Can also help with private accommodation.

Varaždin Concert Bureau (p110) You can get tickets for Varaždin Baroque Evenings here.

Getting There & Around

BUS

The **bus station** (Zrinskih i Frankopana bb) lies just to the southwest of the town centre. You can leave your luggage at the station's **garderoba** (left-luggage office; per bag 7KN; 4.30am-8.30pm Mon-Fri, 6.30am-8.30pm Sat & Sun).

Northbound buses originate in Zagreb and make a stop at Varaždin, but they cost the same whether you buy the ticket in Zagreb or Varaždin. Most buses to the coast go through Zagreb. Note that service to Trakošćan Castle and Varaždinske Toplice is greatly reduced on weekends.

Minibuses (5KN to 15KN) from the bus station serve the town and nearby villages from Monday to Saturday.

TRAIN

The **train station** (Kolodvorska 17) is to the east, at the opposite end of town to the bus station. Leave luggage at the train station's **garderoba** (per day 15KN; 6.25am-6.25pm).

There are 12 daily trains to Zagreb (65KN, 2¾ hours), where you can change for trains to the coast. There are also two daily trains to Budapest (Hungary; 222KN, 6½ hours) with a change in Koprivnica.

MEĐIMURJE

The undulating landscapes of Međimurje stretch northeast of Varaždin, towards the borders with Hungary and Slovenia. Road-tripping through this fertile corner of patchwork fields, teensy villages, and hills lined with regimented vineyards makes for a great countryside escape where visitors are few and far between. A handful of up-and-coming wine cellars provide interesting stopoffs and the thermal pools in the spa village of Sveti Martin are good for a soak at the end of the day's drive.

OFF THE BEATEN TRACK

LONJSKO POLJE NATURE PARK

Nominated for World Heritage Site status, **Lonjsko Polje Nature Park** (044-672 080; www.pp-lonjsko-polje.hr; Krapje 18, Čigoč 26; 10KN; 9am-5pm Apr-Oct) is a 506-sq-km stretch of swampland (*polje* means 'field') in the Posavina region, between the Sava River and Mt Moslavačka Gora. Situated along Lonja River, a Sava tributary that gives the park its name, this huge retention basin is famed for the diversity of its flora and fauna. Surrounding villages are home to traditional 19th-century wooden architecture, and birdwatchers (well, stork lovers) can have a field day here during spring and summer.

The area is divided into several villages. **Čigoć** is a world-famous 'stork meeting point' – the white storks nest on top of Čigoć's lovely wooden houses. The birds flock here in late March and early April, hanging around and munching on the swampland insects up until late August, when they start their two- to three-month flight back towards southern Africa. Čigoć is home to the park's information point and ticket office, and a small ethnographic collection owned by the Sučić family (5KN).

The heritage village of **Krapje** is known for its well-preserved traditional wooden houses and rich fishing and hunting areas. Check out the covered external staircases, porches and pillars, and various farm buildings with their barns, drying sheds, pigsties and hen houses. The Palaić family has a small ethnographic collection you should see (and a couple of apartments to boot). From April through October an information centre in one of the wooden houses has a guide who will be happy to enlighten you about the cultural heritage of the area. Look out for the *posavski* horse, a local breed that grazes in the oak forests of Lonjsko Polje. Also worth a visit is the village of **Mužilovčica**, known for its swallows. Don't miss a meal at the Ravlić family farm here.

There are three entrances to the park: at Čigoč, Krapje and Repušnica. The visitor centres at Krapje and Repušnica offer bike and canoe rentals (80KN per day for bikes, 50KN per canoe for up to three hours).

Lonjsko Polje is 50km southeast of Zagreb. The best way to visit is with your own transport or on a tour, as public transport is poor and makes moving around the park quite difficult. Private accommodation is available in various wooden houses inside the park; more information is available on the website. Our recommendations for hideaways that feature both lodging and food include Tradicije Čigoć, Etno Selo Stara Lonja and Ekoetno Selo Strug.

Activities

Lovrec Vineyard WINE
(040-830 171; www.vino-lovrec.hr; Sveti Urban 133, Štrigova; tour & tasting 80KN; by appointment) To sample the region's top wines in an authentic family environment, head to Lovrec Vineyard in the village of Sveti Urban, 20km northwest of Čakovec, the region's capital. The guided tour (in English, French or German) of this country estate walks you through its fascinating history of boutique wine production which spans six generations of winemakers.

You'll peek into the 300-year-old wine cellar, with its old wine presses and barrels, rest in the shade of two towering plane trees, take in the vistas of the 6-hectare vineyards, and top it off with tasting around 10 wine varieties, from chardonnay to local *graševina*. For 20KN extra you can have some snacks, like cheese, salami and bread sticks, and a bottle of wine to take home.

Cmrečnjak WINE
(098 295 206; www.cmrecnjak.hr; Sveti Urban 273, Štrigova; 8am-4pm Mon-Sat by appointment) One of the area's best family-run cellars, where the wine production dates back to 1884. The winery offers tours, and tastings in a rustic room with a panoramic terrace.

LifeClass Terme Sveti Martin THERMAL BATHS
(www.spa-sport.hr; Izvorska, Sveti Martin Na Muri; pool day use adult/child weekday 60/35KN, weekend 80/52KN; 8am-8pm Mon-Thu & Sun, to 11pm Fri & Sat) The village of Sveti Martin Na Muri is home to the four-star LifeClass Terme Sveti Martin, with its series of outdoor, indoor and thermal pools, water park, tennis courts, forest trails, shops, restaurants and golf course. The wellness centre here has a sauna complex and focuses on various body therapies including mud wraps and Vichy massages.

Sleeping & Eating

Regina Apartments RESORT €€
(☎040-371 111; www.spa-sport.hr; Grkaveščak bb, Sveti Martin Na Muri; apt d/q from €45/70; P ❄ 🛜 🏊 🐾) The nicest accommodation option at Sveti Martin Na Muri's spa and thermal baths complex are these apartments, very popular with Zagreb families on weekends. The apartments have well-equipped kitchens (including a filter coffee-maker) and all come with terrace or balcony. Bigger apartments can comfortably fit a family of four.

★**Mala Hiža** CROATIAN €€
(☎040-341 101; www.mala-hiza.hr; Balogovec 1, Mačkovec; mains 65-135KN; ⏲10am-10pm Mon-Sat, noon-6pm Sun) Foodies from Zagreb travel to Mala Hiža in the village of Mačkovec, 4km north of Čakovec, for its lauded and awarded seasonal cuisine done up with flair. Served in an old wooden Međimurje cottage, the menu features snails, *štrukli* and creative takes on local mainstays, plus over 150 wine labels, at least 30 of which from Međimurje.

Getting There & Away

You'll need your own car to explore this area; public transport is virtually nonexistent.

SLAVONIA

Pancake-flat, river-rich Slavonia is the agricultural heartbeat of Croatia. Chequerboards of green crops and yellow rapeseed roll out for kilometres beside the roadside and you may well spot an eagle or two hanging out near the fields if you keep your eyes peeled as you drive through. The small but vibrant city of Osijek makes for the most obvious base. From here, head out boating on the wetlands of Kopački Rit or hit the wineries of the Baranja region (p120).

The impact of the war hit hardest in southeast Slavonia, where historic Vukovar is slowly attracting more visitors thanks to its two museums and Illok, on the Serbian border, is being discovered by wine fans..

Bordered by three major rivers (Sava, Drava and Danube), this region holds strong connections with Hungary, Serbia and Germany. Slavonia's key appeal lies in this culturally intriguing mix that makes it closer to central Europe than coastal Croatia.

History

Before the 1991 war displaced tens of thousands of inhabitants, Slavonia contained one of the most ethnically diverse populations in Europe. Settled by Slavic tribes in the 7th century, the region was conquered by the Turks in the 16th century. Catholic residents fled, and Serbian Orthodox settlers, who were better received by the Turks, arrived en masse.

In 1690 Serb supporters of Vienna, in their battles with the Turks, left Kosovo and settled in the Srijem region around Vukovar. The Turks ceded the land to Austria in 1699 and the Habsburgs turned a large part of the region into a Vojna Krajina (Military Frontier).

The Muslim population left but more Serbs arrived, joined by German merchants; Hungarian, Slovak and Ukrainian peasants; Catholic Albanians and Jews. Much land was sold to German and Hungarian aristocrats who built huge baroque and classical mansions around the towns of Osijek, Vukovar and Ilok.

The large Serbian community prompted Slobodan Milošević to attempt to incorporate the region into a 'Greater Serbia'. This assault began with the destruction of Vukovar and the shelling of Osijek in 1991. A ceasefire prevailed in 1992, but it wasn't until January 1998 that the region was returned to Croatia as part of the Dayton peace agreement.

The fighting may be over but the war's impact remains profound. In towns such as Vukovar, Serbs and Croats lead almost totally separate lives. Efforts are being made to bring the communities together, but with limited success so far.

Đakovo

☎031 / POP 26,400

Surrounded by patchwork fields, Đakovo is a bustling provincial town that makes a good day trip from Osijek, just 35km to the north. Its impressive neo-Romanesque cathedral, towering over the vast main square, is Đakovo's calling card, decorated toe-to-tip inside with colourful frescos (and unlike many Croatian churches, easy to visit thanks to regular opening hours). After craning your neck at religious art, check out the town's Lipizzaner horse heritage at Ergela where these sought-after pure-breds are trained.

Sights

★Đakovo Cathedral of St Peter CATHEDRAL
(☎031-802 306; Strossmayerov Trg 6; ⌚6.30am-noon & 3-7.30pm) Đakovo's pride and glory is this red-brick cathedral, with its twin 84m-high belfries looming over town. Commissioned by Bishop Strossmayer in 1862, the cathedral took four years to construct and another 12 to decorate. Once you enter this neo-Romanesque structure, you'll see what the dilly-dallying was about. The interior is a dazzling plethora of bright frescos depicting both Old Testament scenes and the life of St Peter.

Ergela FARM
(☎031-822 535; www.ergela-djakovo.hr; Auga Šenoe 45; adult/child 20/10KN; ⌚7am-5pm Mon-Fri, 9am-1pm Sat & Sun Mar-Oct, 7am-3pm Mon-Fri Nov-Feb) Đakovo is famous for its Lipizzaner horses, a noble pure-bred with a lineage that can be traced back to the 16th century. These horses are trained in dressage here at Ergela for their eventual work as high-class carriage and riding horses. About 30 horses undergo daily training and visitors are welcome to visit the facilities. Thirty-minute guided tours are available for 30/20KN adult/child, as are short rides (150KN) in an old-fashioned carriage.

If you're really into horses, it will be worthwhile adding in a trip to **Ivandor**, its horse stud farm, 6km out of town where the foals and colts are kept before they're ready for training. There are around 150 Lipizzaner horses in the paddocks here. Guided tours of these facilities are also available.

Festivals & Events

Đakovački Vezovi CULTURAL
(Đakovo Embroidery; ⌚Jul) Đakovački Vezovi features a display by the Lipizzaner horses and a folklore show on the first weekend in July each year, complete with dancing and traditional songs.

Eating

Bistro Mon Ami CROATIAN €
(Luke Botića 12; mains 30-90KN; ⌚9am-11pm; ❄) Slap-up Slavonian feasting just behind the cathedral. This place dishes up hearty, rustic plates of grilled meat goodness. For folk who prefer meals big on flavour rather than particularly Instagrammable.

Information

Tourist Office (www.tz-djakovo.hr; Kralja Tomislava 3; ⌚7am-3pm Mon-Fri, 8am-1pm Sat) Enthusiastic staff will ply you with maps, brochures, tips and advice at this small office.

Getting There & Away

It's easy to do a day or half-day trip from Osijek to Đakovo (34KN, 45 minutes) with buses running roughly hourly until 9pm on weekdays and six services daily on weekends. Check up-to-date bus timetables on www.panturist.hr. The **bus station** (Splitska bb) is in the centre of town, a two minute stroll to the cathedral.

All buses plying the main Zagreb–Osijek route pull in here.

Osijek

☎031 / POP 104,600

The historic, leafy university town of Osijek, with its waterfront promenade along the broad Drava River and imposing 18th-century fortress area, is the most interesting destination in Slavonia.

The city suffered terribly in the 1990s from Serb shelling and pock-marks still scar some structures, but most of Osijek's grand buildings have now been restored. A walk through town is an architectural feast, from the art nouveau frippery of secessionist mansions to fine baroque buildings squaring off across the plaza in the citadel area.

If buildings aren't enough, though, this regional capital also has the buzziest atmosphere you'll find east of Zagreb, boosted by a booming student population that pack out the cafes nightly. It makes for a enjoyable place to base yourself while exploring the wider region.

History

Osijek's location on the Drava River, near its junction with the Danube (Dunav in Croatian), has made it strategically important for more than two millenniums. It was the Slavic settlers that gave Osijek its name; by the 12th century it was a thriving market town. In 1526 the Turks destroyed Osijek, rebuilt it in Ottoman style and made it into an administrative centre.

Austrians chased the Turks out in 1687, the Muslims fled into Bosnia, and the city was repopulated with Serbs, Croats, Germans and Hungarians. Still wary of Turkish attacks, the Austrians built Tvrđa, the fortress that still stands today, in the early 18th century.

Until the 1990s war, Osijek was a powerful industrial centre of former Yugoslavia. When the war broke out in 1991, the federal Yugoslav army and Serbian paramilitary units overran the Baranja region north of Osijek. The first shells were dropped in July 1991 from Serbian positions across the Drava River. When Vukovar fell in November of that year, federal and Serbian forces made Osijek the object of their undivided attention, pounding it with artillery as thousands of residents poured out of the city. This devastating shelling continued until May 1992, but the city never fell.

Sights

Tvrđa HISTORIC SITE

Built under Habsburg rule as a defence against Turkish attacks, Osijek's compact 18th-century citadel was relatively undamaged during the war in the 1990s. This baroque complex of cobblestone streets, spacious squares and stately mansions reveals a remarkable architectural unity, lending it the feel of an open-air museum, yet one still very much in use today. Many of the mansions are now used by various university faculties and as secondary schools so there's a lively, youthful buzz to the cafe-bars here.

➡ **Water Gate & Northern Battlements**

(Fakultelska) Trvđa's water gate was built into the northern wall in 1715. Just beside it, steps lead up onto the grassy top of the ramparts from where you can walk west to the brick water tower (wear closed shoes, there's broken glass and a fair amount of rubbish along the path up here) or east, following the ramparts until they taper downwards onto Jagića street.

➡ **Museum of Slavonia Archaeology Department**

(Muzej Slavonije; www.mso.hr; Trg Svetog Trojstva 2; adult/child 20/15; ⏲10am-6pm Tue-Sat) The oldest museum in Croatia, the Museum of Slavonia is housed in the renovated city-guard building with a glass dome over an arcaded patio. It showcases Slavonian history through the ages. Start on the 2nd floor with the Neolithic section and work your way down. Exhibits – gorgeous anthropomorphic figurines, burial goods, ceramics, metalware – are thoughtfully curated and, except for the last few rooms on the 1st floor, displays have English explanations.

Afterwards, hop across the square to the museum's second building, housed in Osijek's old Magistrates building. The ground floor here is home to the Lapidarium, with plenty of Roman stelae and tombs, and the 1st floor hosts exhibits on Trvđa's history as well as temporary exhibitions.

➡ **Holy Trinity Monument**

(Trg Svetog Trojstva) This elaborate baroque pillar, erected in 1729, commemorates the victims of the 18th-century plague that swept the city.

➡ **Gloria Maris**

(www.gloria-maris.hr; Svodovi bb; adult/child 20/10KN; ⏲10am-4pm Tue, Wed & Fri, to 8pm Thu, to 1pm Sat & Sun) Inside the vaults of the old citadel, this museum is dedicated to seashells and marine and freshwater life. It's the labour of love of Vladimir Filipović, who has amassed around one million shells in his 48 years of collecting, from all corners of the globe. Enter through the arched alleyway to the right side of the church.

Check out the most poisonous creature in the ocean (the remains of an octopus from the Philippines), fossils from 650 million years ago, a megalodon tooth and a vast array of exotic shells.

Europska Avenija ARCHITECTURE

If you're a fan of early-20th-century architecture, take a stroll down Europska Avenija, lined by ornate art nouveau mansions. Along this stretch you'll also see the grand **Post Office** (Kardinala Alojzija Stepinca 17; ⏲7am-8pm Mon-Sat), built in 1912, and the powder-pink art nouveau **Cinema Urania** (Stjepana Radića bb).

CYCLING SLAVONIA

Cycling is an increasingly popular activity in the region, and a cycle path connects Bilje with Osijek. The **Pannonian Peace Route** is an 80km ride from Osijek to the Serbian city of Sombor, along the Danube and through Kopački Rit. For more info and a map, browse www.zeleni-osijek.hr, the website of a local association for environmental protection. Also popular is the 138km-long **Danube Route**, which traces easternmost Croatia along its borders with Hungary and Serbia.

Osijek

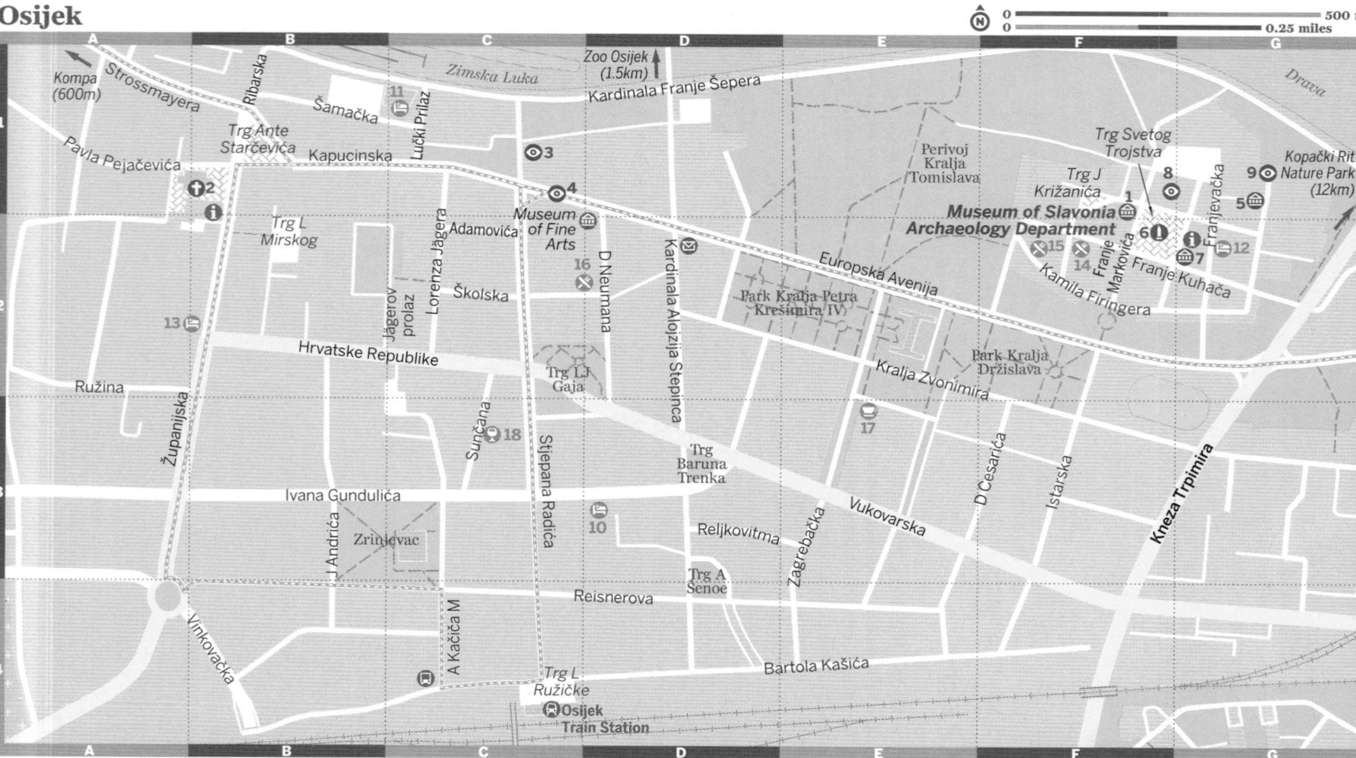

0.25 miles
500 m
Kompa (600m)
Zoo Osijek (1.5km)
Kopački Rit Nature Park (12km)
Drava
Zimska Luka
Strossmayera
Pavla Pejačevića
Ribarska
Trg Ante Starčevića
Šamačka
Kapucinska
Lučki Prilaz
Kardinala Franje Šepera
Trg L Mirskog
Adamovića
Museum of Fine Arts
Lorenza Jägera
Jägerov prolaz
Školska
D Neumana
Kardinala Alojzija Stepinca
Europska Avenija
Perivoj Kralja Tomislava
Museum of Slavonia Archaeology Department
Trg J Križanića
Trg Svetog Trojstva
Franjevačka
Franje Markovića
Franje Kuhača
Kamila Firingera
Park Kralja Petra Krešimira IV
Park Kralja Držislava
Kralja Zvonimira
Hrvatske Republike
Trg LJ Gaja
Stjepana Radića
Sunčana
Trg Baruna Trenka
Ivana Gundulića
Zrinjevac
J Andrića
Županijska
Ružina
Vinkovačka
Reisnerova
A Kačića M
Trg L Ružičke
Osijek Train Station
Trg A Šenoe
Reljkovitma
Vukovarska
Zagrebačka
D Cesarića
Istarska
Kneza Trpimira
Bartola Kašića

Osijek

Church of St Peter & Paul CHURCH

(☎031-310 020; Pavla Pejačevića 1; ⏰1-7pm Mon, 7am-7pm Tue-Sun) This red-brick neo-Gothic church's 90m-high tower is surpassed in height only by the cathedral in Zagreb and dominates downtown Osijek. Built in the 1890s, the interior has 40 elaborate stained-glass windows in Viennese style and vividly coloured frescos by Croatian painter Mirko Rački.

Zoo Osijek ZOO

(www.zoo-osijek.hr; Sjevernodravska Obala 1; adult/child 20/10KN; ⏰9am-8pm) As an escape from the museums and churches, take a free ride on the emblematic *kompa* (a wooden pedestrian ferry propelled by the water current) from the shore of Gornji Grad to Zoo Osijek, on the other side of the Drava. Croatia's largest zoo spreads over 11 verdant riverside hectares, with 80 animal species and a reptile-filled aquarium. The *kompa* operates from 9am to 7pm April to October.

Sleeping

★Maksimilian GUESTHOUSE €

(☎031-497 567; www.maksimilian.hr; Franjevačka 12; s 250-350KN, d 350-450KN, f 550KN, all incl breakfast; ❄@☜) In the heart of the old town, this superb guesthouse is run by a hospitable, English-speaking team. All 14 rooms in the historic 1860 building are cosy and simply styled with high ceilings and satellite TV. Full kudos for providing a fully accessible room for wheelchair users at this price point, too.

There are plenty of extras: kitchen, free coffee and tea, generous breakfast, bike rental and lots of info on cycling in the region.

Hostel Street Osijek HOSTEL €

(☎031-327 743; www.hostel-street-osijek.com; Ivana Gundulića 5; dm/s/d/tr without bath 145/180/290/390KN; ❄☜) Seven bright and well-maintained triple rooms which can be used either as dorms or as privates, all sharing superclean, modern bathrooms. It's popular with cyclists and the bus and train stations are both only a walk away. The hostel is accessed through a courtyard off the street.

Waldinger HOTEL €€

(☎031-250 450; www.waldinger.hr; Županijska 8; pension s/d 290/340KN, hotel s 550-650KN, d 750-850KN; P❄@☜) This is a grand little hotel of two halves. In the main street-facing building, rooms offer lashings of old-school charm, with high beds, plush furnishings and oil paintings on the walls. The pension out back is a humbler abode with functional rooms and a charming garden with fish pond and willow tree. Room rates drop substantially during quiet periods.

A fine breakfast is served in the stately dining room plus there's an upscale restaurant and atmospheric cafe.

Hotel Osijek BUSINESS HOTEL €€€

(☎031-230 333; www.hotelosijek.hr; Šamačka 4; s/d standard 850/955KN, superior 900/1015; P❄@☜) Right on the river, this glass-and-concrete tower is as swanky as Osijek gets. Standard doubles have Drava views, classic styling and all the bells and whistles you'd expect, though the bathrooms are on the small side. Superior rooms get bigger bathrooms (with tub) but most view the city. The 14th-floor wellness centre has a Turkish bath, jacuzzi and sauna.

Eating

Food here is strongly influenced by neighbouring Hungary, with liberal paprika usage. The two restaurants inside the Tvrđa quarter are the best places to try specialities like *fiš paprikaš* (river-fish stew in a paprika sauce, served with noodles). For Drava River views, there are a couple of floating restaurants along the waterfront promenade but in general the food isn't the greatest.

Vege Lege VEGETARIAN €
(Trg Ljudevita Gaja 4; mains 18-32KN; 9am-7pm Mon-Sat) Vegie and vegan burgers, good salads and delicious felafel wraps (they call them tortillas) are all served up at this tiny place with just a few counters with bar stools to perch on.

Slavonska Kuća SLAVONIAN €
(031-369 955; Kamila Firingera 26; mains 45-70KN; 10am-11pm Mon-Sat, 11am-5pm Sun) This is a great choice for authentic Slavonian food, with lots of *pečena riba* (baked fish), including delicious catfish. Prices are moderate and portions hearty. Wash your meal down with *graševina,* a fruity white wine.

★ **Kod Ruže** SLAVONIAN €€
(031-206 066; Kuhačeva 25a; mains 40-135KN; 10am-11pm;) We never turn down a chance to sit at a table under stuffed eagles, goblet in hand, while being served by waiters wearing old-school braces. This is an atmospheric place to try out Slavonian flavours, especially at weekends when a band plays folk music. Try the *čobanac* (traditional meat stew) or the *alas salata* (salad with river fish).

SIPPING SLAVONIAN WINE

Vines have been cultivated in Slavonia for millenniums – it's thought that the name Baranja is derived from the Hungarian for 'wine mother' – and after a period of stagnation the region is undergoing a serious renaissance. White wines made from local grapes, including *graševina,* are justifiably renowned, and earthy reds are also produced, primarily from *frankovka (blaufränkisch),* merlot and cabernet sauvignon. You should call ahead at all these cellars to make sure somebody is there to show you around.

Kutjevo (034-255 075; www.kutjevo.com; Kralja Tomislava 1, Kutjevo; guided tour & tasting 30KN; by appointment), in the town of the same name, is home to a medieval wine cellar dating from 1232, formerly of the Cistercian Abbey. You can visit on a guided tour and sample its wines.

Nearby are two of Slavonia's top wineries: **Krauthaker** (034-315 000; www.krauthaker.hr; Ivana Jambrovića 6, Kutjevo; tasting 40KN; by appointment), whose *graševina* and sweet wines regularly win top awards, and **Enjingi** (034-267 200; www.enjingi.hr; Hrnjevac 87, Vetovo; tasting & tour 50KN; by appointment), one of Croatia's leading ecological producers, with winemaking experience dating back to 1890; try the award-winning Venje white blend. For a complete selection of Kutjevo's wines, visit **Vina Čamak – Kolijevka Graševine** (034-255 689; Republike Hrvatske 56, Kutjevo; by appointment), a wine shop and tasting room in the town centre.

In Baranja, grape cultivation has been revived on the gentle hills around Kneževi Vinogradi. Up-and-coming winegrowers, mainly in the villages of Zmajevac and Suza, work along well-marked wine trails. Traditionalist in its approach to winemaking, **Gerstmajer** (091 35 15 586; www.vina-gerstmajer.weebly.com; Petefi Šandora 31, Zmajevac; by appointment) offers tasting tours of its cellar and 11 hectares of vineyards. Just down the hill is the area's biggest producer, **Josić** (031-734 410; www.josic.hr; Planina 194, Zmajevac; by appointment), which also has a fine restaurant (p122). **Kolar** (031-733 006; Maršala Tita 94, Suza; tastings 24KN; by appointment) offers a restaurant, shop and wine tastings in its 100-year-old cellar, located on the main road in nearby Suza. Don't miss a visit to **Vina Belje** (091 17 90 118; www.vinabelje.hr; Šandora Petefija 2, Kneževi Vinogradi; tour & tasting of 3-4 wines 45-90KN; 10am-5pm), with its ancient cellars and gorgeous viewpoint amid vineyards.

Slavonia also boasts ancient cellars in Ilok at Ilok Wine Cellar (p124), as well as wineries in Dalj and Erdut north of Vukovar, the best of which is **Vina Antunović** (031-590 350; www.vina-antunovic.hr; Braće Radić 17, Dalj; by appointment), which has a lovely tasting room where you can savour their white-wine varieties.

Lumiere EUROPEAN €€

(Franje Šepera 8; mains 70-220KN; ⏲11am-11pm; ❄📶) Beloved by Osijek's fashionable set, this restaurant offers up classic seafood and meaty mains such as octopus cooked under a *peka* and Viennese-style steak with an accompanying impressive wine list from across the country. The interior is contemporary casual-chic with big comfy grey chairs and chunky tables but we prefer the small streetside terrace.

Drinking & Nightlife

Cafe-bar hot spots are along the riverfront around Hotel Osijek, the section of Stjepana Radića north of Ivana Gundulića, and in Tvrđa, on Trg Svetog Trojstva. The Tvrđa bars are a favourite haunt of Osijek's student population.

Caffe Bar Kafka CAFE

(Zagrebačka 1; ⏲7am-10pm Mon-Sat; 📶) This neighbourhood cafe-bar with a small outdoor terrace does good coffee and is a mellow choice for an early evening beer.

Gajba CRAFT BEER

(Sunčana 3; ⏲noon-11pm Mon-Sat) Great little spot for beer lovers, with a small terrace on an off-the-radar pedestrian strip. Try some local craft beers, like Black Hat from Osijek.

Information

For safety information regarding landmines in the area, see the boxed text on p121.

Main Tourist Office (☎031-203 755; www.tzosijek.hr; Županijska 2; ⏲8am-6pm Mon-Fri, to noon Sat mid-Jun–mid-Sep, 8am-4pm Mon-Fri, to noon Sat mid-Sep–mid-Jun) This well-briefed office has bundles of brochures, booklets and maps and is a good first point of call.

Osijek Clinical Medical Centre (Klinički Bolnički Centar; ☎031-511 511; Josipa Huttlera 4; ⏲24hr) East of the centre.

Tourist Office (☎031-210 120; www.tzosijek.hr; Trg Svetog Trojstva 5; ⏲10am-4pm Mon-Fri, 9am-1pm Sat) Friendly info-point in Tvrđa, though it's not always open.

Getting There & Away

AIR

Osijek Airport (☎060 339 339; www.osijek-airport.hr) is located 20km from Osijek on the road to Vukovar; it's a very minor airport with only a few Croatia Airlines flights to Dubrovnik and Zagreb.

BUS

Osijek's **bus station** (☎060 353 353; Bartola Kašića bb) has good connections to local destinations and regular services to Zagreb. Check up-to-date timetables on the websites of local bus companies Panturist (www.panturist.hr) and Čazmatrans (www.cazmatrans.hr).

DOMESTIC DESTINATIONS	COST (KN)	TIME	SERVICES
Đakovo	34	40min	at least hourly weekdays; 6 daily on weekends
Ilok	61	1½hr	2 daily except Sunday
Kopačevo	23	20min	7 daily weekdays
Rijeka	265-277	7hr	9 daily
Slavonski Brod	64	1¾hr	12 daily
Split	290	11½hr	2 daily
Vukovar	34	50min	7 daily weekdays; 2 daily on weekends
Zagreb	125-133	3¾-4¼hr	15 daily

OUTSIDE CROATIA	COST (KN)	TIME	SERVICES
Belgrade	134	3½hr	4 daily
Vienna	185-230	10hr	3 daily
Zürich	386-480	19hr	1-3 daily

TRAIN

Osijek's **train station** (Bartola Kašića) is just south of the centre. Four daily services on weekdays and three daily on weekends go to Zagreb (132KN to 150KN, 4½ to five hours) and one daily service goes to Rijeka (232KN, 8¾ hours).

Getting Around

TO/FROM THE AIRPORT

A shuttle bus meets arrivals at the airport and heads to the city centre. It departs from the bus station 2½ hours before scheduled flights and costs 30KN. The taxi company Sunce departs from the same spot and charges 50KN per ride.

PUBLIC TRANSPORT, TAXI & BICYCLE

Osijek has two tram lines. Line 2 connects the train and bus station with Trg Ante Starčevića in the centre (but in a roundabout way, which takes you to the outer edge of town first), and line 1 goes to Tvrđa. The fare is 10KN, which you pay to the driver.

Buses connect Osijek to nearby Bilje; from the bus station take a Panturist bus for Beli Manastir or Batina and get off in Bilje (16KN, 20m) minutes).

Taxi service **Cammeo** (☎031-205 205; www.taxi-cammeo.hr; basic tariff & first 5km 20KN, additional km 5KN) has modern cars and is very affordable; most rides in town cost just 20KN.

For bike trips to Kopački Rit Nature Park, try **Šport za Sve** (☎031-208 135; Istarska 1; bicycle hire per day 40KN; ⏰9am-1pm Mon-Fri).

Baranja

☎031

A small triangle in the far northeast of Croatia at the confluence of the Drava and Danube Rivers, Baranja stretches east of Osijek towards Serbia, north towards the town of Beli Manastir and southwest towards Đakovo. The Hungarian influence is strongly felt here: all the towns have bilingual names.

Although flying well below the tourist radar, this largely agricultural area of wetlands, vineyards, orchards and wheat fields has been growing in popularity thanks to some good cycling routes, a clutch of wineries and the star attraction, the bird sanctuary of Kopački Rit. Anyone who fancies a slice of far-from-the-crowds appeal will enjoy a trip here.

Kopački Rit Nature Park

Situated 12km northeast of Osijek, **Kopački Rit Nature Park** (Park Prirode Kopački Rit; www.pp-kopacki-rit.hr; adult 10KN, child under 2yr free; ⏰9am-5pm Apr-Oct, 8am-4pm Nov-Mar) is one of Europe's largest wetlands, home to more than 290 bird species and rich aquatic and grassland flora showcasing water lilies, irises, duckweeds and ryegrass, as well as oak and poplar forests. Comprised of a series of ponds, backwaters and two main lakes, Sakadaško and Kopačevo, this massive floodplain was created by the meeting of the Drava and Danube Rivers. These two rivers, together with the Mura, are a Unesco biosphere reserve.

Sights

Beneath Kopački Rit's waters lie 44 species of fish, including carp, bream, pike, catfish and perch. Above the water buzz 21 kinds of mosquito (bring repellent!) and on land roam red deer, wild boar, beaver, pine marten and foxes. But it's really about the birds here – look for the rare black storks, white-tailed eagles, great crested grebes, purple herons, spoonbills and wild geese. The best time to come is during the autumn migration.

The park was heavily mined during the war and closed for many years as a result. Most mines have now been cleared and safe trails have been marked. The park **visitor centre** (☎031-445 445; https://pp-kopacki-rit.hr; ⏰9am-5pm Apr-Oct, 8am-4pm Nov-Mar), located at the main entrance, along the Bilje–Kopačevo road, features a lovely interpretation centre in a string of straw-roofed wooden huts that house interactive exhibits and a cafe. You can walk the 2km series of wooden boardwalks and then take a boat tour on Sakadaško lake. A tour by big boat, taking in a castle complex along the way, costs 80KN for adults and 60KN for children and students; a wildlife tour in a small boat is 100KN per hour (maximum four people) and by canoe 80KN. Tours depart from an embarkation point on the lake about 1km from the visitor centre (at the end of the boardwalk area). Book at the visitor centre when you arrive.

At the northern end of the park, 12km from the visitor centre, is an Austro-Hungarian castle complex and bio-ecological research station, Dvorac Tikveš. Once used by Tito as a hunting lodge, the castle was occupied by Serbs during the 1990s and forests around the complex are still mined – don't wander off by yourself.

Activities

Kopački Rit Nature Park visitor centre rents bikes (20/100KN per hour/day) so that you can explore the rural area surrounding the inner wetlands.

Zlatna Greda ADVENTURE
(☎031-565 181; www.zlatna-greda.org; Zlatna Greda 16; hiking photo safari tour per person €23; ⏰by appointment) Zlatna Greda runs superb tours of Kopački Rit and has its own ecocentre in a deserted village – now a protected cultural heritage site – on the border of Kopački Rit, 28km north of Osijek. Hikes, birdwatching trips, photo safaris and canoe adventures begin here. There's also an adrenalin park with a zipline (weekends only).

Sleeping & Eating

Bilje, 5km north of Osijek, is a dormitory suburb for the city, with a clutch of accommodation options. It makes an alternative base for exploring Kopački Rit. Both family-run B&Bs **Mazur** (031-750 294; Kneza Branimira 2, Bilje; s/d 240/360KN; P) and **Crvendać** (091 55 15 711; www.crvendac.com; Biljske satnije ZNG RH 5, Bilje; r per person 154KN) are good bets here. **Zlatna Greda** (031-565 181; www.zlatna-greda.org; Zlatna Greda 16; dm per person €17, s/d €25/42; P) is a nature-lover's alternative on the park's edge, with hostel-type accommodation.

Kormoran SLAVONIAN €
(031-753 099; www.restorankormoran.com; Podunavlje bb; mains 50-98KN; 10am-10pm) Lots of local flavours are served up here with a menu big on carp, catfish and venison dishes. It's located on the northern side of Kopački Rit Nature Park.

Didin Konak SLAVONIAN €€
(031-752 100; www.didinkonak.hr; Petefi Šandora 93, Kopačevo; mains 55-150KN; 8am-10pm) The quiet village of Kopačevo, on the edge of Kopački Rit, is home to this outstanding regional restaurant. The vibe is rustic and real, and the food delicious. Don't miss the fish skewers of catfish and perch. Some of the dishes, like the venison stew and meats under the *peka*, require advance booking.

Getting There & Away

On weekdays there are seven buses from Osijek to Kopačevo (23KN, 20 minutes), the village on the edge of Kopački Rit. They go via Bilje and some then carry on to Batina. From the bus stop in Kopačevo, it's an easy 1.5km stroll to Kopački Rit's visitor centre.

Alternatively, you can rent a bike in Osijek at Šport za Sve (p120).

Northern Baranja

The northern stretch of Baranja is a land of gently rolling hills, pretty roadside villages and *surduci*, as the traditional wine roads are called. Several of the villages have excellent wine cellars and regional restaurants, including Karanac, Suza, Zmajevac and Kneževi Vinogradi. This area was made for renting a car and simply tootling around for the day.

Sights

Located 8km east of Beli Manastir, the ethno-village and farming community of **Karanac** provides an authentic slice of Slavonian village life and is well set up to welcome visitors. Lined with cherry trees and lovingly tended gardens, it is home to three churches (Reformist, Catholic and Orthodox) and some well-preserved Pannonian architecture.

SAFE TRAVEL

Osijek and its surrounds were heavily laid with landmines during the war in the 1990s. Although the city and its outskirts along the main road have been de-mined and are completely safe, it would be unwise to wander through the swampland north of the Drava River, which leads to Kopački Rit. Most mined areas are marked; be on the lookout for signs.

In summer Kopački Rit is besieged by mosquitoes. Wear long sleeves and trousers or slather on plenty of repellent.

Batina Monument MONUMENT
In Batina, right on the tripartite border where Croatia touches Serbia and Hungary, is this striking communist-era memorial by well-known Croatian sculptor Antun Augustinčić; it commemorates a key victory by Soviet-led forces over the Nazis in WWII. The high ground here offers spectacular views over the Danube and the wine bar near the monument serves a good choice of local wines.

Sleeping & Eating

Ivica i Marica FARMSTAY €
(091 13 73 793; www.ivica-marica.com; Ivo Lola Ribara 8a, Karanac; s/d 350/450KN; P) On the edge of Karanac village, this upmarket working farm is run by a friendly couple and offers spacious, pine-and-brick-clad rooms and suites, as well as bike rental (100KN per day) and farm fun for the kids such as horse-drawn carriage rides (350KN per hour).

Tri Mudraca SLAVONIAN €
(091 21 01 212; www.trimudraca.com; Ive Lole Ribara 27, Karanac; mains 40-90KN; 10am-11pm Thu-Sun) Set on a traditional Slavonian *salaš* (farm), this lovely spot does elaborate dishes, if you call ahead, such as duck glazed with honey, and pork neck in a sauce of reduced merlot and root vegies. Or else just show up and eat whatever the cook has whipped up that day. Sit in the back garden for a view of rolling fields and vineyards.

The family who runs Tri Mudraca also offer **adventure tours** (091 21 01 212;

www.trimudraca.com; Ive Lole Ribara 27, Karanac) on request.

Kovač Čarda SLAVONIAN €
(Maršala Tita 215, Suza; mains 40-60KN; ⌚10am-11pm) In the small village of Suza, the Hungarian-run Kovač Čarda is a no-frills roadside eatery known for Baranja's best *fiš paprikaš*. They make it spicy, so if that's not your thing, ask for the paprika on the side.

★**Josić** SLAVONIAN €€
(☎031-734 410; www.josic.hr; Planina 194, Zmajevac; mains 29-90KN; ⌚1-10pm Tue-Thu & Sun, to midnight Fri & Sat) In the village of Zmajevac, Josić is on a historic *surduk* (wine road) that leads up a steep hill. It's an upmarket restaurant with tables set in vaulted cellars. Meat is the strong suit here – try the duck *perkelt* stew – and tastings of local *graševina* in the wine cellar shouldn't be missed. Reserve ahead in September and October.

Piroš Čizma SLAVONIAN €€
(☎031-733 806; Maršala Tita 101, Suza; mains 50-95KN; ⌚7am-10pm Mon-Thu & Sun, 1pm-midnight Fri & Sat) Located on the roadside when you enter Suza, this restaurant serves up Slavonian dishes prepared with a twist – think marinated catfish on an endive base with lemon, honey and mustard emulsion, and beef steak in a sauce of grapes with *frankovka* wine reduction.

It doubles as a hotel, with 25 pleasant rooms (singles/doubles 280/480KN) in two buildings, all well equipped and featuring breakfasts of local fresh cheeses, jams and cold cuts such as *kulen* (spicy paprika-flavoured sausage).

Baranjska Kuća SLAVONIAN €€
(☎031-720 180; www.baranjska-kuca.com; Kolodvorska 99, Karanac; mains 45-95KN; ⌚11am-10pm Mon-Thu, to 1am Fri & Sat, to 5pm Sun) Baranjska Kuća is an excellent restaurant that serves many traditional dishes, such as meat and fish stews. There's a chestnut-tree-shaded backyard with a barn, a blacksmith's workshop and other huts with old-fashioned crafts. On weekend nights there's live folk music.

Getting There & Around

Bus connections within northern Baranja are limited. Batina has five bus connections to Osijek on weekdays (32KN, 1¼ hours), which go via Bilje, Kopačevo, Suza and Zmajevac. To fully explore this area, though, you need your own wheels.

Vukovar

☎032 / POP 24,200

When you visit Vukovar today, it's a challenge to visualise this town as the pretty town on the Danube it was before the war. Its streets were once rimmed with elegant baroque mansions, art galleries and museums, but all that changed with the siege of 1991, which destroyed its economy, culture, infrastructure, civic harmony and soul.

Since the return of Vukovar to Croatia in 1998, there has been much progress in repairing the damage. Today its two fantastic museums – the Vučedol Culture Museum and Castle Eltz – have restored some of the town's cultural sheen and are well worth the trip south to visit. Many pock-marked and blasted facades remain though, and the former water tower on the road to Ilok has been left as a testament to the destruction.

Sights & Activities

Vukovar offers a combined 60KN pass for entry to both Castle Eltz (Gradski Musej Vukovar) and the Vučedol Culture Museum. Ask for it at either museum ticket office.

★**Vučedol Culture Museum** MUSEUM
(☎032-373 930; www.vucedol.hr; Vučedol 252; adult/child/family 40/30/60KN; ⌚10am-6pm Tue-Sun) Located 5km downriver from Vukovar, this museum sits on one of Europe's most significant archaeological sites and provides an introduction to the most important ancient culture you're likely to have never heard of. The chalcolithic era Vučedol Culture created Europe's first calendar and brewed Europe's first beer. The state-of-the-art exhibits, featuring engrossing animations which re-create the settlement during its golden age, include graves found in situ, symbol-stamped ceramics, a Vučedol house replica and a room of cleverly curated skulls.

This riverside location was first inhabited by farmers in 6000 BC, while the Vučedol culture flourished here between 3000 BC and 2500 BC. All exhibits in the 19 rooms are well marked with bilingual boards, and guided tours (40KN per person) in English are available. After viewing the main museum you can stroll five minutes to the Megaron – a bunker-like building with skylights that houses skeletons in a sand pit, including a grave of a deer that was used on shamanic journeys. The Megaron's rooftop has lovely views out to the river and the leafy surroundings.

A taxi from central Vukovar should cost about 20KN; museum staff are happy to call a taxi for you, for pick-up, when you're finished.

Castle Eltz MUSEUM

(Gradski Musej Vukovar; www.muzej-vukovar.hr; Županijska 2; adult/child/family 40/30/60KN; ⏲10am-6pm Tue-Sun) Closed for several years following the war, the 18th-century Eltz Palace reopened in 2014 as this brilliant museum. Head up the stairs to the 1st floor for a whirlwind tour of Slavonian history, from mammoth fossils through to Bronze Age horde finds and burial goods unearthed from the medieval Bijelo Brdo culture, all the way up to the mid-20th century. On the 2nd floor a moving video exhibit plays footage of the siege of Vukovar and the town's destruction.

All the displays are well curated and have English explanations. You can also take a guided tour in English (100KN).

Place of Memory: Vukovar Hospital 1991 MUSEUM

(☎091 45 21 222; www.mcdrvu.hr/en; Županijska 37; adult/child 15/7KN; ⏲8am-3pm Mon-Fri) This multimedia museum recounts the tragic events that took place in the hospital during the 1991 siege. The stirring tour takes you through a series of sandbag-protected corridors, with video projections of war footage, bomb holes and the claustrophobic atomic shelter where newborn babies and the nurses' children were kept. There are small cubicles where you can listen to interviews and speeches by the victims and survivors.

Ovčara Memorial MEMORIAL

(Ovčara bb; 5KN; ⏲10am-5pm) Around 6km out of town, en route to Ilok, there's a turn-off to the Ovčara Memorial, another 4km down the road. This is the hangar where 194 victims from Vukovar's hospital were beaten and tortured after the town's surrender in November 1991. Inside the dark room are projections of victims' photos, with a single candle burning in the middle. The victims met their deaths in a cornfield another 1.5km down the road, now marked with a black marble gravestone covered with candles and flowers.

Vukovar Waterbus Bajadera BOATING

(☎098 344 741; www.danubiumtours.hr/redplovidbe; Parobrodska bb; adult/child 55/45KN) Run by **Danubium Tours** (☎032-445 455; www.danubiumtours.hr; Olajnica 6/21; ⏲9am-5pm Mon-Fri), a glass-topped boat plies the Danube every evening at 5pm for a scenic 45-minute trip. You'll need to reserve on weekends.

THE SIEGE OF VUKOVAR

Before the war, Vukovar had a multi-ethnic population of about 44,000, of which Croats comprised 44% and Serbs 37%. As Croatia edged away from the former Yugoslavia in early 1991, tensions mounted between the two groups. In August 1991 the federal Yugoslav force launched a full-scale artillery and infantry assault in an attempt to seize the town.

By the end of August all but 15,000 of Vukovar's original inhabitants had fled. Those who remained cowered in bomb-proof cellars, living on tinned food and rationed water while bodies piled up in the streets above them. For several months of the siege, the city held out as its pitifully outnumbered defenders warded off the attacks.

After weeks of hand-to-hand fighting, Vukovar surrendered on 18 November. On 20 November Serb-Yugoslav soldiers entered Vukovar's hospital and removed 400 patients, staff and their families, 194 of whom were massacred near the village of Ovčara, their bodies dumped in a mass grave nearby. In 2007 at the War Tribunal in the Hague, two Yugoslav army officers, Mile Mrkšić and Veselin Šljivančanin, were sentenced to 20 and 10 years in prison, respectively, for their role in this massacre.

In all, it's estimated that 2000 people – including 1100 civilians – were killed in the defence of Vukovar. There were 4000 wounded, several thousand who disappeared (presumably into mass graves) and 22,000 who were forced into exile.

Today in Vukovar, Serbs and Croats live in parallel and hostile universes, socialising in separate spheres. Children attend separate schools and their parents drink in either Serb or Croat cafes. International organisations are trying to encourage more integration, but forgiveness comes hard to those who lost family members and livelihoods.

Sleeping & Eating

Pansion Villa Vanda GUESTHOUSE €€
(☎098 896 507; Dalmatinska 3; s 380-430KN, d 490-530KN; 📶) This family-run guesthouse is in a quiet side street, still within strolling distance to the centre. The place has a certain quirky character with friendly cats roaming around, an aviary with parrots downstairs and old knick-knacks in the hallways. Most of the spacious rooms come with balconies. German (and very minimal English) is spoken by the friendly hosts.

Hotel Lav HOTEL €€
(☎032-445 100; www.hotel-lav.hr; JJ Strossmayera 18; s/d/tr from 490/780/1050KN; P❄📶) Vukovar's only proper hotel is a well-run and friendly place, slap in the centre of town. The very generously sized rooms are a bit retro with their blue carpets and lemon-yellow walls but everything's kept shipshape and scrupulously clean. There's a good bar, coffee room, restaurant, small fitness room and terrace facing the river.

Stari Toranj CROATIAN €
(Trg Republike Hrvatske 7; mains 35-65KN; ⊙11am-11pm) This local joint ain't going to win any 'pretty dish' awards with massive plates of grilled seafood and meats and thick chips piled so high they're nearly toppling off the plate, but you won't leave hungry. There's pasta and a range of – again, huge – pizzas as well.

Information

Tourist Office (☎032-442 889; www.turizam-vukovar.hr; JJ Strossmayera 15; ⊙7am-3pm Mon-Fri, 8am-1pm Sat) Hands out a decent map of the town.

Getting There & Around

Vukovar's **bus station** (Kardinala Alojzija Stepinca bb) has decent connections to nearby towns and to the capital as well as a couple of international services. Services go to Zagreb (165KN, five hours, three daily), Ilok (34KN, one hour, eight daily) and Osijek (34KN, 50 minutes, eight daily weekdays, three daily weekends). There is also a service to Belgrade (99KN, 2½ hours, two daily) in Serbia.

Vukovar's **Cammeo** (☎032-330 040; www.taxi-cammeo.hr; basic tariff & first 5km 20KN, additional km 5KN) taxi service is efficient, well priced and useful for getting to or from the Vučedol Culture Museum if you don't have your own wheels. There's no central taxi stand so phone them for pick-up.

Ilok

☎032 / POP 7000

The easternmost town in Croatia, teensy medieval Ilok is a leafy place perched on a hill overlooking the Danube and the Serbian region of Vojvodina, across the river. It's part of the Srijem region of Croatia, together with Vukovar, 37km to the west. Surrounded by the wine-growing hills of Fruška Gora, famous for viniculture since Roman times, Ilok has managed to cling on to a couple of grand chunks of its once-sturdy city walls, its well-preserved Odescalchi Palace (now the city museum) and two rare specimens of Ottoman heritage: a 16th-century *hammam* (Turkish bath) and a *turbe* (grave) of a Turkish nobleman.

Occupied by Serbia in the early 1990s, Ilok was reintegrated into Croatia in 1998. Wine production has since been revived – the area now has 20 wineries you can tour – and the fortified town centre is being renovated following recent archaeological excavations.

Sights

City Museum MUSEUM
(Muzej Grada Iloka; www.mgi.hr; Šetalište Oca Mladena Barbarića 5; adult/child 40/20KN; ⊙9am-3pm Tue-Thu, to 6pm Fri, 11am-6pm Sat) Ilok's principal attraction is this municipal museum located in the Odescalchi Palace high above the Danube, with spectacular river views. The castle was built on the foundations of a 15th-century structure, which the Italian family Odescalchi later rebuilt in today's baroque-classicist style. The museum's displays are well presented with information panels in English, walking you through Ilok's history under different rulers right up to the present day. The ethnographic section, on the top floor, has a beautiful collection of costumes.

Activities

Ilok Wine Cellar WINE
(Iločki Podrumi; ☎032-590 088; www.ilocki-podrumi.hr; Šetalište OM Barbarića 4; tours 30KN; ⊙7am-11pm) The old wine cellars adjacent to the castle are well worth a look. Be sure to taste the *traminac,* a dry white wine served at the coronation of Queen Elizabeth II. A 30-minute tour takes you to the atmospheric underground cellar with its oak barrels. There's also a terrific wine store. Tours in English need to be arranged in advance.

Čobanković Winery WINE
(Vinarija Čobanković; Vladimira Nazora 59; ⌚9am-5pm Mon-Fri by appointment) The Čobanković family has been producing wine from their 50 hectares of vineyards for generations and they are today known for their green-hued *silvaner* and full-bodied blue *franconian*. Call to make an appointment if you want to do a tasting.

Rakije Barbarić DISTILLERY
(☎032-593 359; www.rakije-barbaric.hr; Vladimira Nazora 27; ⌚tasting 8am-5pm Thu & Fri) For a break from wine tasting, head to this family-run *rakija* distillery to sample a whole gamut of *rakija* flavours, from grape and honey to cherry and plum. Call ahead to make sure someone's there to walk you through *rakije* 101. Tasting prices change, depending on the number of samples you try.

Sleeping

Stari Podrum HOTEL €
(☎032-590 088; www.ilocki-podrumi.hr; Šetalište OM Barbarića 4; s/d 250/430KN; P❄📶) The motel-style accommodation block in the back of the Ilok Wine Cellar has 18 large, modern rooms, all with Danube views. There's also a restaurant here, lined with wood panelling and giant oak barrels – a splendid setting for a hearty meal of Ilok pork sausages and shepherd's stew with dumplings (mains 30KN to 95KN). The wine list is superb.

Hotel Dunav HOTEL €€
(☎032-596 500; www.hoteldunavilok.com; Julija Benešića 62; s/d 300/500KN; P❄📶) Right on the Danube, this fine hotel has 16 attractive rooms with verdant views, some with balconies overlooking the river, and a lovely terrace cafe on the riverfront.

Information

Tourist Office (☎032-590 020; www.turizamilok.hr; Trg Sv Ivana Kapistrana 5; ⌚8am-4pm Mon-Fri) Can recommend rural hotels and walking routes around Ilok and has a lot of local information. Call ahead, as opening hours are sporadic.

Getting There & Away

Buses arrive and depart from an unmarked **car park** (Vladimira Nazora bb) at the bottom of Ilok's hill, an easy walk (back up the hill) to the museum. Check the latest bus schedule at www.cazmatrans.hr.

There are three daily buses on weekdays and one on Saturday to Osijek (61KN, 1¾ hours). Nine daily services on weekdays and four on Saturday head to Vukovar (34KN, one hour).

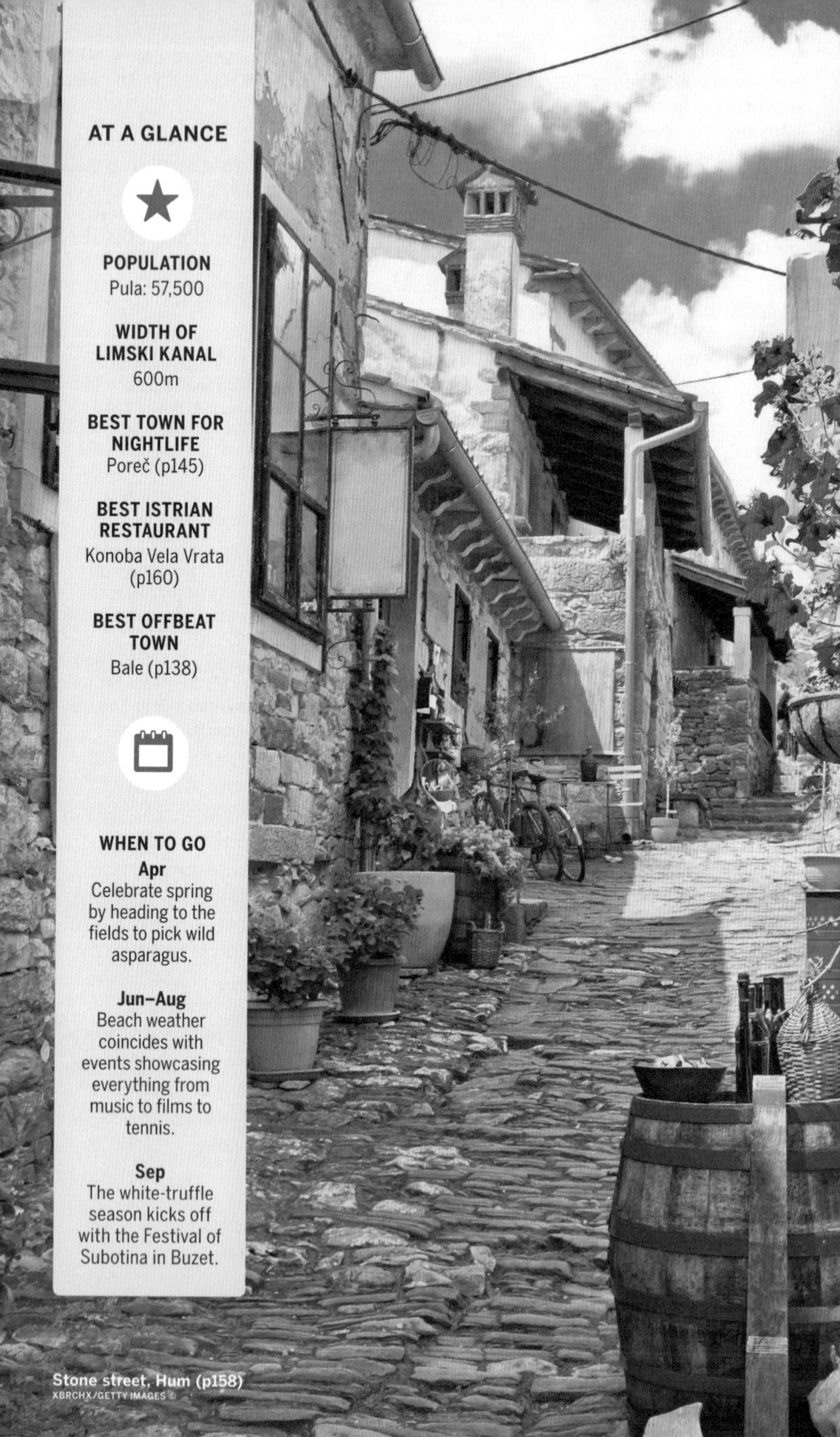

AT A GLANCE

POPULATION
Pula: 57,500

WIDTH OF LIMSKI KANAL
600m

BEST TOWN FOR NIGHTLIFE
Poreč (p145)

BEST ISTRIAN RESTAURANT
Konoba Vela Vrata (p160)

BEST OFFBEAT TOWN
Bale (p138)

WHEN TO GO

Apr
Celebrate spring by heading to the fields to pick wild asparagus.

Jun–Aug
Beach weather coincides with events showcasing everything from music to films to tennis.

Sep
The white-truffle season kicks off with the Festival of Subotina in Buzet.

Stone street, Hum (p158)

Istria

Continental Croatia meets the Adriatic in Istria (Istra to Croats), the heart-shaped, 3600-sq-km peninsula in the country's northwest. The hilltop villages, rural hotels and farmhouse restaurants attract food- and culture-focused visitors, while the indented coastline is madly popular with the sun-and-sea set. Though vast hotel complexes line much of the coast and the rocky beaches are not Croatia's best, facilities are wide-ranging, the sea is clean and secluded spots are still plentiful. The coast gets flooded with central European tourists in summer, but you can still feel alone and undisturbed in the peninsula's interior, even in mid-August. Add acclaimed gastronomy (starring fresh seafood, prime white truffles, wild asparagus, top-rated olive oils and award-winning wines), sprinkle it with historical charm and you have a little slice of heaven.

INCLUDES

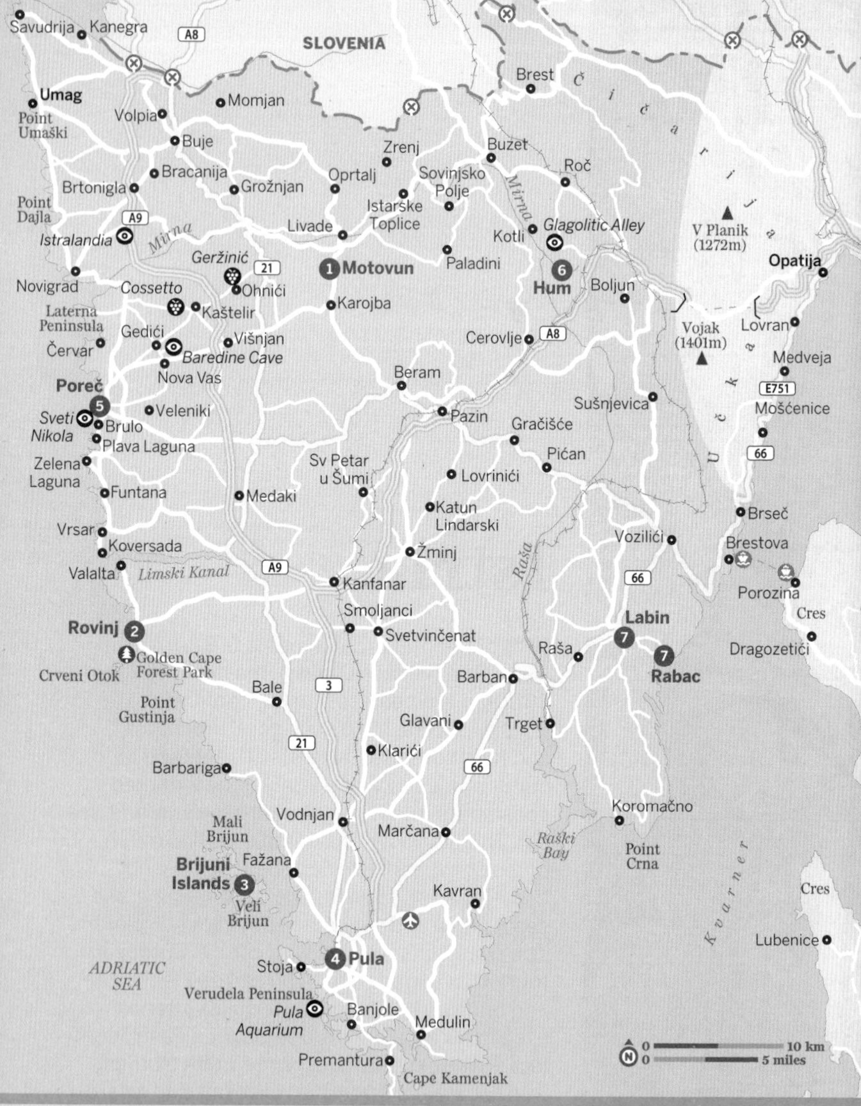

Istria Highlights

❶ **Motovun** (p154) Being wowed by the verdant views and lost-in-time charms of Istria's most atmospheric hill town, then delving deep into the forest on a truffle hunt.

❷ **Rovinj** (p139) Watching the sun set over the coast's prettiest old town.

❸ **Brijuni Islands** (p136) Soaking up the communist chic at Tito's island playground.

❹ **Pula** (p129) Stumbling over ancient ruins throughout the city, en route to the Roman Amphitheatre.

❺ **Poreč** (p145) Admiring the golden mosaics of the extra-ordinary Euphrasian Basilica before heading to the beach.

❻ **Hum** (p158) Hiking and biking around this tiny hilltop village, then soaking up the peaceful vibe.

❼ **Labin & Rabac** (p162) Ping-ponging between a historic hilltown and some of Istria's best beaches.

History

Towards the end of the 2nd millennium BCE, the Illyrian Histrian tribe settled the region and built fortified villages on top of the coastal and interior hills. The Romans swept into Istria in 177 BCE and began building roads and more hill forts as strategic strongholds.

From 539 to 751 CE, Istria was under Byzantine rule, the most impressive remnant of which is the Euphrasian Basilica in Poreč. In the period that followed, power switched between Slavic tribes, the Franks and German rulers until an increasingly powerful Venice wrestled control of the Istrian coast in the early 13th century.

With the fall of Venice in 1797, Istria came under Austrian rule, followed by the French (1809–13) and then the Austrians. During the 19th and early 20th centuries, most of Istria was little more than a neglected outpost of the Austro-Hungarian Empire.

When the empire disintegrated at the end of WWI, Italy moved quickly to secure Istria. Italian troops occupied Pula in November 1918 and, in the 1922 Treaty of Rapallo, the Kingdom of Serbs, Croats and Slovenes ceded Istria along with Zadar and several islands to Italy, as a reward for joining the Allied powers in WWI.

A massive population shift followed as 30,000 to 40,000 Italians arrived from Mussolini's Italy and many Croats left, fearing fascism. Their fears were not misplaced, as Istria's Italian masters attempted to consolidate their hold by banning Slavic speech, education and cultural activities. There was a ban on giving Slavic names to newborns, and adults were forced to use Italian forms of their first names.

Italy retained the region until its defeat in WWII when Istria became part of Yugoslavia, causing another mass exodus, as Italians and many Croats fled Tito's communists. Trieste and the peninsula's northwestern tip were points of contention between Italy and Yugoslavia until 1954, when the region was finally awarded to Italy. As a result of Tito's reorganisation of Yugoslavia, the northern part of the peninsula was incorporated into Slovenia, where it remains.

ISTRIA'S WEST COAST

The west coast is Istria's tourist showcase, with numerous beaches, a trio of fascinating historic towns and Tito's former playground, the gorgeous Brijuni Islands National Park. Tourism infrastructure is well developed here, with plenty of accommodation options and some great restaurants. Just across the water is Italy, and the pervasive Italian influence makes it seem even closer. Italian is a second language in Istria, many Istrians have Italian passports and each town name has an Italian counterpart.

Pula

POP 57,500

A wealth of Roman architecture lifts otherwise-workaday Pula (ancient Polensium; Pola in Italian) from the humdrum. The star of the show is the remarkably well-preserved Roman amphitheatre, smack in the heart of the city, which dominates the streetscape and doubles as a venue for summer concerts and festivals.

Historical attractions aside, Pula is a busy commercial city on the sea that has managed to retain a friendly small-town appeal. Just a short bus ride away, a series of beaches awaits at the resorts that occupy the Verudela Peninsula to the south. Although marred with residential and holiday developments, the coast is dotted with fragrant pine groves, seaside cafes and a clutch of good restaurants.

Pula is also a good base for exploring the protected Cape Kamenjak nature park, to the south, and the Brijuni Islands National Park, to the north.

History

Following the Roman conquest of Istria in 177 BCE, Pula became an important colonial centre and, by the time of Julius Caesar, it was a great city of around 30,000 people.

After the fall of the Western Roman Empire it was ruled by the Ostrogoths, Byzantines and Franks before Venice took control in 1148. Apart from a spell when it was ruled by Pisa, Genoa and the Patriarchate of Aquileia, the Venetians held onto it until 1797.

During the period of Austro-Hungarian rule which followed, the monarchy chose Pula, in 1853, as the empire's main naval centre. The construction of the port and the opening of its large shipyard in 1886 unleashed a demographic and economic expansion that transformed Pula into a military and industrial powerhouse.

The city fell into decline once again under Italian rule, which lasted from 1918 to 1943, when it was occupied by the Germans. At the end of WWII, Pula was administered

Pula

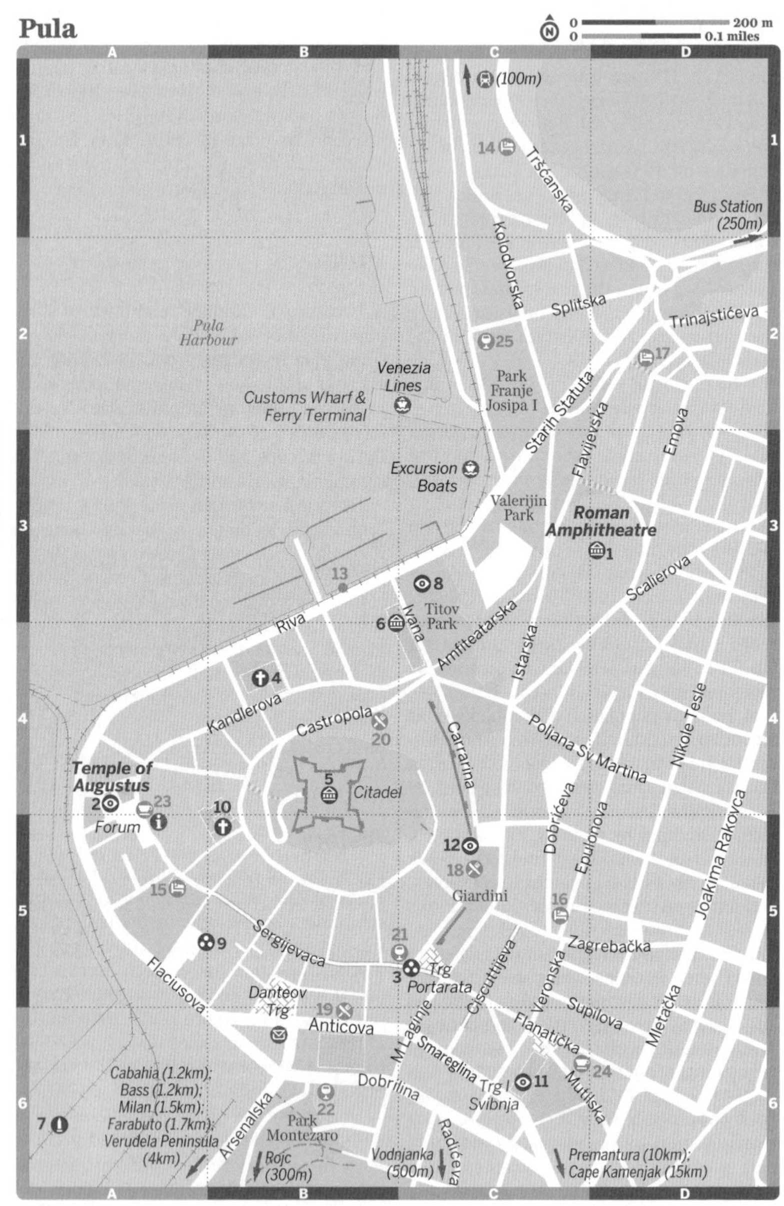

by Anglo-American forces until it became part of postwar Yugoslavia in 1947. Pula's industrial base weathered the Balkan wars relatively well and the city remains an important centre for shipbuilding, textiles, metals and glass.

Sights

The oldest part of the city follows the ancient Roman street plan circling the central citadel. The best beaches are to the south, on the Verudela Peninsula.

Pula

City Centre

★ Roman Amphitheatre HISTORIC BUILDING

(Flavijevska bb; adult/child 50/25KN, audio guide 40KN; 8am-midnight Jul & Aug, to 8pm Apr-Jun, Sep & Oct, 9am-5pm Nov-Mar) Pula's most famous and imposing sight is this 1st-century oval amphitheatre, overlooking the harbour northeast of the old town. It's a huge and truly magnificent structure, slotted together entirely from local limestone and known locally as the Arena. Designed to host gladiatorial contests and seating up to 20,000 spectators, it still serves the mass-entertainment needs of the local populace in the shape of concerts and film-festival screenings.

At 133m long, 105m wide and 32m high, Pula's amphitheatre is the sixth largest of its kind. On the top of the walls is a gutter that collected rainwater, and you can still see the slabs used to secure the fabric canopy, which protected spectators from the sun. You can get a decent view of the Arena from just walking around the outside, but the entrance fee enables you to clamber around the stones and visit the underground chambers. Once used to house the wild beasts and to drag away dead gladiators, they now contain rather more genteel displays of amphorae and equipment used in the production of olive oil.

In summer, check out the **Spectacvla Antiqva** (adult/child 80/40KN), an evening event held at least once a week, featuring gladiator fights and Roman-style clothing, hairstyles, food and drinks.

★ Temple of Augustus TEMPLE

(Augustov hram; Forum; adult/child 10/5KN; 9am-7pm) Fronted by a high porch supported by six Corinthian columns, this small but perfectly proportioned temple was built sometime between 2 BCE and 14 CE. It survived the Christian era by being converted into a church, only for it to be destroyed by a bomb in 1944. The subsequent stone-by-stone reconstruction has brought it back to something closely approaching its former glory, and it now houses a small archaeological display.

It was once one of a pair of matching temples fronting the Forum – the civic heart of Roman and medieval Pula – but all that survives of its twin, the Temple of Diana, can be seen incorporated into the rear wall of the 13th-century city hall next door.

Istria Historical & Maritime Museum MUSEUM

(Povijesni i pomorski muzej Istre; 052-211 566; www.ppmi.hr; Gradinski uspon 6; adult/child 20/5KN; 8am-9pm Apr-Sep, 9am-5pm Oct-Mar) Since ancient times the 34m hill at the centre of Pula's old town has been fortified. The current star-shaped fortress was built by the Venetians in the 1630s. It's now a moody backdrop to exhibitions on an eclectic range of historic themes (the antifascist struggle and a local boxing club at the time of research), but it's worth visiting for the views alone. Hidden around the back of the castle are the ruins of a small ancient Roman theatre.

St Francis' Monastery & Church CHRISTIAN MONASTERY

(Samostan i crkva sv Franje; Uspon sv Franje Asiškog 9; adult/child 9KN/free; ⏲9am-6pm) Built in 1285, Pula's Franciscan monastery has an extraordinary 15th-century gilded altarpiece behind the altar of its cavernous church – but that's not its only, or even its oldest, treasure. Set into the floor of a Gothic chamber accessed via the Romanesque cloister is a Roman mosaic featuring a hippocampus (fish-tailed horse) and a swastika.

Arch of the Sergii RUINS

(Slavoluk Sergijevaca; Sergijevaca) Also known as the Golden Gate (Zlatna vrata), this majestic arch was erected around 27 BCE to commemorate three brothers from the Sergius family who fought in the naval battle of Actium (where the future emperor Augustus defeated Marc Antony and Cleopatra). It stood at the entrance to the Roman town, the walls of which can still be partly seen nearby on Trg Portarata and along Carrarina.

Tržnica MARKET

(☎052-218-122; www.trznica-pula.hr; Narodni trg 9; ⏲7am-1pm Mon-Sat, to noon Sun) City life in Pula revolves around its gorgeous 1903 succession-style market building, and the produce stalls and cafes that surround it.

Lighting Giants PUBLIC ART

(Pula harbour; ⏲dusk-10pm) Don't miss Pula's star evening attraction, an amazing lighting display at the city's 19th-century Uljanik shipyard, one of the world's oldest working docks. Renowned lighting designer Dean Skira has lit up the shipyard's iconic cranes in 16,000 different colour schemes, which come alive on the hour for 15 minutes.

Partisan Memorial MEMORIAL

(Titov Park) Officially known as the 'National Liberation Resistance Fighters & Fascist Terror Victims in Istria Memorial', this monument honours the many thousands of partisans and their supporters killed in Istria during WWII. Behind the main sculptural piece is a set of busts of prominent figures led, naturally, by Tito. Look for Ruža Petrović, depicted wearing a headscarf. In 1944 she was tortured by Italian fascists and had her eyes gouged out; after the war she founded a society for the blind.

Istria Museum of Contemporary Art GALLERY

(Muzej suvremene umjetnosti Istre; ☎052-351 541; www.msu-istre.hr; Sv Ivana 1; adult/child 10KN/free; ⏲10am-10pm Jun-Aug, to 7pm Sep-May) The suitably dishevelled, cavernous confines of an 1862 printing house are a fitting environment for this edgy gallery.

Cathedral of the Assumption of the Blessed Virgin Mary CATHEDRAL

(Katedrala uznesenja Blažene Djevice Marije; Trg Sv Tome 2; ⏲hours vary) Founded in the 4th century and added to until the 15th, Pula's cathedral still has fragments of 5th- and 6th-century mosaics in its floor. The main altar is a Roman sarcophagus holding relics of saints from the 3rd century. Stones from the amphitheatre were used to build the bell tower in 1707.

Roman Floor Mosaic RUINS

(rear Sergijevaca 12) FREE One of the intriguing things about Pula is the way that Roman relics pop up in the most unlikely of places. This remarkably well-preserved 3rd-century floor mosaic is hidden behind a car park on Flaciusova (look for the brown signs). In the midst of geometric motifs is a central panel depicting bad girl Dirce from Greek mythology being punished by being tied to the horns of a bull.

Zerostrasse TUNNEL

(☎052-211 566; www.ppmi.hr; Carrarina 3a; adult/child 15/5KN; ⏲10am-10pm mid-Jun–mid-Sep) This underground system of tunnels was built before and during WWI to shelter the city's population and serve as storage for ammunition. Now you can walk through several of its branches, which all lead to the middle where there's a photo exhibition on early aviation in Pula. There are three entrances, the easiest of which to find is by the taxi stand on Giardini.

Verudela

Pula Aquarium AQUARIUM

(☎052-381 402; www.aquarium.hr; Verudella bb; adult/child 100/70KN; ⏲9am-9pm May-Oct, to 4pm Nov-Mar, to 6pm Apr) Not just any fish tank, this extraordinary aquarium occupies an entire 19th-century military fort – one of 55 built to defend the Austro-Hungarian Empire's main naval base. There are even sharks in an old artillery unit. The displays are well laid out and themed, with an emphasis on environmental issues. The aquar-

WORTH A TRIP

CAPE KAMENJAK

Wild Cape Kamenjak on the **Premantura Peninsula**, 10km south of Pula, is Istria's southernmost point. This gorgeous, entirely uninhabited cape has lovely rolling hills, wild flowers (including 30 species of orchid), low Mediterranean shrubs, fruit trees and medicinal herbs, and around 30km of beaches and rugged swimming spots. It's criss-crossed with a maze of gravel roads and paths, making it easy to get around on foot or by bike.

Near the southern tip of the peninsula is a **viewpoint** providing an incredible vista out over the island of Cres and the peaks of Velebit. Nearby is a wonderfully ramshackle beach bar, half-hidden in the bushes, seemingly cobbled together out of flotsam. The adjacent cliffs are popular with daredevils who dive from them and swim through the shallow caves at the water's edge. Watch out for strong currents if swimming off the southern cape.

Getting to Cape Kamenjak by car is the easiest option, but drive slowly to avoid generating dust, which is detrimental to the environment. From May to September, you'll be charged 40KN for bringing a car onto the cape; this can be paid from 7am to 9pm at the entrance.

Another option is taking city bus 28 from Pula to Premantura (15KN, 35 minutes, five to nine daily), at the entrance to the cape, then walking or renting a bike from **Windsurf Centar Premantura** (☎091 51 23 646; www.windsurfing.hr; Arena Stupice Campsite, Selo 250; windsurfing equipment/courses per hour from 80/200KN).

ium does its bit, operating a sea-turtle rescue centre. Other attractions include rays, crabs, eels, starfish, anemones, seahorses, jellyfish, caimans, octopuses and a huge Indian python.

Activities

The Istria Bike (www.istria-bike.com) website outlines trails, bike shops and agencies that offer cycling trips. The tourist office stocks the Istria Bike map of Pula and its surrounds, outlining 29 trails including a 60km route hugging the coast from Pula to Medulin.

Orca Diving Center DIVING
(☎098 99 04 246; www.orcadiving.hr; Verudella 17) Arranges boat and wreck dives at this centre underneath the Hotel Plaza Histria on the Verudela Peninsula. It also rents kayaks and stand-up paddleboards.

Eat Istria COOKING
(☎095 85 51 962; www.eatistria.com) Eat Istria offers cooking classes with food blogger Goran Zgrablić on a family farm between Medulin and the village of Ližnjan (transfers from Pula included), and wine tours around the peninsula.

Martinabela BOATING
(☎098 99 75 875; www.martinabela.hr; Riva bb) This one-boat company is one of a few Pula-based operators offering trips to Brijuni Islands National Park that is actually permitted to stop on the main island. Summer only.

Festivals & Events

Pula Film Festival FILM
(www.pulafilmfestival.hr; ⏲Jul) Running for well over six decades, this July film festival is the town's most important event, with screenings of mainly Croatian and some international films in the Roman Amphitheatre (p131) and other locations around town.

Seasplash Festival MUSIC
(www.seasplash.net; ⏲late Jul) In the last week in July, this four-day music fest (featuring wide-ranging live performances, from reggae and ska to dancehall and dub) lights up Štinjan's Punta Christo Fort, just northwest of Pula.

Outlook Festival MUSIC
(www.outlookfestival.com; tickets €150-175; ⏲Sep) Europe's largest bass and sound-system culture festival takes place over five days in early September in Punta Christo Fort in Štinjan, just outside Pula. The opening event takes place in the Roman Amphitheatre (p131).

Sleeping

Pula's busy throughout summer but the absolute peak is in July and August. Smaller hotels are clustered in the old town while the large beach resorts are all on the Verudela Peninsula, 3km to the south. Private apartments and villas usually offer better value, though you might need a car for some places; see www.pulainfo.hr for options.

Crazy House Hotel HOSTEL €
(☎091 51 84 200; www.crazyhousehostel.com; Tršćanska 1; dm/d from €20/58;) Crazy? Hardly. Tucked into the bottom floor of an old apartment block, this bright hostel has six- to 10-bed dorms with privacy curtains and lots of lockers, as well as a handful of private doubles and twins. All bathrooms are shared, and there's a communal kitchen and large terrace.

★**Guest House City Centre** GUESTHOUSE €€
(☎099 44 05 575; Sergijevaca 4; r from €84; P) Feel like a local as you ascend the wonky stone stairs in this wonderful building right by the Forum. The rooms are spacious, stylish and surprisingly quiet at night, and the hostess couldn't be more helpful. It doesn't have its own website; reservations are handled through Booking.com.

Hotel Galija HOTEL €€
(☎052-383 802; www.hotelgalija.hr; Epulonova 3; s/d from 608/798KN; P) Well maintained, this two-part hotel sits a stone's throw from the central market. The more exclusive rooms are in a building across the road but the more affordable rooms, above the reception, are tidy and well maintained if not overly large.

Hotel Scaletta HOTEL €€
(☎052-541 599; www.hotel-scaletta.com; Škaleta 1; s/d incl breakfast 512/746KN; P) There's a family vibe at this cosy hotel. The rooms are small but pleasant and there's a buffet breakfast. Plus it's a short walk from the Arena.

Park Plaza Arena Pula RESORT €€€
(☎052-375 000; www.parkplaza.com/arena; Verudella 31; s/d 1006/1320KN; May-Sep; P) Hidden amid pines and manicured lawns facing a gorgeous pebbly cove, this upmarket hotel is the best of the Verudela resorts. As well as the low-slung main hotel block there's a set of two-bedroom suites in the garden.

Park Plaza Histria Pula RESORT €€€
(☎052-590 000; www.parkplaza.com; Verudella 17; r from €157; Apr-Dec; P@) The exterior is a little 'former Yugoslav' but the swanky rooms inside have been thoroughly renovated, and there's a beach right on the doorstep. The hotel offers indoor and outdoor swimming pools, a gym and a spa, and easy access to all of the facilities of the sprawling Verudela Peninsula resort complex – tennis courts, supermarket, hairdresser, cafes and all.

Eating

Corso INTERNATIONAL €
(Giardini 2; mains 40-70KN; 7am-midnight Mon-Wed, to 2am Thu-Sat;) The upstairs dining room of this popular cafe-bar serves tacos, pork ribs, stir fries and spring rolls – but it's included here on the strength of its mighty Corso burger, and the delicious hot chips (fries) that accompany it. Expect to get messy.

Fresh SANDWICHES €
(☎052-418 888; Anticova 5; snacks 21-26KN; 8.30am-4.30pm Mon-Fri;) Best for a quick and wholesome bite, this tiny sandwich-and-salad bar serves sandwiches, toasted panini, tortillas and extremely fresh-looking salads. If you're feeling shady, start the day with a juiced 'Imuno' smoothie.

★**Konoba Batelina** SEAFOOD €€
(☎052-573 767; Čimulje 25, Banjole; mains 75-125KN; 5-11pm Mon-Sat) This family-run tavern is well worth a trek to Banjole, 6km south of central Pula. It only serves seafood, and it's some of the best, most creative and lovingly prepared you'll find in Istria. There's no menu; instead the staff will rattle off the specials and present fresh fish for you to choose from. Book ahead; cash only.

Farabuto MEDITERRANEAN €€
(☎052-386 074; www.farabuto.hr; Sisplac 15, Veruda; mains 75-160KN; noon-11pm Mon-Sat;) It's worth a trek to this nondescript residential area, about 1.5km southwest of the centre, for stylish decor, but more importantly, finely executed Mediterranean fare with a creative touch. There are daily specials and a well-curated wine list; save room for the chocolate mousse with truffle ice cream.

Vodnjanka ISTRIAN €€
(☎052-210 655; D Vitezića 4, Monte Zaro; mains 40-100KN; noon-5pm & 7-10pm Mon-Sat) Locals swear by the real-deal home cooking at this no-frills spot. It's cheap, casual and cash-only, and there's a reassuringly brief menu that focuses on simple, hearty Istrian cuisine. Nothing is frozen and even the pasta is made the night before. It's a bit of a trek out of town – to get here, walk south on Radićeva to Vitezića.

Jupiter PIZZA €€
(☎052-214 333; www.pizzeriajupiter.com; Castropola 42; mains 30-150KN; 11am-11pm Mon-

Fri, from 1pm Sat & Sun) Respectable Croatian thin-crust pizzas and decent pasta dishes served on an upstairs terrace.

Milan ISTRIAN €€€

(052-300 200; www.milanpula.com; Stoja 4, Stoja; mains 95-295KN; noon-11pm) An upmarket vibe, seasonal specialities, clued-up sommeliers and an olive-oil expert make this hotel restaurant, in an oddly dingy part of town, one of the city's best fine-dining options. Various set menus are offered (195KN–385KN), including a four-course Istrian option loaded with prosciutto.

Drinking & Nightlife

Most of the best nightlife is outside of the town centre, but in mild weather the cafes on the Forum and Trg Portarata are lively people-watching spots. Pula's hippest bars are on Širolina in the residential Veruda neighbourhood. For beach-bar action, head to Verudela. To mix with Pula's young crowd, grab some beers and head to the Lungomare coastal strip.

★ **Cabahia** BAR

(www.facebook.com/CabahiaPula; Širolina 4, Veruda; 7am-midnight Mon-Sat, 10am-midnight Sun;) This artsy hideaway, 2km south of the centre in Veruda, has a cosy wood-beamed interior, eclectic objects and rock portraits on the walls, dim lighting, South American tiling and a great garden terrace out the back. It hosts live music and gets packed on weekends.

★ **Bass** BAR

(099 83 19 051; www.facebook.com/basscaffe; Širolina 3, Veruda; 8am-midnight Mon-Sat, from 10am Sun;) Occupying the porch of a decaying Habsburg-era mansion, this hip, dishevelled bar is an oasis of boho cool with a long cocktail menu and a laid-back clientele.

Cvajner CAFE

(Forum 2; 8am-midnight) Housed in a former bank on the Forum (the huge safe is used as a storeroom), this is Pula's hippest cafe, scattered with random Tito-era furniture, the remnants of wall frescos, painted ceiling beams, art by up-and-coming locals and chilled staff. In the warmer months most miss the joys of the interior by plumping for an alfresco seat out front.

Caffe Uliks BAR

(052-219 158; www.facebook.com/caffe.uliks; Trg Portarata 1; 7am-midnight Sun-Wed, to 2am Thu-Sat) A statue of James Joyce greets you at the entrance to this bar named after his famous novel (which occupies the ground floor of a building where Joyce taught English). Inside it's all brass, backlit stained glass, dark wood and maritime knick-knacks – which would be pleasant if it weren't for the thick fug of cigarette smoke.

Cyber Cafe CAFE

(www.facebook.com/cybercafepula; Flanatička 14; 8am-midnight Mon-Sat, to 10pm Sun;) The name marks it as one of a dying breed, but this colourful, art-strewn cafe is no digital dinosaur. Yes, there are a couple of free internet terminals, but most people come here to sip on a coffee or a beer in the huge garden hidden away at the rear.

Club Uljanik CLUB

(095 90 18 811; www.clubuljanik.hr; Dobrilina 2; 9pm-6am Thu-Sat) Going strong since the 1960s, the legendary Pula club these days caters to a young party crowd who come for its range of themed weekend parties and Thursday student nights.

Pietas Julia BAR

(098 181 19 11; www.pietasjulia.com; Riva 20; 8am-9pm Sun-Thu, to 10pm Fri & Sat;) This slick bar on the harbour, next to the rowing club, really comes into its own late on summer weekends when it stays open till 5am. During the day, there are breakfasts and snacks. The seats on the footpath are nice spots for a sundowner.

Zeppelin BEACH BAR

(Saccorgiana bb, Verudella; 9am-midnight Mon-Thu, to 5am Fri & Sat, to 10pm Sun;) Après-beach fun is on the menu at this beach bar in Saccorgiana Bay on Verudela. Inside, large photos of revolutionaries (Che, Tito, Ho Chi Minh, Michael Collins) form a backdrop to table football matches and late-night parties.

Entertainment

Try to catch a concert in the spectacular amphitheatre (p131). The tourist office has schedules and there are posters around Pula advertising live performances.

Rojc ARTS CENTRE

(http://rojcnet.pula.org; Gajeva 3) For an arty underground experience, check out the program at Rojc, a converted army barracks that houses a multimedia arts centre and studios with occasional concerts, exhibitions and other events.

Information

There's free wi-fi all around town – on the Forum, Portarata, Giardini, Flanatička street, Kaštel and Narodni trg.

Pula General Hospital (Opća bolnica Pula; 052-376 500; www.obpula.hr; Alda Negrija 6; 24hr)

Tourist Office (052-219 197; www.pulainfo.hr; Forum 3; 8am-9pm Jul & Aug, 8am-6pm Mon-Fri, 10am-4pm Sat Apr-Jun & Sep, 9am-4pm Mon-Sat Oct-Mar) Knowledgable and friendly staff provide maps, brochures and schedules of events. Pick up two useful booklets: Domus Bonus, which lists the best-quality private accommodation in Istria, and Istra Gourmet, with a list of restaurants. From mid-June to mid-September it also sells the Pula Card (adult/child 90/40KN), which allows free entry to key sights.

Getting There & Away

AIR

Pula Airport (PUY; 052-550 926; www.airport-pula.hr) is located 6km northeast of town. Dozens of airlines fly here in summer but the only year-round operators are Croatia Airlines (to Zagreb and Zadar), Trade Air (to Split and Osijek) and Eurowings (to Düsseldorf).

BOAT

Venezia Lines (052-422 896; www.venezialines.com; Riječki Gat, Sv Petra bb; adult/child from €62/40) operates a fast catamaran to Venice (3¾ hours) two to four times a week between June and September.

Excursion boats leave from nearby.

BUS

Pula's **bus station** (052-544 537; Trg 1 istarske brigade 1) is 1km north of the town centre. Daily connections include Rovinj (37KN, 40 minutes, hourly), Rijeka (100KN, 2½ hours, at least 13 daily), Zagreb (164KN, 5½ hours, at least nine daily), Zadar (235KN, seven hours, at least two daily) and Split (345KN, 10½ hours, at least two daily).

TRAIN

There are direct connections between Pula's **train station** (052-541 982; www.hzpp.hr; Kolodvorska 7) and Vodnjan (12KN, 16 minutes, eight daily), Pazin (36KN, 1¼ hours, eight daily) and Roč (54KN, 1¾ hours, four daily).

Getting Around

An airport bus (30KN) operated by **Brioni Pula** (052-356 500; www.brioni.hr), is timed around flights and departs from the bus station, heading to Pula, Rovinj, Poreč, Novigrad, Umag and Rabac. Taxis to the airport cost from 180KN to 200KN.

Local buses are operated by **Pulapromet** (052-222 677; www.pulapromet.com). Routes of use to visitors are 1, which runs to Camping Stoja, and 2A and 3A to Verudela. The frequency varies from every 15 minutes to every half-hour (from 5am to 11.30pm). Tickets are bought from the driver for 11KN–15KN.

Brijuni Islands

The Brijuni archipelago (Brioni in Italian) consists of two main pine-covered islands and 12 islets off the coast of Istria, just northwest of Pula across the 3km-wide Fažana Channel. Covered by meadows, parks, and oak and laurel forests (including rare plants such as wild cucumber and marine poppy) the islands were pronounced a national park in 1983.

The largest island, **Veli Brijun**, can be visited on boats booked through the **National Park Office** (052-525 882; www.np-brijuni.hr; Brijunska 10, Fažana; boat & tour adult/child 210/105KN; 8am-7pm) in Fažana; prices include a guided tour and entry to various sights. **Mali Brijun** can only be visited during the summertime **Ulysses Theatre** (052-525 829; www.ulysses.hr) season, when performances are staged in an abandoned fort.

Note that most boat tours departing from Pula dock at the islet of **Sveti Jerolim** for a picnic lunch but then only cruise around the main islands, as they're not permitted to land.

Sights

As you arrive on Veli Brijun, after a 15-minute boat ride from Fažana, you'll dock in front of the conjoined Hotel Neptun (1912) and Hotel Istra (1962), where Tito's illustrious guests once stayed. A guide will take you on a four-hour island tour on a miniature **Tourist Train**, beginning with a visit to the 9-hectare **Safari Park** containing animals given to Tito by various famous individuals. Other stops on the tour include the ruins of a **Roman Country House**, dating from the 1st century BCE, an **Archaeological Museum** inside a 16th-century Venetian summerhouse, and **St Germain Church** (1481), now a gallery displaying copies of medieval frescos in Istrian churches.

Most interesting is the **Tito on Brijuni Exhibition** in a building behind Hotel Karmen. A collection of stuffed animals occupies the ground floor, all of which died naturally in the Safari Park. Upstairs are photos of Tito with stars such as Josephine Baker, Sophia

Loren, Elizabeth Taylor and Richard Burton, and world leaders including Indira Gandhi and Fidel Castro. Outside is a 1953 Cadillac that Tito used to show the island to his eminent guests.

Activities

After taking the tour of Veli Brijun, most summertime visitors head to the beaches. **Snorkelling** and **scuba diving** is on offer, and there's a **golf course** (founded in 1921) that's open to the public (260KN for a round).

Sleeping

The national park (p136) operates Veli Brijun's two mediocre hotel complexes – the Hotel Netpun-Istra and Hotel Karmen – and three luxurious villas with their own private beaches, golf carts and bikes. Rates include parking and boat transfers from Fažana. There is nowhere to stay on Mali Brijun.

Getting There & Away

From Pula, you can catch bus 21 to Fažana (15KN, 25 minutes, seven to 14 daily).

National-park boats head from Fažana to Veli Brijun 10 or 11 times a day from March to October, falling to three times a day from November to February. It's best to book in advance, especially in summer, and request an English-speaking tour guide.

Summer theatre performances on Mali Brijun have a boat trip included in the ticket.

Various travel and tour agencies offer day trips from Pula, Rovinj and Poreč.

Getting Around

The only ways to get around Veli Brijun are by bike (35KN per hour or 110KN per day) and electric cart (300KN per hour).

Vodnjan

POP 6120

Connoisseurs of the macabre shouldn't miss Vodnjan (Dignano in Italian), 10km north of Pula. Displayed inside a sober church are the saintly mummies that constitute this somewhat-ramshackle town's primary tourist attraction.

Vodnjan's other claim to fame is as a stop on the Cesta Maslinova Ulica (Olive Oil Hwy), a tourist trail taking in various local producers; grab a brochure from the tourist office. Some have shops and some offer tours, but mostly they're just family homes where, if you knock on the door, you should be able to buy a bottle of their homemade product.

There's not much going on in the rest of the town, which has Istria's largest Roma population. The centre is Narodni trg, composed of several neo-Gothic palaces in varying stages of decay and restoration. There's interesting graffiti scattered around, both modern and historic, in the form of fading Partisan slogans daubed in red paint.

Sights

St Blaise's Church CHURCH

(Crkva sv Blaža; ☎052-511 420; www.zupavodnjan.com; Župni trg 1; entire complex adult/child €10/5, mummies €7/3.50, museum €7/3.50, church €2/1; ⏰9.30am-7pm Mon-Sat, noon-5pm Sun Jun-Sep, by arrangement Oct-May) This handsome neobaroque church was completed in 1800 but commenced 40 years earlier, when Venice was still the style-setter for Istria. With its 63m-high **bell tower** modelled on St Mark's in Venice, it's the largest parish church in Istria, and worth a visit for its magnificent altars alone.

TITO & THE BRIJUNI ISLANDS

Even though traces of habitation go back to Roman times, the islands really owe their fame to Tito, the charismatic Yugoslav leader who turned them into his private retreat.

Each year from 1947 until just before his death in 1980, Tito spent six months in Brijuni at his hideaway. To create a lush comfort zone, he introduced subtropical plant species and created a safari park to house the exotic animals gifted to him by world leaders. The Somali sheep you'll see roaming around came from Ethiopia, while a Zambian leader gave a gift of waterbuck.

At his summer playground, Tito received 90 heads of state and a bevy of movie stars in lavish style. Bijela Vila on Veli Brijun was Tito's 'White House': the place for issuing edicts and declarations as well as entertaining. The islands are still used for official state visits, but are increasingly a favourite on the international yachting circuit. They're also a holiday spot of choice for royalty from obscure kingdoms and random billionaires who love its bygone aura of glamour.

The **mummies** are in a curtained-off area behind the main altar.

In the dim lighting, the complete bodies of Nikolosa Bursa, Giovanni Olini and Leon Bembo resemble wooden dolls in their glass cases. Assorted body parts of three other saints complete the display. As you examine the skin, hair and fingernails of these long-dead people, a tape in English narrates their life stories. Considered to be Europe's best-preserved mummy, the body of Nikolosa is said to emit a 32m bioenergy circle that has caused 50 miraculous healings.

If the mummies have whetted your appetite for saintly relics, head to the **Collection of Sacral Art** (Zbirka Sakralne Umjetnosti) in the sacristy. Here there are hundreds of relics belonging to 150 different saints, including the casket with St Mary of Egypt's tongue.

Eating

Vodnjanka ISTRIAN €€

(☎052-511 435; www.vodnjanka.com; Istarska 22; mains 65-150KN; ⏲11am-11pm Mon-Sat; ☑) This excellent regional restaurant offers personable service and delicious food in several rustic rooms. Specialities include *fuži* (homemade egg pasta) topped with truffles, steak with porcini and truffles, and various kinds of *fritaja* (omelette). The terrace has pretty views of the old-town rooftops and the church tower.

Shopping

Brist FOOD

(☎095 56 24 111; www.brist-olive.hr; Trgovačka 40; tour 150KN; ⏲10am-4pm Mon-Fri, to 2pm Sat Jun-Sep, 10am-2pm Mon-Sat Oct-May) Unlike Vodnjan's many back-door operations, Brist sells its range of five excellent extra virgin olive oils from a cute little shop on the main street. Pop in for a tasting and to arrange a tour of the olive grove with Paul O'Grady, the lucky Irishman who has married into the clan.

Cadenela FOOD

(☎099 64 93 844; www.cadenela.com; 1 Maja 5; ⏲9am-9pm) Operating out of an ordinary-looking house on the outskirts of town, Cadenela sells top-quality extra virgin olive oils from the family orchard. Call ahead in winter, or to arrange a private tour of the olive grove.

Chiavalon FOOD

(☎052-511 906; www.chiavalon.hr; Vladimira Nazora 16; ⏲10am-6pm Mon-Fri, to 2pm Sun) Drop in to this olive-oil producer to stock up on the top-notch product (knock on the door and try your luck in winter), or phone ahead to arrange a tour (from 85KN). Options include a 45-minute tour and oil tasting, or a 60-minute version including cheese and cured meats. Five-course meals can also be arranged.

Information

Tourist Office (☎052-511 700; www.istra.hr/vodnjan; Narodni trg 10; ⏲8am-8pm Mon-Sat, 9am-1pm Sun May-Sep, 8am-4pm Mon-Fri Oct-Apr)

Getting There & Away

Vodnjan is well connected by bus with Pula (24KN, 10 minutes, 14 daily), Rovinj (37KN, 30 minutes, 14 daily), Poreč (50KN, 1¼ hours, five daily), Rijeka (115KN, 2½ hours, five daily) and Zagreb (150KN, five hours, seven daily).

There are direct train connections to Pula (12KN, 16 minutes, eight daily), Pazin (27KN, 55 minutes, eight daily) and Roč (45KN, 1½ hours, four daily).

Bale

POP 936

You could be forgiven for thinking you've stumbled onto a film set as you wander the narrow cobblestone streets of Bale (Valle in Italian). Its crop of medieval town houses developed around a Gothic-Renaissance castle belonging to the Bembo family. However, Bale's origins are much older than that: the Romans had a fort here and, before them, the Illyrians.

The little town is dominated by the oversized Church of the Visitation, with its 36m-high belfry. There are various other historic churches scattered about, along with a town hall with a 14th-century loggia. The closest beaches are 6km away on a stretch of coast that rates as the most pristine in Istria.

Bale draws a bohemian crowd for its apparently very powerful energy – a fact you won't find in the tourist brochures. Come here to meet kindred spirits and spend endless hours talking, drinking, dreaming and scribbling.

Sleeping & Eating

★**Meneghetti** BOUTIQUE HOTEL €€€

(☎052-528 800; www.meneghetti.hr; Stancija Meneghetti 1; r from €279, mains 190-290KN; ⏲Apr-Dec; P❄☜≋) The focus is firmly on quality at this rural retreat – whether that be the estate's top-notch wine and olive oil, the architecture of the guest blocks, which sympathetically embrace the historic house at its core, or the exquisite modern Istrian cuisine served at the restaurant. Plus there's a private beach, accessed by a 25-minute walk through the vineyard. Sheer bliss.

It's located 8.5km southwest of Bale.

Hotel La Grisa BOUTIQUE HOTEL €€€
(052-824 501; www.la-grisa.com; La Grisa 23; s/d/ste from 694/945/1672KN; P ❄ 🛜 ≋) This boutique hotel has 28 tasteful rooms and suites in eight interconnected buildings on the edge of the old town, with an ambitious restaurant (try the dishes with *boškarin*) and a small spa with a sauna (160KN per hour), jacuzzi and massages.

Kamene Priče ISTRIAN €€
(052-824 235; www.kameneprice.com; Castel 57; mains 90-160KN; 10am-2pm & 6-11pm) Enjoy the whimsical decor of this artsy oasis while tucking into dishes brimming with seasonal and local ingredients, named after jazz greats. If you're lucky you may stumble upon a poetry reading, theatre performance or stand-up comedy show. You can even stay the night in the upstairs rooms, where Casanova seduced a local lady in the 1740s.

Getting There & Away

Buses head to Bale from Pula (31KN, 20 minutes, 11 daily), Vodnjan (26KN, 12 minutes, 11 daily), Rovinj (30KN, 18 minutes, 12 daily), Rijeka (124KN, three hours, three daily) and Zagreb (150KN, 5½ hours, three daily).

Rovinj

POP 14,300

Rovinj (Rovigno in Italian) is coastal Istria's star attraction. While it can get overrun with tourists in summer and there aren't a lot of actual sights, it remains an intensely charming place. The old town is contained within an egg-shaped peninsula, webbed with steep cobbled streets and small squares, and punctuated by a tall church tower rising from the highest point. Originally an island, it was only connected to the mainland in 1763 when the narrow channel separating it was filled.

The main residential part of Rovinj spreads back from the old town and up the low hills that surround it, while resort-style hotels hug the coast to the north and south. When the crowds get too much, the 14 islands of the Rovinj archipelago make for a pleasant afternoon away.

History

Rovinj bounced between Illyrian, Roman and Byzantine hands before the first Slavs arrived in the 7th century. It proceeded to develop a strong fishing and maritime industry and, in 1199, the town signed an important pact with Dubrovnik to protect its shipping trade. In the 13th century the threat of piracy forced it to turn to Venice for protection.

From the 16th to 18th centuries, its population expanded dramatically with an influx of immigrants fleeing Turkish invasions of Bosnia and continental Croatia. The town began to develop outside the walls put up by the Venetians, and in 1763 the islet was connected to the mainland and the old town became a peninsula.

Although the town's maritime industry thrived in the 17th century, Austria's 1719 decision to make Trieste and Rijeka free ports dealt Rovinj a blow. The decline of sailing ships further damaged its shipbuilding industry, and in the middle of the 19th century it was supplanted by the shipyard in Pula. Like the rest of Istria, Rovinj passed from Austrian to French to Austrian to Italian rule before finally becoming part of postwar Yugoslavia. There's still a considerable Italian community here, who speak a particular dialect.

Sights

Rovinj City Museum MUSEUM
(Muzej grada Rovinj; 052-816 720; www.muzej-rovinj.hr; Trg Maršala Tita 11; adult/child Jun-Aug 65/40KN, Sep-May 15/10KN; 10am-10pm Jun-Aug, to 1pm Tue-Sat Sep-May) Housed in a 17th-century baroque palace, this museum displays temporary exhibitions on the ground floor, 20th-century and contemporary art on the 1st floor, and 16th- to 19th-century works on the top floor. Croatian artists are well represented, along with Venetian luminaries such as Jacopo Bassano.

★**St Euphemia's Church** CHURCH
(Crkva Sv Eufemije; Trg sv Eufemije bb; tower 20KN; 10am-6pm Jun-Sep, to 4pm May, to 2pm Apr) FREE Built from 1725 to 1736, this imposing structure – the largest baroque church in Istria – dominates Rovinj from its central hilltop location in the the old town. Its 61m-high bell tower is older than the present church; construction commenced in 1654 and lasted 26 years. It's modelled on

Rovinj

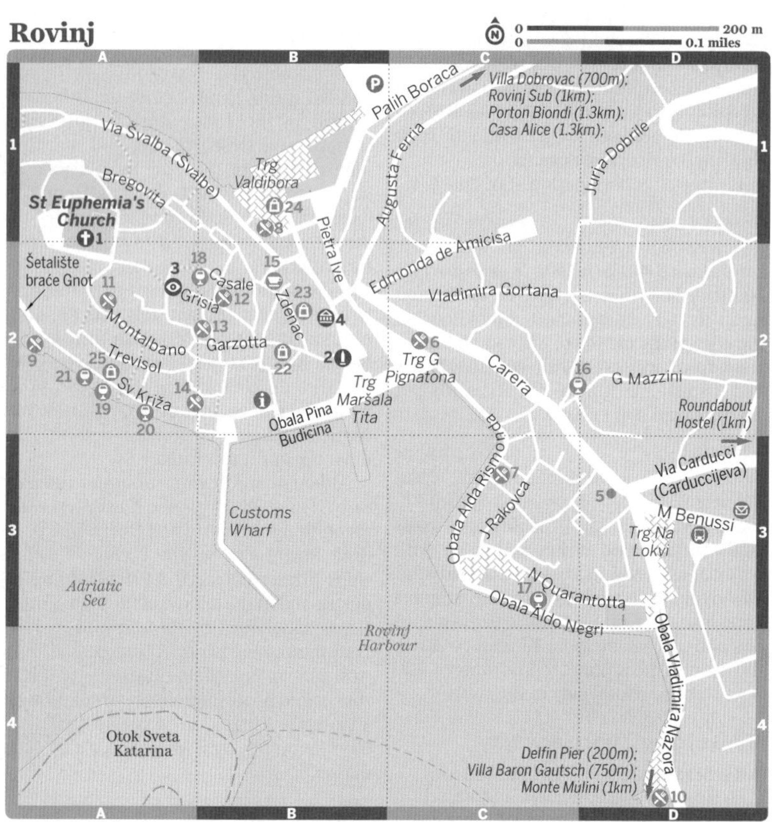

Rovinj

the campanile of St Mark's in Venice, and is topped by a 4m copper statue of St Euphemia, who shows the direction of the wind by turning on a spindle. Inside the church, there are various notable artworks and ceiling frescoes above the sanctuary.

The body of St Euphemia is said to rest in the ancient Roman sarcophagus behind the right-hand altar. Rovinj's patron saint was tortured for her faith by the Emperor Diocletian before being thrown to the lions in 304 CE. Her body was kept in Constantinople (present-day Istanbul) until the 7th century, when it was removed to protect it from iconoclasts. According to local legend, it then appeared off the coast of Rovinj in a spectral boat. The townspeople were unable to budge the heavy sarcophagus until a small boy appeared with two calves and moved it to the top of the hill.

Balbi Arch MONUMENT

(Garzotto bb) This elaborate arch was built in 1679 as the main town gate. The top of the arch is ornamented with a Turkish head on the outside and a Venetian head on the inside. The winged lion at the top is a symbol of Venice, although this one is unusual in that it has visible genitalia.

Grisia STREET

Lined with galleries and souvenir stores, this cobbled street leads uphill through the old town to St Euphemia. Windows, balconies, portals and squares are a pleasant confusion of styles – Gothic, Renaissance, baroque and neoclassical. Notice the unique *fumaioli* (exterior chimneys), built during the population boom when entire families lived in a single room with a fireplace.

Golden Cape Forest Park PARK

(Park šuma Zlatni Rt) Covered in oak and pine groves and boasting 10 species of cypress, this verdant expanse was established in 1890 by Baron Hütterott, an Austrian admiral who kept a villa on Crveni Otok. You can swim off the rocks in the bays nestled between the park's three capes: Punta Montauro, Punta Corrente and Punta Scaraba. It's easily reached on foot or bike by following the waterfront south from the harbour.

Activities & Tours

In summer, boat trips to the islands, such as Crveni Otok and Sveta Katarina (p142), and Limski Kanal (p143) are easily arranged through operators along the waterfront. The main diving attraction is the *Baron Gautsch* wreck, an Austrian passenger steamer sunk in 1914 by a mine in 40m of water. There's good cycling to be had in the surrounding area, along with rock climbing and birdwatching.

Rovinj Sub DIVING

(☎052-821 202; www.rovinj-sub.hr; Braće Brajkovića bb) Professional diving outfit running boat dives down to the many wrecks that lie just offshore. Prices range from 75KN for a shore dive to 338KN for some of the trickier wrecks; equipment is an additional 188KN.

Stupica Excursions CRUISE

(☎091 90 37 805; www.stupica-excursions.com; ⌚half-/full day €20/40) This family-run operation offers full-day 'fish picnic' tours taking in the Limski Kanal, a pirate's cave and the Rovinj archipelago on a small boat, including three swimming stops, breakfast, lunch and unlimited drinks. There's also a half-day sunset-cruise option.

Excursions Delfin CRUISE

(☎091 51 42 169; www.excursion-delfin.com; Šetalište vijeća Europe bb) Offers boat trips to the Limski Kanal (150KN) and around the Rovinj archipelago (75KN), including sunset tours.

Adistra KAYAKING

(☎095 83 83 797; www.adistra.hr; Carera 69) Adistra runs kayaking tours, including 9km jaunts around the Rovinj archipelago and a 14km outing along the Limski Kanal; both cost 280KN and include picnic lunch and snorkelling gear. It also offers a sunset paddle (190KN) with wine, cheese and olives, and rents boats, bikes, scooters and snorkelling gear.

Festivals & Events

Summer Atmosphere with Music & Traditions CULTURAL

(Ljetni ugođaj uz glazbu i tradiciju; ⌚Jun-Aug) Throughout summer the main square hosts a series of events showcasing local music, folk traditions and food.

Rovinj Summer Music Festival MUSIC

(⌚Jun-Aug) A series of four big concerts held at Porton Biondi beach and Crveni Otok, featuring well-known names in the world of jazz, pop and soul.

Grisia Art Show ART

(⌚Aug) The second Sunday in August sees the town's most renowned event, when narrow Grisia becomes an open-air art exhibition. Everyone from children to professional painters displays their work in churches, studios and on the street.

Sleeping

Roundabout Hostel HOSTEL €
(☎052-817 387; www.roundabouthostel.com; Trg na križu 6; dm 140-187KN; P ❄ 📶) This simple budget option has bunks with individual reading lights, lockers and a small shared kitchen. It's located on the big roundabout as you come into Rovinj, about a kilometre from the old town.

Porton Biondi CAMPGROUND €
(☎052-813 557; www.portonbiondirovinj.com; Aleja Porton Biondi 1; per person/tent/campervan 54/46/90KN; ⏲Apr-Oct; 🐾) This 7-hectare beachside campground, which sleeps 1000, is about 700m north of the old town. It has a restaurant, snack bar and plenty of shade.

Villa Dobravac HOTEL €€
(☎052-813 006; www.villa-dobravac.com; Karmelo 1; r €100-128; P ❄ 📶) As well as making wine and olive oil, the Dobravac family rent a set of 10 spacious, modern rooms in this lovely old peach-coloured villa in the residential part of Rovinj. Most have a terrace and a sea view.

Villa Baron Gautsch B&B €€
(☎052-840 538; www.villabarongautsch.com; IM Ronjgova 7; r from 730KN; ⏲Apr-Oct; ❄ 📶) This German-owned guesthouse on a leafy street has 17 spick-and-span rooms, some with terraces and views of the sea and the old town. Breakfast is served on the small terrace out the back.

★ **Casa Alice** HOTEL €€€
(☎052-821 104; www.casaalice.com; Paola Deperisa 1; r €200-220; P ❄ 📶 ≋) Escape the masses in this lovely 10-room hotel in Rovinj's suburban fringes, a 20-minute walk from the centre but only five minutes from the sea. If walking sounds too hard you can always laze around the blue-tiled pool and help yourself to coffee and cake. Some of the rooms have terraces and most have a spa bath.

Monte Mulini HOTEL €€€
(☎052-636 000; www.montemulinihotel.com; Antonija Smareglia 3; r from €550; P ❄ 📶 ≋ 🐾) This swanky and extremely pricey hotel slopes down towards Lone Bay, a 10-minute stroll from the old town along the Lungomare. Rooms all have balconies, sea views and upscale trimmings. The spa and Wine Vault restaurant are tops, and there are three outdoor pools.

Amarin Family Hotel RESORT €€€
(☎052-805 500; www.maistra.com; Val de Lesso 5; r from €272; P ❄ 📶 ≋) While parents love the stylish facilities and pebbly beach, that's beside the point. Here it's all about the kids, right down to rocking horses in reception, swimming pools with slides, play equipment galore and a kids' disco, theatre and gym. Parents may struggle to get them to leave. It's located 4km north of central Rovinj; prices include full board.

Eating

Rovinj has some of Istria's most famous restaurants, and some of its priciest. Establishments line the harbour and there are some excellent places in the old town. For a cheap bite, grab a *burek* (pastry stuffed with meat or cheese) from a kiosk near the green market (p144).

WORTH A TRIP

CRVENI OTOK & SVETA KATARINA

Lovely Crveni Otok (Red Island) is only 2km from Rovinj's harbour and is popular with day trippers. Only 1.9km long, the island is actually comprised of two islets, **Sveti Andrija** (St Andrew) and **Maškin**, connected by a causeway. In the 19th century, Sveti Andrija became the property of Baron Hütterott, who transformed it into a luxuriantly wooded park. Small gravel beaches, a playground and the massive resort-style **Island Hotel Istra** (☎052-800 250; www.maistra.com; Crveni Otok 1; r from €224; ⏲May-Sep; ❄ 📶 ≋) make it popular with families. Maškin is quieter, more wooded and has plenty of secluded coves. Bring a mask for snorkelling around the rocks.

Nearer to Rovinj, just outside the harbour, lies Sveta Katarina (St Catherine), a small island forested by a Polish count in 1905 and now also home to a large hotel.

In summer there are hourly boats from Rovinj from 5.30am till midnight to Crveni Otok (40/20KN, 20 minutes) and to Sveta Katarina (adult/child 30/15KN, 10 minutes). Both depart from the Delfin pier (p145).

Town Centre

Pizzeria Da Sergio PIZZA €
(052-816 949; www.facebook.com/DaSergioRv; Grisia 11; pizzas 35-82KN; 11am-3pm & 6-11pm;) It's worth waiting in line to get a table at this old-fashioned two-floor pizzeria. It dishes out Rovinj's best thin-crust pizza, with a huge range of toppings to choose between. It also serves decent house wine.

Bookeria CAFE €
(052-817 399; www.bookeria.net; Trg Pignaton 7; 40-80KN; 9am-9pm May-Sep, to 6pm Oct-Apr) With little flower-adorned tables spilling onto the square, this sweet little cafe is a favourite Rovinj breakfast spot. Options include eggs, toast, muffins and croissants served with eggplant mousse. As the day progresses the menu expands to include burgers and pasta.

Grota SANDWICHES €
(Valdibora bb; sandwiches 15-20KN; 7am-8pm Mon-Sat, to 2pm Sun) Right by the green market, this tiny place is a great spot for coffee, sandwiches and people-watching. Or come back after the beach for a glass of wine with local cheese and prosciutto, propped up on one of the wine-barrel tables.

Kantinon ISTRIAN €€
(052-816 075; Alda Rismonda bb; mains 60-180KN; noon-10pm Tue-Sun) Located right on the harbourside, this excellent restaurant is headed up by a stellar team. The food is as local and fresh as it gets, with lots of seafood dishes based on traditional recipes. The seafood stew with polenta is a real treat.

Veli Jože ISTRIAN, SEAFOOD €€
(052-816 337; www.velijoze.net; Sv Križa 3; mains 59-190KN; 11am-midnight) Graze on good Istrian standards, either in the eclectic interior crammed with marine knick-knacks or at the clutch of outdoor tables with water views.

Maestral ISTRIAN €€
(052-830 565; Vladimira Nazora bb; mains 65-160KN; 11am-midnight Apr-Oct) Grab an alfresco table at this tavern on the water's edge for simple food and great views of the old town; it's a wonderful place to watch the sunset. If you're just after a snack, try the *ribarska pogača* – a pizzalike pie from the Dalmatian island of Vis, filled with salted fish and tomatoes.

Monte ISTRIAN €€€
(052-830 203; www.monte.hr; Montalbano 75; 3-/4-/6-course menu 619/719/849KN; 6.30-11pm May-Sep;) The first restaurant in Croatia to be awarded a Michelin star, Monte offers a choice of three differently themed six-course Modern Istrian menus (one focused on local ingredients, one exclusively vegetarian and the last emphasising modern techniques). Or you can build your own three- or four-course meal, mixing and matching from all three.

WORTH A TRIP

LIMSKI KANAL

About 10km long, 600m wide and with steep valley walls that rise to a height of 100m, the Limski Kanal is the most dramatic geological sight in Istria. The inlet was formed when the Istrian coastline sank during the last Ice Age, allowing the sea to rush in and fill the Draga Valley. The deep-green waters are used for fishing, oyster and mussel farming, and for tourist excursions.

To get here, you can take an excursion from Rovinj, Pula or Poreč, or follow the signs to Limski Kanal past the village of Sveti Lovreč. Small excursion boats will take you on a one-hour cruise along the canal for 80KN per person (negotiable); these run frequently in July and August, and sporadically in June and September.

Puntulina ISTRIAN €€€
(052-813 186; www.puntulina.eu; Sv Križa 38; mains 100-220KN; noon-10pm;) For an added burst of romance, book ahead at this family-run restaurant and request a table on one of the rocky terraces clinging to the cliffs circling the old town, mere steps from the water; it's especially pretty at sunset. The menu emphasises the Venetian influences on Istrian cuisine, with lots of pasta and seafood dishes.

Ulika MEDITERRANEAN €€€
(098 92 97 541; Porečka 6; mains 120-200KN; 12.30-3pm & 6pm-midnight) Tucked away in an old-town alleyway, this small, pretty tavern serves well-prepared if pricey Mediterranean fare. If it isn't in season, you probably won't find it on the menu. The service is good, too.

Surrounds

Barba Danilo MEDITERRANEAN €€
(052-830 002; www.barbadanilo.com; Polari 5; mains 110-125KN; 6-11pm Mon-Sat) The last place you might expect to find one of Rovinj's best restaurants is on a campsite

3.5km from the centre. Only a handful of choices are offered on the ever-changing menu, with fresh seafood the main focus. With just 45 seats in summer, booking ahead is essential.

Konoba Bruna ISTRIAN €€
(☎098 95 67 836; Monsena 7a; mains 50-130KN; ⏲5-11pm Tue-Sun May-Sep) A 4km taxi ride out of town, this family-run, summer-only tavern serves seasonal dishes using its own veggies, fish and meat, including *peka* dishes (baked under a domed metal lid). The tables are scattered around an olive grove.

Drinking & Nightlife

Rovinj has everything from quiet drinking spots to full-on cocktail bars, though there are few nightclubs as such. Things gather pace in the summer months.

Mediterraneo COCKTAIL BAR
(www.facebook.com/mediterraneo.rovinj; Sv Križa 24; ⏲9am-2am Apr-Sep;) Clinging to the old-town sea cliffs, this gorgeous little bar feels like a secret. It's not, of course – Rovinj's fashionable set are already here, holding court on the pastel-coloured stools right by the water. It's a very relaxed Adriatic scene, with friendly waitstaff and good cocktails, too.

Batel CAFE
(☎052-813 360; Zdenac 22; ⏲7am-1am;) Locals grab a seat outside this old-town cafe-bar for their morning caffeine hit, then return later for a drink in one of the booths in the cosy, dimly lit interior.

Circolo Aperitiv Bar BAR
(www.facebook.com/aperitivbarcircolo; Trg Campitelli 1; ⏲8am-2pm & 5pm-2am Apr-Sep, 8am-2pm & 6pm-1am Mon-Sat Oct-Mar;) Rovinj's rowdiest live-music bar has the most rarified of settings, occupying a grand old building with a very pleasant front yard. In summer there's a DJ, band, quiz or comedian on every night, but you can be guaranteed a Friday-night gig throughout the year.

Valentino COCKTAIL BAR
(☎052-830 683; www.valentino-rovinj.com; Sv Križa 28; ⏲6pm-midnight May-Sep) Premium cocktails and champagne seem like the appropriate poison at this high-end spot. There are fantastic views from the cushions scattered on the water's edge.

Havana COCKTAIL BAR
(☎091 58 83 470; www.facebook.com/havanarovinj; Aldo Negri bb; ⏲9am-2am Jun-Sep) Rum-based cocktails, Cuban cigars, straw parasols and the shade of tall pine trees make this open-air bar a popular spot.

Limbo BAR
(Casale 22b; ⏲11am-midnight Mon-Sat, from 4pm Sun May-Sep) Cosy cafe-bar with small candlelit tables and cushions laid out on the stairs leading to the old town's hilltop. It serves tasty snacks and good Prosecco.

Monte Carlo COCKTAIL BAR
(Sv Križa 21; ⏲10am-1am May-Sep) Perched right on the water's edge, this low-key cafe-bar has unsurpassed views of the Adriatic and Sveta Katarina across the way.

Shopping

Sirena JEWELLERY
(Sv Križa 39) Heed the siren's call to this aquamarine-painted and mermaid-adorned grotto. Inside you'll find contemporary pearl bracelets and necklaces, all designed in-house.

Galerija Brek ART
(Fontika 2; ⏲10am-midnight Jun-Sep) Galerija Brek sells photos of Rovinj and Istria and a small selection of diverse works by local artists.

Galerija Zdenac CERAMICS
(☎095 547 735; www.facebook.com/brakovicceramics; Zdenac 13; ⏲10am-8pm May-Sep) Sells beautiful ceramic pieces from the ground floor of a gorgeous old town house.

Green Market MARKET
(Trg Valdibora; ⏲7am-6pm) Although it's still a fresh-produce market, many of the stalls in this open-sided covered space now sell products aimed at visiting foodies: olive oils, jams, truffle products etc.

Information

Medical Centre (☎052-840 702; Istarska bb; ⏲24hr)

Tourist Office (☎052-811 566; www.rovinj-tourism.com; Pina Budicina 12; ⏲8am-10pm Jul & Aug, to 8pm mid-May–Jun & Sep)

Getting There & Away

BOAT

Venezia Lines (☎052-422 896; www.venezialines.com; Giordana Paliage bb; adult/child from €57/37) operates a fast catamaran to Venice (3¾ hours) between May and September.

Boats to Crveni Otok and Sveta Katarina leave from the Delfin Pier.

BUS

The **bus station** (☎060 333 111; Trg na lokvi 6) is just to the southeast of the old town. Destinations include Pula (37KN, 40 minutes, hourly), Poreč (43KN, 45 minutes, four daily), Rijeka (100KN, 2¼ hours, five daily), Zagreb (150KN, 4½ hours, 10 daily) and Varaždin (208KN, seven hours, two daily).

Poreč

POP 16,700

The ancient Roman town of Poreč (Parenzo in Italian) and the surrounding region are entirely devoted to summer tourism. Poreč is the centrepiece of a vast system of tourist resorts that stretches north and south along the west coast of Istria, attracting holidaymakers in their tens of thousands from June to September.

Mass tourism means this is definitely not the place for a quiet getaway (unless you come out of season). However there's a World Heritage–listed basilica, a medley of Gothic, Romanesque and baroque buildings and a well-developed tourist infrastructure, and the verdant Istrian interior is within easy reach. It's also become the party hub of Istria in the last couple of years, drawing in young partygoers from all corners of Europe.

History

The Romans conquered this region in the 2nd century BCE and laid out the town of Parentium on a peninsula 400m long and 200m wide, dividing it into rectangular parcels marked by the longitudinal Decumanus and the latitudinal Cardo. This street plan survives to the present day.

With the collapse of the Western Roman Empire, Poreč came under Byzantine rule between the 6th and 8th centuries. It was during this time that the Euphrasian Basilica, with its magnificent frescoes, was erected. In 1267 Poreč was forced to submit to Venetian rule.

With the decline of Venice, the town oscillated between Austrian and French dominance before the Italian occupation, which lasted from 1918 to 1943. Upon the capitulation of Italy, Poreč was occupied by the Germans and damaged by Allied bombing in 1944 before becoming part of postwar Yugoslavia.

Sights

The compact old town is squeezed on to a small peninsula, packed with shops and restaurants. Three 15th-century, Venetian-built towers outline the position of the city's eastern wall: the Round Tower (Narodni trg), the Gothic Pentagonal Tower (Decumanus) and the Northern Tower. The

WORTH A TRIP

CAVES & CABERNET

If you can drag yourself off the beach, take a couple of hours to explore the Poreč hinterland. These caves and wineries can easily be combined into a morning or afternoon trip.

Baredine Cave (Baredine jama-grotta; ☎052-421 333; www.baredine.com; Gedići 55, Nova Vas; adult/child 75/45KN; ⏲11am-2pm Mar, 10am-5pm Apr-Oct, at 11am on request Nov-Feb) Within easy reach of Poreč, Baredine Cave has subterranean chambers with stalagmites and stalactites. The standard admission is by way of a 30-minute guided tour which takes you 60m below the surface on well-lit walkways. There's also a cave-climbing centre on-site (www.speleolit.com) and, for added thrills, a tractor museum.

Cossetto (☎052-455 204; www.cossetto.net; Roškići 10, Kaštelir) This winery, 12km northeast of Poreč, produces some of Istria's finest reds and whites. Its *malvazija* is of particularly high quality, and it also produces chardonnay and cabernet sauvignon. Call ahead for a tasting session.

Geržinić (☎052-446 285; www.gerzinic.com; Ohnići 9) This award-winning winery in the hamlet of Ohnići, 14km northeast of Poreč, has been in the same family for a century. It cultivates 10 hectares of vineyards producing a range of varieties (chardonnay, *teran*, syrah and a particularly good *malvazija*, yellow muscat and cabernet sauvignon), along with *rakija* (grappa) and an olive oil rated among the top 100 in the world. It's a great place to stop for a tasting, though you're best to call ahead.

Poreč

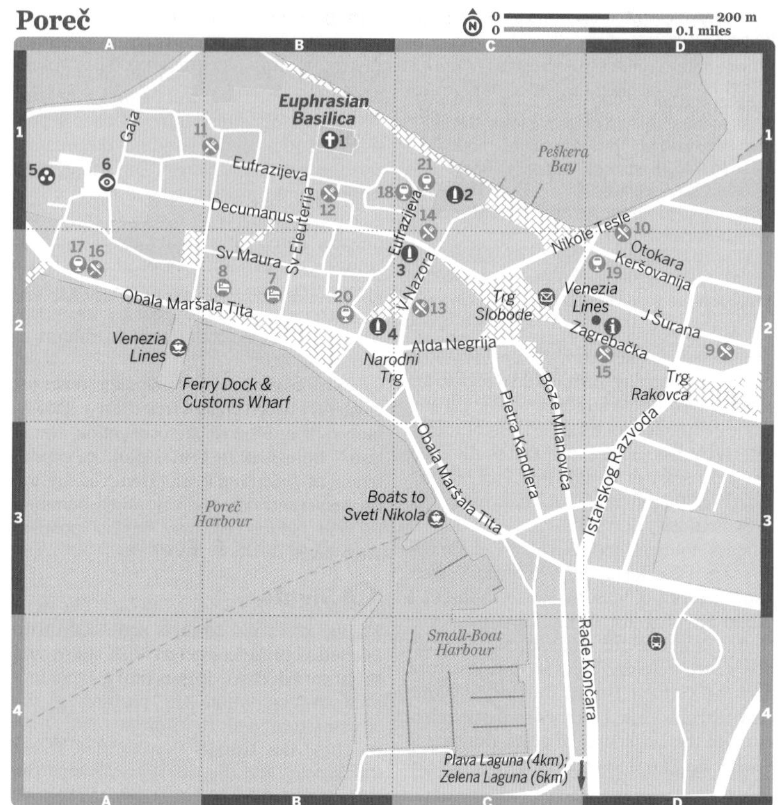

Poreč

Top Sights
1 Euphrasian Basilica ... B1

Sights
2 Northern Tower ... C1
3 Pentagonal Tower ... C2
4 Round Tower ... B2
5 Temple of Neptune ... A1
6 Trg Marafor ... A1

Sleeping
7 Hotel Mauro ... B2
8 Valamar Riviera ... B2

Eating
9 Artha Bistro ... D2
10 Burgerija ... D2
11 Gourmet ... B1
12 Konoba Aba ... B1
13 Konoba Ćakula ... C2
14 Konoba Ulixes ... C2
15 Nono ... D2
Restoran Peterokutna Kula ... (see 3)
16 Sv. Nikola ... A2

Drinking & Nightlife
17 Epoca ... A2
18 Fuego Wine & Bites ... C1
19 Le Mat Corner ... D2
20 Saint & Sinner ... B2
Torre Rotonda ... (see 4)
21 Vinoteka Bacchus ... C1

ancient Roman street Decumanus, with its polished stones, is still the main street running through the peninsula's middle.

★ **Euphrasian Basilica** BASILICA
(Eufrazijeva 22; adult/child 40/20KN; ⏲9am-4pm Mon-Fri, to 2pm Sat Nov-Mar, to 6pm Mon-Sat Apr-Jun, Sep & Oct, to 9pm Jul & Aug) Top billing in

Poreč goes to the 6th-century Euphrasian Basilica, a World Heritage Site and one of Europe's finest intact examples of Byzantine art. Built on the site of a 4th-century oratory, the complex includes a church, an atrium and a baptistery. The glittering 6th-century **mosaics** in the apse of the church are the highlights. The **belfry**, accessed through the octagonal **baptistery**, affords an intimate view of the old town.

Gazing at the mosaics, note how Jesus and the Apostles on the top row are balanced by a set of 12 female saints in the arch, with the Lamb of God at their apex. The main group, in the curve of the apse itself, is centred on the Madonna and Child flanked by angels, saints and Bishop Euphrasius (to the left, holding a model of the church), who commissioned the basilica. Beneath the mosaics, the sanctuary is enclosed by beautifully inlaid marble arranged in geometric patterns. Also note the capitals of the columns supporting the Romanesque arches of the nave; each matched pair is different, carved with birds, flowers and fruit.

Make sure to pop into the adjacent **Bishop's Palace**, which contains a display of ancient stone sculptures, religious paintings and 4th-century mosaics from the original oratory.

Trg Marafor SQUARE

The Roman Forum, where public gatherings took place, once stood on the site of the present-day Trg Marafor. The original pavement has been preserved along the northern row of houses on the square.

Temple of Neptune RUINS

(Romanieka bb) FREE Dating from the 1st century CE, only fragments of this great Roman temple, dedicated to the sea god, have survived.

Sveti Nikola ISLAND

The island of Sveti Nikola lies just short of 500m south of the peninsula. From May to October small passenger **boats** (adult/child 25/15KN; every 30min May-Oct) make the crossing from the wharf on Maršala Tita. Once there, pebble and concrete beaches, rocky breakwaters, shady pine forests and great views of the town across the way await.

Activities & Tours

Nearly every activity you might want to enjoy is on offer in either Plava Laguna or Zelena Laguna, south of the town centre, including tennis, basketball, volleyball, windsurfing, rowing, bungee jumping, paintball, golf, waterskiing, parasailing, boat rentals, go-karting and canoeing. For details, pick up the annual booklet which lists all the recreational facilities in the area from the tourist office (p150).

Fiore Tours OUTDOORS

(052-431 397; www.fiore.hr; Mate Vlašića 6) Offers a range of multiday self- or fully guided hiking, cycling, kayaking and multisports tours through Istria, including accommodation. Themed day trips (Active, Cultural, Art, Gastro) are also available.

Diving Center Poreč DIVING

(052-433 606; www.divingcenter-porec.com; Brulo 4) Offers boat dives (from 135KN, more for caves and wrecks), rents equipment (full set 220KN) and takes speedboat trips to snorkelling spots (140KN including equipment).

Festivals & Events

Concerts in Euphrasiana MUSIC

(www.poup.hr; 50KN; Jul & Aug) Classical-music concerts, run by Poreč University, take place at the Euphrasian Basilica several times a week during summer.

Poreč Open Air Festival PERFORMING ARTS

(www.porecopenair.com; Jul–mid-Sep) Concerts, theatre and film screenings take place on alfresco stages around town and on Sveti Nikola island.

Jazz in Lap MUSIC

(www.poup.hr; mid-Jul–late Aug) These free jazz concerts are held once a week in the lapidarium of the regional museum.

Poreč Annale ART

(Aug–mid-Sep) One of the oldest Croatian contemporary-art exhibitions takes place at the Istrian Parliament and is curated around a single theme.

Sleeping

Accommodation in Poreč is plentiful but gets booked in advance; reservations are essential in July or August. The old town has a handful of hotels, though most campgrounds, hotels, apartment complexes and resorts are spread along the coast north and south of Poreč. Some impose a 20% surcharge if you stay less than three nights.

Polidor CAMPGROUND €
(052-219 495; www.campingpolidor.com; Bijela uvala 12, Funtana; per person/site/cabin from €9/20/45;) Tiny by Croatian standards and tightly packed, nevertheless Polidor crams a lot in. The ablutions block has underfloor heating and a slide to get kids down to the lower level. There's even a dedicated children's bathroom and pets' shower. Submerged bar stools mean you can order cocktails without having to leave the pool. It's 5km south of central Poreč.

Camping Zelena Laguna CAMPGROUND €
(052-410 700; www.lagunaporec.com; Zelena Laguna; per adult/site from €8/14; mid-Apr–Sep;) This huge campground, 5km from the old town, can accommodate up to 2700 people – but you'll still need to book ahead at peak times. Among the activities on offer, there's a pool with a waterslide, and various beaches, including a naturist one.

Valamar Riviera HOTEL €€€
(052-465 000; www.valamar.com; Obala Maršala Tita 15; s/d from €135/186; Apr-Oct;) This rather swanky four-star pad right on the harbourside offers friendly service and some rooms with sea-gazing balconies. There's also a restaurant and bar, plus a long list of guest facilities. The hotel has a private beach on Sveti Nikola island that you can reach by a free boat, departing every 30 minutes.

Hotel Mauro BOUTIQUE HOTEL €€€
(052-219 500; www.hotelmauro.com; Obala Maršala Tita 15; s/d from €159/259; ) With its central location, tasteful rooms, cool marble bathrooms and balconies with Adriatic views, this Austrian-era hotel maintains its elegant caché. There's also a restaurant and lobby bar, and free shuttles to whisk you to its private beach and swimming pools, 2km away.

Eating

Artha Bistro VEGETARIAN €
(052-435 495; Jože Šurana 10; mains 40-80KN; 11am-3pm & 6-10pm Mon-Sat, 10am-3pm Sun May-Oct;) Vegetarians, vegans and broad-minded omnivores will be spoilt for choice at this meat-free restaurant, tucked away on a side street near the main square. Opt for something Istrian, like the classic pasta with truffles, or tuck into a tasty tofu, tempeh or seitan dish. It also serves cheap and filling sandwiches at lunchtime (from 22KN).

Burgerija BURGERS €
(095 51 49 703; www.facebook.com/burgerija; Nikole Tesle 8; mains 16-59KN; noon-11pm;)

TAKING IT ALL OFF IN ISTRIA

Naturism in Croatia enjoys a long and venerable history that began on Rab Island around the turn of the 20th century. It quickly became a fad among Austrians influenced by the growing German *freikörperkultur* (FKK) movement, which loosely translates as 'free body culture'. Later, Austrian Richard Ehrmann opened the first naturist camp on Paradise Beach in Lopar (on Rab), but the real trailblazers of Adriatic naturism were Edward VIII and Wallis Simpson, who popularised it by going skinny-dipping along the Rab coast in 1936.

The coast of Istria now has many of Croatia's largest and most well-developed naturist resorts and campgrounds.

Valalta Naturist Camp (052-804 800; www.valalta.hr; Cesta za Valaltu, Lim 7; per person/site/cabin from 95/258/372KN;) A vast, well-equipped and friendly naturist site on the Lim Channel, north of Rovinj.

Naturist Camping Ulika (052-410 102; www.lagunaporec.com; Červar bb; per person/site from 59/129KN; mid-Apr–Sep;) This vast naturist complex, 5km north of Poreč, occupies an entire headland, with beaches, bars, restaurants and even a supermarket. There are 559 pitches, as well as caravans and mobile homes available for rent.

Naturist Resort Solaris (052-404 000; www.valamar.hr; Solaris 1, Tar; s/d from €86/93; May-Sep;) For naturists who prefer to stay in an apartment, this 49-hectare resort is the ideal choice – although the blocks are a little tired looking. It's located on the Lanterna Peninsula, 12km north of Poreč, and camping is also available.

CampingIN Kanegra FKK (052-709 000; www.istracamping.com; Kanegra 2; per person/site from 50/33/109KN; May–mid-Sep;) There are 193 pitches at this naturist camp, spread along a long pebbly beach 8km northeast of Umag, by the Slovenian border.

Loud rock music fills this bright little joint, where a dozen different meaty burgers are served, and one vegetarian one, with local craft beer to wash it all down. Meat lovers can choose between a 50g, 130g and a whopping 160g patty.

Nono PIZZA €
(052-453 088; Zagrebačka 4; pizzas 35-70KN; noon-11pm;) Be warned – the wheels of pizza here are supersized and one is enough for two, especially if you order a salad to go with it. Some of the creations are topped with truffle shavings but all are scrumptious, and pasta is served, and some grills as well. The vibe is informal, friendly and very local.

★ **Konoba Daniela** ISTRIAN €€
(052-460 519; www.konobadaniela.com; Veleniki 15a; mains 65-150KN; noon-midnight) In the sweet little village of Veleniki, 5km east of Poreč, this rustic, family-run tavern is known for its steak tartare, huge beefsteaks, ravioli stuffed with mushrooms, and seasonal Istrian mainstays. Finish up with cinnamon dumplings with jam. It also rents two rooms (from 480KN).

Konoba Aba MEDITERRANEAN €€
(Matka Vlačića 2; mains 75-185KN; noon-midnight May-Oct) For the best seafood in Poreč, head down the narrow alleyway to find this small place that specialises in local seafood, risottos and truffle dishes. The food is delicious and the staff polite, but the portion sizes of some mains are on the miserly side.

Konoba Ćakula ISTRIAN €€
(052-427 701; www.konobacakula.com; Vladimira Nazora 7; mains 65-180KN; 10am-11pm;) This tavern does interesting cold appetisers and solid mains. Try the fish platter for two, which contains only freshly caught ingredients. It's also a great spot to come for tapas, paired with a glass of wine.

Gourmet ITALIAN €€
(098 255 164; Eufrazijeva 26; mains 63-160KN; 11am-1am) Comforting Italian concoctions come in all shapes and forms here – penne, tagliatelle, fusilli, gnocchi and so on. There are also pizzas from a wood-fired oven as well as meat and seafood dishes. On a summer's eve there's a superb atmosphere, with tables spilling out onto the piazza.

Konoba Ulixes MEDITERRANEAN €€
(052-451 132; Decumanus 2; mains 85-165KN; noon-4pm & 6pm-midnight Jun-Sep) Tucked away just off the main street, this lovely tavern serves great fish and shellfish dishes in a cosy setting. The food is usually spot on but some complain of lazy service. However, there's a good selection of Istrian wines to take your mind off it.

TWO WHEELS, THREE COUNTRIES

The popular **Parenzana Bike Trail** (052-351 603; www.parenzana.net) runs along a defunct narrow-gauge railway that operated from 1902 to 1935 between Trieste and Poreč. Today, it traverses three countries, Italy, Slovenia and Croatia (the Croatian stretch is 78km), and has become quite a popular way to take in the highlights of Istria, especially in spring and autumn.

Sv. Nikola MEDITERRANEAN €€€
(052-423 018; www.svnikola.com; Obala Maršala Tita 23; mains 77-179; 11am-1am;) Gazing out towards the island of the same name, St Nick's is the swankiest restaurant on the waterfront strip but it's not remotely snooty – the service is charming and there's even a kid's menu. The homemade tagliatelle with wild asparagus and truffle has a lot of fans, but the restaurant also serves steaks, duck and various seafood specialities.

Restoran Peterokutna Kula ISTRIAN €€€
(098 97 79 222; www.kula-porec.com.hr; Decumanus 1; mains 80-220KN; noon-midnight) Inside the medieval Pentagonal Tower, this upmarket restaurant has two alfresco patios in a stone vault, and a roof terrace with great views. It serves a full spectrum of pasta, fish and meat dishes in very memorable surroundings.

Drinking & Nightlife

Le Mat Corner BAR
(095 87 82 366; www.facebook.com/TheCornerCaffe; Otokara Keršovanija 2; 7am-2am) Poreč's hippest bar is a dimly lit den with oddball art, mismatched chairs, little round tables, big metal-dome lamps, mezzanine seating, a fridge full of craft beer and PJ Harvey on the stereo. The slightly surly service somehow only adds to the bohemian atmosphere.

Fuego Wine & Bites WINE BAR
(Eufrazijeva 7; 10am-1am) Grab a seat on the lane and give in to its charms, and those of the wine and waitstaff at this bar. Snacks

such as toasted sandwiches, bruschetta and truffle-filled meat-and-cheese platters are also served.

Vinoteka Bacchus WINE BAR

(052-433 539; Eufrazijeva 10; 10am-1am;) This sweet little wine shop has a clutch of tables on an atmospheric lane, where you can try local wine varietals such as *malvazija* and *refošk*, cure any ailments with *biska* (mistletoe grappa), and nibble on antipasti.

Torre Rotonda BAR

(098 255 731; www.torrerotonda.com; Narodni trg 3a; 10am-1am;) There's no more atmospheric place for a glass of wine in winter than the cosy, candlelit interior of this medieval tower. In summer take the steep stairs to the roof for action-packed views of the passing parade.

Byblos CLUB

(091 29 25 678; www.byblos.hr; Zelena Laguna 1; 11pm-6am event nights May-Aug) On summer weekends, celebrity guest DJs crank out electro house tunes at this humongous open-air club, 3km south of town. Expect to pay up to €25 for admission on a big night.

Saint & Sinner BAR, CLUB

(099 22 11 811; www.saint-sinner.net; Obala Maršala Tita 12; 8pm-4am) A black-and-white plastic theme runs throughout this waterfront hang-out, where the young and beautiful sip caffeine-based beverages by day, and alcoholic ones late into the night. As you might guess from the name, the vibe's a little cheesy and sleazy. It also has a beach bar by the Hotel Delfin in Zelena Laguna, and sister establishments in Umag and Rovinj.

Epoca BAR

(098 367 942; www.epoca.hr; Obala Maršala Tita 24; 8am-2am;) Kick back by the water and watch the sun go down, grab a quick espresso or have a leisurely nightcap cocktail at this low-key cafe-bar.

Information

The entire town centre has free wi-fi access.

Main Post Office (Trg Slobode 14; 8am-9pm Mon-Sat Jun-Sep, 8.30am-5.30pm Mon-Fri Oct-May)

Poreč Medical Centre (052-451 611; Maura Gioseffija 2)

Tourist Office (052-451 293; www.myporec.com; Zagrebačka 9; 8am-9pm Jun-Sep, to 6pm Mon-Sat Oct-May)

Getting There & Away

BOAT

Venezia Lines (052-422 896; www.venezialines.com; Zagrebačka 7; adult/child from €57/37; 8am-8pm May-Sep, to 3pm Mon-Fri Oct-Apr) operates a fast catamaran to Venice (2¾ hours) most days between May and September, departing from the **Ferry Dock & Customs Wharf** (Obala Maršala Tita 5).

BUS

The **bus station** (060 333 111; Karla Huguesa 2) is just outside the old town, and has a left-luggage facility at the station. Between Poreč and Rovinj, the bus runs along the Limski Kanal (p143). To see it clearly, sit on the right-hand side if you're travelling south, or on the left if you're northbound.

Connections include Pula (60KN, 1½ hours, at least five daily), Rovinj (43KN, 45 minutes, at least four daily), Rijeka (100KN, 1½ hours, at least four daily), Zagreb (160KN, four hours, at least six daily) and Osijek (300KN, 8¼ hours, two daily).

Getting Around

You can rent bikes for about 100KN per day. From April to October, tourist road trains run up and down the coastal promenades to the surrounding resorts, costing from 15KN to 25KN.

Umag

POP 13,500

Tight by the border with Slovenia, Umag (Umago in Italian) has a compact old town which protrudes out into the Adriatic surrounded by the scant remains of its 13th- to 18th-century walls. It doesn't have the prettiness of Rovinj or the historical sights of Pula or Poreč, but the pace here is slower and there are some secluded beaches to be found in the rocky coves up and down the coast.

Umag has been around since Roman times and has pretty much gone with the Istrian flow since, passing through the hands of various European powers (Byzantium, Venice, Austria, France, Italy) before finally ending up in Yugoslavia in 1954. Before WWI Italians made up the majority of the town's population, but today this figure is down to just over 18%.

Sights

St Peregrine's Church CHURCH

(Crkva sv Peregrina) Abutting Umag's surprisingly large main square is this baroque-style church and its 33m-tall free-standing bell

WORTH A TRIP

NOVIGRAD SEAFOOD STOPS

Halfway between Poreč and Umag, the seaside town of Novigrad has a busy little fishing harbour and marina, and a couple of excellent seafood restaurants.

Marina (052-726 691; Sv Antona 38, Novigrad; set menu from 350KN; noon-3pm & 7-11pm Wed-Mon) Both situated by and helmed by a Marina (hot-shot chef Marina Gaši), this inventive restaurant serves seafood dishes that manage to be both playful and sophisticated at the same time. The serves are a manageable size, making the eight-course set menu feasible with only a modicum of belt loosening. The wine list is excellent, too.

Damir & Ornella (052-758 134; www.damir-ornella.com; Zidine 5, Novigrad; set menu 500-650KN; 12.30-3.30pm & 6.30-11.30pm Tue-Sun) This 28-seat tavern – located down an unlikely lane near the harbour – is famous for its twitchingly fresh, raw-fish specialities. The Mediterranean-style sashimi is particularly good.

tower (built 1651). If the door's locked you can usually peer through the glass foyer to the pretty pastel paintwork and ceiling frescos of the interior.

Umag Municipal Museum MUSEUM
(Muzej grada Umaga; 052-720 386; www.mgu-mcu.hr; Trg sv Martina 1; 15KN; 10am-1pm & 6-9pm Tue-Sat, 10am-1pm Sun Jun-Sep, 10am-noon Tue, Wed, Sat & Sun, 10am-noon & 5-8pm Thu & Fri Oct-May) Located almost at the tip of the old-town peninsula, Umag's small but well-curated museum displays archaeological finds from the wider area dating from Roman times to the 17th century. There are also photographs of the Umago of yesteryear and a sculpture collection.

Festivals & Events

Croatia Open SPORTS
(www.croatiaopen.hr; Jul) Part of the ATP World Tour, the nation's premier men's tennis tournament takes place here over 10 days in mid-July. Previous winners have included Marin Čilić and Carlos Moyá.

Sleeping

CampingIN Park Umag CAMPGROUND €
(052-713 740; www.istracamping.com; Ladin gaj 132a; per person/pitch from 53/142KN; May-Sep; P@) Vast doesn't do justice to this sprawling beachfront campsite, 8km south of Umag. The mammoth scale means that there are plenty of sporting and entertainment options on offer, not least a pirate ship in the swimming pool.

Villa Badi HOTEL €€
(052-756 402; www.badi.hr; Umaška 12, Lovrečica; r from 738KN; P) This intimate family-run hotel in the fishing village of Lovrečica, around 6km south of Umag, has 22 contemporary rooms, an illuminated outdoor pool, a small spa area and buffet breakfasts. It's just 200m from the sea and the same distance from the centre of the village.

Villa La Rossa B&B €€
(052-720 626; Istarska 19, Punta; r from €63; P) A personable alternative to the huge resort hotels that line the coast, La Rossa boasts comfortable rooms, big balconies and friendly staff. The buffet breakfast could do with an upgrade but is always included. It doesn't have its own website; reservations are handled through Booking.com.

Eating & Drinking

Konoba Rustica MEDITERRANEAN €€
(052-732 053; www.konoba-rustica.com; Sv Marija na Krasu 41; mains 50-195KN; noon-11pm Thu-Tue) Located 5km out of Umag on the road towards the Slovenian border, this much-lauded tavern serves the best thin-crust pizza, pastas and dry-aged steaks in the area. As the name suggests, the interior is done out in a rustic style and the setting is suitably rural.

Konoba Lorenzo MEDITERRANEAN €€€
(095 90 74 762; www.konoba-dalorenzo.com; Šetalište Vladimira Gortana 72, Punta; mains 75-175KN; noon-11pm) Situated just back from the marina, a 20-minute walk north of the old town, this relaxed restaurant crafts delicious dishes using local ingredients wherever possible. The Adriatic fish carpaccio and truffle ice cream are real treats.

Buoni Amici BAR
(095 90 48 583; www.facebook.com/BuoniAmici2016; G Garibaldi 15; 9am-2am;) Facing

the water on the old town's southern edge, this hip bar has a good selection craft beer, photos of Bowie and Lou Reed on the wall, and a collection of brass instruments hanging from the ceiling. Look out for live music and DJ sets.

Information

Tourist Office (☎052-741 363; www.coloursofistria.com; Trgovačka 6; ⊙8am-8pm May-Sep, 8am-3pm Mon-Fri, 9am-noon Sat & Sun Oct-Apr)

Getting There & Away

BOAT

In July and August, **Venezia Lines** (☎052-422 896; www.venezialines.com; Obala Josipa Broza Tita 1; adult/child €67/42) operates a weekly fast catamaran to Venice (2½ hours).

BUS

The **bus station** (☎060 317 060; Joakima Rakovca 11) is 800m east of the old town. Connections include Pula (90KN, 2½ hours, five daily), Rovinj (78KN, 1¾ hours, six daily), Poreč (42KN, 50 minutes, six daily), Rijeka (98KN, 2½ hours, five daily) and Zagreb (225KN, five hours, seven daily).

> **OFF THE BEATEN TRACK**
>
> ### BAŠANIJA
>
> If you're in Umag with a car and time to kill, Istria's northwestern tip has a couple of low-key sights worth visiting.
>
> **Savudrija Lighthouse** (Savudrijski svjetionik; www.lighthouses-croatia.com; Svjetionicarska 1, Bašanija) Positioned at Croatia's westernmost point, this elegant stone lighthouse is Istria's oldest, built in 1818. It's not open to the public but a set of apartments within the attached keepers' cottage is available for rent (from 760KN).
>
> **Degrassi** (☎052-759 250; www.degrassi.hr; Podrumarska 3, Bašanija; tour 128KN; ⊙9am-4pm Mon-Sat Feb-Dec) The Degrassi winery, 6km north of Umag, produces a wide range of varietals, including local stalwarts *malvazija*, *teran* and *refosco*. Book ahead for a tour, which includes tastings of five wines and a snack platter, or you can buy by the glass at the charming on-site *enoteca*.

CENTRAL & EASTERN ISTRIA

Head inland from the Istrian coast and you'll notice that crowds dissipate, hotel complexes disappear and what emerges is an unspoilt countryside of medieval hilltop towns, pine forests, fertile valleys and vineyard-dotted hills. The pace slows down considerably, defined less by the needs of tourists and more by the demands of harvesting grapes, hunting for truffles, picking wild asparagus and cultivating olive groves. Farmhouses open their doors to visitors looking for authentic holiday experiences, remote rustic taverns serve up slow-food delights and Croatia's top winemakers provide tastings in their cellars. Hilltop villages that once seemed doomed to ruin are attracting colonies of artists and artisans as well as well-heeled foreigners. While many compare the region to Tuscany (and the Italian influence can't be denied), it's a world all of its own.

Momjan

POP 283

The oft-skipped-over town of Momjan (Momiano in Italian) in northwestern Istria, just south of the Slovenian border, is situated on a hilltop commanding incredible vistas of Istria's interior and the sea. A 15th-century church and the ruins of a 13th-century clifftop castle offer mild historical interest – otherwise it's worth a quick stopoff for a meal, wine tasting and a spot of aimless wandering on the way elsewhere.

Sights

Kozlović WINERY

(☎052-779 177; www.kozlovic.hr; Vale 78; ⊙10am-7pm Mon-Sat Apr-Oct, to 4pm Nov-Mar) The setting, down in a verdant valley by a bubbling river, and the striking architecture of its tasting room make this Istria's most impressive winery to visit. Various 'wine experiences' are on offer, including tastings and winery tours (price on application) – or you can just call in to buy a bottle of the signature muscat, *malvazija*, sauvignon blanc or *teran*.

Sleeping

★**B&B Tinka** B&B €€

(☎098 17 58 279; www.bb-tinka.com; Dolinja Vas 23; s/d €55/90; P❄📶) Three immaculate and imaginatively decorated rooms are on offer here, each themed around a local grape variety. The bathrooms are excellent, and the breakfast, served in the restaurant downstairs, is a veritable feast of homemade and local produce.

Agroturizam San Mauro B&B €€
(052-779 033; www.sinkovic.hr; San Mauro 157; s/d 297/475KN; P) Just up the hill from Momjan, this farmhouse rents eight rooms with kitchenettes, some of which have terraces and sea vistas. Breakfasts include homemade jams, honey and juices. Part of the Senković family winery, it's worth visiting just to sample the extraordinary muscat and for a meal on the terrace. Say hi to Pepa, the friendly truffle pig.

Eating

Konoba Rino ISTRIAN €
(052-779 170; Dolinja Vas 23; mains 60-150KN; noon-10pm Wed-Mon;) This rustic tavern, with heavy beams and stone archways, serves local specialities such as truffle gnocchi and pasta with *boškarin* or *pulićem* (young donkey).

Stari Podrum ISTRIAN €€€
(www.staripodrum.info; Most 52; mains 70-200KN; noon-10pm Thu-Tue) Istrian mainstays are served with a creative touch at this upmarket restaurant, located in a beautiful valley a five-minute drive out of Momjan. The prices are higher than average, hence the flashier-than-usual cars parked outside. As might be expected, truffles feature heavily on the menu but you can't go wrong with the renowned tenderloin steak.

Getting There & Away

You'll need your own wheels to reach Momjan, as there's no bus service.

Grožnjan

POP 736

Until the mid-1960s, tiny Grožnjan (Italian: Grisignana), 27km northeast of Poreč, was slipping towards oblivion. First mentioned in 1102, this hilltop town was a strategically important fortress for the 14th-century Venetians. They created a system of ramparts and gates, and built a loggia, a granary and several fine churches. With the collapse of the Venetian empire in the 18th century, Grožnjan suffered a decline in its importance and population.

In 1965, sculptor Aleksandar Rukavina and a small group of artists 'discovered' the crumbling medieval appeal of Grožnjan and began setting up studios in the abandoned buildings. As the town crawled back to life, it attracted the attention of Jeunesses Musicales International, an international training program for young musicians. In 1969 a summer school for musicians was established here and it has been operating ever since with annual summer courses, recitals and concerts taking place in the castle and leafy squares.

WORTH A TRIP

ISTRALANDIA

If you're travelling with kids who are bored with the beach, head to **Istralandia** (052-866 900; www.istralandia.hr; off the A9; adult/child 210/160KN; 10am-6pm Jun-Sep;), a massive water park, 7km northeast of Novigrad. There's a wave pool and slides galore, and regular entertainment during the day. Tickets are a little cheaper if you arrive after 2pm.

Sights

All the town's sights are marked with plaques that have English explanations. There are more than 30 galleries and studios scattered around town, most open in summer only.

Church of Sts Vitus, Modest & Crescentia CHURCH
(Župna crkva sv Vida, Modesta i Krešencije; Trg Jozip Broza Tita) The town's skyline is dominated by the yellow sandstone bell tower of its large parish church, which was first mentioned in 1310 and renovated in baroque style from 1748 to 1770. When its closed you can usually peer through the porch windows. A large painting above the altar shows the three early martyrs meeting their maker in a Roman arena.

Fonticus Gallery GALLERY
(Gradska galerija Fonticus; Trg Lođe 3; 10am-1pm & 5-8pm Tue-Sun) Housed in a 1597 building which once served as a court, prison and granary, the town's main gallery promotes recent works of mainly Croatian artists. Though it doesn't have a permanent collection, it does have a small display of heraldic paraphernalia.

Festivals & Events

Summertime concerts are organised by the local branch of Jeunesses Musicales (www.hgm.hr). The concerts are free and no reservations are necessary. They are usually held in the church, the main square, the loggia or the castle.

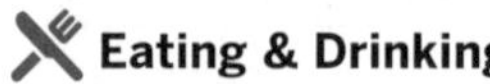

Eating & Drinking

The few restaurants that call Grožnjan home serve superbly authentic Istrian cuisine.

Konoba Pintur ISTRIAN €
(052-776 397; Mate Gorjana 9; mains 35-100KN; 10am-8pm) On the main square, this family-run place has tables outside and acceptable, affordable food and cheap beer. It also rents rooms upstairs.

Bastia ISTRIAN €€
(052-776 370; 1 Svibnja 1; mains 65-180KN; 8am-midnight May-Sep, noon-9pm Wed-Mon Oct-Apr) A bit hit-and-miss, the town's oldest restaurant sits on the verdant main square. The decor is bright and cheerful, and the menu extensive and heavy on truffles.

Cafe Vero BAR
(Trg Cornera 3; 8am-2am Jun-Aug, to midnight Sep-May;) The spectacular valley views from the terrace are the main draw of this cafe-bar at the end of the village. It also serves ice cream.

Information

Tourist Office (052-776 131; www.tz-groznjan.hr; Umberta Gorjana 3; 10am-1pm & 5-8pm Tue-Sun)

Getting There & Away

You will have to rely on private transport to get to Grožnjan, as there are no buses. If you're driving from Motovun, do not take the first marked turn-off for Grožnjan as it's unsealed and takes a lot longer. Continue along the road for another kilometre or so until you get to another sign – this is a far-better approach.

Motovun

POP 484

Motovun (Montona in Italian) is a captivating little walled town perched on a 277m hill in the Mirna River valley. The setting is astonishingly gorgeous and a large part of its appeal is in the lost-in-time views over the verdant valley, with the town rising above it like something from a fairy tale. The damp, dark Motovun Forest at its base also has a mythical quality, especially as it contains hidden treasure in the form of Istria's famous truffles.

It was the Venetians who decided to fortify the town in the 14th century, building two sets of thick walls. Within the walls, an atmospheric cluster of Romanesque and Gothic buildings houses a smattering of artist studios, restaurants and tourist-oriented shops. Newer houses and shops have sprung up on the slopes leading to the old town.

Motovun's main claim to fame is its popular film festival, which takes place every summer.

Sights

Motovun: A History in Motion MUSEUM
(Motovun: Povijest u pokretu; Trg Andrea Antico 7; adult/child 25/15KN; 9am-5pm) Tucked away in a courtyard of the Hotel Kaštel, this small museum has interesting displays on the legendary giant of Motovun Forest, the grim lot of the local peasants forced to work as rowers on Venetian galleons, the truffle and olive-oil industries, the film festival, and Motovun-born motor-sport legend Mario Andretti.

Town Walls WALLS
(Gradske zidine; 091 26 81 616; Trg Andrea Antico bb; adult/family 25/40KN; 9am-9pm Jun-Aug, to 7pm Apr, May & Sep, to 5pm Mar, Oct & Nov) It only takes about 10 minutes to circle Motovun's ramparts and you can get similar views of the surrounding countryside for free, just by walking around town. But visiting the walls does give you the chance to peek into some lovely hidden gardens, as well as access to an exhibition of local landscape photographs housed in the tower above the outer gate. Buy your ticket at the tourist office.

Church of St Stephen CHURCH
(Crkva svetog Stjepana; Trg Andrea Antico bb; hours vary) The town's centrepiece is this large Renaissance church, thought to have been designed by Venetian architect Andrea Palladio. The interior is a restrained affair, typical of churches of the period.

Activities

Montona Tours CYCLING
(052-681 970; www.montonatours.com; Kanal 10; hours vary) This local travel agency rents a fleet of bikes – and it's perfectly located (at the bottom of the hill, mercifully) for day rides on the Parenzana Bike Trail (p149), which passes right through here. Plus it takes bookings for truffle hunts, boats to Venice, accommodation and car rental.

Festivals & Events

Motovun Film Festival FILM

(www.motovunfilmfestival.com; Jul) Around 40,000 people flock to this five-day festival, held in late July. Founded in 1999, it presents a roster of independent and avant-garde films, with nonstop outdoor and indoor screenings, concerts and parties.

Sleeping

There are a few private rooms for rent in Motovun itself plus more formal digs in and around the town.

Motovun Camping CAMPGROUND €

(052-681 557; www.motovun-camping.com; Rižanske skupštine 1a; tent/campervan sites 123/195KN; P) Right below town, this small campground has a gravel parking area for campervans and a small grassy field for tents. There's not much shade, but there is a little swimming pool.

★ **Villa Borgo** B&B €€

(052-681 708; www.villaborgo.com; Borgo 4; s/d/apt from 485/647/811KN; P) Perched on the edge of the old town, this gorgeous place has 10 rooms of different styles and configurations – some with shared baths, some with panoramic views, others overlooking the street – plus a ground-floor apartment that sleeps four. There's a lovely shared terrace with sweeping valley views, perfect for sharing a bottle of wine and watching the sunset.

Hotel Kaštel HOTEL €€

(052-681 607; www.hotel-kastel-motovun.hr; Trg Andrea Antico 7; r from €105; P) The town's only real hotel occupies a restored 17th-century palazzo, with 32 simply furnished rooms and one extraordinary one, sporting a four-poster bed and original moulded reliefs on the walls and ceiling. There's a good restaurant, bike rental (110KN per day), a spa centre, and a lovely indoor pool and outdoor sun deck.

Eating

Pod Napun ISTRIAN €€

(052-681 767; www.antique-motovun.com.hr; Gradizol 33; mains 53-205KN; noon-10pm;) A great choice on the approach to the outer gate, this intimate and friendly restaurant has a terrace with sweeping valley views. It whips up well-prepared traditional dishes from the area. The owners also rent out rooms and houses around the town.

★ **Konoba Mondo** ISTRIAN €€€

(052-681 791; www.konoba-mondo.com; Barbacan 1; mains 75-195KN; noon-3.30pm & 6-10pm;) Just before the outer town gate, this little tavern with a small side terrace serves imaginatively conceived and poshly presented Istrian mainstays, many featuring truffles. And if you just can't get enough of truffles, you can order a top up! Wash it all down with wines from local producers.

Shopping

Miro Tartufi FOOD & DRINKS

(052-681 724; www.miro-tartufi.com; Kanal 27) Truffles infuse olive oil, cheese and sausage in this cute wee shop. However, the main reason to visit is to arrange a truffle hunt (around €65 per person for a three-hour experience, including lunch). The family also rents four apartments upstairs.

Information

Tourist Office (052-681 726; www.tz-motovun.hr; Trg Andrea Antico 1; 9am-9pm Jun-Aug, to 7pm Apr, May & Sep, to 5pm Mar, Oct & Nov) Located on the main square.

Getting There & Away

It's not easy to visit Motovun without your own car or bike. Buses are limited to a daily service to Poreč (37KN, 42 minutes) and Rovinj (69KN, 1¾ hours).

Getting Around

There are three parking areas in town. The first is at the foot of the village, from where it's a steep 2km hike up to the city gates. Another is 300m below the old town. These both charge 20KN per day from April to October. The last one is within the cobbled streets of the old town itself, and is restricted to residents and hotel guests.

Buzet

POP 1680

Its hill isn't as high, or its surroundings as spectacular as Motovun's, but the sleepy old hilltop town of Buzet (*Pinguete* in Italian) offers a taste of the timeless grace of old Istria. Settled by the Romans in 177 BCE, Buzet achieved real prominence under the Venetians, who endowed it with walls, gates and churches. Its present-day claim to fame is as the self-proclaimed 'City of Truffles', sitting at the gateway to Istria's prime truffle-hunting region.

WORTH A TRIP

IDYLLIC INDULGENCE

Motovun and Buzet may be less than 20km apart, but the gorgeous countryside between them offers an extraordinary range of opportunities for self-indulgence, including delicious food, fine wine and a venerable spa resort.

Restaurant Zigante (052-664 302; www.zigantetartufi.com; Livade 7; 3-6 course menu 435-900KN; noon-10pm) Foodies from afar come to this destination restaurant belonging to Istria's top truffle company, located a few kilometres below Motovun in the village of Livade. Expect five-star fancy dining, with truffles as the showcase in a seasonally evolving menu. Amid all of the impressive nods to molecular gastronomy, the simple homemade fettuccine topped with shaved-at-the-table truffle is a showstopper.

Ipša Estate (052-664 010; www.ipsa-maslinovaulja.hr; Ipši 10; 10am-7pm Jul-Sep, 11am-4pm Mon-Sat Oct-Jun) In 2018 the Oscars of olive oil, Flos Olei, rated this family estate's oil among its top 20. The 8km scenic drive up into the hills north of Motovun is well worth it for the views, let alone the opportunity to take a free tasting and to purchase oil directly from the producers. It pays to call ahead.

Konoba Dolina (091 89 32 847; www.konobadolina.hr; Gradinje 59/1; mains 50-110KN; noon-9pm Wed-Mon) This low-key locals' favourite is worth the drive for its unassuming vibe and honest, simple fare featuring Istrian dishes, many with truffles. From Motovun, turn right towards Buzet, continuing till the left turn-off for Gradinje; it's 2.5km from here.

Agroturizam Nežić (052-644 285; Zrenj 11; mains from 50KN; noon-8pm Sun) For a light Sunday meal of truffle-infused antipasti – such as cheese drowned in olive oil, Istrian prosciutto and truffle *fritaja* (frittata) – served with homemade bread, head to this traditional stone tavern in the village of Zrenj, in the mountains between Motovun and Buzet. Be sure to book ahead; accommodation is also available.

Agroturizam Tončić (052-644 146; www.agroturizam-toncic.com; Čabarnica 42; mains from 50KN; 12.30-11pm Fri-Sun;) For a solid meal featuring the best lamb and potatoes cooked under a *peka* (domed baking lid), head to this tavern in the hamlet of Čabarnica, near Zrenj. Food is served in the rustic interior or on the terrace with views of the mountains. Book ahead, as it's hugely popular and sometimes receives big groups.

Toklarija (091 92 66 769; Sovinjsko Polje 11; 6-course meal incl wine 400-500KN; 1-10pm Wed-Mon) At this beautifully converted 600-year-old olive mill in the mountains south of Buzet, eccentric owner Nevio Sirotić serves delectable, homemade slow food (a meal can take up to four hours!). All fruit and vegetables come from the family's gardens, and even the bread and pasta are homemade; 90% of the food is local. Book ahead.

Karlić Tartufi (052-667 304; www.karlictartufi.hr; Paladini 14; per person €65) If you want to experience truffle hunting, join the friendly Karlić family on a tour which includes cheese and truffle tasting, many a truffly tale and a hopeful hunt in the forest that lasts up to two hours. The business is based in the village of Paladini, 13km southwest of Buzet. Book well in advance.

Istarske Toplice (052-603 000; www.istarske-toplice.hr; Sv Stjepana 60; pool adult/child 40/20KN, pool, sauna & steam 120KN; 2-9pm Mon, 9am-9pm Tue-Sun) A relaxing alternative to eating and drinking that dates all the way back to the Roman era, Istarske Toplice is one of Croatia's oldest and most scenic thermal spas. Beneath an 85m-high cliff surrounded by greenery, the complex features a concrete-box-style hotel, a wellness centre and, like most spas in Croatia, a slightly geriatric touch. The rotten-egg smell is from the high sulphur content of the large pool, where temperatures reach 34°C.

The old town is quiet but charming, with stone buildings in various stages of decay and restoration, and cobblestone streets nearly deserted (most of Buzet's residents resettled at the foot of the hill in the unbecoming new part of town long ago). Enjoy a wander around the maze of narrow streets and squares, with sights all well signposted in English.

Sights

Church of the Blessed Virgin CHURCH

(Župna crkva Blažene Djevice; Titov trg bb; ⊙ hours vary) Built by the Venetians in 1784, Buzet's pretty parish church has a pale-yellow ceiling with frescos, an elaborate pulpit and baroque altars. There's also a 15th-century silver salver, an 18th-century organ and a huge canvas depicting the *Madonna and Child* framed by the 15 mysteries of the Rosary.

Local History Museum MUSEUM

(Zavičajni muzej Buzet; ☎052-662 792; Rašporskih kapetana 5; adult/child 15/10KN; ⊙9am-3pm & 5-8pm Mon-Fri, 9am-noon Sat & Sun Jul & Aug, 10am-3pm Mon-Fri Sep-Jun) Housed in the grand Bigatto Palace (built 1639), this museum displays a collection of prehistoric and Roman artefacts as well as some ethnological items such as field tools and folk costumes.

Large Well LANDMARK

(Trg Vela Šterna) At the centre of the old town is an ornate cistern topped with a well, built in 1789 in the rococo style. Look out for the carved lion, the symbol of Venice.

St George's Church CHURCH

(Sv Jurja bb) Positioned by the cliffs at the far end of the old town, this church (completed in 1611) was in the throes of a major restoration during research but it usually contains gilded altars, and paintings of the life of St Anthony produced in the workshop of Venetian master Tiepolo.

Activities

Pick up a guide from the tourist office to wine, olive-oil and truffle routes throughout the region, as well as various activities such as hiking (check out the seven trails in the area), cycling (there are 14 trails around town), free climbing, caving and paragliding.

Tours

Istriana Travel TOURS

(☎091 54 12 099; www.istrianatravel.hr) This local travel company offers truffle-hunting excursions, fresco-painting workshops, wine and olive-oil tours, bike jaunts, hiking, caving, paragliding and much more.

Festivals & Events

Festival of Subotina FOOD & DRINK

(www.facebook.com/subotinabuzet; ⊙Sep) Buzet's top truffle event is on the second Saturday in September, marking the start of the white-truffle season (which lasts through December). The pinnacle of it all is the preparation of a giant truffle omelette – with more than 2000 eggs and 10kg of truffles – in a 1000kg pan.

Sleeping

Vela Vrata BOUTIQUE HOTEL €€

(☎052-494 750; www.velavrata.net; Šetalište Vladimira Gortana 7; s/d from €59/84, mains 70-190KN;) Offering panoramic views of the encircling hills, this lovely boutique hotel has revitalised Buzet's old town. Twenty tasteful antique-strewn rooms are spread through five interconnected buildings, along with an indoor swimming pool and a small spa. Its restaurant is the best place to eat in Buzet, serving adventurous, truffle-loaded takes on traditional cuisine.

Shopping

★ **Destilerija Aura** FOOD & DRINKS

(☎052-694 250; www.aura.hr; II Istarske brigade 2/1; ⊙9am-8pm May-Oct, to 6pm Nov-Apr, closed Sun Jan & Feb;) Occupying the extensive cellars of the elegant 1907-built Narodni Dom (People's House), this Aladdin's cave is filled with glistening bottles, hip flasks and jars of the *rakije* (grappas), liqueurs and jams that are made in the shiny vats on-site. It's a great place to stock up on *biska*, Istria's traditional mistletoe grappa. Tastings and tours are also available.

Zigante Tartufi FOOD

(☎052-663 340; www.zigantetartufi.com; Trg Fontana 3; ⊙9am-8pm) Hidden away in a cave near the main roundabout in the bottom part of town, this little store stocks truffles in various shapes and forms – in olive oil, cheese, tapenades and sausages. It also stocks wine and *rakija* (grappa), and offers tastings. There are further branches in Buje, Livade, Motovun and Grožnjan.

Information

Tourist Office (☎052-662 343; www.tz-buzet.hr; Šetalište Vladimira Gortana 9; ⊙8am-3pm Mon-Fri) In a swanky space next to Vela Vrata, with info about accommodation and plentiful maps and brochures about regional activities.

Getting There & Around

➡ Connections from Buzet's **bus station** (☎052-663 285; Riječka 26/1) include Roč (26KN, 14 minutes, two daily), Poreč (51KN, one hour, two daily), Rovinj (89KN, 2¾ hours, daily), Rijeka (60KN, one hour, two daily) and Zagreb (146KN, four hours, two daily).

➡ Buzet train station is so far out of town it is impractical for travellers.

➡ Parking is restricted in the old town and charged, even in winter. There's a car park by the cemetery, halfway up the hill.

Roč

POP 153

Wee Roč, 8km southeast of Buzet, sleeps snugly within its 15th-century walls. A meander will reveal 11th-century St Anthony's Church, 14th-century St Bartholomew's Church and St Roč's Church, a 15th-century Renaissance house and a collection of inscribed Roman masonry within the 15th-century town gate.

There are a couple of taverns offering local food. One of the town's stone buildings houses Ročka Konoba (☎091 72 99 716; www.facebook.com/rockakonoba; Roč 14; mains 30-130KN; ⊙noon-10pm Tue-Sun May-Sep, Fri-Sun Oct-Apr), a worthwhile regional restaurant with outdoor tables and a fireplace indoors. It's a great place to discover Istrian specialities such as *fuži* (Istrian pasta), homemade sausages and *maneštra* (vegetable stew).

The only accommodation options in the village are private rooms; the tourist office has the full list.

Information

Tourist Office (☎092 16 94 598; www.istria-buzet.com; Roč bb; ⊙9am-5pm May-Oct) Has keys to all the town's churches, so call in here first if you want to see the interiors.

Getting There & Away

Buses stop at the highway junction, 400m from town, heading to Buzet (26KN, 14 minutes, two daily), Rijeka (50KN, 50 minutes, two daily) and Zagreb (146KN, 3½ hours, daily).

Roč train station is 1km northwest of town, with four trains a day to Pula (54KN, 1¾ hours, four daily), Vodnjan (45KN, 1½ hours, four daily) and Pazin (23KN, 38 minutes, six daily).

Hum

POP 28

The self-proclaimed 'world's smallest town' is a mere speck on the map, consisting of basically one street that loops around within its historic walls. Yet, in terms of atmosphere, it's huge. Legend has it that the giants who built Istria had only a few stones left over and they used them to build Hum.

It doesn't take many people for Hum to feel overrun; to experience it at its cosy best, visit in the off season or stay overnight.

Sights

It only takes around five minutes to circle the town – 30 minutes if you stop to read all of the informative multilingual plaques on the significant buildings.

St Jerome's Chapel CHURCH
(Crkvica svetog Jeronima) Positioned in a cemetery just outside the town walls, this little 12th-century Romanesque chapel still has the remains of its original frescoes on the walls, along with graffiti in the archaic Glagolitic script dating from sometime before the 16th century. If it's locked, enquire at the tavern for the key.

Glagolitic Alley LANDMARK
(Aleja Glagoljaša) The road from Roč to Hum has been dubbed Glagolitic Alley in reference to a series of 11 sculptures placed alongside it, commemorating the area's importance as a centre of the Glagolitic alphabet (an archaic Slavic script which survived in parts of Croatia until the 19th century).

Kotli VILLAGE
Don't miss this almost-abandoned village, 2.5km off the road to Roč. It's set on a stream which all but dries up in summer, but at other times bubbles through a series of shallow hollows, perfect for swimming in. Over the bridge are the picturesque ruins of substantial buildings, including preserved courtyards, outer staircases, arched passages and chimneys.

Sleeping

Most people choose to visit on a day trip from elsewhere but Hum has some excellent private rooms.

★**Apartments & Rooms Dores** GUESTHOUSE €
(☎091 56 66 661; www.facebook.com/app.rooms.doresHum; Hum 9; r/apt from €50/65; P❄📶) As petite and gorgeous as Hum itself, this charming guesthouse has two fresh and modern en-suite rooms in a historic block, with a souvenir shop below and the young owners living above. The owners also rent

three self-contained units in Hum (one's a darling free-standing cottage) and another in Roč with its own swimming pool.

Eating & Drinking

Humska Konoba ISTRIAN €

(☎052-660 005; www.hum.hr; Hum 2; mains 32-55KN; ⏰11am-10pm Jun-Sep, Tue-Sun Apr, May & Oct, Mon-Fri Nov-Mar; 📶) The town's tavern serves first-rate Istrian mainstays on a lovely outdoor terrace offering panoramic views. Start with a shot of *biska* (white mistletoe grappa). Next try *maneštra s kukuruzom* (bean and corn soup); continue with truffle-topped *fuži* (homemade egg pasta twisted into unique shapes); and end with *kroštuli* (fried crispy pastry covered in sugar).

Getting There & Away

You'll need your own car to reach Hum as no public transport passes this way.

Pazin

POP 4390

Most famous for a gaping chasm that inspired Jules Verne, and for its medieval castle, Pazin is a workaday provincial town slap bang in the middle of Istria. It deserves a stop mainly for the chasm and the castle, but part of the appeal is its small-town feel and the lack of international tourists stomping its streets. Most of the town centre is given over to pedestrian-only areas, while rolling Istrian countryside surrounds the slightly unsightly outskirts.

Pazin is Istria's administrative seat and is well connected by road and rail to virtually every other destination on the peninsula. However, hotel and restaurant pickings are skimpy, meaning you're better off visiting on a day trip – Pazin is within an hour of most other Istrian towns by car. The countryside around Pazin offers plentiful activities, such as hiking, free climbing, zip-lining, cycling and visiting local honey-makers.

FANTASTIC FUNGUS

The truffle trade is less like a business than a highly profitable cult. It revolves around an expensive subterranean fungus allegedly endowed with semimagical powers, which is picked in dark woods and then sent across borders to be sold for a small fortune. Devotees claim that once you've tasted this small, nut-shaped delicacy, all other flavours seem insipid.

There are 70 sorts of truffle in the world, of which 34 come from Europe. The traditional truffle-producing countries are Italy, France and Spain, but Istrian forests boast three sorts of black truffles (summer, winter and noble) as well as the big white truffle – one of the most prized in the world, which sells at around €4500 per kilogram. Croatia's largest exporter of Istrian truffles is Zigante Tartufi (p157), with its share of the overall Croatian export market being about 90%. In 1999 the company's owner, Giancarlo Zigante, along with his dog Diana, found what was then the world's largest-ever truffle, weighing 1.31kg and making it into Guinness World Records. You can see a model of this whopper in the Zigante restaurant (p156) in Livade.

The Istrian truffle business is relatively young. In 1932, when Istria was occupied by Italy, an Italian soldier from the truffle capital of Alba allegedly noticed similarities in vegetation between his region and Istria. He returned after his military service with specially trained dogs, which, after enough sniffing and digging, eventually uncovered the precious commodity.

Because no sign of the truffle appears above ground, no human can spot it, so dogs (or, traditionally, pigs) are the key to a successful truffle hunt. Istrian *breks* (dogs) may be mongrels, but they are highly trained. Puppies begin their training at two months, but only about 20% of them go on to have fully fledged careers as truffle trackers.

Black truffles can be found most of the year, but the white-truffle-hunting season starts in September and continues to January. During this time at least 3000 people and 9000 to 12,000 dogs wander around the damp Motovun forests.

Some people believe truffles are an aphrodisiac, though scientific research has failed to prove this. Conduct your own experiment!

Sights

Castle CASTLE

(Kaštel; ☎052-622 220; Trg Istarskog Razvoda 1; adult/child 25/15KN; ⏰10am-6pm May-Sep, to 3pm Oct-Apr) Looming over the chasm, Pazin's castle is the largest and best-preserved medieval structure in all of Istria. First mentioned in 983 CE, the castle has had different architectural styles added to it over the centuries. The entrance ticket includes access to its two moderately interesting museums – the **Pazin Town Museum** (www.muzej-pazin.hr) and the **Istrian Ethnographic Museum** (www.emi.hr).

The Town Museum has a collection of medieval church bells, stamps, banknotes, musical instruments, weapons, armor and, in the dungeon, torture instruments. There's also an interesting display on the peasant revolts of 1407 and 1570.

The Ethnographic Museum possesses around 4000 artefacts which give an idea of traditional Istrian village life through the ages. Collections include furniture, national dress, tools and pottery, and there are sections on Slavic festivals and migration.

Pazin Chasm CAVE

(Pazinska jama) Pazin's most renowned site is undoubtedly this 100m-deep abyss, through which the Pazinčica River sinks into subterranean passages forming three underground lakes. Its shadowy depths inspired the imagination of Jules Verne, as well as numerous Croatian writers. Visitors can walk the 1.3km marked path inside the natural canyon, which takes about 45 minutes and involves a gentle winding climb.

There are two entrances, one by Hotel Lovac and one by the footbridge that spans the abyss, 100m from the castle. You can enter the **cave** with an expert speleologist (190KN), if arranged in advance through the tourist office. If the trip into the abyss doesn't appeal, there's a viewing point just outside the castle.

Activities

The Pazin tourist office distributes a map of hiking trails and honey spots (you can visit beekeepers and taste their delicious acacia honey), and a brochure about local wineries.

★**ZipLine Pazinska Jama** ADVENTURE SPORTS

(☎091 54 37 718; Šime Kurelića 4; 2 short lines 80KN, 2 long lines 120KN, all 160KN; ⏰10am-7pm May-Aug) Hurtle across the abyss on two 80m lines, or reach speeds of 40km/hr on the 220m line and 50km/hr on the 280m line.

Eating

★**Konoba Vela Vrata** ISTRIAN €€

(☎052-622 801; Beram 41; mains 45-100KN; ⏰noon-11pm Tue-Sun) Located 5km northwest of Pazin in the hilltop village of Beram, this rural tavern serves some of the best handmade pasta, gnocchi and truffle dishes you'll taste in Istria. In winter the interior is a cosy affair; in summer head for the terrace with amazing views of the central Istrian countryside. And don't miss the incredible truffle chocolate cake.

Information

Tourist Office (☎052-622 460; www.central-istria.com; Velog Jože 1; ⏰10am-5pm Mon-Fri, to 1pm Sat)

A LITERARY CHASM

The writer famous for going around the world in 80 days, into the centre of the earth and 20,000 leagues under the sea found inspiration in the centre of Istria. The French futurist-fantasist Jules Verne (1828–1905) set *Mathias Sandorf* (1885), one of his 27 books in the series Voyages Extraordinaires, in the castle and chasm of Pazin.

In the novel, later made into a movie, Count Mathias Sandorf and two cohorts are arrested by Austrian police for revolutionary activity and imprisoned in Pazin's castle. Sandorf escapes by climbing down a lightning rod but, struck by lightning, he tumbles down into the roaring Pazinčica River. He's carried along into the murky depths of the chasm, but our plucky hero holds on fast to a tree trunk and (phew!) six hours later the churning river deposits him at the tranquil entrance to the Limska Draga Fjord. He walks to Rovinj and is last seen jumping from a cliff into the sea amid a hail of bullets.

Verne never actually visited Pazin – he spun Sandorf's adventure from photos and travellers' accounts – but that hasn't stopped Pazin from celebrating him at every opportunity. There's even a street named after him.

Getting There & Away

BUS

Services from the main **bus station** (☎060 306 040; Miroslava Bulešića 2) include Poreč (42KN, 35 minutes, six daily), Pula (55KN, 50 minutes, five daily), Rovinj (47KN, one hour, four daily), Rijeka (47KN, one hour, five daily) and Zagreb (124KN, three to four hours, 10 daily). Services are reduced on weekends.

TRAIN

The **train station** (☎052-624 310; www.hzpp.hr; Od stareh kostanji 3) is east of the town centre. Connections from Pazin include Pula (36KN, 1¼ hours, eight daily), Vodnjan (27KN, 55 minutes, eight daily) and Roč (23KN, 38 minutes, six daily).

Getting Around

The town is relatively compact, stretching little more than 1km from the train station on the eastern end to the Kaštel on the western end. The bus station is 200m west of the train station and the old part of town is comprised of the 200m leading up to the Kaštel.

Svetvinčenat

POP 267

Situated about halfway between Pazin and Pula in southern Istria, Svetvinčenat is a pretty little town centred on a Renaissance square. With its surrounding cypress trees, harmoniously positioned buildings and laid-back ambience, it's a pleasant place for an aimless wander en route to somewhere else.

Sights

Morosini-Grimani Castle CASTLE
(☎052-384 318; www.grimanicastle.com; Svetvinčenat 47; adult/child 50/25KN; ⏲10am-8pm May-Sep) The northern part of the main square is occupied by this beautiful 13th-century fortified palace. Its present appearance, including its towers, are a legacy of a Venetian makeover in the 16th century. In summertime, the entire castle becomes one big escape room, where groups explore the complex while solving the puzzle. You can also book in for a medieval meal (150KN–400KN) or an evening show featuring sword fights and a witch-burning (80KN).

Church of the Annunciation CHURCH
(Župna crkva Navještenja; Gradski trg; ⏲hours vary) This 16th-century parish church on the east side of the main square has a Renaissance facade made of local cut stone, and five elaborate Venetian marble altars inside.

WORTH A TRIP

GLAVANI PARK

At **Glavani Park** (☎099 85 60 626; www.glavanipark.com; Glavani 10; per activity 50KN; ⏲9am-8pm May-Sep, to 5pm Oct-Apr), you can zoom along ziplines, swoop on the giant swing, pedal a unicycle along a wire and tackle Istria's highest outdoor climbing wall – either as individual activities or as part of a seven-attraction ticket (300KN). However, that's all but a warm-up for the 75m human slingshot (250KN). It's located in the village of Glavani, 13km southeast of Svetvinčenat.

Festivals & Events

Dance & Nonverbal Theatre Festival PERFORMING ARTS
(Festival plesa i neverbalnog kazališta; www.svetvincenatfestival.com; ⏲Jul) This four-day festival in late July showcases contemporary dance, street theatre, circus and mime acts, and various other nonverbal forms of expression, with performers from all over Europe.

Sleeping & Eating

The best places to sleep and eat are a little out of town but, if you don't have a car, you won't go hungry in the town centre.

Stancija 1904 APARTMENT €€€
(☎098 738 974; www.stancija.com; Smoljanci 2; apt/house 1220/3550KN; P) In the village of Smoljanci, 3km west of Svetvinčenat, this traditional Istrian stone house is the residence of the Swiss honorary consul. Two stylish apartments and a separate vacation house are available, and the complex is surrounded by fragrant herb gardens and shaded by tall old-growth trees. It also runs cooking courses.

Konoba Klarići ISTRIAN €
(☎052-579 137; www.konobaklarici.fullbusiness.com; Klarići 83; mains 35-60KN; ⏲11am-11pm Tue-Sun) This delightful stone tavern in the hamlet of Klarići, 10km south of Svetvinčenat, serves superb homemade Istrian pastas and its own exquisite wines. In winter the roaring fire can be a very welcoming sight.

Konoba puli Pineta ISTRIAN €€
(☎098 99 11 795; www.konoba-pulipineta.com; Karlov vrt 1, Žminj; mains 60-120KN; ⌚5-10pm Jul & Aug, 4-10pm Mon-Fri, 1-10pm Sat & Sun Sep-Jun) Located on the edge of the town of Žminj, 7km north of Svetvinčenat, this tavern is known around Istria for its superb homemade pasta and grilled meats.

Information

Tourist Office (☎052-560 349; www.tz-svetvincenat.hr; Svetvinčenat 20; ⌚8am-4pm Mon-Fri, 11am-1pm Sun Jun-Sep, 8am-4pm Mon-Fri Oct-May) Private accommodation bookings, brochures and a map of a bike path outlining a 35km circuit from Svetvinčenat, with information boards explaining the local history, flora and fauna in English.

Getting There & Away

There's a daily bus to Svetvinčenat from Pula (37KN, 25 minutes), Vodnjan (30KN, 15 minutes), Rovinj (38KN, 1¼ hours), Pazin (35KN, 25 minutes) and Zagreb (132KN, 3½ hours).

Labin & Rabac

Perched on a hilltop near the coast, Labin is the heritage highlight of eastern Istria, as well as its administrative centre. The showcase here is the labyrinthine old town, a beguiling maze of steep streets, cobbled alleys and pastel houses festooned with stone ornamentation.

Below is Podlabin, a charmless new town that sprouted as a result of the coal-mining industry. Labin was the mining capital of Istria until the 1970s, its hill mined so extensively that the town began to collapse. Mining stopped in 1999, the necessary repairs were undertaken and the town surfaced with a new sense of itself as a tourist destination.

Labin's coastal resort is Rabac, a former fishing village 5km to the southeast hugging a shallow cove hemmed with beautiful pebble beaches. An ever-expanding array of ritzy resort-style hotels is a reflection of its increasing popularity, especially with German-speaking tourists.

Sights

The hilltop old town contains most of the sights and attractions: wandering the medieval streets is the highlight of any visit. Newer Podlabin offers most of the town's shops and services.

Loggia HISTORIC BUILDING
(Titov trg bb) This 1550 loggia served as the community centre of Labin in the 16th century. News and court verdicts were announced here, fairs were held and wayward people were punished on the pillar of shame.

Church of the Nativity of the Blessed Virgin Mary CHURCH
(Župna crkva rođenja Blažene Djevice Marije; 1 Maja bb; ⌚hours vary) Labin's parish church – originally built in the 11th century but tinkered with until the 18th – has a Venetian lion over the main door and baroque marble altars inside. Note the trompe-l'œil effect on the ceiling, painted to look like it's coffered.

Labin Public Museum MUSEUM
(Narodni muzej Labin; 1 Maja 6; adult/child 15/10KN; ⌚10am-1pm & 6-10pm Mon-Sat Jul & Aug, 10am-1pm & 5-8pm Mon-Sat Jun & Sep, 10am-1pm Mon-Sat May) The ground floor of this museum, housed in the baroque 18th-century Battiala-Lazzarini Palace, is devoted to archaeological finds. Upstairs is a collection of musical instruments with some fun interactive features. So far, so typical regional museum. However, this one's built over a coal pit, which has been turned into a realistic re-creation of an actual coal mine. The town's art gallery is directly across the square.

Fortress VIEWPOINT
(Fortica bb) Labin's fortress once stood at the highest point of the old town. There's no longer a fort to speak of (although there is a canon) but it's well worth wandering up through the cobbled streets for the sweeping view of the coast, the Učka mountain range and Cres island.

Plaža Girandella BEACH
Rabac's best beach is this series of pebbly coves in front of the immense Valamar Girandella resort complex. It's well maintained by the resort, but most of it is open to nonguests. Some areas are designated for families while others are strictly adults only.

Festivals & Events

Labin Art Republika ART
(www.labin-art-republika.com; ⌚Jul-Aug) There are more than 30 artists living and working in Labin and, in summer, the 'Art Republic' takes over the streets. During the festival the town comes alive with street theatre, concerts, plays, clown performances and open studios. Every Tuesday at 9.30pm, free

guided tours (in various languages) depart from the tourist office (p164) in the old town.

Sleeping

There are no hotels in Labin itself but choices abound just below in Rabac. Most of the lodging is of the large hotel-resort kind, with a few smaller properties. There are also plenty of private rooms in the area – contact the tourist office (p164) for these.

★**Valamar Sanfior** RESORT **€€€**
(052-465 000; www.valamar.com; Lanterna 2; s/d from €147/195; P ❄ ☎ ≋ 🐾) Set on a beautiful stretch of pebbly and rocky shore, this large Rabac resort ticks all of the family-holiday boxes. The rooms are swish and modern, there's a choice of indoor and outdoor pools, and the prices include an extensive breakfast and dinner buffet. Add to this playgrounds, a babysitting service and live music in the bar at night.

Villa Annette HOTEL **€€€**
(052-884 222; www.villa-annette.com; Raška 24; ste from €155; P ❄ ☎ ≋) This luxe, art-filled hideaway up on the hill above Rabac has 12 large, modern suites and a wonderful outdoor pool providing dramatic bay views. Half board is an extra €29, with meals taken either in the hotel restaurant or under the olive trees.

RURAL RETREATS

Agritourism is an increasingly popular accommodation option in Istria's interior. Some of these residences are working farms engaged in producing wine, vegetables and poultry; some are country houses with apartments to let; while others are plush modern villas with swimming pools.

The Istrian tourist office (www.istra.hr) has a brochure with photos and information about rural holidays throughout Istria. You'll need your own car to reach most of these lodgings, as many are located in the middle of nowhere. There's often a supplement for stays of less than three nights.

Casa Matiki (098 299 040; www.matiki.com; Matiki 14; apt €90; P ☎ ≋) Three friendly dogs, a charming hostess and a clutch of chickens (in that order) will welcome you to this large rural property near the small town of Žminj, right at the heart of Istria. There are three spacious apartments in the main house, plus two sweet little guest cottages and a lovely pool tucked behind the olive grove.

Agroturizam Ograde (052-693 035; www.agroturizam-ograde.hr; Katun Lindarski 60; house per week €1500; P ☎ ≋) Two separate houses (sleeping eight in one, 12 in the other) are available for rent at this animal-filled farm in the village of Katun Lindarski, 10km south of Pazin. In July and August a minimum week's booking applies. The food is the real deal: veggies from the garden, home-cured meats and wine from the cellar.

Pruga (091 78 17 263; www.apartments-pruga.com; Lovrinići 14; apt €100 incl breakfast; May-Oct; P ☎ ≋) In the village of Lovrinići, 8km south of Pazin, this is a lovely rustic choice for a quiet getaway. Choose one of two beautifully renovated apartments in a traditional limestone Istrian house, each with original details and fully equipped kitchens. Breakfast of local cheese, homemade jams and cakes is served outside among fruit trees.

Hotel Parenzana (052-777 458; www.hotelparenzana.com; Volpija 3; s/d/tr €49/76/95; P ❄ ☎) In the sleepy village of Volpia, 3km north of Buje, this rural inn has 16 simple rooms with rustic wood-and-stone decor, and a *konoba* (tavern) popular for its Istrian food. It's extremely handy if you're touring on the Parenzana cycle trail.

San Rocco (052-725 000; www.san-rocco.hr; Srednja 2, Brtonigla; r/ste from €199/390; P ❄ ☎ ≋) This boutique hotel in the village of Brtonigla, 5km southeast of Buje, is a rural hideaway with 14 stylish rooms. No two are alike, but all are equipped with modern conveniences and graced with original details such as heavy wooden beams and exposed stone walls. There's an outdoor swimming pool, a top-rated restaurant and a small spa.

OFF THE BEATEN TRACK

GRAČIŠĆE

Situated amid rolling countryside, 8km southeast of Pazin, this sleepy medieval hill town is one of Istria's well-kept secrets. Its collection of ancient buildings includes the unassuming Romanesque **St Euphemia's Church** (built 1383), tiny **St Mary's Church** (1425), fronted by a graceful stone loggia, and the ruined shell of the 15th-century Venetian-Gothic **Salamon Palace**. The large **Parish Church of St Vitus** is a relative newbie (1769), but the views from its churchyard are extraordinary.

You won't need more than 30 minutes to circle the tiny town, but the ambience is truly lovely. A well-marked 11.5km circular hiking trail, the **Path of St Simeon** (Pješačka staza sv Šimuna), leads from here.

Eating

Labin is known for its *krafi*, ravioli-like pasta which is served either sweet or savoury. Rabac has plenty of seasonal restaurants serving seafood standards, but most cater to the unfussy tourist crowds.

Velo Kafe CAFE €€

(Titov trg 12; mains 55-125KN; 7am-11pm;) Dominating Labin's Tito Square, this popular, vine-shaded, multitasking spot serves everything from brunch to beefsteaks. Grab a seat on the street for coffee and cake, or sit down to a meal of local pasta or other truffle-infused dishes.

Restaurant Kvarner ISTRIAN €€€

(052-852 336; www.kvarnerlabin.com; Šetalište San Marco bb; mains 75-195KN; 10am-11pm) This Labin old-town restaurant has a terrace overlooking the sea, a menu of authentic Istrian fare and a loyal local following. Handmade *fuži* (Istrian pasta) is the main speciality here but almost anything you order is guaranteed to be packed with local flavour, especially in the form of truffles. It also has rooms and apartments to rent.

Drinking & Nightlife

Rabac is the place to head for a drink or any semblance of after-dark entertainment. A string of cafe-bars lines its pretty harbour.

Movie Bar BAR

(099 50 89 460; www.moviebar.hr; Maršala Tita 81; 10am-1am May-Aug) The best place for a drink on the Rabac strip is this open-air bar under the pines by pebbly Sv Andrija beach. There's often live music at night.

Beat BAR

(052-388 304; www.facebook.com/TheBeatBeachClubRabac; Obala Maršala Tita 75; 10am-1am May-Sep) This slick Rabac beach club serves cocktails on a wooden terrace set around a small pool.

Information

Tourist Office (052-852 399; www.rabac-labin.com; Titov trg 2/1; 8am-9pm Mon-Fri, 10am-2pm & 6-9pm Sat & Sun May-Sep, 9am-3pm Mon-Sat Oct-Apr) At the entrance to the old town.

Getting There & Away

Labin is well connected by bus with Pula (48KN, 55 minutes, 14 daily), Rijeka (54KN, 1½ hours, 15 daily), Zagreb (146KN, 4¼ hours, eight daily), Zadar (205KN, seven hours, five daily) and Split (280KN, 9½ hours, five daily).

Getting Around

Buses stop at Trg 2 Marta in Podlabin, from where you can catch a local bus to the old town. This bus continues on to Rabac in the peak season.

Croatia's Coast

From the tip of Istria to dazzling Dubrovnik, Croatia is blessed with one of the most unrelentingly gorgeous stretches of coast in the entire Mediterranean region. The crystalline waters provide a constant presence as the backdrop changes from mountains to walled towns to low-slung islands and back again.

Contents

Above: A boat moored off Pag Island (p216)

Walled Towns

Since ancient times the people of this coast have encased their towns in sturdy walls of stone as a protection against the attacks that came all too frequently. Although the purpose may have been purely defensive, the end result is spectacular; the sight of these stone bastions rising from the sea is one of the most memorable images of the Adriatic coast. Even when the walls themselves have been largely removed, exposing the nest of medieval streets within, they still make for an impressive sight.

Most people know all about Dubrovnik, but there are many mini-Dubrovniks scattered all along the coast. One of the most magical is Trogir, west of Split, occupying a little islet anchored by bridges to the mainland. Split itself has at its heart an ancient fortress growing out of the remains of a Roman imperial palace – although from the water it's hard to distinguish from the sprawl surrounding it. Šibenik's fortified old town arcs up a hill to an imposing castle, while at Ston the fortifications rise up and over the mountainous terminus of the Pelješac Peninsula.

Historic Rovinj was once an island, separated from the mainland by a narrow channel that was subsequently filled in – much like Dubrovnik itself. In Zadar's case the walls enclosed the tip of a peninsula – although these days only about half of them remain. The islands, too, have many such impressive sites; the old towns of Cres, Krk, Rab, Pag and Korčula being principal among them.

Apart from all the well-known places, you might find yourself stumbling on your own little walled treasure. Like sleepy wee Osor, watching over the channel separating the islands of Cres and Lošinj. Or pretty little Primošten, jutting out over a rocky shore south of Šibenik.

1. Medieval street, Šibenik (p235) **2.** Ston Walls (p323) **3.** Kamerlengo Castle (p264), Trogir

2

BORISB17/SHUTTERSTOCK ©

Island Life

Croatia's 1244 islands range from little more than rocks in the sea, to large, populated places supporting agriculture and small towns. Two of the biggest, Krk and Pag, are joined to the mainland by bridges, yet they still maintain their own distinct island culture and way of life.

The more popular and populated islands are well served by ferries all year round, although there can be lengthy queues for the car ferries in July and August, and during weekends in June and September. If you're planning on island-hopping at those times, you're better off doing so as a foot passenger and hiring a car or scooter when you arrive. Note: locals only tend to use the term 'ferries' when talking about car ferries; the faster passenger-only boats are generally listed on schedules as 'catamarans'.

For the clusters of smaller islands, such as the Kornatis, organised tours are popular; enquire at travel agencies, tourist offices and marinas anywhere along the coast. Yachties will find themselves in sailing heaven, with plenty of deserted bays on unpopulated islets to seek out. If you haven't managed to bring your own yacht with you, it's possible to hire one, either with a skipper or without (provided you have a licence). There are numerous island-hopping package sailing tours available, including some targeted at backpackers.

Beaches

Although it's only about 600km long as the crow flies, Croatia's Adriatic coastline would stretch for 1778km if someone were to iron out all the indentations and unwind the numerous islands. The lure of the clear water and the balmy weather sees literally millions of tourists descend on the beaches each summer, with the peak being during the European school holidays in July and August.

1. Jadrolinija ferries operate from the mainland to Hvar Island (p277)
2. Krk Island (p194) is connected to the mainland by bridge

If you're expecting long sandy beaches to compete with Bondi, Malibu or Copacabana, you'll be disappointed. Mostly you'll find pretty little rocky or pebbly coves, edged by pines, olives or low scrub. There are some beautiful sandy beaches – mainly on the islands – but the water is often painfully shallow, requiring a lengthy walk to get even your knees wet. It's partly for this reason that the locals tend to prefer the rocky bays.

What is particularly striking all the way along the coast is the clarity and colour of the water, at times seeming almost unnaturally blue or green. Currently there are 89 Blue Flag–rated beaches in the country (a measure of water quality and environmental standards), with the majority in Istria and the Kvarner region.

Swimmers should watch out for sea urchins, which are common along the coast. The sharp spines are painful to tread on and can break off in your skin and become infected. If you're planning on swimming, you're well advised to wear water shoes, which are easily purchased on urchin-infested beaches.

Croatia is not short of places to let it all hang out, with naturist beaches all along the coast, often accompanied by campsites. Look for the signs reading 'FKK', which stands for *freikörperkultur,* meaning 'free body culture' in German. Just don't forget those water shoes!

Snorkelling & Diving

Do yourself a favour and pack your mask and snorkel – the clear, warm waters and the abundance of small fish make for lots to see. Serious divers will also find plenty to keep them busy, with numerous wrecks (dating from ancient times to WWII), drop-offs and caves. Popular sites include the wreck of the *Taranto* near Dubrovnik, the Margarita Reef off the Susak, the wreck of the *Rosa* off Rab and around the islands of Brač, Vis, Dugi Otok and Lošinj.

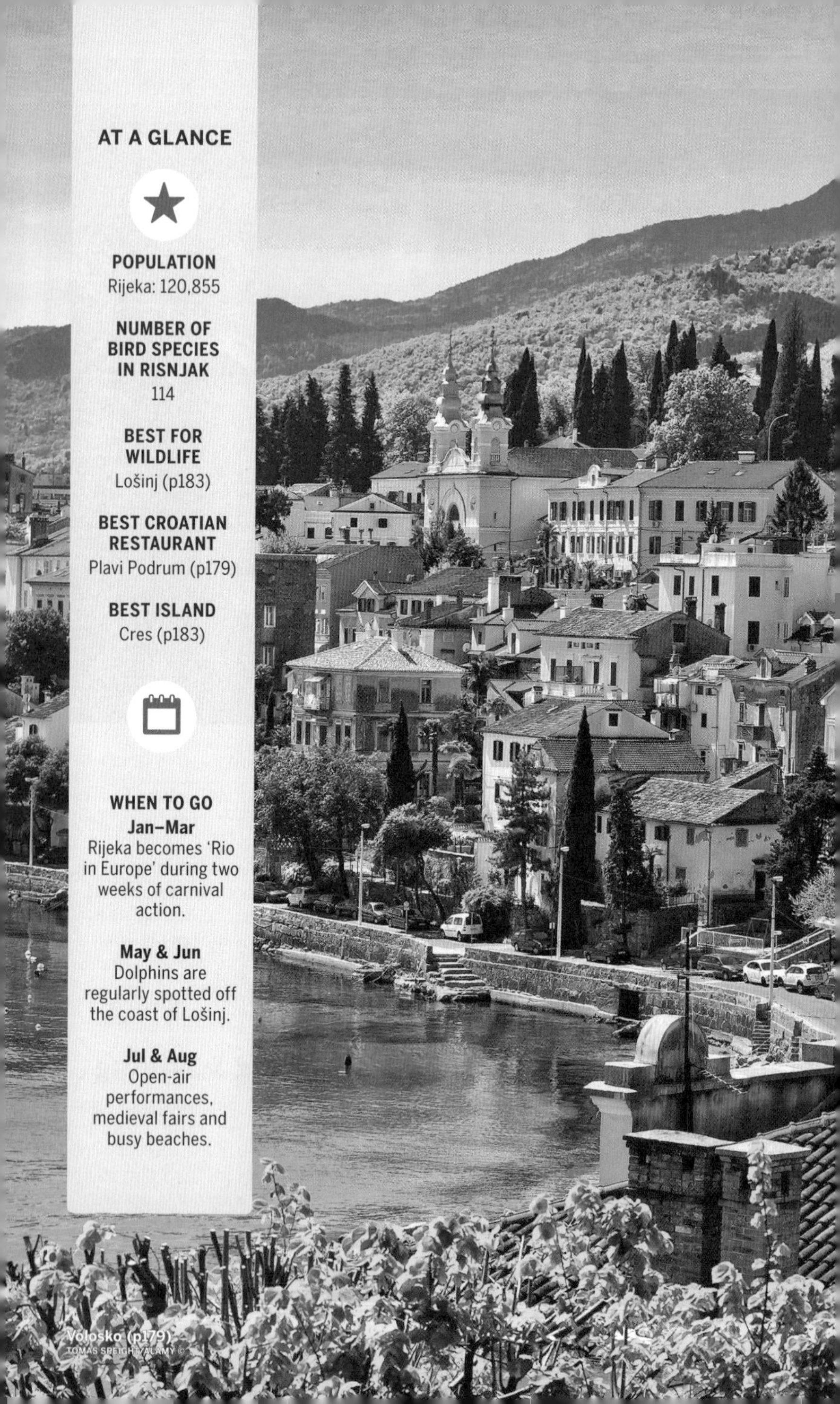

AT A GLANCE

POPULATION
Rijeka: 120,855

NUMBER OF BIRD SPECIES IN RISNJAK
114

BEST FOR WILDLIFE
Lošinj (p183)

BEST CROATIAN RESTAURANT
Plavi Podrum (p179)

BEST ISLAND
Cres (p183)

WHEN TO GO

Jan–Mar
Rijeka becomes 'Rio in Europe' during two weeks of carnival action.

May & Jun
Dolphins are regularly spotted off the coast of Lošinj.

Jul & Aug
Open-air performances, medieval fairs and busy beaches.

Volosko (p179)

Kvarner

Sheltered by soaring mountains, the Kvarner Gulf has long been loved by visitors for its mild climate and cobalt waters. In the days of the Austro-Hungarian Empire, the wealthy built holiday homes here, bestowing places like Rijeka and Opatija with a rich legacy of stately Habsburg-era architecture. From both of these neighbouring towns you can easily connect to hiking trails inside the protected forests of Učka Nature Park and Risnjak National Park. The islands of Cres, Lošinj, Krk and Rab all have highly atmospheric old port towns and stretches of unspoilt coastline dotted with remote coves for superb swimming. Wildlife puts in an appearance, too: Cres has an important griffon-vulture population, Lošinj has a marine centre devoted to preserving the Adriatic's dolphins and turtles, while bears (though elusive) may be sighted in both Učka and Risnjak.

INCLUDES

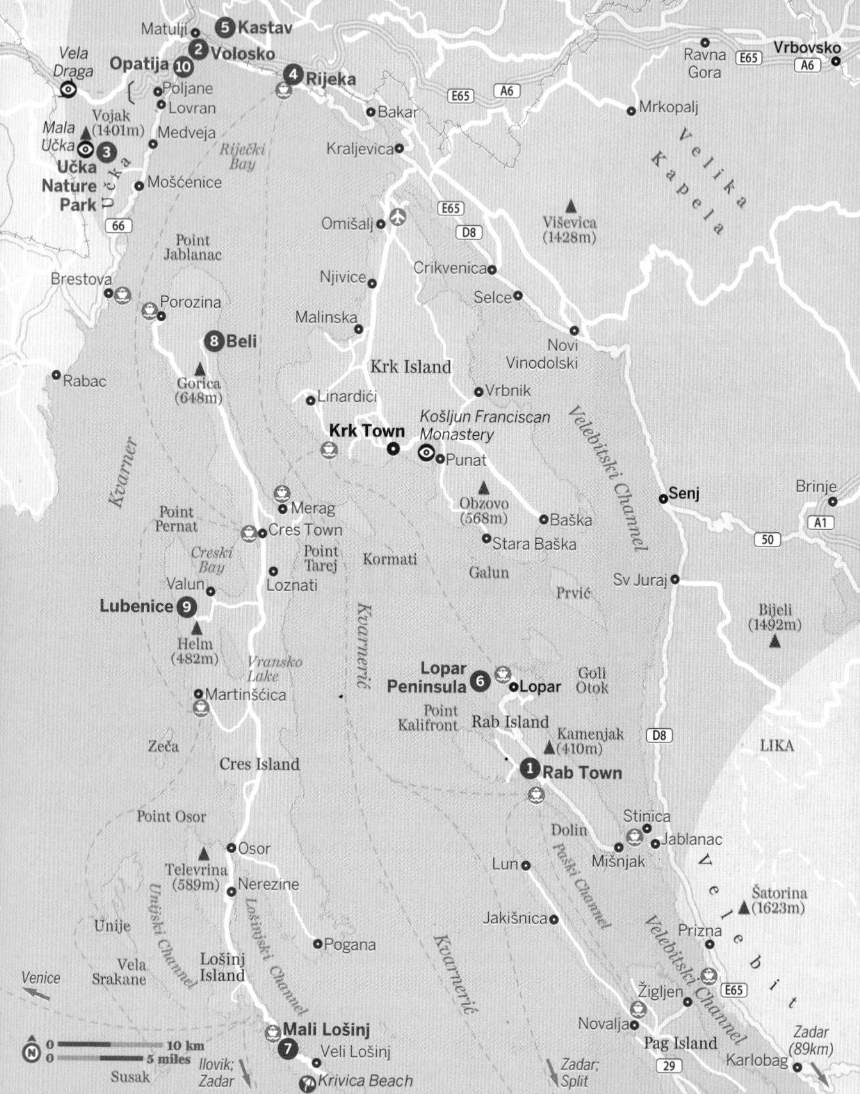

Kvarner Highlights

1 **Rab Town** (p204) Wandering the cobbled streets of this ancient town.

2 **Volosko** (p179) Sampling Croatian specialities in this diner's delight.

3 **Učka Nature Park** (p182) Finding bears and views in the high country.

4 **Trsat Castle** (p173) Admiring the panoramic views from Rijeka's castle.

5 **Kukuriku** (p180) Heading to the hills for a memorable meal in Kastav.

6 **Lopar** (p207) Seeking out remote Peninsula beaches.

7 **Mali Lošinj** (p189) Soaking up the buzzy waterfront vibe in summer.

8 **Beli** (p184) Losing yourself in this quiet corner of wonderful Cres Island.

9 **Lubenice** (p188) Swimming at one of Croatia's most secluded coves far below the dramatic village.

10 **Opatija** (p180) Adopting a Habsburg swagger as you stroll along the promenade.

RIJEKA

051 / POP 120,855

Croatia's third-largest city, Rijeka is a bustling blend of gritty 20th-century port and Italianate Habsburg grandeur. Most people speed through en route to the islands or Dalmatia, but those who pause will discover charm, culture, good nightlife, intriguing festivals and Croatia's most colourful carnival.

Despite some regrettable architectural ventures in the outskirts, much of the centre is replete with ornate Austro-Hungarian-style buildings. It's a surprisingly verdant city once you've left its concrete core, which contains Croatia's largest port, with ships, cargo and cranes lining the waterfront.

Rijeka is a vital transport hub, but as there's no real beach in the city most people base themselves in nearby Opatija.

History

Following their successful conquest of the indigenous Illyrian Liburnians, the Romans established a port here called Tarsaticae. Slavic tribes migrated to the region in the 7th century and built a new settlement within the old Roman town.

The town changed feudal masters – from German nobility to the Frankopan dukes of Krk – before becoming part of the Austrian empire in the late 15th century. Rijeka was an important outlet to the sea for the Austrians and a new road was built in 1725 connecting Vienna with the Kvarner coast. This spurred economic development, especially shipbuilding, the industry that has remained the centrepiece of Rijeka's economy ever since.

In 1750 Rijeka was hit by a devastating earthquake that destroyed much of its medieval heart. Thirty years later the old-town walls were removed to allow for the construction of a more modern commercial centre. Korzo, Rijeka's main pedestrian strip, was built as a grand avenue on the site of the demolished walls.

With the birth of the Austro-Hungarian dual monarchy in 1867, Rijeka was given over to the jurisdiction of the Hungarian government. Imposing municipal buildings were constructed and a new railway linked the city to Zagreb, Budapest and Vienna, bringing the first tourists to the Kvarner Gulf.

Between 1918, when Italian troops seized Rijeka and Istria, and 1945, when Rijeka became part of postwar Yugoslavia, it changed hands several times, with sporadic periods as a free city (known under its Italian name, Fiume). In 1991 Rijeka became part of independent Croatia, but it retains a sizeable, well-organised Italian minority who have their own newspaper, *La Voce del Popolo*.

Sights

The labyrinthine streets and squares in the ancient core of Rijeka have excellent multilingual plaques explaining the history of each sight.

★Trsat Castle CASTLE

(Trsatska Gradina; Petra Zrinskoga bb; adult/child 15/5KN; 9am-8pm Jun-Oct, to 5pm Nov-May) High on a hill above the city, this semiruined 13th-century fortress offers magnificent vistas from its bastions and ramparts, looking down the Rječina River valley to the docks, the Adriatic and the distant island of Krk. The present structure was built by the Frankopan dukes of Krk, but its latest facelift was in 1824, when Irish-born count Laval Nugent, a commander in the Austrian army, bought the castle and had it restored in a romantic neoclassical Biedermeier design.

Guarded by basilisks, the ancient-Greek-style Nugent family mausoleum houses a gallery, while underground a former dungeon hosts occasional exhibits. In summer the fortress stages concerts, theatre performances and fashion shows. The open-air cafe-bar (open until midnight in summer) is a wonderful spot to take in the views.

St Vitus' Cathedral CATHEDRAL

(Katedrala Sv Vida; Trg Grivica 11; 6am-5pm Mon-Fri, to noon Sat, 9am-1pm Sun) FREE North of Rijeka's **Roman Arch** (Rimski Luk; Stara Vrata) is this unusual round cathedral, built by the Jesuit order in 1638 on the site of an older church and dedicated to Rijeka's patron saint. If it looks familiar, it's probably because it features on the reverse of the 100KN note. Massive marble pillars support the central dome, under which are housed baroque altars and a 13th-century Gothic crucifix.

Maritime & History Museum MUSEUM

(Pomorski i Povijesni Muzej; 051-553 667; www.ppmhp.hr; Muzejski trg 1; adult/child 20/15KN; 9am-4pm Mon, to 8pm Tue-Sat, 4-8pm Sun) The star of this museum is the building itself, the former palace of the Austro-Hungarian governor. It's a splendid showcase of Hungarian architecture, with grand staircases, glittering chandeliers and many sumptuously restored rooms. The maritime collection includes Roman amphorae, model ships, sea charts, navigation instruments and portraits of captains; little of it is captioned in English.

Rijeka

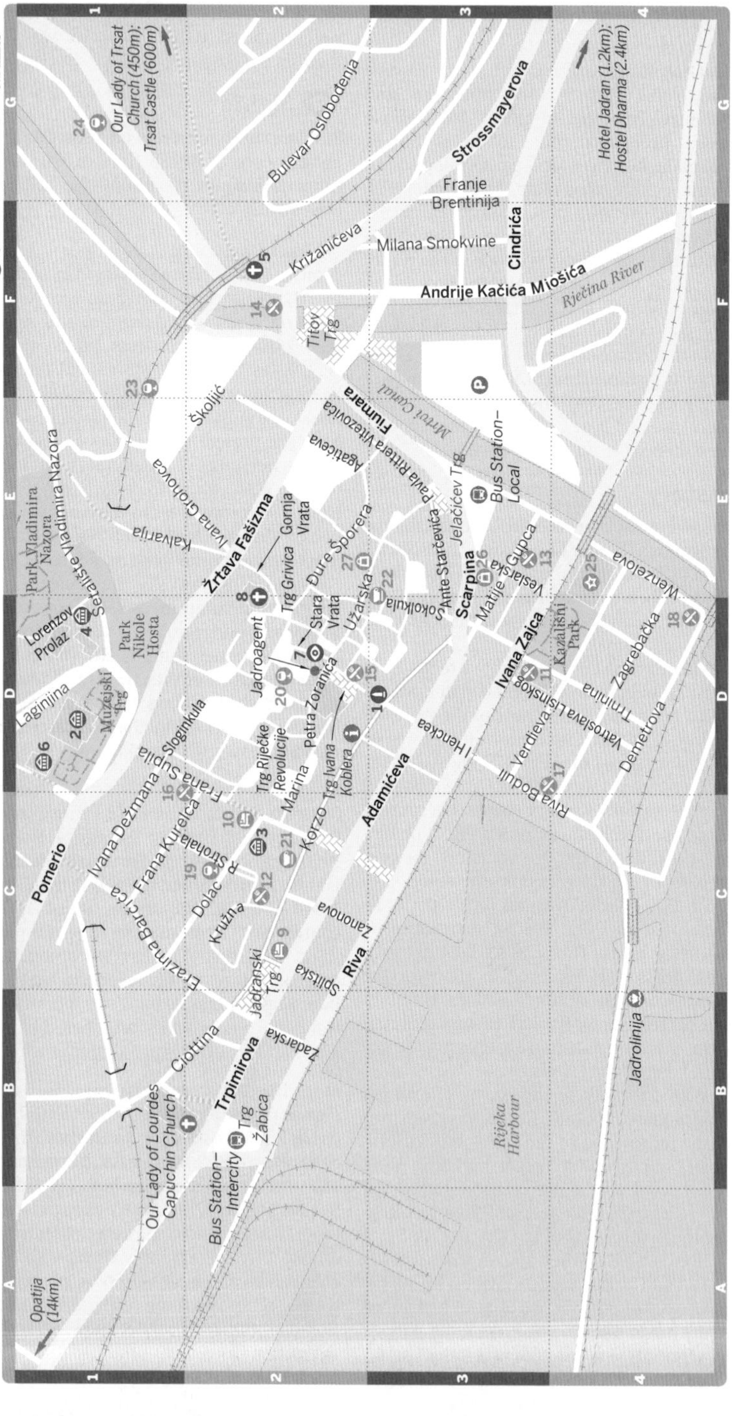

0 200 m
0 0.1 miles
Opatija (14km)
Pomerio
6
2
Laginjina
Muzejski Trg
Lorenzov Prolaz
4
Park Vladimira Nazora
Šetalište Vladimira Nazora
Park Nikole Hosta
24
Our Lady of Trsat Church (450m); Trsat Castle (600m)
23
Our Lady of Lourdes Capuchin Church
Ivana Dežmana
Erazima Barčića
Frana Kurelca
16
Frana Supila
Sloginkula
Kalvarija
Ivana Grohovca
Školjić
Ciottina
19
Dolac
R Strohala
Kružna
10
Bus Station–Intercity
Trg Žabica
Trpimirova
Jadranski Trg
12
3
Trg Riječke Revolucije
20
Jadroagent
8
Žrtava Fašizma
14
5
Trg Grivica
Gornja Vrata
Bulevar Oslobođenja
Križanićeva
9
21
Marina
7
Stara Vrata
Petra Zoranića
Đure Šporera
Titov Trg
Zadarska
Splitska
Zanonova
Korzo
Trg Ivana Koblera
15
1
Užarska
27
22
Agatićeva
Pavla Rittera Vitezovića
Fiumara
Riva
Adamićeva
Mrtvi Canal
Milana Smokvine
Franje Brentinija
Sokolkula
Ante Starčevića
Jelačićev Trg
Scarpina
I Henckea
26
Bus Station–Local
Andrije Kačića Miošića
Strossmayerova
Cindrića
Matije Gupca
Vešlarska
Rijeka Harbour
Riva Boduli
Verdieva
Ivana Zajca
11
13
17
Kazališni Park
25
Rječina River
Hotel Jadran (1.2km); Hostel Dharma (2.4km)
Vatroslava Lisinskog
Trninina
Zagrebačka
Demetrova
Wenzelova
Jadrolinija
18

Rijeka

Sights

1 City Tower D3
2 Maritime & History Museum D1
3 Museum of Modern & Contemporary Art C2
4 Natural History Museum D1
5 Petar Kružić Stairway F2
6 Rijeka City Museum D1
7 Roman Arch D2
8 St Vitus' Cathedral D2

Sleeping

9 Carnevale C2
10 Grand Hotel Bonavia C2

Eating

11 City Market D3
12 Conca D'Oro C2
13 Feral E3
14 Konoba Nebuloza F2
15 Maslina Na Zelenom Trgu D2
16 Mlinar C1
17 Mornar D3
18 Na Kantunu D4

Drinking & Nightlife

19 Bačva C2
20 CukariKafe D2
21 Filodrammatica Bookshop Cafe C2
22 Samovar Bar E3
23 Tunel F1
24 Život G1

Entertainment

25 Croatian National Theatre Ivan Zajc E4

Shopping

26 Paška Sirana E3
27 Šta Da? E2
VBZ .... (see 21)

Natural History Museum MUSEUM
(Prirodoslovni Muzej; www.prirodoslovni.com; Lorenzov Prolaz 1; adult/child 10/5KN; 9am-7pm Mon-Sat, to 3pm Sun) Located in a very grand 19th-century villa, this museum is devoted to the geology, botany and sea life of the Adriatic area. There's a small aquarium, exhibits on sharks, taxidermic animals and lots of insects. Don't miss the adjacent botanical garden, with more than 2000 native plant species.

Our Lady of Trsat Church CHURCH
(Crkva Gospe Trsatske; Frankopanski trg; 8am-5pm) According to legend, the angels carrying the house of Jesus' mother from Nazareth rested here in the late 13th century before moving it to Loreto across the Adriatic in Le Marche. Pilgrims started trickling into the chapel erected on the site, and then pouring in when the Pope donated an icon of St Mary in 1367 (it's located on the main altar, behind a magnificent wrought-iron gate). The church still attracts thousands of pilgrims each year.

View offerings of votive gifts in the baroque cloister and make an appointment to see the valuable sacral-art collection in the treasury, where you can watch a 15-minute film about the church.

To follow in the pilgrims' footsteps, climb the **Petar Kružić Stairway** from Titov trg. It was built in 1531 for the faithful to use on their way to the church, and it's lined with chapels once used as rest stops for the pilgrims. Alternatively, take a quick ride on city bus 2 to Trsat.

Museum of Modern & Contemporary Art GALLERY
(Muzej Moderne i Suvremene Umjetnosti; 051-334 280; www.mmsu.hr; Dolac 1; adult/child 20/10KN; 11am-8pm Tue-Fri, 11am-1pm & 5-8pm Sat & Sun) On the 2nd floor of the university library, this small museum puts on high-quality rotating shows, from street photography to contemporary drawings and sculptures.

City Tower TOWER
(Gradski Toranj; Korzo) One of the few buildings to have survived the 1750 earthquake, the distinctive yellow City Tower was originally a gate from the waterfront to the old town centre. The Habsburgs added the baroque decorations after the disaster, including the portal with coats of arms and busts of emperors. The still-functioning clock was mounted in 1873.

Rijeka City Museum MUSEUM
(Muzej Grada Rijeke; 051-336 711; www.muzej-rijeka.hr; Muzejski trg 1; adult/child 15/10KN; 10am-8pm Mon-Sat, to 3pm Sun) Housed in a boxy 1970s structure, this small museum houses ever-changing themed exhibitions ranging from art to aspects of local history. It's not worth crossing town for, but look in if you're up here to see the adjacent museums.

Festivals & Events

★ **Rijeka Carnival** CARNIVAL
(Riječki Karneval; www.rijecki-karneval.hr; mid-Jan–early Mar) Rio it isn't, but the largest

carnival in Croatia provides a good excuse to tarry in Rijeka between mid-January and Ash Wednesday. The festivities include pageants, street dances, concerts, masked balls, exhibitions and a parade. Check out the *zvončari,* masked men clad in animal skins who dance and ring loud bells to frighten off evil spirits.

Rijeka Summer Nights THEATRE
(Riječke Ljetne Noći; ⏲ Jun & Jul) Theatre performances and concerts are held at the Croatian National Theatre and on outdoor stages set up on the Korso and the beaches.

Sleeping

★ Hostel Dharma HOSTEL €
(☎051-562 108; www.dharmahostels.com; Spinčićeva 2; dm/s/tw 136/270/372KN; P ❄ 📶) A clever conversion of what was once an iron smelter on the eastern edge of town has produced this highly recommended hostel, with a yoga studio and vegetarian restaurant attached. Start your day with a free yoga class and tuck into a substantial vegetarian breakfast before chilling out in the large, verdant garden.

★ Carnevale HOSTEL €
(☎051-410 555; www.hostelcarnevale.com; Jadranski trg 1; dm/r 200/365KN; ❄ 📶) With metallic paint on the walls, billowing fabric on the ceilings, animal-print bed linen and art scattered everywhere, this supercentral hostel should put you in a festive mood. Towels are provided (and changed regularly) and there are big suitcase-size lockers. The only downside is that there's no kitchen.

Grand Hotel Bonavia HOTEL €€
(☎051-357 100; www.bonavia.hr; Dolac 4; r from 475KN; P ❄ 📶) Around for almost 140 years, this striking glass-fronted box of a hotel right in the heart of town offers well-equipped, comfortable, 21st-century rooms that are much more stylish than you might expect. There's also a restaurant, a spa and a small gym.

Hotel Jadran HOTEL €€€
(☎051-216 600; www.jadran-hoteli.hr; Šetalište XIII Divizije 46; s/d from 625/780KN; P ❄ @ 📶) Located 2km east of the centre, this immaculate four-star hotel clings to a cliff above the Adriatic: book a sea-view room and revel in the tremendous vistas from your balcony right above the water. There's a concrete-edged beach below, too.

Eating

★ Mlinar BAKERY €
(☎091 23 88 555; www.mlinar.hr; Frana Supila; snacks from 8KN; ⏲ 5.30am-8pm Mon-Fri, 6.30am-3pm Sat) The best bakery in town, with delicious filled baguettes, wholemeal bread, croissants and *burek* (pastry stuffed with meat, spinach or cheese). There are several branches around town and across Croatia.

Maslina Na Zelenom Trgu ITALIAN €
(☎051-563 563; www.pizzeria-maslina.hr; Koblerov trg bb; pizzas 32-65KN, mains 27-135KN; ⏲ 11am-midnight Mon-Sat) For the best pizza in the city centre head to this small Italian place with wobbly art nouveau decor and tiled tables. The wheels of pizza here are popular among Rijeka's Italian population. Grab an outdoor table in summer and enjoy the views of Rijeka's City Tower (p175).

City Market MARKET €
(Tržnica; Ivana Zajca 3; ⏲ 7am-2pm Mon-Sat, to noon Sun) This local market is one of the best places in town for seasonal fruit and vegetables.

★ Konoba Nebuloza CROATIAN €€
(☎051-374 501; www.konobanebuloza.com; Titov trg 2b; mains 50-120KN; ⏲ 11am-midnight Mon-Fri, from noon Sat) Straddling the line between modern and traditional Croatian fare, this slightly upmarket riverside restaurant serves lots of seafood along with selected beef and turkey dishes. Specialities include sous-vide swordfish and baby rump steak with prosciutto and cheese. The chef seems to have a thing about mangel-wurzel, a vegetable you may never have eaten (or heard of).

★ Mornar BISTRO €€
(☎051-312 222; www.facebook.com/bistromornar; Riva Boduli 5a; mains 40-115KN; ⏲ noon-11pm) Amid the unappealing industrial surrounds of Rijeka's port, this lovely little white-wood bistro serves up excellent fish dishes, as well as a few grilled meats and pasta plates. The service is friendly, the cooking assured. The fish soup is particularly enjoyable.

Na Kantunu CROATIAN, SEAFOOD €€
(☎051-313 271; Demetrova 2; mains 50-110KN; ⏲ 8am-11pm Mon-Sat) Fresh fish and seafood are the stars of the show at this bright and breezy restaurant in a somewhat-grimy location by the port. It's a good place to try

traditional fish or octopus stews, followed by crispy fruit pastries.

Conca D'Oro SEAFOOD, ITALIAN €€
(☎051-213 782; www.facebook.com/concadorori; Kružna 12; mains 50-150KN; ⏰11am-11pm Mon-Sat; 🐾) Savour superbly prepared seafood, Italian pasta and risottos, and choice Croatian wines at this formal though oddly decorated restaurant (the interior features Gaudí-esque columns and stones implanted into the walls). Daily specials such as *pečena hobotnica* (roast octopus) are chalked up on a board.

Feral CROATIAN €€
(☎051-212 274; www.konoba-feral.com; Matije Gupca 5b; mains 60-180KN; ⏰8am-midnight Mon-Sat, noon-6pm Sat) This unassuming restaurant is popular with locals during the day as a cafe, but its meals are particularly good – try the grilled vegetables or the smoked sardines, but don't miss the grilled fish and seafood, cooked to perfection.

Drinking & Entertainment

The main drags of Riva and Korzo are the best bet for a drink, with everything from lounge bars to no-nonsense pubs.

★Samovar Bar CAFE
(☎051-215 521; www.samovar.hr; Trg Matije Vlačića Flaciusa; ⏰7am-10pm Mon-Sat) This warmly eclectic place has a wonderful array of teas, terrific coffees and other drinks such as a stellar rose lemonade. The decoration is delightfully retro, with everything from chandeliers to teddy bears.

★Tunel BAR, CLUB
(Školjić 12; ⏰9am-midnight Tue & Wed, to 2am Thu, to 3am Fri, 7pm-3am Sat; 📶) Tucked beneath the railway tracks in an actual tunnel, this popular place morphs from daytime cafe to comedy and live-music venue to late-night club. It gets rammed at weekends.

Bačva BAR
(Rudolfa Strohala 3; ⏰noon-midnight Mon-Wed, to 1am Thu, to 2am Fri & Sat) Craft and foreign beers, great music and fun decor add up to a good central night-time option. There's also live music some weekends, and then the atmosphere really rocks.

Život CLUB
(☎051-335 882; www.facebook.com/KlubZivot; Ružićeva 2; ⏰10pm-5am Fri & Sat) Funky, retro weekend-only nightclub for the over 25s playing '80s and '90s hits and much more. The decor is an eclectic mix of grandmotherly antiques and hipster junk.

CukariKafe BAR
(☎099 58 38 276; Trg Jurja Klovica 2; ⏰7am-midnight Mon-Thu, to 2am Fri & Sat, 10am-10pm Sun) Tucked into a tiny lane in the old part of town, this is Rijeka's coolest cafe-bar. Grab a seat on the oversized white wooden furniture on the covered deck or head inside to admire the oddball art nouveau–style knick-knacks. Enjoy great coffee and cakes along with a soothing soundtrack.

Filodrammatica Bookshop Cafe CAFE, BAR
(☎051-211 696; Korzo 28; ⏰7am-11pm) A cafe-bar with luxurious decor, comfy sofas and a **VBZ** (☎051-324 010; www.vbz.hr; Korzo 32; ⏰7.30am-7.30pm Mon-Fri, to 5pm Sat) – Croatia's biggest publisher – bookshop at the back, Filodrammatica prides itself on specialist coffees and fresh, single-source coffee beans. It also serves sandwiches and snacks.

Entertainment

Croatian National Theatre Ivan Zajc THEATRE
(Hrvatsko Narodnog Kažalište Ivana pl Zajca; ☎051-337 114; www.hnk-zajc.hr; Verdieva 5a) In 1885 the inaugural performance at this imposing theatre was lit by the city's first lightbulb. These days you can catch dramas in Croatian and Italian, as well as opera and ballet. Gustav Klimt painted some of the ceiling frescos.

Shopping

★Paška Sirana CHEESE
(☎051-734 205; www.paskasirana.hr; Scarpina 3) Shopping for a picnic? This fine little shop sells all manner of Croatian cheeses and you can usually try some before you buy.

TOURIST CARD

The **Rijeka&Opatija Tourist Card** (www.touristcard.hr) offers a 24-/48-/72-hour discount card for 45/75/105KN. It includes free admission to museums in both cities, as well as some free parking and public transport. Buy it at the tourist offices in Rijeka (p178) or Opatija (p182).

Šta Da? GIFTS & SOUVENIRS

(Užarska 14; ⌚10am-8pm Mon-Fri, to 1pm Sat) Literally translating as 'what yes?', *'šta da'* is an idiom peculiar to Rijeka meaning something like 'you what!?' or 'really, you don't say!'. This cool little store stocks T-shirts, jewellery and clocks, including many emblazoned with images of its logo and of the distinctive orange local buses.

Information

Clinical Hospital Center Rijeka (Klinički Bolnički Centar Rijeka; ☎051-658 111; www.kbc-rijeka.hr; Krešimirova 42)

Tourist Office (☎051-335 882; www.visitrijeka.hr; Korzo 14; ⌚8am-8pm Mon-Sat, to 2pm Sun) Has good colour city maps, a few brochures and private accommodation lists.

Getting There & Away

AIR

Rijeka Airport (Zračna Luka Rijeka; ☎051-841 222; www.rijeka-airport.hr; Hamec 1, Omišalj), located 30km from town on the island of Krk, is only used for seasonal flights from April to October. There are international flights to London, Oslo, Warsaw and more. The only domestic routes are **Trade Air** (☎091 62 65 111; www.trade-air.com) services to Dubrovnik, Split and Osijek.

BOAT

Jadroagent (☎051-212 466; www.jadroagent.hr; Trg Ivana Koblera 2;) Has information on all boats around Croatia.

Jadrolinija (☎051-211 444; www.jadrolinija.hr; Riječki Lukobran bb) A daily catamaran connects Rijeka to Rab Town (80KN, 1¾ hours) and Novalja on Pag (80KN, 2¾ hours).

BUS

The **intercity bus station** (☎051-660 300; Trg Žabica 1) is in the town centre. Buses for Opatija (28KN, 20 minutes) leave from the **local bus station** (Jelačićev trg).

Based in Rijeka, **Autotrans** (☎051-660 660; www.autotrans.hr) has connections to Istria, Zagreb, Varaždin and Kvarner. Try also **Flixbus** (https://www.flixbus.com).

Cres 110KN, two hours 20 minutes, up to four daily

Dubrovnik From 348KN, 12½ hours, two daily

Krk 64KN, one hour 20 minutes, hourly

Pula 89KN, 2½ hours, up to 18 daily

Rovinj 115KN, two hours 20 minutes, up to five daily

Split From 236KN, eight hours, up to seven daily

Zadar 156KN, four hours, nine daily

Zagreb From 85KN, 2½ hours, at least hourly

TRAIN

The **train station** (Željeznički Kolodvor; www.hzpp.hr; Trg Kralja Tomislava 1) is a 10-minute walk east of the city centre. Direct services include the following:

Ljubljana 129KN, three hours, two daily

Osijek 232KN, nine hours, daily

Zagreb 119KN, 3¾ hours, three daily

Getting Around

TO/FROM THE AIRPORT

Rijeka Airport is on Krk Island, 30km from Rijeka.

An airport bus meets all flights for the 30-minute ride to the intercity bus station; it leaves for the airport two hours and 20 minutes before flight times. You can buy a ticket (50KN) on the bus.

Taxis from the airport charge 255KN for up to four people to the centre.

BUS

Rijeka has an extensive network of orange city buses run by **Autotrolej** (☎051-311 400; www.autotrolej.hr), operating from the local bus station. Buy two-trip tickets for 15.50KN from any *tisak* (news-stand). A single ticket from the driver costs 10KN.

The same company also operates a 24-hour, colourful, open-topped, double-decker, hop-on, hop-off sightseeing bus (adult/child 50/35KN) that runs between central Rijeka, Trsat and Opatija. The ticket is also valid for travel on all city buses.

TAXI

Taxis are very reasonable in Rijeka (if you use the right firm). **Cammeo** (☎051-313 313; www.taxi-cammeo.hr) cabs are modern and inexpensive, have meters and are highly recommended; a ride in the central area costs 25KN.

AROUND RIJEKA

Rijeka's mountainous surrounds are home to wolfs, bears, lynx and abundant birdlife. You might spot silver foxes in upmarket Opatija, but strictly of the two-legged variety.

Risnjak National Park

Relatively isolated and rarely visited, despite being only 32km northeast of Rijeka, **Risnjak National Park** (Nacionalni Park Risnjak; ☎051-836 133; www.np-risnjak.hr; 2-day pass adult/child 45/25KN) covers an area of 63 sq km and rises up to 1528m at its highest peak, Veliki Risnjak. The landscape linking the Alps with the Balkan ranges is thickly forested with beech and pine trees, and carpeted with meadows and wildflowers. The bracing alpine breezes make it the perfect hideaway when the coastal heat and crowds become overpowering. Most of the park is virgin forest, with only a few settlements. Wildlife-watching is a highlight.

Activities

Most visitors come here to hike, with the easy Leska Path of most appeal to day visitors. To hike further in to scale the minor summits of Risnjak or Snježnik, contact the park office for advice. Trekking to Kupa Spring is another highlight.

Sport fishing and mountain biking are also possible.

Leska Path HIKING

The starting point for the Leska Path, an easy and shady 4.2km trail, is at the Park Information Office. The route is punctuated by several dozen explanatory panels (with English translations) telling you all about the park's history, topography, geology, flora and fauna. Allow around two hours to complete the route.

You'll pass crystal-clear streams, forests of tall fir trees, bizarre rock formations, a feeding station for the deer and a mountain hut with a picnic table.

Sleeping

Hotel Risnjak HOTEL €€

(☎051-508 160; www.hotel-risnjak.hr; Lujzinska 36; s/d 370/620KN; P 📶) This yellow three-storey building has its charm, and inside there are 21 slightly tired rooms, a restaurant (known for its game dishes), a cafe-bar and a gym. The hotel organises activities (paragliding, rafting, canoeing, paintball, archery, skiing, canyon visits) for groups of 10 or more; ask if there are any you can join.

Information

Park Information Office (☎051-836 133; www.np-risnjak.hr; Bijela Vodica 48, Crni Lug; ⏰9am-5pm; 📶) The park information office is just west of the village of Crni Lug. There's a restaurant attached and five simple, clean B&B rooms above, costing 300/480KN per single/double; half- or full-board rates are possible.

Getting There & Away

To access the park by car, exit the main Zagreb–Rijeka motorway at Delnice and follow the signs.

RISNJAK WILDLIFE

The park is home to three charismatic mammal species: the brown bear, wolf and Eurasian lynx, a fluffy-eared, medium-sized wild cat. The park is considered one of the last refuges in the country for the latter, which gives its name to the park (lynx is *ris* in Croatian). All three animals are difficult to see and you'll need to visit with a guide or visit over a number of days to stand any chance. Other wildlife includes wild cats, wild boar, deer, chamois and 500 species of butterfly.

At last count, 114 bird species have been recorded in Risnjak; birders get particularly excited about the capercaillie, peregrine falcon, pygmy owl, Ural owl, tawny owl, white-backed woodpecker and three-toed woodpecker.

There's no public transport to the park, but Delnice has the following bus connections:

Opatija 60KN, one hour 10 minutes, two daily
Pula 139KN, 3½ hours, two daily
Rijeka 48KN, 45 minutes, roughly hourly
Zagreb 99KN, two hours, nine daily

There are also trains to Delnice (43KN, 1¼ hours, six daily) from Rijeka.

Volosko

☎051 / POP 315

Some 2km east of Opatija, Volosko is one of the prettiest places on this section of the Kvarner coastline, a fishing village that has also become something of a restaurant hot spot in recent decades. This is no tourist resort, though, and it's very scenic indeed: fishers repair nets in the tiny harbour, while stone houses with flower-laden balconies rise up from the coast via a warren of narrow alleyways. Whether you're passing through for a drink or having a gourmet meal, you're sure to enjoy the local ambience and wonderful setting.

Sleeping & Eating

★ **Design Hotel Navis** DESIGN HOTEL €€€

(☎051-444 600; www.hotel-navis.hr; Ivana Matetića Ronjgova 10; s/d 1400/1900KN; P ❄ @ 📶) Seeming to cling to the cliff face, this stunning place has achingly stylish rooms with floor-to-ceiling windows looking out over the Adriatic. There's a spa and wellness centre, and a good restaurant.

DON'T MISS

GOING KUKURIKU IN KASTAV

If food is your thing, it's well worth taking a drive to Kastav, an atmospheric fortified hilltop town filled with stone churches and squares, 10km from Rijeka and 7km from Opatija.

At slow-food pioneer Nenad Kukurin's wonderful hotel-restaurant, **Kukuriku** (051-691 519; www.kukuriku.hr; Trg Lokvina 3, Kastav; 6-course meal 420-600KN; 7am-midnight; P ❄), there's no menu, so you need to be prepared to place your trust in the staff. Tell them whether you prefer meat, fish or vegetarian, and whether you have any particular dislikes or dietary requirements (or budget constraints). Then prepare for course after course of delicious, beautifully presented, innovative, local cuisine.

To top it all off, there are 15 extremely chic rooms here – handy if you're planning to partake in the recommended matches from the excellent wine list. And if you're wondering about the rooster-themed paraphernalia scattered about, *kukuriku* is the Croatian take on 'cock-a-doodle-doo'.

★**Konoba Valle Losca** CROATIAN €€
(095 58 03 757; Andrije Štangera 2; mains 90-100KN; 11.30am-2pm & 5pm-midnight) The word *konoba* usually denotes a little family-run eatery – most of which have identikit menus. Here, French and Italian techniques combine with top-notch local ingredients to take things to another level entirely. But don't come here if you're in a hurry – it takes time to fully savour the deliciously rustic dishes, served by multilingual staff in the stone-walled dining room.

Skalinada CROATIAN €€
(051-701 109; www.skalinada.org; Uz Dol 17; snacks & mains from 25-110KN; 1pm-midnight Sun, Mon, Wed & Thu, 3pm-2am Fri & Sat) An intimate, highly atmospheric, wholly unpretentious little restaurant-bar with sensitive lighting, exposed stone walls and a creative menu of Croatian food (small dishes or mains) using seasonal and local ingredients. Many local wines available by the glass.

★**Plavi Podrum** CROATIAN €€€
(051-701 223; www.plavipodrum.com; Obala Frana Supila 6; mains from 220KN; noon-midnight) One of Kvarner's best restaurants, Plavi Podrum does wonderful, innovative cooking perfectly paired with great wines and olive oils. Its standout dishes include risotto with scampi and truffle (or wild asparagus); sea bass, foie gras and pumpkin-and-coriander purée; and scampi skewers with a dusting of coffee and black Istrian truffle accompanied by monkfish reduction and apple purée.

Getting There & Away

From Opatija, walk along the coastal promenade, a 30-minute stroll past bay trees, palms, figs, oaks and magnificent villas. If travelling on public transport, take any bus between Rijeka (25KN, 25 minutes) and Opatija; make sure your bus isn't running express, thereby skipping Volosko.

Opatija

051 / POP 11,145

Genteel Opatija, 13km west of Rijeka, was the most chic seaside resort for the Austro-Hungarian elite during the days of the Austro-Hungarian Empire – as evidenced by the many handsome belle époque villas that the period bequeathed the town. Although it lost a lot of its sheen during the Yugoslav period, Opatija has spruced itself up in the last decade and once again attracts a mainly mature crowd, drawn to its grand spa hotels, spectacular location and agreeable year-round climate. Some excellent restaurants have sprung up to cater to them, with a particularly good cluster in pretty Volosko, just up the road.

The town sprawls along the coast between forested hills and the sparkling Adriatic, and the whole waterfront is connected by a promenade. Don't expect great beaches (there aren't any), but there's still excellent swimming in the sheltered bays.

History

Until the 1840s Opatija was a minuscule fishing village with 35 houses and a church, but the arrival of wealthy Iginio Scarpa from Rijeka turned things around. He built Villa Angiolina (named after his wife) and surrounded it with exotic subtropical plants. The villa hosted European aristocrats aplenty (including the Austrian queen Maria Anna, wife of emperor Ferdinand I) and Opatija's classy reputation was sealed.

Opatija's development was also assisted by the completion of a direct rail link to Vienna, which opened in 1873. Construction of Opatija's first hotel, the Quarnero (today the Hotel Kvarner), began and wealthy visitors arrived en masse. It seemed that everyone who was anyone was compelled to visit Opatija, including kings from Romania and Sweden, Russian tsars and celebrities of the day.

Today Opatija remains a refined (some would say conservative) resort that's very popular with German and Austrian seniors.

Sights

Croatian Museum of Tourism MUSEUM
(Hrvatski Muzej Turizma; ☎051-603 636; www.hrmt.hr; Park Angiolina 1; adult/child 15/7KN; ⏰10am-1pm & 5-9pm Tue-Sun Jul & Aug, 10am-6pm Tue-Sun Apr-Jun, Sep, Oct & Dec, 10am-5pm Tue-Sun Nov & Jan-Mar) Spread between three historic buildings, this excellent museum houses a permanent collection of old photographs, postcards, brochures and posters tracing the history of tourism, and there's always a well-presented travel-themed exhibition as well. But it's the buildings themselves that are the main attraction. The restored **Villa Angiolina** is one of Opatija's grandest structures – a marvel of trompe l'œil frescos, Corinthian capitals, gilded mirrors and geometric floor mosaics – though the addition of modern windows is a crime against architecture.

Verdant gardens surround the villa, replete with ginkgo trees, sequoias, holm oaks, Japanese camellias (Opatija's symbol) and even a little open-air theatre where costumed recitals are held. Neighbouring **Swiss House** (1875) was an outbuilding of the main villa, used partly as a buttery. Further west, past St James' Church, the **Juraj Šporer Artistic Pavillion** (1900) was originally built as a patisserie.

Lungomare WATERFRONT
Lined with majestic villas and ample gardens, this wonderful path (more formally known as the Franz Joseph I Promenade) is a people-watcher's dream and stroller's delight. It winds along the coast, past villa after villa, for 12km from Volosko to Lovran via the villages of Ičići and Ika. Along the way you can peer into the homes of the wealthy and marvel at their seafront palaces.

The path weaves through exotic bushes, thickets of bamboo, a marina and rocky bays where you can throw down a towel and jump into the sea – a better option than Opatija's concrete beach.

Sleeping

Autocamp Medveja CAMPGROUND €
(☎051-710 444; www.liburnia.hr/en/camping-medveja; Medveja bb; pitch for 3 people 400KN, units 1100KN; ⏰Easter–mid-Oct; P❄@) Given the lack of affordable hotels in Opatija, the new mobile homes and simple en suite rooms at this peaceful campground are worth considering. It's set in a cleft in the mountains in a leafy valley leading to a pretty pebbly cove, 10km south of Opatija. You can pay for full and half board, and facilities are well maintained.

Borka B&B €€
(☎051-712 118; Maršala Tita 192; s/d 420/525KN; 📶) Just about the only cheapish formal accommodation provider in Opatija, this old B&B in a pink villa has basic rooms, brown-tiled bathrooms and a flower-filled garden.

★ **Hotel Miramar** HOTEL €€€
(☎051-280 000; www.hotel-miramar.info; Ive Kaline 11; r from 1800KN; P❄@📶🏊) Marketed primarily to a German-speaking clientele, the Miramar is glam almost to the point of kitsch, but it's fabulous nonetheless. The space-rich rooms are spread between five pastel buildings, set amid lovely gardens, and there's a rocky little beach, indoor and outdoor pools, a spa centre and a surfeit of chandeliers.

Villa Ariston HOTEL €€€
(☎051-271 379; www.villa-ariston.hr; Maršala Tita 179; r 1500-2000KN; P❄📶) With a gorgeous location beside a rocky cove, this historic hotel has celebrity cachet in spades (Coco Chanel and the Kennedys were guests here). The interior remains grand and impressive, with a sweeping staircase, chandeliers and plenty of period charm. Many rooms have sea views, though the mansard rooms are a bit poky for these prices.

Eating & Drinking

★ **Kaneta** ISTRIAN €€
(☎051-291 643; Nova 80; mains 50-120KN; ⏰10am-11pm Mon-Sat, noon-7pm Sun) This unassuming family-run restaurant specialises in big flavours and generous portions: feast on roast veal shanks, roast octopus, game stew, turkey, homemade pasta and risotto. The wine list is well chosen.

Pizzeria Roko PIZZA €€
(☎051-711 500; www.roko-opatija.com; Maršala Tita 114; mains 45-110KN; ⏰11am-midnight) Not just great wheels of heavily laden pizza but also

risottos, salads, seafood and cakes are on offer at this rare treat of an affordable Opatija eatery. The food is imaginatively served, portions are large and service is superb. The dining room is simple whitewashed brick and the kitchen is open for anyone to view the food being prepared.

★**Bevanda** EUROPEAN €€€
(051-493 888; www.bevanda.hr; Zert 8; set menus 690-390KN, mains 210-385KN) A marble pathway leads to this striking restaurant, which enjoys a huge ocean-facing terrace complete with Grecian columns and hip monochrome seating. The contemporary menu features terrific fresh-fish and meat dishes, including lots of indulgences (lobster and the like). It was ranked seventh in the whole country in Croatia's prestigious Good Restaurants awards in 2017.

Hemingway COCKTAIL BAR
(051-711 205; www.hemingway.hr/opatija; Zert 2; noon-late) A very sleek bar ideal for a cocktail session, with cool seating and distant views of the Rijeka skyline. It's the original venue of what's now a nationwide chain; there's an adjoining restaurant, too.

Shopping

Kredenca GIFTS & SOUVENIRS
(091 54 47 294; www.kredenca.com; Maršala Tita; 9am-6pm) Wines, olive oils, jams, and a few Croatian handicrafts, cosmetics and accessories make this one of the better places in town to go shopping.

Information

The free 'Discover Opatija Riviera' app is available from app stores.

Da Riva (051-272 990; www.da-riva.hr; Nova 10) A good source of private accommodation and excursions around Croatia.

Kvarner Touristik (051-703 723; www.kvarner-touristik.com; Maršala Tita 162) Books accommodation in Opatija and northern Croatia as well as offering a range of activities and hire services.

Tourist Office (051-271 310; www.visitopatija.com; Maršala Tita 128; 8am-8pm Mon-Sat, 11am-7pm Sun mid-Jun–Aug, shorter hours rest of year) This office has knowledgeable staff and lots of maps, leaflets and brochures.

Getting There & Away

Bus 32 runs roughly every half-hour from Rijeka to Opatija (25KN, 20 minutes) and as far as Lovran; some services continue further south along the coast.

Other destinations include the following:

Pula 90KN, two hours, six daily
Rovinj 124KN, three hours, two daily
Zagreb 112KN, 3¼ hours, four daily

Učka Nature Park

One of Croatia's best-kept natural secrets, this 160-sq-km rarely visited park lies just 30 minutes from the Opatija riviera. Comprising the Učka mountain massif and the adjacent Ćićarija plateau, it's officially split between Kvarner and Istria. On clear days Vojak (1401m), its highest peak, affords sublime views of the Italian Alps and the Bay of Trieste.

Much of the area is covered by beech forest, but there are also sweet-chestnut trees, oaks and hornbeams, as well as 40 species of orchid. Sheep graze the alpine meadows, golden eagles fly overhead, brown bears roam, as do wild boar and roe deer, and endemic bellflowers blossom.

The main access point is the Poklon pass.

Sights

Vela Draga CANYON
The spectacular canyon of Vela Draga on the eastern side of the park is an astounding sight, its valley floor scattered with limestone pillars or 'fairy chimneys'. Raptors, including kestrels and peregrine falcons, can be seen cruising the thermals here, and eagle owls and wallcreepers are also present. From the highway it's a lovely 15-minute descent along an interpretive trail to a viewpoint over the canyon.

Mala Učka VILLAGE
This half-abandoned village at over 995m above sea level is an intriguing place. A few shepherds live here from May to October, and you can buy delicious sheep cheese from the house with green windows by the stream at the village's end. Just ask for *sir* (cheese).

Activities & Tours

For mountain-biking trails, download the park's Učka-Bike pdf from www.pp-ucka.hr.

★**Day With Ranger** TOURS
(051-299 643; www.pp-ucka.hr/en/information-for-visitors/guided-tours; Poklon Information Centre; per person 200KN; 10am-4pm May-Oct) On the six-hour 'Day With Ranger', you explore the park with one of its rangers, both on foot and in a 4WD. It's a wonderful way to get to know the park and go where no other visi-

tors can reach. It begins and ends at the Poklon Information Centre at 10am. Advance bookings essential.

Electric Bike Rental CYCLING
(☎051-299 643; www.pp-ucka.hr; 1/3/6/9hr rental 40/90/150/180KN; ⏲9am-7pm Jul & Aug, 9am-5pm Mon-Fri, to 7pm Sat & Sun Jun & Sep, 9am-5pm May & Oct) Rent an electric bike to scale those hills from either the Poklon Information Centre or the main park information office .

Sleeping & Eating

There are seven guesthouses and weekend-only mountain refuges within the park boundaries. See the park website (www.pp-ucka.hr), under 'Information for Visitors', for details.

Dopolavoro CROATIAN €€
(☎051-299 641; www.dopolavoro.hr; Učka 9; mains 59-145KN; ⏲noon-11pm) Dopolavoro offers excellent game – deer steak with blueberries, wild boar with forest mushrooms, venison stew – as well as homemade pasta and delicious sweet platters.

Information

Staff at the **park office** (☎051-293 753; www.pp-ucka.hr; Liganj 42, Lovran; ⏲8am-4.30pm Mon-Fri) will help plan your trip. There are also two seasonal info points, one at **Poklon** (☎051-299 643; ⏲9am-6pm mid-Jun–mid-Sep) and another at **Vojak** (☎091 89 59 669; ⏲9am-6pm mid-Jun–mid-Sep).

Getting There & Away

Local bus 32 leaves Opatija for Poklon at 9.30am and 2.05pm, returning at 10.30am and 3.45pm. Lovran, at the eastern edge of the park, is served by bus from Rijeka (32KN, 30 minutes, nine daily). There's a car park at the **Poklon Information Centre**.

LOŠINJ & CRES ISLANDS

Separated only by an 11m-wide canal and joined by a bridge, these two sparsely populated and scenic islands in the Kvarner archipelago are often treated as a single entity. Although their topography is different, the islands' identities are blurred by a shared history.

Nature lovers will be in heaven here. Both islands are criss-crossed by hiking and biking trails, and the surrounding waters are home to the only known resident population of dolphins in the Adriatic. Much of the sea off the eastern coast is protected by the Lošinj Dolphin Reserve, the first of its kind in the Mediterranean.

Wilder, greener and more mountainous Cres (Cherso in Italian) has remote campgrounds, pristine beaches, a handful of medieval villages and a real off-the-beaten-track feel. The 31km-long Lošinj (Lussino in Italian) is more populated and touristy and offers more lush vegetation.

History

Excavations indicate that a prehistoric culture spread out over both Lošinj Island and Cres Island from the Stone Age to the Bronze Age. The ancient Greeks called the islands the Apsyrtides. The islands were in turn conquered by the Romans, then put under Byzantine rule and settled by Slavic tribes in the 6th and 7th centuries.

The islands subsequently came under rule of the Venetians, then the Croatian-Hungarian kings, then the Venetians again. By the time Venice fell in 1797, the towns of Veli Lošinj and Mali Lošinj had become important maritime centres, while Cres devoted itself to wine and olive production.

CYCLING THE KVARNER

The Kvarner region offers a variety of options for biking enthusiasts, from gentle rides to heart-pumping climbs on steep island roads. There are several trails around Opatija: two easier paths depart from Mt Kastav (360m), while a challenging 4½-hour adventure goes from Lovran to Učka Nature Park. Lošinj offers a moderately difficult 2½-hour route that starts and ends in Mali Lošinj. On Krk, a leisurely two-hour ride from Krk Town shows you the meadows, fields and hamlets of the island's little-visited interior. A biking route from Rab Town explores the virgin forests of the Kalifront Peninsula. On Cres, a 50km trail takes you from the marina at Cres Town past the medieval hilltop village of Lubenice and the seaside gem of Valun.

For details of these itineraries, ask at any tourist office for the *Kvarner by Bicycle* brochure, which outlines 19 routes across the region. The websites www.kvarner.hr and www.pedala.hr both have details of rides in this region.

During the 19th century shipbuilding flourished in Lošinj, but with the advent of steamships health tourism overtook shipbuilding as the major industry. Meanwhile, Cres had its own problems in the form of a phylloxera epidemic that wiped out its vineyards. Both islands were poor when they were annexed to Italy as part of the 1922 Treaty of Rapallo. They became part of Yugoslavia in 1945 and, most recently, Croatia in 1991.

Today, apart from a small shipyard in Nerezine in north Lošinj and some olive cultivation, sheep farming and fishing on Cres, the main source of income on both islands is tourism. Until very recently one of Cres' main income sources was rearing sheep (the island's lamb is famed for its flavour), but the introduction of wild boar for hunting has upset the unique environment and an age-old culture is now waning.

Getting There & Away

BOAT

Jadrolinija (051-231 765; www.jadrolinija.hr; Riva Lošinjskih Kapetana 22, Mali Lošinj) runs the main car ferries between Brestova (on the mainland, 29km south of Opatija) and Porozina on Cres (adult/child/car 18/9/115KN, 20 minutes, seven to 13 daily), and between Valbiska on Krk and Merag on Cres (adult/child/car 18/9/115KN, 25 minutes, nine to 13 daily). A weekly (daily in July and August) car ferry runs between Mali Lošinj and Zadar (adult/child/car 59/30/271KN, seven hours), stopping at some of the smaller islands en route.

A daily passenger-only catamaran connects Mali Lošinj and Rijeka (60KN, four hours) via Cres Town (45KN, 2½ hours). There's also a passenger-only ferry that loops from Mali Lošinj to the islands of Unije (1½ hours) and Susak (one hour) twice daily.

BUS

Most bus services in the islands begin (or end) in Veli Lošinj and stop in Mali Lošinj and Cres. Off-island destinations include Malinska on Krk (130KN, 2¾ hours, two daily), Opatija (185KN, 3¾ hours, two daily), Rijeka (154KN, four hours, three daily) and Zagreb (from 175KN, seven hours, three daily).

Beli

051 / POP 35

Clinging to a 130m hill above a lovely pebbly beach, Beli is one of Cres' oldest settlements. Its 4000-year history can be felt in its twisting lanes and austere stone town houses overgrown with plants. You can walk a loop around this evocative but diminutive settlement in five minutes or so, stopping at a viewpoint to take in incredible views over the Adriatic to the mainland mountains.

Even with its tiny population, Beli is the main settlement in the Tramuntana region, which covers the island's northern tip. It's a place that time forgot, with ancient virgin forests, abandoned villages, lone chapels and myths of good elves. Much of it is covered with dense oak, hornbeam and chestnut forest and it's prime cruising terrain for the protected griffon vulture.

Sights

Beli Beach BEACH

An archetypal Adriatic beach – secluded, wonderfully quiet and strewn with pebbles – 130m below the pretty village of Beli.

Rescue Centre for Griffon Vultures ANIMAL SANCTUARY

(095 50 61 116; www.facebook.com/BeliVisitorCentre; Beli 4; adult/child 40/20KN; 10am-4pm)

TRAMUNTANA SHEEP

Cres' semiwild Tramuntana sheep are unique to the island and perfectly adapted to the karst pastures that were first developed by the Illyrians more than 1000 years ago. But now the island's culture of free-range sheep farming is on the slide. A couple of decades ago Cres had 100,000 Tramuntana sheep; now it's around 15,000. One of the main factors in this decline has been the introduction of wild boar by Croatia's powerful hunting lobby. Boar numbers have grown exponentially (they have even spread as far as the campsites in Mali Lošinj). Wild boar prey on sheep and lambs.

Declining sheep numbers have an impact on the environment in many ways. Griffon vultures now don't have enough sheep carrion to survive on, and they have to be fed at feeding sites by volunteers. As pastureland has dwindled, juniper and thornbush have replaced native grasses and wildflowers, with a resulting drop in plant biodiversity. *Gromače* (low stone walls used by sheep farmers) used to criss-cross Cres, acting as windbreaks and preventing soil erosion, but these are no longer maintained and many are crumbling away.

Housed at the Beli Visitor Centre, this place is home to, at last count, six juvenile griffon vultures that are being prepared for tagging and release into the wild. There are interesting displays on the species, and you can wander out to look at the enclosures.

Activities & Tours

Beli Visitor Centre has information on seven hikes, ranging from 1km to 8km, six themed tourist-trail walks, and three cycling trails (from 8.5km to 18km). Ask at the visitor centre about bicycle rental, or contact Tramontana Outdoor.

Birdwatchers should also contact the visitor centre to find out where to spot wild griffon vultures.

Tramontana Outdoor TOURS
(☎051-840 519; www.tramontana-outdoor.com; Beli 2) Offering a range of tours of the Tramuntana area, this well-run outfit has a few interesting options alongside its more standard tours: stand-up paddleboarding, a half-day gastronomic tour of the region, and a 'Choose Your Own Beach' excursion. It also organises bicycle rental.

Sleeping & Eating

Pansion Tramontana B&B €€
(☎051-840 519; www.beli-tramontana.com; s 375-563KN, d 450-675KN; ⏲Mar-Dec; P ❄ @ ☎) On the approach to Beli, this attractive place has 12 comfortable rooms upstairs and a fine rustic restaurant (mains 55KN to 175KN) below, where great chunks of meat are barbecued. Fish, pasta, risotto and superb organic salads are available, too. Staff can also organise various adventure activities, from griffon-vulture-watching to mountain climbing.

Konoba Beli CROATIAN €€
(☎051-840 515; www.beli-cres.com; Beli 6; mains 45-120KN; ⏲10am-10pm) The stone dining room bedecked with the agricultural implements of yesteryear creates a suitably rustic setting in which to enjoy locally flavoured grilled fish and meat dishes. When the mercury pushes north, take a seat on the large terrace.

Information

Beli Visitor Centre (☎095 50 61 116; www.facebook.com/BeliVisitorCentre; Beli 4; ⏲10am-4pm) In addition to information on griffon vultures, the visitor centre has info on activities in the area.

Getting There & Away

Two Autotrans (www.autotrans.hr) buses run between Beli and Cres (36KN, 30 minutes); check the website for departure times. Otherwise, you'll need a car to reach Beli.

Cres Town

☎051 / POP 2879

Pastel-hued terrace houses and Venetian mansions embrace the medieval harbour of Cres Town, a beautiful sheltered bay wrapped in vivid green hills of pine and Adriatic scrub. As you amble along the seaside promenade and explore the atmospheric maze of old-town streets, you cannot fail to notice reminders of Italian rule, including the coats of arms of powerful Venetian families and Renaissance loggias.

The town's strong Italian influence dates to the 15th century, when Venetians relocated here after Osor fell victim to plague and pestilence. Public buildings and patricians' palaces were built along the harbour and a town wall was added in the 16th century.

Sights

Trg Frane Petrića SQUARE
Right by the harbour, the main town square was the scene of public announcements, financial transactions and festivals under Venetian rule. It's now the site of a morning fruit-and-vegetable market. Look for the graceful 16th-century **gate**, topped by a blue-faced clock and coats of arms.

St Mary of the Snow Church CHURCH
(Sv Marije Snježne; Trg Frane Petrića; ⏲Mass only) Just inside the main harbour gate, this church is notable for its Renaissance portal with a relief of the Virgin and Child. A glassed-in foyer allows you to peer inside, but the church is only open during Mass. If you do find it open, look for the carved wooden pietà from the 15th century (now under protective glass) at the left altar.

Cres Museum MUSEUM
(Creski Muzej; ☎051-344 963; Ribarska 7; 10KN; ⏲10am-1pm & 7-11pm Tue-Sun mid-Jun–mid-Sep, 9am-noon Tue-Sat Apr–mid-Jun & mid-Sep–mid-Oct) Housed in the Arsan Renaissance palace just off the harbour front, this local museum is worth the modest entry fee for its 16th-century Venetian architecture and its displays on various aspects of local life.

THE THREATENED GRIFFON VULTURE

With a wingspan of almost 3m, measuring about 1m from end to end, and weighing 7kg to 9kg, the Eurasian griffon vulture looks big enough to take passengers. It cruises comfortably at 40km/h to 75km/h, reaching speeds of up to 160km/h. The vulture's powerful beak and long neck are ideally suited to rummaging around the entrails of its meal, which is most likely to be a dead sheep.

Finding precious sheep carcasses is a team effort for griffon vultures. Usually a colony of birds will set out and fly in a comb formation of up to 1km apart. When one of the vultures spots a carcass, it circles as a signal for its neighbours to join the feast. Shepherds don't mind griffons, reasoning that the birds prevent whatever disease or infection killed the sheep from spreading to other livestock.

According to a 2017 census, the total known number of griffon vultures in Croatia was 108 breeding pairs (down from 140 a few years earlier) and 76 nestlings. More than half of them live on the coastal cliffs of Cres, the others in small colonies on Krk and Prvić Islands. The birds' dietary preferences mean that they tend to follow sheep, although they will eat other dead mammals, though this is perilous: the last remaining birds in Paklenica National Park died after eating poisoned foxes.

The griffon population enjoys legal protection as an endangered species in Croatia. Killing a bird or disturbing it while nesting carries a €5000 fine. Intentional killing is rare, but because the young birds cannot fly more than 500m on a windless day, tourists on speedboats who provoke them into flight often end up threatening their lives: the exhausted birds drop into the water and drown.

Breeding habits discourage a large population, as a pair of griffons only produces one fledgling a year and it takes five years for the young bird to reach maturity. During that time the growing griffons travel widely: one tagged in Paklenica National Park was found in Chad, 4000km away. When they're about five, the vultures head home to Cres (sometimes to the same rock where they were born) to find a mate, who will be a partner for life.

Captive vultures can live for more than 55 years, but in the wild 20 to 30 years is more normal. The dangers facing young Cres vultures include the guns of Italian hunters, poison and power lines, but by far the biggest issue is the massive decline in sheep farming in Cres (p184), which is reducing the birds' food source day by day.

If you want to find out more about Croatia's griffon vultures, visit the Rescue Centre for Griffon Vultures (p185) in Beli.

Activities

There's an attractive promenade on the western side of the bay with sunbathing zones and good swimming, plus good beaches around Hotel Kimen. Drop by the tourist office for a map of walking and cycling trails around Cres.

Diving Cres DIVING
(051-571 706; www.divingcres.de; Melin 1/20; boat dive incl equipment €40) Based in Kamp Kovačine, this German crew offers Professional Association of Diving Instructors (PADI) and Scuba Schools International (SSI) courses and wreck dives.

Sleeping

Kamp Kovačine CAMPGROUND €
(051-573 150; www.camp-kovacine.com; Melin 1/20; camping per adult/site 104/100KN, s/d 400/745KN, cabins 700KN; Easter–mid-Oct; P@) With a fine location on the tip of a little wooded peninsula about 1km southwest of town, this large campground offers excellent shower blocks, beachside bathing platforms, a restaurant and activities galore. A quarter of the area, including some of the beach, is reserved for naturists. Private rooms are available in Tamaris, a small guesthouse near the water.

Villa Neho B&B €€
(051-571 868; www.villaneho.com; Zazid 5; r 625KN;) This guesthouse just back from the harbour front offers smart, crisp but smallish rooms with trendy features. Though it lacks any local colour, its standards are a cut above those of the average Croatian B&B, breakfast is a substantial affair and half board is available for a reasonable 110KN a day. Cash only.

Hotel Kimen HOTEL €€€
(☎051-573 305; www.hotel-kimen.com; Melin 1/16; s €59-112, d €70-134; P ❄ ☜) With a prime spot by a beach and grounds pleasantly shaded by pine trees, this large Yugoslav-era 128-room slab was comprehensively renovated a decade or so ago and offers fresh-looking rooms with balconies. Rooms in the neighbouring 'Depandance' are cheaper, but the main hotel is much nicer.

Eating

★ **Konoba Bukaleta** CROATIAN €€
(☎051-571 606; Loznati 99; mains 42-120KN; ⊙noon-11pm Apr-Sep) Cres lamb gets top billing at this down-to-earth village restaurant, which has been run by the same family for well over three decades. Try the lamb breaded, grilled or roasted on the spit, or tuck into homemade gnocchi and pasta instead. Bukaleta is in Loznati, 5km south of Cres Town, and signposted from the highway.

Gostionica Belona CROATIAN €€
(Šetalište 23, Travnja 24; mains 55-150KN; ⊙11am-11pm) This excellent local tavern plates up Cres seafood, lamb dishes, grilled meat and salads. The roadside terrace isn't in the prettiest location, so try instead for a seat indoors. It has excellent service and a good Croatian wine list, and it's just a short walk from the harbour.

Information

Cresanka (☎051-750 600; www.cresanka.hr; Varozina 25) Books private rooms, apartments, campsites and hotels.

Tourist Agency Croatia (☎051-573 053; www.cres-travel.com; Cons 10; ⊙8am-1pm & 4-7pm Mon-Sat, 10am-1pm Sun) Arranges private accommodation, offers internet access, and hires out boats, bikes, cars and scooters.

Tourist Office (☎051-571 535; www.tzg-cres.hr; Cons 10; ⊙8am-noon & 3.30-8pm Mon-Sat, 9am-1pm Sun Jun-Aug, 8am-2pm Mon-Fri Sep-May) Well stocked with maps and brochures, including accommodation listings with photographs.

Getting There & Away

Cres has the following bus connections:

Beli 36KN, 30 minutes, two daily
Mali Lošinj 60KN, 1¼ hours, up to seven daily
Osor 44KN, 45 minutes, four daily
Rijeka 110KN, 2¼ hours, three daily
Valun 32KN, 20 minutes, daily
Veli Lošinj 65KN, 1½ hours, four daily

Getting Around

Gonzo Bikes (☎051-573 107; Turion 8; per hour/day 25/100KN; ⊙9am-4pm Mar-Dec) Rents out good-quality bikes and camping equipment from its Cres base, as well as bikes from Hotel Kimen and various campgrounds.

Valun

☎051 / POP 72

The pretty seaside hamlet of Valun, 14km southwest of Cres Town, is tucked at the foot of cliffs and surrounded by pebbly beaches. Its appeal lies in its tranquillity: its restaurants are rarely crowded, and there's a refreshing lack of souvenir stalls.

Park in the lot above the village and take the steep steps down. To the right of the harbour, a path leads to a beach and campground. About 700m in the other direction there's another lovely pebble beach bordered by pines.

Sights

St Mark's Church CHURCH
The parish church houses the village's main sight: the 11th-century Valun Tablet. Inscribed in both Glagolitic and Latin, this tombstone reflects the ethnic composition of the island at the time it was made. At that point, Cres was inhabited by Roman descendants and newcomers who spoke Croatian. Sadly, the church's opening hours are erratic.

Valun Beach BEACH
Around the headland to the northwest of the village, you'll find a lovely pebble beach bordered by pines. It's much quieter than the beach just east of town.

Sleeping & Eating

Camping Zdovice CAMPGROUND €
(☎051-571 161; per adult/child 115/55KN; ⊙May-Sep; 🐾) This idyllic camping ground is a small affair, with pitches occupying old terraced fields right by a great swimming beach. There's also a volleyball court and a clean toilet block. The Cresanka agency in Cres Town handles bookings.

Konoba Toš-Juna SEAFOOD €€
(Obala Stjepan Mesić; mains 45-100KN; ⊙10am-11pm) Of Valun's handful of restaurants, this one stands out for its seafood and its attractive terrace emblazoned with Glagolitic writing. It's inside a converted olive mill with exposed stone walls, right by the harbour and the church.

Getting There & Away

Valun is not well served by public transport. Buses head to and from Cres Town (32KN, 20 minutes) once a day.

Lubenice

051 / POP 25

Perched on an exposed rocky ridge 378m above the western shore of the island, this medieval hilltop hamlet is one of the most evocative places on Cres. Semiabandoned, Lubenice's maze of ancient, austere stone-built houses and churches seems fused to the very bedrock of the island. The narrow road here is lined with stone fences, olive groves and stands of pine trees.

Sights

The best view of the town is from high on the rocks above the western edge of the car park: you can see the beach from here.

★Lubenice Beach BEACH

One of Kvarner's most remote and beautiful beaches, this secluded cove is accessed by following a steep path through the scrub. The 45-minute descent is a breeze, but coming back up is more of a challenge (you might want to take a taxi boat from Valun or Cres).

Eating

Konoba Hibernicia CROATIAN €

(Lubenice 17; mains 45-100KN; noon-10pm) Extremely rustic, with stone walls and a terrace popular with the village cats, this humble eatery is notable for its lamb dishes and local ham.

BEACHSIDE CAMPING

Tucked away on the west coast of Cres near a nondescript fishing village called Martinšćica, **Campsite Slatina** (051-661 124; www.camps-cres-losinj.com; Martinšcica; camping per adult/site from 67/63KN, units from 850KN; May-Sep) offers access to two lovely pebbly beaches. The complex includes restaurants, a pizzeria, cafes, a grocery shop, a dive school, and boat and bike hire. Despite its large size (500 sites), it's well spaced out and doesn't feel too cramped. Minimum seven-night stay in July and August.

Getting There & Away

If you have the time and the inclination, the best way to get here is on foot: it's a one-hour hike from Valun.

If you're driving up, note that the road is narrow and winding. You'll need to park at the entrance to the village, which costs 10/15/30 per day for motorcycles/cars/campervans.

In summer buses connect Lubenice with Cres Town (34KN, 30 minutes, twice daily Monday to Saturday).

Osor

051 / POP 60

The tiny walled town of Osor is one of the most peaceful places you could imagine, despite its grand and troubled past. The village sits on the narrow channel dividing Cres and Lošinj, which is thought to have been dug by the Romans. Because of it, Osor was able to control a key navigational route. Today it's becoming a kind of museum-town of churches, open-air sculptures and lanes that meander from its 15th-century centre.

History

In the 6th century a bishopric was established here, with authority over both islands throughout the Middle Ages. Until the 15th century Osor was a strong commercial, religious and political presence in the region, but a combination of plague, malaria and new sea routes devastated the town's economy and Osor slowly decayed.

Sights

Entering through the gate on the canal, you pass old city walls and the remains of a castle before you hit the centre of town. Look out for the Ivan Meštrović statue *Daleki Akordi* (Distant Chords), one of the town's many modern sculptures on a musical theme.

Church of the Assumption CHURCH

(Crkva Uznešenja; 10am-noon & 7-9pm Jun-Sep) Completed in 1498, this large church has a rich Renaissance portal facing onto the main square. The baroque altar inside has relics of St Gaudentius, Osor's patron saint.

Osor Archaeological Collection MUSEUM

(Arheološka Zbirka Osor; 051-237 346; www.muzej.losinj.hr; Gradska Vijećnica; adult/child 35/25KN; 10am-1pm & 7-10pm Tue-Sun mid-Jun–mid Sep, shorter hours rest of year, by appointment only Oct-Easter) On the main square in the 15th-century town hall, this outpost of the Lošinj Museum contains a collection of stone fragments, reliefs, ceramics and sculptures from the Roman, early Christian and medieval periods.

Festivals & Events

Osor Musical Evenings MUSIC
(Osorske Glazbene Večeri; 051-237 110; www.osorfestival.eu; mid-Jul–mid-Aug) Well into its fifth decade, this festival sees high-calibre Croatian artists perform classical music in the cathedral and on the main square.

Sleeping & Eating

Camping Bijar CAMPGROUND €
(051-237 147; www.camps-cres-losinj.com; per adult/site 67/79KN; May-Sep; P) Set among the pines on a lovely pebbly cove 500m from Osor, this attractive campground offers fabulous swimming as well as table tennis, volleyball and basketball. There's also a restaurant and wi-fi at reception.

Konoba Bonifačić CROATIAN €€
(Osor 64; mains 50-110KN; noon-11pm) Tuck into home cooking – such as dependable risottos, grilled meat and fish, and traditional pork with sage – in a particularly lovely garden setting. Have a shot of elderflower grappa while you're at it.

Getting There & Away

Depending on the time of year and the day of the week, between two and eight buses a day pass through Osor en route to Cres Town (44KN, 45 minutes), Nerezine (20KN, five minutes), Mali Lošinj (37KN, 30 minutes) and Veli Lošinj (40KN, 45 minutes).

When crossing from Lošinj to Osor by car you may have to wait at the drawbridge spanning the Kavuada Canal – the bridge is raised twice a day (at 9am and 5pm) to allow boats to pass.

Nerezine

051 / POP 415

The first town on the Lošinj side of the bridge from Cres Island, little Nerezine has a pretty harbour lined with pastel houses and a few cafe-bars. It's Lošinj's third-biggest settlement – which isn't saying much. All buses heading along the main highway stop here, and if you're travelling by car the town makes a relaxing halt between Rijeka, Cres and all points south. There's little to do here other than grab a coffee or lunch and watch the Adriatic world meander by.

Sleeping & Eating

Hotel Manora HOTEL €€€
(051-237 460; www.manora-losinj.hr; Magdalenska 26b; s 465-660KN, d 680-1315KN; P) Hidden in the outskirts of Nerezine, cheerful Hotel Manora is brightly painted inside and out, and well set up for families. There's a beautiful swimming pool, a sauna, an outdoor playground and even an indoor playroom for when the weather turns bad. Rooms have attractive parquet floors and stylish lighting.

Konoba Bonaparte CROATIAN €€
(Trg Studenac 1; mains 45-130KN; 11am-11pm) The best place to eat during a stopover in Nerezine is this cosy, rustically themed tavern on the town's main square. If you don't fancy the net-fresh fish and seafood dishes, the steaks and schnitzel are superb. Bookings may be necessary for dinner in July and August.

Getting There & Away

Nerezine has the following bus connections:

Cres 46KN, one hour, up to seven daily

Mali Lošinj 34KN, 30 minutes, up to eight daily

Rijeka 154KN, three to 3½ hours, up to four daily

Veli Lošinj 37KN, 40 minutes, up to eight daily

Mali Lošinj

051 / POP 8200

Mali Lošinj, the largest town on Lošinj Island, is a stunner. Set at the apex of a long natural harbour and ringed by graceful, gently weathered Mediterranean town houses and green hills, the town straddles both coasts on the narrowest section of the island. A string of imposing 19th-century sea-captains' houses lines the seafront, and even with the summer tourist commotion, this historic quarter retains its charm and atmosphere.

You'll find the resort hotels just out of town by the pebbly beaches **Sunčana Uvala** (meaning 'Sunny Bay') and **Čikat**. This leafy area began to flourish in the late 19th century, when the wealthy Vienna and Budapest elite, who gravitated to the 'healthy air' of Mali Lošinj, started building villas and luxurious hotels around Čikat. Some of these grand residences remain, but most of the current hotels are modern developments surrounded by pine forests.

Sights & Activities

Cycling and hiking are increasingly popular on Lošinj. The island also has good diving, with excellent visibility and good sea life. There's a wreck dating from 1917, a large, relatively shallow cave suitable for beginners, and the wonderful Margarita Reef off the island of Susak. Čikat is a good spot for windsurfing, with a narrow shingle beach and great wind exposure.

Fritzy Palace MUSEUM
(Palača Fritzy; www.muzej.losinj.hr; Vladimira Gortana 35; adult/child 35/25KN; ⏲10am-1pm & 7-10pm Tue-Sun mid-Jun–mid-Sep, shorter hours rest of year) The largest branch of the three-headed Lošinj Museum (the others are in Osor, p189; and Veli Lošinj. p193), this grand mansion houses a trio of distinct collections: a moderately interesting set of mainly 17th- and 18th-century paintings, a more interesting array of early-20th-century photographs, and a fascinating display of 20th-century art.

The most intriguing exhibit is one of the smallest: a 10cm-high, possibly Etruscan, clay statue dating from the 7th century BCE known as the 'Lady of Čikat'. In the modern section, look out for works by Croatia's three most important 20th-century sculptors: Ivan Meštrović, Frano Kršinić and Antun Augustinčić.

Garden of Fine Scents GARDENS
(Miomirisni Otočki Vrt; www.miomirisni-vrt.hr; Bukovica 6; ⏲8.30am-12.30pm & 6-9pm Jul & Aug, 8am-3pm Mar-Jun & Sep-Dec) FREE This fragrant paradise on the southern edge of town has more than 250 native plant varieties plus 100 exotic species, all framed with *gromače* (traditional stone fences). Natural fragrances, salts and liquors are sold, too.

Sea Turtle Rescue Centre WILDLIFE RESERVE
(Oporavilište za Morske Kornjače; www.blue-world.org; Sunčana Uvala bb; ⏲10am-2pm Mon-Fri Jun-Sep) FREE Small but extremely interesting, this centre is dedicated to rehabilitating injured sea turtles, most of which have been entangled in plastic or fishing nets. There aren't a lot of displays, but the staff on hand will talk you through the centre's work. You might even get to see some of the patients. It's located between the Adriatic and Vespera hotels, just up from the promenade.

Church of the Nativity CHURCH
(Župna Crkva Male Gospe; Sv Marije bb) The parish church (built 1696–1775) towers over the town from the ridge. Inside are some notable artworks, including a painting of the Nativity by an 18th-century Venetian artist, and relics of St Romulus. It's usually only open during Mass.

WORTH A TRIP

LOŠINJ'S SOUTH END

South of Mali Lošinj the island forms a glorious, barely inhabited, thumb-shaped peninsula that's blessed with exquisite bays and is perfect for hiking; pick up a map from the tourist office (p192). One lonely road snakes down the spine of this hilly, wooded land mass, eventually fizzling out at Mrtvaška, Lošinj's land's end. You can circumnavigate the entire peninsula on foot in a full day, stopping to swim at deserted coves. If you only want to hit one beach, drive 5km to the turn-off for **Krivica**. It's a 30-minute descent from the parking area to this idyllic, sheltered bay, which is ringed by pine trees. The water is emerald tinged and superb for swimming.

Courses

Sunbird WATER SPORTS
(☎095 83 77 142; www.sunbird.de) This German outfit, based on the beach near the Hotel Bellevue, offers courses in windsurfing (from 1000KN) and sailing catamarans (from 675KN). It also rents windsurfers (from 70KN per hour), kayaks (per hour/day 35/150KN) and bikes (25/100KN).

Subseason DIVING
(☎098 294 887; Del Conte Giovanni 1) Based by the water at Čikat, this centre offers a 'Discovery' course and SSI Open Water certification.

Sleeping

Camping Village Poljana CAMPGROUND €
(☎051-231 726; www.campingpoljana.com; Rujnica 9a; camping per site 160KN, units from 550KN; P❄📶) Surrounded by mature trees, this complex on the northern approach to Mali Lošinj has power-fitted sites, air-conditioned units, a restaurant and a supermarket. There's also a small pebble beach and a rocky area for nude bathers.

Alaburić B&B €€
(☎051-231 343; Stjepana Radića 17; r from 450KN; P📶🐾) This welcoming family-run guesthouse has simple, well-equipped rooms and

WORTH A TRIP

ISLANDS OFF LOŠINJ

The nearby car-free islands of Susak, Ilovik and Unije are the most popular day trips from Mali Lošinj. Tiny **Susak** (population 150, area 3.8 sq km) is unique for the thick layer of fine sand that blankets the underlying limestone and creates excellent beaches. The island's unusual culture makes it particularly interesting. Islanders speak their own dialect, which is nearly incomprehensible to other Croats. On feast days and at weddings you can see the local women dressed in traditional multicoloured skirts (a little like tutus) and red leggings. When you see the old stone houses on the island, consider that each stone had to be brought over from Mali Lošinj and carried by hand to its destination. The island has steadily lost its population in the last few decades (it had more than 1600 inhabitants in 1948), with, strangely, many of its citizens settling in Hoboken, New Jersey.

In contrast to flat Susak, **Ilovik** (population 85, area 5.8 sq km) is a hilly island known for its profusion of flowers. Overgrown with oleanders, roses and eucalyptus trees, it's popular with boaters and has some secluded swimming coves.

The largest of the islands, **Unije** (population 85, area 18 sq km) has an undulating landscape that abounds with Mediterranean shrubs, pebble beaches and numerous coves and inlets. The island's only settlement is a picturesque fishing village of gabled stone houses.

Travel agencies in Mali Lošinj sell excursions to the islands or you can peruse the boats moored along the harbour and see which deal takes your fancy.

Otherwise, Jadrolinija (p184) has a passenger-only ferry that loops from Mali Lošinj to Unije (adult/child 16/8KN, 1½ hours) and Susak (adult/child 16/8 KN, one hour) twice daily. A daily morning catamaran leaves Mali Lošinj for Rijeka and stops in Unije (20KN, 30 minutes) en route.

apartments, all with bathrooms – two have distant sea views. It's in a suburban street just below the Garden of Fine Scents. Breakfast is 50KN extra.

★ **Boutique Hotel Alhambra** HOTEL €€€
(051-260 700; www.losinj-hotels.com; Čikat 16; r from 3900KN; P ❄ @ ☎ ≋) Luxury rooms here – especially those with water views – may come at a premium price, but there's a real sense of style, space and sophistication that you just don't find elsewhere. The look is elegant without being overdone, and the service is excellent.

★ **Mare Mare Suites** HOTEL €€€
(051-232 010; www.mare-mare.com; Riva Lošinjskih Kapetana 36; s/d/apt 900/950/1400KN; P ❄ @ ☎) Enjoying a prime position towards the northern end of the harbour, this historic town house has been converted into immaculately presented, individually styled rooms and an apartment with a private terrace. There's a rooftop spa pool and free use of kayaks and bikes. Ask about management's other options nearby.

Eating & Drinking

Porto CROATIAN, SEAFOOD €€
(Sv Martin 33; mains 45-130KN; 8am-11pm) Up over the hill on the eastern side of town, this fine, family-run seafood buffet enjoys a pretty bay location next to a church. Fish fillet with sea urchins is the signature dish, but all seafood is expertly prepared and presented.

Baracuda CROATIAN, SEAFOOD €€
(051-233 309; Priko 31; mains 59-159KN; noon-midnight) The cosy and elegant Baracuda is highly rated for the freshness of its fish, the skill of its chefs and the cheeky charm of its waitstaff. There's a large terrace and usually a daily special or two chalked up on the blackboard. Much of the fish is priced per kilo.

Restaurant Rosemary SEAFOOD €€€
(051-231 837; www.facebook.com/restaurant.rosemary; Čikat 15; mains 110-220KN; noon-11pm) This terrific, welcoming little place does fishy accents in all manner of guises, from pasta with truffles and fish to a perfectly executed tuna tartar. The homemade bread and pretty garden setting are other pluses.

Priko BAR
(Priko 2; 11am-11pm Mon-Thu, to late Fri & Sat; ☎) On summer evenings the terrace of this harbourside bar is the place to be, with live music most nights.

ISLAND HIKES

The tourist office has an excellent brochure, *Promenades and Footpaths*, with maps of 250km of trails and accurate walking times. All five islands of the archipelago (Lošinj, Cres, Ilovik, Susak and Unije) are covered. Climb the highest peak of Televrina (589m) for great views, hike to the remote coves south of Mali Lošinj (p190), or access secret bays on Susak.

Information

Cappelli (☎051-231 582; www.cappelli-tourist.hr; Lošinjskih Brodograditelja 57) Books private accommodation on Cres and Lošinj, and offers cruises and excursions.

Manora (☎051-520 100; www.manora-losinj.hr; Priko 29) Friendly agency associated with Nerezine's Hotel Manora (p189) that hires scooters and mountain bikes.

Tourist Office (☎051-231 547; www.visitlosinj.hr; Priko 42; ⏱8am-8pm Mon-Sat, 9am-1pm Sun Jun-Sep, 8am-3pm Mon-Fri Oct-May) A very useful office, with knowledgable staff and tons of (practical and glossy) leaflets and maps, plus a comprehensive accommodation list with owners' emails and websites.

Getting There & Away

Island buses head to/from Veli Lošinj (12KN, 12 minutes, at least hourly), Nerezine (34KN, 30 minutes, two to nine daily), Osor (37KN, 20 to 30 minutes, eight daily) and Cres Town (60KN, 1¼ hours, up to seven daily).

Getting Around

Between late April and mid-October an hourly shuttle bus (10KN) runs from the town centre to the hotel district in Sunčana Uvala and Čikat.

You must pay to enter the centre of Mali Lošinj in a car (two hours 20KN).

Veli Lošinj

☎051 / POP 915

Despite the name (in Croatian, *veli* means 'big' and *mali* means 'small'), Veli Lošinj is much smaller, more languid and somewhat less crowded than Mali Lošinj, 4km to the northwest. It's a scenic place with a huddle of pastel-coloured houses, cafes, hotels and stores around a tiny harbour. Dolphins sometimes enter the narrow mouth of the bay in April and May. Don't miss a walk to Rovenska, another idyllic little bay that's a 10-minute stroll southeast along a coastal path.

Like its neighbour, Veli Lošinj had its share of rich sea captains who built villas and surrounded them with gardens of exotic plants that they brought from afar. You can glimpse these villas on a walk up the steep streets from the harbour.

Sights

★Lošinj Marine Education Centre MUSEUM

(☎051-604 666; www.blue-world.org; Kaštel 24; adult/child 20/15KN; ⏱10am-9pm Jul & Aug, to 8pm Jun, 10am-6pm Mon-Fri, to 2pm Sat May & Sep, 10am-2pm Mon-Fri Oct-Apr) A companion piece to the practical conservation work of Blue World, this enlightening attraction aims to educate locals and visitors about the marine environment and the threats it's facing. Inside this swanky modern centre there's a highly informative video (in a variety of languages), the vertebrae of an 11m fin whale (a baby) and some multimedia displays, including an acoustic room where you can hear dolphin-click communications.

Church of St Anthony the Hermit CHURCH

(Obala Maršala Tita) Built in baroque style in 1774 and funded by local seafarers, this pretty pink church is elaborately decked out with marble altars, a rich collection of Italian paintings (including on the ceiling), a pipe organ and relics of St Gregory. It's normally only open for Sunday Mass, but you can catch a glimpse of the interior through its metal gate.

Tower Museum MUSEUM

(Kula-Lošinjski Muzej; Kula Kastel bb; adult/child 35/25KN; ⏱10am-1pm & 7-10pm Tue-Sun Jul & Aug, shorter hours rest of year) This striking defence tower, in the maze of streets set back from the harbour, was built by the Venetians in 1455 to defend the town from pirates. It now contains a branch of the Lošinj Museum (the other being in Mali Lošinj, p190), dedicated to the island's maritime history. Browse the Roman ceramic fragments, sabres and old postcards before climbing up to the battlements for unrivalled views of the old town.

Sleeping

Youth Hostel Veli Lošinj HOSTEL €

(051-236 234; www.hfhs.hr; Kaciol 4; dm 135KN; May-Oct;) One of Croatia's best YHA-associated hostels, this converted town house has a friendly vibe and hospitable management. Dorms (all with lockers) are spacious, the pine-trimmed private rooms are quite classy and the front terrace is a great place to meet up for an evening beer.

Hotel Vila Conte HOTEL €€

(051-268 697; www.hotel-vilaconte.com; Garina 14; r 445-1180KN;) This elegant place with whitewashed rooms is the pick of the midrange options in town. You're a stone's throw from the harbour, service is excellent and there's a decent restaurant.

Villa Mozart B&B €€

(098 97 80 051; www.villamozartvelilosinj.com; Kaciol 3; r 600-740KN;) The 18 character-packed rooms at this attractive guesthouse may all be smallish, but they have TVs and tiny bathrooms, and some have harbour views that are worth paying extra for. The breakfast terrace overlooks the shimmering harbour waters and the church. There's a 120KN surcharge for one-night stays in July and August.

Eating & Drinking

★ Bora Bar ITALIAN €€

(051-867 544; www.borabar.net; Rovenska Bay 3; mains 65-174KN; noon-10pm Mar-Oct) Truffle heaven, this casual-chic restaurant, Veli Lošinj's best, has an Italian chef and a passion for the mysterious fungi. Feast on delicious homemade pasta with a generous shaving of truffle, and finish with panna cotta with truffle honey. Istrian wines put in a strong appearance.

Restaurant Mol SEAFOOD €€

(051-236 008; Rovenska 1; mains 65-140KN; 10am-midnight) This excellent family-run restaurant serves up splendid seafood, from a fine fish soup or octopus salad for starters to sea bass or grilled squid for main. It's worth passing by earlier in the day to reserve a seaside table – otherwise they'll all be gone by the time you arrive.

Saturn BAR

(Obala Maršala Tita bb; 8am-2am;) The best bar in town, this atmospheric little place has harbour-facing tables and an eclectic playlist of Western and Croatian music. It can get very noisy at weekends or when the Croatian national football team is in action.

BLUE WORLD

The **Blue World Institute of Marine Research & Conservation** (www.blue-world.org) is a Veli Lošinj–based NGO founded in 1999 to protect the Adriatic's marine environment. As well as hands-on research and conservation work, including running the Sea Turtle Rescue Centre (p190) in Mali Lošinj, it promotes environmental awareness through lectures, media presentations and the organisation of the annual **Dolphin Day**, held in Veli Lošinj on 1 July. It's quite an event, involving photography exhibitions, an eco fair, street performances, water-polo contests, treasure hunts, and displays of hundreds of children's drawings and paintings.

As part of the Adriatic Dolphin Project, Blue World studies bottlenose dolphins that frequent the Lošinj-Cres area. Each dolphin is named and catalogued by photos taken of the natural marks that can be seen on its dorsal fin.

Dolphins were hunted here in the 1960s and '70s, when each kill was rewarded by the local government – fishers were paid by the tail. Protection began in 1995, but a steep decline in bottlenose dolphins was recorded between 1995 and 2003. Subsequently, Blue World worked to establish the Lošinj Dolphin Reserve. Bottlenose-dolphin numbers are now believed to be stable, at around 10,000 individuals. Occasionally, other dolphin species are seen, too, including striped dolphins. The giant basking shark has also been spotted.

The biggest threat to Lošinj's dolphins is boat traffic, which brings noise and disturbance. During July and August dolphins are never seen close to the shore and avoid their main feeding grounds south and east of Cres where hake is common. Overfishing is another big concern as it reduces available prey.

You can get involved by adopting a dolphin (from €30), which supports the Adriatic Dolphin Project, or volunteering. From May to September it's possible to join a 10-day program; programs start at €900 per person (with discounts available for students) and include food and accommodation.

Information

Palma Tourist Agency (051-236 179; www.losinj.com; Vladimira Nazora 22) Offers information, currency exchange, internet access and private accommodation rentals.

Turist (051-236 256; www.island-losinj.com; Obala Maršala Tita 17) Runs excursions to Susak and Ilovik (650KN), rents private accommodation, changes money, and rents bikes and scooters.

Val Tourist Agency (051-236 604; www.val-losinj.hr; Vladimira Nazora 29) Books private accommodation, runs excursions, offers internet access, and rents bikes and scooters.

Getting There & Away

Veli Lošinj has the following bus connections:

Cres Town 65KN, 1½ hours, up to seven daily
Mali Lošinj 12KN, 12 minutes, 13 daily
Nerezine 37KN, 40 minutes, up to eight daily
Osor 40KN, 45 minutes, up to eight daily
Rijeka 154KN, four hours, up to four daily

If arriving by car you'll have to park above the bay and walk down the narrow cobblestone streets in summer.

KRK ISLAND

Krk Island (Veglia in Italian) is connected to the mainland by a toll bridge. It is Croatia's largest island, and also one of the busiest – in summer, hundreds of thousands of central Europeans stream to its holiday houses, campsites and hotels. It's not the lushest or the most beautiful island, though its landscape is quite varied, ranging from forests in the west to sunburnt ridges in the east. Vrbnik, on the east coast, is a charming village away from the tourist hordes. The island's northwestern coast is rocky and steep, with few settlements, because of the fierce *bura* (cold northeasterly wind) that whips the coast in winter. The climate is milder in the southwest and can be scorching in the southeast.

You'll find Krk an easy place to visit, with good transport connections and infrastructure. Rijeka Airport is at its northernmost tip, though flights only land here from April to October.

History

The earliest known inhabitants of Krk were the Illyrian Liburnian tribe, followed by the Romans, who settled on the northern coast. Krk was later incorporated into the Byzantine Empire, then passed between Venice and the Croatian-Hungarian kings.

In the 11th century Krk became a leading centre for the preservation of the Glagolitic alphabet (p199), the original Slavic script introduced by Sts Cyril and Methodius in the 9th century. When the church in Rome demanded that the Croatian church fall into line and use Latin script and language for divine services, the clergy in Krk staged a short-lived revolt. However, Rome eventually granted an exemption for some Croatian dioceses to continue using the vernacular (a rarity in the Catholic tradition until the reforms of the 1960s), and the Glagolitic alphabet was used here until the 19th century.

In 1358 Venice granted rule over the island to the dukes of Krk, later known as the Frankopans, who became one of the richest and most powerful families in Croatia. Although they were vassals of Venice, they ruled with a measure of independence until 1480, when the last member of the line put the island back under Venetian protection.

Although tourism is the dominant activity on the island today, there are two small shipyards (in Punat and Krk), and some agriculture and fishing.

Getting There & Away

Ferries come and go from the Valbiska jetty, with services to the islands of Cres and Rab.

Buses head across the bridge from Rijeka to Malinska (50KN, one hour, at least hourly), Krk Town (64KN, 1¾ hours, hourly), Punat (71KN, 1¾ hours, 11 daily) and Baška (84KN, 2¼ hours, seven daily).

There are also services from Zagreb to Malinska (105KN, three hours, 12 daily), Krk Town (105KN, three hours, eight daily), Punat (115KN, 3½ hours, six daily) and Baška (115KN, four hours, six daily).

There are buses from Malinska to both Cres Town (79KN, 1¼ hours, two to three daily) and Mali Lošinj (129KN, 2½ hours, three daily).

Malinska

051 / POP 3471

Once the main port for the export of wood on the island, Malinska is now essentially a sprawl of colourful holiday apartments grouped around a little marina. Sheltered from the winds and averaging 260 sunny days per year, it became a popular holiday destination with the Viennese aristocracy back in the dying days of the Austro-Hungarian Empire. Now the tidy gardens and well-kept abodes speak to a large population of retirees. The surrounding Dubašnica area is scattered with little villages.

Although it's a little removed from the island's main sights, and there are more attractive towns elsewhere, the location is handy for the Cres–Rijeka buses and for its proximity to the ferry and airport.

Sleeping & Eating

Villa Haya APARTMENT €€
(051-604 021; www.villahaya.com; Linardići 28/4, Linardići; apt 480-950KN; P ❄ 🛜 🏊) Located in a middle-of-nowhere village between Malinska and the ferry port, this block of nine apartments makes a good-value, relaxing base, provided you have your own car. It has its own little blue-tiled pool and there are remote beaches within a 40-minute walk.

Pinia HOTEL €€€
(051-866 333; www.hotel-pinia.hr; Porat bb; d incl half board 950-2000KN; P ❄ 🛜 🏊) This curvy hotel gazes over a dining terrace and lush lawns to the beach, 4km west of the harbour. The rooms are very well fitted out, and there's an indoor pool and spa centre to enjoy. All rates are for half board.

★ **Bistro Bukarica** EUROPEAN €€
(051-859 022; www.bistrobukarica.com; Nikole Tesle 61; mains 70-180KN; 11am-11pm) Tucked away up the hill in an unlikely residential street, this inventive restaurant is well worth seeking out. Asian flavours make their way onto a solidly European menu, highlighting the best Croatian produce. The desserts are sensational, too.

Information

Tourist Office (051-859 207; www.tz-malinska.hr; Obala 46; 8am-9pm Mon-Sat, 9am-1pm & 5-8pm Sun Jul & Aug, shorter hours rest of year)

Getting There & Away

Malinska is something of a bus hub for the island. Destinations include the following:

Cres Town 79KN, 1¼ hours, two to three daily
Krk Town 32KN, 20 minutes, hourly in summer
Mali Lošinj 129KN, 2½ hours, three daily
Rijeka 50KN, one hour, six to 15 daily

Krk Town

051 / POP 6281

On the island's southern coast, Krk Town clusters around an ancient walled centre. The newer part of town spreads out over the surrounding hills and bays, and includes a port, beaches, campgrounds and hotels. The seafront promenade can get seriously crowded in summer with tourists and weekending Croats, who spill into the narrow cobbled streets that make up the pretty old quarter.

Minus the crowds, this stone labyrinth is the highlight of Krk Town. The former Roman settlement still retains sections of the ancient city walls and gates, as well as a grand Romanesque cathedral and a 12th-century Frankopan castle.

You won't need more than a couple of hours to see the sights, but Krk Town is a good base from which to explore the rest of the island.

> **BROWSING BEACHES**
>
> To find your favourite beach on Krk Island, pick up the full-colour brochure *Plaža & Uvale* (Beaches & Bays) from any of the island's tourist offices. It has photos of 31 Krk beaches and five enticing coves, complete with GPS coordinates.

Sights

Cathedral of the Assumption CATHEDRAL
(Katedrala Uznešenja; Trg Sv Kvirina; 9am-1pm & 5.30-7.30pm Easter-Sep, 8.30am-12.30pm & 5-6.30pm Oct-Easter) FREE This imposing 12th-century Romanesque structure was built on the site of Roman baths and an early Christian basilica. Inside, note the rare early Christian carving of two birds eating a fish on the first column next to the apse. The left nave features a Gothic chapel from the 15th century, with the coats of arms of the Frankopan princes who used it as a place of worship. Grafted onto the side is an 18th-century **campanile** with onion dome and angel statue.

Next door, the adjoining **St Quirinus' Church** is another Romanesque church built of white stone and dedicated to the island's patron saint. Among the art and vestments stored in its treasury is a silver altarpiece depicting the Madonna that dates to 1477.

Kaštel FORTRESS
(098 726 884; www.kastel-krk.com; Trg Kamplin; adult/child 22/15KN; 9am-9pm Mon-Sat Jun-Aug, shorter hours rest of year) This crumbling seafront fortress guarded the old town from pirate attacks. Check out the inscribed Liburnian and Roman stones displayed in the courtyard before scrambling up the newly

renovated 12th-century tower that was once used as a Frankopan courtroom – the views from the top are worth the climb.

Activities

Pick up an island map from the tourist office and get out and explore the lanes around Krk Town by bike – there are a few bike-rental places at the bus station with bikes for around 100KN a day.

Cable Krk Wakeboard Center WATER SPORTS
(091 26 27 303; www.wakeboarder.hr; per hour/day 104/230KN; 10am-dark May-Sep) Adrenalin junkies can get their fix at this 650m-long cableway for wakeboarding and waterskiing, running at a speed of 32km/h. It's located just off the main road at the head of the bay (before the turn-off to Punat). The complex includes restaurant, bar and board shop.

Fun Diving Krk DIVING
(051-222 563; www.fun-diving.com; Braće Juras 3; day tour incl 2 dives 433KN; Easter-Oct) This German crew offers courses and dives around the island. Some of the best dive sites include *Peltastis,* the wreck of a 60m Greek cargo ship, and the Punta Silo and Kamenjak reefs, which are rich with sea life, including sea snails and octopuses.

Festivals & Events

Krk Fair CULTURAL
(8-10 Aug) This Venetian-inspired event takes over the town for three days, with concerts on four stages, people dressed in medieval costumes, and around 200 stalls selling traditional food and handicrafts.

Sleeping & Eating

Hotel Marina HOTEL €€€
(051-221 128; www.hotelmarina.hr; Obala Hrvatske Mornarice 8; s/d from 850/1350KN; P ❄) Four-star Marina is the only hotel in the old town, and it's a good one, too. The prime waterfront location allows you to gaze out over the yachts from the balconies of all 10 plush units (book one with a terrace for the best views). All boast stylish but understated contemporary decor and hip bathrooms, plus there's a good restaurant.

★ **Konoba Nono** CROATIAN €€
(051-222 221; www.nono-krk.com; Krčkih Iseljenika 8; mains 35-150KN; 11am-late) Just outside the old town, this rustic place is renowned for its Krk cooking and produces its own olive oil, as evidenced by the large traditional press around which tables are arranged. It also hangs its own prosciutto, which goes into some of the dishes. Big portions and incredibly knowledgable and polite staff make Nono worth seeking out.

There's a smaller branch, Mali Nono, in the old town.

Citta Vecchia CROATIAN €€
(095 50 63 179; JJ Strossmayera 36; mains 49-160KN; noon-11pm) Travellers rave about this place – for its perfectly grilled seafood and meat dishes, for its friendly service, for its local wines, and for its intimate garden setting. It's one of the best places for a meal in town.

Drinking & Nightlife

★ **Volsonis** BAR, CLUB
(051-880 249; www.volsonis.hr; Vela Placa 8; 7am-midnight Sun-Thu, to 1am Fri & Sat) This dark, cool, cave-like place has a terrace, a pool table, a delicious secret garden and even a collection of archaeological relics that were uncovered during renovations. Live bands and DJs do their thing on weekend nights, or you can just chill on the terrace with a coffee or cocktail.

Caffettaria XVIII st. BAR
(Vela Placa 1; 7am-2am May-Sep, to midnight Oct-Apr;) Located right on the main square in the erstwhile entrance of the historic town hall, this is the place for a bit of people-watching and a delicious coffee in the shade. It has good wi-fi and nice sofas to lounge on.

Information

Aurea (051-221 777; www.aurea-krk.com; Vršanska 26l; 8am-2pm & 3-8pm) Local agency offering island excursions and private accommodation bookings.

Tourist Office (051-220 226; www.tz-krk.hr; JJ Strossmayera 9; 8am-9pm daily Jun, to 10pm Jul & Aug, reduced hours rest of year) Useful islandwide information.

Getting There & Away

The bus station is near the water, only 350m west of the old town. Destinations include the following:

Baška 37KN, 45 minutes, 12 daily in summer

Malinska 32KN, 20 minutes, hourly in summer

Punat 28KN, 15 minutes, at least hourly in summer

Rijeka 64KN, 1½ hours, 12 daily

Punat

051 / POP 2010

Six kilometres southeast of Krk, the small town of Punat has an attractive promenade lined with gelaterias, a marina much loved by yachties, and decent beaches on its outskirts. The main attraction here is the monastery islet of Košljun, only a 10-minute boat ride away. Otherwise, it's a standard, if fairly quiet, Croatian beach town.

Sights

Košljun Franciscan Monastery MONASTERY
(Franjevački Samostan Košljun; 051-854 017; www.kosljun.hr; 20KN; 9.30am-5pm Mon-Sat, 10.30am-12.30pm Sun) The tiny island of Košljun contains a 16th-century Franciscan monastery built on the site of a 12th-century Benedictine abbey. Taxi boats wait at Punat harbour, ready to shuttle people across to the island (25KN return); in summer there'll be plenty of interested parties with whom you can share a ride. Visitors should dress modestly.

Highlights include a large, appropriately chilling *Last Judgment,* painted in 1653 and housed in the monastery church. There's also a small museum with religious paintings, an ethnographic collection and a rare copy of Ptolemy's *Atlas* printed in Venice in the late 16th century. Allow extra time to stroll around the forested island and admire its 400 plant species. There are no beaches or swimming on the island.

Getting There & Away

Buses to/from Punat:

Baška 36KN, 30 minutes, 12 daily in summer

Krk Town 28KN, 15 minutes, at least hourly in summer

Malinska 37KN, 40 minutes, at least hourly in summer

Rijeka 71KN, 1½ hours, four to nine daily

Vrbnik

051 / POP 975

Perched on a 48m cliff overlooking the sea, Vrbnik is a beguiling medieval village of steep, arched streets. It's not a real secret (tour groups pass through from time to time), but most of the year it's a peaceful, unhurried place.

Vrbnik was once the main centre where the Glagolitic script was used and was the repository for many Glagolitic manuscripts. The script was kept alive by priests, who were always plentiful in the town since many young men entered the priesthood to avoid serving on Venetian galleys.

Now the town is a terrific place to soak up the vistas and sample the *žlahtina* white wine produced in the surrounding region. After wandering the tightly packed cobbled alleyways, head down to the town beach for a swim.

Sights & Activities

Wander to get lost in the uneven cobblestone lanes that climb the hill to the bell tower (p198). Information panels in Croatian and English explain other buildings of minor significance nearby.

Not far away, signs lead to the **Klančić**, which claims to be the narrowest street in the world (although a street in Reutlingen, Germany, officially holds that honour).

Bell Tower HISTORIC BUILDING
At the summit of a hill, this bell tower has a Glagolitic inscription above the entrance stating that it was built in 1527 and was, for a time, used as a prison.

Katunar WINE
(091 53 21 224; www.kucavina-ivankatunar.com; Braće Trinajstić 3; by appointment) Part wine shop, part shopfront for Ivan Katunar, one of the region's most respected family wineries, Katunar can arrange tastings and tours of the vineyard and can also sell you as many bottles as you please.

OFF THE BEATEN TRACK

STARA BAŠKA

Many of Krk's best beaches are heavily developed and crowded in summer. For more tranquillity, head south of Punat on the lonely road that heads to **Stara Baška** (not southeast to Baška). It's a superlative drive, through steep, parched hills and lunar scenery. Stara Baška itself is a run-of-the-mill tourist sprawl of holiday homes and caravan parks, but if you pull up 500m before the first campsite there's a series of gorgeous pebble-and-sand coves with wonderful swimming. You'll have to park on the road and then walk down one of the rocky paths for five minutes to get to the coast.

Toljanić-Gospoja WINE
(☎051-857 201; www.gospoja.hr; Frankopanska 1; ⊙noon-6pm) This local winery is the best place in town to sample the crisp local *žlahtina* white. You can also try other Croatian wines and even locally made brandies.

Sleeping

★Hotel-Vinotel Gospoja HOTEL €€€
(☎051-669 350; www.gospoja.hr; Frankopanska 1; d from 1025KN) Beautifully designed rooms with lavishly painted walls and ceilings that follow a wine theme make this place a real contemporary standout; each room is named after a Croatian wine. It's part of the growing Gospoja wine portfolio. It's all very classy, with a good restaurant, too.

★Luce BOUTIQUE HOTEL €€€
(☎091 28 57 083; www.konoba-luce.hr; Braće Trinajstić 15; r 960KN) Four-star style has come late to Vrbnik, but this place is part of the new wave. Rooms are stunners, with exposed brickwork, splashes of bright colours, and stunning contemporary photographs. There's also a good tavern-restaurant. Minimum two-night stay in summer.

Eating

★Gospoja – Konoba Žlahtina CROATIAN €€
(☎051-857 142; www.gospoja.hr; Trg Pred Sparov zid 9; mains 50-110KN) Part of the Gospoja wine empire, this elegant place does the usual range of grilled fish and meat dishes, as well as an excellent seafood risotto. But it also serves local specialities, such as lamb or beef stew with *šurlice* (noodles), and rump steak stuffed with prosciutto and cheese, with fig sauce and gnocchi.

★Restaurant Nada CROATIAN €€
(☎051-857 065; www.nada-vrbnik.hr; Glavača 22; mains 60-180KN; ⊙11am-midnight Apr-Oct) Nada is a great place to sample local favourites such as Krk lamb or *šurlice* topped with meat goulash. There are two attractive dining terraces – one shaded and one overlooking the sea – plus a cellar where you can snack on deli treats surrounded by wine barrels. It also has some classy stone houses for rent.

Shopping

★AurA FOOD & DRINKS
(Placa Vrbničkog Statuta 1; ⊙9am-6pm) This excellent little shop in the old town sells local wines, grappa, olive oils and truffles, as well as its homemade brandy and jams. Everything has an organic focus.

Information

Mare Tours (☎051-604 400; www.mare-vrbnik.com; Pojana 4; ⊙8am-8pm Mon-Sat, 9am-4pm Sun) Travel agency offering tourist information and renting private rooms.

Tourist Office (☎051-857 479; Placa Vrbničkog Statuta 4; ⊙10am-4pm) Small office; don't count on the official opening hours.

Getting There & Away

Buses to/from Vrbnik include the following:

Krk Town 32KN, 30 minutes, two daily

Malinska 37KN, 40 minutes, two daily

If you're driving, you'll need to park at the base of the old town; it costs 5KN per hour.

Baška

☎051 / POP 1674

The drive to the southern end of Krk Island is dramatic, passing through a fertile valley that's bordered by eroded mountains. Eventually the road peters out at Baška, where there's a fine crescent beach set below barren hills. With the peaks of the mainland directly opposite, you're effectively enveloped by soaring highlands, making the sea seem like an alpine lake.

However (and this is a considerable caveat), in summer tourists are spread towel-to-towel and what's otherwise a pretty, if slimline, pebble beach turns into a fight for your place in the sun.

Baška's small 16th-century core of Venetian town houses is pleasant enough, but what surrounds it is a bland tourist development of modern apartment blocks and generic restaurants. Facilities are plentiful and there are nice hiking trails into the surrounding mountains, and more secluded beaches to the east of town, reachable on foot or by water taxi.

Sights

St Lucy's Church CHURCH, MUSEUM
(Crkva Sv Lucija; 25KN; ⊙9am-9pm Jun-Aug, 10am-5pm Sep-May) More than just a village church, little St Lucy's was the site of one of the most important cultural discoveries in Croatia – the 11th-century Baška Tablet – which was found in the floor of the church in 1851. Written in Glagolitic, it contains the earliest reference in the Croatian language to a Croatian king. Visitors are invited to watch a video that tells the fascinating story of the tablet's discovery and eventual

THE GLAGOLITIC ALPHABET

The Glagolitic script is generally considered to be the oldest known Slavic alphabet, having been created in the 9th century by Byzantine monks from Thessaloniki. Its original purpose was a missionary one: by rendering the Slavic languages in written form, they hoped to have greater success in converting the locals. In the 13th century the Pope granted to the Bishop of Senj the unusual privilege of being allowed to celebrate Mass in the local language, although centuries later it became a symbol of resistance – a statement by the local Catholic Church that it intended to worship in its local tongue rather than Latin.

Originally, the Glagolitic alphabet had 41 letters, although this was later simplified to 30. There are significant similarities between it and the Greek alphabet. That said, a number of the letters represented non-Greek sounds. Linguists have also traced Hebrew and Armenian influences.

The earliest known Glagolitic inscription, the **Baška Tablet**, dates to the 11th century. It is an 800kg stone slab inscribed with details of a donation of land by King Zvonimir to the local Byzantine community, followed by a description of the church's construction. The original resides in the Strossmayer Gallery of Old Masters in Zagreb. A video tells the story of the tablet in the church where it was found, St Lucy's Church in Baška, on the island of Krk. The valley that leads down from the Krk uplands to Baška was considered a stronghold of Glagolitic traditions and the alphabet was used here until the 19th century, long after it had died out elsewhere; a towering letter 'A' from the alphabet marks the point where the road descends, next to Zipline Edison. Other places where the script can be seen include St Mark's Church in Valun, the village of Nin near Zadar, and the Bell Tower in Vrbnik; the latter small town was another Glagolitic stronghold.

translation, and are then shown around the church itself.

The squat, early Romanesque church was built on the foundations of a 4th-century villa and has a Roman column and gravestone built into its porch. The famous stone tablet is now in the Strossmayer Gallery of Old Masters (p75) in Zagreb, but a replica has been positioned in its original place, where the rood screen would once have stood. On the feast of St Lucy (13 December), the sun strikes the inscription referring to the saint. Look out for the statue of St Lucy, depicted with an angel holding her gouged-out eyes on a plate – a reference to her gruesome martyrdom.

The church is in the village of Jurandvor and well signposted from the approach to Baška; it's only 2km from town, so is easily reached on foot.

Baška Beach BEACH

Baška's beach arcs around the coastline south of the main drag, with fine views over towards the mainland. It can get crowded in summer, but there's usually space to spread your towel.

Activities

Several popular **trails** begin around Camping Zablaće, including an 8km walk over the stark, salt-washed limestone hills to Stara Baška. Along the way you'll see the flower-shaped stone pens traditionally used for mustering and shearing sheep. There are also two **rock-climbing** sites in the area.

Zipline Edison OUTDOORS

(☎098 626 061; www.zipline-edison-krk.com; 2hr 390KN; ⏰10am-7pm) At the head of the valley that leads down towards Baška, and next to a lookout marked by a sculpture in the shape of the Glagolitic letter 'A', this place offers 2km of ziplines. You can just turn up most of the year, but book ahead in summer.

Sleeping

Naturist Camp Bunculuka CAMPGROUND €

(☎051-656 223; camping per adult/site 85/200KN, units from 1650KN; ⏰Apr-Oct; P@📶🏊) This shady 400-pitch naturist camp is a 15-minute walk over the hill east of the harbour on a lovely beach. It's equipped with good facilities for kids, including minigolf and a playground, as well as restaurant, fruit-and-veg market, bakery and internet cafe. Minimum five-night stay in summer.

Camping Zablaće CAMPGROUND €

(☎051-656 223; Zablača 40; camping per adult/site 80/230KN, mobile homes 950KN; ⏰Apr–mid-Oct; P❄📶) Voted one of Croatia's best campgrounds in 2015, this well-equipped site extends along the long pebble beach and has excellent showers, laundry facilities and snazzy mobile homes with barbecues.

★**Heritage Hotel Forza** HOTEL €€€
(☎051-864 036; www.hotelforza.hr; Zvonimira 98; r from 1400KN; P ❄ @ 📶) The quality here is excellent. Rooms have wooden floors and/or exposed stone walls and larger-than-life artworks that bring a real sense of personality and style.

Hotel Tamaris HOTEL €€€
(☎051-864 200; www.baska-tamaris.com; Emila Geistlicha bb; r from 900KN; ⊙Easter-Sep; P ❄ @ 📶) Right on the beach on the western side of town, this small, well-run hotel started life as an Austro-Hungarian army barracks. The emperor's troops have long since departed and today it's the tourists who enjoy the decent, if smallish, carpeted rooms and apartments. Dinner is a very reasonable extra 100KN and breakfast a less attractive 65KN.

Eating

★**Bistro Francesca** CROATIAN €€
(☎099 65 47 538; www.bistrofrancesca.com; Zvonimira 56; mains 59-180KN; ⊙noon-3.30pm & 6pm-midnight) Quality seafood dishes are on offer here – the black seafood risotto is something of a local institution. Try the scallops with cauliflower cream and the mixed seafood platter, too. Friendly service.

Cicibela CROATIAN €€€
(☎051-856 013; www.cicibela.hr; Emila Geistlicha 22a; mains 55-235KN; ⊙9am-midnight Mar-Oct) At the heart of the beach promenade, this is Baška's top cat, with stylish seating, a maritime theme and a massive and tempting menu of seafood and meat dishes, just steps from the lapping Jadran (Adriatic). If you're ordering fish by the kilogram, ask for the price in advance to avoid postmeal awkwardness.

ℹ Information

PDM Guliver (☎051-864 007; www.pdm-guliver.hr; Zvonimira 98) Travel agency letting private rooms and apartments.

Primaturist (☎051-856 132; www.primaturist.hr; Zvonimira 98) Agency dealing in private rooms and apartments.

Tourist Office (☎051-856 817; www.tz-baska.hr; Zvonimira 114; ⊙8am-9pm Mon-Sat Jun-Aug, to 2pm Mon-Fri Sep-May) Just down the street from the bus station, between the beach and the harbour. Walkers should head here to pick up its hiking-path map. Staff are multilingual.

ℹ Getting There & Away

Buses heading to/from Baška:

Krk Town 37KN, 45 minutes, 12 daily in summer
Malinska 44KN, 1¼ hours, 10 daily in summer
Punat 36KN, 30 minutes, 12 daily in summer
Rijeka 84KN, 2¼ hours, four to seven daily

EAST KVARNER COAST

Heading south from Rijeka, the coastal road passes through a couple of interesting historic towns.

Crikvenica

☎051 / POP 11,400

You could easily miss Crikvenica as you speed along the coast road, but drop down to the water's edge and you'll encounter one of the Croatian coast's fastest-growing yet most appealing destinations. The waterfront area and the streets just back from it have a lovely mix of stone architecture, colourful facades and art nouveau buildings, while the climb up the steep hillside has its own appeal. The pebbly beaches offer front-row views of Krk Island, and the town attracts a mix of local and international visitors. As a base for the Kvarner coast, it's a terrific choice.

Activities

Paragliding Kvarner PARAGLIDING
(☎095 85 49 995; www.paragliding-kvarner.com) This crew offers tandem flights taking off from 770m above the Kvarner Gulf. Choose between a 15-minute panoramic flight (€90) and 30 minutes riding the thermals (€140).

Sleeping

Guesthouse Barica GUESTHOUSE €€
(☎091 298 63 59; www.pansion-barica.com; Dolac 29; r 770-1150KN, apt from KN1500; P ❄ 📶) Up in the hills above town, this quiet place gets good reviews from travellers for its friendly service and fine views from most rooms – the elevated location means you have an uninterrupted vista to the island of Krk from the sea-facing ones. Rooms have dark-wood furnishings and a sense of style that's missing from many similarly priced places.

Hotel Crikvenica HOTEL €€€
(☎051-505 800; www.hotel-crikvenica.com; Strossmayerovo Šetalište 8; s/d 600/915KN; P ❄ @ 📶)

There's a certain playfulness about this multi-storey waterfront hotel. The chic rooms are dominated by soothing earth tones and an understated sense of contemporary style, but there are splashes of colour throughout. Supremely comfortable and well run, it's a good choice.

Eating

Restaurant Dida Crikvenica CROATIAN €€
(051-761 070; www.facebook.com/restaurantdida; Šetalište Vladimira Nazora 77; mains 70-180KN; noon-11pm) The pretty garden setting of this family restaurant allows you to watch the water through the trees while you dine on excellent steaks and seafood, complemented by fine local wines.

Gostionica Zrinski CROATIAN, SEAFOOD €€
(051-241 116; Kralja Tomislava 43; mains 50-160KN; 11.30am-11pm) With a dining area more stylish than at your average Croatian tavern (which goes some way towards compensating for the lack of sea views), and with nicely prepared, artfully presented seafood, Gostionica Zrinski is an excellent choice for a meal.

Information

Tourist Information Centre (051-241 051; www.rivieracrikvenica.com; Trg Stjepana Radića 1c; 8am-9pm daily Jun–mid-Sep, shorter hours & closed Sun rest of year) Has a good range of brochures and information on local accommodation options.

Getting There & Away

Buses connect Crikvenica with Rijeka (47KN, 45 minutes, at least hourly), Krk Town (from 62KN, 2¾ hours, at least four daily), Zagreb (105KN, three to four hours, at least hourly) and Šibenik (182KN, five to six hours, at least four daily).

Senj

053 / POP 7200

The historic walled town of Senj is the largest town on the coast between Rijeka and Zadar. In the 16th century it became a base for the Uskoks: Croats driven from their homes by the Ottoman invasion. They became a feared fighting force, harassing both Turkish and Venetian vessels with their own pirate fleet, painted red and black – the colours of blood and death. Their castle is the main reason to stop here en route to somewhere else.

If you travel along the Dalmatian coast by bus, you're sure to spend at least some time in Senj, as it's a popular coffee or *burek* halt.

Sights

Nehaj Castle CASTLE
(Tvrđava Nehaj; www.muzej-senj.hr; adult/child 20/10KN; 10am-9pm Jul & Aug, to 6pm May, Jun, Sep & Oct) The story of the Uskoks is showcased in the dramatic setting of Nehaj Castle, a sturdy stone cube that looms above the town from a 62m-high hill to the south. It was completed in 1558 with funds supplied by the Austrian emperor; the current structure was largely reconstructed in 1970. Head up to the parapets for fine views along the coast and over the island of Krk.

Municipal Museum MUSEUM
(053-881 141; www.senj.hr/muzej; Milana Ogrizovića 5; adult/child 20/10KN; 7am-3pm & 6-8pm Mon-Fri, 10am-noon & 6-8pm Sat, 10am-noon Sun Jul & Aug, 7am-3pm Mon-Fri rest of year) The local museum, housed in a Gothic-Renaissance 15th-century palace built by Senj's medieval first family, the Vukasovićs, is a mixed bag of local history from the past 2000 years. The most interesting sections for Slavophiles are the exhibition dealing with the erstwhile printing house that produced religious texts in the Glagolitic script and the ethnographic section with its colourful folk costumes.

Eating

Kod Veska CROATIAN, SEAFOOD €€
(053-884 056; Ruminja Vrata; mains 39-155KN; noon-11.30pm) Grilled fish or meat, preceded by a damned-fine fish soup, will ensure you leave happy. Friendly service, pleasing decor and a good central location round out an excellent experience.

Information

Tourist Office (053-881 068; www.visitsenj.com; Stara 2; 8am-9pm daily Jun–mid-Sep, shorter hours & closed Sun rest of year) Useful for information on the town and wider region.

Getting There & Away

Senj is a stop on the Rijeka–Split route – often a long stop involving caffeine. Connections from Senj:

Rijeka 73KN, 1½ hours, 13 daily
Split 206KN, 6½ hours, seven daily
Zadar 114KN, 2¾ to 3½ hours, seven daily
Zagreb 130KN, 2¾ to 4½ hours, five daily

RAB ISLAND

Madly popular, Rab (Arbe in Italian) has some of the most diverse landscapes in the Kvarner region, leading to its declaration as a geopark in 2008.

The more densely populated southwest coast has pine forests and beaches, while the northeast coast is a windswept region with few settlements, high cliffs and a barren look. In the interior, fertile land is protected from cold winds by mountains, allowing the cultivation of olives, grapes and vegetables. The Lopar Peninsula offers the best sandy beaches.

The cultural and historical highlight of the island is enchanting Rab Town, characterised by four elegant bell towers rising from the ancient stone streets. Even at the peak of the summer season, when the island is overrun with visitors, you still get a sense of discovery wandering its old quarter and escaping to nearly deserted beaches just a quick boat ride away.

History

After being governed by the Romans, Rab underwent periods of Byzantine and Croatian rule before being sold to Venice, along with Dalmatia, in 1409. Farming, fishing, vineyards and salt production were the economic mainstays, but most income ended up in Venice. Two plague epidemics in the 15th century nearly wiped out the population and brought the economy to a standstill.

When Venice fell in 1797, there was a short period of Austrian rule until the French arrived in 1805. After the fall of Napoleon in 1813, power returned to the Austrians, who favoured the Italianised elite, and it was not until 1897 that Croatian was made an official language. The tourism industry began at the turn of the 20th century.

After the fall of the Austro-Hungarian Empire in 1918, Rab eventually became part of the Kingdom of Yugoslavia. Occupied by Italian and then German troops in the early 1940s, it was liberated in 1945. During Tito's rule Goli Otok (Barren Island), off the Lopar Peninsula, served as a notorious prison camp for fascists, Stalinists and other political opponents.

These days tourism is Rab's bread and butter. Even during the 1990s war, Rab managed to hold on to its German and Austrian visitors.

Getting There & Away

BOAT

Jadrolinija (☎051-666 111; www.jadrolinija.hr) A daily catamaran stops in Rab Town en route between Rijeka (80KN, 1¾ hours) and Novalja on Pag (45KN, 45 minutes). The company also runs a handy car ferry between Valbiska on Krk and Lopar (adult/child/car 37/19/225KN, 1½ hours) twice daily October to May, four times daily in high season.

Rapska Plovidba (☎051-724 122; www.rapska-plovidba.hr) A car ferry shuttles back and forth between Mišnjak on the island's southeastern tip and Stinica (adult/child/car 17/7/98KN, 15 minutes) on the mainland; even in winter there are a dozen boats a day, increasing to nearly double that in high season. There's also a passenger boat from Rab Town to Lun on the island of Pag, operating three days a week (daily June to August).

BUS

Buses head to Rab Town from Rijeka (125KN, three hours, two daily) and Senj (74KN, 1½ hours, five daily); from Zadar you'll need to change at Senj. In high season there are four direct buses a day from Zagreb to Rab (230KN, five to six hours); book ahead on this busy route.

Getting Around

There are 11 buses a day (nine on Sunday) between Rab Town and Lopar (22KN, 15 minutes); some are timed to meet the Valbiska–Lopar ferry.

Taxi boats will take you to any island beach.

Rab Town

☎051 / POP 8027

Crowded onto a narrow peninsula, walled Rab Town is among the northern Adriatic's most spectacular sights. Its four instantly recognisable bell towers rise like exclamation marks from a red-roofed huddle of stone buildings. A maze of streets leads to the upper town, where there are ancient churches and dramatic lookout points. It's quite a scene, the glinting azure waters of Rab's pocket-sized harbour set against the island's backbone of hills that shelter the bay from cool *bura* winds. Once you've soaked up the town vibe, there are excursion and taxi boats waiting to whisk you off to the lovely beaches scattered around the island.

A five-minute walk north of the old town is the ageing, down-at-heel commercial centre, with shops and the bus station. Along the coast sprawl built-up suburbs, including Banjol and Barbat in the south and Palit and Kampor in the north.

History

Originally settled by the Illyrian Liburnian people in around 360 BCE, Rab was declared a city in 10 BCE by the Roman emperor Augustus. It was Augustus who ordered the first walls to be built. The town first made its way into the history books in 70 CE, when Pliny the Elder referred to it as Arba (meaning 'Dark', 'Obscure' or 'Green'). It later became known as Felix Arba (Happy Arba).

Sights

It's a delight to meander through the narrow old alleys of Rab and explore the harbour, upper town and parks. Rab's principal sights are its historic churches and towers, which are clustered on the narrow lane of Gornja (Upper St), which runs parallel to Srednja (Central) and Donja (Lower) streets. Most of the churches are usually only open for morning and evening Mass, but even when they're closed you can often peer through metal railings to view their interiors.

A long, pebbly beach stretches all around Rab Town, so take a towel and freshen up after sightseeing – just mind those sea urchins!

★St Mary's Campanile TOWER
(Toranj Sv Marije; Ivana Rabljanina bb; 15KN; 9.30am-1pm & 7-9pm May-Sep) Dating from the 12th century, this is Rab's tallest bell tower and one of the most beautiful on the entire Croatian coast. The 26m edifice is topped with an octagonal pyramid surrounded by a Romanesque balustrade, and features a cross with five small globes and reliquaries of several saints. Climb up the very steep wooden staircase for glorious views over old-town rooftops and sea. You'll emerge right by the chiming mechanism itself.

Viewpoint VIEWPOINT
For a great view over Rab's rooftops, including all four bell towers, head to the northwesternmost corner of the old town and look for a small courtyard containing fragments of old monuments. Stone stairs lead up from here on to the walls and a lookout – take care with children, as the drops are steep and the railings past their best.

Holy Cross Church CHURCH
(Crkva Sv Križa; Gornja bb) This 13th-century church takes its present name from a crucifix upon which, in 1556, the image of Christ was said to have wept due to the immoral conduct of the people of Rab. Sadly, the miraculous cross was lost in the early 20th century. Today the church is a venue for summer concerts during Rab Musical Evenings.

WORTH A TRIP

SVETI ILIJA HIKE

From Rab Town a trail leads northeast to the mountain peak of Sveti Ilija. It only takes about 30 minutes on foot and the view is well worth the effort.

St Andrew's Monastery CHURCH
(Samostan Sv Andrije; Ivana Rabljanina bb) Founded in 1018, this Benedictine monastery has Rab's oldest bell tower (1181) and a still-functioning bell dating from 1396. Peer through the railings at the church's triple nave; some of the plasterwork has been removed to reveal the original stonework. Nearby, the monks run a monastery shop selling oils and honey.

Church of the Assumption CHURCH
(Crkva Uznesenjca; Ivana Rabljanina bb) It hasn't been a cathedral since 1828, when the diocese was dissolved, but locals still refer to this, their grandest church, as the *katedrala*. Its striking facade has stripes of pink and cream stone, and a Gothic-style pietà over the door. Inside, key features include 15th-century choir stalls and weathered pillars. It's been remodelled a lot over the years, but mosaics found here indicate that this has been a Christian place of worship since the 4th or 5th century.

Its opening hours are erratic, but you can usually peer in through the metal grille.

St Anthony the Abbot's Church CHURCH
(Crkva Sv Antuna Opata; Ivana Rabljanina bb) At the eastern tip of the old town, this church attached to a still-operating Franciscan convent has lots of inlaid marble and a carving of a seated St Anthony decorating the altar. It's the final resting place of St Marin of Rab, whose statue graces a beautifully landscaped park below, a relaxing stop during a sightseeing tour.

Komrčar Park PARK
(Banjol/Obala Kralja Petra Krešimira IV) This 8.3-hectare park abuts the old town and stretches along the coast to the marina at Palit. It was originally used to graze cattle but was planted in forest in the 19th century, much to the consternation of the townsfolk. It's leafy and deliciously cool on a summer day – pack a picnic from the supermarket

Rab Town

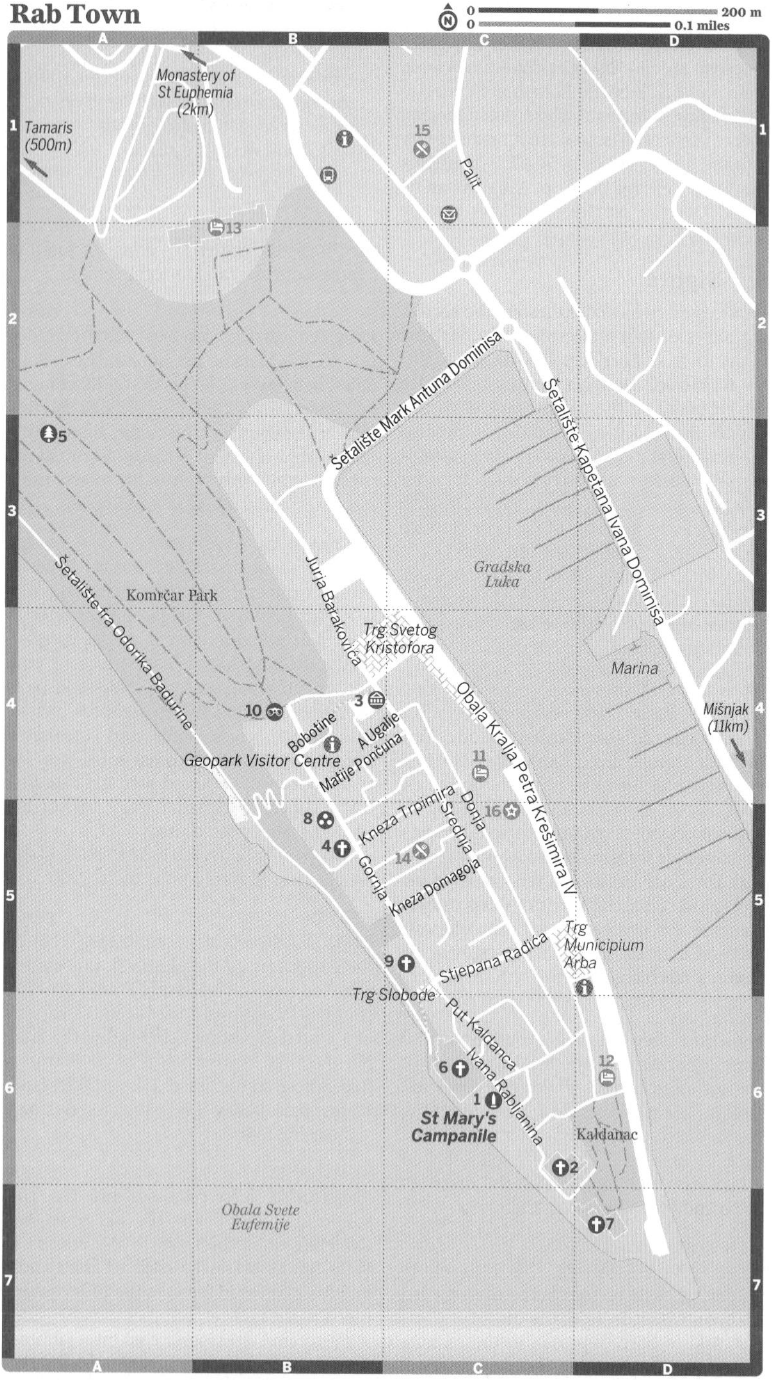

0 200 m
0 0.1 miles

A B C D
1 2 3 4 5 6 7

Monastery of St Euphemia (2km)
Tamaris (500m)
15
Palit
13
5
Šetalište Mark Antuna Dominisa
Šetalište Kapetana Ivana Dominisa
Gradska Luka
Jurja Barakovića
Komrčar Park
Šetalište fra Odorika Badurine
Trg Svetog Kristofora
Marina
Obala Kralja Petra Krešimira IV
10
3
Bobotine
A Ugalje
Geopark Visitor Centre
Matije Pončuna
Mišnjak (11km)
11
Kneza Trpimira
Donja
16
8
4
14
Srednja
Gornja
Kneza Domagoja
Trg Municipium Arba
9
Stjepana Radića
Trg Slobode
Put Kaldanca
6
Ivana Rabljanina
12
1
St Mary's Campanile
Kaldanac
2
7
Obala Svete Eufemije

Rab Town

at the harbour and enjoy a couple of hours chilling on the grass. There's a good children's playground at the harbour end.

Dominis Palace HISTORIC BUILDING
(Srednja bb) Built at the end of the 15th century for a prominent patrician family who taught the public to read and write here, this building is worth noting for its Renaissance windows and striking doorway decorated with the family coat of arms.

St John the Evangelist's Church RUINS
(Crkva Sv Ivana Evanđelista; Gornja bb) It's thought that parts of this atmospherically ruined Romanesque basilica date as far back as the 5th century. Today, amid assorted rubble, only a handful of columns are still standing, along with the restored 12th-century bell tower.

St Justine's Church CHURCH
(Crkva Sv Justine; Gornja bb) This semiderelict church has a bell tower dating from 1672. It's located beside pretty Trg Slobode, which has a holm oak tree and sea vistas. Below is an easily accessible stretch of shingle/concrete beach for foot-soothing, midsightseeing paddles.

Activities

Rab has 100km of hiking trails and 80km of biking trails; several can be accessed from Rab Town. Pick up the *Biking and Trekking* map from the tourist office (p207) or call into the Geopark Visitor Centre (p207) for information on the new 'geotrails'. Bikes can be rented from several travel agencies.

Mirko Diving Centre DIVING
(051-721 154; Barbat 710; 2 dives from 450KN) Mirko Diving Centre, based in nearby Barbat, offers courses and fun dives as well as trips to well-known dive sites such as the wreck of the *Rosa* and a protected amphora field off the cape of Sorinj.

Tours

Day tours of the island by boat, including swim stops and visits to nearby islands such as Sveti Grgur and the infamous Goli Otok, once used as a prison, are offered by many travel agents; expect to pay about 200KN to 275KN, which includes lunch. You can also chat directly with skippers about trips: in the evening the main harbour front is lined with excursion boats. Trips to the islands of Lošinj and Krk are also possible.

Festivals & Events

Rab Musical Evenings MUSIC
(Rapske Glazbene Večeri; mid-Jun–mid-Sep) This top-notch classical-music festival revolves around Thursday-night concerts at venues including Holy Cross Church.

Rab Fair FIESTA
(Rapska Fjera; Jul) Witness Rab transporting itself back to the Middle Ages. Residents dress in period garb and there are drummers, processions, fireworks, medieval dancing and crossbow competitions.

Summer Festival MUSIC
(early Aug) Croatian pop stars and international DJs perform in the old town.

Sleeping

Hostel Rab International HOSTEL €
(051-602 000; Obala Kralja Petra Krešimira IV 4; dm 225KN; P) This five-room hostel right in the centre of the peninsula features clean bunks in spacious if slightly characterless dorms with crisp linen and spotless bathrooms. Some rooms have harbour views, but

WORTH A TRIP

MONASTERY OF ST EUPHEMIA

A 2.5km walk heading north along the seaside promenade from Rab's old town brings you to the **Monastery of St Euphemia** (Samostan Sv Eufemije; Kampor; adult/child 20/10KN; ⏲10am-noon & 4-7pm Mon-Sat), a peaceful Franciscan monastery, dating from the 13th century. The monks have a small museum with old manuscripts and religious paintings. Check out the pleasant cloister and, inside the baroque church of St Bernardine, the ethereal painted ceiling – a stark contrast to the visceral agony depicted on the late-Gothic wooden crucifix in the side chapel. Note also the 15th-century polyptych by the Vivarini brothers.

there are no cooking facilities. As it's Rab's only true hostel of note, beds fill up fast.

Tamaris HOTEL €€
(☎051-724 925; www.tamaris-rab.com; Palit 285; s/d 575/850KN; P❄☜) A 10-minute walk north of town, this is a well-run little hotel with attentive staff and a peaceful location near the sea. Rooms are simple but quite comfortable, with laminate floors and soft linen. Some have sea views from their balconies.

Valamar Imperial Hotel HOTEL €€
(☎052 465 000; www.valamar.com; Šetalište Mark Antuna Dominisa 9; r 640-1035KN; P❄☜≋) A recent overhaul has brought style and substance to this well-located hotel amid the trees of Komrčar Park. Facilities include tennis courts, a gym, a spa and a very appealing outdoor swimming pool. Rooms have soothing yet contemporary steely-grey colour schemes.

Hotel Arbiana BOUTIQUE HOTEL €€€
(☎051-725 563; www.arbianahotel.com; Obala Kralja Petra Krešimira IV 12; r 1150-2220KN; P❄☜) The classiest address in Rab, this historic hotel dates to 1924 and retains plenty of period character and formal elegance. All 27 rooms are perfectly maintained and come with 21st-century TVs, sturdy desks and good-quality retro furnishings. Most have balconies. The hotel restaurant is also worth a try, even if you're not staying here.

Eating

Restaurant Velum SEAFOOD €€
(☎051-774 855; www.velum.hr; Palit 71; mains 60-170KN) Steak, pizza, grilled meats and fish – there's nothing too surprising on the menu here, but the cooking is assured and the service excellent, and the kitchen does wonderful things with wild asparagus.

Konoba Rab CROATIAN €€
(☎051-725 666; Kneza Branimira 3; mains 75-130KN; ⏲10am-2pm & 5-11pm Mon-Sat, 5-11pm Sun) For real country cooking – albeit in a multilevel, faux-rural setting – this place excels. Find one of the many nooks and crannies containing tables and order mains of grilled meat and fish staples, or the lamb baked under a *peka* (traditional domed baking lid) in advance. Fish is priced by the kilo.

Entertainment

Santos Beach Club CLUB
(☎051-724 145; www.sanantonio-club.com; Pudarica Beach; ⏲10am-dawn late Jun-early Sep) This summer-only beach club is about 10km from Rab Town, far away from any complaining neighbours in a remote spot near the Mišnjak car ferry (shuttle boats run at night). DJs spin to a lively party crowd and there are live concerts and fashion shows. It doubles as a daytime beach hang-out, with loungers and volleyball.

Dock 69 BAR, CLUB
(Obala Kralja Petra Krešimira IV; ⏲8am-3pm & 7pm-midnight Sun-Thu, to 3am Fri & Sat) This slick lounge bar has a harbour-facing cafe terrace and a clubby interior where DJs ramp up the volume at weekends.

ℹ Information

There's free wi-fi around the tourist office and the bus station.

Geopark Visitor Centre (Bobotine bb; ⏲10am-5pm Mon, Tue & Thu-Sat, 3-8pm Sun) Call in for information on 'geotrail' paths that explore the island's unique geology. There are also interactive information screens and samples of local rocks.

Numero Uno (☎092 16 94 399; www.numero-uno.hr; Banjol 30) Books private accommodation, rents bicycles, and offers trekking trips and kayak and bike tours.

Post Office (☎072 303 304; www.posta.hr; Mali Palit 67; ⏲7.30am-9pm Mon-Sat Jun-Sep, 7am-8pm Mon-Fri, to 2pm Sat Oct-May)

Stay in Rab (☎051-724 495; www.stayinrab.com; Šetalište Markantuna Dominisa 5) Organises private accommodation, money exchange, bike rental, boat excursions and even tours to distant places such as Plitvice Lakes National Park.

Tourist Office (☎051-724 064; www.rab-visit.com; Trg Municipium Arba 8; ⏰8am-9pm Mon-Sat, to 1pm Sun Easter-Oct, 8am-3pm Mon-Fri Nov-Easter) A well-organised office with helpful staff and loads of useful maps, brochures and leaflets. In summer it operates a second **branch** (⏰8am-3pm Jun-Sep) around the corner from the **bus station** (Banjol).

Lopar

☎051 / POP 1288

At the northern tip of the island, the beach town of Lopar is semirural around the edges, with garden plots and roses growing in front gardens. It's sleepy even in early June, but in the school holidays Central European families flock here, as the sea is very shallow and perfect for small children. This is particularly so with 1500m-long Paradise Beach on Crnika Bay, right in the centre of town, where you can almost wade across to a little offshore island.

There are 22 sandy beaches bordered by shady pine groves scattered around the peninsula, including Livačina Beach and Sahara Beach.

Sights

★Paradise Beach BEACH

(Rajska Plaža) One of Croatia's best beaches, this sickle of fine sand hems Lopar's southern flank and is the biggest attraction in these parts. Backed by all sorts of attractions, from minigolf to ice-cream parlours, this is the ideal spot for a family holiday. The beach hardly shelves as it goes out into the warm Adriatic, and a small offshore island makes for a great swimming or kayaking destination.

Livačina Beach BEACH

This popular beach is one cove east of Lopar town. It can get busy, but it's a good alternative to the even busier main town beach. Backed by pine trees and with sheltered waters, it's popular with families.

Sahara Beach BEACH

Sahara Beach is a popular nudist spot in a gorgeous but shallow bay. Look for the signpost pointing off the main road before you reach Paradise Beach; it's a 1.8km (half-hour) walk from here, or you can drive along the narrow lane and walk for 15 minutes from the parking area.

Sleeping

Hotel Epario HOTEL €€

(☎051-777 500; www.epario.net; Lopar 456a; incl half board s 266-488KN, d 415-976KN; P ❄ 📶) Just about the only real hotel in Lopar, the laid-back Epario is a modern block facing the fields on the main road leading towards Paradise Beach. Rooms have desks, balconies and good bathrooms. It's a short walk to the beach and to the large Konzum supermarket at the nearby crossroads.

Eating & Drinking

Gostionica Laguna MEDITERRANEAN €€

(☎051-775 177; www.laguna-lopar.com; Lopar 547; mains 85-190KN; ⏰noon-10pm; P ❄ 📶) The greenery-trimmed, wooden-roofed terrace at this friendly tavern is by far the nicest place to eat at this end of the island. Specialities include spit-roast suckling pig, *peka*-cooked lamb or octopus, but there's also a large menu of pasta, monster pizzas, and grilled meat and fish. Inside there's a soft playroom where the kids can make international friends as you kick back.

Bamboocho BAR

(Rajska Plaža; ⏰noon-late) Among the pine trees lining the eastern end of Paradise Beach, this open-air beach bar has been quirkily sculpted from bits of scrap metal and chunky bamboo. It's a wonderful spot for a sundowner.

Information

Sahara Tours (☎051-775 633; www.sahara-lopar.com; Lopar 53) Has dozens of private rooms, houses and apartments on its books. Look for it opposite the tennis courts.

Tourist Office (☎051-775 508; www.lopar.com; Lopar 248; ⏰8am-10pm Mon-Sat, to 2pm Sun Jul & Aug, to 11am Mon-Fri Sep-Jun) Helpful little office next to the Konzum supermarket.

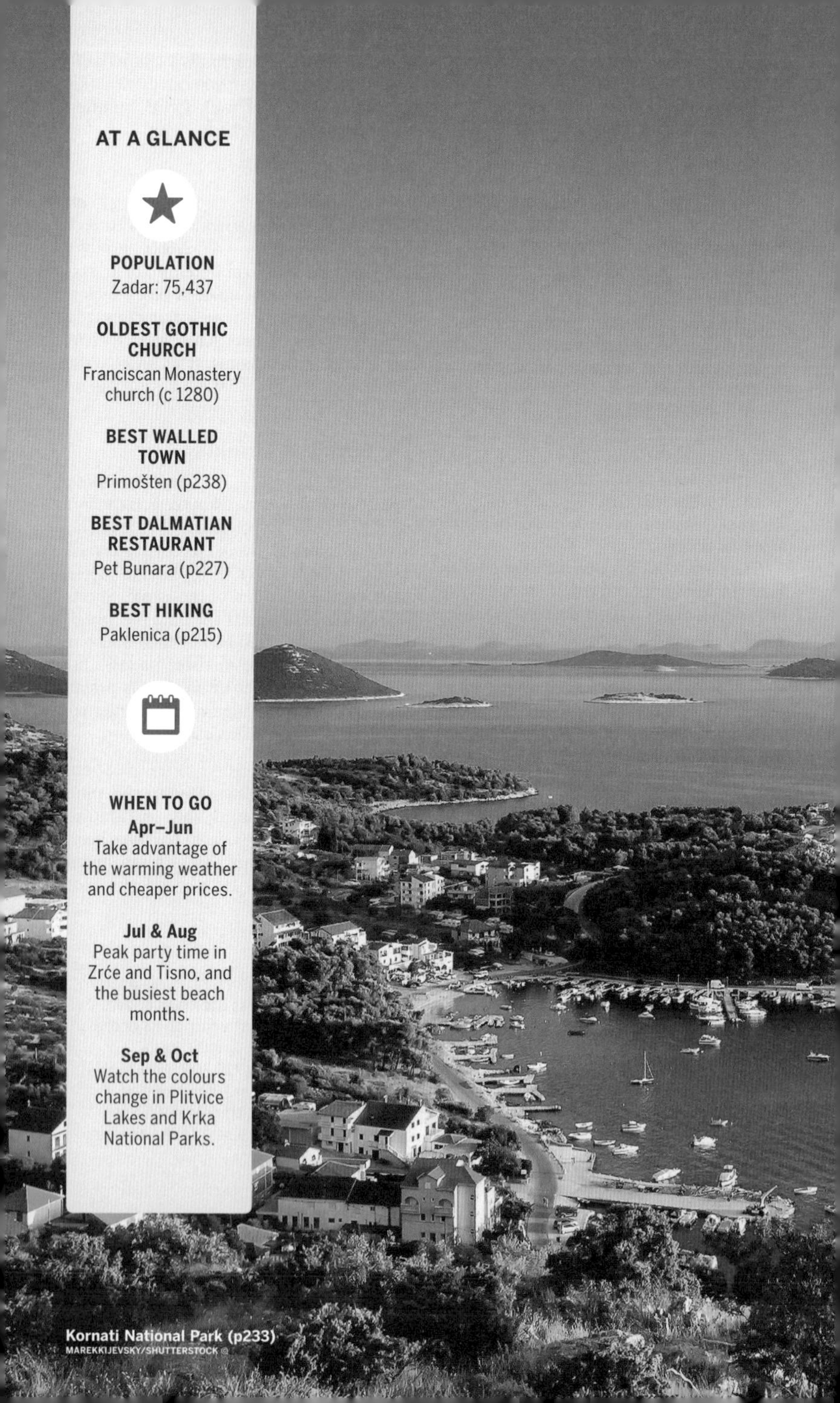

AT A GLANCE

POPULATION
Zadar: 75,437

OLDEST GOTHIC CHURCH
Franciscan Monastery church (c 1280)

BEST WALLED TOWN
Primošten (p238)

BEST DALMATIAN RESTAURANT
Pet Bunara (p227)

BEST HIKING
Paklenica (p215)

WHEN TO GO

Apr–Jun
Take advantage of the warming weather and cheaper prices.

Jul & Aug
Peak party time in Zrće and Tisno, and the busiest beach months.

Sep & Oct
Watch the colours change in Plitvice Lakes and Krka National Parks.

Kornati National Park (p233)
MAREKKIJEVSKY/SHUTTERSTOCK ©

Northern Dalmatia

Serving the classic Dalmatian cocktail of historic towns, jewel-like waters, rugged limestone mountains, sun-kissed islands, gorgeous climate and Mediterranean cuisine, this region is a holidaymaker's dream. Yet it's the cities and islands further south that hog all the limelight, leaving Northern Dalmatia, if not quite undiscovered, then certainly less overrun. Yachties can sail between unpopulated islands without a shred of development, lost in dreams of the Mediterranean of old, while hikers can wander lonely trails where bears and wolves still dwell, and explore three of Croatia's most impressive national parks, which shelter in the hinterland. By contrast, Zadar is a cultured city rich in museums, Roman ruins, restaurants and hip bars. Summertime clubbers gravitate to Zrće Beach and Tisno, which together form the nucleus of Croatia's premier clubbing scene.

INCLUDES

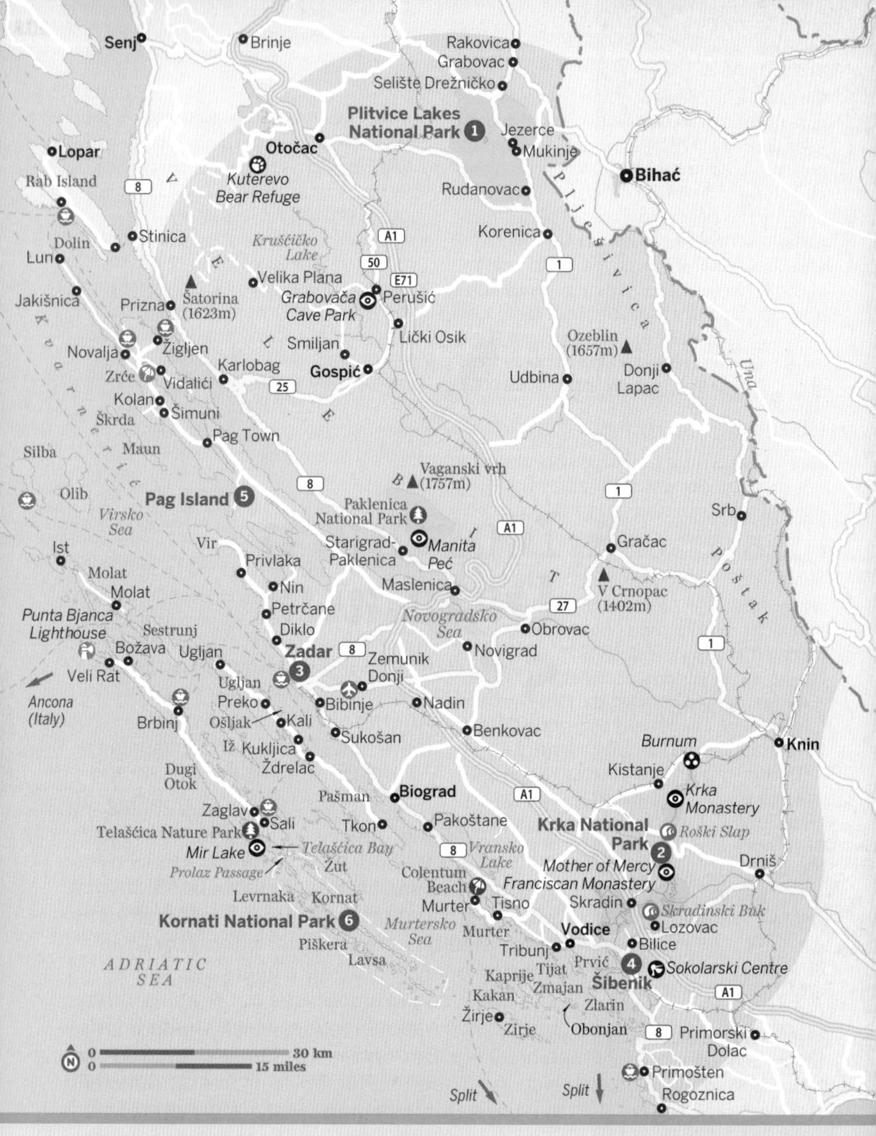

Northern Dalmatia Highlights

❶ **Plitvice Lakes National Park** (p211) Marvelling at the other-worldly turquoise lakes and dramatic waterfalls of Croatia's top natural attraction.

❷ **Krka National Park** (p233) Strolling alongside crystalline streams, swimming in a waterfall-fed lake and exploring historic monasteries.

❸ **Zadar** (p223) Exploring Roman ruins, intriguing museums, local eateries and hip bars within the marbled streets of the old town.

❹ **Šibenik** (p235) Stopping to admire the celebrated architecture of St James' Cathedral while wandering the medieval streets.

❺ **Pag Island** (p216) Enjoying the sensory delights of sun-scorched scenery, fine wine, rustic cooking, pungent cheese and partying in the sun.

❻ **Kornati National Park** (p233) Seeing the Mediterranean as it looked to the ancients while boating between unpopulated islands.

LIKA

Covering a large swath of the Northern Dalmatian interior between the coastal mountains and the Bosnian border, this lightly populated region has blissful scenery ranging from bucolic farmland to dense forest and craggy uplands. If you're looking for an alternative to beaches and islands, it's a wonderful area to explore. In parts, the karstic nature of the underlying limestone has bequeathed a wonderland of caves, canyons, lakes and waterfalls. The most dramatic of these natural attractions is Plitvice Lakes National Park, one of Croatia's unmissable experiences.

History

Part of the Croatian heartland since the early 7th century, Lika was attacked by the Ottomans in the 16th century and was incorporated into the military frontier *(vojna krajina)*. Vlach and Serb refugees, driven from Bosnia by the encroaching Ottomans, settled in the region with the blessing of the Habsburg monarchy, on the condition that they were prepared to fight to defend their new home. By the 1910 census the population was almost evenly split between the Orthodox and Catholic faiths, with many districts in the east having an outright Serbian majority.

During WWII, Lika's Serbian population suffered greatly at the hands of the Ustaše regime. In 1991, following Croatia's declaration of independence, the Serbs of the Krajina declared themselves an autonomous republic and it was in Lika that the first shots of the war rang out. Much of the local Croatian population was forced to abandon their homes and flee. When Croatian forces regained the area in 1995, most of the Serb population fled – leaving in their wake many abandoned homes and villages. Some, however, chose to return, and today the ethnic make-up of the region is 86% Croat and 12% Serb.

Plitvice Lakes & Around

053

By far Croatia's top natural attraction and the absolute highlight of Croatia's Adriatic hinterland, this glorious expanse of forested hills and turquoise lakes is exquisitely scenic – so much so that in 1979 Unesco proclaimed it a World Heritage Site. The name is, however, slightly misleading, as it's not so much the lakes that are the attraction here but the hundreds of waterfalls that link them. It's as though Croatia decided to gather all its waterfalls in one place and charge admission to view them.

The extraordinary natural beauty of the park merits a full day's exploration, but you can still experience a lot on a half-day trip from Zadar or Zagreb. You must be able to walk a fair distance to get the most out of the place.

WHEN TO VISIT

While the park is beautiful year-round, spring and autumn are the best times to visit. In spring and early summer the falls are flush with water, while in autumn the changing leaves put on a colourful display. Winter is also spectacular, although snow can limit access and the free park transport doesn't operate. Unquestionably the worst time to visit is in the peak months of July and August, when the falls reduce to a trickle, parking is problematic and the sheer volume of visitors can turn the walking tracks into a conga line and cause lengthy waits for the buses and boats that ferry people around the park.

History

A preservation society was founded in 1893 to ensure the protection of the lakes, and the first hotel was built here in 1896. The boundaries of the national park were set in 1951 and the lakes became a major tourist attraction until the civil war (which actually began in Plitvice on 31 March 1991, when rebel Serbs took control of the park headquarters). Croatian police officer Josip Jović became the war's first victim when he was killed here in the park. The Serbs held the area for the war's duration, turning the hotels into barracks. The Croatian army retook the park in August 1995, and subsequently the park's facilities have been fully restored.

Sights

★Plitvice Lakes National Park NATIONAL PARK

(053-751 015; www.np-plitvicka-jezera.hr; adult/child Jul & Aug 250/110KN, Apr-Jun, Sep & Oct 150/80KN, Nov-Mar 55/35KN; 7am-8pm) Within the boundaries of this heavily forested national park, 16 crystalline lakes tumble into each other via a series of waterfalls and cascades. The mineral-rich waters carve through the rock, depositing tufa in continually changing formations. Clouds of butterflies drift above the 18km of wooden footbridges and pathways that snake around the edges and across the rumbling water.

It takes upwards of six hours to explore the lakes on foot, or you can slice two hours off by taking advantage of the park's free boats and buses (departing every 30 minutes from April to October). From Entrance 2, catch the bus to the top of the upper lakes and wander back down to the shore of 4km-long **Kozjak**, the park's largest lake. A boat will whisk you from here to the lower lakes, where the circuit culminates in the aptly named **Veliki Slap**, the tallest waterfall in Croatia (78m). The path then climbs steeply (offering great views and photo opportunities) to a bus stop, where you can grab a lift back to Entrance 2.

If you've got limited time, the upper lake section can be completed in two hours. The lower section takes about three, although it's best to start with the bus ride and end with the boat to save yourself a climb. Swimming is not permitted in any of the lakes.

Sleeping & Eating

The four hotels operated by the national park are relatively charmless institutions, but they're conveniently positioned right on the park's borders (see the park website, www.np-plitvicka-jezera.hr, for details). Otherwise, there are excellent guesthouses within walking distance in surrounding villages. For a particularly atmospheric alternative, hunt for private rooms in tiny Korana, an idyllic village set by a gurgling stream and reached by a narrow road north of the Korana bridge.

Plitvice Backpackers HOSTEL €
(☎053-774 777; www.plitvicebackpackers.com; Jezerce 62, Jezerce; dm/tw 150/340KN;) Located in Jezerce, the nearest village to the lakes, just 3km from Plitvice Lakes National Park's Entrance 2, this well-run hostel occupies a large house on the main highway. Rooms are clean, lockers are big and there's a fully equipped kitchen. The owners really look after their guests, even shuttling them to and from the park and local supermarket.

★**House Župan** GUESTHOUSE €€
(☎047-784 057; www.sobe-zupan.com; Rakovica 35, Rakovica; s/d 250/370KN; P) With an exceptionally welcoming hostess and clean, contemporary and reasonably priced rooms, this is a superb choice. There's even a guest kitchen and plenty of other diversions when you want to relax after a hike. It's set back from the highway in the small town

PLITVICE'S WONDROUS NATURE

The Plitvice lake system is divided into upper and lower sections. The upper lakes, lying in a dolomite valley, are surrounded by dense forests and are linked by several gushing waterfalls. The lower lakes are smaller and shallower. Most of the water comes from the Bijela and Crna (White and Black) Rivers, which join south of Prošćansko Lake, but the lakes are also fed by underground springs. In turn, water disappears into the porous limestone at some points, only to reemerge in other places. All the water empties into the Korana River near Sastavci Falls.

The upper lakes are separated by dolomite barriers, which expand with the mosses and algae that absorb calcium carbonate as river water rushes through the karst. The encrusted plants grow on top of each other, forming travertine barriers and creating waterfalls. The lower lakes were formed by cavities created by the water of the upper lakes. They undergo a similar process, as travertine is constantly forming and reforming itself into new combinations so that the landscape is ever changing. This unique interaction of water, rock and plant life has continued more or less undisturbed since the last ice age.

The lakes' colours also change constantly. Most of the time they're a surreal shade of turquoise, but hues shift with the quantity of minerals and organisms in the water, rainfall and the angle of sunlight. On some days the lakes can appear more jade green or steely grey.

The luxuriant vegetation of the national park includes beech, fir, spruce and white pine forests, dotted with patches of whitebeam, hornbeam and flowering ash, which change colour in autumn.

The mammalian stars of the park are bears (there are an estimated 50) and wolves, but there are also deer, boar, rabbits, foxes and badgers. Look out for bird species including hawks, owls, cuckoos, kingfishers, wild ducks and herons, and occasionally black storks and ospreys.

of Rakovica, 11km north of Plitvice Lakes National Park.

Plitvice Mirić Inn GUESTHOUSE €€
(☎098 93 06 508; www.plitvice-croatia.com; Jezerce 18/1, Jezerce; s/d 550/780KN; ⊙Apr-Oct; P ❄ 🛜) Run by a delightful family, this flower-strewn guesthouse has 13 well-cared-for rooms divided between neighbouring buildings, conveniently located a mere 1.5km from Plitvice Lakes National Park's Entrance 2. Rooms boast slightly more floor space in the newer annexe, but they're all very comfortable. Try the home baking if you get a chance.

House Tina GUESTHOUSE €€
(☎047-784 197; www.housetina.com; Grabovac 175, Grabovac; d/bungalows 560/875KN; P ❄ 🛜) Smart and modern, but with a rural ambience, this large, family-run guesthouse offers first-rate family-friendly accommodation both in the main house and in two rustic wooden bungalows in the yard. It's 9km from Plitvice Lakes National Park's Entrance 1, but the owners can organise transport for a relatively small cost.

Villa Lika GUESTHOUSE €€€
(☎053-774 302; www.villa-lika.com; Mukinje 63, Mukinje; r from 950KN; ⊙Apr-Oct; P ❄ 🛜 🏊) Right by the bus stop in Mukinje, these two large houses have shiny white rooms punctuated with brightly coloured curtains and tiles. There are 15 rooms in total, all set around a beautifully landscaped pool, and a recently opened restaurant offering international and Croatian dishes (portion sizes are small).

Hotel Degenija HOTEL €€€
(☎047-782 143; www.hotel-degenija.com; Selište Drežničko 57a, Selište Drežničko; s/d from 700/990KN; P ❄ 🛜) With a crisp, newish feel, this 20-room roadside hotel, 4km north of Plitvice Lakes National Park's Entrance 1, has smart international-standard rooms and an attractive **restaurant** (mains 55-140KN; ⊙7am-11pm; 🛜).

★ **Lička Kuća** CROATIAN €€
(☎053-751 024; Rastovača; mains 70-195KN; ⊙11am-10pm Mar-Nov) Built in 1972 and fully rebuilt in traditional stone-walled style in 2015 after burning to the ground three years earlier, Lička Kuća is touristy and extremely busy in high season, but the food is excellent. Specialities include slow-cooked lamb, dry-cured local prosciutto, and mountain trout, making it one of the best places for traditional dishes in the Northern Dalmatian interior.

Information

Both of the park's two main entrances have parking (7/70KN per hour/day) and an information office stocking brochures and maps. The main park **office** (☎053-751 014; www.np-plitvicka-jezera.hr; Josipa Jovića 19, Plitvička Jezera) is in Plitvička Jezera.

Getting There & Away

Buses stop at both park entrances; there's a small ticket office at the stop near Entrance 2. Destinations include the following:

Šibenik 118KN, four hours, three daily
Split 174KN, 4½ hours, six daily
Zadar 95KN, 2½ hours, seven daily
Zagreb 89KN, two hours, many daily

Gospić

☎053 / POP 6575

One of the prettiest among inland Northern Dalmatian towns, riverside Gospić is surrounded by the craggy mountains so typical of the region. The main reason to visit is the nearby Nikola Tesla Memorial Centre, but the town, too, is worth a wander. The terracotta roofs and pretty church steeple give it a skyline that's matched at street level by handsome architecture. It's a fine place to break your journey between north and south, or as a detour from the coast.

History

Although the first record of a settlement here dates to 1263, it was not until the early 17th century that the name Gospić was used. The town gained notoriety in the 20th century: a Nazi-backed concentration camp was established nearby during WWII, and more than 42,000 people are believed to have been killed at the camp.

That anything at all survives here is remarkable – in 1991 the town came under frequent bombardment as the Croatian army fought for control against Serbian forces backing the Republic of Serbian Krajina. It was not until 1995 that peace was restored.

Sights

Nikola Tesla Memorial Centre MUSEUM
(☎053-746 530; www.mcnikolatesla.hr; Smiljan; adult/child 50/20KN; ⊙8am-8pm Tue-Sun Apr-Oct, 9am-3pm Tue-Sun Nov-Mar) It's extraordinary to think that one of the greatest minds of the modern world came from such a peaceful and obscure place as the tiny village of Smiljan, 5km west of Gospić. Yet it

OFF THE BEATEN TRACK

LIKA'S HIDDEN GEMS

With the exception of the Plitvice Lakes, almost all of the Lika region could accurately be described as 'off the beaten track'. If you've got a vehicle and don't mind taking your time to get around, it's a profitable place to explore.

Kuterevo Bear Refuge (☎053-799 001; www.kuterevo-medvjedi.org; Pod Crikvon 109, Kuterevo; admission by donation; ⊙hours vary) Founded in 2002, the bear refuge works with villagers to protect orphaned bears that are endangered due to traffic, hunting and poaching. From spring to late autumn, volunteers will happily take you around the large enclosures, explaining the history of each bear and touching on the wider issues of bear conservation. Your best chance of seeing the bears in an active state is in the couple of hours before sunset.

Kuterevo village is in the northern Velebit Range, 48km southeast of Senj along the D23 and D50. The website is in Croatian, but emails will be answered in English.

Zipline Beware of the Bear (☎095 846 41 71; www.ziplineplitvice.com; Rudopolje-Vrhovine; adult/child Jun-Sep 280/140KN, Oct-May 240/120KN; ⊙10am-7pm) At 1700m, Beware of the Bear is Europe's longest one-piece zipline. Under the right wind conditions, you'll reach speeds of up to 120km/h as you zip 80m above the earth. It really does feel like flying.

The zipline is in Rudopolje-Vrhovine, 44km by road west of Plitvice Lakes National Park's Entrance 1. You'll need your own car to get here.

Linden Tree Retreat & Ranch (☎053-685 616; www.lindenretreat.com; Velika Plana 3, Velika Plana; r per person 590-900KN) Nestled within the wild reaches of the Velebit Range 27km northwest of Gospić, this remote dude ranch offers atmospheric accommodation in tepees or wooden chalets. The highlight here is horse riding (390KN for a two-hour jaunt, 1280KN for a day trip), but you can also partake in wagon rides, guided hikes to nearby caves, mountain biking and mountain climbing.

Grabovača Cave Park (Pećinski Park Grabovača; ☎053-679 233; www.pp-grabovaca.hr; Perušić; tours adult/child 50/35KN; ⊙10am-6pm Jun, to 9pm Jul & Aug, 9am-5pm Apr, May, Sep & Oct, 8am-3pm Nov, closed Dec-Mar) Samograd, the largest cave of this extraordinary complex, has four beautiful chambers – the biggest is large enough to host a concert every Easter Monday. Tours (not suitable for small children) descend 480 handmade stairs into the depths; check the website for departure times. Wear warm clothes and sensible shoes. The cave complex lies on the edge of Perušić, a small town 12km north of Gospić. Perušić is also notable for its pretty onion-domed church and its perfect chess-piece Turkish castle.

was here that Nikola Tesla – the man responsible for bringing electricity into our homes and inventing wireless technology – was born. This fascinating museum includes displays about his life and working replicas of some of his most famous inventions.

Tesla's father was a Serbian Orthodox priest and, sadly, the family house, barn and church on this site were torched during the 1990s war. What stands here today is a reconstruction, financed by the Croatian government.

Sleeping & Eating

Hotel Stara Lika HOTEL €€
(☎053-658 160; www.hotelstaralika.hr; Dr Franje Tudjmana 1; r/ste from 355/460KN; P ❄ 📶) An excellent choice in a quietly elegant building, the Stara Lika has classically styled rooms with wooden desks and leather-studded armchairs. It's reassuringly warm in winter and otherwise supremely comfortable, with good service. It will appear to be fabulous value (which it is) if you're used to summer coastal prices.

Bistro Travel BISTRO €€
(☎099 779 00 59; www.facebook.com/bistrowinetravel; Smiljanska 32; mains 50-130KN; ⊙noon-11pm) Quite a find out here in the back blocks, Bistro Travel does excellent pizzas, as well as tasty inland fare (the steaks are especially good) and some seafood-based nods to the coast. Service is friendly.

Information

Tourist Information Centre (☎053-560 754; www.visitgospic.com/hr; Karlovića 1; ⊙7am-3pm)

Getting There & Away

One daily bus connects Gospić with Šibenik (135KN, 3¼ hours), Zagreb (115KN, 3½ hours) and Split (189KN, five hours).

Paklenica National Park

Stretching for 145km and creating a natural barrier between inland and coastal Croatia, the rugged peaks of the Velebit Range are an impressive sight. **Paklenica National Park** (☎023-369 155; www.np-paklenica.hr; adult/child Jun-Sep 60/30KN, Mar-May & Oct 40/20KN, Nov-Feb 20/10KN; ⏲entrance booths 6am-8.30pm Jun-Sep, 7am-3pm Oct-May) takes up 95 sq km of these limestone mountains and boasts some of Croatia's most dramatic alpine vistas. It's a superb place to trek gorges, do a bit of climbing or just amble along one of the many streams that score the land.

The park's two biggest attractions are the gorges of Velika Paklenica (Great Paklenica) and Mala Paklenica (Small Paklenica), where cliffs rise 400m into the azure skies. Animals you might spot along the way include golden eagles, striped eagles, peregrine falcons and, if you're extremely lucky, lynx and bears. Chamois gather near the park entrances.

Sights

Manita Peć CAVE

(adult/child 30/15KN; ⏲10am-1pm Jul-Sep, reduced days Apr-Jun & Oct) The only cave in Paklenica National Park that's open to the public, Manita Peć has a wealth of stalagmites and stalactites enhanced by strategically placed lighting in the main chamber (40m long and 32m high). Entry is by 30-minute tour.

The cave is about 90 minutes' walk from the park's Entrance 1 car park. The path heads right up and into the Velika Paklenica gorge. When you pass a rocky waterfall with a stream on your right, you'll be at Anića Luka, a green, semicircular plateau. After another kilometre a steep trail leads up to the cave.

Activities

Hiking

Most hikes in the park are one-day affairs from either of the two main park entrances (accessed from Starigrad-Paklenica on the coast), or from one of the mountain huts. Given the nature of the terrain, most hikes are reasonably challenging, but there are shorter routes suitable for novices. It's a good idea to ask at the park office (p216) about walks that will suit your level of ability. The park's website has an overview of nine popular hikes, from 1½-hour walks to seven-hour trails with a 1250m vertical drop.

Rock Climbing

Paklenica has rock-climbing routes ranging from beginner level to borderline suicidal. The firm, occasionally sharp limestone offers graded climbs, including 72 short sports routes and 250 longer routes. You'll see beginners' routes at the entrances to the park, with cliffs reaching about 40m, but the best and most advanced climbing is on **Anića Kuk**. Most of the routes are bolted.

Otherwise, the most popular climbs here are Mosoraški (350m), Velebitaški (350m) and Klin (300m).

Spring is the best climbing season, as summers can be hot and winters too windy. A rescue service is also available. Boris Čulić's *Paklenica* climber's guide offers the complete rundown; it's available from the park office.

Sleeping & Eating

There's some rustic accommodation for hikers and climbers within the park's boundaries, but most people base themselves in the relative comfort of Starigrad-Paklenica, the small settlement that sprawls along the coastal road near the park entrances. It's neither particularly *stari* (old) or much of a *grad* (town), but it does have access to the sea for a cooling dip after a day's exertions.

National Park

Rugged types can avail themselves of three basic free-of-charge mountain shelters: Ivine Vodice, Struge and Vlaški Grad. There's no electricity and you'll need your own sleeping bag, but each has a spring that's a reliable source of water in all but the height of summer; check with the park office or at Planinarski Dom Paklenica lodge before setting out.

Planinarski Dom Paklenica HUT €

(☎023-301 636; www.pdpaklenica.hr; dm 100KN; ⏲Sat & Sun year-round, daily mid-Jun–mid-Sep) Offering such luxuries as running water, a toilet and electricity, this lodge crams 50 beds into four rooms; bring a sleeping bag.

SAFE HIKING IN PAKLENICA

Landmines left over from the 1990s are still a risk in some of Paklenica National Park's higher zones. Follow only clearly marked paths and check with the park office before attempting any unusual routes.

There's also a kitchen and dining room. The hut is a two-hour walk up from the Velika Paklenica gorge. Reservations are recommended on summer weekends.

Starigrad-Paklenica

Camp 'National Park' CAMPGROUND €
(☎023-369 155; www.paklenica.hr; camping per adult/site 40/35KN; ⏰mid-Mar–mid-Nov) On a bit of gravelly Adriatic beach next to the park's admin building, this basic 100-person campground is a favourite among climbers and other adventurers heading into the limestone canyons of Paklenica National Park. The swimming is great. No reservations are taken.

Pansion Kiko GUESTHOUSE €€
(☎023-369 784; www.pansion-kiko.com; Ante Starčevića bb, Seline; r 813KN; P ❄ 📶) Just outside Starigrad-Paklenica, in the coastal village of Seline, this superb guesthouse offers 12 balconied rooms as well as access to a private beach and a decent restaurant. The friendly family owners will go out of their way to make sure your stay is as comfortable as possible, and this is a great base for exploring Paklenica National Park.

Buffet Dinko CROATIAN €€
(☎091 51 29 445; www.dinko-paklenica.com; Pakleničke 1; mains 59-135KN; ⏰7am-11pm) At the junction of the coastal highway and the access road in Starigrad to Entrance 1 for Paklenica National Park, this popular restaurant has a shady terrace and a hefty menu of grilled meat and seafood. Helpings are normally huge. The owners also have **rooms** (☎098 402 007; Selina 10; r 260KN, apt 295-370KN) to rent.

Information

Croatian Mountaineering Association (p37) Has up-to-date information and publishes a useful map of the park. The association's office is in Zagreb.

Paklenica National Park Office (☎023-369 155; www.paklenica.hr; Dr Franje Tuđmana 14a, Starigrad-Paklenica; ⏰7am-3pm Mon-Fri) Sells booklets and maps. The *Paklenica National Park* guide gives an excellent overview of the park and details on walks. Rock-climbing permits cost 60KN to 80KN depending on the season; climbers should talk to guides at the park office for advice. Main office in Starigrad-Paklenica; other offices at park entrances.

Starigrad Tourist Office (☎023-369 245; www.rivijera-paklenica.hr; Trg Tome Marasovića 1, Starigrad-Paklenica; ⏰8am-9.30pm Jul & Aug, to 8pm Jun & Sep, to 2pm Mon-Fri Oct-May) In the Starigrad-Paklenica town centre, across from the small marina.

Getting There & Around

Most buses travelling along the coastal highway stop at Starigrad-Paklenica. Destinations include Rijeka (135KN, 3¾ hours, five daily), Zadar (28KN, one hour, five daily), Split (118KN, four hours, five daily) and Dubrovnik (from 221KN, nine hours, three daily).

There are generally no taxis in Starigrad-Paklenica. Some hotels will drop off and pick up guests at the park's entrance gates.

PAG ISLAND

Pag is like something from a 1950s Italian film, perfect for a broody black-and-white Antonioni set – it's barren, rocky, and sepia coloured, with vast, empty landscapes. The Adriatic is a steely blue around it and, when the sky is stormy, the island is the most dramatic-looking place in the whole of Croatia. Its karstic rock forms a moonscape defined by two mountain ridges, patches of shrubs, and a dozen or so villages and hamlets.

Modern Pag is an unusual mix. The island has long-standing traditions of cheese- and winemaking; *paški sir* (Pag cheese) is one of Croatia's most celebrated culinary exports, its source the otherwise unremarkable village of Kolan. The famous intricate Pag lace is framed on many a Croat's wall. And yet Novalja is a party town and the island has become a clubbing mecca, with Zrće Beach a summer nightlife hot spot.

Getting There & Around

BOAT

A daily **Jadrolinija** (☎in Rijeka 051-666 111; www.jadrolinija.hr) catamaran connects Novalja to Rab (40KN, 55 minutes) and Rijeka (60KN, 2¾ hours).

Regular Jadrolinija car ferries also link Žigljen on Pag's northeast coast to Prizna on the mainland (adult/child/car 14/7/80KN, 15 minutes); these run roughly every 90 minutes, increasing to hourly in July and August. If you're coming from the north, this will save you at least 1½ hours' driving time as opposed to taking the bridge.

BUS

Buses connect Novalja and Pag Town year-round with Zadar, with summer-only services to/from Šibenik, Split, Rijeka and Zagreb.

Three to 11 buses a day make the 40-minute trip between Pag Town and Novalja (from 39KN).

Pag Town

023 / POP 3700

Historic Pag Town enjoys a lovely setting, fringing a narrow spit of land between sun-scorched hills, with an azure bay on its eastern flank and shimmering salt pans to its west. It's an intimate grid of narrow lanes and bleak-looking stone houses with pebble beaches close by.

History

In the early 15th century the prosperous salt business (Pag sea salt can still be bought in any supermarket) prompted the construction of Pag Town when adjacent Stari Grad could no longer meet the demands of its burgeoning population. Venetian rulers engaged the finest builder of the time, Juraj Dalmatinac, to design a new city – the first cornerstone was laid in 1443. In the centre, there's a square with a cathedral, a ducal palace and an unfinished bishop's palace. In 1499 Dalmatinac began working on the city walls, but only the northern corner, with parts of a castle, remains.

Sights

Collegiate Church of the Assumption CHURCH

(Zborna Crkva Marijinog Uznesenja; Trg Kralja Petra Krešimira IV; 9am-noon & 5-7pm May-Sep, Mass only Oct-Apr) FREE Juraj Dalmatinac's Gothic church sits in perfect harmony with the modest structures surrounding it on the pretty main square. The lunette over the portal shows the Virgin with women of Pag in medieval blouses and headdresses, and there are two rows of unfinished sculptures of saints. Completed in the 16th century, the interior was renovated with baroque stucco ceiling decorations in the 18th century.

Pag Lace Gallery MUSEUM

(Galerija paške čipke; Trg Kralja Petra Krešimira IV; 10KN; 9am-noon & 7-10pm Jul & Aug, 9am-noon Jun & Sep, 10am-1pm May, call tourist office for access Oct-Apr) Housed in the spectacular restored Ducal Palace (Kneževa Palača), designed by Juraj Dalmatinac, this museum showcases some remarkably intricate designs. The history of lacemaking in Pag and its importance to the community is skilfully illustrated with photographs and information panels.

PAG CHEESE

There's no other cheese quite like the distinctive *paški sir* (Pag cheese). Salty and sharp, its taste easily recalls the island that makes it. As sea winds whip through the low slopes of Pag Island, a thin deposit of salt permeates the ground and the flora it sprouts. The 35,000 free-range sheep of Pag Island graze freely on the salty herbs and plants, transmitting the flavour to their meat and milk.

The milk for Pag cheese is gathered in May when the flavour is at its peak. It takes 20L of sheep's milk to make a single wheel and each sheep yields half a litre per day. The milk is left unpasteurised, which allows a stronger flavour to emerge during the fermentation process. When the cheese finally ferments, it's rubbed with sea salt, coated with olive oil and left to age for anywhere from six months to two years. The result is a tangy, firm product that matures into an aromatic, dry, crumbly cheese. As a starter, it's served in thin slices with black olives, but it can also be grated and used as a topping instead of parmesan. It's a favourite at Croatian weddings, where it's served with prosciutto and Croatian wine.

The cheesemakers of Pag Island have won numerous awards. Sirana Gligora's *paški sir* won has been awarded the gold medal for 'Best Hard Sheep Cheese' at the International Cheese Awards three times.

Otherwise, look out, too, for the ricotta-like *skuta*, a subtly flavoured (though rare) soft cheese found in restaurants including Boškinac (p219), near Novalja.

Numerous places across the island sell the cheese, including **Sirana Gligora** (023-698 052; www.gligora.com; Figurica 20; 7.30am-8pm) and **Sirana Mih** (023-698 011; www.siranamih.hr; Stanić 29; 8am-8pm) in Kolan, and **Paška Sirana** (023-600 810; www.paskasirana.hr; Zadarska 5; 7am-3pm Mon-Sat) and **Siroteka** (Vela 12; 10am-5pm Tue-Sat, 9am-2pm Sun) in Pag Town. **Sirana Gligora** (Figurica 22; per person 84KN; by appointment Mon-Fri) also runs excellent tours and tastings.

Tours

★ Pag Tours TOURS
(☎091 42 28 868, 023-318 593; www.pagtours.hr; Petra Rumore) This place offers tours that are a little out of the ordinary, such as a Friday tour that explores the town's lace, salt and stone heritage (100KN per person) or Tuesday's 'Pag by Bike' (100KN). Other possibilities include a UFO tour, birdwatching, or a gastronomic tour of the island. It can also arrange kayak and boat rental.

Festivals & Events

Pag Carnival CULTURAL
(⌚last weekend Jul) The Pag Carnival is a tradition that's been 80 years in the making. Watch the *kolo* (a lively Slavic circle dance) and appreciate the elaborate traditional dress of Pag. The main square fills with dancers and musicians, and a theatre troupe presents the folk play *Paška Robinja* (The Slave Girl of Pag).

Sleeping & Eating

Camping Šimuni CAMPGROUND €
(☎023-697 441; www.camping-simuni.hr; Šimuni bb; camping per adult/child/site 89/60/215KN, units from 880KN; P ❄ 📶) On a gorgeous cove with a shingle beach, about 12km from Pag Town in the direction of Novalja, this large complex has a good vibe and lots of activities on offer. All local buses stop here.

Hotel Pagus HOTEL €€€
(☎023-611 310; www.hotel-pagus.hr; Ante Starčevića 1; r from 1380KN) The low-slung, four-star Pagus has attractive rooms with leather armchairs and fine views from the sea-facing rooms. It's a short and rather pleasant walk into town, and service is professional and attentive.

★ Trapula Wine & Cheese Bar CROATIAN €€
(☎099 27 19 014; www.facebook.com/TrapulaWineAndCheeseBar; Trg Kralja Petra Krešimira IV; tapas from 40KN; ⌚8am-10pm) Eateries on the main square of a town are usually best avoided: they don't have to work as hard to bring in diners as places elsewhere. But this fine bar on the main square has an excellent list of local wines (by the glass or bottle) and a range of tapas; order a board with local Pag cheese and prosciutto. Bliss!

Shopping

It would be a shame to leave the island without buying lace, since the prices are relatively cheap and buying a piece helps keep the tradition alive. A small circle or star about 10cm in diameter takes a good 24 hours to make. If you walk down Kralja Tomislava or Kralja Dmitra Zvonimira you can buy directly from the lacemakers, virtually all of whom have fixed prices.

Information

Mediteran Pag (☎023-611 238; www.mediteranpag.com; Golija 43; ⌚hours vary) Has a very wide selection of private accommodation and excursions.

Meridian 15 (☎023-612 162; www.meridijan15.hr; Ante Starčevića 1; ⌚hours vary) Runs island excursions and trips to national parks including **Paklenica** (p215). Also books accommodation.

Tourist Office (☎023-611 286; www.tzgpag.hr; Vela bb; ⌚8am-10pm Jul & Aug, 8am-8pm Mon-Fri, to 1pm Sat & Sun Jun & Sep, 8am-3pm Mon-Fri Oct-May) Has a small number of brochures and information on the town and island.

Zrće Beach

☎053

About 3km southeast of Novalja, Zrće Beach is staking its claim as the Ibiza of Croatia. Unlike in Ibiza, all of the clubs and bars are right on the beach – but in terms of scale, it's got a long way to go. Basically, there are three main clubs and a scattering of bars in between, all of which open in June and close by mid-September. Entrance prices very much depend on the event: nights are usually free at the beginning of the season but cost as much as €40 for big-name DJs in mid-August.

The beach itself is a picturesque 1km-long treeless crescent of pebbles overlooking a parched strip of eastern Pag, with the mountains of the mainland rearing up on the horizon – rent an umbrella for shade. Out of season you'll have this otherwise-lonely place to yourself.

Festivals & Events

Hideout MUSIC
(www.hideoutfestival.com; ⌚late Jun/early Jul) The festival that put Zrće on the electronic dance music (EDM) map takes over the beach bars and clubs in late June/early July. Expect big-name DJs and multiple nights of mayhem.

Sonus MUSIC
(www.sonus-festival.com; ⌚mid-Aug) Five days and nights of EDM on Zrće. In previous years the event has featured the likes of John Digweed and Laurent Garnier.

Drinking & Nightlife

★ Papaya CLUB

(www.papaya.com.hr; ⏲10am-6am Jun-Sep) Rated one of the best clubs in the world (it came in at number six in *DJ Mag*'s 2017 list), Papaya is the kingpin of the Zrće scene, complete with palm trees, waterfalls and a shell-like roof over the dance floor. On big nights it can cram 5000 people onto its terraces.

Kalypso CLUB

(www.kalypso-zrce.com; ⏲10am-6am Jun-Sep) Kalypso is the coolest-looking club on the strip, built into a cove at the northern end of the beach with myriad cabana-like bars surrounded by palm trees. While the sun shines you can chill out on day beds by a small pool; after dark, DJs spin deep house mixes to a sophisticated crowd.

Aquarius CLUB

(www.aquarius.hr; ⏲Jun-Sep) Repeatedly voted one of the top 100 clubs in the world, Aquarius is a huge space with stylish alcoves, great views and a glassed-off area. Top DJs and festivals come here, as well as a beautiful crowd.

Getting There & Away

In summer shuttle buses run from Novalja to Zrće Beach (12KN). If you fancy the walk or bike ride, it's 4.1km from Novalja's centre.

Novalja

☎053 / POP 3961

In a nation of sedate resorts, Novalja bucks the trend big time. Its thumping bars and clubs offer nightlife as raucous as you'll find in Croatia and as a consequence it attracts a noticeably younger crowd. Depending on which side of 35 you sit, this could be heaven or it could be hell. Cultural interest is confined to the incendiary club scene based at nearby Zrće Beach; there are no historic sights. That said, the promenade has a real buzz in summer, and there are fine beaches close by. In winter it reverts to being a cold, virtually uninhabited backwater.

Sleeping & Eating

Most of the best places to stay are a little out of the town centre. Accommodation is incredibly hard to find during the summer party season, especially during the big events, so make sure you book ahead.

OFF THE BEATEN TRACK

OLIVE GARDENS OF LUN

Close to the northern tip of Pag Island, where the road begins its descent into the quiet village of Lun, signed walking trails lead between the stone fences and stone houses associated with ancient olive-growing traditions. Signposts point out some of the more venerable trees (up to 1600 years old!) and centuries-old walls held together with not a drop of mortar. There's also an amphitheatre for occasional presentations, and in summer you may also come across locals selling olive oils and other olive-based products.

Barbati HOTEL €€

(☎091 12 11 233; www.barbati.hr; Vidalići 39; r/apt from 720/1800KN; P❄@🛜🏊) Located across the bay from Zrće (you'll hear it in the distance) within a scrappy development of beach apartments 6km from Novalja, this chic little hotel has well-designed rooms, a tiny covered pool and an attractive waterside bar-restaurant.

★ Boškinac HOTEL €€€

(☎053-663 500; www.facebook.com/hotel.boskinac; Škopaljska 120; r 1750KN; P❄🛜🏊) The most sophisticated place to stay, eat and drink on Pag, this wonderful little winery-hotel offers eight huge rooms and three suites in a blissful rural location surrounded by vines. Even if you're not staying here, be sure to sample the wine (cellar hours are noon to 1am) and dine at the acclaimed restaurant (mains 70KN to 160KN).

The winery's cabernet-merlot blend is excellent and it's the only place in the world growing and making wine from Gegić, a grape endemic to Pag (producing an elegant white). It's about 3km north of Novalja; follow the signs towards Stara Novalja.

Starac i More SEAFOOD €€

(☎053-662 423; Braće Radić bb; mains 49-120KN; ⏲noon-11.30pm) For a bit of sober Croatian authenticity in clubbing Novalja, head to this characterful tavern (the name translates as The Old Man and the Sea) set just back from the seafront and bedecked in fishing paraphernalia (and the odd giant fish). The seafood here is the best in town. Waiters will recommend wine to go with your meal.

SIMONE SIMONE/GETTY IMAGES ©

1. Kornati National Park (p233)
Comprising 89 of Kornati's 140 islands, this park shelters part of the largest and densest archipelago in the Adriatic.

2. Plitvice Lakes National Park (p211)
This Unesco World Heritage site is 16 gorgeous turquoise lakes linked by a series of waterfalls and cascades.

3. Cheese (p217)
There's no other cheese quite like the distinctive *paški sir* (Pag cheese) from Pag Island (p216).

4. St James' Cathedral (p235), Šibenik
This World Heritage Site is local builder and sculptor Juraj Dalmatinac's most outstanding work.

FESUS ROBERT/SHUTTERSTOCK ©

ISA_OZDERE/SHUTTERSTOCK ©

3

LAURA EDWARDS/LONELY PLANET ©

Information

Aurora (053-663 493; www.aurora-novalja.com; Slatinska 9; 9am-8pm) Well-organised agency with rental apartments and rooms on its books. Excursions, too.

Sunturist (053-661 211; www.sunturist.hr; Silvija Strahimira Kranjčevićeva bb; hours vary) Books private accommodation and trips.

Tourist Office (053-661 404; www.visitnovalja.hr; Trg Briščić 1; 8am-8pm Jun-Sep, to 3pm Mon-Fri Oct-May) Stocks free town maps and timetables for boats and buses.

NIN

023 / POP 2825

One of the loveliest towns in the Zadar hinterland, Nin has as its centrepiece a tiny islet, where the old town is located. Also known for its significance as a seat of bishops and kings, who left behind two of the prettiest small churches in Dalmatia, it's a lovely place that combines pretty coastal scenery and considerable cultural interest. Keep an eye out for Glagolitic inscriptions (p199) on some of the older buildings around town.

History

A settlement was first established on the site of the old town almost 3000 years ago. From the 9th century BCE and the centuries that followed, Nin was a centre for trade with the Romans and Greeks; Roman villas have been discovered in the area, suggesting a prosperous and well-established trading community. Apart from its strategic significance, the town also prospered as a major source of salt.

Nin came under Croatian rule in the 7th century CE, and by 900 it was the seat of a Croatian bishop. It is also considered to have been the first Croatian royal town. It came under Venetian rule in 1409, and its strategic position was so important that the Venetians destroyed the town rather than abandon it to the Ottomans in 1571 and again in 1646.

Sights

Church of the Holy Cross CHURCH

(Crkva Svetog Križa; Petra Zoranića 8; 6am-9pm Jun-Aug, shorter hours rest of year) FREE This appealing little pre-Romanesque white church, often called 'the smallest cathedral in the world' in recognition of its role as the ancient seat of bishops, dates to the 9th century. Before the 14th century it was used as a royal chapel, although it remains pleasingly unadorned. The windows are perfectly placed to allow the sun's rays to enter and the church to act as a sundial.

Museum of Salt MUSEUM

(Solana Nin; 023-264 021; www.solananin.hr; Ilirska 7; tours adult/child 65/20KN; 8am-10pm) Nin's salt was prized in ancient times for its high iodine content, making it sought after for both culinary and medicinal purposes. This small museum takes you through the town's salty story with the aid of a multimedia presentation. The industry is enjoying something of a revival, and local salt is once again for sale here. Forty-five-minute tours run on the hour, taking in a crumbling Roman gateway and skirting the salt pools, and enlivened by fascinating expert commentary.

Church of St Nicholas CHURCH

(Sveti Nicola; Prahulje; hours vary) This unusual early Romanesque church crowns its own hill off Rte 306 southwest of Nin. The small, pretty edifice was built in the late 11th or early 12th century, and the crenellations on the roof reflect its strategic significance in ancient times – it was here that seven Croatian kings were crowned (hence its unofficial name: the Coronation Church). The church was built with a fortress aspect to guard against Ottoman invasion; it served as a lookout in times of war.

Sleeping & Eating

Mendula Zadar Eco Village HOTEL €€€

(Žerava 1; apt 2100KN; P) Almost as close to Zadar as to Nin (9km either way), this attractive hotel has a quiet countryside location and is handy for both towns. The apartments are stylish and contemporary, with exposed brick, concrete floors and lovely feature walls. Most look out over the swimming pool. Reserve through travel agencies or booking websites.

Konoba Bepo SEAFOOD, CROATIAN €€

(023-280 336; www.konoba-bepo.hr; Dražnikova 76; mains 45-160KN; noon-11pm May-Sep) With its sea-facing terrace and fresh seafood, Konoba Bepo has picked up on an enduringly successful Croatian theme. Service is fast and friendly, and the food – a mix of grilled seafood and fish, pasta and other coastal staples – is reliably good.

Information

Tourist Information Centre (023-265 247; www.nin.hr; Trg Braće Radića 3; 8am-8pm Jun-Aug, shorter hours rest of year) Town and accommodation information.

Getting There & Away

Getting to Nin usually requires your own wheels – public transport is sometimes infrequent but more often nonexistent.

ZADAR

023 / POP 75,437

Boasting a historic old town of Roman ruins, medieval churches, cosmopolitan cafes and quality museums set on a small peninsula, Zadar is an intriguing city. It's not too crowded and its two unique attractions – the sound-and-light spectacle of the *Sea Organ* and the *Sun Salutation* – need to be seen and heard to be believed.

While it's not a picture-postcard kind of place from every angle, the mix of ancient relics, Habsburg elegance and coastal setting all offset the unsightly tower blocks climbing up the hilly hinterland. It's no Dubrovnik, but it's not a museum town either – this is a living, vibrant city, enjoyed by residents and visitors alike.

Zadar is also a key transport hub, with superb ferry connections to the surrounding islands.

History

Zadar was inhabited by the Illyrian Liburnian tribe as early as the 9th century BCE. By the 1st century BCE it had become a minor Roman colony. Slavs settled here in the 6th and 7th centuries CE, and Zadar eventually fell under the authority of Croatian-Hungarian kings.

The rise of Venetian power in the mid-12th century was bitterly contested – there was a succession of citizens' uprisings over the next 200 years – but the city was finally acquired by Venice in 1409, along with the rest of Dalmatia.

Frequent Veneto-Turkish wars resulted in the building of Zadar's famous city walls in the 16th century, partly on the remains of the earlier Roman fortifications. With the fall of Venice in 1797, the city passed to Austrian rulers, who administered the city with the assistance of their Italianised ruling aristocracy. Italian influence endured well into the 20th century, with Zadar (or Zara, as the Italians call it) captured by Italy at the end of WWI and officially ceded to Italy with the Treaty of Rapallo in 1922.

When Italy capitulated to the Allies in 1943, the city was occupied by the Germans and then bombed to smithereens by the Allies, with almost 60% of the old town destroyed. The city was rebuilt following the original street plan.

History repeated itself in November 1991 when Yugoslav rockets kept Zadar under siege for three months. Few war wounds are now visible, however, and Zadar has reemerged as one of Croatia's most dynamic towns.

Sights

★ Sea Organ MONUMENT

(Morske orgulje; Istarska Obala) FREE Zadar's incredible *Sea Organ*, designed by local architect Nikola Bašić, is unique. Set within the perforated stone stairs that descend into the sea is a system of pipes and whistles that exudes wistful sighs when the movement of the sea pushes air through it. The effect is hypnotic, the mellifluous tones increasing in volume when a boat or ferry passes by. You can swim from the steps off the promenade while listening to the sounds.

This is a superb spot to peacefully watch the sun go down to the mesmerising tones of Zadar's most popular attraction.

★ Sun Salutation MONUMENT

(Pozdrav Suncu; Istarska Obala) Another wacky and wonderful creation by Nikola Bašić (the local architect who designed the nearby Sea Organ), this 22m-wide circle set into the pavement is filled with 300 multilayered glass plates that collect the sun's energy during the day. Together with the wave energy that makes the *Sea Organ's* sound, it produces a trippy light show from sunset to sunrise that's meant to simulate the solar system. It also collects enough energy to power the entire harbour-front lighting system.

The place is packed with tourists, excited children and locals every night, especially at sunset, when the gorgeous sea views and the illuminated pavement make for a spectacular sight.

Museum of Ancient Glass MUSEUM

(Muzej antičkog stakla; 023-363 831; www.mas-zadar.hr; Poljana Zemaljskog Odbora 1; adult/child 30/10KN; 9am-9pm Mon-Sat May-Sep, to 4pm Oct-Apr) It's baffling that a medium as delicate as glass could survive the earthquakes and wars that have plagued this region over the millenniums, but this impressive museum has thousands of objects on display: goblets, jars, vials, jewellery and amulets. Many of the larger glass urns were removed from the local Roman necropolis (cemetery), where they held cremated remains. The layout is superb,

Zadar

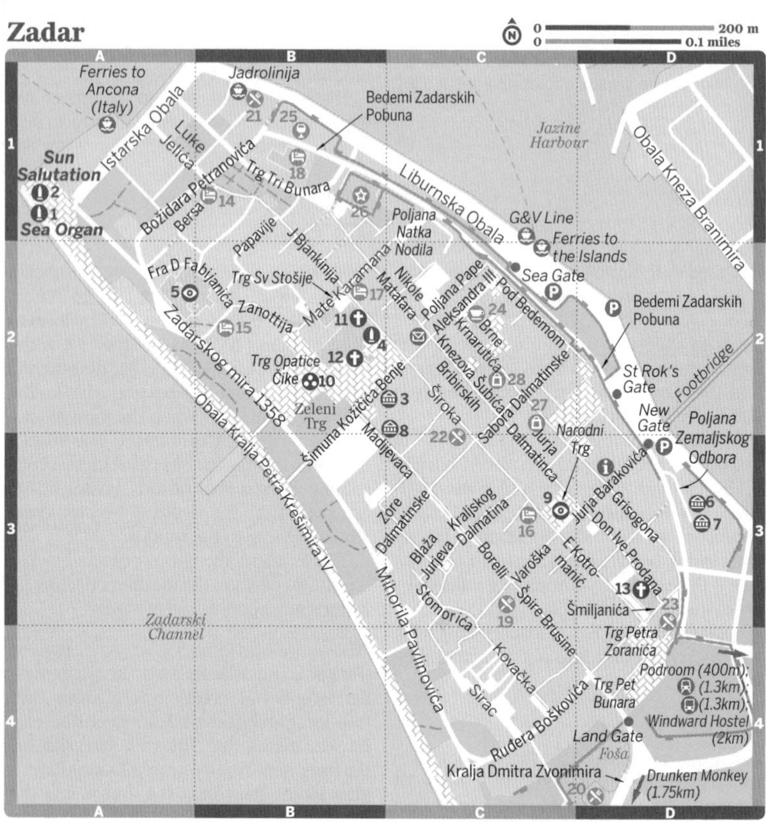

with large light boxes and ethereal music to heighten the experience.

There are also daily demonstrations of glass-blowing, bead making and miniature-bottle production, usually between 10am and 2pm.

St Simeon's Church CHURCH

(Crkva Sv Šime; Poljana Šime Budinića bb; ⌚8.30am-noon & 5-7pm Mon-Fri, 8.30am-noon Sat May-Oct) While this 17th-century baroque church is pretty enough, it's what lies inside that makes it truly noteworthy. Taking pride of place above the main altar, the sarcophagus of St Simeon is a masterpiece of medieval goldsmithery. Commissioned in 1377, the coffin is made of cedar and covered inside and out with finely executed gold-plated silver reliefs.

The middle relief, showing the presentation of Jesus to Simeon at the temple, is a copy of Giotto's fresco from Cappella dell'Arena in Padua, Italy. Other reliefs depict scenes from the lives of the saints and King Ludovic's visit to Zadar.

Narodni trg SQUARE

(People's Square) Traditionally the centre of public life, this pretty little square is constantly abuzz with chatter from its many cafe-bars. The western side is dominated by the late-Renaissance **City Guard** building, dating from 1562; the clock tower was added under the Austrian administration in 1798. Public proclamations and judgments were announced from the **loggia** opposite (1565), which is now an art-exhibition space.

Archaeological Museum MUSEUM

(Arheološki Muzej; ☎023-250 516; www.amzd.hr; Trg Opatice Čike 1; adult/child 30/15KN; ⌚9am-9pm Jun & Sep, to 10pm Jul & Aug, to 3pm Apr, May & Oct, 9am-2pm Mon-Fri, to 1pm Sat Nov-Mar) A wealth of prehistoric, ancient and medieval relics, mainly from Zadar and its surrounds, awaits at this fascinating museum. Highlights in-

Zadar

Top Sights
1 Sea Organ ... A1
2 Sun Salutation ... A1

Sights
3 Archaeological Museum ... C2
4 Bell Tower ... B2
5 Franciscan Monastery ... A2
6 Museum of Ancient Glass ... D3
7 Museum of Illusions ... D3
8 Museum of Religious Art ... C2
9 Narodni trg ... C3
10 Roman Forum ... B2
11 St Anastasia's Cathedral ... B2
12 St Donatus' Church ... B2
13 St Simeon's Church ... D3

Activities, Courses & Tours
Zadar Walking Tours ... (see 9)

Sleeping
14 Almayer - Art & Heritage Hotel ... B1
15 Apartments Donat ... B2
16 Art Hotel Kalelarga ... C3
17 Boutique Hostel Forum ... B2
18 Hotel Bastion ... B1

Eating
19 4 Kantuna ... C3
Corte Vino & More ... (see 14)
20 Foša ... D4
Gourmet Kalelarga ... (see 16)
Kaštel ... (see 18)
21 Kornat ... B1
22 Mlinar ... C3
23 Pet Bunara ... D3

Drinking & Nightlife
24 Cogito Coffee ... C2
25 Garden Lounge ... B1

Entertainment
26 Arsenal ... B1

Shopping
27 Gligora ... C2
28 Natura Zara ... C2

clude a 2.5m-high marble statue of Augustus from the 1st century CE, and a model of the Forum as it once looked.

Roman Forum RUINS

(Zeleni trg) One of the most intriguing things about Zadar is the way Roman ruins seem to sprout randomly from the city's streets. Nowhere is this more evident than at the site of the ancient Forum, constructed between the 1st century BCE and the 3rd century CE. As in Roman times, it's the centre of civic and religious life, with St Donatus' Church dominating one side of it.

Among the ruins of temples and colonnades stands one intact Roman column, which in the Middle Ages served as a shame post where wrongdoers were chained and publicly humiliated. Nearby are more Roman remains, including altars with reliefs of the mythical figures Jupiter Ammon and Medusa. On the top you can see the hollows used in blood sacrifices. It is believed that this area was a temple dedicated to Jupiter, Juno and Minerva dating from the 1st century BCE.

St Donatus' Church CHURCH

(Crkva Sv Donata; Šimuna Kožičića Benje bb; 20KN; 9am-9pm May-Sep, to 4pm Oct-Apr) Dating from the beginning of the 9th century, this unusual circular Byzantine-style church was named after the bishop who commissioned it. As one of only a handful of buildings from the early Croatian kingdom to have survived the Mongol invasion of the 13th century, it's a particularly important cultural relic. The simple and unadorned interior includes two complete Roman columns, recycled from the Forum. Also from the Forum are the paving slabs that were revealed after the original floor was removed.

The church hasn't been used for services for around 200 years and these days it often serves as a concert hall or exhibition space.

St Anastasia's Cathedral CATHEDRAL

(Katedrala Sv Stošije; Trg Sv Stošije; 6.30-7pm Mon-Fri, 8-9am Sat, 8-9am & 6-7pm Sun) FREE Built in the 12th and 13th centuries, Zadar's cathedral has a richly decorated facade and an impressive three-nave interior with the remains of frescos in the side apses. The cathedral was badly bombed during WWII and has since been reconstructed. On the altar in the left apse is a marble sarcophagus containing the relics of St Anastasia, while the choir contains lavishly carved stalls. A glass vestibule allows you to peer inside when the cathedral's closed, which is often.

Climb the **bell tower** (Široka; 15KN; 9am-10pm Mon-Sat Jun-Aug, shorter hours rest of year) for old-town views.

Museum of Illusions MUSEUM

(Muzej Iluzija; 023-316 803; www.zadar.muzejiluzija.com; Poljana Zemaljskog Odbora 2; adult/

child 60/40KN; ⏲9am-midnight Jun-Sep, 10am-8pm Apr, May, Oct & Nov, 10am-4pm Dec-Mar) This fun museum is devoted to optical and other illusions. There's a vortex tunnel, holograms, a mirror room, an infinity room and loads of interactive exhibits that will have you scratching your head trying to work it all out.

Museum of Religious Art MUSEUM
(Trg Opatice Čike bb; adult/child 30/10KN; ⏲10am-1pm & 5-7pm Mon-Sat, 10am-1pm Sun) This impressive museum in a Benedictine convent boasts a fine collection of reliquaries, sculpture, embroidery and paintings. Of particular note are works by Venetian masters Paolo Veneziano and Vittore Carpaccio.

Franciscan Monastery MONASTERY
(Franjevački Samostan; www.svetifrane.org; Trg Sv Frane 1; adult/child 10/5KN; ⏲9am-6pm) Entry to this historic monastery includes access to a lovely Renaissance cloister, the Gothic church (the oldest of its kind in Dalmatia, consecrated in 1280), the sacristy (where the 1358 treaty under which Venice relinquished its rights to Dalmatia in favour of the Croatian-Hungarian king Ludovic was signed) and a small treasury. Highlights of the last include a large 12th-century painted wooden crucifix, a 15th-century polyptych from the island of Ugljan and a 16th-century painting of the dead Christ by Jacopo Bassano.

Activities

There's a **swimming area** with diving boards, a park and a cafe on the coastal promenade south of the old town; from the Land Gate, follow the road as it curves to the right and continue on Kralja Dmitra Zvonimira. The promenade takes you to a beach in front of Hotel Kolovare and then winds on for about 1km along the coast.

Tours

Local travel agencies offer boat cruises to Telašćica Bay and the beautiful Kornati Islands; tours generally include lunch and a swim in the sea or a salt lake. Ask around on Liburnska Obala (where the excursion boats are moored) or contact **Aquarius Travel Agency** (☎023-212 919; www.aquariuszadar.com; Nova Vrata bb; ⏲hours vary). Organised trips to the national parks of Paklenica, Krka and Plitvice Lakes are also very popular, making it easy for visitors to access the parks without having to worry about organising transport.

Zadar Walking Tours TOURS
(☎091 32 79 777; www.zadarwalkingtour.com; per person 100KN; ⏲10am, noon & 6pm) These 100-minute tours are a terrific way to get an overview of the city and its history. The guides are excellent and have a full portfolio of Zadar legends and anecdotes, as well as plenty of historical detail. Book in advance or just turn up 10 minutes before the departure time at the lamp post on Narodni trg (People's Sq).

Festivals & Events

Full Moon Festival CULTURAL
(Noć Punog Miseca; ⏲late Jul) During this festival (held on the night of the full moon in July), Zadar's quays are lit with torches and candles, stalls sell local delicacies and boats lining the quays become floating fish markets.

St Donatus Musical Evenings MUSIC
(Glazbene večeri u Sv Donatu; ☎023-627 762; www.donat-festival.com; ⏲late Jul & early Aug) Classical-music performances featuring prominent artists from across the globe, held in St Donatus' Church.

Sleeping

Windward Hostel HOSTEL €
(☎091 62 19 197; www.facebook.com/windward.hostel.zadar; Gazića 12; dm/d 112/450KN; ❄📶) Just 1.5km from the old town, this 20-bed, yachting-themed hostel is run by a passionate sailor. Rooms are immaculate, with big lockers, electric window blinds and private reading lights. There's a supermarket and bakery nearby, and staff can organise sailing tours and lessons.

Drunken Monkey HOSTEL €
(☎023-314 406; www.themonkeytroophostels.com; Jure Kastriotica Skenderbega 21; dm/r from 175/450KN; ❄@📶🏊) Tucked away in a suburban neighbourhood, this friendly little hostel has brightly coloured rooms, a small pool, a guest barbecue and an all-round funky vibe. Staff can arrange trips to the Plitvice Lakes and Krka National Park. When full, the Drunken Monkey has a nearby sister, the Lazy Monkey, with similar standards and rates.

★**Boutique Hostel Forum** HOSTEL €€
(☎023-253 031; www.hostelforumzadar.com; Široka 20; dm/d/ste from 155/665/725KN) Wonderfully colourful dorm rooms and stylish, white-and-black doubles and suites, some with top skyline and partial water views, make this easily the best hostel and midrange hotel in the old centre. The location couldn't be better and the rooms are terrific for the price.

OFF THE BEATEN TRACK

SILBA ISLAND

In the outer reaches of the archipelago that stutters out into the Adriatic from the Northern Dalmatian coast, Silba Island is a pretty detour if you're keen to escape the crowds (although it's all relative in summer). Covering just 15 sq km, Silba is quite flat, but it has its scenic corners and is otherwise lovely and quiet with very little motorised traffic. Among the numerous pretty beaches, try the uncharacteristically steep and rocky **Vele Stene (Large Rocks)**, **Dobre Vode** with its shallow sandy bottom, and the more expansive **Nozdre** with distinctive rock forms.

And don't miss the **Toreta** in Silba, the island's only town. This narrow, cylindrical stone tower with an external spiral staircase is attached to a local love legend – a sailor built it for his sweetheart to watch for his return, but she grew tired of waiting and married another – and affords splendid views.

If you'd like to stay after the day trippers return home, rent a boat, or otherwise get further information, visit www.silba.org.

Silba Island can only be reached by **Jadrolinija** (www.jadrolinija.hr) ferries to/from Zadar (adult/child 31/15.50KN, four hours, daily) and Mali Lošinj (adult/child/car 31/15.50/170KN, 2½ hours, daily).

Apartments Donat APARTMENT €€
(☎095 82 56 390; www.apartmentsdonat.com; Nadbiskupa Mate Karamana 12; apt from 700KN) Appealing modern apartments in a good old-town location make this an excellent choice. Some are attic rooms and most have artwork feature walls or exposed modern brickwork.

★**Art Hotel Kalelarga** HOTEL €€€
(☎023-233 000; www.arthotel-kalelarga.com; Majke Margarite 3; s/d incl breakfast 1515/1810KN; ❄📶) Built and designed under strict conservation rules due to its old-town location, this 10-room boutique hotel is an understated and luxurious beauty. Exposed stonework and mushroom hues imbue the spacious rooms with plenty of style and character. The gourmet breakfast is served in the hotel's own stylish cafe, Gourmet Kalelarga.

★**Almayer - Art & Heritage Hotel** HERITAGE HOTEL €€€
(☎023-335 357; www.almayer.hr; Braće Bersa 2; d/ste 1745/2200KN; P❄@📶) This elegant hotel, tucked away near the tip of the old town's peninsula, has classy rooms in a wonderful stone-walled heritage building. Discreet service and marvellous breakfasts are all part of the deal.

★**Hotel Bastion** HOTEL €€€
(☎023-494 950; www.hotel-bastion.hr; Bedemi Zadarskih Pobuna 13; r 1320-2730KN; P❄📶) Built over the remains of a Venetian fortress, the Bastion radiates character and sophistication. The 23 rooms and five suites successfully combine a classic early-20th-century feel with a contemporary sensibility. It also boasts a top-drawer restaurant and a basement spa. It's a classy place and the location is brilliant.

Eating

Mlinar BAKERY €
(☎091 23 88 620; www.mlinar.hr; Široka 1; snacks from 8KN; ⏰6.30am-11pm Mon-Fri, 7am-11pm Sat & Sun) The Zadar outpost of this nationwide chain is the best bakery in town. It's great for a snack or breakfast on the run, with wholemeal bread, croissants, sweet pastries and *burek* (pastry stuffed with meat, spinach or cheese).

★**Kaštel** MEDITERRANEAN €€
(☎023-494 950; www.hotel-bastion.hr; Bedemi Zadarskih Pobuna 13; mains 70-190KN; ⏰7am-11pm) Hotel Bastion's fine-dining restaurant offers contemporary takes on classic Croatian cuisine (octopus stew, stuffed squid, Pag cheese). France and Italy also make their presence felt, particularly in the delectable dessert list. Opt for the white-linen experience inside or dine on the battlements overlooking the harbour for a memorable evening.

★**Pet Bunara** DALMATIAN €€
(☎023-224 010; www.petbunara.com; Stratico 1; mains 65-160KN; ⏰noon-11pm) With exposed stone walls inside and a pretty terrace lined with olive trees, this is an atmospheric place to tuck into Dalmatian soups and stews, homemade pasta and local faves such as octopus and turkey. Save room for a traditional Zadar fig cake or cherry torte.

4 Kantuna ITALIAN, INTERNATIONAL €€

(☎091 31 35 382; www.restaurant4kantuna.com; Varoshka 1; pizzas 48-63KN, mains 68-175KN; ⊙11am-11pm) With a cool laneway setting as well as a stylish interior dining area, 4 Kantuna gets the simple things right – good service and high-quality cooking without asking you to pay over the odds for the privilege. There's pizza, pasta, risotto and a handful of carefully chosen meat and fish mains.

Gourmet Kalelarga CAFE €€

(☎023-233 000; www.arthotel-kalelarga.com/gourmet; Široka 23; breakfast 28-60KN, mains 59-155KN; ⊙7am-10pm) Beneath the Art Hotel Kalelarga, this chic little beige cafe is your best option for a cooked breakfast or a decadent cake. As the day progresses, the focus shifts towards more substantial Dalmatian fare. Service is very good.

Restaurant Niko SEAFOOD €€

(☎023-337 888; www.hotel-niko.hr; Obala Kneza Domagoja 9; mains 70-170KN; ⊙noon-midnight) This wildly popular **hotel** (s/d 8250/1140KN; P❄📶) restaurant is great for grilled fish and other seafood, though the menu has red meat and vegetarian dishes, too. It's your best bet down the Borik end of the city.

★ **Corte Vino & More** INTERNATIONAL €€€

(☎023-335 357; www.facebook.com/cortevinomore; Braće Bersa 2; mains 80-180KN; ⊙noon-2.30pm & 7-10.30pm) One of the classiest dining experiences in Zadar, Corte Vino & More in the Al Mayer Heritage Hotel has a gorgeous setting, wonderfully attentive service and high-quality food that changes with the seasons, taking Croatian traditional dishes and riffing in subtle new and creative directions. Fabulous wine list and knowledgeable waiters, too.

Foša SEAFOOD €€€

(☎023-314 421; www.fosa.hr; Kralja Dmitra Zvonimira 2; mains 130-270KN; ⊙noon-1am) Classy Foša boasts a gorgeous terrace that juts into the harbour and a sleek interior that combines ancient stone walls with 21st-century style. The main focus of chef Damir Tomljanović is fresh fish, plucked from the Adriatic and served grilled or salt baked; the beef tenderloin with truffles is another star. Also try the Adriatic shrimp with smoked-mussel gnocchi.

Kornat MEDITERRANEAN €€€

(☎023-254 501; www.restaurant-kornat.hr; Liburnska Obala 6; mains 120-190KN; ⊙noon-midnight Mon-Sat) Sitting pretty in a prime harbourfront spot, this elegant place has always been one of Zadar's best restaurants. The cooking marries fresh Croatian produce, rich French-style sauces and plenty of Italian touches. It was closed for renovations at research time.

Drinking & Entertainment

Zadar has a lively and diverse bar scene, buoyed by a large student population. Head to the Varoš neighbourhood, on the southwestern side of the old town, for interesting little cafe-bars popular with arty types.

Podroom CLUB

(☎099 74 98 451; www.podroom.club; Marka Marulića bb; ⊙midnight-6am Fri, 1-6.30am Sat) One of Zadar's biggest clubs, Podroom draws a regular cast of Croatian and international DJs, especially in summer. It's within staggering distance of the old town and really only gets going around 2am. Live acts also take to the stage to get things going. Admission prices vary depending on who's on the bill.

Cogito Coffee CAFE

(Poljana Pape Aleksandra III B; ⊙8am-4pm Tue-Sun) Many locals swear that this is the best coffee in the old town. It also does cocktails and craft beers, and it's far enough off the main tourist drag to feel like a neighbourhood cafe.

Garden Lounge BAR

(☎023-250 631; http://thegarden.hr/the-garden-lounge; Liburnska Obala 6; ⊙10am-1am late May-Oct) Perched on top of the old city walls, this exceedingly cool bar-club-garden is very Ibiza-esque, with harbour views, day beds, secluded alcoves, billowing fabric and contemporary electronic music. All. Very. Chilled.

Arsenal CONCERT VENUE

(☎023-253 821; www.arsenalzadar.com; Trg Tri Bunara 1) This huge former shipping warehouse is now mainly used for concerts, art exhibitions and private functions. Check the website to see what's on when you're in town.

Shopping

★ **Natura Zara** FOOD & DRINKS

(☎098 888 585; www.facebook.com/Naturazara; Brne Karnarutića 7; ⊙8am-9pm Mar-Oct) This gorgeous little shop, tucked away on a quiet old-city street, sells high-quality Croatian wines, olive oils, honeys, truffles and liqueurs, all from small family producers, and all with an ecological focus.

Gligora FOOD & DRINKS

(☎023-700 730; www.gligora.com; Hrvoja Vukčić Hrvatinića 5; ⊙7am-8pm Mon-Fri, to 2pm Sat &

OFF THE BEATEN TRACK

NADIN

The tiny village of Nadin is 32km east of Zadar and has a couple of worthwhile stops if you're interested in olive oil and wine.

Uljara Nadin (023-663 114, 091 569 97 82; www.uljara-nadin.hr; Nadin 58b, Nadin; tour & tasting from 75KN; by appointment) This fine place offers olive-oil tasting (including advice on how to tell the difference between good and bad olive oil), a tour of its production processes, and a shop where you can purchase the real thing. It's a wonderful introduction to what is something of a Croatian obsession.

Vinarija Škaulj (091 389 14 21; www.vinarija-skaulj.hr; Nadin; by appointment) Tours, tastings and cellar-door sales make this a fine detour just off the E71. The organic winery is best known for its reds (cabernet sauvignon, merlot and syrah), but make sure you try the *maraština*, an indigenous local white particular to the Dalmatian coast and hinterland. Contact the winery in advance for tastings; you could just turn up, but there may be noone to show you around.

Sun) Sheep cheese from the island of Pag is a celebrated Croatian culinary tradition. This is the Zadar shopfront for its multi-award-winning cheeses, as well as olive oils, wines and other goodies.

Information

Tourist Office (023-316 166; www.zadar.travel; Jurja Barakovića 5; 8am-11pm May-Jul & Sep, to midnight Aug, 8am-8pm Mon-Fri, 9am-2pm Sat & Sun Oct-Apr;) Publishes a good colour map and rents audioguides (40KN) for a self-guided tour around the town.

Zadar General Hospital (Opća Bolnica Zadar; 023-505 505; www.bolnica-zadar.hr; Bože Peričića 5)

Getting There & Away

AIR

Zadar Airport (023-205 800; www.zadar-airport.hr) is 12km east of the town centre. Croatia Airlines flies to Zadar from Zagreb. There are international flights to Brussels, Dublin, London, Munich, Paris, Warsaw and many more destinations, often with budget airlines.

BOAT

G&V Line (www.gv-zadar.hr) Has three daily passenger ferries to Dugi Otok, stopping at both Sali (25KN to 40KN, 45 minutes) and Zaglav (25KN to 40KN, 40 minutes).

Jadrolinija (023-254 800; www.jadrolinija.hr; Liburnska Obala 7) Ferries pull right up to the old town, with the large international boats mooring on Istarska Obala and the smaller boats on Liburnska Obala (where you'll also find the ticket office). Six ferries per week head to/from the Italian port of Ancona from June to September, increasing to 14 in July and August (passenger/car from 407/510KN).

Local ferries Sail to destinations including Mali Lošinj (adult/child/car 59/30/250KN, 6¾ hours, daily July and August), Brbinj on Dugi Otok (30/15/176KN, 1¼ hours, two to three daily) and Preko on Ugljan (18/9/103KN, 25 minutes, 11 to 17 daily). Passenger-only catamarans also head to Božava on Dugi Otok (40KN, 1¼ hours, three daily).

BUS

The **bus station** (060 305 305; www.liburnija-zadar.hr; Ante Starčevića 1) is about 1km southeast of the old town. In addition to standard buses, try **FlixBus** (www.flixbus.com).

Domestic destinations include the following:

Dubrovnik 182KN, eight hours, up to six daily

Rijeka 156KN, 4½ hours, 12 daily

Šibenik 43KN, 1½ hours, at least hourly

Split 86KN, three hours, hourly

Zagreb 110KN, 3½ hours, hourly

Getting Around

TO/FROM THE AIRPORT

Timed around all Croatia Airlines flights, buses (25KN one way) depart from outside the main terminal, and from the old town (Liburnska Obala) and the bus station one hour prior to flights.

A taxi will cost around 150KN to the old town and 180KN to Borik.

BIKE

Calimero (023-311 010; www.rent-a-bike-zadar.com; Zasjedanja Zavnoh 1; per hour/day from 40/120KN; 8am-8pm Mon-Fri, to 1pm Sat) Zadar's best place to rent a bicycle. It's an easy walk from the old town.

BUS

Liburnija (www.liburnija-zadar.hr) Liburnija runs buses on 10 routes, which all loop through the bus station. Tickets cost 10KN on board, or 16KN for two from a *tisak* (news-stand). Buses 5 and 8 (usually marked 'Puntamika') head to/from Borik regularly.

DUGI OTOK

☎023 / POP 1625

The largest island in the Zadar area, Dugi Otok has a lost-in-time feel, with plenty of relatively untouched natural beauty to enjoy. The name means 'Long Island': stretching from northwest to southeast, it's 43km long and just 4km wide at its narrowest point. The southeastern coast is marked by steep hills and cliffs, while the northern half is cultivated with vineyards, orchards and sheep pastures. In between is a series of karstic hills rising to 338m at Vela Straža, the island's highest point.

History

Ruins on the island reveal early settlement by Illyrians, Romans and then early Christians, but the island wasn't documented until the mid-10th century. It later became the property of the monasteries of Zadar. Settlement expanded with the 16th-century Turkish invasions, which prompted immigration from elsewhere along the coast.

Dugi Otok's fortunes have largely been linked with Zadar as it changed hands between Venetians, Austrians and the French, but when Northern Dalmatia was handed over to Mussolini the island stayed within Croatia. Old-timers still recall the hardships they endured when the nearest medical and administrative centre was Šibenik, a long, hard boat ride along the coast.

Economic development has always been hampered by the lack of any freshwater supply – drinking water must be collected from rainwater or brought over by boat from Zadar. The population has drifted away over the last few decades, leaving only the hardiest souls to brave the dry summers and *bura*-chilled winters.

Getting There & Away

G&V Line (☎023-250 733; www.gv-zadar.com) runs three daily passenger ferries from Zadar, stopping at Sali (25KN to 40KN, 45 minutes) and Zaglav (25KN to 40KN, one hour).

Jadrolinija (www.jadrolinija.hr) has daily catamarans from Zadar to Božava (40KN, 1¼ hours) and Brbinj (40KN, 1¾ hours). The company also runs a car ferry to Brbinj (adult/child/car 30/15/176KN) three times a day in summer.

Getting Around

The only bus services in Dugi Otok run between Božava and Brbinj in the north and are timed to coincide with boat connections. You can rent scooters in Sali and Božava. Having your own wheels, be that a bike or hire car, is essential if you want to explore the island.

Veli Rat & Punta Bjanca

POP 62

Veli Rat is a pretty village with a marina on a sheltered bay close to the northwestern point of Dugi Otok. Aside from a solitary store-bar, there's not a lot here. However, if you continue for 3km towards the tip of the island you'll reach the striking Punta Bjanca lighthouse.

Sights

Punta Bjanca Lighthouse LIGHTHOUSE

Close to the northern tip of Dugi Otok you'll find Punta Bjanca lighthouse (built 1849). At 42m, it's the largest such beacon on the Adriatic. A small chapel dedicated to St Nicholas, patron saint of sailors, is positioned nearby. As the lighthouse faces nearly due west, it's hard to imagine a more sublime spot to watch a sunset.

Sleeping

Camp Kargita CAMPGROUND €

(☎098 532 333; www.camp-kargita.hr; adult/child/site 70/42/155KN; ⏲Apr-Oct) Virtually in the shadow of the Punta Bjanca lighthouse, this friendly little campground has a terrifically remote feel to it and a rocky beach nearby. It's of fairly recent vintage, so the facilities are in good shape.

Božava

POP 125

Božava is a peaceful little place huddled around a lovely natural harbour that's changed from fishing village to holiday resort in a couple of generations. The village is overgrown with lush, flowering trees and there are appealing shady paths along the coast. Tourism now dominates the local economy in the shape of the four hotels of the Božava 'tourist village' and a couple of harbourside restaurants.

During the summer season a little land 'train' (10KN) tootles between the hotels and Sakarun Bay. Mainly pebbly, with a small strip of sand, this is one of the island's prettiest beaches – although there's not much shade and the water's painfully shallow (but it's great for families with

OFF THE BEATEN TRACK

VRANSKO LAKE NATURE PARK

Lovely Vransko Lake is Croatia's largest natural lake and one of the Mediterranean's best-preserved wetlands. Birdwatching is a particular highlight, with 261 species recorded here, and migratory wetland species – herons, cormorants, sandpipers, grebes and warblers – present in their tens of thousands from August to October. The northern end of the lake is a dedicated ornithological reserve, with boardwalks, bird hides and hiking trails. Cycling, horse riding and kayaking are also possible.

The Vransko Lake Nature Park Office (023-383 181; www.pp-vransko-jezero.hr; Kralja P Svačića 2, Biograd Na Moru; hours vary), in the gateway town of Biograd Na Moru, can arrange guides and organise other activities. The lake is on the southeastern outskirts of town.

Just off the northeastern tip of the lake, in the small settlement of Vrana, Maškovića Han (023-333 230; www.maskovicahan.hr; Marina 1, Vrana, Pakoštane; r 890KN; P ❄ @) is one of Dalmatia's best places to stay. Inhabiting a restored, 370-year-old sandstone compound, it has a small museum, a fabulous restaurant and delightful rooms.

small children). To get to the beach by car from Božava, turn right onto the main island road and look for the turn-off on the left after 3km.

Sleeping

Hotel Maxim HOTEL €€€
(023-291 291; www.hoteli-bozava.hr; Božava 46; s/d from 775/1550KN; P ❄ @) The four-star Maxim is Božava's most upmarket option. The smart rooms and apartments all have satellite TVs, fridges, and balconies overlooking the sea. There's an appealing little pool terrace and access to floodlit tennis courts and a small spa centre.

Information

Tourist Office (023-377 607; www.dugiotok.hr; Božava bb; 9am-1pm & 5-8pm Mon-Fri, to 2pm Sat Jun-Sep) Just above the tiny harbour; can help with bike, scooter and car rental, and with finding private accommodation.

Sali

POP 750

As the largest town on Dugi Otok, Sali is a positive metropolis compared to the rest of the settlements scattered around the island. Named after a now-defunct salt works, the town has a rumpled, lived-in look. Its little harbour is a working fishing port and in summer it fills up with the small passenger boats and yachts that dock here on their way to and from Telašćica Bay and the Kornati Islands.

Activities

Tome BOATING
(023-377 489; www.tome.hr) Offers a full-day cruise to Telašćica Bay and the Kornati Islands (2500KN; maximum of six people), including food and entry fees, or you can hire a boat and skipper and set your own itinerary (1500KN). Fishing trips (from 2500KN) can also be arranged.

Eating & Drinking

Spageritimo CROATIAN €€
(023-377 227; Sali bb; mains 45-135KN; 11am-10pm) Sali's best place to eat is this harbourside tavern specialising in local seafood fresh off the boat. The service is excellent and the owners produce their own olive oil, but some travellers complain about small portion sizes.

Maritimo BAR
(Obala Petra Lorinija bb; 11am-1am) The heart and soul of Sali, this bar has a vibrant buzz about it, rain or shine. It's got plenty of character, with a long wooden bar and photographs of yesteryear decorating the walls, plus a popular terrace that's good for a cocktail, coffee or draught beer.

Information

Tourist Office (023-377 094; www.dugiotok.hr; Obala Kralja Tomislava bb; 8am-8pm Mon-Sat, 11am-1pm Sun Jul & Aug, 8am-3pm Mon-Fri Sep-Jun) On the harbour front.

Getting Around

Louvre (098 650 026; Obala Kralja Tomislava bb) Hires out scooters and mountain bikes.

Telašćica Bay

The southeastern tip of Dugi Otok is split in two by the deeply indented Telašćica Bay (Park prirode Telašćica; www.telascica.hr; 25KN), dotted with five small islands and five even tinier islets. With superb, sheltered azure waters, it's one of the largest, most beautiful and least spoilt natural harbours in the Adriatic. Consequently, it's very popular with yachties.

The Kornati Islands extend nearly to the edge of Telašćica Bay and the topography of the two island groups is identical – stark white limestone with patches of brush. The tip of the western side of the island faces the sea, where the wind and waves have carved out sheer cliffs dropping 166m. There are no towns, settlements or roads on this part of Dugi Otok.

Sights

Mir Lake LAKE

Saltwater Mir Lake is fed by underground channels that run through limestone to the sea; it's home to an endemic species of eel. The lake, which is clear but has a muddy bottom, is surrounded by pine forests and its water is much warmer than the sea. Like most mud in unusual places, it's supposed to be very good for your skin.

Getting There & Away

The only ways to reach Telašćica Bay are by boat or on foot from Sali, a hike of around 3km. **Adamo Travel** (023-377 208; www.adamo.hr; Obala Kralja Tomislava bb; 8am-6pm Mon-Sat) in Sali runs trips here.

ŠIBENIK-KNIN REGION

Wedged between the bigger, more attention-grabbing cities of Zadar and Split, this slice of Croatia is often unfairly overlooked. Yet it's loaded with interesting attractions, including the incredible medieval heart of Šibenik and two national parks – the pristine Kornati Islands and the inland watery wonderland of Krka.

Tisno & Murter Island

022 / POP 5220

Tisno is a cute little town that straddles the bridge connecting the island of Murter to the mainland. Its relatively new-found fame as host to a series of high-profile music festivals is totally out of keeping with its otherwise-sleepy appeal.

On the island proper, the main settlement is Murter village, which although unremarkable in itself is an excellent base from which to explore the Kornati Islands. Murter's steep southwestern coast is indented by small coves, most notably Slanica, which is great for swimming.

Sights

★ **Colentum Beach** BEACH

FREE On Murter's northern coast, along the western edge of the Gradina Peninsula north of the settlement of Marina Hramina, is one of Dalmatia's most unusual beaches. Opened to the public in 2017, Colentum Beach (sometimes spelled Kolentum) is a 200m arc of sand with a very special attraction: tumbling into the sea at the southern end are the remains of a Roman villa that

TISNO'S FESTIVAL SEASON

Between July and August Tisno is imbued with some of the globe's most celebrated electronic music. Styles are myriad and music is eclectic: cosmic disco, soul and funk, folk-tinged electronica, deep house and jazzy lounge. The ringmaster for all of these festivals is the Zadar-based Garden bar.

The festival site is a grand affair, only 1km from town, with a private sandy beach, 80 apartments and a luxury campsite – with 30-sq-metre Indian Shikar cotton tents that have electric fans and lighting, real beds, mosquito nets, and even a separate dressing room. These are all for the revellers to stay in and make as much noise as they like without annoying the locals. There are shady chill-out zones and three music areas, including the open-air Barbarella's club, a short bus or water-taxi ride away. Chuck in the infamous Argonaughty boat parties on the sparkling Adriatic and you have yourself quite a scene.

Things were in a state of flux at research time; check out www.thegarden.hr/events for upcoming summer scheduling.

WORTH A TRIP

KORNATI ISLANDS

Composed of 89 of the Kornati's 140 islands, **Kornati National Park** (022-435 740; www.np-kornati.hr) shelters part of the largest and densest archipelago in the Adriatic. Due to the typically karstic terrain, the islands are riddled with cracks, caves, grottoes and rugged cliffs. The evergreens and holm oaks that used to be found here were long ago burned down. Far from stripping the islands of their beauty, the deforestation has highlighted startling rock formations, whose stark whiteness against the deep-blue Adriatic is an eerie and wonderful sight.

The two series of islands facing the open sea comprise Kornati National Park and have the most dramatically rugged coastline. Kornat is by far the largest island in the park, extending 25km in length but only 2.5km in width. Both the land and surrounding sea are protected. Fishing is strictly limited in order to allow the regeneration of fish shoals. The island of Piškera, also within the park, was inhabited during the Middle Ages and served as a fishing collection and storage point.

The **Kornati National Park Office** (022-435 740; www.kornati.hr; Butina 2, Murter; 8.30am-5pm Mon-Fri) is located in Murter, and is well stocked with information.

Unless you have your own boat, you'll have to book an excursion from Zadar, Sali, Šibenik, Split or another coastal city, or arrange a private transfer from Sali or Murter.

dates to the 1st century CE. It's an evocative sight, not to mention a lovely place to swim.

Sleeping

Heritage Hotel Tisno HOTEL €€€

(022-438 182; www.hoteltisno.com; Zapadna Gomilica 8, Tisno; r 500-1500KN;) Creating a rather grand impression on the Tisno waterfront, this late-19th-century house has been converted into a stylish little hotel. The rooms are in keeping with the era, with gathered crimson curtains and lots of polished wood, but the ambience isn't even remotely stuffy.

Information

Tourist Office (022-434 995; www.tzo-murter.hr; Butina 2, Murter; 8am-10pm Jun-Aug, to 3pm Sep-May) Moderately helpful tourist office.

Getting There & Away

Buses on the coastal highway stop at the Tisno turn-off, 6km from the centre. There are at least five daily buses between Tisno and Šibenik (19KN, 25 minutes). Otherwise, you'll need your own car.

Krka National Park

022

Extending along the 73km Krka River, **Krka National Park** (022-201 777; www.npkrka.hr; adult/child Jul & Aug 200/120KN, Apr-Jun, Sep & Oct 110/80KN, Nov-Mar 30/20KN) runs from the Adriatic near Šibenik inland to the mountains of the Croatian interior. It's a magical place of waterfalls and gorges, with the river gushing through a karstic canyon 200m deep. Sights built by humans are also a major draw of the region, the area's remoteness attracting monks who constructed their monasteries here.

The park has five main entrances, at Skradin, Lozovac, Roški Slap, Krka Monastery and Burnum – all are accessible by car.

Sights

★**Krka Monastery** MONASTERY

(Manastir Krka; 10am-6pm) This isn't just the most important Serbian Orthodox monastery in Croatia; it's one of the faith's most important sites full stop. Featuring a unique combination of Byzantine and Mediterranean architecture, it occupies a peaceful position above the river and a small lake. From mid-June to mid-October a national-park guide is at hand to show you around. At other times you're welcome to visit the church and wander the lakeside path.

Dedicated to the Archangel Michael, the monastery was founded in 1345 by Jelena Šubić, the wife of a local Croatian noble and half-sister to Emperor Dušan of Serbia. However, its Christian origins are much older than that. Beneath the complex in a natural cave system are catacombs bearing early Christian graffiti, possibly from the 1st century. Local lore has it that this hidden church was visited by St Titus and possibly even St Paul. The guided tours only visit a small section of cave, where the graffiti and human bones can be seen; the cave system continues for at least 100m and possibly for a couple of kilometres.

During the war of the 1990s, the monastery's substantial treasury – including priceless manuscripts and religious paraphernalia – was moved to Belgrade for safekeeping. A new museum has been constructed to display the items. The monastery itself was protected during the fighting by the UN. The complex is also home to the Serbian Orthodox church's oldest seminary. It reopened in 2001 and now has 50 theological students.

From Roški Slap, boats to Krka Monastery leave by arrangement (2½ hours, April to October only).

Skradinski Buk WATERFALL

The highlight of Krka National Park, an hour-long loop follows boardwalks, connects little islands in the emerald-green, fish-filled river and terminates at the park's largest waterfall. Skradinski Buk's 800m-long cascade descends by almost 46m before crashing into the lower lake, which is a popular swimming spot. Nearby, a cluster of historic mill cottages have been converted into craft workshops, souvenir stores and eateries. The whole area gets insanely busy in summer.

From the Lozovac entrance, buses (free with park admission) shuttle visitors from the large car park (also free) down a serpentine road to Skradinski Buk. Neither the free boats nor the buses operate from November to February, but in those months you can drive right down to the falls.

Mother of Mercy Franciscan Monastery MONASTERY

(Franjevački samostan Majke od Milosti; ☎022-775 730) Upstream of Skradinski Buk waterfall the Krka River broadens into Lake Viskovac, a habitat for marsh birds. At its centre is a tree-fringed island, the perfect place for a monastery. Founded in the 14th century by Augustinian hermits, the monastery was expanded in 1445 by Franciscans escaping the Ottoman invasion of Bosnia. The church was extensively remodelled in the 17th century and the bell tower added in 1728. Boat trips head here from Skradinski Buk and include 30 minutes on the island.

Skradin VILLAGE

Skradin is a pretty little riverside town with a combination of brightly painted and bare stone houses on its main street and a ruined fortress towering above. Apart from the opportunity to see the town itself, the advantage to starting your visit to Krka National Park in Skradin is that the park admission fee includes a boat ride through the canyon to Skradinski Buk waterfall. The disadvantage is that there can be long queues for the boats in summer.

Roški Slap WATERFALL

(adult/child Jul & Aug 100/55KN, Apr-Jun, Sep & Oct 60/40KN, Nov-Mar 30/20KN, with Krka National Park entry free; ⏲9am-8pm Jul & Aug, shorter hours rest of year) Beginning with shallow steps and continuing in a series of branches and islets to become 23m-high cascades, this 650m-long stretch is a flamboyantly pretty part of the Krka River. On the eastern side you can visit the water mills that used to grind wheat. Boats leave from Skradinski Buk waterfall (adult/child 140/95KN, 3½ hours).

Burnum RUINS

(adult/child 40/30KN, with Krka National Park entry free; ⏲10am-6pm Apr-Jun, Sep & Oct, 9am-8pm Jul & Aug) Just off the main road from Kistanje to Knin, 6km past the monastery turn-off, lie the remains of the only Roman military amphitheatre in Croatia. Earth mounds lined with brick form the distinctive oval shape of the structure, which once entertained the troops stationed here. A little further along the road, look out for the two elegant white arches of a ruined aqueduct. There are also a couple of waterfall **viewpoints** in the vicinity.

Sleeping

Guest House Ankora GUESTHOUSE €€

(☎095 910 70 68; www.guesthouseankora.com; Mesarska 5a, Skradin; r/apt 490/950KN) Simple but lovingly looked-after rooms and apartments in a good, central Skradin location make this an excellent base for Krka National Park. The stone walls in some rooms, the outdoor hot tub and the friendly service are all bonuses. Three-night minimum stay in summer.

Vila Barbara APARTMENT €€€

(☎095 884 58 01; www.vilabarbara.com; Zagrađe 17, Skradin; apt 1200KN; P 📶) This excellent place has colourful, almost whimsically painted apartments, a quiet terrace and a hot tub. The welcome is warm and the location, not far from the water's edge, is excellent.

Information

There are information offices at each of the park entrances.

Krka National Park Office (☎022-771 688; www.npkrka.hr; Skradin; ⏲8am-8pm) Near the harbour in Skradin; provides good maps and information, and can arrange excursions.

Skradin Tourist Office (☎022-771 329; www.skradin.hr; Trg Male Gospe 3; ⊙9am-5pm Mon-Fri) The main tourist office is in the town hall, but from Easter to October it also staffs a kiosk by the national-park office.

Getting There & Away

Numerous agencies sell excursions to Krka from Šibenik, Zadar and other coastal cities, but it's not difficult to visit independently. In summer seven daily buses (three on Sunday) with **Autotransport Šibenik** (☎022-212 557; www.atpsi.hr) depart from Šibenik for Lozovac and Skradin (28KN, 25 minutes). In winter the only buses are timed around the school run.

Šibenik

☎022 / POP 34,500

Šibenik has a magnificent medieval heart, gleaming white against the placid waters of the bay, something that may not be immediately apparent as you drive through the somewhat-shabby outskirts. The stone labyrinth of steep backstreets and alleys is a joy to explore. Šibenik is also an important access point for Krka National Park and the Kornati Islands.

History

Unlike many other Dalmatian coastal communities, Šibenik was founded not by Illyrians, Greeks or Romans but by the Croatian king Petar Krešimir IV in the 11th century. The city was conquered by Venice in 1116, and tossed around between Venice, Hungary, Byzantium and Bosnia until Venice ultimately seized control in 1412. Ottomans periodically attacked the town, disrupting trade and agriculture in the 16th and 17th centuries.

Venetian control was usurped in 1797 by Austrian rule, which continued until 1918. Following on from the discoveries of compatriot Nikola Tesla, local engineer and inventor (and later mayor) Ante Šupak built one of the world's first hydroelectric plants on the Krka River in 1895, and Šibenik became only the third city in the world with an alternating current (AC) street-lighting system.

Šibenik fell under attack in 1991 from Yugoslav federal forces and was subject to shelling until its liberation as part of 'Operation Storm' by the Croatian army in 1995. Little physical damage is evident, but the city's aluminium industry was shattered and unemployment grew to over 50%. But Šibenik has made a serious comeback in the past few years, and tourism has slowly become a vital part of the local economy.

Sights

Many of Šibenik's beautiful smaller churches are only open around Mass times.

★**St James' Cathedral** CATHEDRAL
(Katedrala Svetog Jakova; Trg Republike Hrvatske; adult/child 20KN/free; ⊙9.30am-6.30pm) The crowning architectural glory of the Dalmatian coast and the undisputed masterpiece of its principal designer, Juraj Dalmatinac, this World Heritage Site is worth a detour to see. It was constructed entirely of stone quarried from the islands of Brač, Korčula, Rab and Krk, and is reputed to be the world's largest church built completely of stone without brick or wooden supports. The structure is also unique in that the interior shape corresponds exactly to the exterior.

Dalmatinac was not the first (nor last) architect to work on the cathedral. Construction began in 1431, but, after 10 years of toying with various Venetian builders, the city appointed Dalmatinac, a Zadar native, who increased the size of the building and transformed the conception of the church into a transitional Gothic-Renaissance style. The unusual domed-roof complex was completed after Dalmatinac's death by Nikola Firentinac, who continued the facade in a pure Renaissance style. It was all finally completed in 1536.

The cathedral's most unusual feature is the **frieze** of 71 heads on the exterior walls at the rear of the building. These portraits – placid, annoyed, comical, proud and fearful – almost appear to be caricatures but are depictions of ordinary 15th-century citizens. The building cost a great deal to construct, and it's said that the stingier the individual, the grosser the caricature.

Note also the **Lion's Portal** on the northern side, created by Dalmatinac and Bonino da Milano, in which two lions support columns containing the figures of Adam and Eve, who appear to be excruciatingly embarrassed by their nakedness.

Pick up the excellent brochure (available in various languages) as you enter the church; it provides a self-guided circuit of the artworks and architectural features inside. A highlight is Dalmatinac's extraordinary **baptistery** in the rear corner, with its exquisitely carved ceiling and font supported by three angels.

Šibenik

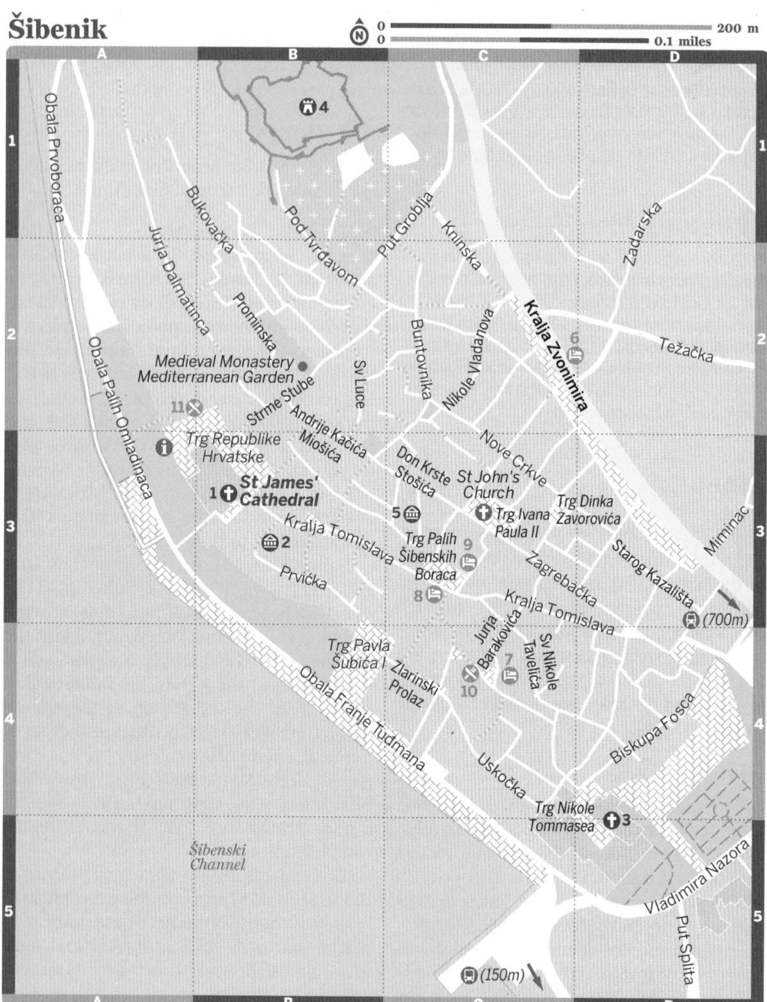

Šibenik

Top Sights
1 St James' Cathedral B3

Sights
2 Šibenik City Museum B3
3 St Francis' Church D5
4 St Michael's Fortress B1
5 Victory Museum C3

Sleeping
6 Hostel Mare C2
7 Indigo C4
8 King Kresimir Heritage Hotel C3
9 Medulic Palace Rooms & Apartments C3

Eating
10 Konoba San Antonio C4
11 Pelegrini A2

Other interior artworks worth noting are the tomb of Bishop Šižigorić (by Dalmatinac), who supported the building of the cathedral; the altar painting of St Fabian and St Sebastian (by Filippo Zaniberti); and a particularly gruesome 15th-century Gothic crucifix (by Juraj Petrović).

Šibenik City Museum MUSEUM

(Muzej grada Šibenika; ☎022-213 880; www.muzej-sibenik.hr; Gradska Vrata 3; adult/child 30/10KN; ⏱8am-8pm Tue-Fri, 10am-8pm Sat & Sun) Housed in the 17th-century Rector's Palace, this well-curated museum focuses on the city and its surrounds. The permanent collection of artefacts dating from prehistory to the end of the Venetian period is split into four clear periods. There are English translations throughout and the odd bit of video to spice things up.

St Michael's Fortress FORTRESS

(Tvrđava Sv Mihovila; adult/child 40/20KN; ⏱8am-10pm) Clamber up to the battlements of this large medieval fort for magnificent views – particularly impressive at sunset – over Šibenik, the Krk River and the Adriatic islands. Parts of the fortress date to the 13th century, but the surviving shell has been shored up with a polished-concrete understructure and converted into a summer stage.

St Francis' Church CHURCH

(Crkva Sv Frane; Trg Nikole Tommasea 1; ⏱7.30am-7.30pm) The Franciscan monastery's mammoth church dates from the end of the 14th century. It has fine frescos and an array of Venetian baroque paintings, but the highlight is the painted wooden ceiling, dating from 1674. It's the principal shrine of St Nikola Tavilić, a Franciscan missionary who became the first Croatian saint when he was martyred in Jerusalem in 1391. In the adjacent courtyard there's an exhibition on the church's history.

Victory Museum MUSEUM

(Muzej Pobjede Šibenik; Fra Nikole Ružića 1; ⏱10am-1pm & 5-7pm Mon-Sat) Also known as the Museum of Victory and Liberation of Dalmatia, this well-presented archive documents the antifascist struggle in Dalmatia. Opened in 2016, and the first museum of its kind in Croatia, its focus is on WWII, with multimedia and photographic exhibits in Croatian and English and some interesting historical footage.

Sleeping

★**Indigo** HOSTEL €

(☎022-200 159; www.hostel-indigo.com; Jurja Barakovića 3; dm 129KN; ❄📶) Lauded by all who stay the night and longer, this friendly little hostel has a four-bed dorm with pine bunks and lockable drawers on each of its four floors. At the very top, the terrace has views over the rooftops to the sea. Blue jeans provide a kooky decoration throughout. Sadly, there's no kitchen.

WORTH A TRIP

OBONJAN ISLAND

The tiny car-free island of **Obonjan** (☎UK +44 203 808 7333; www.obonjan-island.com; ⏱late Jul-early Sep), around 10km off Šibenik, has been transformed into a holiday resort, but one with a twist. Accommodation is in safari-style tents, some with views straight across the Adriatic, but the main attraction is the month-long cultural program, packed with DJs, film screenings, talks, workshops, art events and sport. There are also four restaurants, three bars, free yoga classes, and boat trips around the region.

Three boats leave Šibenik daily when the resort is open. The fare is 105KN each way. Booking ahead is essential. Check the website for prices and packages if you plan to stay.

Hostel Mare HOSTEL €

(☎022-215 269; www.hostel-mare.com; Kralja Zvonimira 40; dm 100-159KN, r 330-450KN; ❄📶) Pass through the heavy door that opens from the busy road onto a cobbled courtyard, and behind lies this breezy hostel. The decor is fresh, bright and IKEA-style modern, the dorms have backpack-sized lockers and there's one double room with its own bathroom. Breakfast is available (for an extra charge). Bike storage available.

★**Medulic Palace Rooms & Apartments** APARTMENT €€

(☎095 53 01 868; www.medulicpalace.com; Ivana Pribislavića 4; r 310-630KN, apt 365-815KN; ❄📶) Wonderfully central and with exposed stone or brick walls, the Medulic is a fabulous deal. The standard rooms have less character, but the apartments and superior rooms are well priced and lovely places to spend a night or more.

King Kresimir Heritage Hotel HERITAGE HOTEL €€€

(☎022-427 461; www.hotel-kingkresimir.com; Dobrić 2; r from 1075KN; ❄@📶) Right on the main square in a former mansion that combines Gothic and baroque touches, this hotel has quietly luxurious rooms. Some rooms have four-poster beds, others have sea views, and the whole place has a classy, professional air.

Eating

★ Pelegrini MEDITERRANEAN €€
(☎022-213 701; www.pelegrini.hr; Jurja Dalmatinca 1; mains 79-185KN, 3-/4-/5-course set menu 440/570/700KN; ⊙noon-midnight) Responsible for upping the culinary ante in Šibenik, this wonderful restaurant raids the globe for flavours, with influences from Japan and France, but its heart is in the Mediterranean. Dalmatian offerings are very well represented on the wine list. Call ahead to bag one of the outside tables.

Konoba San Antonio CROATIAN €€
(☎098 16 42 141; Dobrić 1; mains 40-160KN; ⊙8am-11pm) This tavern has a pleasant old-town terrace and a tradition of well-prepared seafood, fish and grilled-meat dishes – try the salmon carpaccio. Owner Antonio adds much warmth and energy to the place.

Information

General Hospital Šibenik (Opća bolnica Šibenik; ☎022-641 641; www.bolnica-sibenik.hr; Stjepana Radića 83)

Tourist Office (☎022-214 411; www.sibenik-tourism.hr; Obala Palih Omladinaca 3; ⊙8am-9pm May-Oct, to 4pm Mon-Fri Nov-Apr) Helpful tourist office in the heart of the old town.

Getting There & Away

Šibenik's **bus station** (☎060 368 368; Draga 14) has plenty of regular services and is only a short walk from the old town.

Destinations include the following:

Dubrovnik 148KN, 6½ hours, at least two daily

Rijeka 200KN, 6½ hours, at least four daily

Split 48KN, 1½ hours, 12 daily

Zadar 43KN, 1½ hours, at least hourly

Zagreb From 132KN, five to seven hours, at least hourly

Primošten

☎022 / POP 3050

Pretty little Primošten occupies what was once an islet just off the coast, 28km south of Šibenik. During the Turkish threat of the 16th century it was fortified, and when the Turks disappeared the drawbridge connecting it to the mainland was replaced by a causeway.

Sleepy to the point of inertia in winter, Primošten comes alive in summer, with bands playing in the main square, interesting gift shops selling their wares and excited kids racing around the cobbled streets. Romantics stroll up the hill to St George's Church to watch the sunset, and loop around the peninsula's perimeter after dark. It's one of the loveliest towns along this stretch of coastline.

Sleeping & Eating

Golden Rays Luxury Resort RESORT €€€
(☎099 20 62 404; www.goldenrays.hr; Tepli bok 69b; apt from 2365KN; P❄@🛜≋) The sweeping Adriatic views from the floor-to-ceiling windows and the contemporary stylishness throughout make this a wonderful choice. Multiple swimming pools, high levels of comfort and professional service round out a terrific package.

★ Mediteran MEDITERRANEAN €€€
(☎022-571 780; www.mediteran-primosten.hr; Briga 13; mains 95-250KN; ⊙1pm-midnight) Mediteran centres on a lovely old stone building, although in summer the action moves into the courtyard and up to the little 1st-floor terrace. Chef Pero Savanović's dishes offer a modern take on Dalmatian traditions and

WORTH A TRIP

RAPTOR RESCUE

Dedicated to protecting birds of prey in Croatia, **Sokolarski Centre** (☎091 50 67 610; www.sokolarskicentar.com; Škugori bb; adult/child 50/40KN; ⊙9am-7pm Apr-Nov) performs a kind of rescue and rehab service for around 150 injured raptors each year. Visitors are treated to a highly entertaining and educational presentation from centre director Emilo Mendušić, who uses a tame eagle owl and Harris hawks to demonstrate these birds' agility and skills. Rescued native birds aren't used for these shows; they're only kept at the centre until they're healthy enough to be released back into the wild.

Most of the patients at the centre have been involved in a collision on Croatian roads. Other threats to the birds include illegal poisoning, shooting and the use of pesticides.

The Sokolarski Centre is about 7km from Šibenik and is not served by public transport. It's a little tricky to find: to get here take the road to Krka National Park, turn east at Bilice and look for the signs.

highlight delicious local produce. Visit when Istrian truffles are in season and you'll be in for a treat – try the monkfish with truffle sauce.

Information

Tourist Office (022-571 111; www.tz-primosten.hr; Trg biskupa Josipa Arnerića 2; 8am-9pm Jul & Aug, shorter hours rest of year)

Getting There & Away

Buses run at least hourly to Primošten from Šibenik (18KN, 30 minutes), normally continuing on to Split (38KN, one hour).

Rogoznica

022 / POP 2450

A well-protected harbour on a peninsula 38km by road south of Šibenik, laid-back Rogoznica is popular with Adriatic yachtspeople in the know and tourists looking for a quiet hideaway. With its pebbly beaches, tranquil, historic streets and some good eating options, the town makes a pleasant base for exploring the Šibenik area if you're not keen on city clamour. It also has one of the best climates in Croatia, with more sunny days per year than most other coastal communities.

Sights

★Dragon's Eye Lake LAKE
(Zmajevo Oko) One of Northern Dalmatia's most striking natural phenomena, Dragon's Eye Lake is a 10,000-sq-metre oval encircled by 4m- to 24m-high cliffs. Connected to the ocean by underwater channels and cracks in the surrounding limestone, the lake is up to 15m deep. What makes it so unusual is its base of hydrogen sulphide – although it's safe to swim here, the water gets hotter the deeper you dive. On occasion the lake 'boils' as the salts and hot water bubble to the surface.

Sleeping & Eating

Hotel Life HOTEL €€€
(022-558 128; www.hotel-life.hr; Rtić 12e; r 1500KN; P ❄ 🛜 ≋) Located in Zečevo Bay between Rogoznica and Primošten, this small, family-run hotel offers minimalist-chic accommodation near a quiet pebble beach. Rooms are studies in grey-and-white 21st-century styling, there's a restaurant, and the small indoor pool is lovely for an early-morning wallow.

Atrium CROATIAN, SEAFOOD €€
(098 170 92 73; www.restaurantatrium.com; Miline 44; mains 65-190KN; noon-midnight) Consistently recommended by travellers for its helpful service and terrific food, Atrium does the simple things well, including grilled calamari, sea bass, vegetables – grilled everything – to perfection. Other good choices include the octopus salad and the tuna carpaccio.

Information

Tourist Office (022-559 253; www.lovero goznica.eu; Obala kneza Domagoja 56) Helpful office with an especially informative website. Also serves the surrounding villages.

Getting There & Away

Buses link Rogoznica to Šibenik (26KN, 45 minutes, at least hourly) and Split (36KN, one hour, at least eight daily).

AT A GLANCE

POPULATION
Split: 178,000

TOURISTS IN HVAR TOWN DURING HIGH SEASON
20,000

BEST FOR WILDLIFE
Kopački Rit Nature Park (p120)

BEST DALMATIAN RESTAURANT
Konoba Marjan (p255)

BEST REMOTE BEACH
Stiniva (p286)

WHEN TO GO

May
Sunny, less crowded, and the sea is already warm enough for swimming.

Jun–Aug
The best weather and a full roster of festivities but overflowing with tourists.

Sep
Come for warm seas and lower prices after the summer hordes have left.

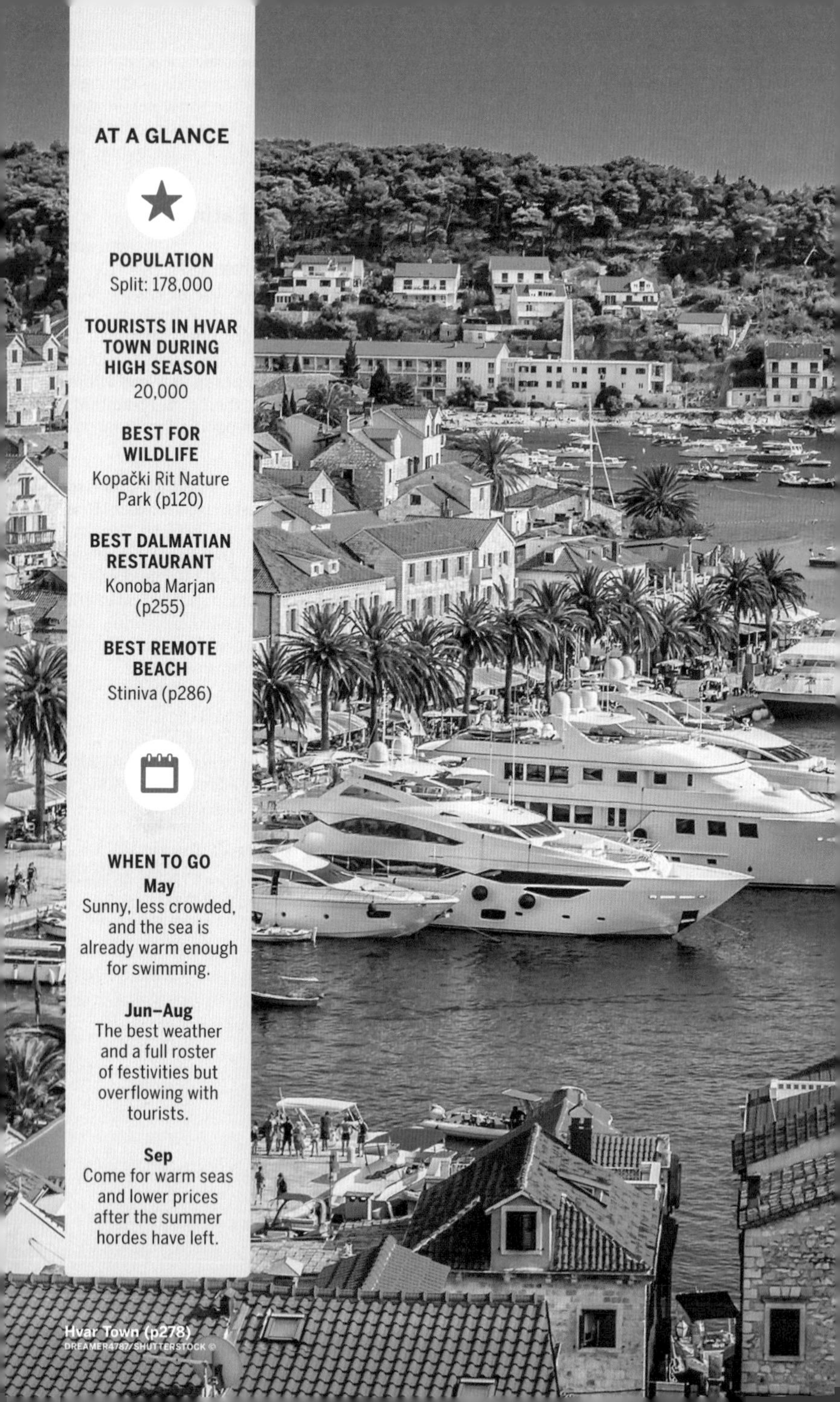

Hvar Town (p278)

Split & Central Dalmatia

Central Dalmatia is the most action-packed and diverse part of Croatia, with pretty islands, quiet ports, rugged mountains, numerous castles and an emerging culinary scene, as well as three Unesco World Heritage Sites: Diocletian's Palace in Split, the medieval walled town of Trogir and the ancient strip fields of the Stari Grad plain on the island of Hvar. Throughout it all, the rugged 1500m-high Dinaric Range provides a dramatic background. Hot spots include the buzzing Mediterranean-flavoured city of Split and gorgeous little Hvar Town, where the cashed meet the trashed on the Adriatic's most glamorous party island. But if it's relaxation you're after, there are seductive sandy beaches and pebbly coves scattered about islands near and far.

INCLUDES

Split & Central Dalmatia Highlights

1 Diocletian's Palace (p244) Discovering Split's ancient heart in Diocletian's Palace, a quarter that buzzes day and night.

2 Vis (p286) Savouring the food and beaches of one of Croatia's remotest islands.

3 Zlatni Rat (p274) Stretching out on Zlatni Rat, Croatia's most photogenic beach, in the pretty town of Bol.

4 Hvar Town (p278) Capping off endless beach days with sunset cocktails and back-lane boogie sessions.

5 Biokovo Nature Park (p271) Hiking up dramatic peaks and enjoying views right across the Adriatic to far-off Italy.

6 Trogir (p262) Taking in the remarkably preserved Romanesque and Renaissance architecture of this tiny World Heritage star.

7 Brač (p272) Exploring the historic hamlets of the island's interior and the sleepy little towns scattered around the coast.

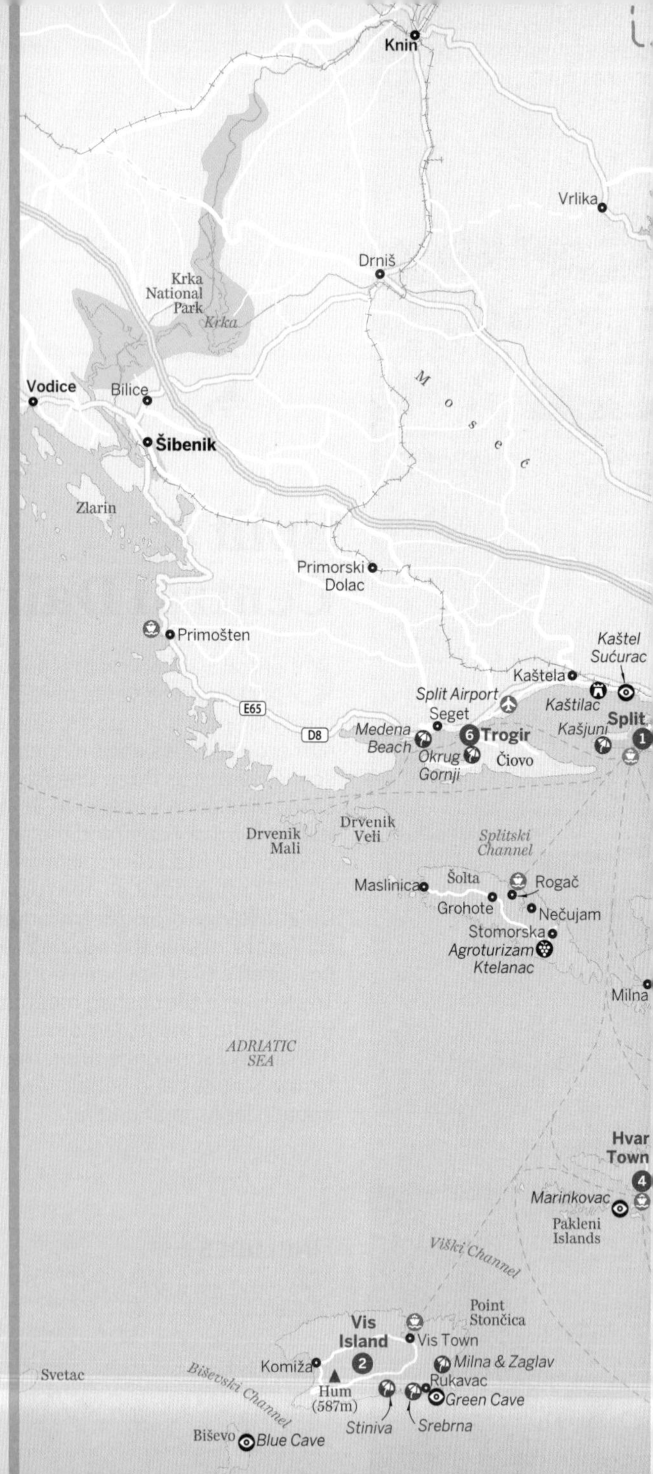

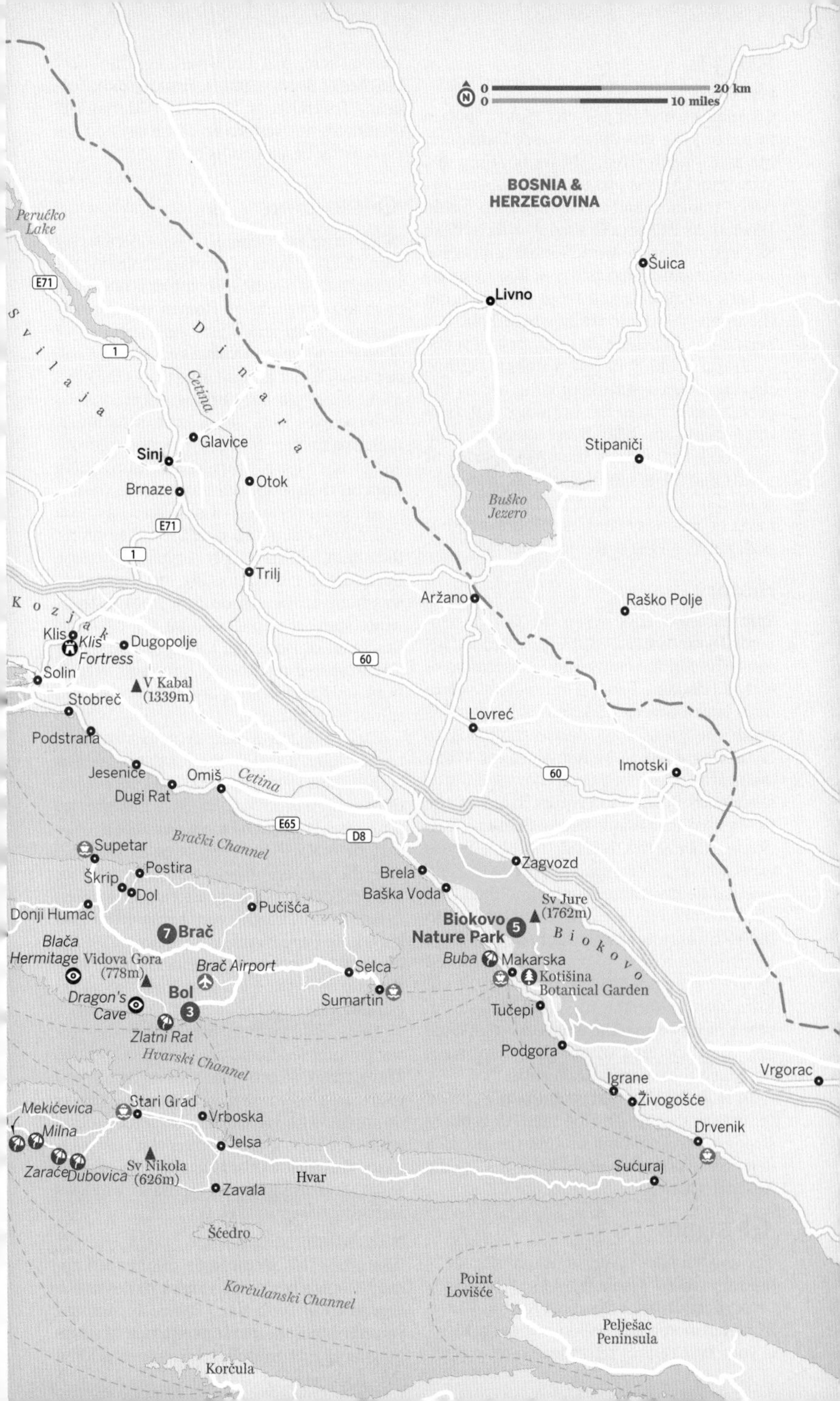

0 20 km
0 10 miles
BOSNIA & HERZEGOVINA
Peručko Lake
E71
Svilaja
Dinara
1
Cetina
Šuica
Livno
Glavice
Sinj
Brnaze
Otok
Stipaniči
Buško Jezero
E71
1
Trilj
Aržano
Raško Polje
Kozjak
Klis
Klis Fortress
Dugopolje
60
Solin
V Kabal (1339m)
Stobreč
Lovreć
Podstrana
Imotski
60
Jesenice
Omiš
Cetina
Dugi Rat
E65
D8
Bračkí Channel
Supetar
Postira
Škrip
Dol
Donji Humac
Pučišća
Brela
Baška Voda
Zagvozd
Sv Jure (1762m)
Biokovo Nature Park
5
7 Brač
Biokovo
Blača Hermitage
Vidova Gora (778m)
Brač Airport
Selca
Buba
Makarska
Kotišina Botanical Garden
Dragon's Cave
Bol
3
Sumartin
Tučepi
Zlatni Rat
Hvarski Channel
Podgora
Vrgorac
Igrane
Živogošće
Mekićevica
Stari Grad
Vrboska
Milna
Drvenik
Jelsa
Zaraće
Dubovica
Sv Nikola (626m)
Hvar
Sućuraj
Zavala
Šćedro
Point Lovišće
Korčulanski Channel
Pelješac Peninsula
Korčula

SPLIT

POP 178,000

Croatia's second-largest city, Split (Spalato in Italian) is a great place to see Dalmatian life as it's really lived. Always buzzing, this exuberant city has just the right balance between tradition and modernity. Step inside Diocletian's Palace (a Unesco World Heritage Site and one of the world's most impressive Roman monuments) and you'll see dozens of bars, restaurants and shops thriving amid the atmospheric old walls where Split has been humming along for thousands of years.

To top it off, Split has a unique setting. Its dramatic coastal mountains act as the perfect backdrop to the turquoise waters of the Adriatic and help divert attention from the dozens of shabby high-rise apartment blocks that fill its suburbs. It's this thoroughly lived-in aspect of Split that means it will never be a fantasy land like Dubrovnik, but perhaps it's all the better for that.

History

Split achieved fame when the Roman emperor Diocletian (245–313 CE), noted for his restructure of the empire and persecution of early Christians, had his retirement palace built here between 295 and 305. After his death the great stone palace continued to be used as a retreat by Roman rulers. When the nearby colony of Salona (now Solin) was abandoned in the 7th century, many of the Romanised inhabitants fled to Split and barricaded themselves behind the high palace walls, where their descendants live to this day.

First the Byzantine Empire and then Croatia controlled the area, but from the 12th to the 14th centuries medieval Split enjoyed a large measure of autonomy, which favoured its development. The western part of the old town around Narodni trg, which dates from this time, became the focus of municipal life, while the area within the palace walls remained the ecclesiastical centre.

In 1420 the Venetian conquest of Split led to its slow decline. During the 17th century, strong walls were built around the city as a defence against the Ottomans. In 1797 the Austrians arrived, remaining until 1918.

Sights

The ever-frenetic waterfront promenade – officially called Obala hrvatskog narodnog preporoda (Croatian National Revival Waterfront) but more commonly known as the Riva – is your best central reference point in Split. East of here, past the wharf, are the buzzy beaches of Bačvice (p256), Firule (p256), Zenta and Trstenik bays. The wooded Marjan Hill dominates the western tip of the city and has even better beaches at its base.

Old Town

★ Diocletian's Palace HISTORIC SITE

(Map p252) Taking up a prime harbourside position, this extraordinary complex is one of the most imposing ancient Roman structures in existence today, and where you'll spend most of your time while in Split. Don't expect a palace, though, nor a museum – this is the city's living heart, its labyrinthine streets packed with people, bars, shops and restaurants. Built as a military fortress, imperial residence and fortified town, the palace measures 215m from north to south and 180m east to west.

Although the original structure has been added to continuously over the millenniums, the alterations have only served to increase the allure of this fascinating site. The palace was built in the 4th century from lustrous white stone transported from the island of Brač, and construction lasted 10 years. Diocletian spared no expense, importing marble from Italy and Greece, and columns and 12 sphinxes from Egypt.

Each wall has a gate at its centre that's named after a metal: the northern **Golden Gate** (Zlatna Vrata; Map p252; Dioklecijanova bb), the southern **Bronze Gate** (Brončana Vrata; Map p252; Obala hrvatskog narodnog preporoda bb), the eastern **Silver Gate** (Srebrna Vrata; Map p252) and the western **Iron Gate** (Željezna Vrata; Map p252). Between the eastern and western gates there's a straight road (Krešimirova, also known as Decumanus), which separated the imperial residence on the southern side, with its state rooms and temples, from the northern side, once used by soldiers and servants.

There are 220 buildings within the palace boundaries, home to about 3000 people. The narrow streets hide passageways and courtyards – some deserted and eerie, others thumping with music from bars and cafes – while residents hang out their washing overhead, kids kick footballs against the ancient walls, and grannies sit in their windows watching the action below.

➡ Peristil

(Map p252) This picturesque colonnaded ancient Roman peristyle (courtyard) lies at the very heart of Diocletian's Palace. In summer you can almost be guaranteed a pair of strapping local lads dressed as legionaries adding to the scene. Notice the black-granite sphinx sitting between the columns near the cathedral; dating from the 15th century BCE, it was one of 12 looted from Egypt when the palace was constructed.

Diocletian's Palace Substructure
(Supstrukcije Dioklecijanove palače; Map p252; www.mgst.net; Obala hrvatskog narodnog preporoda bb; adult/child 42/22KN; ⌚8.30am-9pm Apr-Sep, to 5pm Sun Oct, 9am-5pm Mon-Sat, to 2pm Sun Nov-Apr) The Bronze Gate of Diocletian's Palace once opened straight from the water into the palace basements, enabling goods to be unloaded and stored here. Now this former tradesman's entrance is the main way into the palace from the Riva. While the central part of the substructure is now a major thoroughfare lined with souvenir stalls, entry to the chambers on either side is ticketed.

Although mostly empty save the odd sarcophagus or bit of column, the basement rooms and corridors exude a haunting timelessness that is worth the price of admission. For fans of *Game of Thrones,* here be dragons – Daenerys Targaryen keeps her scaly brood here when she's in Meereen.

Cathedral of St Domnius
(Katedrala sv Duje; Map p252; Peristil bb; cathedral/belfry 35/20KN; ⌚8am-8pm Jun-Sep, 7am-noon & 5-7pm May & Oct, 7am-noon Nov-Feb, 8am-5pm Mar & Apr) Split's octagonal cathedral is one of the best-preserved ancient Roman buildings still standing. It was built as a mausoleum for Diocletian, the last famous persecutor of the Christians, who was interred here in 311 CE. In the 5th century the Christians got the last laugh, destroying the emperor's sarcophagus and converting his tomb into a church dedicated to one of his victims. Note that a ticket for the cathedral includes admission to its crypt, treasury and baptistery (Temple of Jupiter).

The exterior of the building is still encircled by an original colonnade of 24 columns. A much later addition, the tall Romanesque **bell tower**, was constructed between the 13th and 16th centuries and reconstructed in 1908 after it collapsed. Tickets are sold separately for those eager to climb up for views over the old town's rooftops. You'll need a head for heights, though, as the steep stone stairs quickly give way to flimsy metal ones suspended over the internal void.

In summer, visitor access to the cathedral is via the sacristy, situated in an annexe around the right-hand side of the building. This structure also houses the cathedral's **treasury**, which is rich in reliquaries, icons, church robes, illuminated manuscripts and documents in Glagolitic script (p199). In the low season, entry is via the front door and the treasury isn't open to the public (tickets are 10KN cheaper when the treasury is closed).

Inside the cathedral itself, the domed interior has two rows of Corinthian columns and a frieze running high up on the walls that, surprisingly, still includes images of the emperor and his wife. To the left of the main altar is the altar of St Anastasius (Sveti Staš; 1448), carved by Juraj Dalmatinac. It features a relief of *The Flagellation of Christ* that is considered one of the finest sculptural works of its time in Dalmatia.

The choir is furnished with 13th-century Romanesque seats, the oldest of their kind in Dalmatia. Other highlights include a 13th-century pulpit; the right-hand altar, carved by Bonino da Milano in 1427; and the vault above the high altar, decorated with murals by Dujam Vušković. As you leave, take a look at the remarkable scenes from the life of Christ on the wooden entrance doors. Carved by Andrija Buvina in the 13th century, the images are presented in 28 squares, 14 on each side, and recall the fashion of Romanesque miniatures of the time.

Don't forget to take a look in the **crypt**, accessed by an exterior door on the right side of the church. Now a chapel dedicated to St Lucy, it's an eerily quiet chamber that stays cool even on the hottest days.

If you're interested in the technical aspects of the building's architecture, check out the free **New Research on Split Cathedral** (Nova istraživanja Splitske katedrale; Map p252; Peristil bb; ⌚10am-1pm & 5-8pm Tue-Sun) FREE exhibition in the building opposite the main entrance.

Temple of Jupiter
(Jupiterov hram; Map p252; 10KN, with cathedral ticket free; ⌚8am-7pm Mon-Sat, 12.30-6.30pm Sun May-Oct, to 5pm Nov-Apr) Although it's now the cathedral's baptistery, this wonderfully intact building was originally an ancient Roman temple dedicated to the king of the gods. It still has its original barrel-vaulted ceiling and decorative frieze, although a striking bronze statue of St John the Baptist by Ivan Meštrović now fills the spot where Jupiter once stood. The font is made from 13th-century carved stones recycled from the cathedral's rood screen.

Of the columns that once supported a porch, only one remains. The black-granite sphinx guarding the entrance was already ancient when the Romans dragged it from

Split

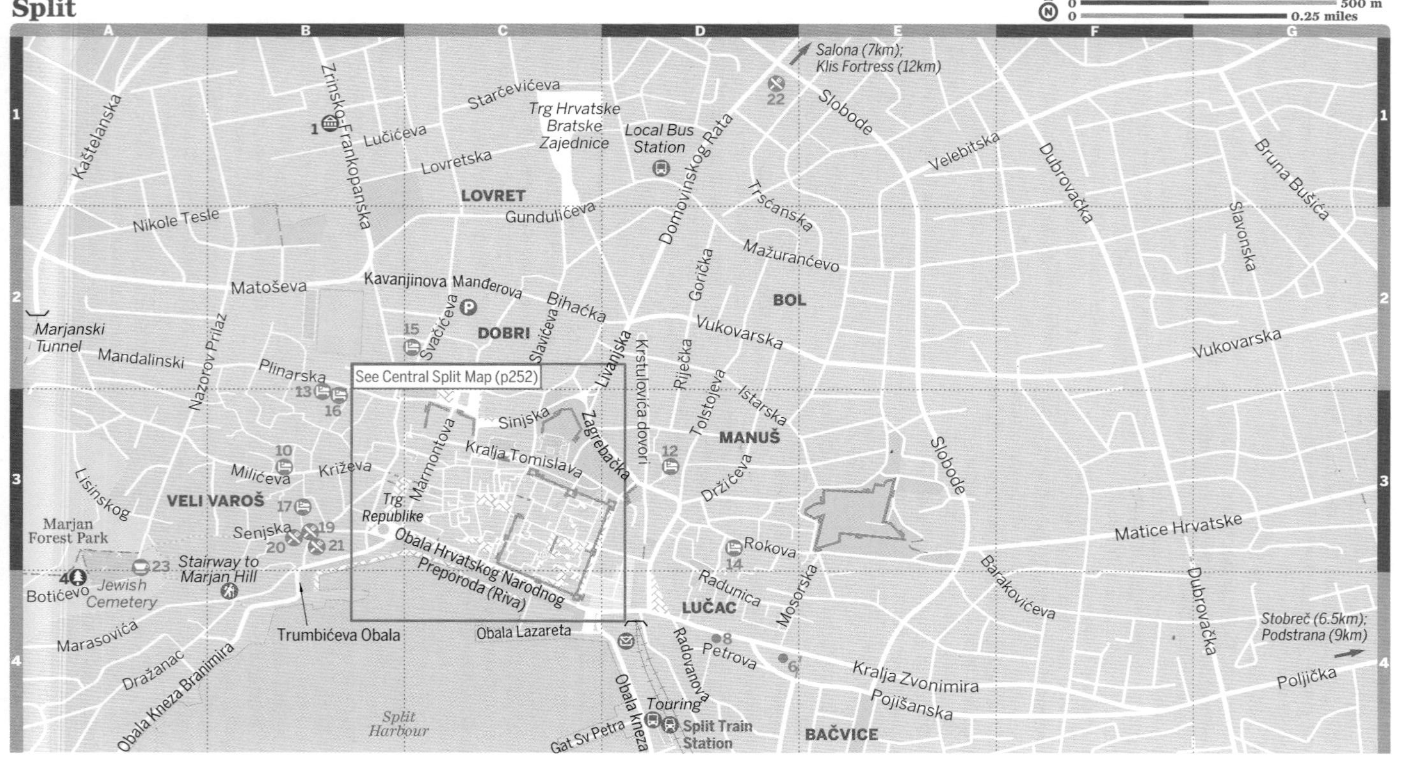
500 m
0.25 miles
Salona (7km); Klis Fortress (12km)
Stobreč (6.5km); Podstrana (9km)
Kaštelanska
Zrinsko-Frankopanska
Lučićeva
Starčevićeva
Lovretska
Trg Hrvatske Bratske Zajednice
Local Bus Station
Domovinskog Rata
Slobode
Velebitska
Dubrovačka
Bruna Bušića
Slavonska
LOVRET
Gundulićeva
Nikole Tesle
Trsćanska
Mažuranćevo
Goriška
Matoševa
Kavanjinova
Manđerova
Bihaćka
Svačićeva
Slavićeva
DOBRI
BOL
Vukovarska
Marjanski Tunnel
Mandalinski
Nazorov Prilaz
Plinarska
Livanjska
Krstulovića dovori
Riječka
Tolstojeva
Istarska
See Central Split Map (p252)
Sinjska
Zagrebačka
Marmontova
Kralja Tomislava
MANUŠ
Križeva
Milićeva
Držićeva
Lisinskog
VELI VAROŠ
Trg Republike
Matice Hrvatske
Marjan Forest Park
Senjska
Obala Hrvatskog Narodnog Preporoda (Riva)
Rokova
Stairway to Marjan Hill
Jewish Cemetery
Botićevo
Radunica
Mosorska
Barakovićeva
LUČAC
Marasovića
Trumbićeva Obala
Obala Lazareta
Radovanova
Petrova
Dražanac
Obala Kneza Branimira
Kralja Zvonimira
Poljička
Pojišanska
Obala kneza
Touring
Split Train Station
Split Harbour
Gat Sv Petra
BAČVICE

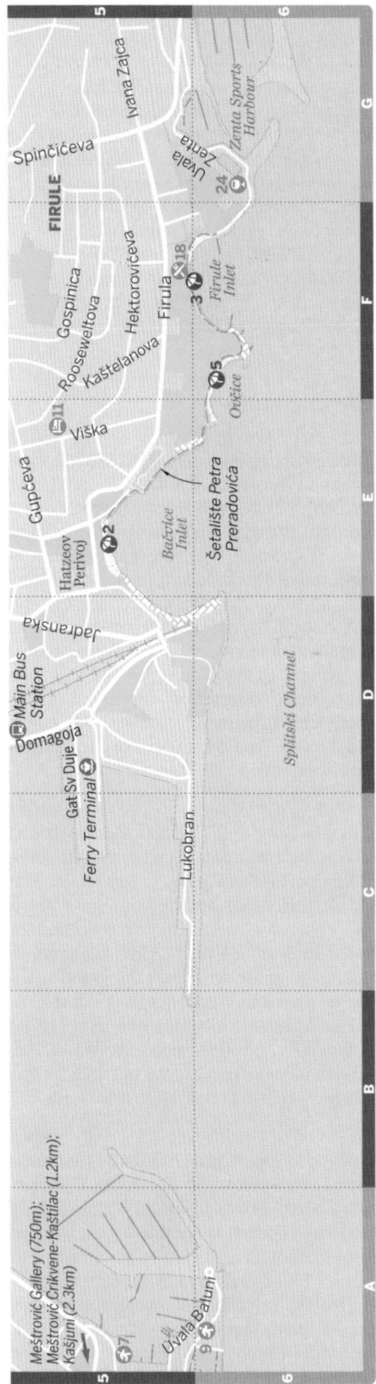

Split

Sights

1 Archaeological Museum B1
2 Bačvice E5
3 Firule F6
4 Marjan Forest Park A4
5 Ovčice F6

Activities, Courses & Tours

6 CroActive & Adventure D4
7 Nautika Centar Nava A5
8 Red Adventures D4
9 Ultra Sailing A6

Sleeping

10 Apartments Magdalena B3
11 Beach Hostel Split E5
12 CroParadise Green Hostel D3
13 Korta B3
14 Splendida Palace D3
15 Tchaikovsky Hostel C2
16 Vila Baguc B3
17 Villa Varoš B3

Eating

18 Dvor F5
19 Konoba Fetivi B3
20 Konoba Marjan B3
21 Konoba Matejuška B3
22 Konoba Stare Grede D1

Drinking & Nightlife

23 Vidilica A3
24 Zenta G6

Egypt in the 3rd century. It was defaced (literally) by early Christians, who considered it a pagan icon.

Split Ethnographic Museum

(Etnografski muzej Split; Map p252; 021-344 161; www.etnografski-muzej-split.hr; Iza Vestibula 4; adult/child 20/10KN; 9.30am-8pm Mon-Sat, to 1pm Sun Jun-Sep, 9.30am-6pm Mon-Fri, 10am-2pm Sat & Sun Oct, 9.30am-4pm Mon-Fri, to 2pm Sat Nov-May) This mildly interesting museum occupies a former convent built within what was originally the emperor's bed chambers. Downstairs are temporary exhibitions, while elsewhere there's a collection of traditional costumes, jewellery, lace, weapons, toys and tools. Make sure you climb the reconstructed Roman staircase that leads to the Renaissance terrace encircling the top of the vestibule; the views are reason enough to visit the museum.

Split City Museum

(Muzej grada Splita; Map p252; 021-360 171; www.mgst.net; Papalićeva 1; adult/child 22/12KN; 8.30am-9pm Apr-Sep, 9am-5pm Tue-Sat, to 2pm Sun Oct-Mar) Built by Juraj Dalmatinac in the

LOCAL KNOWLEDGE

PICIGIN

For a bit of fun, join the locals at the beach and play the very Dalmatian sport of *picigin*. The rules are simple: stand in the water up to your knees or waist and pass a small ball (the size of a squash ball) to other players by whacking it with the palm of your hand. The idea is to keep the ball from falling and touching the water's surface. It is imperative that you throw yourself about and generally attract as much attention to your sporting vigour as is humanly possible. It's also essential to splash all the people standing around you.

Check out the *picigin* 'headquarters' page at www.picigin.org or the several YouTube videos demonstrating *picigin* techniques (which vary between Split, Krk and other parts of the coast). Have a go at the special New Year's Eve *picigin* game if you think you're tough enough, or come in June to watch the best players splash about during the ironically named **World Championship** (Prvenstvo Svita u Piciginu; ⏲Jun).

15th century for one of the many noblemen who lived within the old town, the Large Papalić Palace is considered a fine example of late-Gothic style, with an elaborately carved entrance gate that proclaimed the importance of its original inhabitants. The interior has been thoroughly restored to house this museum, which has interesting displays on Diocletian's Palace (p244) and on the development of the city.

Captions are in Croatian, but wall panels in a variety of languages provide a historical framework for the displays of medieval sculpture, 17th-century weapons, fine furniture, coins, documents and drawings.

Grgur Ninski Statue STATUE

(Map p252; Kralja Tomislava bb) Sculpted by Ivan Meštrović, this gargantuan statue is one of the defining images of Split. Its subject, a 10th-century Croatian bishop, fought for the right to use old Croatian in liturgical services instead of Latin. Notice that his left big toe has been polished to a shine – it's said that rubbing the toe brings good luck and guarantees that you'll come back to Split.

Gallery of Fine Arts GALLERY

(Galerija umjetnina Split; Map p252; ☎021-350 110; www.galum.hr; Kralja Tomislava 15; adult/child 40/20KN; ⏲10am-6pm Tue-Fri, to 2pm Sat & Sun) Housed in a building that was the city's first hospital (1792), this gallery exhibits 400 works of art spanning 700 years. Upstairs is the permanent collection – a chronological journey that starts with religious icons and continues with works by the likes of Paolo Veneziano, Albrecht Dürer and Guido Reni, alongside the work of locals such as Vlaho Bukovac, Ivan Meštrović and Cata Dujšin-Ribar. The temporary exhibits downstairs change every few months.

Surrounds

Archaeological Museum MUSEUM

(Arheološki muzej; Map p246; ☎021-329 340; www.armus.hr; Zrinsko-Frankopanska 25; adult/child 20/10KN; ⏲9am-2pm & 4-8pm Mon-Sat Jun-Sep, closed Sat afternoon & Sun Oct-May) A treasure trove of classical sculpture and mosaics is displayed at this excellent museum, a short walk north of the town centre. Most of the vast collection originated from the ancient Roman settlements of Split and neighbouring Salona (p266; Solin), and there's also some Greek pottery from the island of Vis. There are displays of jewellery and coins, and a room filled with artefacts dating from the Palaeolithic to the Iron Age.

Meštrović Gallery GALLERY

(Galerija Meštrović; ☎021-340 800; www.mestrovic.hr; Šetalište Ivana Meštrovića 46; adult/child 40/20KN; ⏲9am-7pm Tue-Sun May-Sep, to 4pm Tue-Sun Oct-Apr) At this stellar art museum you'll see a comprehensive, well-arranged collection of works by Ivan Meštrović, Croatia's premier modern sculptor, who built the grand mansion as a personal residence in the 1930s. Although Meštrović intended to retire here, he emigrated to the USA soon after WWII. Admission includes entry to the nearby Kaštilac, a fortress housing other Meštrović works.

Our-Lady-of-Health Church CHURCH

(Gospa od zdravlja; Map p252; ☎021-344 988; www.gospa-od-zdravlja.com; Trg Gaje Bulata 3; ⏲7am-noon & 5-8pm) Completed in 1937, this striking Modernist church is notable for the simple, clean lines of its architecture. It's attached to a friary, founded in 1723 by Franciscans fleeing Turkish-ruled Bosnia. Inside, tall, square, granite-lined columns support a soaring ceiling, while a vast 1959 fresco by Ivo Dulčić fills the entire back wall. It depicts a stylised

Christ rising above a multitude of peasants in folk costumes, milling about on a outline of the Adriatic Coast.

Marjan Forest Park PARK
(Park-šuma Marjan; Map p246; www.marjan-parksuma.hr) Looming up to 178m over Split's western fringes, this nature reserve occupies a big space in Split's psyche. The views over the city and surrounding islands are extraordinary, and the shady paths provide a welcome reprieve from both the heat and the summertime tourist throngs. Trails pass through fragrant pine forests to scenic lookouts, a 16th-century Jewish cemetery, medieval chapels and cave dwellings once inhabited by Christian hermits. Climbers take to the cliffs near the end of the peninsula.

Meštrović Crikvene-Kaštilac MUSEUM
(☎021-340 800; www.mestrovic.hr; Šetalište Ivana Meštrovića 39; adult/child 40/20KN, with Meštrović Gallery free; ⏲9am-7pm Tue-Sun May-Sep) This 16th-century fortified home, set in an olive grove near the Meštrović Gallery, was bought by Ivan Meštrović in 1939 and restored to house his powerful *Life of Christ* cycle of wood reliefs in the chapel. At the centre of the complex, a large stone sculpture entitled *Author of the Apocalypse* looks over a lovely quadrangle.

Tours

Connecto Tours TOURS
(☎021-312 594; www.connectotours.com; ⏲Apr-Oct) Private tours, plus scheduled day trips to Krka National Park (€27), Bol (€49 including picnic), Dubrovnik (€67), Mostar and Međugorje (€67), the Kornati Islands (€69), Plitvice Lakes (€65), Trogir and Zadar (€79), the Blue Cave and Hvar (€125), and a Zrće all-nighter (€89). It also offers Cetina River rafting (€45), quad biking (€90) and a jet-ski safari (€130).

Portal TOURS
(Map p252; ☎021-360 061; www.split-excursions.com; Trg Republike 1; ⏲7am-9pm May-Sep, 8am-3pm Mon-Fri, to 1pm Sat Oct-Apr) A one-stop shop for booking excursions and activities, this local agency can arrange rafting (320KN), canyoning (350KN), quad biking (350KN), diving (300KN) and cruises to the Blue Cave (940KN). Coach destinations include Šibenik and Krka (450KN), Dubrovnik (500KN), Mostar and Međugorje (500KN), and the Plitvice Lakes (710KN). It also has a popular transfer to Zagreb via the Plitvice Lakes (140KN).

Ziggy Star TOURS
(Map p252; ☎099 54 97 385; www.pubcrawlsplit.net; crawl €15; ⏲from 10pm) Named, presumably, after the mythical rocker who took it all too far, Ziggy Star offers an opportunity to push your limits in a guided all-night bender. Starting with a 'power hour' of cocktails and shooters, the trail leads to a bar on the Riva, then a club, then breakfast.

Red Adventures ADVENTURE
(Map p246; ☎091 79 03 747; www.red-adventures.com; Kralja Zvonimira 8) Specialising in active excursions, this crew offers sea kayaking (from €38), rock climbing (from €50), custom hikes (from €30) and bike tours around Split (from €35). It also rents bikes, kayaks and cars, charters yachts, provides transfers and arranges private accommodation.

CroActive & Adventure OUTDOORS
(Map p246; ☎021-277 344; www.croactive-holidays.com; Kralja Zvonimira 14) Runs a scenic half-day Marjan peninsula kayak (300KN) as well as rafting on the Cetina River (350KN plus 125KN transfer), hiking, rock climbing, cycling, canyoning, sailing, zip-lining and stand-up paddleboarding trips, and wine and culinary tours. Multiday excursions are also available.

Split Walking Tours TOURS
(Map p252; ☎099 82 15 383; www.splitwalkingtour.com; Dioklecijanova 3) Leads walking tours in English, Spanish, Italian, German and French, departing from the Golden Gate at set times during the day (check the website). Options include the 75-minute Diocletian's Palace Tour (100KN) and the two-hour Split Walking Tour (160KN), which includes the palace and the medieval part of town. It also offers kayaking, diving, cycling tours, boat trips and excursions.

Festivals & Events

Sudamja RELIGIOUS
(⏲May) Festivities celebrating Split's patron saint, St Domnius (Sv Duje), start at the beginning of May. They include concerts, poetry readings, exhibitions and a rowing regatta. On the actual 7 May feast day (aka Split Day) there's a religious procession, Mass and fair on the Riva, with fireworks filling the skies.

Summer Colours of Split MUSIC
(Splitski litnji koluri; ⏲mid-Jun–mid-Sep) Live music nightly on the Riva, concerts below Diocletian's Palace, a rock weekend, a techno weekend, and the Days of Diocletian: three

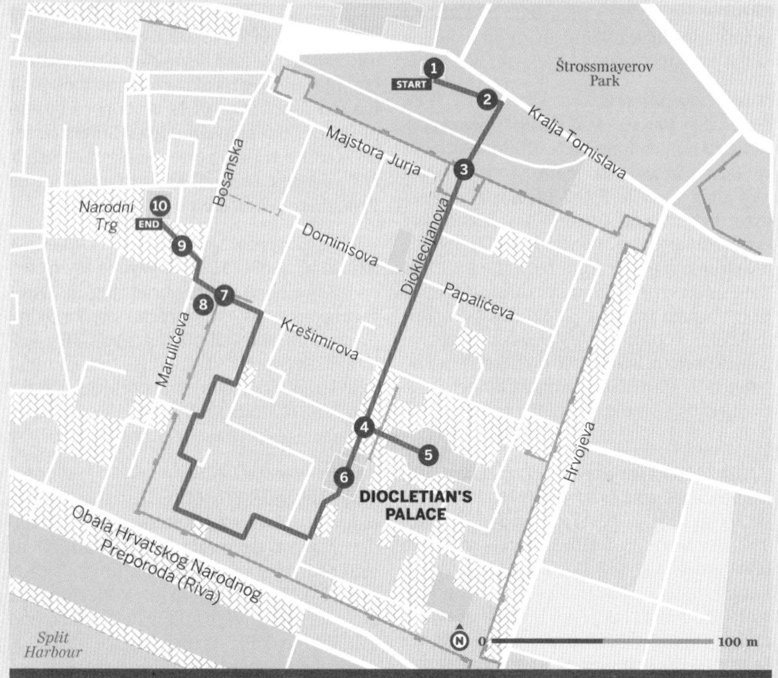

City Walk
Split's Old Town

START CHAPEL OF ARNERIUS
END NARODNI TRG
LENGTH 500M; ONE HOUR

Begin outside the well-preserved northwestern corner tower of Diocletian's Palace at the remains of the ❶ **Chapel of Arnerius**, once part of St Euphemia's Church. Through the protective glass you'll see the altar slab and sarcophagus carved by the early Renaissance master Juraj Dalmatinac.

Head in the direction of the imposing statue of ❷ **Grgur Ninski** (p248), and stop to rub his toe for good luck. Take the stairs down to the ❸ **Golden Gate** (p244), the grandest of the palace's portals. This was the main processional entrance into the palace, decorated with statues, columns and arches, the remains of which are still visible.

Enter the palace and walk along its main north–south street, Dioklecijanova, to the ❹ **peristil** (p244), the ceremonial court at the approach to the imperial apartments. Behind this is Diocletian's magnificent mausoleum, now the ❺ **Cathedral of St Domnius** (p245).

At the far end, take the stairs up into the well-preserved ❻ **vestibule** (p259), a grand and cavernous domed room, open to the sky, which was once the formal entrance to the retired emperor's personal quarters.

Step through the vestibule, head to the far right-hand corner of the little square and turn right onto Andrije Alješija. Work your way around the maze of streets, lined with medieval buildings housing some of Split's best bars, until you reach Krešimirova, the palace's main east–west axis.

Turn left and exit the palace through the high arches of the ❼ **Iron Gate** (p244). As you pass through the outer part of the double gate, the building immediately to your left, easily spotted by the sculptural relief of St Anthony the Hermit on the corner, is the late-Romanesque ❽ **Ciprianis-Beneditti Palace**, built in 1394.

You're now on ❾ **Narodni trg**, which has been Split's main civic square since medieval times. It was once lined with Venetian Gothic buildings, but the only one that has survived is the 15th-century ❿ **Old City Hall (Vjećnica)**.

days of tunics, togas, legionaries and barely dressed gladiators.

Ultra Europe MUSIC

(www.ultraeurope.com; Poljud Stadium; 3-day ticket from €129; Jul) One of the world's largest electronic-music festivals takes over the city's Poljud stadium for three days in July before heading to the islands for the rest of Destination Ultra Croatia Music Week. People from across the world swarm to rave to the tunes of celebrity DJs.

Split Summer PERFORMING ARTS

(Splitsko Ljeto; www.splitsko-ljeto.hr; mid-Jul–mid-Aug) This festival features art exhibitions, opera, drama, ballet and concerts.

Sleeping

As you'd expect in a big city that is also a tourist hub, prices in Split tend to be higher than the national average – but not as high as in the likes of Dubrovnik or Hvar. That said, Split has a good range of hostels and some excellent apartment-style providers catering to the midrange market.

Old Town

★Heritage Hotel Antique Split HERITAGE HOTEL €€€

(Map p252; 021-785 208; www.antique-split.com; Poljana Grgura Ninskog 1; r from €267;) Palace living at its most palatial, this boutique complex has eight chic rooms with stone walls and impressive bathrooms. In some you'll wake up to incredible views over the cathedral.

★Villa Split B&B €€€

(Map p252; 091 40 34 403; www.villasplitluxury.com; Bajamontijeva 5; r from €215;) Built into the Roman-built wall of Diocletian's Palace, this wonderful boutique B&B has only three rooms, the best of which is the slightly larger one in the attic. If you're happy to swap the ancient for the merely medieval, there are six larger rooms in a 10th-century building on the main square.

Surrounds

Tchaikovsky Hostel HOSTEL €

(Map p246; 021-317 124; www.tchaikovskyhostel.com; Čajkovskoga 4; dm 170-240KN;) Hidden away in a residential block in the Dobri neighbourhood, this converted apartment has four tidy dorms with wooden bunks featuring built-in shelves. There's only one bathroom, and a small kitchen.

Beach Hostel Split HOSTEL €

(Map p246; 092 17 67 599; www.facebook.com/splitbeachhostel; Viška 9; dm 197-205KN; Apr-Oct;) A hop and a skip from Bačvice beach (p256), this cosy hostel is managed by a friendly Norwegian called Ladybird, who imbues the place with a chilled-out vibe. There's free coffee and tea, colourful cartoons on the walls and a terrace with a guitar ready.

CroParadise Green Hostel HOSTEL €

(Map p246; 091 44 44 194; www.croparadise.com; Čulića Dvori 29; dm 200KN, r 500KN, without bathroom 460KN;) This crowd-pleasing hostel (winner of Hostelworld's 'most popular' award 2016–18) offers a range of brightly coloured dorm rooms and small apartments, spread between three apartment buildings in the central neighbourhood of Manuš. Each dorm has access to lockers and a small kitchen; other facilities include laundry, and bike and scooter rental.

★Korta APARTMENT €€

(Map p246; 021-571 226; www.kortasplit.com; Plinarska 31; apt from €94;) Set around a courtyard in the historic Veli Varoš neighbourhood, these simple but elegant apartments have stone-tiled bathrooms and white walls hung with huge TVs and photos of rustic Croatian scenes. Many have balconies.

★Apartments Magdalena APARTMENT €€

(Map p246; 098 423 087; www.magdalena-apartments.com; Milićeva 18; apt 465-611KN;) You may never want to leave Magdalena's top-floor apartment once you see the old-town view from the dormer window. The three apartments are comfortable and fully furnished, and the hospitality offered by the off-site owners is exceptional: beer and juice, a back-up toothbrush in the cupboard and even a mobile phone with credit on it.

Villa Varoš GUESTHOUSE €€

(Map p246; 021-483 469; www.villavaros.hr; Miljenka Smoje 1; s/d/apt from €50/80/121;) Owned by a New York–dwelling Croat, Villa Varoš offers simple, clean rooms with wooden furniture, en suite bathrooms and TVs in a quiet but central location. There are also a couple of bikes to rent.

★Splendida Palace BOUTIQUE HOTEL €€€

(Map p246; 021-838 485; www.splendidapalace.com; Rokova 26; r incl breakfast from €239; Apr-Oct;) Get in quick to secure one of the 10 rooms in this family-run hotel in a 19th-century house on a quiet street. Rooms are named after Split landmarks, with large-scale

Central Split

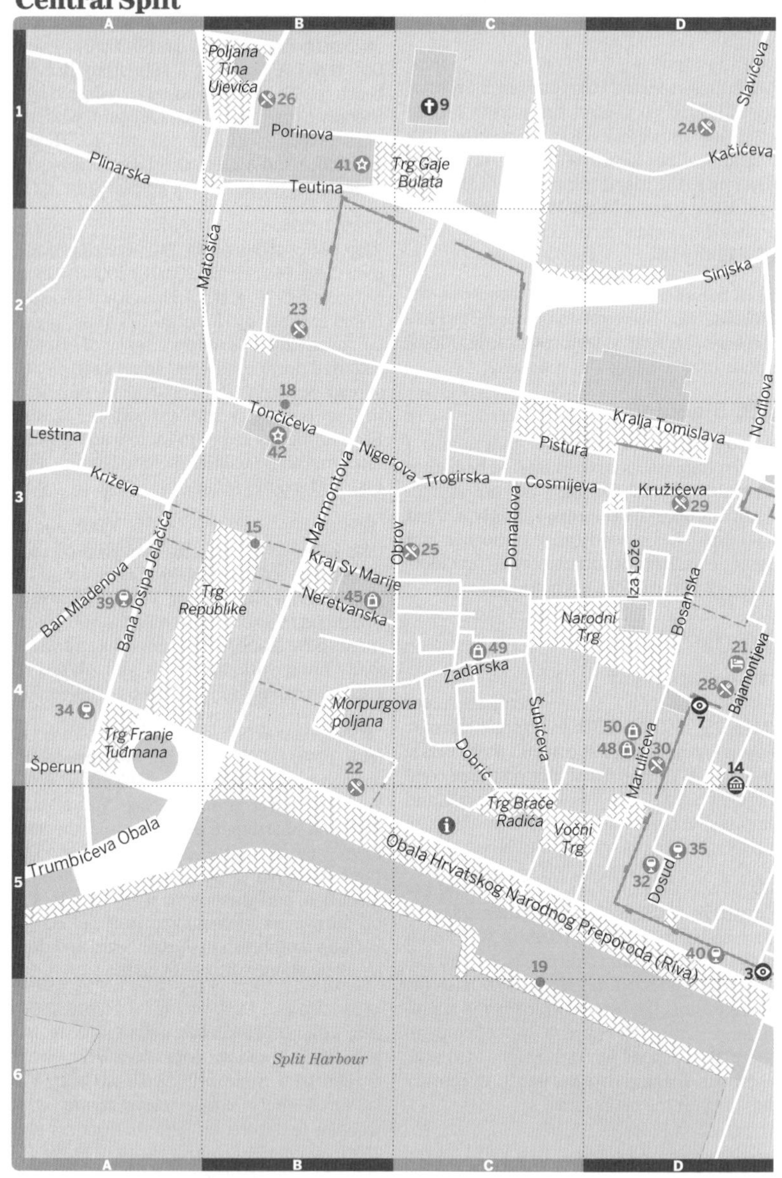

black-and-white photographs to reinforce the theme. The breakfast is buffet-style and there's a small plunge pool in the rear courtyard.

Vila Baguc B&B €€€
(Map p246; ☎021-770 456; www.baguc.com; Plinarska 29/2; r from €145; ❄ 📶) Oozing character, this restored 150-year-old family house in Veli Varoš has four guest rooms on four floors, with modern fittings combined with original details such as exposed stone walls. The villa is tucked back from the street, only a five-minute walk from the town centre.

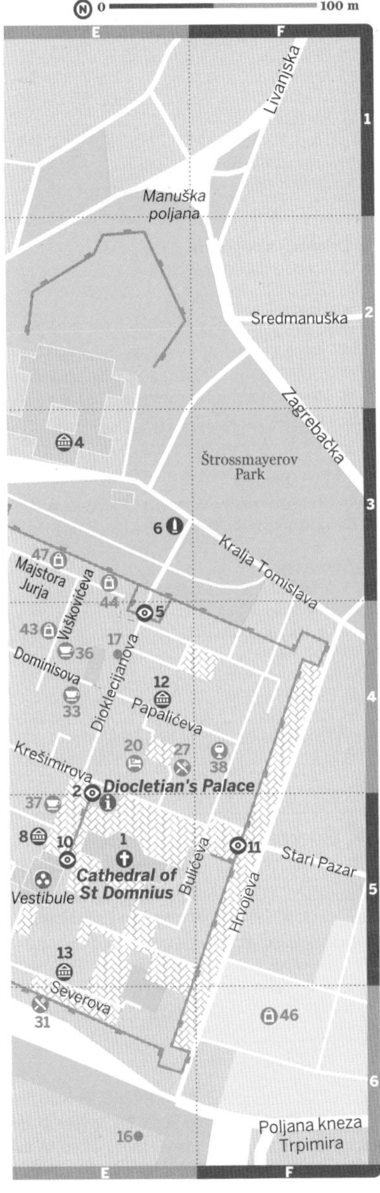

Eating

Old Town

Kruščić BAKERY €
(Map p252; ☎099 26 12 345; www.facebook.com/Kruscic.Split; Obrov 6; items 6-15KN; ⏰8am-2pm) Spit's best bakery serves delicious bread, pastries and pizza slices. The focus is more savoury than sweet, although you'll find sweet things, too.

Villa Spiza DALMATIAN €€
(Map p252; Kružićeva 3; mains 50-100KN; ⏰noon-midnight Mon-Sat) A locals' favourite, just outside the walls of Diocletian's Palace, this low-key joint offers daily-changing, great-quality Dalmatian mainstays – calamari, risotto, veal – at reasonable prices. The colourful interior has only one table and some bench seating, so be prepared to wait.

Trattoria Bajamont DALMATIAN, SEAFOOD €€
(Map p252; ☎099 54 26 675; www.trattoriabajamont.fullbusiness.com; Bajamontijeva 3; mains 60-150KN; ⏰8am-11pm Mon-Sat) This tiny joint within the walls of Diocletian's Palace is like a granny's living room, with old-school sewing-machine tables. There's no sign above the door, and the daily menu is written out in marker pen; traditional seafood dishes, such as *brujet* (seafood stew with wine, onions and herbs, served with polenta), feature. There's an annexe across the alley.

★ **Zoi** MEDITERRANEAN €€€
(Map p252; ☎021-637 491; www.zoi.hr; Obala hrvatskog narodnog preporoda 23; mains 120-180KN; ⏰6.30pm-midnight) Accessed by a discreet door on the waterfront promenade, this upstairs restaurant serves sophisticated modern Mediterranean dishes that look as divine as they taste. The decor is simultaneously elegant and extremely hip, with the exposed walls of Diocletian's Palace offset with bright bursts of magenta. Head up to the roof terrace for one of Split's most memorable dining spaces.

★ **Portofino** ITALIAN €€€
(Map p252; ☎091 38 97 784; www.facebook.com/portofinosplit; Poljana Grgura Ninskog 7; mains 95-250KN; ⏰5-11pm) Spilling onto a surprisingly quiet square at the heart of Diocletian's Palace, Portofino will charm the pants off you with its friendly service, elegant decor, complimentary *amuse-bouches* and delicious pasta , steak and seafood dishes.

Zinfandel EUROPEAN €€€
(Map p252; ☎021-355 135; www.zinfandelfoodandwinebar.com; Marulićeva 2; mains 140-270KN; ⏰8am-midnight Mon-Sat) The vibe might be more like that of an upmarket wine bar, but the food here is top notch. The menu includes delicious risotto, homemade pasta with fresh truffles, burgers, steaks and fish, and to wash it down there's a huge choice of local wine by the glass. Good beer selection, too.

Central Split

Top Sights
1 Cathedral of St Domnius....E5
2 Diocletian's Palace....E4

Sights
3 Bronze Gate....D5
Diocletian's Palace Substructure....(see 3)
4 Gallery of Fine Arts....E3
5 Golden Gate....E4
6 Grgur Ninski statue....E3
7 Iron Gate....D4
8 New Research on Split Cathedral....E5
9 Our-Lady-of-Health Church....C1
10 Peristil....E5
11 Silver Gate....F5
12 Split City Museum....E4
13 Split Ethnographic Museum....E5
14 Temple of Jupiter....D4

Activities, Courses & Tours
15 Portal....B3
16 Split Rent Agency....E6
17 Split Walking Tours....E4
18 Summer Blues....B3
19 Ziggy Star....C6

Sleeping
20 Heritage Hotel Antique Split....E4
21 Villa Split....D4

Eating
22 Brasserie on 7....B5
23 Chops.Grill....B2
24 Gušt....D1
25 Kruščić....C3
26 Luka....B1
27 Portofino....E4
28 Trattoria Bajamont....D4
29 Villa Spiza....D3
30 Zinfandel....D4
31 Zoi....E6

Drinking & Nightlife
32 Academia Ghetto Club....D5
33 D16....E4
34 Fabrique....A4
35 Fluid....D5
36 Galerija....E4
37 Luxor....E5
38 Marcvs Marvlvs Spalatensis....F4
39 Paradox....A4
40 St Riva....D5

Entertainment
41 Croatian National Theatre Split....B1
42 Split City Puppet Theatre....B3

Shopping
43 Arterija....E4
44 Bag & Co....E3
Diocletian's Cellars....(see 3)
45 Fish Market....B4
46 Green Market....F6
47 Studio Naranča....E3
48 Think Pink....D4
49 Think Pink....C4
50 Uje....D4

Chops.Grill GRILL €€€
(Map p252; ☎091 36 50 000; www.chops-grill.com; Tončićeva 4; mains 90-250KN; ⏰8am-midnight) Chops, steak, chicken breast, duck breast, tuna, sea bass, lobster, scampi – you name it, they'll grill it. Don't skimp on the sides; the truffle mash is delicious. Gas flames lend a flash of colour and movement to this simple, modern space.

Brasserie on 7 MODERN EUROPEAN €€€
(Map p252; ☎021-278 233; www.brasserieon7.com; Obala hrvatskog narodnog preporoda 7; mains breakfast 68-94KN, lunch 88-150KN, dinner 105-240KN; ⏰7.30am-11.30pm Apr-Sep, 8am-4pm Oct-Mar) The best of the Riva eateries, this waterfront brasserie's outdoor tables are the perfect vantage point for watching the passing parade. Start the day with a cooked breakfast, end it with a cocktail, and fill the hours in between with a light lunch, a more substantial dinner, or wine and a cheese platter. The service is excellent, too.

Surrounds

Gušt PIZZA €
(Map p252; ☎021-486 333; www.pizzeria-gust.hr; Slavićeva 1; pizzas 40-62KN; ⏰9am-11pm Mon-Sat) Split's diehard pizza fans swear by this joint – it's cheap and very local, serving delicious pizza with Neapolitan-style chewy bases. The stone and brick walls make it a cosy retreat in winter.

Luka SWEETS €
(Map p252; Svačićeva 2; items 8-12KN; ⏰8.30am-11pm Mon-Sat, 10am-11pm Sun; 📶) Sweet little Luka serves muffins, cakes and coffee to locals on one of the inner city's least touristy squares. In summer there are queues out the door for the homemade ice cream.

★ **Konoba Fetivi** DALMATIAN, SEAFOOD €€
(Map p246; ☎021-355 152; www.facebook.com/KonobaFetivi; Tomića stine 4; mains 70-95KN; ⏰noon-11pm Tue-Sun) Informal and family run, with a TV screening sports in the corner, Fetivi feels more like a tavern than most

that bear the '*konoba*' name. However, that doesn't detract from the food, which is first rate. Seafood is the focus here. The cuttlefish stew with polenta is highly recommended, but the whole fish is wonderfully fresh, too.

★ **Konoba Matejuška** DALMATIAN, SEAFOOD €€
(Map p246; ☎021-814 099; www.konobamatejuska.hr; Tomića Stine 3; mains 75-140KN; ⏲noon-11pm Apr-Oct, to 9pm Wed-Mon Nov-Mar) This cosy, rustic tavern, in an alleyway minutes from the seafront, specialises in seafood – as epitomised in its perfectly cooked fish platter for two. The grilled squid is also excellent, served with the archetypal Dalmatian side dish, *blitva* (Swiss chard with slightly mushy potato, drenched in olive oil). Book ahead.

Dvor EUROPEAN €€
(Map p246; ☎021-571 513; www.facebook.com/Dvor.Split; Firula 14; breakfast 30-35KN, lunch 70-90KN, 5-course dinner 170KN; ⏲8am-midnight) There's no better way to start a Split day than coffee and an omelette on the garden terrace of this upmarket restaurant, overlooking Firule beach (p256). However, Dvor is more famous for its sophisticated evening fare, such as just-so sirloin steaks, *confit* pork belly and crispy sea bass.

Konoba Stare Grede DALMATIAN €€
(Map p246; ☎021-643 901; Domovinskog rata 46; mains 49-145KN; ⏲9am-11pm Mon-Fri, noon-11pm Sat & Sun; 📶) Located 1km up the busy main street out of town, this is a blue-collar hang-out for *marenda*, a Dalmatian midday meal, with a rustic vibe – old beams, wooden benches and stone walls.

★ **Konoba Marjan** DALMATIAN, SEAFOOD €€€
(Map p246; ☎098 93 46 848; www.facebook.com/konobamarjan; Senjska 1; mains 84-160KN; ⏲noon-11pm Mon-Sat; 📶) Offering great-quality Dalmatian fare, this friendly little Veli Varoš tavern features daily specials such as cuttlefish *brujet* (a flavour-packed seafood stew – highly recommended), *gregada* (fish stew with potato) and prawn pasta. The wine list is excellent, showcasing some local boutique wineries, and there are a few seats outside on the street leading up to Marjan Hill.

Drinking & Nightlife

Split is great for nightlife, especially in spring and summer. The palace walls throb with loud music on Friday and Saturday nights, and you can wander the mazelike streets discovering new places. The palace bars go quiet at 1am (as people live within the palace walls), but the beach bars and clubs to the east stay open till the wee hours.

Old Town

★ **Marcvs Marvlvs Spalatensis** WINE BAR
(Map p252; www.facebook.com/marvlvs; Papalićeva 4; ⏲11am-midnight Jun-Aug, to 11pm Mon-Sat Sep-May; 📶) Fittingly, the 15th-century Gothic home of the 'Dante of Croatia', Marko Marulić, now houses this wonderful little 'library jazz bar' – small rooms crammed with books and frequented by ageless bohemians, tortured poets and wistful academics. Cheese, chess, cards and cigars are all on offer, and there's often live music.

★ **Paradox** WINE BAR
(Map p252; ☎021-787 778; www.paradox.hr; Bana Josipa Jelačića 3; ⏲8am-midnight; 📶) This stylish wine and cheese bar has a fantastic rooftop terrace, a massive selection of Croatian wines (more than 120, including 40 by the glass) and an array of local cheeses to go with them. The clued-up staff members really know their stuff, and there's live music most weekends.

D16 CAFE
(Map p252; ☎091 79 00 705; www.d16coffee.com; Dominisova 16; ⏲7am-7pm Mon-Sat, 9am-7pm Sun; 📶) D16's baristas are serious about coffee. Hidden away in the back lanes of Diocletian's Palace, this hip little speciality roaster is your best bet for a superbly executed flat white, cold brew or espresso with almond milk. Just be prepared to pay double the price you'd pay at a local-style cafe.

Academia Ghetto Club BAR, CLUB
(Map p252; ☎099 67 18 308; Dosud 10; ⏲4pm-midnight; 📶) Split's most bohemian bar has ancient Roman walls, a large courtyard with a trickling fountain, a chandelier-bedecked piano lounge and a red-walled club space with poetry on the walls. The music is great, but the service can be shockingly bad.

Fluid BAR
(Map p252; ☎095 67 00 002; www.facebook.com/fluid.split; Dosud 1; ⏲9am-1am Jun-Aug, 6pm-1am Fri & Sat Sep-May) This chic little place, with cushions on the lane, is great for a cocktail and a spot of people-watching.

Galerija CAFE, BAR
(Map p252; Vuškovićeva 3; ⏲8am-midnight Mon-Sat, 10am-midnight Sun) Locals come here to catch up with friends without loud music drowning out the conversation – except during the weekend DJ sessions. Plus it stocks

LAZY DAYS IN SPLIT

KAŠJUNI

Kašjuni (Šetalište Ivana Meštrovića bb) is Split's most appealing beach due largely to its green surroundings and upmarket beach bar. It can be reached by a long, rewarding walk through Marjan Forest Park (p249) but, if you're feeling lazy, catch a cab.

BAČVICE

Sandy **Bačvice** (Map p246) is Split's busiest beach, lined with restaurants, bars, late-night clubs and a whole heap of concrete. Keep an eye out for people thrashing about in the shallows, whacking a squash ball to each other with the palms of their hands: this is the very Dalmatian sport of *picigin* (p248), a prime showing-off opportunity for Split's young bucks.

OVČICE

The next bay along the promenade, **Ovčice** (Map p246; Šetalište Petra Preradovića bb) has a little less concrete, a beach bar and a pleasant strip of fine pebbles.

FIRULE

The horseshoe cove of **Firule** (Map p246) has a slimline sandy beach with a bar down the far end. There's not much space to spread out, but the cliffs and pine trees make for a much more appealing backdrop than Bačvice's concrete jungle.

1. Bačvice
2. Marjan Forest Park (p249)
3. Kašjuni

MRAK.HR/SHUTTERSTOCK ©

ALEX RINKUS/SHUTTERSTOCK ©

In the summertime, the Splitčani leave their ancient city centre to the tourists and head to the beaches abutting their home suburbs, to socialise and to cool off. A younger crowd returns in the evening for the bars and clubs.

soy milk – a rarity in these parts. The interior is cosy and elegant, with printed cushions, interesting art, chandeliers, bentwood chairs and a velveteen couch. In summer the action spills out onto a tiny square.

St Riva BAR
(Map p252; Obala hrvatskog narodnog preporoda 18; ⌚7am-midnight; 📶) Bad techno and tacky cocktails don't stop St Riva being a great place to hang out. Grab a perch on the narrow terrace built into the walls of Diocletian's Palace and watch the mayhem on the Riva below. Later in the night, a fair bit of booty-shaking happens in the small, clubby space inside.

Fabrique BAR
(Map p252; ☎098 17 51 271; www.fgroup.hr; Trg Franje Tuđmana 3; ⌚9am-2am May-Oct, to midnight Nov-Apr; 📶) Big, bright and brash, this large industrial-style bar has offset its brick arches with kooky light fixtures and elegant little tables where the Splitćani glitterati hold court over beer and barbecue. Local craft beers feature heavily on the extensive list, alongside a range of speciality gins and tonics. The vibe gets clubby as the night progresses.

Luxor CAFE
(Map p252; ☎021-341 082; www.facebook.com/Lvxor1700; Peristil bb; ⌚8am-midnight; 📶) Touristy, yes, but this cafe-bar is a great place to have coffee and cake right in the ceremonial heart of Diocletian's Palace. Cushions are laid out on the steps and there's live music nightly.

Surrounds

Zenta CLUB
(Map p246; ☎099 33 51 979; www.zentasplit.com; Uvala Zenta 3; 20-80KN; ⌚from 11pm, nights vary) With a waterfront terrace and two floors inside, Split's top nightclub cranks up several notches in summer, with nights such as Monday Trash and Friday's Recesija (cheap drinks, R & B, electronica and Balkan pop).

Vidilica CAFE, BAR
(Map p246; Nazorov Prilaz 1; ⌚8am-midnight; 📶) It's worth the climb up the stone stairs through the ancient Veli Varoš quarter for a sunset drink on the terrace of this cafe with glorious city, harbour and mountain views.

Entertainment

Split hosts plenty of free performances in summer; check at the tourist office whether anything's happening during your stay. The city has a couple of prominent theatres, but most performances are in Croatian.

Croatian National Theatre Split THEATRE
(Hrvatsko narodno kazalište Split; Map p252; ☎021-306 908; www.hnk-split.hr; Trg Gaje Bulata 1) Theatre, opera, ballet and concerts are presented at this gorgeous theatre, built in 1891. Tickets can be bought at the box office or online.

Split City Puppet Theatre THEATRE
(Gradsko kazalište lutaka Split; Map p252; ☎021-395 958; www.gkl-split.hr; Tončićeva 1) Although shows are mainly in Croatian, there's a fair chance your toddlers can speak fluent puppet.

Shopping

Central Split is filled with stores catering to the tourist market and cashed-up locals. Marmontova is the main shopping strip, with the biggest names, but you'll find some interesting local boutiques scattered around Diocletian's Palace.

Arterija FASHION & ACCESSORIES
(Map p252; ☎091 54 77 141; Vuškovićeva 5; ⌚10am-9pm May-Oct, 10am-2pm & 4-8pm Mon-Fri, 10am-2pm Sat Nov-Apr) A showcase for local designer Gorana Gulišija (and a curated selection of the work of others from the region), this little store stocks interesting women's clothes, jewellery and shoes.

Bag & Co FASHION & ACCESSORIES
(Map p252; ☎091 51 43 126; www.bagbyag.com; Majstora Jurja 17; ⌚9am-9pm Apr-Nov) Call into this little shop to check out Ana Gjivoje's range of bright and patterned handbags, tote bags and shoulder bags, many of which are made from recycled materials.

Think Pink FASHION & ACCESSORIES
(Map p252; Zadarska 4; ⌚9am-9pm) Boho women's clothing and jewellery made by homegrown designers. There's a second **store** (Map p252; Marulićeva 1; ⌚9am-9pm) around the corner.

Uje FOOD & DRINKS
(Map p252; ☎021-342 719; www.uje.hr; Marulićeva 1; ⌚8am-8.30pm Mon-Fri, to 2pm Sat) For a little place, Uje stocks a large range of top-quality Croatian olive oil, along with locally made jam, pasta sauce, *rakija* (grappa), wine, soap and wooden products.

Studio Naranča DESIGN
(Map p252; ☎021-344 118; www.studionaranca.com; Majstora Jurja 5; ⌚10am-7pm Mon-Sat, to 2pm Sun May-Sep) Showcasing the work of local artist Pavo Majić, 'Studio Orange' sells original art and very cool T-shirts, tote bags and postcards featuring his designs.

Diocletian's Cellars MARKET
(Map p252; Obala hrvatskog narodnog preporoda bb; ⌚9am-9pm) The main passage through the basement of Diocletian's Palace is lined with stalls selling jewellery, gifts made from Brač stone, scarves, T-shirts, handmade soap and prints. For a touristy souvenir strip, the quality's actually pretty good.

Fish Market MARKET
(Ribarnica; Map p252; Obrov 5; ⌚6.30am-2pm) As stinky and chaotic a scene as you could possibly imagine, Split's indoor-outdoor fish market is a spectacle to behold. Locals head here on a daily basis to haggle for all their scaly and slimy requirements from their favourite chain-smoking vendors. It's all over by about 11am, bar the dregs.

Green Market MARKET
(Map p252; Hrvojeva bb; ⌚6.30am-2pm) This open-air market is the place to come to stock up on fruit, vegetables and cut flowers. While it's busiest in the mornings, a few stallholders stay open to sell cherries and strawberries to tourists throughout the afternoon in summer.

Information

MEDICAL SERVICES

KBC Split (Klinički bolnički centar Split; ☎021-556 111; www.kbsplit.hr; Spinčićeva 1) Hospital.

TOURIST INFORMATION

Split's tourist offices stock the free 72-hour **Split Card**, which offers free or discounted access to attractions, car rental, restaurants, shops and theatres. You're eligible for the card if you're staying in Split more than four nights from April to September, or staying in designated hotels for more than two nights at other times.

Tourist Office Peristil (Map p252; ☎021-345 606; www.visitsplit.com; Peristil bb; ⌚8am-9pm Jun-Sep, 8am-8pm Mon-Sat, to 5pm Sun Apr, May & Oct, 9am-4pm Mon-Fri, to 2pm Sat Nov-Mar)

Tourist Office Riva (Map p252; ☎021-360 066; www.visitsplit.com; Obala hrvatskog narodnog preporoda 9; ⌚8am-9pm Jun-Sep, 8am-8pm Mon-Sat, to 5pm Sun Apr, May & Oct, 9am-4pm Mon-Fri, to 2pm Sat Nov-Mar)

TRAVEL AGENCIES

Daluma Travel (☎021-338 424; www.daluma-travel.hr; Obala kneza Domagoja 1) Books excursions and boat trips, and arranges private accommodation and car, scooter and bike rental.

Turistički Biro (☎021-347 100; www.turistbiro-split.hr; Obala hrvatskog narodnog preporoda 12) Excursions and private accommodation.

KLAPA YOUR HANDS!

Few visitors to Dalmatia will leave without at some point being mesmerised by the dulcet tones of a *klapa* song. This a cappella tradition involves a bunch of burly men in a circle, singing tear jerkers about love, betrayal, patriotism, death, beauty and other life-affirming subjects in honeyed multitonal harmonies.

In Split, the best place to catch a *klapa* group doing its thing is the **vestibule** (Peristil bb) FREE, the emperor's circular foyer on the south side of the peristil (p244) within the palace walls.

Getting There & Away

The bus, train and ferry terminals are clustered on the eastern side of the harbour, a short walk from the old town.

AIR

Split Airport (Zračna luka Split; ☎021-203 555; www.split-airport.hr; Dr Franje Tuđmana 1270, Kaštel Štafilić) is in Kaštela, 24km northwest of central Split. In summer, dozens of airlines fly here from all over Europe (including Austrian Airlines, British Airways, easyJet, Norwegian Air Shuttle and Scandinavian Airlines). The following airlines operate all year round:

Croatia Airlines (☎021-203 305; www.croatiaairlines.com) The national carrier has flights to Zagreb, Rome, Munich and Frankfurt year-round. In summer there are also domestic flights to Dubrovnik and Osijek, and international flights to many European cities.

Eurowings (www.eurowings.com) Year-round flights to Cologne/Bonn, Düsseldorf and Stuttgart, and seasonal flights to other German and Austrian cities.

Trade Air (www.trade-air.com) Flies to Dubrovnik, Pula and Rijeka.

BOAT

Split's ferry harbour is extremely busy and can be hard to negotiate, so you're best to arrive early. Most domestic ferries depart from Gat Sv Petra, the first of the three major piers, which has ticket booths for both Jadrolinija and Kapetan Luka. The giant international ferries depart from Gat Sv Duje, the second of the piers, where there's a large **ferry terminal** (Map p246) with ticketing offices for the major lines.

In July and August, and at weekends, it's often necessary to appear hours before departure for a car ferry, and put your car in the line for boarding. There is rarely a problem or a long wait obtaining a space in the low season.

Jadrolinija (☎021-338 333; www.jadrolinija.hr; Gat Sv Duje bb) operates most of the ferries between Split and the islands, as well as overnight ferries to **Ancona** in Italy.

Kapetan Luka (Krilo; ☎021-645 476; www.krilo.hr) has the following high-speed catamaran services:

- Daily to **Hvar** (90KN, one hour) and **Korčula** (130KN, 2½ hours) twice daily June to September.
- From April to October, an additional daily boat to **Hvar,** twice daily May to September.
- From May to mid-October, daily to **Milna on Brač** (40KN, 25 minutes), **Hvar**, **Korčula** (130KN, 2¼ hours), **Pomena on Mljet** (140KN, three hours) and **Dubrovnik** (210KN, 4¼ hours);
- From June to September, daily to **Bol on Brač** (80KN, 50 minutes), **Makarska** (100KN, 1½ hours), **Korčula** (130KN, 2¾ hours), **Sobra on Mljet** (140KN, four hours) and **Dubrovnik** (210KN, five hours).

Bura Line (☎095 83 74 320; www.buraline.com; Obala kralja Zvonimira bb; adult/child 35/18KN) heads backwards and forwards to **Trogir** on a small boat four to six times a day from May to September.

SNAV (www.snav.it) has overnight car ferries to/from **Ancona** (from €34, 11 hours) from April to October.

BUS

Most intercity and international buses arrive at and depart from the **main bus station** (Autobusni Kolodvor Split; Map p246; ☎060 327 777; www.ak-split.hr; Obala kneza Domagoja bb) beside the harbour. In summer it's best to purchase bus tickets with seat reservations in advance. If you need to store bags, there's a **garderoba** (left-luggage office; Obala kneza Domagoja 12; 1st hour 5KN, additional hours 1.50KN; ⏲6am-10pm May-Sep) nearby.

Domestic destinations include Zagreb (157KN, five hours, at least hourly), Pula (300KN, 10 hours, five daily), Rijeka (244KN, eight hours, eight daily), Zadar (90KN, three hours, at least hourly) and Dubrovnik (127KN, 4½ hours, at least 11 daily). Note that Split–Dubrovnik buses pass briefly through Bosnian territory, so keep your passport handy.

Touring (Map p246; ☎021-338 503; www.touring.hr; Obala kneza Domagoja 10; ⏲8am-8pm Mon-Fri, 9am-3pm Sat & Sun), located near the bus station, represents Deutsche Touring and sells bus tickets to German cities.

JADROLINIJA SERVICES FROM SPLIT

Note that the schedules listed for these ferries are for services between June and September. Service is reduced outside these months.

Car Ferries

DESTINATION	COST (PER PERSON/CAR KN)	DURATION (HR)	FREQUENCY
Ancona (Italy)	from 300/440	11	3-4 weekly
Drvenik Mali	30/150	2¼	weekly
Drvenik Veli	30/150	2	weekly
Rogač (Šolta)	33/154	1	5-6 daily
Stari Grad (Hvar)	47/310	2	5-7 daily
Supetar (Brač)	33/154	¾	12-14 daily
Ubli (Lastovo)	68/470	4½	daily
Vela Luka (Korčula)	60/470	2¾	2 daily
Vis (Vis)	54/340	2¼	2-3 daily

Catamarans

DESTINATION	COST (KN)	DURATION (HR)	FREQUENCY
Bol (Brač)	55-80	1	2 daily
Dubrovnik	210	6	daily
Hvar (Hvar)	55-110	1-2	4-8 daily
Jelsa (Hvar)	55	1½	daily
Korčula (Korčula)	160	3¾	daily
Milna (Brač)	40	½	weekly
Ubli (Lastovo)	70	3¼	daily
Vela Luka (Korčula)	60	2¼	daily
Vis (Vis)	55	1½-2½	daily

CAR

Various car-hire companies have desks at the airport, including **Dollar Thrifty** (☎021-399 000; www.subrosa.hr; Trumbićeva obala 17), which also has a city office. You can also rent cars, scooters and motorbikes through Daluma Travel (p259) and **Split Rent Agency** (Map p252; ☎091 59 17 111; www.split-rent.com; Obala Lazareta 3).

TRAIN

Trains head to **Split Train Station** (Željeznica stanica Split; ☎021-338 525; www.hzpp.hr; Obala kneza Domagoja 9; ⏰6am-10pm) from Zagreb (194KN, 6½ hours, four daily) and Knin (65KN, 2¼ hours, three daily). The station has lockers (15KN per day) that will fit suitcases, but you can't leave bags overnight. There's another **garderoba** (☎098 446 780; Obala kneza Domagoja 5; per day 15KN; ⏰6am-10pm Jul & Aug, 7.30am-9pm Sep-Jun) nearby, out on the street.

Getting Around

TO/FROM THE AIRPORT

Airport Shuttle Bus (☎021-203 119; www.plesoprijevoz.hr; 1 way 30KN) Makes the 30-minute journey between the airport and Split's main bus station (platform 1) at least 14 times a day.

City buses 37 & 38 The regular Split–Trogir bus stops near the airport every 20 minutes. The journey takes 50 minutes from the **local bus station** on Domovinskog Rata, making it a slower option than the shuttle but also cheaper (17KN from Split, 13KN from Trogir).

Taxi A cab to central Split costs between 250KN and 300KN.

PUBLIC TRANSPORT

Promet Split (☎021-407 888; www.promet-split.hr) operates local buses on an extensive network throughout Split (per journey 11KN) and as far afield as Klis (13KN), Solin (13KN), Kaštela (17KN), Trogir (17KN) and Omiš (22KN). You can buy tickets on the bus, but if you buy from the **local bus station** (Map p246) or from a kiosk, a two-journey (ie return, known as a 'duplo') central-zone ticket costs only 17KN. Buses run about every 15 minutes from 5.30am to 11.30pm.

AROUND SPLIT

Kaštela

POP 38,700

If you're looking to hunker down in safety, you can't do much better than having the mountains behind you and the sea in front. At least that's what the Dalmatian nobility thought when faced with the threat of Ottoman invasion in the 15th and 16th centuries. One after the other, rich families from Split headed to the 20km stretch of coast between Trogir and Split to build their sturdy mansions, until a total of 17 castles and towers were built, some with fortified villages attached. The Turks never reached them and many of the castles remain today.

Kaštela is now a municipality in its own right, incorporating seven separate little harbour towns, each named after a castle, which together form the second-largest settlement in Split-Dalmatia County. Running from Split to Trogir, they are Kaštel Sućurac, Kaštel Gomilica, Kaštel Kambelovac, Kaštel Lukšić, Kaštel Stari, Kaštel Novi and Kaštel Štafilić.

Sights & Activities

The main highway heads through Kaštela's industrial fringes, leaving a less-than-positive impression, but turn off towards the water and a different Kaštela comes into view – one of historic villages clinging to rocky bays. Confusingly, the names of the seven settlements don't always match up with the castles they contain. Some have more than one castle and some no longer have any at all.

If you visit just one part of Kaštela, make it **Kaštel Lukšić**, home to Dvorac Vitturi, the largest and best preserved of Kaštela's castles. It now houses a museum and tourist office. The village also has a big baroque church and the most un-castle-like Kaštel Rušinac, a private house and garden enclosed by sturdy walls.

Kaštilac CASTLE
(Kaštel Gomilica) At the centre of the Kaštel Gomilica waterfront is this square-shaped fortified island, linked to the mainland by a bridge. It was built for a community of Benedictine nuns and is now filled with private dwellings. *Game of Thrones* fans will recognise it as one of the locations used for the town of Braavos. The island is flanked by shallow, sandy beaches.

Kaštela Town Museum MUSEUM, CASTLE
(Muzej grada Kaštela; ☎021-260 245; www.muzej-grada-kastela.hr; Lušiško Brce 1, Kaštel Lukšić; adult/child 15/5KN; ⏰9am-8pm Mon-Fri, 6-9pm Sat, 9am-1pm Sun Jun-Sep, 9am-4pm Mon-Fri, to 1pm Sat Oct-May) Built in the late 15th and early 16th centuries, Dvorac Vitturi was home to the Vitturi family right up until 1943, when it was converted into a school. Now it's a small museum, with one of the upstairs rooms devoted to archaeology (containing Roman coins,

jewellery and pottery) and another to the lifestyles of the local nobility (with displays of furniture, weapons and clothing).

Kaštel Sućurac OLD TOWN
Kaštel Sućurac has an appealing strip of waterfront cafes and a historic core set around the ruins of a Gothic-style 15th-century bishop's palace. The bell tower is all that remains of the 16th-century parish church, which was destroyed in an Allied bombing raid in 1943 that claimed 67 lives.

Kaštel Štafilić OLD TOWN
Kaštel Štafilić has two squat fortifications on its waterfront: Kaštel Štafileo-Rotondo (1508) and the Nehaj Fort (1558). There's also a large Renaissance church and, in the backstreets (off Sv Lucije), a 1500-year-old olive tree.

Putalj Winery WINE
(☎092 37 41 545; www.putalj.com; Putaljski, Kaštel Sućurac; per person €80) High in the mountains (with phenomenal views), this family-run winery offers a three-hour early-evening tour of its vineyard and production facilities, followed by tastings of its wine and olive oil – accompanied by bread, prosciutto and cheese – on a terrace set among the vines. The price includes transfers from Split. Market tours and cooking classes can also be arranged.

Information

Tourist Office (☎021-227 933; www.kastela-info.hr; Dvorac Vitturi, Lušiško Brce 5, Kaštel Lukšić; ⊙8am-8pm Mon-Fri, 8am-noon & 5-8pm Sat, 8am-noon Sun Jun-Oct)

Getting There & Away

Bus 37 heads between Split and Trogir every 20 minutes and stops in all the Kaštela towns. Kaštela is best explored on foot or by bike, as the streets are narrow, parking is terrible and the road signage isn't great.

Trogir

POP 13,200

Gorgeous Trogir (called Trau by the Venetians) is set within medieval walls on a tiny island, linked by bridges to both the mainland and to the far larger Čiovo Island. On summer nights everyone gravitates to the wide seaside promenade, lined with bars, cafes and yachts, leaving the knotted, mazelike marble streets gleaming mysteriously under old-fashioned streetlights.

The old town has retained many intact and beautiful buildings from its age of glory between the 13th and 15th centuries. In 1997 its profuse collection of Romanesque and Renaissance buildings earned it World Heritage status.

While it's easily reached on a day trip from Split, Trogir also makes a good alternative base to the big city and a relaxing place to spend a few days.

History

Backed by high hills in the north, surrounded by water on all sides and snug within its walls, Trogir proved an attractive place to settlers. It was founded in the 3rd century BCE by Greek colonists and later became Romanised. Its defensive position allowed Trogir to maintain a degree of autonomy throughout Croatian and Byzantine rule, while trade and nearby mines ensured its economic viability.

In the 13th century sculpture and architecture flourished, reflecting a vibrant, dynamic culture. When Venice bought Dalmatia in 1409, Trogir refused to accept the new ruler and the Venetians bombarded the town into submission. While the rest of Dalmatia stagnated under Venetian rule, Trogir continued to produce great artists who enhanced the beauty of the town.

Sights

★**St Lawrence's Cathedral** CATHEDRAL
(Katedrala svetog Lovre; ☎021-881 426; Trg Ivana Pavla II; 25KN; ⊙8am-8pm Mon-Sat, noon-6pm Sun Jun-Aug, to 6pm Sep-May) Trogir's show-stopping attraction is its three-naved Venetian cathedral, one of the finest architectural works in Croatia, built between the 13th and 15th centuries. Master Radovan carved the grand Romanesque **portal** in 1240, flanked by a nude Adam and Eve standing on the backs of lions. At the end of the portico is another fine piece of sculpture: the 1464 cherub-filled **baptistery** sculpted by Andrija Aleši.

Inside, don't miss the richly decorated 15th-century **Chapel of Blessed Ivan Orsini**, Trogir's first bishop, halfway along the left-hand wall. Be sure to take a look at the **treasury**, which contains an ivory triptych and various silver reliquaries. You can also climb the 47m-high cathedral **bell tower** for views over the old town.

Sacred Art Museum MUSEUM
(Muzej sakralne umjetnosti; ☎021-881 426; Trg Ivana Pavla II 6; 10KN; ⊙8am-8pm Mon-Sat, 11.30am-7pm Sun Jun-Sep) Highlights of this small museum include illuminated manuscripts, a large painting of St Jerome and St John the Baptist by Bellini, an almost life-size, bright-

WORTH A TRIP

CHASING DRAGONS TO KLIS

Controlling the valley leading into Split, **Klis Fortress** (Tvrđava Klis; ☎021-240 578; www.tvrdavaklis.com; Klis bb; adult/child 40/15KN; ⏲9.30am-4pm) spreads along a limestone bluff, reaching 385m at its highest point. Its long and narrow form (304m by 53m) derives from constant extensions over the course of millenniums. Inside, you can clamber all over the fortifications and visit the small museum, which has displays of swords and costumes and detailed information on the castle's brutal past.

Klis' real history (in a nutshell) goes like this: founded by the Illyrians in the 2nd century BC; taken by the Romans; became a stronghold of medieval Croatian duke Trpimir; resisted attacks for 25 years before falling to the Turks in 1537; briefly retaken in 1596; finally fell to the Venetians in 1648. *Game of Thrones* fans will probably recognise the fortress as Meereen, where Daenerys Targaryen had all those nasty slave-masters crucified in season four. If you're having trouble visualising it, there's a room with stills from the show to jog your memory.

Klis is located 12km northeast of the city centre, and can be reached by city bus 22 (13KN) from Trg Gaje Bulata or Split's local bus station.

Klis is famous for its spit-roasted lamb restaurants, and Split residents have been heading to **Restoran Perlica** (☎021-240 004; www.restoran-perlica.hr; Trg Grlo 1, Klis; mains 50-150KN; ⏲9am-10pm; P ᯤ 👪) for a meaty, fatty, smoky, garlicky fix since 1877. To get here from the fortress, continue along the main road, away from Split, for 1.7km (about 20 minutes on foot). Order the 'Plata Perlica', a heaped plate of lamb, potatoes and vegetables.

ly painted *Crucifix with Triumphant Christ* and the darkly lit fragments of a 13th-century icon that once adorned the cathedral's altar.

St Nicholas's Convent CONVENT
(Samostan svetog Nikole; ☎02-881 631; Gradska 2; adult/child 10/5KN; ⏲10am-1pm & 4.15-5.45pm Jun-Sep, by appointment other times) The treasury of this Benedictine convent is home to a dazzling 3rd-century relief of Kairos, the Greek god of opportunity, carved out of orange marble.

Okrug Gornji BEACH
(Copacabana; Šetalište Stjepana Radića bb) Trogir's most popular beach lies 1.7km south of the old town on the island of Čiovo and can be reached by road or boat. It's a 2km-long stretch of pebbles, lined with cafe-bars, ice-cream parlours and holiday apartments.

Medena Beach BEACH
On the Seget Riviera, 4km west of the old town, this stretch of beach has a long promenade lined with bars, tennis courts, minigolf, ice-cream parlours and stands renting jet skis, kayaks and windsurfers. While it's in the grounds of the faded Hotel Medena megaresort, it's open to the general public and there's parking on-site.

Trogir Town Museum MUSEUM
(Muzej grada Trogira; ☎021-881 406; www.muzejgradatrogira.blogspot.com; Gradska vrata 4; adult/child 20/15KN; ⏲10am-1pm & 6-9pm daily Jul & Aug, Mon-Sat Jun & Sep, 9am-2pm Mon-Fri Oct-May) Housed in the former Garagnin-Fanfogna palace, this museum exhibits books, documents, drawings and period costumes from Trogir's long history.

Grand Cipiko Palace PALACE
(Velika palača Cipiko; Gradska 41) This palatial house, opposite the cathedral, was home to a prominent family during the 15th century. It's not open to the public, but you can stop to admire the intricately carved Gothic triforium encasing the windows on the facade, the work of Andrija Aleši.

Town Hall HISTORIC BUILDING
(Gradska vijećnica; Trg Ivana Pavla II 1; ⏲7am-7pm Mon-Fri) This 15th-century building beside the cathedral has a Gothic courtyard decorated with coats of arms, a monumental staircase and a well carved with the winged lion of St Mark, the symbol of the Venetian Republic.

St Sebastian's Church CHURCH
(Crkva Sv Sebastijana; Trg Ivana Pavla II) No longer used for services, this 1476 church shelters stone sarcophagi and the photos of locals killed in the 1990s war. It's topped by a large, blue-faced Renaissance clock.

Town Loggia HISTORIC BUILDING
(Gradska loža; Trg Ivana Pavla II) On the main square, this 13th-century open-sided structure contains an interesting relief by famous Croatian sculptor Ivan Meštrović.

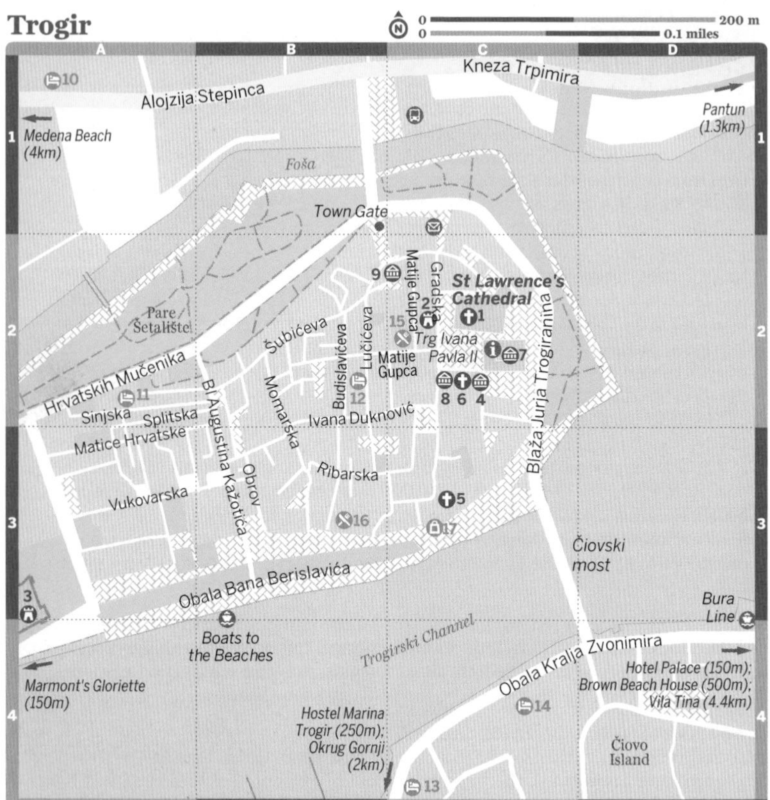

Trogir

Top Sights

1 St Lawrence's Cathedral C2

Sights

2 Grand Cipiko Palace C2
3 Kamerlengo Castle A3
4 Sacred Art Museum C2
5 St Nicholas's Convent C3
6 St Sebastian's Church C2
7 Town Hall C2
8 Town Loggia C2
9 Trogir Town Museum C2

Sleeping

10 ApartHotel Bellevue A1
11 Hotel Pašike A2
12 Hotel Tragos B2
13 Villa Moretti C4
14 Villa Tudor C4

Eating

15 Konoba Trs C2
16 Pizzeria Mirkec B3

Shopping

17 Small Loggia C3

Kamerlengo Castle CASTLE

(Kaštel Kamerlengo; Hrvatskog proljeća 1971 bb; adult/child 25/20KN; ⏲9am-7pm) Built by the Venetians in around 1420, this fortress was once connected to the city walls. Inside it's basically an empty shell, but you can climb up and circle the walls. Concerts are held here during the Trogir Summer festival.

Marmont's Gloriette HISTORIC BUILDING

(Marmontov glorijet) Right at the western tip of Trogir island, this elegant gazebo was built by the French during the Napoleonic occupation of Dalmatia. At the time it jutted out into a marshy lagoon and Marshal Marmont used to sit within the circle of columns, surrounded by water, and play cards.

Festivals & Events

Trogir Summer MUSIC

(Trogirsko ljeto; Jul & Aug) Classical and folk music concerts presented in churches, squares and the fortress. Posters advertising the events are displayed all around town.

Sleeping

Hostel Marina Trogir HOSTEL €

(021-883 075; www.hostelmarina-trogir.com; Cumbrijana 16; dm 175KN; May-Oct;) Run by an expat German couple, this excellent hostel has only four dorms, each sleeping seven or eight people. The custom-built wooden bunks have suitcase-sized lockers underneath, reading lights and privacy curtains for the lower bunk (but not the top one). Plus there's a communal kitchen and separate men's and women's bathrooms.

Villa Moretti HISTORIC HOTEL €€

(021-885 326; www.villamoretti.com; Lučica 1; r €90-120; P) Owned by the same family since 1792, this 17th-century palazzo has five spacious, antique-filled rooms accessed by a grand marble and wrought-iron stairway. Two rooms open onto a large rear terrace, but all have million-dollar views over the old town. The bathrooms are large but a tad dated.

Villa Tudor HOTEL €€

(091 25 26 652; www.facebook.com/VillaTudorTrogir; Obala kralja Zvonimira 12; r/apt from €104/171; P) With exposed stone offset with baby-blue walls in the stylish bedrooms, and the best water-framed views of Trogir's old town that you could imagine, this little family-run hotel is quite exceptional. The double glazing really does its job on what's a busy strip.

Hotel Tragos HERITAGE HOTEL €€

(021-884 729; www.tragos.hr; Budislavićeva 3; r from €105; May-Oct;) This medieval family house has been well restored, with lots of exposed stone and original details. Its 12 sleek, nicely decorated rooms come with satellite TV and minibars. Even if you don't stay here, come for the wonderful home cooking served in the restaurant (mains from 55KN); try the *trogirska pašticada* (Trogir-style beef stew).

Vila Tina HOTEL €€

(021-888 001; www.vila-tina.com; Domovinske zahvalnosti 63, Arbanija; r from €85; P@) Out on a limb in a small seaside settlement 5km east of Trogir, Vila Tina will suit those travelling with a car who value having a little concrete-lined swimming spot at their doorstep. Some of the spacious, tidy rooms have big, sea-facing balconies. Plus there's a hot tub and infrared sauna.

ApartHotel Bellevue HOTEL €€

(021-492 000; www.bellevue.com.hr; Alojzija Stepnica 42; r/apt from €116/139; Apr-Oct; P) On the landward side of Trogir, this painfully 1990s-looking block has spacious, simply furnished rooms and apartments. Some have curved balconies overlooking the old town, although the rear rooms are quieter and the views aren't quite as *belle* from this side of Trogir anyway.

Brown Beach House HOTEL €€€

(021-355 400; www.brownhotels.com; Gradine 66; s/d from €208/260; Mar-Oct; P) Much more swanky than the name implies, this luxurious property is the first from this mini chain outside Israel. You would never guess that this vast stone building started life as a tobacco factory; the 42 rooms have style and space to spare. That sense of sophisticated glamour continues down to the chequer-board pool and the private beach.

Hotel Pašike HERITAGE HOTEL €€€

(021-885 185; www.hotelpasike.com; Splitska 4; r from €143;) This delightful hotel accentuates its 15th-century heritage with antique furniture, dark timber and elaborate beds. The friendly staff members wear traditional outfits, adding to the days-gone-by vibe. Head up to the little roof terrace for views over the old town.

Hotel Palace HOTEL €€€

(021-685 555; www.hotel-palace.net; Gradine 8; s/d €125/165; P@) A gaudy reception with brass columns and bright ceiling panels greets guests at this large, peach-coloured palace on Čiovo island. The decor of the bedrooms is, thankfully, much more restrained. There's also a small spa complex and fitness room.

Eating

Pizzeria Mirkec PIZZA €€

(021-883 042; www.pizzeria-mirkec.hr; Budislavićeva 15; mains 45-180KN; 9am-midnight) With dozens of tables spilling out onto the waterfront promenade and the main restaurant tucked around the corner, this relaxed joint serves tasty wood-fired pizza along with omelettes, steaks, pasta, grilled fish and, if preordered, traditional meals slow-roasted under a *peka* (domed metal lid). There's also a good-value set breakfast option (50KN).

WORTH A TRIP

ROAMING A ROMAN CITY

The ruins of the ancient city of **Salona** (☎021-213 358; Don Frane Bulića bb, Solin; adult/child 30/15KN; ⊙9am-7pm Mon-Sat, to 2pm Sun), situated at the foot of the mountains just northeast of Split, are the most archaeologically important in Croatia. Start by paying your admission fee at Tusculum, near the northern entrance to the reserve. Built in 1898 by the site's ground-breaking archaeologist Monsignor Frane Bulić as a base for his research, it has a Roman-style drawing room with displays on the early archaeology undertaken here.

Salona was first mentioned as an Illyrian town in 119 BC and it's thought that it already had walls by then. The Romans seized the site in 78 BC and under the rule of Augustus it became the administrative headquarters of the empire's Dalmatian province. When Emperor Diocletian built his palace in Split at the end of the 3rd century CE, it was the proximity to Salona that attracted him. That grand history all came to a crashing halt in the 7th century, when the city was levelled by the invading Avars and then the Slavs. The inhabitants fled to take refuge within Diocletian's old palace walls and on the neighbouring islands, leaving Salona to decay.

While many of Salona's ancient treasures are now on display in Split's Archaeological Museum (p248), there's a surprising amount in situ. Numerous sarcophagi are scattered about the area known as Manastirine, between the car park and the museum. This was a burial place for Christian martyrs prior to the decriminalisation of Christianity and includes the substantial remains of an early basilica.

From Tusculum, a path bordered by cypresses runs south to the northern city wall. From here you can get an overview of the foundations of buildings that compose the Episcopal Centre, including a three-aisled 5th-century cathedral with an octagonal baptistery, and the remains of Bishop Honorius' basilica, with a ground plan in the form of a Greek cross. The ruins of public **baths** (Thermae) sit across the narrow lane at the rear of the basilica.

Just beyond this complex and slightly to the right is the monumental 1st-century eastern city gate, Porta Caesarea, later engulfed by the city as it spread eastward. Grooves in the stone road left by ancient wheels can still be seen here, along with the remains of a covered aqueduct that ran along the top of the wall. It was probably built around the 1st century CE and supplied both Salona and Diocletian's Palace with water from the Jadro River.

The original city spread west from here to the huge 2nd-century amphitheatre, destroyed in the 17th century by the Venetians to prevent it from being used as a refuge by Turkish raiders. At one time it could accommodate 18,000 spectators, which gives an idea of the size and importance of ancient Salona.

The main path leading to the amphitheatre follows the line of the ancient wall. Just to the right of the path (ie outside the wall) you'll pass another early Christian cemetery, where the remains of some of those killed in the amphitheatre were once buried, along with the ruins of the **Five Martyrs Basilica** (Kapljuč basilica), built in their honour.

Further ruins can be found among the vineyards and orchards to the left of the path, including the scant remains of the Forum and, nearby, a theatre and a Temple of Dionysus.

Salona is easily accessible on Split city bus 1 (single/return 13/22KN), which goes all the way to the parking lot every half-hour, departing from Trg Gaje Bulata.

Konoba Trs DALMATIAN €€€
(☎021-796 956; www.konoba-trs.com; Matije Gupca 14; mains 105-230KN; ⊙11am-midnight Mon-Sat, 5pm-midnight Sun) As traditional-looking as they come, this rustic little tavern has wooden benches and old stone walls inside, and an inviting courtyard shaded by grapevines. Yet the menu adds clever, contemporary twists to Dalmatian classics, featuring the likes of panko-crumbed octopus tentacles, and the signature dish, nutmeg-spiced lamb *pašticada* (stew), served with savoury pancakes.

Shopping

Small Loggia MARKET
(Mala loža; Obala Bana Berislavića 11; ⊙9am-9pm May-Sep) This historic open-sided market is still used by street traders, although these days they mainly deal in jewellery. It's a good place to buy interesting pieces showcasing local stone and pearls.

Information

Portal Trogir (p42) Arranges private accommodation; rents bikes, scooters and kayaks;

and books excursions and adventure activities (quad safaris, rafting, diving, canyoning).

Tourist Office (☎021-885 628; www.tztrogir.hr; Trg Ivana Pavla II 1; ⏰8am-8pm May-Sep, 9am-5pm Mon-Fri Oct-Apr) Inside the town hall; distributes town maps.

Getting There & Around

BOAT

Bura Line (p260) has a small boat heading backwards and forwards to Split four to six times a day from May to September.

Jadrolinija (p260) has three daily car ferries (per passenger/car 16/150KN) heading from Trogir to Drvenik Veli (one hour) and on to Drvenik Mali (a further 20 minutes).

In summer, small passenger boats depart from Obala Bana Berislavića, right in front of Hotel Concordia, heading to the beaches of Okrug Gornji (25KN) and Medena (20KN). The journey takes about 45 minutes.

BUS

Intercity buses stop at the **bus station** (☎021-882 947; Kneza Tripimira bb) on the mainland near the bridge to Trogir. Destinations include Zagreb (148KN, 6½ hours, 10 daily), Rijeka (230KN, 7½ hours, three daily), Zadar (73KN, 2½ hours, 11 daily), Split (20KN, 30 minutes, frequent) and Dubrovnik (137KN, 5½ hours, five daily).

Split city bus 37 (17KN) takes the coastal road through Kaštela every 20 minutes, also stopping at the airport. This is a much slower option than the intercity buses, which take the highway.

Šolta Island

This lovely, wooded island (59 sq km) is a popular getaway for Split inhabitants escaping the sultry summer heat. The Romans called it Solentia (The Sun), but it first entered written history in the 4th century BCE under its Greek name, Olynthia.

The island's main entry point is Rogač, where ferries from Split tie up at the edge of a large bay. A road leads around the bay to smaller coves with rocky beaches, and another leads uphill to the island's administrative centre of Grohote.

Maslinica is the island's prettiest settlement, with seven islets offshore. Another gorgeous village is Stomorska; its sheltered harbour is popular with yachties. The island's interior has several worthwhile family-run, farm-based 'agroturizam' ventures, where visitors can sample and buy olive oil, *rakija* (grappa) and wine.

Šolta shuts up shop in the low season; it can be hard to hire cars or find a place to eat.

Agroturizam Ktelanac WINERY
(☎098 385 376; www.agroturizamkastelanac.com; Duga gomila 7, Gornje Selo; ⏰8am-10pm Jun-Oct, by arrangement Nov-May) Call into this family farm in Gornje Selo (Upper Village) to sample some excellent olive oil and the island's indigenous red-wine variety, *dobričić,* accompanied by a platter of homemade bread and olives.

Martinis Marchi HOTEL €€€
(☎021-572 768; www.martinis-marchi.com; Sv Nikole 51, Maslinica; ste from €311; ⏰Apr-Sep; ❄🏊) Built in 1703, this seaside castle has been converted into a luxurious heritage hotel, with seven suites, gardens, a marina, a terrace restaurant and a spa centre.

Konoba Momčin Dvor DALMATIAN €€
(Šoltanskih žrtava 18, Grohote; mains 110KN; ⏰10am-2pm & 6-10pm; 📶) Accessed via a cobbled back lane, this highly atmospheric tavern is as traditional as they come, with a loyal local following. There's no menu and choices are limited to just a couple of options; expect the likes of grilled fish served with *blitva* or lamb cooked under a *peka.*

Information

Maslinica Tourist Office (☎021-659 220; www.visitsolta.com; Briga bb; ⏰8am-3pm Sun-Wed, 3-9pm Fri & Sat Jun-Sep)

Rogač Tourist Office (☎021-654 491; www.visitsolta.com; Obala Sv Terezije 1; ⏰8am-2pm Thu-Tue, to 12.30pm Wed Jun-Sep)

Stomorska Tourist Office (☎021-658 192; www.visitsolta.com; Riva Pelegrin 8; ⏰8am-2pm Mon, Fri & Sat, 2.30-9pm Wed, Thu & Sun Jun-Sep)

Getting There & Around

Four to six **Jadrolinija** (☎021-654 664; www.jadrolinija.hr; Obala Sv Tereze bb) car ferries run between Split and Rogač every day (passenger/car 33/154KN, one hour). Three buses a day head between Rogač and Stomorska via Gornje Selo, with an additional three between Rogač and Maslinica (all 12KN).

Stobreč & Podstrana

Positioned under the mountains at the foot of the Split peninsula, these neighbouring settlements mark the beginning of long chain of beach towns heading southeast along the coast. They sit on opposite sides of a sheltered bay, divided by the Žrnovnica River.

Stobreč is the prettier of the two, with a marina and partly sandy beach. It started life in the 3rd century BCE as the Greek town of Epetion. Podstrana has the disadvantage of the coastal highway passing right through it, but it has some nice beaches.

Camping Stobreč CAMPGROUND €
(☎021-325 426; www.campingsplit.com; Sv Lovre 6, Stobreč; per adult/child/site from 60/33/74KN, cabins from 418KN;) Occupying a pretty pine-shaded spit at the end of the Stobreč waterfront, this well-equipped place has two beaches, bars, a restaurant, a shop, a playground and a gazillion activities on offer nearby. It's the best place to camp within striking distance of Split and, unlike most Croatian campgrounds, it's open year-round.

Le Méridien Lav HOTEL €€€
(☎021-500 500; www.lemeridienlavsplit.com; Grljevačka 2a, Podstrana; r/ste from €248/478;) This five-star giant straddles 800m of beach, five interlinking buildings, 381 neutrally decorated rooms, a marina, a casino and luscious gardens. The views back towards Split are wonderful.

Kaša Grill & Bar CROATIAN €€
(☎021-325 083; www.facebook.com/kasagrillbar; Alojzija Stepinca 17, Stobreč; mains 50-120KN; noon-3pm & 6pm-midnight;) Grilled meat takes centre stage at this friendly family-run restaurant, tucked away on a residential street set back from the water in Stobreč. Local oddities such as steak stuffed with cheese and proscuitto sit alongside the likes of lamb chops, veal livers, chicken fillets and burgers.

Information

Podstrana Tourist Office (☎091 33 38 440; www.visitpodstrana.hr; Jurasova 2; 8am-noon & 4-8pm Mon-Sat Jul & Aug, 8am-4pm Mon-Fri Sep-Jun)

Stobreč Tourist Office (☎021-324 016; www.visitstobrec.com; Sv Lovre 4; 8am-9pm Apr-Oct, 9am-4pm Mon-Fri, to 2pm Sat Nov-Mar)

Getting There & Away

Bus 25 heads to Podstrana regularly, departing from the stop outside Split's Green Market.

Omiš

POP 15,000

The legendary pirates' lair of Omiš has one of the most dramatic locations of any town on the Dalmatian coast. Situated at the mouth of the Cetina River, at the end of a picturesque canyon, it's backed by sheer walls of mottled grey rock topped with craggy peaks.

The coastal-highway traffic slows to a crawl as the road narrows into the leafy oak-lined main street. On the landward side is a small but atmospheric maze of old streets capped by a little castle. A sandy-shingly beach stretches out on its other flank, attracting scores of perky families in summer.

Sights & Activities

Omiš' enviable location lends itself to plenty of activities. The most gentle option is a cruise up the river canyon to pretty Radmanove Mlinice (Radman's Mills; around 100KN). Small boats line up alongside the bridge and depart when full. Hiking, rafting and zip-lining are also popular.

St Michael's Church CHURCH
(Župna crkva sv Mihovila; Trg Sv Mihovila; hours vary) Abutting a sunny square at the centre of the old town, Omiš' early-17th-century parish church has an ornate entrance carved from Brač stone, including Corinthian columns decorated in an interesting fish-scale pattern. Inside there's a single nave with a high vaulted ceiling, a gilded high altar and some beautiful paintings.

Mirabela Fortress CASTLE
(Tvrđava Mirabela; 20KN; 9am-9pm May-Oct) Also known as Peovica, this little tower was built in the 13th century on 9th-century Byzantine foundations. It's reached by a steep set of steps, and while there's not a lot inside, it's worth trudging up the internal staircase and taking the final ladder to the top for the views over the town.

Zipline ADVENTURE SPORTS
(☎095 82 22 221; www.zipline-croatia.com; Josipa Pupačića 4; ride 400KN) Blast along a set of eight wires strung high above the Cetina canyon – up to 150m high, to be exact. The longest runs for 700m. The price includes transfers from Omiš.

Sleeping & Eating

Hotel Plaža HOTEL €€€
(☎021-755 260; www.hotelplaza.hr; Trg kralja Tomislava 6; r from €122;) Right by the beach, this large, modern hotel has richly coloured rooms, many with balconies and sea views. Facilities include a restaurant, a small fitness room and a spa centre, and the friendly staff can help arrange local activities.

La Fabbrica GASTROPUB €€
(☎091 89 00 212; www.facebook.com/lafabbricaomis; Fošal 19; mains 50-120KN; 9am-midnight Sun-Thu, to 2am Fri & Sat;) Omiš' hippest eatery serves the likes of burgers and steaks alongside such traditional dishes as *pašticada*, pasta and grilled fish, and more adventurous fare like truffle cappuccino soup. The

vibe is relaxed and bar-like, and there's regular live music in summer.

Drinking & Nightlife

Lix BAR
(Ivana Katušića 5; 9am-midnight) Omiš' more bohemian types gravitate to this tiny old-town bar, and hold court at the scattering of tables on the marbled lane or inside the stone-walled interior.

Turjun BAR
(Fošal 9; 7am-2am May-Sep, to 10pm Oct-Apr;) Locals congregate inside this tower, which is all that remains of the historic town gate, or they soak up the afternoon sun from the footpath in front.

Information

Tourist Office (021-861 350; www.visitomis.hr; Fošal 1a)

Getting There & Away

Split city bus 60 heads here every half-hour (22KN). Other destinations include Makarska (32KN, 45 minutes, hourly), Dubrovnik (121KN, four hours, four daily), Šibenik (62KN, 2½ hours, two daily) and Zagreb (140KN, six hours, nine daily).

CETINA RIVER RAFTING

The Cetina is the longest river in Central Dalmatia, stretching 105km from the eponymous village. It flows through the Dinara mountains, through the fields around Sinj and gathers steam until it pours into a power plant near Nova Sela. It's an extraordinarily scenic journey, as the limpid blue river is bordered by high rocky walls, thick with vegetation. Rafting is possible upstream from Omiš from spring to autumn, but the rapids can become quite fast after heavy rains. Summer is best for inexperienced rafters.

Rafting operators tout their trips from the riverside on the old-town side of the Omiš bridge. The better operators charge upwards of 200KN. Some are cheaper, but they're not as good.

MAKARSKA RIVIERA

The Makarska Riviera is a 58km stretch of coast at the foot of the Biokovo mountain range, where a series of cliffs and ridges forms a dramatic backdrop to a string of beautiful pebbly beaches. The foothills are protected from harsh winds and covered with lush Mediterranean greenery, including pine forests, olive groves and fruit trees.

If you're mainly interested in a beach holiday without too many historical sights to distract you, the crystal-clear waters of this strip are hard to beat. However, this is one of the most developed stretches of the Dalmatian coast, and popular with package tours. Note that in July and August the entire riviera is jam-packed with holidaymakers, and many hotels impose a seven-night minimum stay.

Brela

POP 1710

The longest and arguably the loveliest coastline in Dalmatia stretches through the holiday town of Brela. Six kilometres of pebble beaches curve around coves thickly forested with pine trees, where you can enjoy beautifully clear seas and fantastic sunsets. A shady promenade lined with bars and cafes winds around the coves, which spread out on both sides of the town. The best beach is **Punta Rata**, a gorgeous spit of pebbles and pines about 300m northwest of the town centre.

Sentido Bluesun Berulia HOTEL €€€
(021-603 599; www.brelahotelberulia.com; Frankopanska 66; r from €212; May-Oct;) This freshly renovated four-star giant has 199 rooms and an outdoor pool, only metres from the beach, 300m east of the town centre.

Del Posto DALMATIAN €€
(021-604 890; Obala Sv Nikole 71, Baška Voda; mains 50-90KN; 7am-11pm;) Take a 20-minute walk to this elegant restaurant and wine bar on the terrace of the flashy Grand Hotel Slavia in Baška Voda, the next town along the coast. The prices are surprisingly reasonable for the somewhat-rarefied ambience.

Information

Berulia Travel (021-618 519; www.beruliatravel-brela.hr; Frankopanska 111) Finds private accommodation, changes money, books excursions and arranges airport transfers.

Tourist Office (021-618 455; www.brela.hr; Trg Alojzija Stepinca bb; 8am-8pm May-Sep, 8am-3pm Mon-Fri Oct-Apr) Provides a town and a regional cycling map.

Getting There & Away

Most buses running along the highway stop near the Brela turn-off, 1km above the town centre. Destinations include Zagreb (170KN, 6¼ hours, nine daily), Šibenik (66KN, three hours, two daily), Split (35KN, one hour, hourly), Makarska (18KN, 20 minutes, hourly) and Dubrovnik (110KN, 3½ hours, four daily).

Free parking is hard to come by, even in the low season.

Makarska

POP 13,900

Makarska is a beach resort with a spectacular natural setting, backed by the glorious Biokovo mountain range. While the outskirts are a little shabby, there's a lovely long waterfront promenade and a pretty limestone centre that turns peachy orange at sunset. Active types base themselves here to take advantage of the nearby hiking, climbing, paragliding, mountain biking, windsurfing and swimming opportunities, and the good transport connections.

Makarska is favoured by tourists from neighbouring Bosnia, who descend on the town's long pebbly beach in huge numbers during summer.

The high season is pretty raucous, with many buzzing nightlife spots, but it's also a lot of fun for those with children. If you're interested in hanging around beach bars and clubs, playing volleyball and generally lounging about, you'll like Makarska. Outside the high season, things are quiet.

Sights & Activities

Makarska's harbour and historic centre are located on a large cove bordered by Cape Osejava in the southeast and the Sveti Petar peninsula in the northwest. The long pebble **town beach**, lined with hotels, stretches from the Sveti Petar park northwest along the bay. For a party atmosphere, head past the town beach to **Buba beach**, near the Hotel Rivijera, where music pumps all day during summer. To the southeast are rockier and lovelier beaches, such as **Nugal**, popular with nudists.

Makarska Municipal Museum MUSEUM
(Gradski muzej Makarska; ☎021-612 302; Obala kralja Tomislava 17; 10KN; ⏰9am-1pm Mon-Sat) Kill time on a rainy day tracing the town's history by checking out this collection of photos, old stones and nautical relics.

Franciscan Monastery & Shell Museum MONASTERY
(Franjevački samostan & Malakološki muzej; ☎099 88 52 165; Franjevački 1; museum 15KN; ⏰museum 10am-noon May-Sep, by arrangement Oct-Apr) There's a huge contemporary mosaic in the apse of the hurch and a well-presented **shell museum** tucked around the back (enter from Alkarska), the labour of love of a past friar.

Wine Club Croatia WINE
(☎091 57 70 053; www.wineclubcroatia.com; workshop 300KN) Enthusiastic and charming wine expert Daniel Čečavac hosts these excellent wine-tasting events in the Park and Osejava hotels (as well as in Baška Voda and Split), pairing five top-notch vintages with local food specialities. He also leads private wine, food and sightseeing tours (two to eight people) to the Pelješac Peninsula (1650KN), Vrgorac (1250KN) and Imotski (850KN).

THE WHOLE PACKAGE

The best of the package hotels, **Sensimar Adriatic Beach Resort** (☎021-681 400; www.sensimaradriaticbeach.com; Porat 136, Živogošće; s/d all-inclusive from €217/288; ⏰May-Sep; P ❄ 📶 🏊) has a pool overlooking the beach and multiple bars and restaurants. Most of the rooms have views, many have balconies and there are even 'swim-up rooms' that open onto a lap pool. The clientele is roughly 90% British and 10% Scandinavian. Rates include breakfast, lunch and dinner.

Sleeping

Vintage Hostel Makarska HOSTEL €
(☎021-615 372; www.hostelmakarska.com; Prvosvibanjska 15; dm 120KN, r from 280KN, without bathroom from 260KN; ⏰May-Sep; P ❄ 📶) Major renovations have converted this long-time favourite into one of the flashest on the Dalmatian coast. The new deluxe rooms have arty stencils on the walls and stylish black-and-white bathrooms. There are separate eight-bed male and female dorms, a small bar that also serves breakfast, and a loveable resident pooch.

★ **Maritimo** HOTEL €€€
(☎021-679 041; www.hotel-maritimo.hr; Cvitačke 2a; r from 930KN; P ❄ 📶) Right by the beach, this excellent hotel has friendly staff and modern rooms with fridges, safes, good bathrooms and balconies with sea views. Breakfast on the terrace by the water is a blissful way to start the day.

Eating & Drinking

Konoba Kalalarga DALMATIAN €
(Kalalarga 40; mains from 50KN; ⏰9am-2am Tue-Sun; 📶) This tavern has dim lighting, dark wood and alfresco bench seating in an alley-

WORTH A TRIP

TASTY TUČEPI

If you have a car, there are a couple of great options in the hills above the village of Tučepi, southeast of Makarska.

Jeny Restaurant (☎091 58 78 078; www.restaurant-jeny.hr; Čovići 1, Gornji Tučepi; menu with/without wine 780/600KN; ⏰6pm-midnight mid-May–Sep; ✎) In this fine-dining restaurant on the slopes of Biokovo mountain, the culinary focus is Mediterranean with a French touch. There's no à la carte option, only a seven-course *degustation*, which can be tailored for vegetarians or those with allergies (let them know when you book). The breathtaking riviera views make up for the passable decor.

Konoba Ranč (☎021-623 563; www.ranc-tucepi.hr; Kamena 62, Tučepi; mains 90-200KN; ⏰6pm-1am Apr-Sep) This rustic spot, away from the tourist buzz, is worth the 10-minute drive from Makarska; follow the sign leading up from the highway. Dine on log chairs under olive trees, feasting on grilled meat and fish, a preordered *peka* (meat or seafood cooked beneath a domed baking lid), house wine and sporadic *klapa* (p259) performances.

way leading up from the main square. It serves food the way *baba* (grandma) would make it, including traditional Dalmatian treats such as *pašticada*. There's no menu – the waiter will run through the specials.

Grabovac WINE BAR
(Kačićev trg 11; ⏰9am-2am Apr-Oct; ☎) Right on the main square in front of the church, this outpost of a famous winery from Imotski (right on the Bosnian border) serves its own wine by the glass, plus tasty titbits such as local cheese and *pršut* (prosciutto).

Deep CLUB
(www.facebook.com/deepmakarska; Šetalište dr fra Jure Radića 5a; ⏰9am-5am Jun–mid-Sep; ☎) Inside a cave near the **Hotel Osejava** (☎021-604 300; www.osejava.com; Šetalište dr fra Jure Radića bb), Deep attracts a fashionable set who sip cocktails as a DJ spins the latest beats. Cover charges kick in after 11pm.

Information

Tourist Office (☎021-612 002; www.makarska-info.hr; Obala kralja Tomislava 16; ⏰8am-8pm) Publishes a useful guide to the city with a map.

Getting There & Away

BOAT

Jadrolinija (☎021-679 515; www.jadrolinija.hr; Obala kralja Tomislava 15) has three car ferries per day to Sumartin on Brač (passenger/car 30/150KN, one hour), increasing to four in June and September, and five in July and August.

From June to September, **Kapetan Luka** (p260) has a daily high-speed catamaran to Dubrovnik (160KN, 3¼ hours), Sobra on Mljet (140KN, 2¼ hours), Korčula Town (130KN, one hour), Bol on Brač (90KN, 35 minutes) and Split (100KN, 1½ hours).

BUS

From the **bus station** (☎021-612 333; Ante Starčevića 30; ⏰5am-10.30pm), 300m uphill from the harbour, there are buses to/from Dubrovnik (105KN, three hours, eight daily), Split (50KN, 1¼ hours, at least hourly), Šibenik (100KN, three hours, at least four daily), Rijeka (275KN, seven hours, two daily) and Zagreb (175KN, six hours, 10 daily).

Biokovo Nature Park

The hulking limestone Biokovo massif, Makarska's moody backdrop, offers hiking opportunities with views aplenty. You can also drive on a rough, single-track, 23km road all the way to Sveti Jure (1762m), its highest peak. Park entry fees apply, payable at the **Biokovo Nature Park** (Park Prirode Biokovo; www.biokovo.com; adult/child 50/25KN; ⏰7am-8pm mid-May–Sep, 8am-4pm Apr–mid-May & Oct–mid-Nov) booth at the beginning of Biokovska, the main road that runs up the mountain.

The nature park's website lists contacts for various mountain huts, mainly used by serious hikers and mountain climbers. Otherwise, base yourself in Makarska for day trips.

Hikers can set off from Makarska or drive up to the park entrance. Enquire at Makarska's tourist office about tracks to suit your ability. Take plenty of water, sunscreen, a hat and waterproof clothes – the weather on the mountain can change suddenly. Various agencies offer guided walks and drives.

Kotišina Botanical Garden NATURE RESERVE
(Botanički vrt Kotišina) FREE Just up from the village of Kotišina, this isn't a traditional botanical garden – more a wild, 16.5-hectare expanse of mountainside filled with well-labelled indigenous flora. Ranging in height from

350m to 500m above sea level, the site offers spectacular views over the islands of Brač and Hvar. Rocky paths lead past a fort built into a cave and up a canyon. Good shoes are a must.

Getting There & Away

To get to the park entrance from Makarska, head southeast and branch off the highway on the road leading to Vrgorac. Look for the entrance to the left after 6km.

BRAČ ISLAND

POP 14,500

Brač is famous for two things: its radiant white stone, used to build Diocletian's Palace in Split (and, depending on whom you believe, the White House in Washington) and Zlatni Rat, the pebbly beach at Bol that extends languidly into the Adriatic and adorns 90% of Croatia's tourism posters.

It's the largest island in central Dalmatia, with several towns and villages, and a dramatic landscape of steep cliffs, inky waters and pine forests. The interior is scattered with piles of rocks – the result of the back-breaking labour of women who, over hundreds of years, gathered the rocks to clear land for vineyards and orchards. The tough living conditions meant that, over time, a lot of people moved to the mainland for work.

The two main centres, Supetar and Bol, are quite different: Supetar is pleasant if unassuming, while Bol revels in its more exclusive appeal.

History

Remnants of a neolithic settlement have been found in Kopačina cave near Supetar, but the first inhabitants to make the historical record were the Illyrians, who built a fort in Škrip to protect against Greek invasion. The Romans arrived in 167 BCE and began exploiting the stone quarries near Škrip and building summer mansions around the island.

From the 11th century, control of the island was passed between Venice, Byzantium, Hungary, Croatia, Venice again, Byzantium again, Omiš, Venice yet again, Bosnia, Dubrovnik and, finally, Venice, which ruled from 1420 until 1797. During this time the interior villages were devastated by plague and the inhabitants moved to the 'healthier' settlements along the coast, revitalising the towns of Supetar, Bol, Sumartin and Milna.

After a brief period under Napoleonic rule, the island passed into Austrian hands. Wine cultivation expanded until the phylloxera epidemic at the turn of the 20th century ravaged the island's vines and people began leaving for the Americas, especially Chile. The island endured a reign of terror during WWII when German and Italian troops looted and burned villages, imprisoning and murdering their inhabitants.

Although the tourism business took a hit in the mid-1990s, it has rebounded well and the island is now a busy place in summer.

Getting There & Away

AIR

Brač Airport (BWK; ☎021-559 711; www.airport-brac.hr) is 14km northeast of Bol and 38km southeast of Supetar.

The airport only has scheduled commercial flights from mid-May to September. Destinations include Zagreb, Ljubljana, Bern, Luxembourg, Brussels and Rotterdam.

BOAT

Jadrolinija (☎021-631 357; www.jadrolinija.hr; Hrvatskih velikana bb) car ferries operate on the following routes:

Split to Supetar (passenger/car 33/154KN, 50 minutes) Roughly every 90 minutes from June to October (every two hours at other times). The ferry drops you off in the centre of Supetar, only steps from the bus station.

Makarska to Sumartin (passenger/car 30/150KN, one hour) Three times daily, increasing to four in June and September, five in July and August. Note: bus connections from Sumartin are infrequent.

Jadrolinija's high-speed catamaran services:

- On Wednesdays to **Milna** from **Split** (40KN, 30 minutes) and **Vis** (55KN, 55 minutes).
- Daily to **Bol** from **Split** (55KN, one hour) and **Jelsa on Hvar** (35KN, 20 minutes). Buy your ticket in advance, as these can sell out quickly in high season.
- From June to September, a second boat to **Bol** from **Split** (80KN, one hour), **Hvar** (80KN, 50 minutes), **Korčula** (130KN, 2½ hours) and **Dubrovnik** (210KN, 4¾ hours).

Kapetan Luka (p260) also operates high-speed catamarans:

- From May to mid-October, daily to **Milna** from **Dubrovnik** (210KN, 3¾ hours), **Pomena on Mljet** (140KN, 2½ hours), **Korčula** (130KN, 1¾ hours), **Hvar** (70KN, 30 minutes) and **Split** (40KN, 25 minutes).
- From June to September, daily to **Bol** from **Dubrovnik** (210KN, four hours), **Sobra on Mljet** (140KN, three hours), **Korčula** (120KN, 1¾ hours), **Makarska** (90KN, 35 minutes) and **Split** (80KN, 50 minutes).

Getting Around

- There's no transport from the airport to Supetar, so you'll need to take a taxi, which costs about 300KN (150KN to Bol).

OFF THE BEATEN TRACK

BRAČ'S QUIET ESCAPES

Sumartin, the entry point to Brač if you're coming from Makarska, is a sleepy port with a few rocky beaches and little to do, but it makes a nice retreat from the busier tourist centres of Bol and Supetar. If you decide to stay, there's a little **tourist office** (021-648 209; www.touristboard-selca.com; Porat 1; 8am-9pm Jul & Aug, 8am-3pm Mon-Fri, to 1pm Sat Sep & Oct, 8am-3pm Mon-Fri Nov-Jun) in the centre of town, next to the ferry and bus stop, which has listings of private accommodation providers.

For a quiet coastal getaway, head to **Pučišća** (try saying that quickly three times after a shot of *rakija!*) on Brač's northern coast. This appealing little town curves around a port lined with blindingly white historic buildings. One of these houses the **tourist office** (021-633 555; www.tzo-pucisca.hr; Trg Hrvatskog skupa 1; 8am-noon Mon-Fri May & Oct, to 2pm Mon-Sat Jun & Sep, to 8pm daily Jul & Aug).

One of Brač's more interesting sites is the village of **Škrip**, the oldest settlement on the island, about 8km southeast of Supetar. Formerly a refuge of the ancient Illyrians, the fort was taken over by the Romans in the 2nd century BC, and then by refugees escaping the fall of Salona (near Split). The **Island of Brač Museum** (Bračkí otoka muzej; 091 63 70 920; Škrip; adult/child 20/10KN; 9am-7pm) is housed in the Kaštil Radojković, a tower built during the Venetian-Turkish wars that incorporates part of an ancient Illyrian wall and a surprisingly intact Roman mausoleum.

Donji Humac, 8km south of Supetar, has a stone quarry and an interesting onion-domed church tower. But the main reason to head here is to enjoy the panoramic valley views at **Konoba Kopačina** (021-647 707; www.konoba-kopacina.com; Donji Humac 7, Donji Humac; mains 40-140KN; 10am-10pm Mon-Thu, to midnight Fri & Sat;) while sampling traditional Brač specialities such as *vitalac* (skewered lamb offal wrapped in lamb meat).

The port of **Milna**, 20km southwest of Supetar, is the kind of lovely intact fishing village that in any other part of the world would have long ago been commandeered by package tourists. For now, though, it's mainly visited by luxury yachts. The 17th-century town is set at the edge of a deep natural harbour that was used by Emperor Diocletian for shipping stone to Split for the construction of his palace. Paths head around the harbour, which is studded with coves containing rocky beaches. Dominating the picture-perfect setting is the tall steeple of the beautiful 18th-century **Church of the Annunciation** (Riva bb, Milna; hours vary), with a baroque facade, pretty painted ceiling and ornate marble altars.

➡ Supetar is the hub for bus transport around the island. Destinations include Milna (30KN, 30 minutes, five daily), Škrip (24KN, 15 minutes, three daily), Pučišća (30KN, 35 minutes, five daily), Bol (43KN, one hour, five daily) and Sumartin (43KN, 1¼ hours, three daily). Services increase in summer and reduce on Sunday.

➡ From Bol, services are much more limited. Aside from the Supetar buses, there are connections to Pučišća (30KN, 35 minutes, three daily).

➡ A car is useful for exploring the smaller settlements on the island. If you want to avoid the car-ferry charges, it's easy enough to hire a car or scooter from travel agencies in Supetar or Bol when you arrive.

Supetar

POP 4080

Although it suffers in comparison to its more glitzy sister, Bol, Supetar is an attractive little town in its own right, with a historic core of old stone streets fanning out from a harbour dominated by an imposing church. It's a popular holiday destination for Croatian families, with pebbly beaches within an easy stroll of the town centre. The views back across the water to Split and the mountains beyond are universally wonderful.

Sights

Supetar Cemetery CEMETERY

(Groblje Supetar; Banj bb) An unexpected highlight of Supetar is its fascinating cemetery, full of striking sculptural monuments. Grandest of all is the over-the-top **Petrinović family mausoleum**. Built from white Brač stone between 1924 and 1927, it has a cluster of five Byzantine-style domes, an ornate bronze door and a fine carved relief in the style of the Vienna Secession. A striking crucifix is visible if you peer through the keyhole.

Just outside the main entrance are the ruins of a 6th-century Roman *villa rustica* (country house).

Church of the Annunciation CHURCH

(Crkva Navještenja Marijina; Radnička 4; hours vary) Built in the 18th century, this elegant triple-naved baroque church and its 35m-high bell tower dominate the historic harbour at the heart of Supetar. Inside, its ornate marble altars are offset by a soothing palette of pale greens and lemons. Set into the pavement to the left of the church is a Roman mosaic that once decorated the floor of an early basilica dedicated to St Peter, from which the town takes its name.

Activities

Swimming beaches are scattered along the pebbly coast in both directions. **Vrilo** is about 100m east of the town centre. Walking west, you'll come first to **Vlačica**, then **Banj** beach, a large eastward-facing curve lined with pine trees and beach bars. Further on, past the cemetery, are **Tri Mosta** and **Bili Rat**. Then, beyond the next bend, is **Vela Luka**, set on a peaceful bay.

Sleeping

Hotel Osam HOTEL €€€

(021-552 333; www.hotel-osam.com; Vlačica 3; r/ste from €138/183;) Swanky Osam offers a child-free escape for those wanting to lounge around the terrace pool in relative harmony. Ask for a room with a sea view and balcony. The rooftop bar offers unbeatable views back towards Split and the mountains.

Eating & Drinking

★**Vinotoka** DALMATIAN €€

(021-630 969; Jobova 6; mains 70-150KN; noon-10pm Apr-Sep;) Sit by the open fire in Vinotoka's stone-walled dining room or, when it warms up, grab a table on the street or in the large, glassed-in terrace across the lane. The seafood is excellent; try the green fettuccine with shellfish. With notice, it also serves lamb or octopus *peka*.

Konoba Luš DALMATIAN €€

(099 80 33 646; www.facebook.com/konobalus; Glavna bb; mains 60-145KN; 5-11.30pm May-Oct) High above town on the main road to Mirca, this rustic, family-run tavern offers good traditional food, brilliant views and a warm welcome. Grab a seat on the terrace under the olive trees and tuck into grilled squid and fish, or (if you order ahead) meat, fish or octopus *peka* or spit-roasted lamb.

Punta CROATIAN €€

(021-631 507; www.vilapunta.com; Punta 1; mains 75-110KN; 8am-midnight Apr-Oct) This fabulously located restaurant has a beach terrace overlooking the sea. As well as Dalmatian favourites (fish, squid and the like), there's also plenty of grilled-meat dishes from continental Croatia. Portions are huge.

Beer Garden PUB

(095 55 67 225; www.facebook.com/beergardensupetar; Petra Jakšića 1; 8am-midnight May-Oct) Head to this stone courtyard, tucked away from the buzz of the coastal promenade, to listen to indie tunes, sample from a big selection of local and imported craft beer, and snack on food such as boar and venison burgers.

Information

Atlas Supetar (021-631 105; www.atlas-supetar.com; Porat 10; 8am-3pm Mon-Fri) Books excursions and private accommodation, rents cars and exchanges foreign cash.

Tourist Office (021-630 551; www.supetar.hr; Porat 1; 8am-10pm Jul & Aug, to 6pm May, Jun, Sep & Oct, to 3pm Mon-Fri Nov-Apr) Near the ferry terminal; has information on activities and sights, lengthy lists of private accommodation, and up-to-date bus and ferry timetables.

Bol

POP 1630

Gathered around a compact marina, the old town of Bol is an attractive place made up of small stone houses and winding streets dotted with pink and purple geraniums. While it's short on actual sights, many buildings are marked with interpretative panels explaining their cultural and historical significance.

The town's major attraction is Zlatni Rat, the seductive pebbly beach that stretches into the Adriatic and draws crowds of swimmers and windsurfers in summer. A long coastal promenade lined with pine trees, sculptures and gardens connects the beach with the old town. Bol is a buzzing place in summer – one of Croatia's favourites – and perennially packed with tourists.

Sights

★**Zlatni Rat** BEACH

Croatia's most photographed beach extends like a tongue into the sea for about 400m. Despite the hype and constant crowds, the 'golden cape' is a gorgeous place. Made up of smooth white pebbles, its elegant tip is constantly shuffled by the wind and waves. Pine trees provide shade and rocky cliffs rise sharply behind it, making the setting one of the loveliest in Dalmatia. There's a small nudist section immediately west of the cape.

OFF THE BEATEN TRACK

BLACA HERMITAGE & VIDOVA GORA

Two of Brač's most extraordinary sights lie nestled in the mountains between Nerežišća and the south coast. If you've got your own wheels, they can easily be combined into one trip; look for the signposted turn-off from the main road 4km southeast of Nerežišća.

The journey to **Blaca Hermitage** (Pustinje Blaca; ☎091 51 64 671; adult/child 40/10KN; ⏲9am-5pm Tue-Sun Jul & Aug, to 3pm Tue-Sun Sep-Jun) is a large part of the experience, involving a rough drive along a narrow, unsealed road and then a 2.5km walk down a steep path (good shoes are recommended).

Things can't have looked too different on the approach to this remote mountain cleft when a small group of priests and their servants, on the run from the Ottoman Turks on the mainland, arrived here in 1551. They initially took shelter in a cave (the walls of which are still visible in the kitchen) and built out from there. You can now take an informative 30-minute tour of the complex, which is full of original furniture, tools and rare manuscripts.

By the 18th century the hermitage ministered to three remote villages, with the priests operating a school from one of the rooms. The school closed in 1963 with the death of the hermitage's last resident priest, the extraordinary Fr Nikola Miličević, who was also a poet and an astronomer of international repute.

If you don't have your own transport, you can arrange a boat from Bol to the bottom of the valley and take a somewhat longer walk up. Otherwise, enquire at the tourist office (p277) about tours.

Vidova Gora is easily reached by a good sealed road through a pine forest, or you can sweat your way up from Bol on foot (two hours) or by mountain bike. At 778m, it's the highest point on the Adriatic islands and the view from the top is astounding. From here the entire island of Hvar is spread out like a map, with Vis and the mountains of the Pelješac Peninsula and Biokovo filling the horizon.

Stina WINERY

(☎021-306 220; www.stina-vino.hr; Riva bb; tastings 75-295KN; ⏲11am-7pm Apr, to 9pm May & Oct, to midnight Jun-Sep) This local winery operates a slick, modern tasting room in the First Dalmatian Wine Co-op warehouse (built in 1903), right on the waterfront. Call in at 5pm for a 30-minute tour and leisurely tasting of its top drops, including indigenous Croatian varietals *pošip, vugava, tribidrag* and *plavac mali*. Otherwise, just drop by for a glass of wine in elegant surrounds.

Branislav Dešković Art Gallery GALLERY

(Galerija umjetnina Branislav Dešković; ☎021-637 092; Trg Sv Petra 1; adult/child 15/5KN; ⏲9am-noon & 6-11pm Tue-Sun Jul & Aug, 9am-3pm Tue-Sat Sep-Jun) In a Renaissance-baroque town house right on the seafront, this excellent gallery displays 20th-century Croatian artworks. It's a prestigious collection for such a small town, including works by the likes of sculptor Ivan Meštrović and expressionist painter Ignjat Job. The gallery is named after Brač-born Dešković (1883–1939), a sculptor who became famous for his depictions of animals – look for his *Scratching Dog* in the courtyard.

Our-Lady-of-Carmel Church CHURCH

(Župna crkva Gospe od Karmela; Uz pjacu bb; ⏲hours vary) Bol's main parish church is a pretty baroque structure built between 1668 and 1788. The sturdy stone exterior is ornamented with a frilly pediment set with a clock, a finely sculpted rose window and a stone angel holding Veronica's veil over the door. Inside there are ornate baroque altars and a delicate marble pulpit.

Dominican Monastery MONASTERY

(Dominikanski samostan; Šetalište Anđelka Rabadana 4; ⏲hours vary) Positioned at the end of a pretty pebbly beach, this monastery was founded in 1475, but it's far from the oldest structure on the site; the little chapel by the beach was built in the 9th or 10th century on 6th-century foundations. Although it's often closed, the main church has a magnificent altar painting from the workshop of Venetian superstar Tintoretto. There's also a museum displaying rare manuscripts, coins, liturgical items and archaeological finds.

Activities

Bol is a windsurfing hot spot. Most of the action takes place at the beaches west of the town centre. Although the maestral (strong, steady westerly wind) blows from April to October, the best times to windsurf are at the end of May, the beginning of June, and at the end of July and beginning of August. The wind

OFF THE BEATEN TRACK

DRAGON'S CAVE

It takes about an hour to hike to **Dragon's Cave** (Zmajeva špilja; 091 51 49 787; per person 50KN, minimum 200KN), a strange cave from Murvica, 5km west of Bol, where an extremely unusual set of reliefs decorates the walls. Believed to have been sculpted by an imaginative 15th-century friar, the carvings include angels, animals and a gaping dragon in a blend of Christian and pagan symbols. The cave can only be accessed on a guided tour; either call Zoran Kojdić directly or ask at the tourist office (p277). You'll need decent walking shoes.

generally reaches its peak in the early afternoon and then dies down at the end of the day.

Alternatively, if you fancy a challenging **hike**, try the two-hour walk up to Vidova Gora or the four-hour track to Blaca Hermitage. There are also **mountain-biking** trails leading up. The local tourist office (p277) can give you advice and basic maps.

Big Blue Diving DIVING
(098 425 496; www.big-blue-diving.hr; Hotel Borak, Zlatnog rata 42; dives with/without equipment 330/220KN; 9am-7pm mid-Apr–Oct) Offers introductory courses and has daily trips for qualified divers to sites including reefs, caves and the remains of a submerged Roman villa with mosaics.

Nautic Center Bol BOATING
(098 361 651; www.nautic-center-bol.com; Zlatnog rata 9a; Jun-Oct) Rents boats from the beach in front of the Bretanide Hotel and offers parasailing, and excursions to Hvar, Korčula and Biševo's Blue Grotto.

Festivals & Events

Imena Culture Festival CULTURAL
(Jun) An annual event gathering writers, artists and musicians for three days of exhibits, readings, concerts and happenings.

Bol Summer CULTURAL
(Bolsko lito; Jun-Sep) The Bol Summer Festival is held from the middle of June through late September each year, with art exhibitions, food events, and dancers and musicians from around the country performing in churches and open spaces.

Destination Ultra Regatta MUSIC
(www.ultraeurope.com; Jul) The only things racing at this 'regatta' are the heart rates of the up-for-it electronic-dance-music fans. This beach party is held at Zlatni Rat (p274) on the Monday after the big Ultra Europe festival (p251) in Split.

Bolska Fjera CULTURAL
(5 Aug) Bol celebrates its patron saint, Our Lady of the Snows, with a procession of residents dressed in traditional costumes, as well as music, dancing and feasting on the streets.

Sleeping

A row of huge resort-style tourist complexes lines the promenade between the old town and Zlatni Rat beach. Most of them are former state hotels run by the Bluesun group (www.bluesunhotels.com); some of them offer all-inclusive (breakfast, lunch and dinner) or half-board (breakfast and dinner) packages. Smaller hotels, guesthouses and apartment complexes are scattered about the streets fanning out from the old town. Local travel agencies can arrange private accommodation.

Villa Ana APARTMENT €
(021-635 022; www.villa-ana-bol.com; David 55a; apt from €51; P) A warm welcome awaits at this friendly, family-run set of apartments on the eastern fringes of Bol. The simple but well-equipped units are spread between two blocks, with a small swimming pool and hot tub in between.

Pansion Ivan & Ivana GUESTHOUSE €
(021-635 262; www.pansionivanandivana.com; Novi 10; r/apt from €47/71; P) A couple with disconcertingly similar names live downstairs, renting out three spacious bedrooms above and a self-contained apartment with its own terrace out the back. Each upstairs bedroom has a private bathroom across the corridor.

Hostel Bol HOSTEL €€
(091 50 32 271; www.facebook.com/HostelBol; Podan glavica 1d; dm/r from 156/466KN; May-Sep; P) Even the dorms get their own bathrooms in this well-run, custom-built hostel, right in the heart of the old town. Some of the private rooms have wonderful sea views, and there's even a small indoor pool and a terrace with an outdoor kitchen.

Hotel Bol BOUTIQUE HOTEL €€€
(021-635 660; www.hotel-bol.com; Hrvatskih domobrana 19; r/ste from €137/215; P) There's an olive theme running through this contemporary boutique hotel – and we're not just talking about the colour scheme: potted trees grace the balconies and oversized fruit hang on the walls. It's a very slick set-up, with swish rooms, a sauna and a small gym.

Eating & Drinking

Ranč DALMATIAN €€

(021-635 635; Hrvatskih domobrana 6; mains 55-190KN; 6-11.30pm) The simple things stand out at Ranč, such as the delicious homemade bread and the traditional fish soup. Call ahead to preorder spit-roasted lamb or a *peka* filled with lamb, veal or octopus.

Taverna Riva DALMATIAN €€€

(021-635 236; www.tavernariva-bol.com; Frane Radića 5; mains 95-370KN; noon-3pm & 6-10pm Mar-Oct;) Bol's most upmarket and expensive restaurant serves fancy Frenchified versions of Dalmatian dishes, including a delicious fish soup, creamy seafood pastas, gnocchi with truffles, lobster and a selection of steaks. Try to leave room for the walnut semifreddo. It's located on a pretty terrace right above the *riva* (seafront promenade).

Varadero COCKTAIL BAR

(091 23 33 471; www.facebook.com/Varadero.Bol; Frane Radića 1; 8am-2am May-Nov;) At this open-air cocktail bar on the seafront you can sip coffee and fresh OJ under straw umbrellas during the day and return in the evening for fab cocktails, DJs and lounging on sofas and armchairs.

Marinero BAR

(021-635 579; www.facebook.com/marinerobol; Rudina 46; 8am-2am;) A popular gathering spot for Bol locals, with a leafy terrace on a square, an upmarket interior, football on the TV, Bon Jovi on the stereo, regular live music and a diverse merry-making crowd.

Information

TOURIST INFORMATION

Tourist Office (021-635 638; www.bol.hr; Porat Bolskih Pomoraca bb; 8.30am-10pm Jul & Aug, hours vary rest of year) Housed in a 15th-century Gothic town house, Bol's helpful tourist office is a good source of information on events, sights and activities.

TRAVEL AGENCIES

Bol has a swag of travel agencies, all of which rent cars and scooters (and sometimes bikes and boats), and book tours, private accommodation and transfers. Options include the following:

Adria Bol (021-635 966; www.adria-bol.hr; Bračka 10; 8am-9pm Jun-Sep, to 8pm Mon-Fri Oct-May)

Bol Tours (021-635 693; www.boltours.com; Vladimira Nazora 18; 10am-1pm & 5-8pm May-Sep)

More (021-642 050; www.more-bol.com; Vladimira Nazora 28; May-Sep)

HVAR ISLAND

POP 11,080

Long, lean Hvar is vaguely shaped like the profile of a holidaymaker reclining on a sun lounger, which is altogether appropriate for the sunniest spot in the country (2724 sunny hours each year) and its most luxurious beach destination.

Hvar Town offers swanky hotels, elegant restaurants and a general sense that, if you care about seeing and being seen, this is the place to be. Rubbing shoulders with the posh yachties are hundreds of young partygoers, dancing on tables at the town's legendary beach bars. The northern coastal towns of Stari Grad and Jelsa are far more subdued and low-key.

Hvar's interior hides abandoned ancient hamlets, craggy peaks, vineyards and the lavender fields that the island is famous for. This region is worth exploring on a day trip, as is the island's southern coast, which has some of Hvar's most beautiful and isolated coves.

Getting There & Away

Hvar has two main car-ferry ports: one near Stari Grad and the other at Sućuraj on the eastern tip of the island. **Jadrolinija** (021-765 048; www.jadrolinija.hr; Trajeknto pristanište 1) operates from both, on the following routes:

- **Split to Stari Grad** (passenger/car 47/310KN, two hours, at least three daily).
- **Drvenik to Sućuraj** (16/108KN, 35 minutes, at least six daily). Note: bus services to/from Sućuraj are extremely limited.
- In August some weekend ferries between Split and Ancona (Italy) stop in **Stari Grad**.

Jadrolinija also operates the following high-speed catamarans:

- Daily to **Jelsa** from Split (55KN, 1½ hours) and Bol on Brač (35KN, 20 minutes).
- Daily to **Hvar Town** from Split (55KN, one hour), Vela Luka on Korčula (40KN, 55 minutes) and Ubli on Lastovo (55KN, two hours).
- Tuesdays only, stopping in **Hvar Town** en route between Split (55KN, 1¼ hours) and Vis (40KN, 50 minutes).
- From May to September, up to five times a day between **Hvar Town** and Split (110KN, one hour).
- From June to September, daily to **Hvar Town** from Split (110KN, two hours), Bol (80KN, 50 minutes), Korčula (120KN, 1½ hours) and Dubrovnik (210KN, 3½ hours).

Kapetan Luka (p260) has the following catamaran services to **Hvar Town**:

- Daily from Split (90KN, one hour) and Korčula (110KN, 1¼ hours), twice daily June to September.
- From April to October, daily from Split, twice daily May to September.

➡ From May to mid-October, daily from Dubrovnik (210KN, three hours), Pomena on Mljet (140KN, 1¾ hours), Korčula (110KN, one hour), Milna on Brač (70KN, 30 minutes) and Split.

Getting Around

Buses meet most ferries that dock at the port near Stari Grad and head to Hvar Town (27KN, 20 minutes), central Stari Grad (13KN, 10 minutes) and Jelsa (33KN, 40 minutes). Buses also connect Hvar Town with Stari Grad (30KN, 30 minutes, nine daily) and Jelsa (33KN, 50 minutes, eight daily), and Stari Grad with Jelsa (30KN, 25 minutes, 13 daily). Services are less frequent in the low season.

Hvar Town

POP 4260

The island's hub and busiest destination, Hvar Town is estimated to draw around 20,000 people a day in the high season. It's amazing that they can all fit in the small bay town, where 13th-century walls surround beautifully ornamented Gothic palaces and traffic-free marble streets, but fit they do.

Visitors wander along the main square, explore the sights on the winding stone streets, swim at the numerous beaches or pop off to the Pakleni Islands to get into their birthday suits – but most of all they come to party. Hvar's reputation as Croatia's premier party town is well deserved.

There are several good restaurants, bars and hotels here, but thanks to the island's appeal to well-heeled guests, the prices can be seriously inflated. Don't be put off if you're on a more limited budget, though, as private accommodation and multiple hostels cater to a younger, more diverse crowd.

Sights

Hvar is such a small, easily navigable town that it only recently obtained street names, although nobody really uses them. The historic part of town, centred on Trg Sv Stjepana (St Stephen's Sq), is closed to traffic, which helps preserve the tranquillity of its tiny medieval lanes. A long seaside promenade winds along the coast in both directions, dotted with small rocky coves, hotels, bars and restaurants.

Fortica FORTRESS

(Tvrđava Španjola; Map p281; ☎021-742 608; Biskupa Jurja Dubokovica bb; adult/child 40/20KN; ⏲8am-9pm Apr-Oct) Looming high above the town and lit with a golden glow at night, this medieval castle occupies the site of an ancient Illyrian settlement dating from before 500 BCE. The views looking down over Hvar and the Pakleni Islands are magnificent, and well worth the trudge up through the old-town streets. Once you clear the town walls it's a gently sloping meander up the tree-shaded hillside to the fortress – or you can drive to the very top (100KN in a taxi).

The Byzantines built a citadel here in the 6th century, and the Venetians began construction of the present fortress in 1278. It was strengthened in 1551, which may have saved the lives of Hvar's population, who sheltered here in 1571 when the Turks sacked their town. The Austrians renovated it in the 19th century, adding barracks. Inside there's a collection of ancient amphorae recovered from the seabed, and a terrace cafe.

Trg Sv Stjepana SQUARE

(Map p281; St Stephen's Sq) Stretching from the harbour to the cathedral, this impressive rectangular square was formed by filling in an inlet that once reached out from the bay. At 4500 sq metres, it's one of the largest old squares in Dalmatia. Hvar Town's walled core, established in the 13th century, covers the slopes to the north. The town didn't spread south until the 15th century.

Look for the well, which is hidden among the umbrellas of the restaurants closest to the cathedral. It was built in 1520 and has a wrought-iron grille dating from 1780.

St Stephen's Cathedral CATHEDRAL

(Katedrala svetog Stjepana; Map p281; Trg Sv Stjepana bb; ⏲hours vary) Providing a grand backdrop to the main square, this baroque cathedral was built in the 16th and 17th centuries at the height of the Dalmatian Renaissance to replace a cathedral destroyed by the Turks. Parts of the older building include stone reliefs of saints near the rear of the nave and carved 15th-century choir stalls. The building's most distinctive feature is its tall, rectangular bell tower, which sprouts an additional window at each level, giving it an oddly top-heavy appearance.

Episcopal Museum MUSEUM

(Biskupski Muzej; Map p281; ☎021-743 126; Trg Sv Stjepana 26; 10KN; ⏲9am-noon & 5-7pm Mon-Fri, 9am-noon Sat Jun-Sep) Adjoining the cathedral, this treasury houses silver vessels, embroidered liturgical robes, numerous Madonnas, a 13th-century icon, an elaborately carved sarcophagus and, intriguingly, a stamp collection. A highlight is a 15th-century golden chalice that was a gift from the last king of Bosnia.

Hvar Town

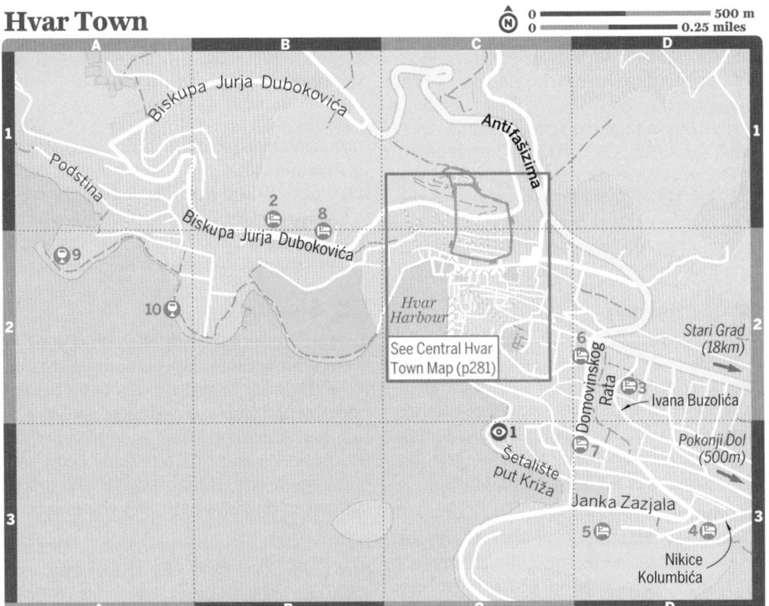

Hvar Town

Sights

1 Franciscan Monastery.........................C3

Sleeping

2 Apartments Ana Dujmović..................B1
3 Apartments Ivanović............................D2
4 Apartments Komazin............................D3
5 Kapa...D3
6 Luka's Lodge...D2
7 Villa Skansi...D3
8 Violeta Hvar..B2

Drinking & Nightlife

9 Falko...A2
10 Hula-Hula Hvar....................................A2

Arsenal HISTORIC BUILDING

(Map p281; Trg Sv Stjepana) Mentioned in Venetian documents as 'the most beautiful and the most useful building in the whole of Dalmatia', the Arsenal once served as a repair and refitting station for war galleons. Its present incarnation was built in 1611 to replace a building destroyed by the Ottomans. Although you can't enter via the large, graceful arch, you can wander up the stairs to the terrace to enjoy the views over Hvar's pretty harbour.

Upstairs is an atmospheric theatre decorated with frescos and baroque loggias. Opened in 1612, it's said to be the first theatre in Europe to have admitted plebeians and aristocrats alike. It remained a regional cultural centre throughout the centuries and plays were still staged here right up until 2008.

In 2016, the remains of a 1st-century Roman building were discovered beneath the floor. The complex has been closed for restoration for years now, but completed parts are occasionally used for special events.

Benedictine Convent CONVENT

(Muzej Hanibal Lucić; Map p281; ☎021-741 052; Kroz Grodu bb; 10KN; ⊙10am-2pm & 5-7pm Mon-Sat May-Oct) Playwright and poet Hanibal Lucić was born here in 1485, but this town house has been home to a community of Benedictine nuns since 1664. Over the centuries the nuns have perfected the art of lacemaking, painstakingly weaving together fibres derived from dried agave leaves. This tradition has now been recognised by Unesco on its Intangible Cultural Heritage of Humanity list. A small museum showcases the nuns' handiwork alongside a collection of paintings and liturgical paraphernalia.

Franciscan Monastery MONASTERY

(Franjevački samostan; Map p278; Šetaliste put Križa 15; museum 30KN; ⊙9am-3pm & 5-7pm Mon-Sat May-Oct) Overlooking a pretty cove, this 15th-century monastery has an elegant bell tower, built in the 16th century by a well-known family of stonemasons from Korčula. Its Renaissance cloister leads to a refectory containing lace, coins, nautical charts and valuable documents, such as an edition of Ptolemy's *Atlas* printed in 1524. Inside, your eye will immediately be drawn to *The Last Supper*, an 8m by 2.5m work by the Venetian Matteo Ingoli that dates from the end of the 16th century.

The adjoining church, dedicated to Our Lady of Mercy, contains more fine paintings, such as the three polyptychs created by Francesco da Santacroce in 1583, which represent the summit of this painter's work.

Activities

Hvar Adventure ADVENTURE SPORTS
(Map p281; ☎021-717 813; www.hvar-adventure.com; Jurja Matijevića 20; ⊙Apr-Sep) This agency is a one-stop shop for travellers, offering kayaking, sailing, cycling, climbing, hiking, skydiving, 4WD safaris, triathlon training and, by way of a breather, wine tours.

Swimming

Most of the swimming spots on the promenade heading west from the centre are tiny, rocky bays, some of which have been augmented with concrete sunbathing platforms. Wander along and take your pick, but check the prices before you settle on a lounger, as some are stupidly expensive (325KN per day at the historic Bonj Les Bains beach club, for instance).

If you don't mind a hike, there are larger pebbly beaches in the opposite direction. A 30-minute walk south and then east from the centre will bring you to the largest of them, **Pokonji Dol**. From here, a further 25 minutes via a scenic but rocky path will bring you to secluded **Mekićevica**.

Otherwise, grab a taxi boat to the Pakleni Islands or to one of the beaches further east along the coast such as **Milna** and **Zaraće**. **Dubovica** is particularly recommended: a tiny cluster of stone houses and a couple of cafe-bars set on a gorgeous grin of beach. The juxtaposition of the white pebbles alongside the brilliant blue-green water is dazzling. If you have your own wheels you can park on the highway, not far from where it turns inland towards the tunnel, and reach Dubovica via a rough stony path.

Hiking & Cycling

There are 120km of hiking trails and 96km of marked biking routes within easy reach of Hvar Town; ask at the tourist office (p284).

Festivals & Events

Hvar Summer Events MUSIC
(Hvarske ljetne priredbe; www.hvarsummerfestival.hr; ⊙Jun-Sep) A summer-long music and cultural festival, with concerts held on Trg Sv Stjepana and in the cloister of the Franciscan Monastery.

Ultra Beach MUSIC
(www.ultraeurope.com; tickets €99; ⊙Jul) Part of Destination Ultra, this massive pool party takes place at the Hotel Amfora in the week following the Ultra Europe (p251) electronic-dance-music festival in Split. The day wraps up with the Resistance party at Carpe Diem.

Sleeping

As Hvar is one of the Adriatic's most popular destinations, don't expect many bargains. Even the hostels nudge out of the budget category and into the midrange category in summer. Accommodation is extremely tight in July and August, despite there being several large hotels, various hostels and lots of family-run holiday-apartment complexes.

Kapa HOSTEL €
(Map p278; ☎091 92 41 068; karmentomasovic@gmail.com; Martina Vučetića 11; dm/r from €28/60; ⊙May-Oct; P✱📶) The advantages of Kapa's south-end-of-town location are the spacious surrounds and the brilliant sunset views. Dorms sleep four to six people, and there are private doubles with their own bathrooms.

Jagoda & Ante Bracanović House GUESTHOUSE €
(Map p281; ☎021-741 416; www.hvar-jagoda.com; Šime Buzolića Tome 21; r/apt 380/560KN) There are three tidy rooms and one apartment for rent in this large private house on a residential street with very quiet neighbours (it's next to the cemetery). Each room and apartment has its own fridge, balcony and bathroom, and there's a kitchen for guests to use.

Hvar Out Hostel HOSTEL €
(Map p281; ☎021-717 375; Kroz Burak 32; dm from 200KN; ⊙May–mid-Oct; ✱📶) Just steps from the harbour, this buzzy backpackers has well-equipped four- to 12-bed dorms with lockers, a small shared kitchen and a terrace on the top floor with views of the water. Book online through www.hostelworld.com.

Hostel Marinero HOSTEL €
(Map p281; ☎091 41 02 751; www.hostel-marinero-hr.book.direct; Sv Marka 7; dm €33-37; ⊙mid-May–Sep; ✱📶) Located in the heart of Hvar's party precinct, this hostel has six basic but clean dorms with big lockers. There's no shared kitchen, but the restaurant downstairs is a good place to mingle. Be ready for some noise, as the Kiva Bar is right next door.

Central Hvar Town

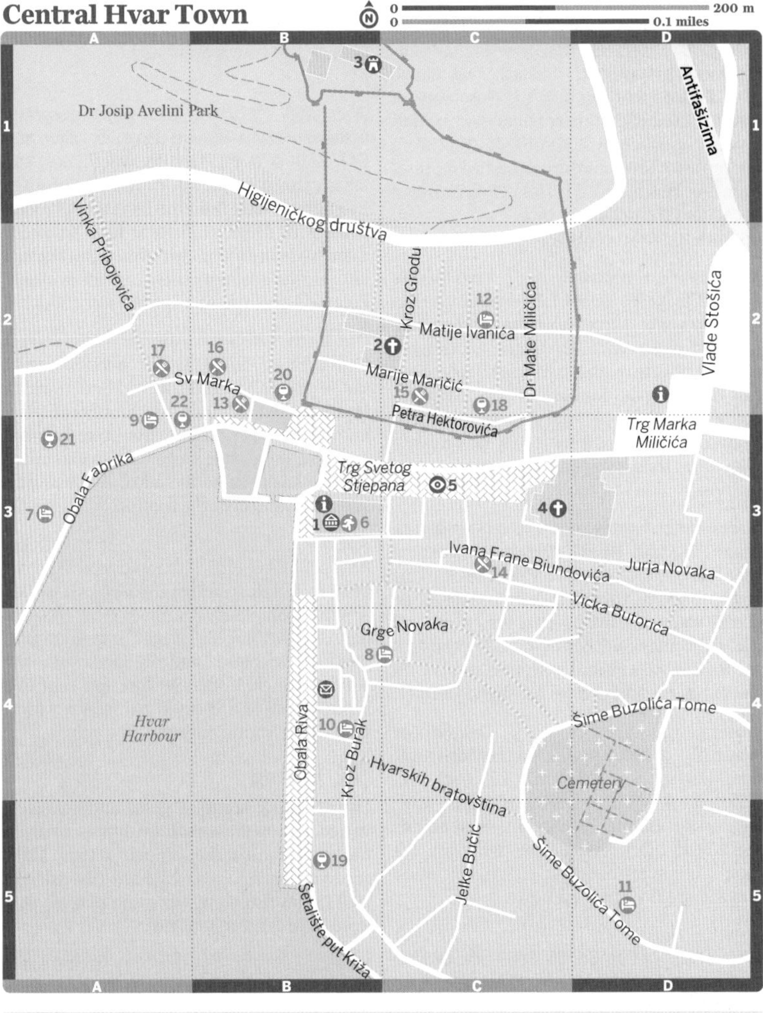

Central Hvar Town

Sights

1 Arsenal B3
2 Benedictine Convent C2
Episcopal Museum .... (see 4)
3 Fortica B1
4 St Stephen's Cathedral C3
5 Trg Sv Stjepana C3

Activities, Courses & Tours

6 Hvar Adventure B3

Sleeping

7 Adriana A3
8 Helvetia House C4
9 Hostel Marinero A3
10 Hvar Out Hostel B4
11 Jagoda & Ante Bracanović House D5
12 Old Town Hvar Apartments C2

Eating

13 Dalmatino B2
14 Fig C3
15 Grande Luna C2
16 Lola B2
17 Mizarola A2

Drinking & Nightlife

18 3 Pršuta C2
19 Carpe Diem B5
20 Central Park Club B2
21 Kiva Bar A3
22 Nautica A3

Apartments Ana Dujmović APARTMENT €€
(Map p278; 098 838 434; www.visit-hvar.com/apartments-ana-dujmovic; Biskupa Jurja Dubokovića 36; apt from €65; P) This brace of comfortable holiday apartments is set behind an olive grove, only a 10-minute walk from the centre of town and, crucially, five minutes from the beach and the Hula-Hula bar. Call ahead and the delightful owner will pick you up from the town centre.

Apartments Komazin APARTMENT €€
(Map p278; 091 60 19 712; www.croatia-hvar-apartments.com; Nikice Kolumbića 2; r/apt from €80/110;) With six bright apartments and two private rooms sharing a kitchen, bougainvillea-draped Komazin is an attractive option near the top of the private-apartment heap. What the apartments may lack in style they more than compensate for in size. And the host couldn't be more welcoming.

Apartments Ivanović APARTMENT €€
(Map p278; 021-741 332; www.ivanovic-hvar.com; Ivana Buzolića 9; r/apt from €87/90; P) This large, modern, three-storey house has one double room and five apartments for rent, all with balconies and bathrooms. The hostess speaks English well and welcomes guests with a drink on the large grapevine-shaded terrace.

Violeta Hvar APARTMENT €€
(Map p278; 099 33 44 779; ursa.lavanda@gmail.com; Biskupa Jurja Dubokovića 22; r/apt from €110/156;) White walls are offset with large-scale island images in this stylish apartment block just above the town. All rooms and apartments have large balconies, and the top floor has sea views.

Helvetia House HOSTEL €€
(Map p281; 091 34 55 556; rino.hajduk@gmail.com; Grge Novaka 6; dm/tw/apt from 190/460/760KN; Apr-Sep;) Run by a friendly islander from his family's old stone house, just behind the waterfront, this hostel has only a handful of dorms and private rooms. The highlight is the rooftop terrace where guests enjoy undisturbed views of the harbour and the Pakleni Islands.

Villa Skansi HOSTEL €€
(Map p278; 021-741 426; hostelvillaskansi1@gmail.com; Domovinskog rata 18; dm/r from 190/700KN; Jun-Sep; @) Hvar's biggest hostel has brightly coloured dorms, fancy bathrooms, a great terrace with sea views, a bar, a book exchange and a laundry service, and rents scooters and boats. The pleasant but overpriced private rooms are in a separate block next door, surrounded by citrus trees, pomegranates and bougainvillea. There are barbecues or pub crawls every night.

Luka's Lodge HOSTEL €€
(Map p278; 021-742 118; www.lukalodgehvar.hostel.com; Šime Buzolića Tome 75; dm/r from €43/69; P@) Friendly owner Luka really takes care of his guests at this cosy hostel, a five-minute walk from the harbour. All rooms come with fridges and some have balconies. There's a living room, two terraces, an outdoor kitchen and a laundry service. If he's available, Luka will pick you up from the ferry dock.

Old Town Hvar Apartments APARTMENT €€€
(Map p281; 097 78 03 700; ivanaukic@net.hr; Matije Ivanića 10; apt €150;) Hidden within Hvar's walled old town, this family-run place has three swish apartments. Apartments 1 and 2 share a 1st-floor terrace, while apartment 3 has a large one all of its own, with sublime views over the rooftops.

Adriana HOTEL €€€
(Map p281; 021-750 200; www.suncanihvar.com; Obala Fabrika 28; r/ste from €380/643; Apr-Dec;) Completely refurbished in 2018, this deluxe spa hotel has bright, swanky rooms overlooking the sea and the medieval town. Facilities include the Sensori spa centre, a rooftop pool and cocktail bar, and a variety of in-house eating options.

Eating

Hvar's eating scene is good and relatively varied, although, as with the hotels, many of the restaurants target affluent diners. Make sure you try *hvarska gregada* (the island's traditional fish stew); in some places you'll need to order it in advance.

Lola STREET FOOD €€
(Map p281; Sv Marak 10; mains 59-119KN; 10am-2pm & 6pm-2am;) Hit this buzzing hole-in-the-wall place for top-notch cocktails and a globetrotting array of tasty snacks: everything from empanadas and burgers to pulled-pork steam buns and lamb curry. Grab a table on the lane and soak up the scene.

Mizarola PIZZA €€
(Map p281; 098 799 978; www.facebook.com/mizarolahvar; Vinka Pribojevića 2; mains 55-180KN; noon-midnight;) Mizarola has a loyal local following, partly because it's one of the only places to open in the low season, but mainly because of its crowd-pleasing Neapolitan-style pizza. It serves other things (pasta, gnocchi, risotto, grilled meat, fish), but nothing rivals the main attraction. Head up to the roof terrace and tuck in.

Fig CAFE €€

(Map p281; ☎099 26 79 890; www.figcafebar.com; Ivana Frane Biundovića 3; mains 65-100KN; ⏱10am-10pm May-Oct; 📶✍) This great little place serves up delicious stuffed flatbreads (fig and ricotta, pear and gorgonzola, brie and prosciutto), vegetarian curries, and a highly recommended Hvar breakfast: spiced eggs. There are even some vegan options – a rarity in these parts.

Dalmatino DALMATIAN €€€

(Map p281; ☎091 52 93 121; www.dalmatino-hvar.com; Sv Marak 1; mains 80-265KN; ⏱11am-midnight Mon-Sat Apr-Nov; 📶) Calling itself a 'steak and fish house', this place is always popular – due, in part, to the handsome waiters and the free-flowing *rakija* (grappa). Thankfully, the food is also excellent; try the *gregada* (fish fillet served on potatoes with a thick, broth-like sauce).

Grande Luna DALMATIAN €€€

(Map p281; ☎021-741 400; www.grandeluna.hr; Petra Hektorovića 1; mains 75-180KN; ⏱11am-2.30pm & 5-10.30pm; 📶) Grande Luna's rooftop terrace doesn't offer views per se, unless you count the blue of the Dalmatian sky offset against the stone of the surrounding buildings. It's an atmospheric setting in which to try traditional dishes, such as *hvarska gregada* (fish stew) and *crni rižoto* (squid-ink risotto). The service is excellent, too.

Drinking & Nightlife

Hvar has some of the best nightlife on the Adriatic coast, mostly centred on the harbour. People come here to party hard, so expect plenty of action come nightfall. Things kick off early, partly due to the popularity of the Hula-Hula beach bar in the hours leading up to sunset.

Hula-Hula Hvar BAR

(Map p278; ☎095 91 11 871; www.hulahulahvar.com; Šetalište Antuna Tomislava Petrića 10; ⏱9am-11pm Apr-Oct) *The* spot to catch the sunset to the sound of techno and house music, Hula-Hula is known for its après-beach party (4pm to 9pm), where all of young, trendy Hvar seems to descend for sundowner cocktails. Dancing on tables is pretty much compulsory.

Kiva Bar BAR

(Map p281; ☎091 51 22 343; www.facebook.com/kivabar.hvar; Obala Fabrika 10; ⏱9pm-2am Apr-Dec) A happening place in an alleyway just off the waterfront, Kiva is packed to the rafters most nights, with patrons spilling out and filling up the lane. DJs spin a popular mix of old-school dance, pop and hip-hop classics to an up-for-it crowd.

3 Pršuta WINE BAR

(Map p281; Petra Hektorovića 5; ⏱6pm-2am May-Oct) Hvar's best wine bar is an unpretentious little place lurking in an alley behind the main square. Sink into the couch by the bar and feel as if you're in a local's living room while sampling some of the best island wines, paired with Dalmatian snacks.

Nautica BAR

(Map p281; www.nautica-bar.com; Obala Fabrika 8; ⏱5pm-2am) It starts slowly, with a mixed crowd enjoying cocktails by the water, but once Hula-Hula winds down and Kiva packs out, Nautica comes into its own as an obligatory stop on Hvar's night-crawl circuit. DJs spin everything from techno to hip hop to Euro-disco.

Carpe Diem COCKTAIL BAR

(Map p281; ☎021-742 369; www.carpe-diem-hvar.com; Obala Riva bb; ⏱9am-2am mid-May–Sep) Look no further – you have arrived at the mother of Croatia's glitzy coastal bars. From a groggy breakfast to (pricey) late-night cocktails, there's no time of day when this swanky place is dull. The house music spun by resident DJs is smooth, the drinks well mixed, and the crowd well heeled.

Central Park Club BAR

(Map p281; ☎021-718 337; www.klubparkhvar.com; Bankete bb; ⏱7am-2am Apr-Oct, to 11pm Nov-Mar) Set behind the cluster of phoenix palms on the waterfront, this large terrace bar is Hvar's main locale for live music. In summer there's something on every night, from jazz to soul, old-time rock and roll and funk. The cocktails are good, too.

Falko BAR

(Map p278; ☎095 23 35 296; www.facebook.com/falkohvar; Šetalište Tonija Petrića 22; ⏱10am-8pm mid-May–mid-Sep; 📶) Walk almost to the end of the seaside promenade and you'll reach this adorable hideaway among the pines, just above the beach. It's an unpretentious alternative to the flashy spots closer to town, with a low-key, beach-shack vibe, hammocks and a chilled-out crowd. Service can be slow.

Shopping

Lavender, lavender and more lavender is sold in bottles, flasks, sachets and little fragrant bags. Depending on the time of year, there will be anywhere from one to 50 stalls along the harbour selling the substance, its aroma saturating the air. Various herbal oils, potions, skin creams and salves are also hawked.

Information

Emergency Clinic (Dom Zdravlja; 021-717 099; Biskupa Jurja Dubokovića 3) About 400m west of the town centre.

Fontana Tours (021-742 133; www.happyhvar.com; Obala Riva 18) Finds private accommodation, runs island tours, books taxi boats, and rents cars, scooters and bicycles.

Pelegrini Tours (021-742 743; www.pelegrini-hvar.hr; Obala Riva 20) Private accommodation, Kapetan Luka ferry tickets, excursions (including popular daily trips to the Pakleni Islands and Vis' Blue and Green Caves), and bike, scooter, car and boat rental. It also offers island tours (around €60, including wine tasting) and walking tours with licensed guides (from 420KN).

Tourist Office (Map p281; 021-741 059; www.tzhvar.hr; Trg Sv Stjepana 42; 8am-10pm Jul & Aug, 8am-8pm Mon-Sat, 8am-1pm & 4-8pm Sun Jun & Sep, 8am-2pm Mon-Fri, to noon Sat Oct-May) In the Arsenal building, right on Trg Sv Stjepana.

Tourist Office Information Point (Map p281; 021-718 109; Trg Marka Miličića 9; 8am-9pm Mon-Sat, 9am-1pm Sun Jun-Sep) In the bus station; a summertime annexe of the main tourist office.

Pakleni Islands

Most visitors to Hvar Town visit the crystal-clear waters, hidden beaches and deserted lagoons of the Pakleni Islands (Pakleni otoci), a gorgeous chain of wooded isles that stretches out immediately in front of the town. Although the name is often translated as 'Hell's Islands', it's thought to derive from *paklina*, a pine resin that was once harvested here to waterproof boats.

The closest of the islands to Hvar is clothing-optional Jerolim. Next up is Marinkovac, best known for the raucous beach club on Stipanska bay. At the opposite end of Marinkovac are pretty Ždrilca and lagoon-like Mlini. Both have seasonal restaurants and a handful of stone cottages.

The largest of the islands by far is Sveti Klement, which supports three villages in its 5 sq km. Palmižana is set on a beautiful horseshoe bay, with a busy marina, accommodation, restaurants and a tiny sandy beach.

Palmižana Meneghello BUNGALOW €€€
(021-717 270; www.palmizana.hr; Palmižana, Sveti Klement; r/apt from €160/180;) The artsy Meneghello family runs this beautiful boutique complex of villas and bungalows, scattered among lush tropical gardens. The complex features two restaurants and an art gallery, and often hosts music recitals.

Zori EUROPEAN €€€
(091 32 22 227; www.zori.hr; Palmižana 19, Palmižana, Sveti Klement; mains 150-380KN; 11.30am-11pm Apr-Oct) Catering to the well-heeled yachties moored in Palmižana bay, this upmarket restaurant serves contemporary European cuisine, including Dalmatian specialities such as *pašticada*, *gregada* and a very pretty octopus salad. The slick service and gorgeous setting, on a terrace shaded by palm trees, will help to distract you from the prices.

Carpe Diem Beach BAR, CLUB
(099 49 68 534; www.carpe-diem-hvar.com; Stipanska, Marinkovac; 10am-7pm & 11pm-5am Jun–mid-Sep) This place offers quite the heady Med-glam experience, with family-friendly beach fun during the day and all-night parties after dark. Boat transfers depart outside the Carpe Diem in Hvar Town; admission varies depending on the night.

Getting There & Away

Taxi boats leave regularly for the islands, departing from in front of the Arsenal in Hvar Town. Expect to pay around 50KN to 60KN for the nearer islands and about 70KN to 80KN for Palmižana (on Sveti Klement).

Alternatively, you can hire a boat and skipper for a two-hour cruise around the nearer islands for about 550KN.

Stari Grad

POP 2790

Stari Grad, on Hvar's north coast, is a quieter, more cultured and altogether more sober affair than Hvar Town, its stylish and sybaritic sister. If you're not after pulsating nightlife and thousands of people crushing each other along the streets in the high season, head here and enjoy Hvar at a more leisurely pace. That said, you can easily see all of the little town's sights in half a day.

The name Stari Grad means 'Old Town', a reference to the fact that it was founded in 384 BCE by the ancient Greeks, who called it Pharos. The surrounding fields are still divided into parcels of land demarcated in antiquity.

The town sits at the end of a deep inlet, with the narrow lanes of the old quarter spreading out on its southern side. The waterfront promenade continues along the northern bank to a small beach.

WORTH A TRIP

VRBOSKA

A single canal and some old stone bridges have earned sweet little Vrboska (www.vrboska.info) the overblown epithet of 'the Venice of Croatia'. It's nothing like Venice – but it's well worth visiting for its enigmatic, crumbling buildings and its curvy harbour, which wiggles its tail into the aforementioned canal.

Up on the hill on the south side of town is a pair of interesting churches. Fifteenth-century **St Lawrence's** (Crkva sv Lovre; Vrboska bb; ⌚hours vary) is crammed with valuable art, including what is believed to be a Veronese triptych above the high altar. At the top of the hill is the highly unusual **Our-Lady-of-Mercy Church-Fortress** (Crkva-tvrđava sv Marije; Vrboska bb; ⌚hours vary). From the outside it's very much a castle, with only the cross and three bells at the top marking it out as a church. It was fortified in 1575 after the town was sacked by the Ottomans four years earlier.

Finish your trip with a wine tasting and snacks at **Vina Carić** (☎098 16 06 276; www.vinohvar.hr; Vrboska 211, Vrboska; ⌚noon-7pm Mon-Sat, 4-7pm Sun May-Oct), on the banks of the canal, by the second bridge.

Tvrdalj GARDENS
(☎021-765 068; Trg Tvrdalj Petra Hektorovića 11; 15KN; ⌚10am-1pm & 5-9pm May-Oct) This fortified house was built by aristocrat and writer Petar Hektorović (1487–1572) in the 16th century. At its heart is a lovely, lush Renaissance garden, set around the green waters of a pond stocked with mullet, as it was in Hektorović's day. It's a reflection of his favourite pastime, as recorded in his most famous poetic work, *Fishing and Fishermen's Chat* (1555).

Quotes from the writer's work are inscribed on the walls in Latin and Croatian. The one above the toilet alcove reads: 'Know what you are and then you can be proud'. You'll find it tucked away in a corner of the entry hall, which is the only part of the interior of the building that's open to the public.

Dominican Monastery of St Peter the Martyr MONASTERY
(Dominikanski samostan sv Petra Mučenika; ☎021-765 442; Kod Sv Petra 3; 20KN; ⌚9.30am-12.30pm & 4-6.30pm May-Oct) Founded in 1482, this monastery was damaged by the Turks in 1571 and later fortified with a tower. Palms, orange trees, hydrangeas and lavender bloom in the cloister garden, and there's an interesting little museum packed with fossils, ancient Greek inscriptions, Greek and Roman coins, and beautiful religious icons dating from the 16th to 18th centuries. The highlight, however, is Tintoretto's engrossing 16th-century painting, *Lamentation of Christ*.

St Stephen's Church CHURCH
(Crkva sv Stjepana; Trg Sv Stjepana; ⌚hours vary) Built in 1605, this large church has a baroque facade and water-damaged paintwork inside in shades of pale green, blue and grey. Note the faux-marble paint effect in the sanctuary, the Venetian high altar from 1702 and the over-the-top rococo organ loft. The freestanding bell tower was constructed in 1753, partly from stones pillaged from the ancient Greek town walls. Look out for a Roman stone relief of Eros facing the street, to the right of the church.

Apolon BOUTIQUE HOTEL **€€€**
(☎021-778 320; www.apolon.hr; Šetalište Don Šime Ljubića 7; r/ste from €169/249; ⌚May-Oct; P ❄ 📶) Named after the terracotta statue of Apollo on the roof, this grand old building was built in 1887 for the local luminary who's buried in the lavish mausoleum next door. The building's now an elegant boutique hotel, with antique-style furniture and a claw-foot bath-tub in the spacious suite. The restaurant is worth checking out, even if you're not staying here.

Jurin Podrum DALMATIAN **€€**
(☎091 75 57 382; Duolnjo kola 9; mains 60-90KN; ⌚5-11pm Mon-Sat) 'George's Cellar' has bucketloads of atmosphere, courtesy of old stone walls, woven wicker lamps and a couple of tables outside in the lane. The menu includes pasta, gnocchi, risotto and grilled fish, along with veal liver and chicken dishes.

ℹ Information

Tourist Office (☎021-765 763; www.stari-grad.eu; Obala dr Franje Tuđmana 1; ⌚8am-8pm Jun-Sep, 8am-2pm Mon-Fri Oct-May) Distributes a good local map.

ℹ Getting There & Away

➡ Although most Jadrolinija (p277) ferries connecting the island to the mainland list Stari Grad as their port of call, the town is actually a couple of kilometres east of the island's main car-ferry terminal.

➡ The bus station (no left-luggage office) is at the foot of the bay. Buses head to/from the ferry (13KN, 10 minutes, seven daily), Hvar Town (30KN, 30 minutes, nine daily) and Jelsa (30KN, 25 minutes, 13 daily).

Jelsa

POP 3590

The small harbour town of Jelsa is a tidy little place surrounded by thick pine forests and tall poplars. While it lacks the Renaissance buildings of Hvar Town, its intimate streets, squares and parks are pleasant, and there are some good swimming spots nearby. Basing yourself here isn't recommended, but it's a nice spot for a short visit.

Church of the Assumption CHURCH
(Trg Križonoše; ⌚hours vary) Jelsa's parish church has an elegant baroque facade and a Renaissance bell tower, while inside there are ceiling frescos and an elaborate marble high altar. It's been tinkered with over the centuries, but a large part of the structure dates from 1535.

Vina Tomić WINERY
(☎021-768 160; www.bastijana.hr; Jelsa 874a; ⌚9am-8pm Jun-Aug, 7am-3pm Mon-Fri Sep-May) A local winery offering tastings in an atmospheric stone cellar above Mina bay.

Flying Pig BURGERS €
(☎095 55 41 179; www.facebook.com/flyingpigjelsa; Obala Ćire Gamulina bb; burgers 60-80KN; ⌚noon-midnight Jun-Sep) For the rest of the year they're busy with their bistro, Beštija, in Zagreb, but come summer this hip young crew heads to Jelsa to celebrate the simple things in life: juicy gourmet burgers and craft beer.

Konoba Nono DALMATIAN €€
(☎021-761 933; Braće Batoš bb; mains 70-150KN; ⌚6pm-midnight Apr-Oct) This charming family-run tavern serves traditional island fare.

FOLLOWING THE CROSS

Included on Unesco's Intangible Cultural Heritage of Humanity list, this 500-year-old **procession** (Za Križen; ⌚Mar or Apr) simultaneously starts from Jelsa and five surrounding towns and villages at 10pm on the night of Holy Thursday. Participants follow a cross bearer and walk through the night in a 25km, eight-hour circuit, stopping in each parish church along the way.

ℹ Information

Tourist Office (☎021-761 017; www.tzjelsa.hr; Strossmayerovo šetalište bb; ⌚8am-10pm Mon-Sat, 10am-noon & 7-9pm Sun Jul & Aug, 8am-1pm & 5.30-8pm Mon-Sat, 9.30am-noon Sun May, Jun, Sep & Oct, 8am-noon Mon-Fri Nov-Apr) Information on sights, activities, private accommodation and hotels.

VIS ISLAND

POP 3620

Of all the inhabited Croatian islands, Vis is the furthest from the coast and the most enigmatic. It spent much of its recent history serving as a Yugoslav military base, cut off from foreign visitors from the 1950s right up until 1989. This isolation preserved the island from development and drove much of the population to move elsewhere in search of work, leaving it underpopulated for many years.

As has happened with impoverished islands across the Mediterranean, Vis' lack of development has become its drawcard as a tourist destination. International and local travellers alike now flock to Vis, seeking authenticity, nature, gourmet delights and peace and quiet. The island also gets its fair share of ABBA pilgrims since *Mamma Mia! Here We Go Again* was filmed on the island in 2017.

Vis has its own distinct grape, *vugava*, a white varietal that's been cultivated here since ancient times.

There are beaches scattered around Vis Town and Komiža, however, some of the island's best are a boat or scooter ride away. The most unspoilt beaches can be found on the southern and eastern sides of the island. Several require some steep downhill walking, so wear comfortable shoes:

Stiniva Tiny Stiniva, in Vis' most perfect cove, is lined with large, smooth pebbles, which blaze white against the blue sea.

Srebrna Backed by a nature reserve, with large white pebbles and clear water.

Milna & Zaglav Sandy Milna has strikingly blue water and small islands forming an idyllic backdrop. Neighbouring Zaglav, also sandy, is even prettier and quieter.

History

Inhabited first in neolithic times, Vis Island was settled by the ancient Illyrians, who brought the Iron Age to Vis in the 1st millennium BCE. In 390 BC a Greek colony was

WORTH A TRIP

RURAL EATS

Vis' gastronomic offering isn't limited to its main towns. The interior of the island and its isolated coves are becoming a foodie's dream. In recent years a number of rural households have started offering local homemade food worth travelling for.

Konoba Stončica (021-784 7188; www.konoba-stoncica.com; Stončica 11; mains 60-140KN; 1-11pm May-Oct) Set on a pretty sandy beach, this relaxed eatery serves excellent grilled squid and fish under the shade of palms, pines and a wooden pergola. Order a side of smashed potatoes with olive oil and garlic – it's a Vis speciality.

Roki's (098 303 483; www.rokis.hr; Plisko Polje 17, Plisko Polje; peka per person 150KN; 7pm-midnight May-Oct) Set amid fields 8km south of Vis Town, this winery restaurant is one of the very best places to try food cooked under a traditional *peka* (metal dome). Four hours' notice is required, so call ahead to order your choice of lamb, veal, octopus or fish. The restaurant also provides free transport for groups of four or more.

formed on the island, known then as Issa, from which the Greek ruler Dionysius the Elder controlled other Adriatic possessions. The island eventually became a powerful city-state and established its own colonies on Korčula and at Trogir and Stobreč. Allying itself with Rome during the Illyrian wars, the island nonetheless lost its autonomy and became part of the Roman Empire in 47 BCE.

By the 10th century Vis had been settled by Slavic tribes, and it was sold to Venice (who called it Lissa) along with other Dalmatian towns in 1420. Fleeing Dalmatian pirates, the population moved inland from the coast.

With the fall of the Venetian empire in 1797, the island fell under the control of Austria, France, the UK, Austria again, Italy, the first Yugoslavia, and then Italy during WWII, as the great powers fought for control of this strategic Adriatic outpost. During the war Vis was an important military base for Josip Broz Tito's Partisans. Tito established his supreme headquarters in a cave on Hum mountain, from where he coordinated military and diplomatic actions with Allied forces.

Getting There & Around

- Two to three large **Jadrolinija** (021-711 032; www.jadrolinija.hr; Šetalište stare Isse 2, Luka) car ferries head between Vis Town and Split daily (per person/car 54/340KN, 2¼ hours).
- There's also a catamaran on this route (55KN, 1½ to 2½ hours, daily), which stops off at Hvar Town (40KN, 50 minutes) on Tuesday and Milna (Brač; 55KN, 55 minutes) on Wednesday.
- The Vis ticket office opens 90 minutes before each boat departs.
- Buses between Komiža and Vis Town (25KN) are timed around the ferry schedule.

Vis Town

POP 1940

The ancient town of Vis sits at the foot of a wide, horseshoe-shaped bay. Ferry arrivals give spurts of activity to an otherwise-peaceful collection of coastal promenades, crumbling 17th-century town houses and narrow lanes twisting gently uphill from the seafront.

The town is a merger of two settlements: 19th-century Luka (meaning 'port'), where the ferry docks, and medieval Kut, on the opposite curve of the horseshoe. A harbourside promenade runs scenically between the two. Vis' long and complicated history has bequeathed it the remains of a Greek cemetery, Roman baths and an English fortress.

Sights

Small beaches line the promenade, but the busiest town beach lies north of the harbour in front of Hotel Issa. Beyond it are nudist coves and a series of wild swimming spots. On the other side, past Kut and the British Naval Cemetery, is the pretty pebble beach of **Grandovac**, which has a beach bar (look out for occasional late-night parties), a small stretch of pebbles and a string of rocky beaches on either side.

Issa Archaeological Museum MUSEUM
(Arheološkog muzeja; Šetalište viški boj 12, Kut; adult/child 20/10KN; 9am-1pm & 5-9pm Mon-Sat Jun-Sep) Housed in a 19th-century Austrian fortress, this small museum has the largest collection of Hellenistic artefacts in Croatia, including ancient Greek pottery, jewellery and sculpture. The highlight is an exquisite 4th-century-BCE bronze head of the goddess Artemis. A room on the other side of the courtyard displays relics from shipwrecks.

Activities

Diving is excellent in the waters around Vis. Fish are plentiful and there are various shipwrecks, an amphorae field and a WWII plane to explore. However, much of the best diving is of a technical nature, requiring a degree of proficiency.

Tours

Most of the travel agencies in town offer a range of tours, which are more or less identical. The most interesting is the tour of the island's top-secret military sights, abandoned by the Yugoslav National Army in 1992. The trip takes in rocket shelters, bunkers, weapon-storage spaces, submarine 'parking lots', Tito's Cave (which housed Partisan leader Josip Broz Tito during WWII) and nuclear shelters that served as communication headquarters for Yugoslavia's secret service. These sites occupy some of the island's most beautiful spots.

Other tour options include caving, trekking, food and wine tasting, and boat trips to outer islands that take in the Blue Cave (p289), the **Green Cave** (Zelena špilja; adult/child Jul & Aug 70/35KN, May, Jun, Sep & Oct 50/25KN) and remote beaches.

Sleeping & Eating

Vis has some wonderful restaurants, scattered around both Luka and Kut. There are a few local specialities to try, including *viška pogača* (flatbread filled with salted fish and onions) and *viški hib* (dried grated figs mixed with aromatic herbs).

Apartments Kuljiš APARTMENT €€
(☎098 460 937; vkuljis@inet.hr; Petra Svačića 41, Kut; apt from €82; P❄📶) With welcoming hosts and a great location just a short walk from the centre of Kut, these four comfortable apartments are a smart choice. All have kitchenettes and either balconies or terraces.

Villa Vis B&B €€€
(☎098 94 87 490; www.villaviscroatia.com; Jakšina 11, Kut; r 995KN; ⏰Jun-Oct; ❄📶) This stylish option has four colour-themed rooms inside a traditional town house with all-modern interiors. The location is great: close to restaurants and bars, and within walking distance of the beach.

Hotel San Giorgio HOTEL €€€
(☎021-607 630; www.hotelsangiorgiovis.com; Petra Hektorovića 2, Kut; s/d from €151/168; ⏰May-Sep; ❄📶) Filled with interesting art, this gorgeous Italian-owned hotel has 10 swish, colourful rooms and suites in two buildings. All have wooden floors, great beds and all sorts of upscale perks. Best of all is room 1, with a large sea-facing terrace and a hot tub.

★ **Pojoda** DALMATIAN, SEAFOOD €€
(☎021-711 575; Don Cvjetka Marasovića 10, Kut; mains 50-115KN; ⏰noon-1am Mar-Oct, 6-10pm Nov-Feb; 📶) Locals in the know rave about this seafood restaurant, its leafy courtyard dotted with bamboo, orange and lemon trees. For a winter warm-up, try the *pojorski bronzinić,* a tasty peasant stew with squid, lentils and barley. In spring and summer the signature dish is *orbiko,* with orzo, peas and shrimp.

Lola MEDITERRANEAN €€€
(☎095 56 33 247; www.lolavisisland.com; Matije Gupca 12, Luka; mains 140-170KN; ⏰6pm-midnight May-Oct) Marked by an old-time bicycle on its wall, Lola is tucked away into a beautiful garden courtyard with old stone walls and a Meštrović fountain. The Croatian chef and his Spanish wife present a short but highly creative menu with a lot of influence from Spain. The wine list and service are excellent as well.

Drinking & Nightlife

Fort George BAR
(☎091 26 56 041; www.fortgeorgecroatia.com; Utvrda Sv Juraj bb; ⏰noon-1am May-Oct) The service can be offhand, but there's no better place to watch the sunset on a summer night than the terrace of this old fort, built by the British in 1811 (see if you can spot the stone Union Jack above the entrance).

Lambik BAR
(☎095 22 24 221; www.facebook.com/LambikBarBistro; Pod Ložu 2, Kut; ⏰8am-2am Jun-Oct) Kut's best bar has alfresco seating both on the square and in a lovely vine-covered stone passageway under the colonnade of a 16th-century house. Acoustic bands and singers perform on some nights.

Information

Ionios Travel Agency (☎021-711 532; www.facebook.com/ionios.vis; Sv Jurja 37, Luka; ⏰Apr-Oct; 📶) Finds private accommodation; rents cars, bikes and scooters; and runs excursions.In the high season (May to September), there's a second branch at Pod Ložu 5, Kut.

Navigator (☎021-717 786; www.navigator.hr; Šetalište stare Isse 1, Luka; ⏰8am-2pm & 4.30-7.30pm daily) Books tours and diving trips, and rents cars, scooters and boats.

Tourist Office (☎021-717 017; www.tz-vis.hr; Šetalište stare Isse 5; ⏰8am-2pm & 5-8pm Jun-Sep, 8am-2pm Mon-Fri Oct-May) Near the Jadrolinija ferry dock.

BLUE MAGIC

Located on the island of Biševo, off Vis' southwestern tip, **Blue Cave** (Modra špilja; adult/child Sep-Jun 70/35KN, Jul & Aug 100/50KN) is one of the region's most famous natural sights. It's at its best between 11am and noon, when the sun's rays pass through an underwater opening, bathing the interior in an unearthly blue light. Beneath the translucent water, rocks glimmer in silver and pink to a depth of 16m. To get here, the easiest, quickest and best option is to take a tour from Komiža.

A huge increase in visitor numbers over recent years has made the experience much less pleasant, and it's no longer possible for boats to linger within the cave or for people to jump out for a swim. Even with the hefty admission charge, the line of boats waiting to get in can be discouragingly long – and many tours don't even attempt to visit when the blue glow is at its peak. Crowding isn't a problem in winter, but it's difficult to find a boat and the water can be too choppy to enter the cave due to the prevailing *jugo* (southern wind).

In summer tours head to the cave from all over Vis, the surrounding islands and as far away as Split. From Komiža, the trips take between an hour and 90 minutes, depending on the waiting time to enter the cave. Expect to pay around 100KN (or 140KN including a lunch stop) for a trip on a rigid-inflatable speedboat, in addition to the admission charge.

Komiža

POP 1530

Set on a picturesque bay at the foot of Hum mountain, this small town has diehard fans among Croats, who swear by its somewhat-bohemian, rough-around-the-edges ambience. Narrow backstreets lined with 17th- and 18th-century stone town houses twist uphill from the port, which has been used by fisherfolk since at least the 12th century.

A friendly rivalry exists between Komiža and Vis Town. The latter was historically associated with the nobility, while Komiža is proud of its working-class fishing heritage and pirate tales.

Komiža has its own little sand-and-pebble beaches, but most visitors head here to catch a boat to the Blue Caveon the nearby island of Biševo. Boat trips can be arranged through any of the local travel agencies, or simply by walking along the harbour.

At the southern end of the harbour is a blocky Renaissance citadel, built in 1585, known as the **Kaštel** (Riva Sv Mikule). The fortresslike church that you'll pass on the eastern approach to the town dates from the 17th century and is attached to a **Benedictine Monastery** (Benediktinaca bb).

Komiža's most popular **beach** is at the northern end of town, right below the Hotel Biševo. It's fringed with pine trees and backed by the triple-naved Gospa Gusarica Church.

Alter Natura (☎021-717 239; www.alter-natura.hr; Hrvatskih mučenika 2) specialises in adventure tourism, including paragliding, caving, kayaking and abseiling, and offers a military tour and boat trips to the Blue Cave, the Green Cave (p288) and various hard-to-get-to beaches.

Villa Nonna APARTMENT €€
(☎098 380 046; www.villa-nonna.com; Ribarska 50; apt €60-120;) This lovely old town house has seven renovated apartments, each with wooden floors and a kitchen; some have balconies or patios. Next door is another gorgeous old house, Casa Nono, which has four bedrooms, three bathrooms, a lovely garden, a living room with exposed stone walls and self-catering facilities.

Slastičarnica Cukar BAKERY €
(☎098 92 94 888; www.facebook.com/cukar.komiza; Hrvatskih mučenika 8; cakes 8-17KN; ⏰8am-2pm Jun-Oct) Head to this tiny cake shop for a delicious sweet treat.

Konoba Bako DALMATIAN €€
(☎021-713 742; www.konobabako.hr; Gundulićeva 1; mains 70-155KN; ⏰4pm-2am Jun-Aug, 5pm-midnight Sep-May) Specialising in seafood (although the grilled lamb is very good, too), Bako has a terrace with water views and a cool stone interior decorated with a collection of Greek and Roman amphorae. It's a good place to try the very localised speciality *komiška pogača* (pastry-like bread stuffed with anchovies).

Information

Darlić & Darlić (☎021-713 760; Hrvatskih mučenika 8) Offers excursions and rents cars, scooters and bikes.

Tourist Office (☎021-713 455; www.tz-komiza.hr; Riva Sv Mikule 1; ⏰8am-9pm Sun-Fri, 9am-3pm Sat Jul & Aug, 8am-noon & 5-7pm May, Jun, Sep & Oct, 8am-2pm Mon-Fri Nov-Apr)

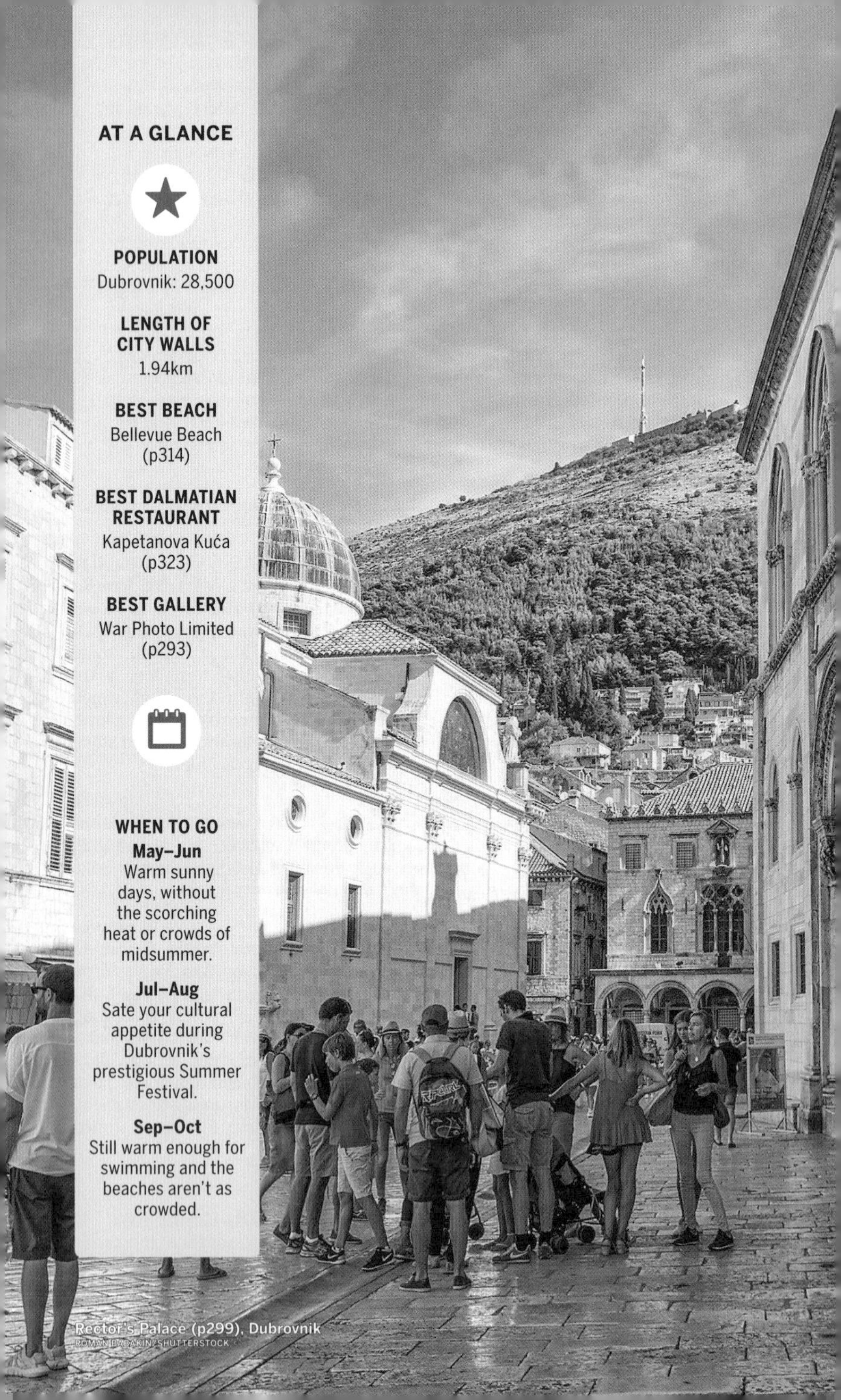

AT A GLANCE

POPULATION
Dubrovnik: 28,500

LENGTH OF CITY WALLS
1.94km

BEST BEACH
Bellevue Beach (p314)

BEST DALMATIAN RESTAURANT
Kapetanova Kuća (p323)

BEST GALLERY
War Photo Limited (p293)

WHEN TO GO

May–Jun
Warm sunny days, without the scorching heat or crowds of midsummer.

Jul–Aug
Sate your cultural appetite during Dubrovnik's prestigious Summer Festival.

Sep–Oct
Still warm enough for swimming and the beaches aren't as crowded.

Rector's Palace (p299), Dubrovnik
ROMAN BABAKIN/SHUTTERSTOCK

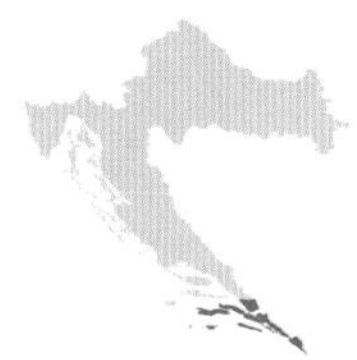

Dubrovnik & Southern Dalmatia

From the island of Korčula in the northwest to the dreamy plains of Konavle in the southeast, Southern Dalmatia is a region to be savoured by beach seekers, wine lovers and history buffs alike. Yet the remarkable old town of Dubrovnik is a show-stealer. Ringed by mighty defensive walls that dip into cerulean sea, the city encapsulates the very essence of a medieval Mediterranean fantasy. Dubrovnik is unique; its beauty is bewitching, its setting sublime. Thousands of visitors walk along its marble streets every day, gazing, gasping and happily snapping away. When Dubrovnik's tourist scrum threatens to overwhelm, a reinvigorating balm is but a quick boat or bus ride away. Refresh yourself on the shady paths of Trsteno Arboretum or, if that doesn't do the trick, the divine wine and oysters of the sparsely populated Pelješac Peninsula surely will.

INCLUDES

Dubrovnik & Southern Dalmatia Highlights

1. **Dubrovnik** (p293) Circling the historic city's mighty walls and then catching the cable car up Mt Srđ for breathtaking views from above.

2. **Korčula Town** (p327) Soaking up the medieval atmosphere amid the marble streets of the walled town.

3. **Mljet Island** (p320) Seeking out secluded beaches down at the island's east end, before joining the throngs at the national park's pretty lakes.

4. **Lokrum** (p296) Exploring the gardens, forest and beaches of Dubrovnik's closest island getaway.

5. **Pelješac Peninsula** (p323) Sampling Croatia's best red wine directly from the cellar door.

6. **Cavtat** (p316) Wandering along the waterfront promenade, stopping for a bite at Bugenvila and a dip at one of the little coves around the headland.

7. **Ston** (p323) Slurping down oysters in Mali Ston and then tracing the extraordinary 13th-century walls up and over the hill to Ston proper.

DUBROVNIK

POP 28,500

Regardless of whether you are visiting Dubrovnik for the first time or the hundredth, the sense of awe never fails to descend when you set eyes on the beauty of the old town. Indeed it's hard to imagine anyone becoming jaded by the city's limestone streets, baroque buildings and the endless shimmer of the Adriatic, or failing to be inspired by a walk along the ancient city walls that protected the capital of a sophisticated republic for centuries.

Although the shelling of Dubrovnik in 1991 horrified the world, the city has bounced back with vigour to enchant visitors again. Marvel at the interplay of light on the old stone buildings; trace the peaks and troughs of Dubrovnik's past in museums replete with art and artefacts; take the cable car up to Mt Srđ; exhaust yourself climbing up and down narrow lanes – then plunge into the azure sea.

History

The story of Dubrovnik begins with the 7th-century onslaught of the Slavs, which had wiped out the Roman city of Epidaurum (site of present-day Cavtat). Residents fled to the safest place they could find, which was the rocky islet of Ragusa, separated from the mainland by a narrow channel. Building walls was a matter of pressing urgency due to the threat of invasion; the city was well fortified by the 9th century when it resisted a Saracen siege for 15 months.

Meanwhile, another settlement emerged on the mainland, which became known as Dubrovnik, named after the *dubrava* (holm oak) that carpeted the region. The two settlements merged in the 12th century, and the channel that separated them was filled in.

By the end of the 12th century Dubrovnik had become a significant trading centre on the coast, providing an important link between the Mediterranean and Balkan states. Dubrovnik came under Venetian authority in 1205, finally breaking away again in 1358.

By the 15th century the Respublica Ragusina (Republic of Ragusa) had extended its borders to include the entire coastal belt from Ston to Cavtat, having previously acquired Lastovo Island, the Pelješac Peninsula and Mljet Island. It was now a force to be reckoned with. The city turned towards sea trade and established a fleet of its own ships, which were dispatched to Egypt, the Levant, Sicily, Spain, France and Istanbul. Through canny diplomacy the city maintained good relations with everyone – even the Ottoman Empire, to which Dubrovnik began paying tribute in the 16th century.

Centuries of peace and prosperity allowed art, science and literature to flourish, but most of the Renaissance art and architecture in Dubrovnik was destroyed in the earthquake of 1667, which killed 5000 people and left the city in ruins. Holy Saviour Church, Sponza Palace and Rector's Palace are the only significant buildings remaining from before this time. The earthquake also marked the beginning of the economic decline of the town.

The final coup de grâce was dealt by Napoleon, whose troops entered Dubrovnik in 1808 and announced the end of the republic. The Vienna Congress of 1815 ceded Dubrovnik to Austria; though the city maintained its shipping, it succumbed to social disintegration. Following WWI the city started to develop its tourist industry, swiftly becoming Yugoslavia's leading attraction.

Dubrovnik was caught in the cross-hairs of the war that followed Croatia's declaration of independence in 1991. For no obvious military or strategic reason, Dubrovnik was pummelled with some 2000 shells in 1991 and 1992 by the Yugoslav military, suffering considerable damage and loss of life. All of the damaged buildings have now been restored.

Sights

Today Dubrovnik is the most prosperous, elegant and expensive city in Croatia. In many ways it still feels like a city state, isolated from the rest of the nation by geography and history. It's become such a tourism magnet that there's even talk of having to limit visitor numbers in the car-free old town – the main thoroughfares can get impossibly crowded, especially when multiple cruise ships disgorge passengers at the same time.

Old Town

City Walls & Forts FORT

See p292.

★ **War Photo Limited** GALLERY

(Map p298; ☎020-322 166; www.warphotoltd.com; Antuninska 6; adult/child 50/40KN; ⏲10am-10pm May-Sep, to 4pm Wed-Mon Apr & Oct) An immensely powerful experience, this gallery features compelling exhibitions curated by

(Continued on page 298)

AMIRRAIZAT/SHUTTERSTOCK ©

TOP SIGHT
CITY WALLS & FORTS

Dubrovnik's defining feature is the imposing ring of walls that encircles its historic core. From the sea, the juxtaposition of pinkish-grey stone and azure waters is mesmerising, while from above, the tight maze of church steeples and terracotta roofs is the setting for a fairy tale – or, at the very least, an HBO series featuring queens and dragons.

Need for Walls

Dubrovnik was originally an island and it was the natural protection afforded by its rocky cliffs that first enticed refugees from the Roman town of Epidaurum (present-day Cavtat) to settle here in the 7th century.

The first set of walls to enclose the city was built in the 9th century and was strong enough to resist a 15-month siege by the Saracens. In the middle of the 14th century the 1.5m-thick defences were fortified with 15 square forts. The threat of attacks from the Turks in the 15th century prompted the city to strengthen the existing forts and add new ones, so that the entire old town was contained within a stone barrier 2km long and up to 25m high. The walls are thicker on the land side – up to 6m – and range from 1.5m to 3m on the sea side.

City Gates

Historically, the entrance to the city was via two elaborate gates: the **Pile Gate** (Gradska vrata Pile; Map p298; pictured above) to the west and the **Ploče Gate** (Vrata od Ploča; Map p298) to the east. Both have drawbridges that were raised at sunset when the doors were locked and the keys handed to the rector. A third entrance, the **Buža Gate**, was added to the northern wall at the top of Boškovićeva street in 1907.

DON'T MISS

- Wall Walk
- Pile Gate (pictured)
- Fort Lawrence

PRACTICALITIES

- Gradske zidine
- Map p298
- 020-638 800
- www.wallsofdubrovnik.com
- adult/child 150/50KN
- 8am-6.30pm Apr-Oct, 9am-3pm Nov-Mar

The most impressive of the three is the Pile Gate, built in 1537, which remains the main entrance to the town. Note the stone **Statue of St Blaise**, holding the city in his hands, set in a niche over the Renaissance portal. This 4th-century Armenian martyr is Dubrovnik's patron saint, and similar images are positioned in various parts of the wall and above all the major entrances. After passing through the outer gate you'll enter a large court with a ramp and stairs heading down to the inner gate, dating from 1460 and topped by a statue of St Blaise by leading Croatian sculptor Ivan Meštrović (1883–1962).

Wall Walk

There are ticketed entrances to the city walls near the Pile Gate, the Ploče Gate and the Maritime Museum. To reduce congestion, you're required to walk the walls in an anticlockwise direction. At busy times it can resemble a sweaty, slow-moving conga line. Don't let that put you off: the views over the old town and the shimmering Adriatic are worth any frustration resulting from a busy period.

One of the most charming aspects of the walk (although perhaps not for Dubrovnik's long-suffering residents) is the glimpses it gives into hidden gardens and courtyards in the residential fringes of the town.

Starting from the Ploče Gate entrance, you'll quickly reach **St Luke's Tower** (built 1467), facing the Old Harbour and Fort Revelin. The northern, landward section of wall is the highest, reaching a peak at rounded **Fort Minčeta** (Tvrđava Minčeta; Map p298) at the city's northwestern corner. This massive structure was completed in 1464 to designs by Juraj Dalmatinac, who is most famous as the creator of Šibenik's extraordinary cathedral. The battlements at the top provide remarkable views over the old town's rooftops.

From here it's mainly downhill as you pass over Pile Gate and then narrow to single file as you climb towards **Fort Bokar** (Tvrđava Bokar; Map p298) at the city's southwestern corner. The seaward stretch of the walls passes a couple of cafe-bars and souvenir stores, before terminating at Fort St John at the entrance to Dubrovnik's Old Harbour.

Fort Lawrence

St Blaise gazes down from the walls of this large, free-standing **fortress** (Tvrđava Lovrjenac; Map p298; www.citywallsdubrovnik.hr; Pile; 50KN, free with city walls ticket; ⌚8am-6.30pm Apr-Oct, 9am-3pm Nov-Mar), constructed atop a 37m-high promontory adjacent to the old town. Built to guard the city's western approach from invasion by land or sea, its walls range from 4m to 12m thick. There's not a lot inside, but the battlements offer wonderful views over the old town and its large courtyard is often used as a venue for summer theatre and concerts.

GAME OF THRONES

Dubrovnik's walls and forts feature prominently in the HBO series *Game of Thrones*. Fort Minčeta was used for the exterior shots of Qarth's House of Undying, Tyrion Lannister commanded the defence of King's Landing from the seaward-facing walls during the Battle of the Blackwater and, if you can look past all of the CGI enhancements, you'll recognise Fort Lawrence as the core of the Red Keep.

The entrance to the walls nearest to the Pile Gate tends to be the busiest. Skip the queues by entering from the Ploče side, which has the added advantage of getting the steepest climbs out of the way first.

WAR DAMAGE

You can get a good impression of the extent of the damage caused by the Yugoslav army's shelling of Dubrovnik in 1991 and 1992 by gazing over the old town's rooftops: those sporting bright new terracotta suffered damage and had to be replaced. The softer-toned original tiles are in a clear minority.

TOP SIGHT
LOKRUM ISLAND

Leave the crush of Dubrovnik's old town a world away with a 10-minute ferry ride to this lush, forested island populated by preening peacocks and over 150 other bird species. The entire island is a protected nature reserve, full of holm oaks, black ash, pines and olive trees. It's a popular swimming destination, although the beaches are rocky.

Boats

Boats leave from Dubrovnik's Old Harbour (Map p298) roughly hourly in summer (half-hourly in July and August). Make sure you check what time the last boat to the mainland departs. The last few boats for the day can get very crowded; to guarantee a place, make sure you get to the wharf early. No one is allowed to stay on the island overnight.

DON'T MISS

- Cloister garden (pictured)
- Botanical Garden
- *Game of Thrones* exhibition

PRACTICALITIES

- 020-311 738
- www.lokrum.hr
- adult/child incl boat 150/25KN
- Apr-Nov

Benedictine Monastery & Gardens

The island's main hub is its large medieval Benedictine monastery (pictured above), located a short stroll from the ferry wharf. It's thought that monks first settled on the island in the early 10th century, although the first definitive mention of the monastery dates from 1023. The last monks were eventually turfed out in 1799, when the cash-strapped republic

decided to sell the island to raise funds; legend has it that the monks cursed the island's future owners.

The island eventually fell into the hands of ill-fated Austrian Archduke Maximilian Ferdinand, the future Emperor of Mexico, who had a summer villa built within the monastery complex in the early 1860s. Maximilian was responsible for reviving the gorgeous **cloister garden** and planting a significant **botanical garden**, featuring giant agaves and exotic palms.

One of the monastery buildings now contains a display on the island's history and the TV show *Game of Thrones*. This is your chance to pose imperiously on a reproduction of the Iron Throne. Fans of the show may recognise the cloister garden as the location used for filming the reception for Daenerys in Qarth.

Fort Royal

Near the centre of the island, at its highest point (97m), is circular Fort Royal. Napoleon's troops started construction of the fort shortly after taking control of Dubrovnik in 1806. Head up to the roof for views over Dubrovnik's old town.

Swimming Spots

The island is mainly surrounded by flat rocky ledges rather than beaches, and most visitors are content to seek a quiet shelf on which to spread out. Another popular place for a swim is the small saltwater lake known as the **Dead Sea**, south of the monastery.

There's a nudist area near the southeastern tip of the island; head left from the ferry and follow the signs marked FKK. The rocks at its far end are Dubrovnik's de facto gay beach.

Dubrovnik Old Town

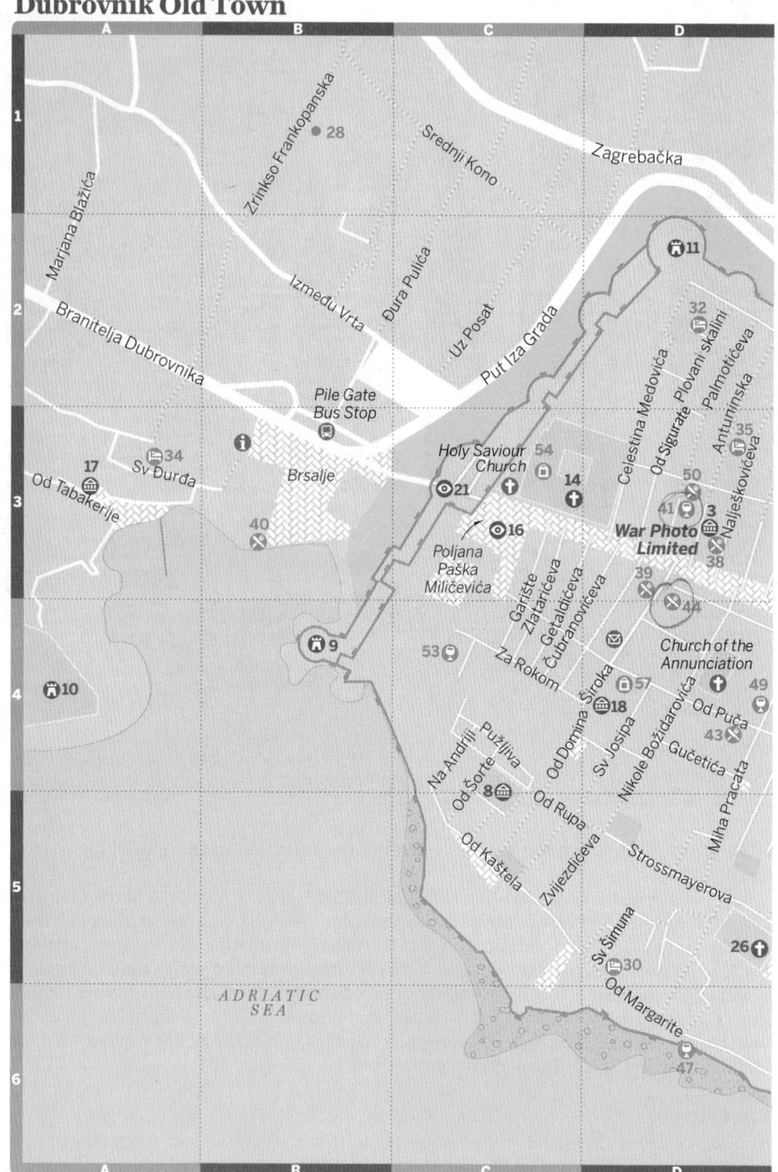

(Continued from page 293)

New Zealand photojournalist Wade Goddard, who worked in the Balkans in the 1990s. Its declared intention is to 'expose the myth of war...to let people see war as it is, raw, venal, frightening, by focusing on how war inflicts injustices on innocents and combatants alike'. There's a permanent exhibition on the upper floor devoted to the wars in Yugoslavia; the changing exhibitions cover a multitude of conflicts.

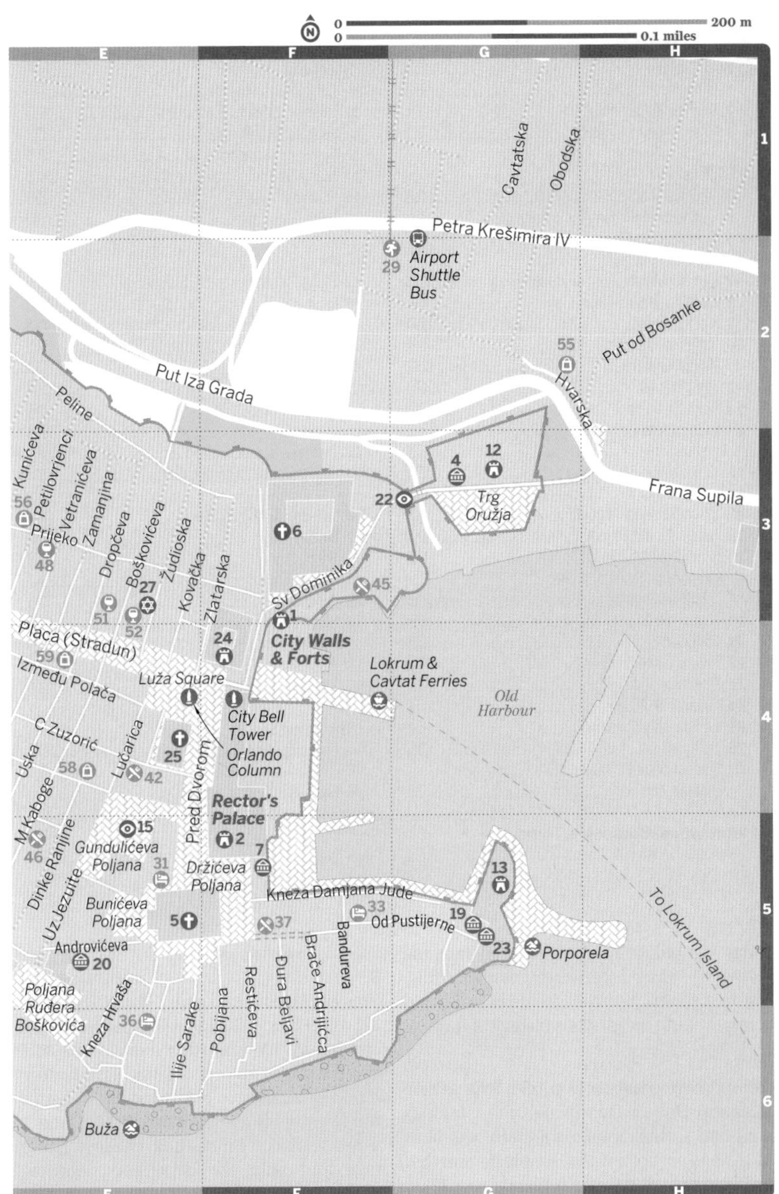

★ **Rector's Palace** PALACE

(Knežev dvor; Map p298; ☎020-321 497; www.dumus.hr; Pred Dvorom 3; adult/child 80/25KN, incl in multimuseum pass adult/child 120/25KN; ⏲9am-6pm Apr-Oct, to 4pm Nov-Mar) Built in the late 15th century for the elected rector who governed Dubrovnik, this Gothic-Renaissance palace contains the rector's office and private chambers, public halls, administrative offices and a dungeon. During their one-month term the rector was unable to leave the building without the permission of the senate.

Dubrovnik Old Town

Top Sights

1	City Walls & Forts	F3
2	Rector's Palace	F5
3	War Photo Limited	D3

Sights

4	Archaeological Museum	G3
5	Cathedral of the Assumption	E5
6	Dominican Monastery & Museum	F3
7	Dulčić Masle Pulitika Gallery	F5
8	Ethnographic Museum	C4
9	Fort Bokar	B4
10	Fort Lawrence	A4
11	Fort Minčeta	D2
12	Fort Revelin	G3
13	Fort St John	G5
14	Franciscan Monastery & Museum	C3
15	Gundulićeva poljana	E5
16	Large Onofrio Fountain	C3
17	Love Stories Museum	A3
18	Marin Držić House	D4
19	Maritime Museum	G5
	Memorial Room of the Dubrovnik Defenders	(see 24)
20	Natural History Museum	E5
21	Pile Gate	C3
22	Ploče Gate	G3
23	Pulitika Studio	G5
24	Sponza Palace	F4
25	St Blaise's Church	E4
26	St Ignatius of Loyola Church	D5
27	Synagogue & Jewish Museum	E3

Activities, Courses & Tours

28	Adriatic Kayak Tours	B1
29	Cable Car	G2

Sleeping

30	City Walls Hostel	D5
31	Fresh* Sheets Kathedral	E5
32	Hostel Angelina	D2
33	Karmen Apartments	F5
34	MirÓ Studio Apartments	A3
35	Rooms Vicelić	D3
36	Villa Sigurata	E6

Eating

37	Bota Šare Oyster & Sushi Bar	F5
38	Dolce Vita	D3
39	Fast Food Republic	D3
40	Nautika	B3
41	Nishta	D3
42	Oliva Pizzeria	E4
43	Peppino's	D4
44	Proto	D4
45	Restaurant 360°	F3
46	Restaurant Dubrovnik	E5

Drinking & Nightlife

47	Buža	D6
48	Buzz Bar	E3
49	Dubrovnik Beer Factory	D4
50	D'vino	D3
51	Malvasija	E3
	Revelin	(see 12)
52	Rock Caffe Exit	E3
53	Tavulin	C4

Shopping

54	Franciscan Pharmacy	C3
55	Kawa	G2
56	Medusa	E3
57	Terra Croatica Dubrovnik	D4
58	Uje	E4
59	Uje	E4

Today the palace has been turned into the **Cultural History Museum**, with artfully restored rooms, portraits, coats of arms and coins, evoking the glorious history of Ragusa.

Large Onofrio Fountain FOUNTAIN
(Velika Onofrijeva fontana; Map p298; Poljana Paska Miličevića) One of Dubrovnik's most famous landmarks, this circular fountain was built in 1438 as part of a water-supply system that involved bringing water from a spring 12km away. Originally the fountain was adorned with sculptures, but it was heavily damaged in the 1667 earthquake and only 16 carved masks remain, with their mouths dribbling drinkable water into a drainage pool. Its sibling, the ornate **Little Onofrio Fountain**, is in Luža Square at the other end of Stradun.

Franciscan Monastery & Museum CHRISTIAN MONASTERY
(Franjevački samostan i muzej; Map p298; 020-321 410; Placa 2; 30KN; 9am-6pm Apr-Oct, to 2pm Nov-Mar) Within this monastery's solid stone walls is a gorgeous mid-14th-century **cloister**, a historic **pharmacy** and a small **museum** with a collection of relics and liturgical objects, including chalices, paintings and gold jewellery, and pharmacy items such as laboratory gear and medical books.

Before you head inside, stop to admire the remarkable pietà over the church door, sculpted by the local masters Petar and Leonard Andrijić in 1498. Unfortunately, the portal is all that remains of a richly decorated church that was destroyed in the 1667 earthquake. Its baroque replacement is adorned with ornate altars capped with large paintings.

Access the cloister and the museum via the small passage between the monastery church and St Saviour's church. The cloister is one of the most beautiful late-Romanesque structures in Dalmatia. Notice how each capital over the incredibly slim dual columns is topped by a different figure, portraying human heads, animals and floral arrangements. At the centre is a small square garden that's shaded by orange and palm trees.

Further inside is the original location of the third-oldest functioning pharmacy in Europe, which has been in business since 1317. It may have been the first pharmacy in Europe open to the general public. The room is now part of the monastery's museum, with pharmacy displays taking up one wall and the rest filled with religious artefacts and art. Highlights include a large painted altar crucifix by Blaž Jurjev Trogiranin (1428) and Vlaho Bukovac's *The New Ring* (1892), one of a handful of secular pieces in the collection.

Moved from its first location several times, the present-day **pharmacy** (Ljekarna kod Mala Braća; Map p298; ☎020-321 411; www.ljekarna-dubrovnik.hr; Placa 2; ⏱7am-7pm Mon-Fri, 7.30am-3pm Sat) sits just before the museum ticket desk by the monastery entrance.

Synagogue & Jewish Museum SYNAGOGUE

(Sinagoga i Židovski muzej; Map p298; Žudioska 5; 50KN; ⏱10am-5pm) With a religious practice that can be traced back to the 14th century, this is said to be the second-oldest still-functioning synagogue in Europe and the oldest Sephardic one. Sitting on a street that was once the Jewish ghetto, the synagogue also houses a small museum exhibiting religious relics and documentation on the local Jewish population, including records relating to their persecution during WWII.

Dominican Monastery & Museum CHRISTIAN MONASTERY

(Dominikanski samostan i muzej; Map p298; ☎020-321 423; www.dominicanmuseum.hr; Sv Dominika 4; adult/child 30/20KN; ⏱9am-5pm) This imposing structure is an architectural highlight, built in a transitional Gothic-Renaissance style and containing an impressive art collection. Constructed around the same time as the city walls in the 14th century, the stark exterior resembles a fortress more than a religious complex. The interior contains a graceful 15th-century **cloister** constructed by local artisans after the designs of the Florentine architect Maso di Bartolomeo.

The large, single-naved church features some bright, modern stained glass and a painting by Vlaho Bukovac (*St Dominic's Miracle,* 1911) above one of the side altars. Other priceless pieces of art are hung in rooms off the cloister, including 15th- and 16th-century works by Lovro Dobričević and Nikola Božidarević, and an exquisite painting of St Blaise and St Mary Magdalene (c 1550) by Venetian luminary Titian.

MUSEUMS OF DUBROVNIK PASS

Perhaps a cunning plan to get you through the doors of some of the town's more marginal museums, a multimuseum pass (adult/child 120/25KN) allows access to nine of Dubrovnik's institutions. The only must-see among them though is the Rector's Palace (p299), which is also the only one ticketed separately (for adult/child 80/25KN).

If you're interested in visiting the excellent Museum of Modern Art (p304), then it's worth buying the pass. The other museums could easily be skipped, but if you want to get your money's worth in a limited amount of time, we suggest you prioritise the rest in the following order: **Maritime Museum** (Pomorski muzej; Map p298; ☎020-323 904; www.dumus.hr; Tvrđava Sv Ivana; ⏱9am-6pm Tue-Sun Apr-Oct, to 4pm Nov-Mar), **Archaeological Museum** (Arheološki muzej; Map p298; ☎020-324 041; www.dumus.hr; Fort Revelin, Sv Dominika 3; ⏱10am-4pm Thu-Tue), **Dulčić Masle Pulitika Gallery** (Map p298; ☎020-612 645; www.ugdubrovnik.hr; Držićeva poljana 1; ⏱9am-8pm Tue-Sun), **Natural History Museum** (Prirodoslovni muzej; Map p298; ☎020-324 888; www.pmd.hr; Androvićeva 1; ⏱10am-6pm Mon-Sat Jun-Oct, to 5pm Mon-Fri, to 2pm Sat Nov-May), **Ethnographic Museum** (Etnografski muzej; Map p298; ☎020-323 056; www.dumus.hr; Od Rupa 3; ⏱9am-4pm Wed-Mon), **Pulitika Studio** (Atelijer Pulitika; Map p298; ☎020-323 104; www.ugdubrovnik.hr; Tvrđava Sv Ivana bb; ⏱9am-3pm Tue-Sun), **Marin Držić House** (Dom Marina Držića; Map p298; ☎020-323 242; www.muzej-marindrzic.eu; Široka 7; ⏱10am-6pm Mon, 9am-10pm Tue-Sun Jun-Sep, 9am-8.30pm Tue-Sun Oct-May).

Dubrovnik

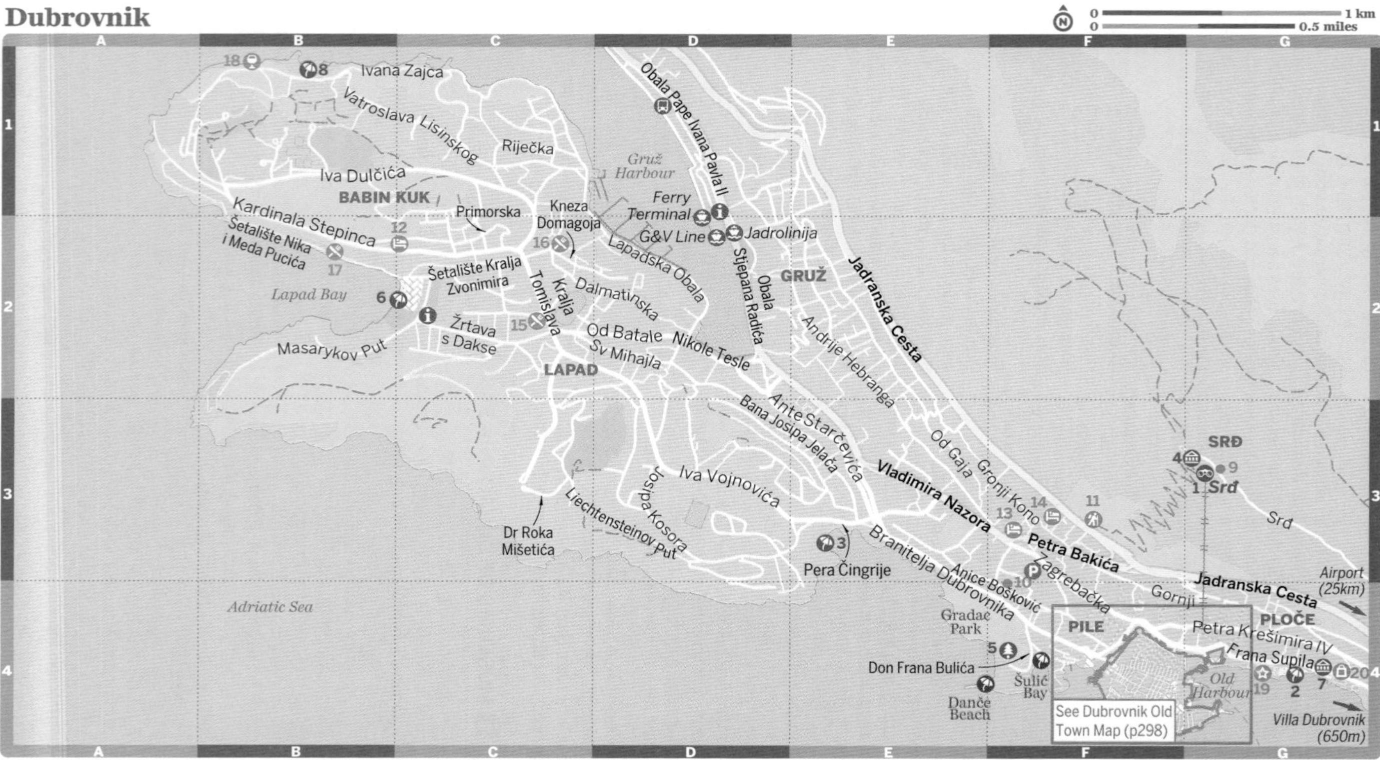
1 km
0.5 miles
Ivana Zajca
Vatroslava Lisinskog
Riječka
Iva Dulčića
BABIN KUK
Primorska
Kardinala Stepinca
Šetalište Nika i Meda Pucića
Lapad Bay
Šetalište Kralja Zvonimira
Kralja Tomislava
Žrtava s Dakse
Masarykov Put
Kneza Domagoja
Gruž Harbour
Ferry Terminal
G&V Line
Jadrolinija
Obala Pape Ivana Pavla II
Lapadska Obala
Obala Stjepana Radića
GRUŽ
Jadranska Cesta
Dalmatinska
Od Batale
Sv Mihajla
Nikole Tesle
LAPAD
Andrije Hebranga
Ante Starčevića
Bana Josipa Jelačića
Iva Vojnovića
Josipa Kosora
Liechtensteinov Put
Dr Roka Mišetića
Od Gaja
Gronji Kono
Vladimira Nazora
Petra Bakića
Pera Čingrije
Branitelja Dubrovnika
Anice Bošković
Zagrebačka
Gornji
SRĐ
Srđ
Airport (25km)
PLOČE
PILE
Petra Krešimira IV
Frana Supila
Old Harbour
Villa Dubrovnik (650m)
Gradac Park
Don Frana Bulića
Šulić Bay
Danče Beach
See Dubrovnik Old Town Map (p298)
Adriatic Sea

Dubrovnik

Top Sights

1 Srđ ... G3

Sights

2 Banje Beach ... G4
3 Bellevue Beach ... E3
4 Dubrovnik During the Homeland War ... G3
5 Gradac Park ... F4
6 Lapad Bay ... C2
7 Museum of Modern Art ... G4
8 Okrug Gornji ... B1

Activities, Courses & Tours

9 Buggy Safari Dubrovnik ... G3
10 Dubrovnik Boat Rentals ... F4
11 Way of the Cross walking trail ... F3

Sleeping

12 Apartments Silva ... C2
13 Guest House Biličić ... F3
14 Villa Klaić ... F3

Eating

15 Pantarul ... C2
16 Shizuku ... C2
17 Slatki Kantun ... B2

Drinking & Nightlife

Cave Bar More ... (see 17)
18 Coral Beach Club ... B1

Entertainment

19 Lazareti ... G4

Shopping

20 Studio Aplika ... G4

Sponza Palace PALACE

(Palača Sponza; Map p298; ☎020-321 031; Placa bb; May-Oct/Nov-Apr free/25KN; ⌚archives display & cloister 10am-10pm May-Oct; cloister 10am-3pm Nov-Apr) One of the few buildings in the old town to survive the 1667 earthquake, the Sponza Palace was built from 1516 to 1522 as a customs house, and it has subsequently been used as a mint, treasury, armoury and bank. Architecturally it's a mixture of styles beginning with an exquisite Renaissance portico resting on six Corinthian columns. The 1st floor has late-Gothic windows and the 2nd-floor windows are in a Renaissance style, with an alcove containing a statue of St Blaise.

Just inside the building, before you enter the cloister, is the **Memorial Room of the Defenders of Dubrovnik** (Spomen soba poginulih Dubrovačkih branitelja; Map p298; ⌚9am-9pm May-Oct, 10am-3pm Nov-Apr) FREE, a heartbreaking collection of black-and-white photographs of the mainly young men who perished between 1991 and 1995.

The 1st and 2nd floors house the State Archives, a priceless collection of manuscripts dating back nearly 1000 years. Though the archives are not open to the public, copies of the most precious and significant pieces are exhibited in a display on the ground floor. There are some English translations, but the displays aren't particularly interesting.

St Blaise's Church CHURCH

(Crkva Sv Vlahe; Map p298; Luža Sq; ⌚8am-noon & 4-5pm Mon-Sat, 7am-1pm Sun) Dedicated to the city's patron saint, this exceptionally beautiful church was built in 1715 in the ornate baroque style. The interior is notable for its marble altars and a 15th-century silver gilt statue of St Blaise within the high altar, who is holding a scale model of pre-earthquake Dubrovnik. Note also the stained glass windows designed by local artist Ivo Dulčić in 1971.

Cathedral of the Assumption CATHEDRAL

(Katedrala Marijina Uznesenja; Map p298; Držićeva poljana; treasury 20KN; ⌚8am-5pm Mon-Sat, 11am-5pm Sun Easter-Oct, 9am-noon & 4-5pm Mon-Sat Nov-Easter) Built on the site of a 7th-century basilica, Dubrovnik's original cathedral was enlarged in the 12th century, supposedly funded by a gift from England's King Richard I, the Lionheart, who was saved from a shipwreck on the nearby island of Lokrum. Soon after the first cathedral was destroyed in the 1667 earthquake, work began on this, its baroque replacement, which was finished in 1713.

The cathedral is notable for its fine altars, especially the altar of St John of Nepomuk, made of violet marble. The most striking of its religious paintings is the polyptych of the *Assumption of the Virgin*, hanging behind the main altar, by 16th-century Venetian painter Titian.

To the left of the main altar is the cathedral's **treasury**. Dripping in gold and silver, it contains relics of St Blaise as well as over 150 other reliquaries largely made in the workshops of Dubrovnik's goldsmiths between the 11th and 17th centuries.

St Ignatius of Loyola Church CHURCH

(Crkva Sv Ignacija Lojolskoga; Map p298; ☎020-323 500; Poljana Ruđera Boškovića 6; ⌚7am-7pm) Dramatically poised at the top of a broad flight of stairs, this Jesuit church was built in the baroque style between 1699 and 1725.

Inside, magnificent frescos display scenes from the life of St Ignatius, founder of the Society of Jesus. Abutting the church is the former Jesuit college Collegium Ragusinum, today the Diocesan Classical high school.

Surrounds

★Srđ VIEWPOINT
(Map p302; Srđ bb) From the top of this 412m-high hill, Dubrovnik's old town looks even more surreal than usual – like a scale model of itself or an illustration on a page. The views take in all of Dubrovnik and Lokrum, with the Elafiti Islands filling the horizon. It's this extraordinary vantage point that made Srđ a key battleground during the 1990s war. That story is told in **Dubrovnik During the Homeland War** (Dubrovnik u Domovinskom ratu; Map p302; ☎020-324 856; Fort Imperial, Srđ; adult/child 30/15KN; ⏲8am-10pm; P), an exhibition housed in Fort Imperial at the summit.

The easiest and quickest way to get to the top is by **cable car** (Žičara; Map p298; ☎020-414 355; www.dubrovnikcablecar.com; Petra Krešimira IV bb, Ploče; adult/child return 140/60KN, one way 85/40KN; ⏲9am-midnight Jun-Aug, to 10pm Sep, to 8pm Apr, May & Oct, to 4pm Nov-Mar), or you can drive (follow the signs to Bosanka), walk via the **Way of the Cross** (Križni put; Map p302; Jadranska cesta, Srđ), or catch bus 17 from the Pile stop to Bosanka and then walk the final 1.5km.

Lokrum ISLAND
See p296.

Museum of Modern Art GALLERY
(Umjetnička galerija; Map p302; ☎020-426 590; www.ugdubrovnik.hr; Frana Supila 23, Ploče; multimuseum pass adult/child 120/25KN; ⏲9am-8pm Tue-Sun) Spread over three floors of a significant modernist building east of the old town, this excellent gallery showcases Croatian artists, particularly painter Vlaho Bukovac from nearby Cavtat. Head up to the sculpture terrace for excellent views.

Love Stories Museum MUSEUM
(Map p298; www.lovestoriesmuseum.com; Od Tabakarije 2, Pile; adult/child 50/35KN; ⏲9am-10pm May-Sep, 10am-6pm Oct-Apr) Providing a sunny Dalmatian counterpoint to Zagreb's popular Museum of Broken Relationships (p68), this unusual museum aims to tug at the heart strings. Exhibits focus on love songs, romantic stories from local history and legend, and smoochy scenes from films and TV series shot in Dubrovnik (*Game of Thrones* without the viscera?). However the museum's real heart is in the collection of sentimental objects donated by ordinary people and the stories behind them.

Activities

For beaches, see Lazy Days in Dubrovnik (p314).

Outdoor Croatia KAYAKING
(☎020-418 282; www.outdoorcroatia.com; day trip 440KN) Rents kayaks and offers day trips around the Elafiti Islands, along with multiday excursions and kayaking-cycling combos.

Tours

Insider Holidays WINE
(☎099 47 73 701; www.insiderholidays.eu) Run by a restaurateur and her writer husband, this agency excels in specialised wine and food tours. Try wine tasting your way through the old town (2½ hours, tasting six wines, 560KN), winery hopping in Pelješac Peninsula (5½ hours, two wineries, 715KN) or a tailored itinerary in the old town or the Dubrovnik region.

Buggy Safari Dubrovnik ADVENTURE
(Map p302; ☎098 16 69 730; www.buggydubrovnik.com; cable-car terminus, Srđ; 1-/2-people trip 400/600KN; ⏲Mar-Nov) Take a trip in a souped-up quad bike through the mountainous nether regions of Srđ, visiting forts and a farm. Expect to come back caked in mud and dust.

Dubrovnik Boat Rentals CRUISE
(Map p302; ☎095 90 45 799; www.dubrovnikboatrentals.com; Anice Bošković 6, Pile) Offers half- or full-day private speedboat trips (prices on enquiry) to Lokrum, Cavtat, the Elafiti Islands, Mljet and Korčula.

Dubrovnik Boats CRUISE
(☎098 757 890; www.dubrovnikboats.com; ACI Marina Dubrovnik, Na Skali 2, Komolac) Private speedboat tours (prices on enquiry) to the Elafiti Islands and as far afield as Mljet and Korčula.

Dubrovnik Day Tours TOURS
(☎098 17 51 775; www.dubrovnikdaytours.net) Private day trips (prices on enquiry) led by licensed guides to as far away as Korčula, Split, Kotor, Budva, Mostar and Sarajevo, as well as sightseeing and *Game of Thrones* tours around Dubrovnik. It also offers

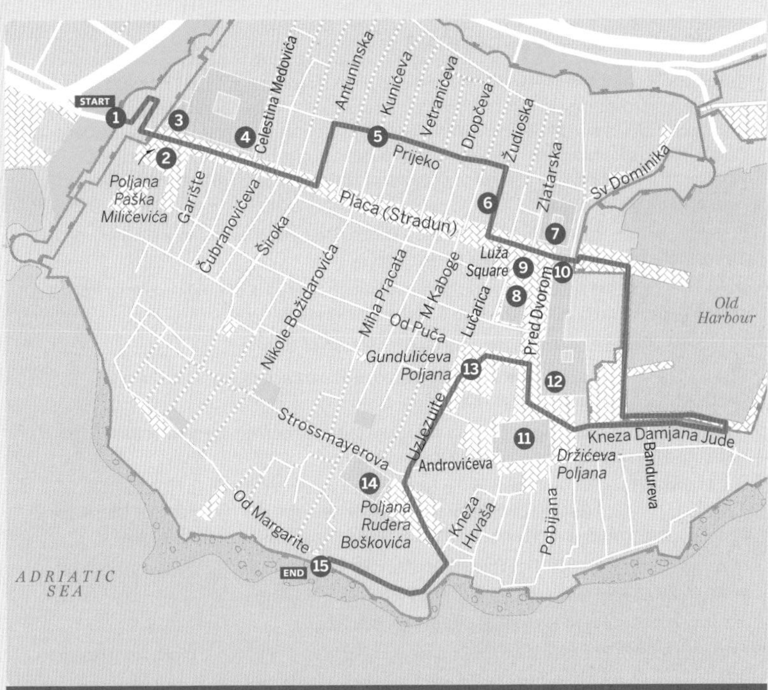

Town Walk
Dubrovnik's Old Town

START PILE GATE
END BUŽA BAR
LENGTH 1.2KM; ONE HOUR

Head through the 1 **Pile Gate** (p294) to the beginning of Placa (aka Stradun), Dubrovnik's marbled main street. It sits roughly where the channel once was that separated the islet of Ragusa from the mainland. Immediately to your right is the 2 **Large Onofrio Fountain** (p300), while opposite it is 16th-century 3 **Holy Saviour Church**.

Continue along past the 4 **Franciscan Monastery** (p300) and take any of the narrow lanes to the left. Turn right at the first side street, 5 **Prijeko**, lined with restaurants of varying quality. Turn right onto Žudioska, Dubrovnik's former Jewish ghetto; its 14th-century 6 **synagogue** (p301) is the oldest still-functioning Sephardic synagogue in Europe.

Back on Placa, continue to Luža Square, a former marketplace lined with beautiful buildings such as the 7 **Sponza Palace** (p303) and 8 **St Blaise's Church** (p303). Edicts, festivities and public verdicts were announced from the 9 **Orlando Column** at its centre. Erected in 1417, it features the image of a medieval knight; the statue's forearm was the official linear measure of the Republic – the ell of Dubrovnik (51.2cm).

Duck through the arch beneath the 10 **City Bell Tower** and turn left, and then right at the arch leading to the Old Harbour. Head to the shade of the walls on the far side, then look back for a great view of the Ploče Gate defenses.

Scoot through the hole in the wall and turn right; straight ahead is the 11 **Cathedral** (p303), with the 12 **Rector's Palace** (p299) diagonally across from it. Head down Od Puča, the main shopping strip, and cut through the market on busy 13 **Gundulićeva poljana** (p306), named after the poet whose statue stands at its centre.

At the far end, head up the Jesuit Stairs to 14 **St Ignatius of Loyola Church** (p303). Cross the square to its far corner and follow the lane as it curves along the inside of the city walls. When you see a metal gate cut through the wall to 15 **Buža** (p311).

GAME OF THRONES LOCATIONS

Dubrovnik is like a fantasy world for most people, but fans of *Game of Thrones* have more reason to indulge in flights of fancy than most, as a large chunk of the immensely popular TV series was filmed here. While Split and Šibenik were also used as locations, Dubrovnik has featured the most prominently, standing in for the cities of King's Landing and Qarth. If you fancy taking your own 'walk of shame' through the streets of Westeros, here are some key spots:

Fort Lawrence (p295) King's Landing's famous Red Keep. Cersei farewelled her daughter Myrcella from the little harbour beneath it.

City Walls (p294) Tyrion Lannister commanded the defence of King's Landing from the seaward-facing walls during the Battle of the Blackwater.

Fort Minčeta (p295) The exterior of Qarth's House of Undying.

Rector's Palace (p299) The atrium featured as the palace of the Spice King of Qarth – they didn't even bother moving the statue!

Sv Dominika street The street and staircase outside the Dominican Monastery (p301) were used for various King's Landing market scenes.

Uz Jezuite The stairs connecting the St Ignatius of Loyola Church (p303) to **Gundulićeva poljana** (Gundulićeva Square; Map p298) were the starting point for Cersei Lannister's memorable naked penitential walk. The walk continued down Stradun.

Gradac Park (Map p302; Don Frana Bulića bb, Pile) The site of the Purple Wedding feast, where King Joffrey finally got his comeuppance.

Ethnographic Museum (p301) Littlefinger's brothel.

Lokrum (p296) The reception for Daenerys in Qarth was held in the monastery cloister.

Trsteno Arboretum (p319) The Red Keep gardens, where the Tyrells chatted and plotted endlessly during seasons three and four.

tailored small-group tours targeted to cruise passengers and marketed as Dubrovnik Shore Tours (www.dubrovnikshoretours.net).

Adriatic Kayak Tours KAYAKING, CYCLING
(Map p298; ☎020-312 770; www.adriatickayaktours.com; Zrinsko Frankopanska 6, Pile; half-day from 280KN; ⏲Apr-Oct) Offers sea-kayak excursions (from a half-day paddle to a week-long trip), hiking and cycling tours, and Montenegro getaways (including rafting).

Festivals & Events

Feast of St Blaise CULTURAL
(⏲3 Feb) A city-wide bash in honour of the town's patron saint, marked by pageants and a procession listed by Unesco as an 'Intangible Cultural Heritage' for remaining largely unchanged for almost a thousand years.

Dubrovnik Summer Festival CULTURAL
(Dubrovačke ljetne igre; ☎020-326 100; www.dubrovnik-festival.hr; ⏲Jul-Aug) The most prestigious summer festival in Croatia presents a program of theatre, opera, concerts and dance on open-air stages throughout the city from 10 July to 25 August. Tickets are available online, from the festival office just off Placa, and at various venues (up to one hour before the performance).

Sleeping

Dubrovnik is the most expensive city in the country, so expect to pay more for a room here (even hostels usually fall into our midrange category) and you should book well in advance, especially in summer. There's limited accommodation in the compact old town itself. If you want to combine a beach holiday with your city stay, consider the leafy Lapad peninsula, 4km west of the centre.

Old Town

Hostel Angelina HOSTEL €
(Map p298; ☎091 89 39 089; www.hostelangelinaoldtowndubrovnik.com; Plovani skalini 17a; dm from €49; ❄📶) Hidden away in a quiet nook of the old town, this cute little hostel offers bunk rooms, a small guest kitchen and a bougainvillea-shaded terrace with memorable views over the rooftops. Plus you'll get a great glute workout every time you walk up

the lane. It also has private rooms in three old-town annexes (from €110).

★**Karmen Apartments** APARTMENT €€
(Map p298; 020-323 433; www.karmendu.com; Bandureva 1; apt from €95;) These four inviting apartments enjoy a great location a stone's throw from Ploče harbour. All have plenty of character with art, splashes of colour, tasteful furnishings and books to browse. Apartment 2 has a little balcony while apartment 1 enjoys sublime port views. Book well ahead.

City Walls Hostel HOSTEL €€
(Map p298; 091 79 92 086; www.citywallshostel.com; Sv Šimuna 15; dm/r from €46/104; @) Tucked away by the city walls, this classic backpackers is warm and welcoming with a lively character. Downstairs there's a small kitchen and a space for socialising. Upstairs you'll find clean and simple dorms and a cosy double with a sea view.

Rooms Vicelić GUESTHOUSE €€
(Map p298; 095 52 78 933; www.rooms-vicelic.com; Antuninska 10; r €80-120;) Situated on one of the steeply stepped old-town streets, this friendly, family-run place has four atmospheric stone-walled rooms with private bathrooms. Guests have use of a shared kitchenette with a microwave and a kettle. There's also a studio apartment for rent two streets down.

Villa Sigurata GUESTHOUSE €€€
(Map p298; 091 57 27 181; www.villasigurata.com; Stulina 4; s/d €110/160) Hidden down a hard-to-find and surprisingly quiet lane behind the cathedral, this 17th-century house has eight atmospheric rooms with exposed stone walls and stylish furnishings. With lanes this tight, it's not surprising that the rooms are dark but you'll appreciate the shade on hot days. It also has two other old-town annexes.

Fresh* Sheets Kathedral GUESTHOUSE €€€
(Map p298; 091 89 67 509; www.freshsheetskathedral.com; Bunićeva poljana 6; r from €188;) Head up the well-worn stairs past corridors adorned with religious art to this friendly little guesthouse, right in the thick of things. The elegant rooms all have en suites, except for one that has a bathroom just across the corridor. Our favourite is spacious room 9, which looks out on Gundulićeva poljana. There's also a guest kitchen.

Surrounds

Villa Klaić B&B €€
(Map p302; 091 73 84 673; www.villaklaic-dubrovnik.com; Šumetska 9, Pile; r from €120; P) Just off the main coastal highway, high above the old town, this outstanding guesthouse offers comfortable modern rooms and wonderful hospitality courtesy of the owner, Milo Klaić. Extras include a small swimming pool, continental breakfast, free pick-ups (for longer stays) and free beer!

Apartments Silva GUESTHOUSE €€
(Map p302; 098 244 639; Kardinala Stepinca 62, Babin Kuk; r from 660KN; P) Lush Mediterranean foliage lines the terraces of this lovely hillside complex, a short hop up from the beach at Lapad. The rooms are comfortable and well priced, but best of all is the spacious top-floor apartment (sleeping five). It doesn't have a website, but you'll find it on major booking sites.

Guest House Biličić GUESTHOUSE €€
(Map p302; 098 802 111; Privežna 2, Pile; r from 740KN;) The main attraction of this long-standing guesthouse is its gorgeous subtropical garden, with a guest kitchen on the terrace. Bedrooms are simple and clean, although you have to cross the corridor to reach your private bathroom. It doesn't have its own website but you can find it on major booking sites.

★**MirÓ Studio Apartments** APARTMENT €€€
(Map p298; 099 42 42 442; www.mirostudioapartmentsdubrovnik.com; Sv Đurđa 16, Pile; apt €145-200;) Located in a quiet residential nook only metres from the sea, hidden between the old-town walls and Fort Lawrence, this schmick complex is an absolute gem. The decor marries ancient stone walls and whitewashed ceiling beams with design features such as uplighting, contemporary bathrooms and sliding glass partitions.

Villa Dubrovnik BOUTIQUE HOTEL €€€
(020-500 300; www.villa-dubrovnik.hr; Vlaha Bukovca 6, Viktorija; r/ste from €720/1260; P) Gazing endlessly at the old town and Lokrum from its prime waterfront position, this elegant, low-slung, boutique hotel gleams white against a backdrop of honey-coloured stone. The windows retract completely to bring the indoor pool into the outdoors, but sun seekers can laze on a lounger by the sea or commandeer a day bed in the rooftop prosciutto-and-wine bar.

Dubrovnik's Old Town

Nothing quite prepares you for your first sight of Dubrovnik's Old Town. From a distance, the compact nest of terracotta roofs enclosed by honey-coloured walls jutting out into the cerulean sea is overwhelmingly picturesque. The effect doesn't diminish as you pass through the ancient gates and stride forth on the marbled lanes.

1

WITR/GETTY IMAGES ©

CGE2010/SHUTTERSTOCK ©

1. Fort Minčeta (p295)
The highest part of the City Walls, this massive structure was completed in 1464 to designs by Juraj Dalmatinac.

2. Views over the Old Town (p293)
Take in stellar views of the Old Town and Adriatic Sea from the city's fort lookouts.

3. Rooftops (p295)
Roofs sporting bright new terracotta suffered damage by the Yugoslav army's shelling of Dubrovnik in 1991 and 1992. The softer-toned original tiles are in a minority.

4. Street Dining (p310)
Relax at an outdoor table and enjoy local cuisine at an Old Town restaurant.

ANDREY OMELYANCHUK/SOOPX ©

Eating

There are some very average restaurants in Dubrovnik, so choose carefully. Many places ride on the assumption that you're here just for a day (as many cruise-ship passengers are) and that you won't be coming back. Prices are also the highest in Croatia. That said, there are some great eateries scattered around the old town, Lapad and Gruž.

Old Town

Dolce Vita SWEETS €
(Map p298; Nalješkovićeva 1a; ice cream/pancakes from 11/22KN; ⊙11am-midnight) Over a dozen different kinds of sumptuous, creamy gelato are on offer at this sweet spot. Alternatively, choose from a substantial menu of cakes and pancakes. You'll have no trouble finding it, as its bright orange chairs and lanterns picturing an ice-cream cone pop out from a narrow side street just off Stradun.

Fast Food Republic FAST FOOD €
(Map p298; www.facebook.com/RepublicDubrovnik; Široka 4; mains 39-100KN; ⊙10am-midnight; 📶) Owned and operated by a friendly young crew, this little burger bar serves a tasty selection of burgers, sandwiches, pizza slices and hot dogs. For a local twist, try an octopus burger.

Peppino's ICE CREAM €
(Map p298; www.peppinos.premis.hr; Od Puča 9; scoops from 14KN; ⊙11am-midnight) With over 20 tempting varieties of thick, delicious gelato on offer, this artisanal ice-cream shop serves everything from your standard chocolate to funky remakes based on popular candy or cakes. The Premium ice cream has an even richer flavour, and gluten-free Bio scoops are also available.

Nishta VEGAN €€
(Map p298; ☎020-322 088; www.nishtarestaurant.com; Prijeko bb; mains 98-108KN; ⊙11.30am-11.30pm Mon-Sat; 🖉) The popularity of this tiny old-town restaurant is testament not just to the paucity of options for vegetarians and vegans in Croatia, but also to the imaginative and beautifully presented food produced within. Each day of the week has its own menu with a separate set of cooked and raw options.

Oliva Pizzeria PIZZA €€
(Map p298; ☎020-324 594; www.pizza-oliva.com; Lučarica 5; mains 74-105KN; ⊙10am-11pm; 📶🖉) There are a few token pasta dishes on the menu, but this attractive little restaurant is really all about pizza. And the pizza is worthy of the attention. Grab a seat on the street and tuck in.

Bota Šare Oyster & Sushi Bar SUSHI €€
(Map p298; ☎020-324 034; www.bota-sare.hr; Od Pustijerne bb; mains 62-120KN; ⊙noon-midnight) It's fair to say that most Croatians don't have much of an interest in or aptitude for Asian cooking, yet fresh seafood is something that they understand very well, as this little place demonstrates. Grab a terrace table with a view of the cathedral and tuck into Ston oysters (fresh or tempura style) and surprisingly good sushi and sashimi.

★**Restaurant 360°** INTERNATIONAL €€€
(Map p298; ☎020-322 222; www.360dubrovnik.com; Sv Dominika bb; 2-/3-/5-courses 520/620/860KN; ⊙6.30-10.30pm Tue-Sun Apr-Sep; 📶) Dubrovnik's glitziest restaurant offers fine dining at its best, with flavoursome, beautifully presented, creative cuisine, an impressive wine list and slick, professional service. The setting is unrivalled – on top of the city walls with tables positioned so you can peer through the battlements over the harbour.

Proto SEAFOOD €€€
(Map p298; ☎020-323 234; www.esculaprestaurants.com; Široka 1; mains 225-356KN; ⊙10.30am-11pm) This elegant place is known for its fresh fish and bags of old-town atmosphere. To say it's 'long-standing' is an understatement – it opened its doors in 1886 and has served the likes of Edward VIII and Wallis Simpson. The menu showcases Dalmatian and Istrian cuisine, including fresh pasta, grilled fish and a few token meat dishes.

Restaurant Dubrovnik EUROPEAN €€€
(Map p298; ☎020-324 810; www.restorandubrovnik.com; Marojice Kaboge 5; mains 110-230KN; ⊙noon-midnight; 📶) One of Dubrovnik's most upmarket restaurants has a wonderfully unstuffy setting, occupying a covered rooftop terrace hidden among the venerable stone buildings of the old town. A strong French influence pervades a menu full of decadent and rich dishes, such as confit duck and perfectly cooked steak.

Surrounds

Slatki Kantun BURGERS, DESSERTS €
(Map p302; ☎020-494 200; www.facebook.com/SlatkiKantun; Hotel More, Nika i Meda Pucića 13, Babin Kuk; desserts 30-45KN; ⊙10am-10pm) Positioned by the pool on the terrace of the

Hotel More, this 'pastry and cocktail bar' offers a seductive selection of sweet treats including the signature (and highly theatrical) white-chocolate bomb with forest fruits. Before 5pm it also serves burgers, fish and chips, and salads (75KN to 85KN).

Shizuku JAPANESE €€
(Map p302; ☎020-311 493; www.facebook.com/ShizukuDubrovnik; Kneza Domagoja 1f, Batala; mains 70-85KN; ⏲5pm-midnight Tue-Sun; 📶) Attentive local wait staff usher you to your table in the clean-lined, modern dining room of this popular restaurant, tucked away in a residential area between Gruž Harbour and Lapad Bay. The Japanese owners will be in the kitchen, preparing authentic sushi, sashimi, udon, crispy *karaage* chicken and gyoza dumplings. Wash it all down with Japanese beer or sake.

Konoba Bonaca DALMATIAN €€
(☎020-450 000; www.konoba-bonaca.info; Sustjepanska Obala 23, Sustjepan; mains 42-130KN; ⏲9am-midnight; 🖉) You'll need to catch a bus or taxi to get to this family-style eatery on the inlet north of the harbour. Being this far from the tourist fray means you'll pay a little less for all the local favourites, such as grilled squid, black risotto and pizza. If it's open, the pretty little church next door is worth a look.

★**Nautika** EUROPEAN €€€
(Map p298; ☎020-442 526; www.nautikarestaurants.com; Brsalje 3, Pile; mains 290-360KN; ⏲6pm-midnight Apr-Oct) Nautika bills itself as 'Dubrovnik's finest restaurant' and it comes pretty close. The setting is sublime, overlooking the sea and the city walls, and the service is faultless: black bow-tie formal but friendly. As for the food, it's sophisticated if not particularly adventurous, with classic techniques applied to the finest local produce. For maximum silver-service drama, order the salt-crusted fish.

★**Pantarul** MEDITERRANEAN €€€
(Map p302; ☎020-333 486; www.pantarul.com; Kralja Tomislava 1, Lapad; mains 108-180KN, 5-course tasting menus 390-410KN; ⏲noon-4pm & 6pm-midnight Tue-Sun; 🅿📶) This breezy bistro aligns its menu with the seasons and has a reputation for exceptional homemade bread, pasta and risotto, alongside the likes of steaks, ox cheeks, burgers and various fish dishes.

Drinking & Nightlife

Old Town

Buža BAR
(Map p298; off Od Margarite; ⏲8am-2am Jun-Aug, to midnight Sep-May) Finding this ramshackle bar-on-a-cliff feels like a real discovery as you duck and dive around the city walls and finally see the entrance tunnel. However, Buža's no secret – it gets insanely busy, especially around sunset. Wait for a space on one of the concrete platforms, grab a cool drink in a plastic cup and enjoy the vibe and views.

D'vino WINE BAR
(Map p298; ☎020-321 130; www.dvino.net; Palmotićeva 4a; ⏲9am-midnight Mar-Nov; 📶) If you're interested in sampling top-notch Croatian wine, this convivial bar is the place to go. As well as a large and varied wine list, it offers tasting flights presented by cool and knowledgeable staff (three wines from 55KN) plus savoury breakfasts, snacks and platters. Sit outside for the authentic old-town-alley ambience, but check out the whimsical wall inscriptions inside.

Malvasija WINE BAR
(Map p298; Dropčeva 4; ⏲5pm-1am; 📶) Named after the white wine produced in the neighbouring Konavle region, this tiny bar is a good spot to sample the local drop. The delicious cheese and charcuterie platters (from 80KN) are a great option for a light, affordable meal in the often-pricey old town. The service is as charming as it is knowledgeable.

Dubrovnik Beer Factory CRAFT BEER
(Map p298; www.facebook.com/dubrovnikbeerfactory; Miha Pracata 6; ⏲9am-1am; 📶) The name might mislead you: this isn't, in fact, a brewery, but the selection of Croatian craft beer is good enough to justify the tag. Still, with huge murals, vaulted ceilings, historic stone details and a large beer garden tucked away in the back, the setting remains the true drawcard. It also serves food and hosts live music.

Rock Caffe Exit BAR
(Map p298; Boškovićeva 3; ⏲6pm-2am) Favoured by local rockers and metalheads, this little wood-lined upstairs bar hosts regular live acts. At other times, it's a surprisingly pleasant place for a quiet drink, away from the main tourist scrum.

Tavulin WINE BAR
(Map p298; ☎099 88 54 197; www.facebook.com/TavulinArtWine; Za Rokom 11; ⏰10.30am-10pm; 📶) Claiming a relatively quiet corner of the old town, this cute little 'wine and art bar' pours a plethora of wine by the glass, sourced from all over the country.

Buzz Bar BAR
(Map p298; ☎020-321 025; www.thebuzzbar.wixsite.com/buzz; Prijeko 21; ⏰8am-2am; 📶) Appropriately named, this buzzy little bar is rocky and relaxed, with craft beer and cocktails being the main poisons – aside from those being exhaled by the recalcitrant smokers in the corner.

Revelin CLUB
(Map p298; www.clubrevelin.com; Sv Dominika 3; ⏰11pm-6am daily Jun-Sep, Sat Oct-May) Housed within the vast vaulted chambers of Fort Revelin, this is Dubrovnik's most impressive club space, with famous international DJs dropping in during summer.

Surrounds

Cave Bar More BAR
(Map p302; www.hotel-more.hr; Šetalište Nika i Meda Pucića bb, Babin Kuk; ⏰10am-midnight Jun-Aug, to 10pm Sep-May) This little beach bar serves coffee, snacks and cocktails to bathers reclining by the dazzlingly clear waters of Lapad Bay, but that's not the half of it – the main bar is set in an actual cave. Cool off beneath the stalactites in the side chamber, where a glass floor exposes a water-filled cavern.

Coral Beach Club BAR
(Map p302; www.coral-beach-club.com; Ivana Zajca 30, Babin Kuk; ⏰9am-9pm May–mid-Sep; 📶) Spreading out along a fine stretch of pebbles, this swanky beach bar rents out luxurious loungers and serves cocktails to the bronzed souls reclining on them.

Entertainment

Summer sees classical concerts, theatre and dance performances popping up in historic fortresses and churches; look out for signs around town or enquire at any of the tourist offices. In the evening, various old-town bars host live music.

Lazareti ARTS CENTRE
(Map p302; www.arl.hr; Frana Supila 8, Ploče) Housed in a former quarantine centre, Lazareti hosts cinema nights, club nights, live music, folk dancing, art exhibitions and pretty much all the best things in town.

Shopping

★ **Kawa** GIFTS & SOUVENIRS
(Map p298; ☎091 89 67 509; www.kawa.life; Hvarska 2, Ploče; ⏰10am-8pm) Selling 'wonderful items made by Croatians', this very cool design store sells everything from wines and craft beers to jewellery, clothing, homewares and even its own line of products under the Happy Čevapi label. Superb service rounds off the experience.

Terra Croatica Dubrovnik GIFTS & SOUVENIRS
(Map p298; ☎020-323 209; www.facebook.com/terracroatica.dubrovnik; Od Puča 17; ⏰9am-9pm) A welcome interlude in a streak of shops with cheesy souvenirs and *Game of Thrones* paraphernalia, Terra Croatica wears its Authentically Croatian Souvenir certification proudly. Pop in for gift-sized foodie treats like olive oils, wines, truffles and gourmet chocolates, but also for handmade ceramics, stone mortars, cosmetics and Dalmatian cookbooks.

Medusa GIFTS & SOUVENIRS
(Map p298; ☎020-322 004; www.medusa.hr; Prijeko 18; ⏰9am-10pm Apr-Oct, 10am-5pm Nov-Mar) This self-described 'charming shop for charming people' sells locally produced soaps, flavoured salt, *rakija* (grappa), neckties, objects made from Brač stone, art prints, chocolate and toiletries.

Studio Aplika DESIGN
(Map p302; ☎099 21 23 469; Frana Supila 27, Ploče; ⏰9am-2pm & 5-10pm Apr-Nov) Interesting printed T-shirts, bags, jewellery, ceramics and art, some of it made on-site.

Uje FOOD & DRINKS
(Map p298; ☎020-321 532; www.uje.hr; Placa 5; ⏰11am-6pm Jan-Mar, 9am-9pm Apr, May & Oct-Dec, 9am-11pm Jun-Sep) Uje specialises in olive oils, along with a wide range of other locally produced epicurean delights, including some excellent jams, pickled capers, local herbs and spices, honey, figs in honey, chocolate, wine and *rakija*. There's another **branch** (Map p298; ☎020-324 865; Od Puča 2; ⏰9am-9pm Sep-Jun, to midnight Jul & Aug) around the corner.

Information

Dubrovnik's tourist board (www.tzdubrovnik.hr) has offices in **Pile** (Map p298; ☎020-312 011; Brsalje 5; ⏰8am-8pm), **Gruž** (Map p302; ☎020-417 983; Obala Pape Ivana Pavla II 1; ⏰8am-8pm Jun-Oct, 8am-3pm Mon-Fri, to 1pm Sat Nov-Mar, 8am-8pm Mon-Fri, to 2pm Sat & Sun Apr & May) and **Lapad** (Map p302; ☎020-437 460; Dvori Lapad, Masarykov put 2; ⏰8am-

8pm Jul & Aug, 8am-noon & 5-8pm Mon-Fri, 9am-2pm Sat Apr-Jun, Sep & Oct) that dispense maps, information and advice.

Dubrovnik General Hospital (Opća bolnica Dubrovnik; ☎020-431 777, emergency 194; www.bolnica-du.hr; Dr Roka Mišetića 2, Lapad) Public hospital with a 24-hour emergency department.

Marin Med Clinic (☎020-400 500; www.marin-med.com; Dr Ante Starčevića 45, Montovjerna; ⏰8am-8pm Mon-Fri, to 1pm Sat) Large private health centre with English-speaking doctors.

Travel Corner (Avansa Travel; ☎020-492 313; www.dubrovnik-travelcorner.com; Obala Stjepana Radića 40, Gruž; internet per hr 25KN, left luggage per 2hr/day 10/40KN) This handy one-stop shop has a left-luggage service and internet terminals, dispenses tourist information, books excursions and sells Kapetan Luka ferry tickets.

Getting There & Away

AIR

Dubrovnik Airport (DBV, Zračna luka Dubrovnik; ☎020-773 100; www.airport-dubrovnik.hr) is in Čilipi, 19km southeast of Dubrovnik. Croatia Airlines, British Airways, Iberica, Turkish Airlines and Vueling fly to Dubrovnik year-round. In summer they're joined by dozens of other airlines flying seasonal routes and charter flights.

Croatia Airlines has domestic flights from Zagreb (year-round), Split and Osijek (both May to October only). Trade Air has seasonal flights to/from Rijeka and Split.

BOAT

The **ferry terminal** (Map p302; Obala Pape Ivana Pavla II 1) is in Gruž, 3km northwest of the old town. Ferries for **Lokrum and Cavtat** (p294) depart from the Old Harbour.

Jadrolinija (Map p302; ☎020-418 000; www.jadrolinija.hr; Obala Stjepana Radića 40, Gruž) has four ferries per day to Koločep (23KN, 30 minutes), Lopud (23KN, 55 minutes) and Suđurađ on Šipan (23KN, 1¼ hours); an additional seven to 10 per week also head to Suđurađ (23KN, one hour), with some stopping at Lopud (23KN, one hour) en route. From June to September, there's also a daily catamaran to Korčula (130KN, two hours), Hvar (210KN, 3½ hours), Bol (210KN, 4¾ hours) and Split (210KN, six hours). From April to November, one to four car ferries per week travel between Dubrovnik and Bari in Italy (passenger/car from €44/59, 10 hours).

G&V Line (Map p302; ☎020-313 119; www.gv-line.hr; Obala Ivana Pavla II 1, Gruž) has a daily catamaran to Šipanska Luka on Šipan (35KN, 50 minutes) and to Sobra on Mljet (55KN, 1¼ hours). On Tuesdays and Thursdays in May a second boat heads directly to Sobra and then on to Ubli on Lastovo (95KN, four hours). In June this boat runs daily to Sobra and Polače on Mljet (70KN, 1¾ hours), continuing to Ubli on Tuesdays and Thursdays. In July and August they also add a stop at Korčula (90KN, 2½ hours) four times a week. Tickets can be purchased from the kiosk by the harbour 30 minutes prior to departure (an hour prior in July and August). A limited batch is released for online purchase, but must be printed to board.

Kapetan Luka (Krilo; ☎021-645 476; www.krilo.hr) has a daily fast boat from May to mid-October to/from Pomena on Mljet (80KN, 1¼ hours), Korčula (130KN, 1¾ hours), Hvar (210KN, three hours), Milna on Brač (210KN, 3¾ hours) and Split (210KN, 4¼ hours). From June to September another daily boat goes to Sobra on Mljet (80KN, 55 minutes), Korčula (130KN, two hours), Makarska (160KN, 3¼ hours), Bol on Brač (210KN, four hours) and Split (210KN, five hours).

BUS

Buses from **Dubrovnik Bus Station** (Autobusni kolodvor; Map p302; ☎060 305 070; www.libertasdubrovnik.hr; Obala Pape Ivana Pavla II 44a, Gruž; ⏰4.30am-10pm; 📶) can be crowded, so purchase tickets online or book in advance in summer. The station has toilets and a *garderoba* for storing luggage. Departure times are detailed online.

Domestic destinations include Makarska (104KN, three hours, eight daily), Split (127KN, 4½ hours, 11 daily), Zadar (182KN, eight hours, five daily), Rijeka (248KN, 12½ hours, daily) and Zagreb (259KN, 11¾ hours, 10 daily). Split–Dubrovnik buses pass briefly through Bosnian territory, so keep your passport handy for border-crossing points.

International destinations include Kotor (145KN, two hours, four daily), Budva (160KN, three hours, four daily), Mostar (125KN, 3¼ hours, three daily), Maribor (340KN, 13 hours, three daily) and Vienna (390KN, 17½ hours, three daily).

Getting Around

TO/FROM THE AIRPORT

Atlas runs the **airport shuttle bus** (Map p298; ☎020-642 286; www.atlas-croatia.com; one-way/return 40/70KN), timed around flight schedules. Buses to Dubrovnik stop at the Pile Gate and the bus station; buses to the airport pick up from the bus station and from the bus stop near the cable car.

City buses 11, 27 and 38 also stop at the airport but are less frequent and take longer (28KN, seven daily, no Sunday service).

LAZY DAYS IN DUBROVNIK

SVETI JAKOV BEACH

Wander past Dubrovnik's grandest houses to the most 'local' of Dubrovnik's beaches, **Sveti Jakov Beach** (Vlaha Bukovca bb, Viktorija), positioned at the eastern end of the coastal strip. Take a late-afternoon swim in the deliciously clear water and stay to watch the sun set over the old town from the terrace of the beach bar.

BELLEVUE BEACH

Below the Hotel Bellevue, this pebbly **cove** (Map p302; Montovjerna) is sheltered by high cliffs that provide a platform for daredevil cliff divers and also cast a shadow over the beach by late afternoon – a boon on a scorching day. Public access is via a steep staircase off Kotorska.

DANČE BEACH

This little rocky **stretch** (Map p302; Don Frana Bulića bb, Pile) has turquoise waters and a series of sunbathing terraces. It's positioned below an old monastery at the foot of Gradac Park, 600m west of the Pile Gate.

BANJE BEACH

Banje Beach is the closest beach to the old town, just beyond the 17th-century Lazareti (a former quarantine station) outside Ploče Gate. Although many people rent lounge chairs and parasols from the beach club, there's no problem with just flinging a towel on the beach if you can find a space.

LAPAD BAY

Bounded by the forested Petka hills on one side and the crest of Babin Kuk on the other, **Lapad Bay** (Uvala Lapad; Map p302; Lapad; 👪) is a busy string of pebble beaches, beachfront hotels and pedestrianised promenades. There are plenty of diversions here, both in and out of the water, including a kids playgrounds and lots of cafes and bars.

1. Banje Beach
2. Lapad Bay
3. Sveti Jakov Beach

1

GORAN JAKUS/SHUTTERSTOCK ©

2

MARTIN CHARLES HATCH/SHUTTERSTOCK ©

If the summer heat saps your enthusiasm for sightseeing, a trip to the beach is the obvious remedy. These are some of our favourites.

3

Allow up to 280KN for a taxi to Dubrovnik. Dubrovnik Transfer Services (www.dubrovnik-transfer-services.com) offers a set-price taxi transfer service to the city (€30) and Cavtat (€16), and to as far away as Zagreb, Sarajevo, Podgorica and Tirana.

CAR & MOTORCYCLE

The entire old town is a pedestrian area, public transport is good and parking is expensive, so you're better off not hiring a car until you're ready to leave the city. All of the street parking surrounding the old town is metered from May to October (40KN per hour). Further out it drops to 20KN or 10KN per hour.

It's a short walk down from the covered **Ilijina Glavica Car Park** (Map p302; ☎020-312 720; Zagrebačka bb, Pile; per hr/day/week 40/480/2400KN; ⏰24 hour) to the old town, but a hard slog back up. Note that the daily and weekly rates are for prepay only; the machines don't make this clear and we've witnessed people being stung with hefty bills as a result.

All of the usual hire-car companies are represented at the airport and most also have city branches.

PUBLIC TRANSPORT

Dubrovnik has a superb bus service; buses run frequently and generally on time. The key tourist routes run until after 2am in summer, so if you're staying in Lapad, there's no need to rush home. The fare is 15KN if you buy from the driver and 12KN if you buy a ticket at a *tisak* (news-stand). Timetables are available at www.libertasdubrovnik.hr.

To get to the old town from the bus station, take buses 1a, 1b, 3 or 8. To get to Lapad, take bus 7.

From the **bus stop** (Map p298) at Pile Gate, take bus 4, 5, 6 or 9 to get to Lapad.

AROUND DUBROVNIK

Dubrovnik is an excellent base for day trips to the surrounding region – and even in the surrounding countries of Montenegro and Bosnia. You can hop over to the Elafiti Islands (p318) for a day of peaceful sunbathing, wander through the gardens at Trsteno (p319) or pop down to Cavtat for sights and swimming.

Cavtat

POP 2150

Set on a petite peninsula embraced by two harbours, the ancient town of Cavtat (pronounced *tsav*-tat) has a pretty waterfront promenade peppered with restaurants, pebbly beaches and an interesting assortment of artsy attractions.

Without Cavtat there would be no Dubrovnik, as it was refugees from Epidaurum (the Roman incarnation of Cavtat) who established the city in 614. The walls of its famous offshoot are visible in the distance and the two are well connected by both boat and bus, making Cavtat either an easy day-trip destination from Dubrovnik or a quieter (not to mention cheaper) alternative base.

History

Founded in the 6th-century BC as a Greek settlement called Epidaurus, Cavtat became a Roman colony in 228 BC (Epidaurum) and was subsequently destroyed by invading Avars and Slavs in the 7th century. Re-established in the Middle Ages under the Republic of Ragusa (Dubrovnik), it shared in the cultural and economic life of the nearby capital.

Sights

St Nicholas' Church CHURCH

(Crkva svetog Nikole; Obala Ante Starčevića bb; ⏰hours vary) Peek inside this 15th-century church to view its impressive wooden altars and the accomplished Bukovac paintings of the four evangelists on either side of the sanctuary. Cavtat landmarks feature prominently in much of the art, including in the 19th-century altarpiece by Carmelo Reggi and in the Stations of the Cross that line the walls.

Bukovac House MUSEUM

(Kuća Bukovac; ☎020-478 646; www.kuca-bukovac.hr; Bukovčeva 5; 30KN; ⏰9am-6pm Mon-Sat, to 2pm Sun Apr-Oct, 10am-6pm Tue-Sat, 9am-1pm Sun Nov-Mar) The house where Cavtat's most famous son, the painter Vlaho Bukovac (1855–1922), was born and raised has been converted into an interesting little museum devoted to his work. The early-19th-century architecture provides a fitting backdrop to his mementoes, drawings and paintings.

Our-Lady-of-the-Snow Monastery MONASTERY

(Samostan Gospe od snijega; ☎020-678 064; www.franjevacki-samostan-cavtat.com; Šetalište Rat 2; ⏰7am-9pm) The church attached to this Franciscan Monastery (founded in 1484) is worth a look for some notable early Renaissance paintings and a wonderful Bukovac canvas depicting the Madonna and Child gazing at Cavtat at dusk. Concerts are regularly held in the cloister.

WORTH A TRIP

CROSS-BORDER JAUNTS

Dubrovnik is an easy bus ride away from **Montenegro** and the towns of Herceg Novi, Perast, Kotor and Budva. All four have wonderful historic centres, with curving marble streets and impressive architecture. If you really want to take your time and explore the region, you should hire a car, but you can also get there by public bus or on a tour. The checkpoint can be very slow in summer; allow two hours to get to Herceg Novi by bus and a further hour to reach Kotor. Citizens of most European nations, Australia, New Zealand, Canada and the US don't need a visa to enter Montenegro; other nationalities should check with their embassy.

Buses also go to **Mostar**, giving you a chance to glance at its emblematic bridge and dip your toe into the world of Bosnia and Hercegovina. It's possible to go by public transport, but easier on an organised day excursion in private minibuses (around 380KN); enquire at local travel agencies. These leave around 8am and travel via the pretty fortified village of Počitelj, arriving in Mostar around 11.30am. After a (typically very brief) guided tour you'll be left to your own devices until 3pm – which doesn't leave a lot of time to have lunch and explore the town. Mostar is still divided along Croat–Bosnian lines (with the river acting as border), but most of the historic sights are on the Bosnian side.

Račić Family Mausoleum MONUMENT
(Mauzolej obitelji Račić; www.migk.hr; Groblje sv Roka, Kvaternikova bb; 20KN; ⌚10am-5pm Mon-Sat Apr-Oct) Built from 1920 to 1921, this octagonal white-stone tomb is the handiwork of preeminent Croatian sculptor Ivan Meštrović. Inside a heavenly host of angelic faces gaze down on stylised saints. It's located in the town cemetery, in the wooded area near the peak of the peninsula.

Sleeping

★**Villa Lukas** APARTMENT €€
(☎098 549 916; www.villalukas.com; Stjepana Radića 2a; apt from 762KN; P❄☜≋) Within the peachy shell of this modern block, elegant white-stone stairs lead up to 12 attractive apartments with balconies and sea views. If you get sick of lounging by the little blue-tiled pool, there's a fitness room and a sauna tucked away in the basement.

Castelletto HOTEL €€
(☎020-479 547; www.dubrovnikexperience.com; Frana Laureana 22; r from €99; P❄@☜≋) This very well-run, family-owned place has 13 spacious rooms in a converted villa. All have tea- and coffee-making facilities, a fridge and satellite TV, and some have balconies and sweeping bay views. Airport transfers are free.

Villa Ivy APARTMENT €€€
(☎020-478 328; www.villaivy-croatia.com; SS Kranjčevića 52; apt from 960KN; P❄≋) If the location seems a little odd, tucked away in a scruffy neighbourhood at the top of the town, it all makes sense once you see the sea views from the pool terrace. Plus, it's quiet. The four apartments within the apricot-hued block are modern and very comfortable. It only accepts weeklong bookings in July and August.

Eating

Peco BAKERY, CAFE €
(Kneza Domagoja 2; pasteries 20-30KN; ⌚6am-midnight May-Sep, to 8pm Oct-Apr; ☜) Few local cafes sell food and even fewer bakeries have seats attached, making Peco a pleasant aberration. Peruse the cabinet then take a seat in the glassed-in terrace and order a sweet or savoury pastry to enjoy with your morning coffee. Return at lunchtime for a sandwich or mini pizza.

★**Bugenvila** EUROPEAN €€€
(☎020-479 949; www.bugenvila.eu; Obala Ante Starčevića 9; mains 90-275KN; ⌚noon-4pm & 6.30-10pm; ☜✍) Not just the best place on Cavtat's seafront strip, Bugenvila is one of the culinary trendsetters of the Dalmatian coast. Local ingredients are showcased in adventurous dishes served with artistic flourishes. Visit at lunchtime to take advantage of the three-course special menu (180KN). A separate vegetarian menu is available on request.

Shopping

Škatulica GIFTS & SOUVENIRS
(☎020-773 505; www.skatulica.weebly.com; Obala Ante Starčevića 36; ⌚9am-10pm Jun-Sep, to 8pm Oct-May) In Dubrovnik's dialect, *škatulica* means 'small treasure box'. Living up to its

name, this little shop serves the best of local knick-knacks in an atmospheric setting. Look for products made of Brač stone, artsy souvenirs and an assortment of foodie gems, from marmalade to wine.

Information

Tourist Office (020-479 025; https://visit.cavtat-konavle.com; Zidine 6; 8am-8pm Mon-Sat, to 2pm Sun Apr-Oct, to 3pm Mon-Fri Nov-Mar) Well stocked with leaflets and a good free map.

Getting There & Away

BOAT

During the tourist season at least three different operators offer boats to Cavtat from Dubrovnik's Old Harbour (one-way/return 100/60KN, 45 minutes), with departures at least every half hour. In winter this reduces to three to five a day, weather dependent.

BUS

Bus 10 runs roughly half-hourly to Cavtat (25KN, 30 minutes) from Dubrovnik's bus station; the closest stop to the Old Town is next to the cable-car terminus.

Konavle

After the dry and rugged coast around Dubrovnik, the lush fields and orderly vineyards of Konavle are quite a surprise. Here, in this hidden nook between the Bosnian and Montenegrin borders, east of Cavtat, the mountains have taken half a step back, providing a dramatic backdrop to the fertile agricultural region. It's best known for *malvazija,* an endemic grape producing a very pleasant white wine.

Sights

Pasjača BEACH

Hidden below high cliffs, Pasjača is one of Dalmatia's most beautiful beaches, with intensely blue and green water lapping at a pebbly shore. It's a little hard to find; head to Popovići and then follow your nose along the narrow village road, keeping an eye out for the few signs pointing the way. From the parking area, a path heads along sheer cliffs and partially through tunnels carved through the rock.

Sokol Grad CASTLE

(020-638 800; www.citywallsdubrovnik.hr; Dunave; adult/child 70/30KN; 10am-6pm Apr-Oct, 10am-4pm Nov, noon-3pm Dec-Mar) Perched atop a 25m-high crag, this fairy-tale castle has a name which literally means 'Falcon Town', and it certainly provides a bird's-eye view of Konavle. Built to guard one of the historic routes leading through the mountains to Hercegovina, the site has been occupied from prehistoric times, with the Romans, Byzantines and various medieval states taking turns to hold it before Dubrovnik wrested control. Restored and partly reconstructed, it now houses interesting displays on medieval weaponry and the castle's history.

Eating

★ **Konoba Koraćeva Kuća** DALMATIAN €€

(020-791 557; www.koracevakuca.com; Gruda 155; mains 75-165KN; 4-10pm Mon-Fri, noon-10pm Sat & Sun mid-Apr–May, 4-10pm Jun–mid-Oct; P) There's no better place to soak up the scenery than the terrace of this exceptional family-run restaurant, specialising in modern takes on Dalmatian traditions. Call ahead for lamb or veal slow-roasted under a *peka* (charcoal-covered metal dome), or just call in to see what's on the menu. Upstairs in the 300-year-old building there are six comfortable en-suite rooms (from €70).

Getting There & Away

This region is best explored by car or bike as public transport is limited. City buses 11 and 38 head from Dubrovnik to Gruda (three or four daily), or there's bus 31 from Cavtat (three to five daily). For Sokol Grad, catch bus 25 from Dubrovnik (three daily).

Elafiti Islands

A day trip to the islands in this archipelago northwest of Dubrovnik makes a perfect escape from the summer crowds. Out of 14 islands only the three largest – Koločep, Lopud and Šipan – are permanently inhabited. You can see all three in one day on a 'Three Islands & Picnic' tour, which is offered by various operators that have desks at Dubrovnik's Old Harbour (expect to pay between 250KN and 300KN, including drinks and lunch).

Sights

Koločep ISLAND

The nearest of the Elafitis to Dubrovnik, this sweet little island is inhabited by a mere 163 people and is covered in centuries-old pine forests, olive groves and orchards filled with orange and lemon trees. A sandy beach

WORTH A TRIP

TRSTENO

Gorgeous whatever the season, **Trsteno Arboretum** (020-751 019; adult/child 50/30KN; 7am-7pm May-Oct, 8am-4pm Nov-Apr), 14km northwest of Dubrovnik, is the oldest of its kind in Croatia. It was during the Renaissance that Dubrovnik's noblesse started to pay extra attention to their gardens. Ivan Gučetić started the trend at his Trsteno estate in 1494, and his descendants maintained the garden throughout the centuries. The land was eventually taken over by the Yugoslav Academy of Sciences & Arts, which turned it into a public arboretum.

The garden has a Renaissance layout, with a set of geometric shapes formed with plants such as lavender, rosemary, fuchsia and bougainvillea, while citrus trees perfume the air. It's set around a stone villa (built around 1500), with a cliff-edge pavilion in front and a chapel behind. There's also a small hedge maze, a fine palm collection (including Chinese windmill palms) and a gorgeous pond overlooked by a statue of Neptune and filled with white waterlilies and dozens of bullfrogs and goldfish. It's only partially landscaped, though – quite a bit of it is wonderfully wild.

Don't miss the two giant plane trees at the entrance to Trsteno village – each is more than 500 years old and around 50m high. They're among the largest of their kind in Europe.

To get to Trsteno, catch local bus 12, 15, 21, 22 or 35 from Dubrovnik's bus station. Otherwise any intercity bus bound for Split will stop here.

stretches out from the main village past a large resort-style hotel. Continue around the corner and you'll reach a pretty but rocky nudist area.

Lopud ISLAND

Car-free Lopud has the prettiest settlement of all the Elafitis, composed of stone houses surrounded by exotic gardens and overlooked by ruined fortresses. There's a little beach in the town, but you're better off walking across the spine of the island to beautiful sandy **Šunj**, where a little bar serves griddled fish. The walk takes about 25 minutes, or you can grab a ride in a golf cart for around 20KN.

The first sight when sailing into the harbour is the immense sea wall and 30m-high bell tower of Lopud's 15th-century **Franciscan Monastery** (Franjevački samostan; hours vary). The only part of the complex that is regularly open to the public is **St Mary-of-the-Cave Church**, built in 1483 and worth a visit for its 16th-century altarpiece and intricately carved choir chairs.

Further along the seaside promenade is shady **Đorđić-Mayneri Park** (Obala Iva Kuljevana 31), laid out in the late 19th-century by the great-granddaughter of Dubrovnik's last rector. Botanical specimens from around the world include North African date palms, North American magnolias and Tasmanian eucalyptus trees.

Dedicated to the patron saint of sailors, **St Nicholas' Church** (Crkva Sv Nikole; Obala Iva Kuljevana bb; hours vary) attests to the times when Lopud was an important seafaring centre. Positioned on the waterfront, this 1482 church is modest in content, but provides an airy environment for a quiet moment.

It's also worth seeking out **Your Black Horizon Art Pavilion** (www.TBA21.org/lopud; 10am-7pm Jun-Sep) FREE, set in an orchard of cypress, carob and olive trees on the edge of the settlement. This amalgamation of contemporary art and architecture was moved here after originally being presented at the Venice Biennale in 2005. Inside is a light installation that showcases the colour changes on the horizon over a 24-hour period, shortened into a 15-minute looping LED display.

Šipan ISLAND

At 16 sq km Šipan is the largest of the Elafiti Islands and was a favourite with the Dubrovnik aristocracy, who built houses here. Most ferries dock in **Suđurađ**, a little harbour lined with stone houses and the large fortified Skočibuha villa and tower, built in the 16th century (not open to the public). On the other side of the island, the village of **Šipanska Luka** has the remains of a Roman villa and a 15th-century Gothic duke's palace.

Buses, mainly timed around the ferries, connect the two settlements.

Sleeping & Eating

★Hotel Božica HOTEL €€€

(☎020-325 400; www.hotel-bozica.hr; Ulica 13 1d, Suđurađ, Šipan; r/apt/ste from €160/290/390; ⏲May-Oct; P❄📶🏊) If it's peace and quiet you're after, you could do a lot worse than this modern 30-room hotel on Šipan. Shuffle from the pool to the beach terrace and back again before plotting your next move. The restaurant perhaps? It also rents kayaks and bikes.

Obala DALMATIAN €€€

(☎020-759 170; www.obalalopud.com; Obala Iva Kuljevana 18, Lopud; mains 120-165KN; ⏲10.30am-6pm Apr, to midnight May-Sep) The finest restaurant on Lopud, Obala has been known for its seafood delicacies since 1938. The prices are as fine as the service and the food, but the ambience surpasses it all; you'll be sitting close enough to the sea to dip your feet in. If in doubt, go for the fresh fish baked in salt, a local speciality.

Getting There & Away

Aside from the numerous boat tours, there are regular ferries to the Elafitis from Dubrovnik's Gruž Harbour.

Jadrolinija (p313) has four ferries per day to Koločep (23KN, 30 minutes), Lopud (23KN, 55 minutes) and Suđurađ on Šipan (23KN, 1¼ hours); an additional seven to 10 car ferries per week also head to Suđurađ (23KN, one hour), with some stopping at Lopud (23KN, one hour) en route.

G&V Line (p313) has a daily catamaran connecting Šipanska Luka (on Šipan) to Dubrovnik (35KN, 50 minutes) and to Sobra on Mljet (30KN, 35 minutes).

MLJET ISLAND

POP 1090

Forest-shrouded Mljet is one of the most seductive of all the Adriatic islands. The establishment of a national park in 1960 at its western end put the island on the tourist map, but Mljet is anything but overrun. Visitors are almost entirely drawn to the tourist enclave around Pomena. The remainder of the island retains the unspoilt air of tranquillity that, according to legend, captivated Odysseus for seven years.

History

Ancient Greeks called the island 'Melita' or 'honey' for the many bees humming in the forests. It appears that Greek sailors came to the island for refuge against storms and to gather fresh water from the springs. At that time the island was populated by Illyrians, who erected hill forts and traded with the mainland. They were conquered by the Romans in 35 BC, who expanded the settlement around Polače by building a palace, baths and servants' quarters.

The island fell under the control of the Byzantine Empire in the 6th century and was later subjected to the 7th-century invasions of Slavs and Avars. After several centuries of regional rule from the mainland, Mljet was given to the Benedictine order in the 13th century. Dubrovnik formally annexed the island in 1410.

Although Mljet's fortunes were thereafter tied to those of Dubrovnik, the inhabitants maintained their traditional activities of farming, viticulture and seafaring. These remain key occupations today.

Information

Sobra Tourist Office (☎020-746 025; www.mljet.hr; ⏲9am-2pm & 4-7pm Mon-Sat, 9am-2pm Sun May-Sep, 9am-2pm Mon-Fri Oct-Apr) Tucked away by the Jadrolinija ticket office at the ferry port.

Getting There & Away

Mljet has three ferry ports: Sobra, near the centre of the island, and Polače and Pomena in the national park. Catamarans head to all three; only Sobra handles car ferries.

➡ The quickest connection from the mainland is the **Jadrolinija** (☎020-746 134; www.jadrolinija.hr; Zaglavac bb) car ferry from Prapratno to Sobra (passenger/car 28/140KN, 45 minutes, four to five daily).

➡ G&V Line (p313) has a catamaran between Sobra and Dubrovnik daily (55KN, 1¼ hours), stopping first at Šipanska Luka (30KN, 35 minutes). On Tuesdays and Thursdays in May a second boat heads directly from Dubrovnik to Sobra and then on to Ubli (70KN, three hours). In June this boat runs to Sobra and Polače daily, continuing on to Ubli twice a week. In July and August it also stops at Korčula (80KN, 55 minutes) four times a week.

➡ From May to mid-October Kapetan Luka (p313) has a daily boat to Pomena from Dubrovnik (80KN, 1¼ hours), Korčula (80KN, 30 minutes), Hvar (140KN, 1¾ hours), Milna (140KN, 2½ hours) and Split (140KN, three hours). From June to September a second daily boat heads to Sobra from Dubrovnik (80KN, 55 minutes), Korčula (80KN, 55 minutes), Makarska (140KN, 2¼ hours), Bol (140KN, three hours) and Split (140KN, four hours).

OFF THE BEATEN TRACK

VID

Huddled on a hill by the sleepy Norin River, tiny Vid stands out amid the lush-green flat lands of the Neretva River valley. Once a thriving Roman settlement named Narona and later ruled by the Neretva pirates, today it is one of the only parts of southern Dalmatia where the economy relies on agriculture, rather than tourism.

An ideal off-the-beaten-path excursion from Dubrovnik, or diversion on the way to Split or Mostar, Vid offers visitors a completely different experience from the nearby Dalmatian coast. The town's unrushed character envelopes you slowly as you stroll around the archaeological museum or take a peaceful boat ride through the surrounding marshland.

Narona Archaeological Museum (Arheološki muzej Narona; ☎020-691 596; www.a-m-narona.hr; Naronski trg 6; adult/student 40/20KN; ⊙9am-7pm Tue-Sun Jun-Sep, to 4pm Tue-Sat, to 1pm Sun Oct-May) In 1995 archaeologists in Vid made the extraordinary discovery of an Augusteum, a temple dedicated to the cult of the Roman Emperors, built around 10 BC. Along with a simple monochromatic floor mosaic they found 17 marble statues of the Imperial family, all of which had been decapitated when the temple was destroyed in the 4th century. The site is now enclosed within an impressive piece of contemporary architecture, showcasing the temple and other exhibits highlighting the area's history.

Đuđa i Mate (☎020-687 500; www.djudjaimate.hr; Velika Riva 2; mains 60-100KN; ⊙9am-11pm) Established by two best friends a quarter of a century ago, this landmark restaurant is famous for its Neretva regional specialities, particularly frogs and eels. Try them fried, grilled or combined in a *Neretva brudet* – a flavourful spiced stew served with polenta. It also offers 45-minute 'safaris' along the Norin River in a shallow, traditional boat called a trupa.

Getting There & Away

From the main coastal D8 road, follow the signs onto the E73 to Metković. In Metković, turn left onto the bridge across the Neretva River and follow the signs to Vid.

There are no regular buses to Vid but many intercity services stop in nearby Metković, 3.5km away, where you can continue by cab.

Getting Around

- **Mini Brum** (☎099 61 15 574; www.rent-a-car-scooter-mljet.hr; ⊙9am-7pm) rents basic cars (five/12/24 hours from 280/320/390KN) and scooters (five/12/24 hours from 190/220/250KN) from the ferry port in Sobra and from Polače.
- Bikes can easily be rented in Polače or Pomena (around 20KN per hour).
- Expect to pay about 300KN for a taxi between Sobra and Polače.
- Bus services on the island are limited to a single bus per day departing from each end of the island at the crack of dawn and heading to Sobra, returning in the evening.

Mljet National Park

Although it covers 54 sq km of land and sea, including the entire westernmost quarter of the island, when most people talk of **Mljet National Park** (Nacionalni park Mljet; ☎020-744 041; www.np-mljet.hr; Pristanište 2; adult/child Jun-Sep 125/70KN, Oct-May 70/50K; ⊙office 8am-8pm Apr-Oct) they're referring to the small section that's ticketed, taking in the gorgeous saltwater lakes Malo Jezero (Little Lake) and Veliko Jezero (Big Lake). The two are connected to each by a short channel, while the larger one empties into the sea via the much longer Soline Channel, which makes the lakes subject to tidal flows.

The main hubs of the park are the small villages of Pomena and Polače, which are packed with visitors on summer days but quieten down again once all the boats leave. Kiosks in both villages sell park admission tickets. From Pomena it's a 400m walk along a forested path to Malo Jezero; from Polače, your ticket includes a transfer to Pristanište on Veliko Jezero, where there's a park information centre.

Sights

Sveta Marija ISLAND

Tiny St Mary's Island lies on Veliko Jezero, not far from its southern shore. Boats (included in the park admission price) head here at least hourly during park opening hours from Mali Most, the bridge near the channel between the two lakes, and from Pristanište. The island's **Benedictine monastery** was founded in 1198 but has been rebuilt several times, adding Renaissance and baroque features to the Romanesque structure.

Roman Palace RUINS

(Rimska palača; Polače) It's hard to miss this impressive structure on the Polače waterfront; it's so large that the road now passes through the centre of it. Built around the 5th century, this palatial residence has a rectangular floor plan and towers on the front corners separated by a pier. Other ancient ruins scattered around the town include a late Antiquity fort and an early Christian church.

Activities

There are walking and cycling paths throughout the national park, and bikes are available to rent from various locations. Cycling is an excellent way to explore but be aware that Pomena and Polače are separated by a steep hill. The lakeside bike path is an easier and very scenic pedal.

You can walk completely around the little lake, but not the larger one, as there's no bridge over the Soline Channel. If you decide to swim it, keep in mind that the current can be strong.

The busiest swimming spot is on the little lake, near the bridge – although we suggest that you stroll along the shore until you find a quiet nook of your own. There's also a nice little beach near Polače.

Eating

Konoba Galija DALMATIAN €€€

(☎095 91 12 588; Pomena 7a; mains 80-220KN; ⏰noon-11pm) Galija is one of a string of seafood restaurants on the Pomena waterfront – each with its own yacht moorings and seawater tank stocked with lobsters. If you don't mind getting messy, order the spaghetti with shrimp; it's big enough for two and absolutely delicious. Otherwise there's grilled fish, *brodet* (fish stew), octopus and all the usual fishy suspects.

Okuklje

POP 30

Basically a single row of houses clinging to an almost-circular bay ringed by green hills, Okuklje is the kind of place that's easy to fall in love with at first sight. There's not a lot to do here apart from relax with a book, take a dip in the harbour and walk up to tiny St Nicholas' Church for the views over the bay and back towards the Pelješac Peninsula.

Sleeping & Eating

Lampalo APARTMENT €

(☎099 62 38 833; Okuklje 8; apt from €39; P ❄ 📶) Despite English not being their strong point, the charming hosts offer a warm welcome and maybe even a beer on arrival. With a bit of notice they'll fire up the charcoal and throw something on the grill for dinner. There are only two simple apartments for rent: a studio and a spacious two-bedroom.

Konoba Maestral DALMATIAN €€€

(☎098 428 890; www.okukljerestaurantmaestral.com; Okuklje 47; mains 110-150KN; ⏰1pm-midnight mid-Apr–mid-Oct; 📶) Maestral is an altogether charming family affair, with the owner's young children helping out front of house and the oldest son sweating away shovelling charcoal onto the pre-ordered *pekas* (metal domes used to roast lamb or octopus). Make sure you try the octopus carpaccio – we can't recommend it highly enough.

Saplunara

POP 70

At Mljet's very eastern tip, the teensy village of Saplunara feels sublimely isolated – despite the views towards the bright lights of Dubrovnik. The main drawcards are an excellent restaurant and a trio of sandy beaches. If you're tempted to stop at the first (**Velika Saplunara**) or second beach (**Mala Saplunara**), resist the urge and continue to the third (**Blace**) – the water's shallow, but this semicircular cove is the most beautiful beach on the island.

Sleeping & Eating

Villa Mirosa B&B €€

(☎099 19 96 270; www.villa-mirosa.com; Saplunara 26; r from €116; ⏰Mar-Dec; P ❄ 📶 🏊) A gorgeous infinity-lipped rooftop pool is what gives this guesthouse the edge over similar places on Mljet. The rooms are perfectly pleasant, and there's a grapevine-shrouded terrace restaurant at the front and access to a rocky cove at the rear.

Stermasi DALMATIAN €€
(098 93 90 362; www.stermasi.hr; Saplunara 2; mains 70-190KN; 8am-midnight;) Stermasi's 11 apartments (from €65) are bright and modern, and either have a terrace or private balcony. But the big draw here is the restaurant, serving flavoursome, authentic Dalmatian food prepared with love and skill. House specialities include vegetables, octopus or kid goat cooked under a *peka,* wild boar with gnocchi and Mljet-style *brodet* (fish stew).

BYPASSING BOSNIA

Jadrolinija (020-743 911; www.jadrolinija.hr; Ribarska obala 1) runs the Ploče–Trpanj car ferry (passenger/car 32/138KN, four to seven daily). If you're coming from (or heading to) the north, this ferry cuts around 90 minutes off the drive, but takes an hour for the crossing. It also avoids having to pass through Bosnian territory. Car ferries for Sobra on Mljet leave from Prapratno, while those for Korčula Town leave from Orebić.

PELJEŠAC PENINSULA

The slender, fingerlike peninsula of Pelješac is coastal Croatia at its most relaxed. Blessed with craggy mountains, sweeping valleys, idyllic coves and fine wines, it's a glorious place to visit. Two historic towns, Ston and Orebić, bookend the peninsula and the slow, winding drive between them is a very pleasant one indeed; allow an hour, or longer if you stop for wine tastings along the way. The peninsula's third-largest settlement is pretty little palm-lined Trpanj on the northern coast, where the car ferry leaves for Ploče.

Ston & Mali Ston

POP 690

Flanking the isthmus that connects the Pelješac Peninsula with the mainland, Ston and Mali ('little') Ston – are famous for three things: salt, oysters and the remarkable 5.5km defensive wall that links them.

The first two have been harvested here since Roman times. The name Ston derives from its Latin name Stagnum, a reference to the marshy nature of the land, which was put to use for the production of salt. The economic importance of this industry to the Republic of Ragusa (Dubrovnik) led, in 1333, to the construction of one of the longest fortifications in Europe, stretching clear across the isthmus.

Within its walls, Ston has an atmospheric medieval town centre with sunny, car-free streets. Mali Ston is a gastronomic destination in its own right, famed for the mussels and large flat oysters that thrive in the narrow channel separating the peninsula from the mainland.

Sights

Ston Walls FORT
(Stonske zidine; adult/child 70/30KN; 8am-6.30pm Apr-Oct, 9am-3pm Nov-Mar) Famous architects, including Juraj Dalmatinac (best known for Šibenik Cathedral), were involved in the design and construction of Ston's extraordinary 14th-century defenses, which originally included 40 towers and five forts, and stretched for 7km. Twenty towers and 5.5km of wall are still standing, arching far up the hill between Ston and Mali Ston. You can walk the Ston section in 15 minutes; allow an extra 30 sweaty minutes to continue up and over the hill to Mali Ston.

Admission includes entry to the substantially reconstructed **Fort St Jerome** (Tvrđava sv Jeronima), a square castle with a tower at each corner positioned on Ston's southeastern flank.

Prapratno BEACH
The closest beach to Ston, this gem of a bay has a sandy shore and clear, calm waters, making it a hit with local families. It's located 4km southwest of Ston, near the ferry to Mljet.

Sleeping & Eating

Ostrea HOTEL €€
(020-754 555; www.ostrea.hr; Mali Ston; s/d from €83/111; P) Behind the stone walls and green shutters of this historic building are elegant rooms with polished timber floors and en suite bathrooms. Staff are welcoming and professional and the hotel is just steps from Mali Ston's pretty harbour.

★ **Kapetanova Kuća** DALMATIAN, SEAFOOD €€
(020-754 264; www.ostrea.hr; Mali Ston; mains 95-140KN; 9am-midnight) The 'Captain's

PELJEŠAC WINE TRAIL

As they zip along the winding road through the centre of the Pelješac Peninsula, travellers may not be aware that they're passing through the realm of the king of Croatian red wines: *plavac mali*.

A descendant of *crljenak kaštelanski* (more commonly known as *zinfandel* or *primitivo*) and little-known *dobričić*, this little *(mali)* blue *(plavac)* grape produces big, flavoursome wine. The more inhospitable the terrain, the more flavour-laden the grapes, which is why the very best *plavac mali* is grown on the barren, sun-baked slopes of **Dingač** and **Postup** on the peninsula's southern coast. The vines are so difficult to access that all of the grapes must be harvested by hand. Both of these regions are now recognised appellations, protected by a 'stamp of geographic origin'.

You couldn't hope for a more authentically rustic spot to sample a local drop than **Taverna Domanoeta** (091 56 01 591; 9am-1am Jul & Aug), a stone-walled cellar bar in **Janjina**, a small village at the very centre of the peninsula. If it's sunny, grab a table in the garden and order some *plavac mali*, accompanied by local cheese and *pršut* (prosciutto).

A little further on is the turn-off for the village of **Trstenik**, where legendary Napa Valley winemaker Mike Grgich has established **Grgić Vina** (020-748 090; www.grgic-vina.com; Trstenik 78; tasting 40KN; 9am-9pm Jun-Aug, to 5pm Mon-Fri Sep-May). Call in to the winery to try and buy the award-winning *plavac mali* and *pošip* (a white varietal that originated on Korčula); phone ahead in winter.

The main road continues through a valley to **Potomje** village, where a 400m tunnel cuts through the mountain to the famed wine-growing slopes of Dingač. Of the many wineries in Potomje, the best to visit is **Matuško** (020-742 393; www.matusko-vina.hr; Potomje 5a; 8am-8pm Mar-Dec), where you can check out the extensive cellars before sitting down to a free tasting.

If all this wine tasting is making you thirsty, stop at **Peninsula** (020-742 503; www.peninsula.hr; Donja Banda; 9am-11pm Apr-Oct;), a roadside wine bar with over 40 high-quality local wines, as well as a selection of *rakija* (grappa) and liqueurs. It's located in **Donja Banda**, near where the road from Trpanj branches off from the main peninsula road.

House' is one of the most venerable seafood restaurants in the region. Feast on Ston oysters and grilled squid on the shady terrace, but try to leave room for the *Stonski makaruli*, a macaroni cake that's a local speciality – it's unusual but surprisingly delicious.

Information

Tourist Office (020-754 452; www.ston.hr; Pelješki put 1, Ston; 8am-7pm Jun-Sep, 8am-2pm Mon-Fri Oct-May) Has brochures and bus timetables and can help you find private accommodation.

Getting There & Away

The bus stop is on the main road in Ston. You can walk from here to Mali Ston in 15 minutes. Destinations include Orebić (51KN, 1½ hours, two daily), Dubrovnik (from 42KN, 1¼ hours, five daily), Split (105KN, 3¼ hours, daily), Zadar (174KN, six hours, daily) and Zagreb (247KN, 9½ hours, daily).

Orebić

POP 1980

Orebić, on the southern coast of the Pelješac Peninsula, has a strip of lovely little beaches, some sandy and some shingly, bordered by groves of tamarisk and pine. Its waterfront is lined with houses and exotic gardens built by the sea captains who made the town prosperous in the 18th century. Only 2.5km across the water from Korčula Town, it makes a perfect day trip or an alternative base.

After lazing on the beach, you can take advantage of some excellent hiking up and around Mt Ilija (961m) or poke around a couple of churches and museums. Mt Ilija protects the town from harsh northern winds, allowing vegetation to flourish. The temperature is usually a few degrees warmer than Korčula; spring arrives early and summer leaves late.

History

The Pelješac Peninsula became part of Dubrovnik in 1333, when it was purchased from Serbia. Until the 16th century the town was known as Trstenica (the name of its eastern bay) and was an important maritime centre. The name Orebić comes from a wealthy seafaring family who, in 1658, built a citadel as a defence against the Turks.

The height of Orebić seafaring was in the 18th and 19th centuries, when it was the seat of one of the largest companies of the day: the Associazione Marittima di Sabbioncello. With the decline of shipping, Orebić began to turn to tourism.

Sights & Activities

Orebić is a great base for hiking, so pick up a trail map from the tourist office. A track through the pine trees leads from the Hotel Bellevue to a 15th-century **Franciscan monastery** on a ridge 152m above the sea. From this vantage point, Dubrovnik patrols could watch the Venetian ships moored on Korčula and notify the authorities of any suspicious movements.

The village of **Karmen** near the monastery is the starting point for walks to picturesque upper villages and the more daring climb up **Mt Ilija**, the bare, grey massif that hangs over Orebić. The reward for climbers is a sweeping view of the entire coast.

On a hill east of the monastery is **Our Lady of Carmel Church**, next to several huge cypresses, as well as a baroque loggia and the ruins of a duke's castle.

Plaža Trstenica BEACH
There's a slim beach west of the dock, but the best beach is the long stretch at Trstenica about 700m east of the dock. A beautiful broad crescent of sand and fine shingle, it's fringed by trees and turquoise waters.

Korta Katarina WINERY
(020-713 817; www.kortakatarinawinery.com; Bana Josipa Jelačića 3; 9am-9pm May-Sep, to 4pm Apr & Oct) Phone ahead to arrange a tasting at this large, schmick winery. Basic sessions include a tour and tastings of three wines (100KN), VIP tastings add an extra reserve wine and snacks (300KN), while degustation tastings include a five-course meal with wine pairings (700KN).

Sleeping

Glavna Plaža CAMPGROUND €
(098 513 634; www.glavnaplaza.com; Šetalište kneza Domogoja 49; camping per adult/child/site/car from €5/2/4/4, apt from €44; Jun-Sep; P) This tiny family-run campground is tucked away at the Orebić end of sandy Trstenica beach. As well as sites, there are four simple apartments available (three studios and one that can sleep six).

Mimbelli B&B €€
(020-713 636; www.peljesac-mimbelli.hr; Trg Mimbelli 6; r from €100; P) This appealing little guesthouse has five romantic rooms set above a reputable restaurant in an atmospheric 18th-century captain's house. Each is tastefully furnished along a rustic theme (olive, grapevine, lavender etc).

Hotel Adriatic HOTEL €€€
(020-714 488; www.hoteladriaticorebic.com; Šetalište kneza Domagoja 8; r €180-210;) Right by the water, this converted ship-captain's mansion has six luxurious rooms with exposed stone walls, wooden floors, ample bathrooms and sea views. An excellent breakfast is served on the seaside terrace. No children are permitted.

Hotel Indijan HOTEL €€€
(020-714 555; www.hotelindijan.hr; Škvar 2; s/d from €110/190; P) A contemporary feel pervades this well-designed hotel. Rooms are modern and well equipped, and some have balconies with views to Korčula. The small circular heated pool has a retractable glass roof, so it's usable year-round.

Eating

Croccantino CAFE €
(098 16 50 777; www.facebook.com/CroccantinoCRO; Obala Pomoraca 30; snacks 8-18KN; 7am-11pm) Satisfy a sweet urge with a strudel, slice of cake or a homemade gelato at this chilled-out cafe on the promenade.

La Casa PIZZA €€
(020-713 847; Obala Pomoraca 40; mains 43-145KN; noon-10pm;) There's a funky garden bar downstairs, but head up to the terrace of this grand old house for sea views and tasty Neapolitan-style pizza. It also serves pasta, risotto, steaks and grilled squid.

Konoba Andiamo DALMATIAN €€
(098 98 38 614; Šetalište kneza Domagoja 28; mains 50-120KN; 1pm-midnight Jun-Oct;) A bright mural of a city street provides a cheerfully anachronistic backdrop for this breezy restaurant, set in a wooden terrace just metres from the sea. We wholeheartedly endorse the seafood platter for two, packed with prawns, mussels, langoustine and two types of fish. With advance notice it'll also roast lamb, pork, veal or octopus under a *peka*.

Information

Tourist Office (☎020-713 718; www.visitorebic-croatia.hr; Zrinsko Frankopanska 2; ⏰8am-10pm Jul & Aug, to 8pm Mon-Sat May, Jun, Sep & Oct, to 1pm Mon-Fri Nov-Apr) Supplies a good hiking and biking map of the peninsula.

Getting There & Away

Jadrolinija (☎020-714 075; www.jadrolinija.hr; Obala pomoraca 32) car ferries from Korčula (passenger/car 16/76KN, 15 minutes) tie up just steps from the tourist office and bus stop.

Buses head to/from Ston (51KN, 1½ hours, three daily), Dubrovnik (81KN, 2¾ hours, two daily), Split (121KN, 4½ hours, daily), Zadar (194KN, 7¼ hours, daily) and Zagreb (258KN, 10¾ hours, daily).

KORČULA ISLAND

POP 15,600

Rich in vineyards, olive groves and small villages, and harbouring a glorious old town, the island of Korčula is the sixth-largest Adriatic island, stretching nearly 47km in length. Dense pine forests led the original Greek settlers to call the island Korkyra Melaina (Black Corfu). Quiet coves and small sandy beaches dot the steep southern coast while the northern shore is flatter and more pebbly.

Tradition is alive and kicking on Korčula, with age-old religious ceremonies, folk music and dances still being performed to the delight of an ever-growing influx of tourists. Oenophiles will adore sampling its wine. Arguably the best of all Croatian whites is produced from the indigenous grape *pošip*, particularly from the areas around the villages of Čara and Smokvica. The *grk* grape, cultivated around Lumbarda, also produces quality dry white wine.

The island's best beach is Pupnatska Luka on the south coast.

History

A neolithic cave (Vela Spila) located near Vela Luka, on the island's western end, points to the existence of a prehistoric settlement, but it was the Greeks who first began spreading over the island sometime around the 6th century BC. Their most important settlement was founded in the area of today's Lumbarda around the 3rd century BC.

Rome conquered Korčula in the 1st century, giving way to the Byzantines in the 6th and Slavs in the 7th century. After the turn of the first millennium, the island passed through the hands of various medieval states before falling to the Venetians in 1420, who remained until 1797. Under Venetian control the island became known for its stone, which was quarried and cut for export. Shipbuilding also flourished.

After the Napoleonic conquest of Venice in 1797, Korčula's fortunes followed those of the region, changing hands among the French, British, Austro-Hungarians and Italians before becoming a part of the first Yugoslavia in 1921. Today Korčula is one of Croatia's most prosperous islands, its historic capital drawing visitors in increasing numbers.

Getting There & Away

BOAT

The island has three major entry ports: Korčula Town's West Harbour, Dominče (3km east of Korčula Town) and Vela Luka.

Jadrolinija (☎020-715 410; www.jadrolinija.hr; Plokata 19 travnja 1921 br 19) has car ferries between Orebić and Dominče (passenger/car 16/76KN, 15 minutes), departing roughly every hour (every 90 minutes from October to May). From June to September, a daily catamaran heads from Korčula Town to Dubrovnik (130KN, two hours), Hvar (120KN, 1½ hours), Bol (130KN, 2¾ hours) and Split (160KN, 3¾ hours).

From Vela Luka, Jadrolinija has two car ferries a day to Split (passenger/car 60/470KN, 2¾ hours) and up to three a day to Ubli on Lastovo (passenger/car 32/180KN, 1¾ hours). There's also a daily catamaran on this route, stopping in Hvar (40KN, 55 minutes) en route between Split (60KN, 2¼ hours) and Ubli (40KN, 55 minutes).

Kapetan Luka (p313) sails a catamaran from Korčula Town to Hvar (110KN, 1¼ hours) and Split (130KN, 2½ hours) at least once a day. From May to mid-October there's a daily boat to/from Dubrovnik (130KN, 1¾ hours), Pomena on Mljet (80KN, 30 minutes), Hvar (110KN, one hour), Milna on Brač (130KN, 1¾ hours) and Split (130KN, 2¼ hours). From June to September there's another boat to Dubrovnik (130KN, two hours), Sobra on Mljet (80KN, 55 minutes), Makarska (130KN, one hour), Bol (120KN, 1¾ hours) and Split (130KN, 2¾ hours).

In July and August, G&V Line (p313) has four catamarans per week to Korčula Town from Dubrovnik (90KN, 2½ hours), Sobra (60KN, 1½ hours) and Polače on Mljet (50KN, 55 minutes). Two of these continue on to Ubli (60KN, 1¼ hours).

BUS

Buses connecting the mainland and Korčula Town use the Orebić car ferry. Destinations include Ston (63KN, two hours, two daily), Dubrovnik (97KN, three hours, daily), Split (129KN, five hours, daily), Zadar (202KN, 7¾ hours, daily) and Zagreb (269KN, 11¼ hours, daily). Book ahead in summer.

Getting Around

Buses head from Korčula Town to Lumbarda (15KN, 15 minutes, at least five daily) and Vela Luka (43KN, one hour, at least three daily); limited Sunday service.

Korčula Town

POP 2860

Korčula Town is a stunner. Ringed by imposing defences, this coastal citadel is dripping with history, with marble streets rich in Renaissance and Gothic architecture.

Its fascinating fishbone layout was cleverly designed for the comfort and safety of its inhabitants: western streets were built straight in order to open the city to the refreshing summer *maestral* (strong, steady westerly wind), while the eastern streets were curved to minimise the force of the winter *bura* (cold, northeasterly wind).

The town cradles a harbour, overlooked by round defensive towers and a compact cluster of red-roofed houses. There are rustling palms all around and several beaches are an easy walk away.

History

Although documents indicate that a walled town existed on this site in the 13th century, it wasn't until the 15th century that the current city was built. Construction coincided with the apogee of stone-carving skills on the island, lending the buildings and streets a distinctive style. In the 16th century masons added decorative flourishes such as ornate columns and coats of arms to building facades, which gave a Renaissance look to the original Gothic core.

People began building houses south of the old town in the 17th and 18th centuries as the threat of invasion diminished. The narrow streets and stone houses in the 'new' suburb attracted merchants and artisans, and this is still where you'll find most commercial activity.

Sights & Activities

There are some excellent biking and hiking trails around Korčula; pick up an island map from the tourist office (p330). In the summer, water taxis offer trips to Badija Island, which has a 15th-century Franciscan monastery, a restaurant and a naturist beach.

★**St Mark's Cathedral** CATHEDRAL
(Katedrala svetog Marka; Trg Sv Marka; church 10KN, bell tower adult/child 20/15KN; ⏲9am-9pm Jul & Aug, hours vary Sep-Jun) Dominating the little square at Korčula's heart is this magnificent 15th-century cathedral, built from Korčula limestone in a Gothic-Renaissance style by Italian and local artisans. The sculptural detail of the facade is intriguing, particularly the naked squatting figures of Adam and Eve on the door pillars, and the two-tailed mermaid and elephant on the triangular gable cornice at the very top. The **bell tower**

SWORD DANCES

One of the island's most colourful traditions, the Moreška sword dance has been performed in Korčula Town since the 15th century. Although it's probably of Spanish origin, the only place in the world that it's performed now is in Korčula. It tells the story of two kings – the White King (dressed in red) and the Black King – who fight for a princess abducted by the Black King. In the spoken introduction the princess declares her love for the White King, and the Black King refuses to relinquish her. The two armies draw swords and 'fight' in an intricate dance accompanied by a band. Although traditionally performed only on Korčula's town day (29 July), the **Moreška Cultural Club** (www.moreska.hr; Ljetno kino, Foša 2; 100KN; ⏲shows 9pm Mon & Thu Jul & Aug, shows 9pm Thu Jun & Sep) now stages it throughout the summer.

Kumpanija dances in the villages of Pupnat, Smokvica, Blato, Čara and the town of Vela Luka also make for a fun night out, but you'll need your own transport to see them. These dances also involve a 'fight' between rival armies and culminate in the unfurling of a huge flag. They're accompanied by the *mišnice* (similar to a bagpipe) and drums. A variation is the *moštra*, performed in the village of Žrnovo only on the evening of the Feast of the Assumption (15 August).

Korčula Town

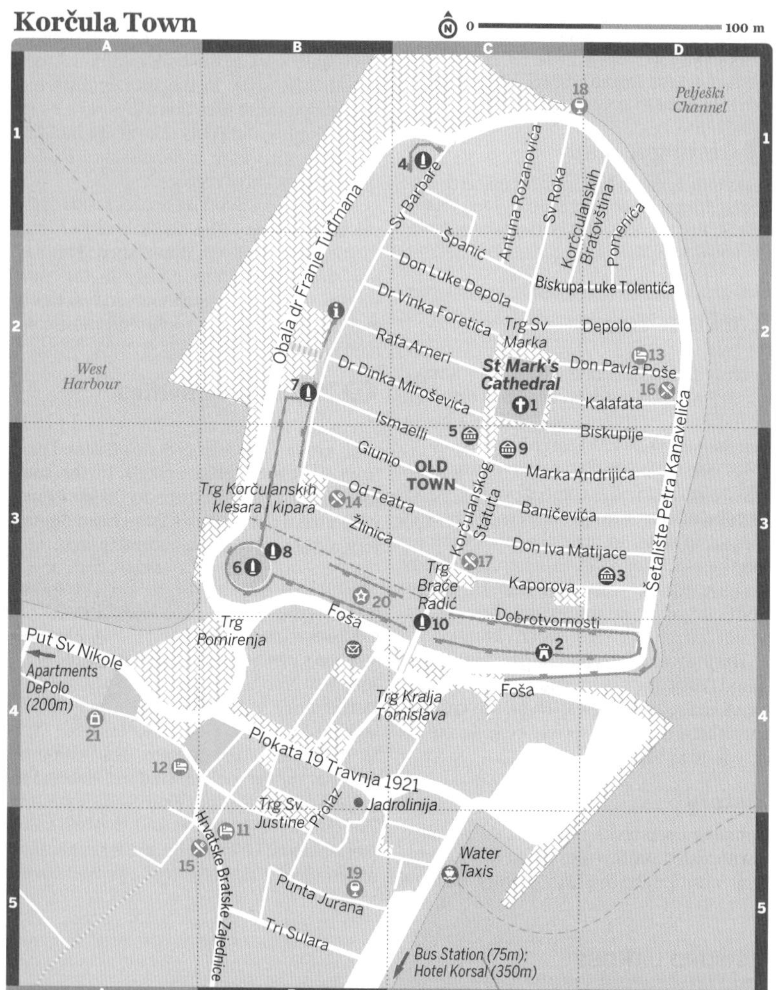

is topped by a balustrade and ornate cupola, beautifully carved by Korčulan Marko Andrijić.

Inside, the nave soars 30m in height and is lined with a twin colonnade of exposed limestone pillars. Look out for the ciborium, also carved by Andrijić, and behind it the altarpiece painting *Three Saints,* by Tintoretto. Another painting attributed to Tintoretto or his workshop, *The Annunciation,* is beside the baroque altar of St Anthony.

Other noteworthy artworks include a bronze statue of St Blaise by Ivan Meštrović, near the altar on the northern aisle, and a painting by the Venetian artist Jacopo Bassano in the apse of the southern aisle. Check out the sculptures in the **baptistery** too.

Before leaving the square, notice the elegantly ornamented **Arneri Palace** opposite the cathedral, at the corner of the narrow street of the same name.

City Defences FORT

Korčula's towers and remaining city walls look particularly striking when approached from the sea, their presence warning pirates the town would be no pushover. Originally

Korčula Town

Top Sights
1 St Mark's Cathedral....C2

Sights
2 City Defences....C4
3 Icon Museum....D3
4 Kanavelić Tower....C1
5 Korčula Town Museum....C3
6 Large Governor's Tower....B3
7 Sea Gate Tower....B2
8 Small Governor's Tower....B3
9 St Mark's Abbey Treasury....C3
10 Veliki Revelin Tower....C4

Sleeping
11 Guest House Korunić....B5
12 Korčula Royal Apartments....A4
13 Lešić Dimitri Palace....D2

Eating
14 Aterina....B3
15 Cukarin....B5
16 LD Terrace....D2
17 Marco's....C3

Drinking & Nightlife
18 Massimo....C1
19 Vinum Bonum....B5

Entertainment
20 Moreška Cultural Club....B3

Shopping
21 Kutak Knjiga....A4

these defences would have been even more foreboding, forming a complete stone barrier against invaders that consisted of 12 towers and 20m-high walls.

The main entrance to the old city is through the southern land gate in the Veliki Revelin Tower (Trg kralja Tomislava). Built in the 14th century and later extended, this fortification is adorned with coats of arms of the Venetian doges and Korčulan governors. There was originally a wooden drawbridge here, but it was replaced in the 18th century by the wide stone steps that give a sense of grandeur to the entrance. The best remaining part of the defensive walls stretches west from here.

On the western side the conical Large Governor's Tower (Obala dr Franje Tuđmana bb), built in 1483, and the Small Governor's Tower, built in 1449, protected the port, shipping and the Governor's Palace, which used to stand next to the town hall. Continuing clockwise around the edge of the old-town peninsula, the small Sea Gate Tower (Sv Barbare bb) has an inscription in Latin from 1592 asserting the fanciful notion that Korčula was founded after the fall of Troy. Next up is the renovated Kanavelić Tower (Sv Barbare bb), its semicircular profile topped with battlements, and then the smaller Zakerjan Tower, which now houses the Massimo cocktail bar (Šetalište Petra Kanavelića 1; ⏲3-11pm May-Oct).

Icon Museum MUSEUM

(Muzej ikona; Trg Svih Svetih; 15KN; ⏲9am-2pm Mon-Sat May-Sep) This modest museum has a collection of interesting Byzantine icons, painted on gilded wood, and 17th- and 18th-century ritual objects. The real highlight is access to gorgeous 15th-century All Saints' Church (Crkva Svih Svetih) next door. This baroque church features a 17th-century painted Cretan crucifix, an extraordinary late-18th-century pietà carved from walnut, and a carved and painted 1439 polyptych altarpiece by Blaž Jurjev of Trogir, considered a Croatian masterpiece.

Korčula Town Museum MUSEUM

(Gradski muzej Korčula; ☎020-711 420; www.gm-korcula.com; Trg Sv Marka 20; adult/child 20/8KN; ⏲9am-9pm Jul-Sep, 10am-1pm Oct-Jun) Occupying the 16th-century Gabriellis Palace, this museum traces the history and culture of Korčula throughout the ages. Displays cover stonemasonry, shipbuilding, archaeology, art, furniture, textiles and examples of Korčulan traditional dress. There are some interesting curios scattered over its four floors –including a tablet recording the Greek presence on the island in the 3rd century BC.

St Mark's Abbey Treasury MUSEUM

(Opatska riznica svetog Marka; Trg Sv Marka; incl cathedral 25KN; ⏲9am-7pm Mon-Sat May-Nov) The 14th-century Abbey Palace houses an important collection of icons and Dalmatian religious art. The most outstanding work is the 1431 polyptych of *The Virgin & Child with Saints* by Blaž Jurjev of Trogir. The 20th century is represented by a sketch by Ivan Meštrović and a painting by Đuro Pulitika. There are also liturgical items, jewellery, coins, furniture and ancient documents relating to the history of Korčula.

Sleeping

Apartments DePolo GUESTHOUSE €
(020-711 621; www.family-depolo.com; Sv Nikole 28; r 330KN;) A great budget option, these four simple but comfortable rooms have their own bathrooms and one has a terrace with amazing views. There's a 30% surcharge in the summer for short stays.

★ **Korčula Royal Apartments** APARTMENT €€
(098 18 40 444; www.korcularoyalapartments.com; Trg Petra Šegedina 4; apt €90-115; May-Sep;) The setting for these smart, well-equipped apartments couldn't be better, occupying an old stone villa facing a little square by the water, just outside the old town.

Guest House Korunić GUESTHOUSE €€
(020-715 108; www.guesthousekorunic.com; Hrvatske bratske zajednice 5; r €80;) This little guesthouse consists of three tidy en suite rooms above the owner's house, one of which has its own kitchenette. They're not very large, but there's a lovely roof terrace with views over the rooftops if you want to spread out.

Lešić Dimitri Palace APARTMENT €€€
(020-715 560; www.ldpalace.com; Don Pavla Poše 1-6; apt from €446;) In a class of its own, this extraordinary place has five 'residences' in an 18th-century bishop's palace. All are themed after Marco Polo's journeys – China, India etc – while original features (including exposed beams, stone walls and flagstones) reflect the old-town setting.

Hotel Korsal HOTEL €€€
(020-715 722; www.hotel-korsal.com; Šetalište Frana Kršinića 80; s/d from €147/194; May-Oct;) Korsal has 18 comfortable rooms spread among three neighbouring buildings near the marina. The two older blocks have been fully renovated and have sea views, while the new one is set back behind the others and has only partial views.

Eating & Drinking

Cukarin DELI €
(020-711 055; www.cukarin.hr; Hrvatske bratske zajednice bb; cakes from 10KN; 8.30am-noon & 5-7.30pm Mon-Sat Apr-Oct) This deli-style place bakes sweet Korčulan creations such as *klajun* (walnut pastry) and *amareta* (a round, rich cake with almonds). It also sells wine, jam and olive oil from the island.

Marco's DALMATIAN €€
(098 275 701; www.marcoskorcula.com; Kaparova 1; mains 65-115KN; 9am-midnight mid-Apr–mid-Oct, 6-11pm Mon-Sat Mar–mid-Apr & mid-Oct–Dec) The hanging filament lights over the bar and the big brass fixtures over the tables mark this out as one of Korčula's most fresh and fun restaurants. The menu joins the party, offering traditional specialities such as *žrnovski makaruni* (hand-rolled pasta) alongside the likes of burgers and couscous salads.

LD Terrace DALMATIAN €€€
(020-601 726; www.ldrestaurant.com; Šetalište Petra Kanavelića bb; mains 190-240KN; 8am-midnight Apr-Oct;) The LD stands for Lešić Dimitri and it's no surprise that Korčula's most elegant accommodation should also have its finest restaurant. The setting is magnificent, with a chic upstairs dining room as well as romantic tables set right above the water. The modern Dalmatian menu is well matched by a fine wine list.

Aterina MEDITERRANEAN €€€
(091 98 61 856; www.facebook.com/aterinakorcula; Trg Korčulanskih klesara i kipara 2; mains 80-180KN; noon-midnight May-Oct) As well as being a brilliant place to watch the sunset, Aterina serves an excellent selection of Italian-influenced seafood dishes. The daily specials are the main show – chalked on a blackboard to reflect the daily catch.

Vinum Bonum WINE BAR
(091 47 70 236; Punta Jurana 66; 6pm-midnight May-Oct;) Tucked away on a car-free lane just off the harbour, this casual place allows you to nibble on antipasti while you sample some of the island's best wine and *rakija*.

Shopping

Kutak Knjiga BOOKS
(020-716 541; http://kutak-knjiga.blogspot.co.nz; Kovački prolaz bb; 9.30am-8pm Mon-Fri May-Oct, to 1.30pm Nov-Apr) It's a mystery how Kutak crams books written in Croatian, English, French, Spanish, Czech, Italian, German, Polish, Swedish and Mandarin into such a small place.

Information

Health Centre (Dom zdravlja; 020-711 700; www.dom-zdravlja-korcula.hr; ul 57 br 5)

Tourist Office (020-715 701; www.visitkorcula.eu; Obala dr Franje Tuđmana 4; 8am-

WORTH A TRIP

RURAL EATS

Some of Korčula's best eating experiences can be found at local taverns in its small villages. If you've got your own transport, it's well worth seeking them out.

Konoba Mate (020-717 109; www.konobamate.hr; Pupnat 28; mains 60-118KN; 11am-2pm & 7pm-midnight Mon-Sat, 7pm-midnight Sun May-Sep;) Our favourite place to eat on the entire island has the unlikely setting of the sleepy farming village of Pupnat, 11km west of Korčula Town. The menu is short but universally tempting, offering unusual twists on true-blue traditions, including kid goat cooked under a *peka* (domed baking lid). The antipasto platter is sublime. And mate, the name's pronounced *ma*-teh.

Konoba Belin (091 50 39 258; www.facebook.com/RestoranBelin; Žrnovo Prvo Selo 50; mains 50-130KN; 10.30am-1.30pm & 6-11.30pm Mon-Sat, 6-11.30pm Sun May-Oct) It's all about the barbecue (which dad is firmly in control of) at this friendly, family-run place in the old part of Žrnovo, 2.5km west of Korčula Town. Expect lots of grilled fish and meat.

Konoba Maslina (020-711 720; www.konobamaslina.com; Lumbarajska cesta bb; mains 65-120KN; 11am-10pm Mon-Sat, to 4pm Sun;) Everything you'd want from a rural *konoba* (simple family-run eatery), this place offers honest country cooking including local specialities such as *žrnovski makaruni* (homemade pasta with a meaty sauce) and *pašticada* (rich beef stew). It's about 3km out of Korčula on the road to Lumbarda.

8pm Jun-Aug, 8am-3pm Mon-Sat May, Sep & Oct, 8am-2pm Mon-Fri Nov-Apr)

Lumbarda

POP 1220

Lumbarda is a laid-back sort of town set around a harbour on the southeastern end of Korčula Island. The sandy soil is perfect for vineyards, and wine from the *grk* grape is Lumbarda's most famous product. In the 16th century, aristocrats from Korčula built summer houses here, and it remains a quieter retreat from the more urbanised Korčula Town. The town beaches are small but sandy.

Information

Tourist Office (020-712 005; www.tz-lumbarda.hr; Prvi žal bb; 8am-9pm Jun–mid-Sep, to 3pm Mon-Fri mid-Sep–May)

Vela Luka

POP 4140

Surrounded by hills covered with olive groves, Vela Luka is a port town set in a lovely natural harbour – but it's hardly the most interesting destination. There are coves for swimming but little in the way of actual beaches. Small boats can take you to the idyllic offshore islands of Proizd and Osjak.

The production and marketing of Korčula's famous olive oil is vital to the local economy. Tourism and fishing are the other main industries.

For a total veg-out at the beach, nothing beats the island of **Proizd** at Korčula's northwestern tip. There's not much here but a single summertime restaurant, but the clear, blue water and white stones are dazzling. Bring plenty of sunscreen as there is little shade on the beaches. In the tourist season, small boats head to the island from Vela Luka. The trip takes about 40 minutes; expect to pay around 50KN per person.

Set within an olive grove 5km northwest of town, **Camp Mindel** (020-813 600; www.mindel.hr; Stani 192; adult/child/tent/car 35/15/30/25KN; May-Oct;) is a compact, inexpensive, friendly site and an ideal base for country walks; the beach is a 10-minute stroll away. There's no bus service.

Information

Tourist Office (020-813 619; www.tzvelaluka.hr; Obala 3 br 19; 8am-9pm Mon-Sat, 9am-2pm Sun Jul & Aug, reduced hours rest of year)

LASTOVO ISLAND

One of the most remote and undeveloped of Croatia's populated islands, little Lastovo sits in quiet isolation south of Korčula and west of Mljet. Like similarly far-flung Vis, the island was used as a military base during the Yugoslav era and was closed to foreign visitors.

Now that it's open for business it has become a favourite destination for yachties, who moor in its blissful wee bays. There's not as much appeal for land-based tourists. The main attraction is Lastovo Town, a striking collection of stone houses and aged churches clinging to a hillside in the interior.

Lastovo and the dozens of islets that surround it are now protected by the Lastovo Archipelago Nature Park, home to shearwaters, sea corals, sponges, lobsters, rare sea snails, dolphins, and loggerhead and green turtles.

Activities

The island is criss-crossed with well-marked cycling and hiking trails. Enquire at the tourist office for a route to suit your interests and abilities.

The only place approaching a proper beach is the small pebbly stretch below the Restaurant Porto Rosso in the deeply inset bay of **Skrivena Luka**.

Sleeping & Eating

Perhaps because many visitors stay on their boats, good accommodation is hard to come by. The pretty village of Pasadur, which straddles two islands connected by a little bridge, has Lastovo's only hotel and some basic holiday apartments. Contact the tourist office for details of private accommodation providers.

Triton DALMATIAN, SEAFOOD **€€**
(☎020-801 161; www.triton.hr; Zaklopatica 15; mains 60-100KN; ⏲11am-10pm May-Sep) Positioned at the centre of the lovely horseshoe cove of Zaklopatica, this excellent family-run seafood restaurant serves delicious fresh fish and lobster.

Information

Tourist Office (☎020-801 018; www.tz-lastovo.hr; Pjevor 7, Lastovo Town; ⏲8am-2pm & 4-8pm Mon-Sat)

Getting There & Away

The ferry port is at Ubli, at the western end of the island.

Jadrolinija (☎020-805 175; www.jadrolinija.hr; Ubli bb) has up to three car ferries a day to Vela Luka on Korčula (passenger/car 32/180KN, 1¾ hours), with one continuing on to Split (passenger/car 68/470KN, 4½ hours). There's also a daily catamaran on this route, stopping at Vela Luka (40KN, 55 minutes), Hvar (55KN, two hours) and Split (70KN, 3¼ hours).

On Tuesdays and Thursdays from May to August, G&V Line (p313) has catamarans to/from Sobra on Mljet (70KN, three hours) and Dubrovnik (95KN, four hours). From June they also stop in Polače on Mljet (70KN, 2¼ hours), while in July and August they add a stop in Korčula Town (60KN, 1¼ hours).

Getting Around

On weekdays there are seven buses between Lastovo Town and Ubli (five on weekends), with four carrying on to Pasadur.

Understand Croatia

Above: Croatian folk dancers perform in Zagreb (p65)

History

Trampled over by invading armies, passed back and forth between empires, split up then put back together again in various different shapes: Croatia's history is more convoluted than most. In this part of the world, echoes of the past are ever present, both in the built environment and as the subtext to any serious discussion about the present – not to mention the future.

The word Adriatic (Jadran in Croatian) is thought to be linked to the ancient Etruscan town of Adria, near Venice, but may also be related to the Illyrian word for water.

Early Inhabitants

Around 30,000 years ago, Croatia was the haunt of Neanderthals (an early human species), who roamed through the hills of Slavonia. The Croatian Natural History Museum in Zagreb displays relics of this distant era, and the Museum of the Krapina Neanderthal in Krapina offers a faithful picture of Neanderthal life. By the end of the last ice age (around 18,000 years ago) modern humans were living in places such as the Vela Spila cave on the island of Korčula.

By around 1000 BCE, the Illyrians took centre stage in the area now comprised of Slovenia, Croatia, Serbia, Kosovo, Montenegro and Albania. It's thought that the modern Albanian language, a linguistic oddity unrelated to any other language, is derived from ancient Illyrian. The often-warring tribes erected hill forts and created distinctive jewellery made from amber and bronze. In time they established a loose federation of tribes.

The Illyrians had to contend with the Greeks, who established trading colonies on the Adriatic coast at Epidaurus (present-day Cavtat) and Korčula in the 6th century BCE, and on the islands of Vis and Hvar in the 4th century BCE. In the meantime Celts were pushing down from the north.

In the 3rd century BCE, Queen Teuta of the Illyrian Ardiaei tribe committed a fatal tactical error in seeking to conquer various Greek colonies. The put-upon Greeks asked the Romans for military support. The Romans pushed their way into the region and by 168 BCE they defeated Gentius, the last Illyrian king. And so, gradually, the Illyrians were Latinised.

TIMELINE

6th century BCE

Greek colonies are founded on the island of Korčula and at Epidaurus (modern-day Cavtat, south of Dubrovnik), within an area already populated by people the Greeks refer to as Ilyrians.

4th century BCE

Illyrian tribes such as the Histri (the old name of Istria) and the Liburnians achieve supremacy in the Balkans, founding several kingdoms and establishing themselves as maritime powers.

229 BCE

Rome goes to war against Illyrian queen Teuta, at the behest of the Greeks who were being harried by state-sponsored Illyrian pirates. Following her defeat, the Illyrians pay annual tributes to Rome.

When in Rome

Following the fall of Gentius, the southern part of Illyria officially became an independent Roman protectorate known as Illyricum. It later became a Roman province and was enlarged as Rome pushed north in what was known as the Pannonian Wars. In 9 CE Illyricum was split into two separate Roman provinces: Pannonia (present-day Slovenia, northern Croatia and Bosnia, and bits of Austria, Slovakia, Hungary and Serbia) and Dalmatia (the rest of modern-day Croatia and Bosnia, Montenegro, and bits of Albania and Serbia).

Roman rule centred on the administrative headquarters of Salona (now Solin, near Split). It eventually brought peace and prosperity to the region, and cities such as Iader (Zadar), Felix Arba (Rab Town), Curicum (Krk Town), Tarsaticae (Rijeka), Parentium (Poreč), Polensium (Pula) and Siscia (Sisak) gained all the cultural accoutrements of Roman life, such as temples, baths and amphitheatres. The Romans built a series of roads reaching to the Aegean and Black Seas and the Danube, facilitating trade and the expansion of Roman culture. The roads also accelerated the later spread of Christianity.

These provinces even produced important figures in Roman history. Diocletian was born near Salona around 244 CE and distinguished himself as a military commander before becoming emperor in 285. As ruler, Diocletian attempted to simplify the unwieldy empire by dividing it into two administrative halves, thus sowing the seeds for the later division into the Eastern and Western Roman Empires. He is also remembered as a great persecutor of the Christians. In 305 he retired to the grand seaside palace he had built for himself near where he was born. Today Diocletian's Palace is Croatia's greatest Roman remnant, forming the heart of the old town of Split. The Christians eventually had the last laugh, turfing the deceased emperor out of his mausoleum and converting it into a cathedral.

Christianity reached this region in its very earliest days. In the Bible, St Paul talks of preaching in Illyricum in his letter to the Romans (written in about 56 CE), while his second letter to Timothy states that St Titus is in Dalmatia. Early Christian catacombs can be found under the Serbian Orthodox Monastery in Krka National Park, and local lore states that Titus, and possibly even Paul himself, visited the community here. In 313, only two years after Diocletian's death, the Emperor Constantine decriminalised Christianity, and in 380 it became the only tolerated religion under Theodosius the Great.

Theodosius was the last Roman leader to rule a united empire. On his death in 395 CE, the empire was formally divided into eastern and western realms. The dividing line fell down the middle of present-day Montenegro, leaving present-day Croatia in the western half and Serbia in the east. The eastern half became the Byzantine Empire, which persisted

Best Roman Ruins

Diocletian's Palace in Split, Central Dalmatia

Salona/Solin on the outskirts of Split

Roman Amphitheatre (Arena) in Pula, Istria

168 BCE

The last Illyrian king, Gentius, is defeated by the Romans near his capital Shkodra (present-day Albania), and Rome takes control over all of Dalmatia.

11 BCE

The Roman province of Illyricum, covering present-day Dalmatia, is extended to the Danube after the defeat of Pannonian tribes. The new province takes in all of modern-day Croatia except Istria.

9 CE

Illyricum is split into two provinces: Dalmatia to the south and Pannonia to the north. What we now call Croatia is split between the two.

257

The city of Salona becomes the first diocese in Roman Dalmatia, thus creating a toehold for the Christian Church in the region; within 30 years the Bishop of Salona becomes pope.

until 1453. The Western Roman Empire fell in 476, following invasions by various 'barbarian' tribes, such as the Visigoths, Huns and Lombards. The Goths took control of Dalmatia until 535 when the Byzantine Emperor Justinian booted them out.

Hello Slavs, Adiós Avars

In the wake of the collapse of the Western Roman Empire, various Slavic tribes headed south from their original territory north of the Carpathians. Around the same time, the Avars (a nomadic central Asian people known for their brutality) were sallying around the Balkan fringes of the Byzantine Empire. The Avars ravaged the former Roman towns of Salona and Epidaurus, whose inhabitants took refuge in Diocletian's Palace and Ragusa (Dubrovnik), respectively. The Avars then progressed all the way to the mighty Byzantine capital of Constantinople itself (present-day Istanbul), where the Byzantines duly crushed them and they faded into history (to 'die away like Avars' is a common Balkan saying).

Controversy surrounds the role that the Slavs had in the defeat of the Avars. Some claim that Byzantium called on the Slavs to help in the fight against the Avar assault, while others think that they merely filled the void left when the Avars disappeared. Whatever the case, the Slavs spread rapidly through the Balkans, reaching the Adriatic by the early 7th century.

Two closely related Slavic tribes settled along the Adriatic Coast and its hinterland: the Croats and the Serbs. The Croats settled in an area roughly equivalent to present-day Croatia and Bosnia. By the 8th century, they had formed two powerful tribal entities, each led by a *knez* (duke). The Duchy of Croatia included most of present-day Dalmatia, parts of Montenegro and western Bosnia, while the Duchy of Pannonia included present-day Slavonia, Zagorje and the area around Zagreb. The Byzantines maintained control of several coastal cities, including Zadar, Split and Dubrovnik, as well as the islands of Hvar and Krk.

While the Croats are clearly related to other Slavic nations, the name by which they know themselves – Hrvat – isn't a Slavic word. One theory posits that Hrvat is a Persian word, and the Croats are a Slavic tribe who were briefly ruled – and named – by a ruling cast of Persian-speaking Alans from central Asia.

Christianity & the Croat Kings

Charlemagne's Franks gradually encroached on central Europe from the west and in 800 CE they seized Dalmatia, baptising the previously pagan Croats en masse. After Charlemagne's death in 814 CE, the Pannonian Croats revolted unsuccessfully against Frankish rule, without the support of the Dalmatian Croats, whose major coastal cities remained under the influence of the Byzantine Empire. The big breakthrough for the Croats happened when Duke Branimir revolted against Byzantine control and won recognition from Pope John VIII. This brought them closer to the Vatican, and Catholicism became a defining feature of Croatian national identity.

Trpimir, who was *knez* from 845 to 864, is widely considered to have founded the first Croatian dynasty, but it was his grandson Tomislav who

395

After Theodosius the Great dies, the Roman Empire is split in two. Slovenia, Croatia and Bosnia fall into the Western Roman Empire, with Serbia, Kosovo and Macedonia in the Byzantine Empire.

614

Central Asian marauders, the Avars, sack Salona and Epidaurus. Some contend that the Croats and Serbs followed in their wake; others that they were invited by Emperor Heraclius to fend off the Avars.

800

The Franks led by their King Charlemagne seize control of Dalmatia and forcibly baptise the pagan Croats. The Byzantines recognise Frankish rule but retain control of several key coastal cities.

845–64

Trpimir establishes Croatia's first royal line. He fights and defeats the powerful Bulgarian state, and inflicts major defeats on the Byzantines. Croatian territory expands well into what is now Bosnia.

first crowned himself *kralj* (king) in 925, and united Pannonia and Dalmatia. His kingdom included virtually all of modern Croatia as well as parts of Bosnia and the coast of Montenegro.

But the glory days were not to last. During the 11th century, the Serbs, Byzantines and Venetians imposed themselves on the Dalmatian coast, and new adversaries, the Hungarians, emerged in the north and advanced into Pannonia. Krešimir IV (r 1058–74) turned the tables and regained control of Dalmatia, but Croatia's rebound was only temporary and Krešimir was succeeded by Zvonimir and Stjepan, neither of whom produced an heir. Seeing an opportunity, the Hungarian King Laszlo claimed the throne by virtue of being the brother of Zvonimir's widow, Queen Jelena. He managed to take control of a large area of northern Croatia, but died before he could cement his claims in the south.

Dalmatian dogs are thought to be one of the oldest breeds, but there's no conclusive evidence that they originated in Dalmatia. Some experts believe the dogs may have been brought to Dalmatia by the Roma.

Covetous Neighbours: Hungary vs Venice

Laszlo's brother Koloman succeeded him to the Hungarian throne and continued in his drive to take the Croatian throne as well. In 1097 he defeated his rival claimant Petar Svačić, thus ending the era of native-born Croat kings. In 1102 he imposed the *Pacta conventa,* ostensibly stating that Hungary and Croatia were separate entities under a single – Hungarian – monarchy. In practice, while Croatia maintained a *ban* (viceroy or governor) and a *sabor* (parliament), the Hungarians steadily marginalised the Croatian nobility. Under Hungarian rule, Pannonia became known as Slavonia, and the interior towns of Zagreb, Vukovar and Varaždin became thriving centres of trade and culture. In 1107 Koloman persuaded the Dalmatian nobility to bring the coast, long coveted by land-locked Hungarian kings, into his realm.

Upon Koloman's death in 1116, Venice launched new assaults on Biograd and the islands of Lošinj, Pag, Rab and Krk. Meanwhile, Zadar had

THE VENETIAN YOKE

For nearly 800 years the doges of Venice sought to control, colonise and exploit the Croatian coast. Coastal and island towns from Rovinj in the north to Korčula in the south still show a marked Venetian influence in architecture, cuisine and culture. However, as in Venice's other dominions, the period was not a happy time.

Venetian rule in Dalmatia and Istria was a record of virtually unbroken economic exploitation. The Venetians systematically denuded the landscape in order to provide timber for their ships. State monopolies set artificially low prices for olive oil, figs, wine, fish and salt, thus ensuring cheap commodities for Venetian buyers, while local merchants and producers were impoverished. Shipbuilding was effectively banned; no roads or schools were built and no investment was made in local industry.

869

At the behest of Byzantium, Macedonian monks Methodius and Cyril create the Glagolitic alphabet, specifically with a view to speeding the spread of Christianity among the Slavic peoples.

910–28

Tomislav proclaims himself king while expanding territory at the expense of the Hungarians and defeating Bulgarian Tsar Simeon in modern Bosnia. Tomislav unites Pannonian and Dalmatian Croats.

1000

Venice capitalises on a lack of stability in Croatia to begin encroaching on the Dalmatian coast. So begins the tussle between Venice and other powers for control of Dalmatia.

1058–74

Soon after the 1054 split of the church into Orthodox and Catholic strands, the pope recognises Krešimir IV as king of Dalmatia and Croatia. This places Croatia within the Catholic sphere.

Best Gothic Buildings

St James' Cathedral, Šibenik

St Mark's Cathedral, Korčula

Cathedral of the Assumption of the Blessed Virgin Mary, Zagreb

St Mark's Church, Zagreb

grown to become the largest and most prosperous Dalmatian city and had successfully fended off two Venetian naval expeditions in the 1190s. But a vengeful Venetian doge in 1202 paid the soldiers of the Fourth Crusade to sack Zadar, despite Pope Innocent III specifically banning the crusaders from attacking Christian states. After this they rumbled on to brutally sack Constantinople, the great bastion of Eastern Christianity.

The Mongolian juggernaut ravaged the Croatian interior in 1242, but not before King Bela IV of Hungary fled the onslaught and took refuge in Trogir. The Venetians used the chaos to consolidate their hold on Zadar, and upon the death of King Bela in 1270, added Šibenik and Trogir to their possessions.

King Ludovic (Louis) I of Hungary (r 1342–82) reestablished control over the country and even persuaded Venice to relinquish Dalmatia. But new conflicts emerged upon his death. The Croatian nobility rallied around Ladislas of Naples, who was crowned king in Zadar in 1403. Short of funds, Ladislas sold Zadar to Venice in 1409 for a paltry 100,000 ducats and renounced his rights to Dalmatia. In the early 15th century, Venice strengthened its grip on the Dalmatian coastline south from Zadar and remained in control until the Napoleonic invasion of 1797. Only the wily citizens of Ragusa managed to retain their independence.

The Ottoman Onslaught

Croatia had plenty to contend with as Venetians, Hungarians and others picked at the remnants of the original Croatian state, yet another threat loomed from the east. The Ottoman Turks had emerged out of Anatolia in the early 14th century and rapidly swallowed up the Balkans.

THE REPUBLIC OF RAGUSA

While most of the Dalmatian coast struggled under Venetian rule, Ragusa (now Dubrovnik) led a charmed life, existing as a republic in its own right. A ruling class, abounding in business acumen and diplomatic skill, ensured that this minuscule city-state punched well above its weight and played a significant role in the immediate region and beyond.

The Ragusans asked the pope for permission to trade with the Turks in 1371 and subsequently established trade centres throughout the Ottoman Empire. Burgeoning trade led to a flowering in the arts and sciences. The Ragusans were extremely liberal for the time, abolishing the slave trade in the 15th century. They were also scientifically advanced, establishing a system of quarantine in 1377.

However, the Ragusans had to maintain a perilous position sandwiched between Ottoman and Venetian interests. An earthquake in 1667 caused a great deal of damage, from which they never fully recovered, and Napoleon finally swallowed up the republic in 1808.

1091–1102

Hungarian King Laszlo, related by marriage to the late King Zvonimir, claims the Croatian throne; his successor, Koloman, defeats the last Croatian king and cements Hungarian control of Croatia with the *Pacta conventa*.

1242

The Mongols devastate the royal houses of Hungary and Croatia. The noble Šubić and Frankopan families step in to assume a degree of political and economic power that persists for centuries.

1300s

The Hungarian Anjou dynasty under Carl (Charles) and Ludovic (Louis) reasserts royal authority in Croatia and seeks to expel the Venetians who had taken Dalmatian territory.

1358

Ragusa (modern Dubrovnik) frees itself of Venice and becomes an independent city republic. It grows to become an advanced and liberal society, while cannily fending off Venetians and Ottomans.

The Serbs were rolled at Kosovo Polje in 1389, a hastily choreographed anti-Turkish crusade was garrotted in Hungary in 1396, and Bosnia was dispatched in 1463. When the Croatian nobility finally faced up to the Ottomans in 1493 in Krbavsko Polje, they too were pummelled.

Despite a sudden show of unity among the remaining noble families, one city after another fell to the Ottoman sultans. The important bishopric at Zagreb heavily fortified the cathedral in Kaptol, which remained untouched, but the gateway town of Knin fell in 1521. Five years later, the Ottomans engaged the Hungarians in Mohács. Again the Turks won and the Hungarian army was destroyed. The Turks threatened the Adriatic coast, but never actually captured it, while Ragusa maintained its independence throughout the turmoil.

Turkish assaults on the Balkans caused massive havoc. Cities and towns were destroyed, people were enslaved and commandeered to the Ottoman war machine, and refugees scattered around the region.

The necktie is a descendant of the cravat, which originated in Croatia as part of military attire and was adopted by the French in the 17th century. The name 'cravat' is a corruption of both Croat and Hrvat.

Enter the Habsburgs

With the Hungarians out of the picture, the Croats turned to the Austrians for protection. The Habsburg Empire, ruled from Vienna, duly absorbed a narrow strip of territory around Zagreb, Karlovac and Varaždin. The Habsburgs sought to build a buffer against the Ottomans, creating the Vojna Krajina (Military Frontier). In this region comprising a string of forts, a standing army, largely of Vlachs and Serbs, faced down the Ottomans.

Exactly a century after their defeat by the Ottomans, the Croats managed to turn the tables on the Turks. At Sisak in 1593 the Habsburg army, including Croat soldiers, finally inflicted a defeat on the Ottomans. In 1699 in Sremski Karlovci the Ottomans sued for peace for the first time and the Turkish stranglehold on central Europe was loosened. Bosnia remained within the Ottoman Empire but Venice regained the coast, apart from a thin strip of land around Neum that gave the Ottomans access to the Adriatic and provided a buffer between the territories of Venice and Ragusa.

The Habsburgs reclaimed Slavonia soon after, thus expanding the Krajina. This period saw a return to stability and advances in agricultural production, but Croatian language and culture languished.

Šibenik-born bishop, inventor and engineer Faust Vrančić (1551–1617) made the first working parachute, based on rough sketches by Leonardo da Vinci.

Napoleon & the Illyrian Provinces

Habsburg support for the restoration of the French monarchy provoked Napoleon to invade the Italian states in 1796. After conquering Venice in 1797 he agreed to transfer Dalmatia to Austria in the Treaty of Campo Formio in exchange for other concessions. The Croats' secret hopes that Dalmatia would be united with Slavonia were soon dashed, as the Habsburgs made it clear that the two territories would retain separate administrations.

1409

Ladislas of Naples assumes the Croatian throne but, scared off by dynastic squabbling, sells Zadar to Venice for 100,000 ducats, renouncing his rights to Dalmatia. Venetian control soon extends from Zadar to Ragusa.

1493

At Krbavsko Polje a joint Croatian-Hungarian army engages the Turks, but is obliterated, leaving Croatia open to Turkish raids. The Turkish advance brings turmoil, as populations flee and famine ensues.

1526–27

The Battle of Mohács sees the Ottoman Turks annihilate the Hungarian nobility, ending Hungarian control of Croatia. Hungarian King Louis dies heirless, allowing the Austrian Habsburgs control.

1537–40

The Turks take Klis, the last Croatian bastion in Dalmatia. The Turkish advance continues to Sisak, just south of Zagreb. For reasons unknown, the Turks never push on to Zagreb.

The Balkans (2000), by noted historian Mark Mazower, is a highly readable short introduction to the region. It offers clearly discussed overviews of geography, culture and the broad historical sweep of the Balkans.

Austrian control of Dalmatia only lasted until Napoleon's 1805 victory over Austrian and Prussian forces at Austerlitz, which forced Austria to cede the Dalmatian coast to France. Ragusa quickly surrendered to French forces, which also swallowed up the Bay of Kotor in present-day Montenegro. Napoleon renamed his conquest the 'Illyrian provinces' and moved swiftly to reform the neglected territory. A tree-planting program was implemented to reforest the barren hills. Roads and hospitals were built and new crops introduced. Since almost the entire population was illiterate, the new government set up primary schools, high schools and a college at Zadar. Yet the French regime remained unpopular.

After Napoleon's Russian campaign and the fall of his empire, the 1815 Congress of Vienna recognised Austria's claims to Dalmatia and placed the rest of Croatia under the jurisdiction of Austria's Hungarian province. For the Dalmatians the new regime meant a return to the status quo, since the Austrians restored the former Italian elite to power, whereas the Hungarians imposed the Hungarian language and culture on the northern Croatian population.

A South Slavic Consciousness

Traditionally, upper-class Dalmatians spoke Italian and the northern Croatian nobility spoke German or Hungarian, but flush with the Enlightenment fervour, Napoleon had sown the seeds of creating a south Slavic consciousness. This sense of a shared identity eventually manifested itself in an 'Illyrian' movement in the 1830s, which centred on the revival of the Croatian language. Napoleon's grand plan was to foster Serbian culture, too, but Serbia remained under Ottoman occupation.

The establishment of the first Illyrian newspaper in 1834, written in the Zagreb dialect, prompted the Croatian *sabor* to call for the teaching of Slavic languages in schools.

Ivan Vučetić (1858–1925), who developed dactyloscopy (fingerprint identification) after migrating to Argentina, was born on the island of Hvar.

Following the 1848 revolution in Paris, the Hungarians began to press for change within the Habsburg Empire. The Croats saw this as an opportunity to regain some control and unify Dalmatia, the Krajina and Slavonia. The Habsburgs paid lip service to Croatian sentiments and appointed Josip Jelačić *ban* (viceroy or governor) of Croatia. Jelačić promptly called elections, claimed a mandate and declared war on Hungarian agitators in order to curry favour with the Habsburgs, but his demands for autonomy fell on deaf ears. Jelačić is immortalised in a martial pose in the heart of Zagreb.

Disillusionment spread after 1848, and amplified after the birth of the Austro-Hungarian Dual Monarchy in 1867. The monarchy placed northern Croatia and Slavonia within the Hungarian administration, while Dalmatia remained within Austria. Whatever limited form of self-government the Croats enjoyed under the Habsburgs disappeared.

1593

At Sisak, previously the Ottoman high-tide mark, the Habsburgs inflict the first major defeat on the Ottomans, thus prefiguring the long, slow Turkish retreat from central Europe.

1671

A deputation led by Franjo Frankopan and Petar Zrinski, with the aim of ridding Croatia of Hungarian domination, is cut short. Both are hanged, their lands confiscated by the Habsburgs.

1699

At the Treaty of Karlovci, the Ottomans renounce all claims to Croatia. Venice and Hungary reclaim all freed lands over the next 20 years.

1780s

The Habsburgs begin a process of Germanisation, ordering all administration be conducted in German. This leads to rising nationalist feelings among the Habsburg's non-German subjects.

Dreams of Yugoslavia

The river of discontent forked into two streams that dominated the political landscape for the next century. The old 'Illyrian' movement became the National Party, dominated by Bishop Josip Juraj Strossmayer. Strossmayer believed that the Habsburgs and the Hungarians set out to emphasise the differences between Serbs and Croats, and that only through Jugoslavenstvo (literally 'Southslavism' – or south Slavic unity) could the aspirations of both peoples be realised. Strossmayer supported the independence struggle in Serbia, but favoured a Yugoslav (ie south Slavic) entity within the Austro-Hungarian Empire rather than complete independence.

By contrast, the Party of Rights, led by the militantly anti-Serb Ante Starčević, envisaged an independent Croatia made up of Slavonia, Dalmatia, the Krajina, Slovenia, Istria, and part of Bosnia and Hercegovina. At the same time, the Orthodox Church was encouraging the Serbs to form a national identity based upon their religion. Until the 19th century, Orthodox inhabitants of Croatia identified themselves as Vlachs, Morlachs, Serbs, Orthodox or even Greeks. With the help of Starčević's attacks, the sense of a separate Serbian Orthodox identity within Croatia developed.

Following the principle of 'divide and rule', the Hungarian-appointed *ban* of Croatia blatantly favoured the Serbs and the Orthodox Church, but his strategy backfired. The first organised resistance formed in Dalmatia. Croats in Rijeka and Serbs in Zadar joined together in 1905 to demand the unification of Dalmatia and Slavonia, with a formal guarantee of Serbian equality as a nation. The spirit of unity mushroomed, and by 1906 Croat–Serb coalitions had taken over local government in Dalmatia and Slavonia, forming a serious threat to the Hungarian power structure.

Dubrovnik: A History (2003), by Robin Harris, is a thoughtful and thorough look at the great city, investigating events, individuals and movements that have contributed to the architectural and cultural fabric of the 'pearl of the Adriatic'.

WWI & the First Yugoslavia

With the outbreak of WWI, Croatia's future was again up for grabs. Sensing that they would once again be pawns to the Great Powers, a Croatian delegation called the 'Yugoslav Committee' talked the Serbian government into establishing a parliamentary monarchy that would rule over the two countries. Although many Croats were unclear about Serbian intentions, they were sure about Italian intentions, since Italy lost no time in seizing Pula, Rijeka and Zadar after the war. Effectively given a choice between throwing in their lot with Italy or Serbia, the Croats chose Serbia.

The Yugoslav Committee became the National Council of Slovenes, Croats and Serbs after the collapse of the Austro-Hungarian Empire in 1918. The council quickly negotiated the establishment of the Kingdom of Serbs, Croats and Slovenes to be based in Belgrade (the unwieldy name was changed to the Kingdom of Yugoslavia in 1929). The previously independent kingdom of Montenegro was also subsumed into the new entity. Montenegro's King Nikola had escaped to France during the war,

1797–1815

Napoleon brings the Venetian Republic to an end; Venetian dominions are initially given to the Habsburgs, but in 1806 Napoleon gains the Adriatic coast, which he dubs the 'Illyrian provinces'.

1867

The Habsburg throne devolves to become the Austro-Hungarian Dual Monarchy. Croatian territory is divided between them: Dalmatia is awarded to Austria, and Slavonia is under Hungarian control.

1905

Burgeoning Croatian national consciousness becomes visible in the Rijeka Resolution, which calls for increased democracy as well as the reunification of Dalmatia and Slavonia.

1908

The Austro-Hungarian Empire takes control of Bosnia and Hercegovina, bringing the Slavic Muslims of the Balkans within its sphere of responsibility, thus creating the nucleus of the future Yugoslav federation.

and France refused to allow him to leave, thus ending the 300-year-old Petrović dynasty.

Problems with the kingdom began almost immediately. As under the Habsburgs, the Croats enjoyed scant autonomy. Currency reforms benefited Serbs at the expense of the Croats. A treaty between Yugoslavia and Italy gave Istria, Zadar and several islands to Italy. The new constitution abolished Croatia's *sabor* and centralised power in Belgrade, while new electoral districts severely underrepresented the Croats.

Opposition to the new regime was led by the Croat Stjepan Radić, who favoured the idea of Yugoslavia, but wished to transform it into a federal democracy. His alliance with the Serb Svetozar Pribićević proved profoundly threatening to the regime and Radić was assassinated in 1928. Exploiting fears of civil war, Yugoslavia's King Aleksandar ended any hope of democratic change by proclaiming a royal dictatorship, abolishing political parties and suspending parliamentary government. Meanwhile, during the 1920s the Yugoslav Communist Party arose; Josip Broz Tito was to become leader in 1937.

The Rise of Ustaše & WWII

One day after the proclamation of the royal dictatorship, a Bosnian Croat, Ante Pavelić, set up the Ustaše Croatian Liberation Movement in Zagreb, inspired by Mussolini. The stated aim was to establish an independent state, by force if necessary. Fearing arrest, he first fled to Sofia in Bulgaria and made contact with anti-Serbian Macedonian revolutionaries. He then moved on to Italy, where he established training camps for his organisation under Mussolini's benevolent eye. In 1934 he and the Macedonians assassinated King Aleksandar in Marseilles. Italy responded by closing down the training camps and imprisoning Pavelić and many of his followers.

When Germany invaded Yugoslavia on 6 April 1941, the exiled Ustaše were quickly installed by the Germans and the Italians, the latter of which hoped to see their own territorial aims in Dalmatia realised. Within days the Nezavisna Država Hrvatska (NDH; Independent State of Croatia), headed by Pavelić, issued a range of decrees designed to persecute and eliminate the regime's 'enemies', a thinly veiled reference to the Jews, Roma and Serbs. The majority of the Jewish population was rounded up and sent to extermination camps between 1941 and 1945.

Serbs fared little better. The Ustaše program explicitly called for 'one-third of Serbs killed, one-third expelled and one-third converted to Catholicism', an agenda that was carried out with appalling brutality. Villages conducted their own pogroms against Serbs and extermination camps were set up, most notoriously at Jasenovac (south of Zagreb), where Serbs, Jews, Roma and antifascist Croats were killed. The exact number of Serb victims is uncertain and controversial, although it is likely to have been in the hundreds of thousands.

1918

The Kingdom of Serbs, Croats and Slovenes is created after the dismantling of the Austro-Hungarian Empire following WWI. Serbian Prince Aleksandar Karađorđević assumes the throne.

1920

Stjepan Radić establishes the Croatian Republican Peasant Party, which becomes the primary voice for Croatian interests in the face of Serb domination.

1934

Ustaše and Macedonian revolutionaries conspire to assassinate Yugoslavia's King Aleksandar. He's shot in Marseilles while on a state visit to France. The crown passes to his 11-year-old son Petar.

1939

Nazi Germany invades Poland and WWII begins. Yugoslavia, headed by the regent Prince Paul, attempts to stay neutral. Two years later, when Hitler pressures him to sign a pact, he is deposed in a coup.

Tito & the Partisans

Not all Croats supported these policies and some spoke out against them. The Ustaše regime drew most of its support from the Lika region, southwest of Zagreb, and western Hercegovina. Pavelić's agreement to cede a good part of Dalmatia to Italy was highly unpopular and the Ustaše had almost no support in that region. Likewise, the Ustaše had little support among Zagreb's intellectuals.

Serbian 'Četnik' formations led by General Draža Mihailović provided armed resistance to the regime. The Četniks began as an antifascist rebellion, but soon retaliated against the Ustaše with in-kind massacres of Croats in eastern Croatia and Bosnia.

TITO

Josip Broz was born in Kumrovec in 1892 to a Croat father and a Slovene mother. When WWI broke out, he was drafted into the Austro-Hungarian army and was taken prisoner by the Russians. He escaped just before the 1917 revolution, became a communist and joined the Red Army. He returned to Croatia in 1920 and became a union organiser while working as a metalworker.

As secretary of the Zagreb committee of the outlawed Communist Party, he worked to unify the party and increase its membership. When the Nazis invaded in 1941, he adopted the name Tito and organised small bands of guerrillas, which formed the core of the Partisan movement. His successful campaigns attracted military support from the British and the Americans, but the Soviet Union, despite sharing his communist ideology, repeatedly rebuffed his requests for aid.

In 1945 he became prime minister of a reconstituted Yugoslavia. Although retaining a communist ideology, and remaining nominally loyal to Russia, Tito had an independent streak. In 1948 he fell out with Stalin and adopted a conciliatory policy towards the West.

Yugoslavia's rival nationalities were Tito's biggest headache, which he dealt with by suppressing all dissent and trying to ensure a rough equality of representation at the upper echelons of government. As a committed communist, he viewed ethnic disputes as unwelcome deviations from the pursuit of the common good.

Yet Tito was well aware of the ethnic tensions that simmered just below the surface in Yugoslavia. Preparations for his succession began in the early 1970s as he aimed to create a balance of power among the ethnic groups of Yugoslavia. He set up a collective presidency that was to rotate annually but the system proved unworkable. Later events revealed how dependent Yugoslavia was on its wily, charismatic leader.

When Tito died in May 1980, his body was carried from Ljubljana (Slovenia) to Belgrade (Serbia). Thousands of mourners flocked to the streets to pay respects to the man who had united a difficult country for 35 years. It was the last communal outpouring of emotion that Yugoslavia's fractious nationalities were able to share.

1941

Germany invades Yugoslavia. Ante Pavelić proclaims the Nezavisna Država Hrvatska (NDH; Independent State of Croatia), a Nazi puppet state. His Ustaše followers begin exterminating Serbs, Roma and Jews.

1943

Tito's communist Partisans achieve military victories and build a popular antifascist front. They reclaim territory from retreating Italian brigades. The British and the USA lend military support.

1945

Germany surrenders, the Partisans enter Zagreb and the Federal People's Republic of Yugoslavia is founded. Croatia becomes a constituent member of a federation of six republics.

1948

Tito breaks with Stalin and Yugoslavia is expelled from the Cominform, the Soviet-dominated forum of Communist states. Tito begins to steer a careful course between the Eastern and Western blocs.

The most effective antifascist struggle was conducted by the National Liberation Partisan units lead by Josip Broz, known as Tito. The Partisans, which had their roots in the outlawed Yugoslav Communist Party, attracted long-suffering Yugoslav intellectuals, Croats disgusted with Četnik massacres, Serbs disgusted with Ustaše massacres, and antifascists of all kinds. The Partisans gained wide popular support with their early manifesto, which envisioned a postwar Yugoslavia based on a loose federation.

Although the Allies initially backed the Serbian Četniks, it became apparent that the Partisans were waging a far more focused and determined fight against the Nazis. With the diplomatic and military support of Churchill and other Allied powers, the Partisans controlled much of Croatia by 1943. They established functioning local governments in the territory they seized, which later eased their transition to power. On 20 October 1944, the Partisans entered Belgrade alongside the Red Army. When Germany surrendered in 1945, Pavelić and the Ustaše fled and the Partisans entered Zagreb.

The remnants of the NDH army, desperate to avoid falling into the hands of the Partisans, attempted to cross into Austria. A small British contingent met a column of the retreating troops but refused to accept their surrender. After eventually surrendering to the Partisans a series of massacres occurred which, along with harsh forced marches, claimed the lives of tens of thousands of NDH troops and Ustaše supporters (the exact number is in doubt but is thought to have been upwards of 50,000 people).

Clearly explaining centuries of complicated events, Marcus Tanner's *Croatia: A Nation Forged in War* (3rd edition, 2010) sallies forth from the arrival of the Slavs to the present day, presenting, in a lively, readable style, the trials and tribulations of Croatian history.

The Second Yugoslavia

Tito's attempt to retain control of the Italian city of Trieste and parts of southern Austria faltered in the face of Allied opposition. Dalmatia and most of Istria did, however, become a permanent part of postwar Yugoslavia. In creating the Federal People's Republic of Yugoslavia, Tito was determined to forge a state in which no ethnic group dominated the political landscape. Croatia became one of six republics – along with Macedonia, Serbia, Montenegro, Bosnia and Hercegovina, and Slovenia – in a tightly configured federation. However, Tito effected this delicate balance by creating a one-party state and rigorously stamping out all opposition.

During the 1960s, the concentration of power in Belgrade was an increasingly complicated issue as it became apparent that money from the more prosperous republics of Slovenia and Croatia was being distributed to the poorer autonomous province of Kosovo and the republic of Bosnia and Hercegovina. The problem seemed particularly blatant in Croatia, which saw money from its prosperous tourist business on the Adriatic coast flow into Belgrade. At the same time, Serbs in Croatia were over-represented in the government, armed forces and police.

In Croatia the unrest reached a crescendo in the 'Croatian Spring' of 1971. Led by reformers within the Communist Party of Croatia, intellec-

1956

Tito is instrumental in forming the Non-Aligned Movement, an alternative grouping of nations distinct from the prevailing Cold War powers. It now comprises 120 member states representing 55% of the world's population.

1960s

Croatian unrest about the centralisation of power in Belgrade builds. The use of Croatian money to support poorer provinces is resented, along with the over-representation of Serbs in the public service and military.

1971

In the 'Croatian Spring', Communist Party reformers, intellectuals, students and nationalists call for greater economic and constitutional autonomy for Croatia.

1980

President Tito dies. There is a genuine outpouring of grief, and tributes are paid from around the world. Yugoslavia is left beset by inflation, unemployment and foreign debt.

tuals and students called for a loosening of Croatia's ties to Yugoslavia. In addition to calls for greater economic autonomy and constitutional reform for Croatia, nationalistic elements manifested themselves, too. Tito fought back, clamping down on the liberalisation that had gradually been gaining momentum in Yugoslavia. Serbs viewed the movement as the Ustaše reborn; in turn, jailed reformers blamed the Serbs for their troubles. The stage was set for the rise of nationalism and the war of the 1990s.

The Death of Yugoslavia

Tito left a shaky Yugoslavia upon his death in May 1980. With the economy in a parlous state, a presidency that rotated among the six republics could not compensate for the loss of Tito's steadying hand at the helm. The authority of the central government sank along with the economy, and long-suppressed mistrust among Yugoslavia's ethnic groups resurfaced, coinciding with the rise to power of nationalist Slobodan Milošević in Serbia.

In 1989 repression of the Albanian majority in Serbia's Kosovo province sparked renewed fears of Serbian hegemony and precipitated the end of the Yugoslav Federation. With political changes sweeping Eastern Europe and in the face of increasing provocations from Milošević, Slovenia embarked on a course for independence. For Croatia, remaining in a Serb-dominated Yugoslavia without the counterweight of Slovenia would have been untenable.

In the Croatian elections of April 1990, Franjo Tuđman's Hrvatska Demokratska Zajednica (Croatian Democratic Union; HDZ) secured 40% of the vote, to the 30% won by the Communist Party, which retained the loyalty of the Serbian community as well as voters in Istria and Rijeka. On 22 December 1990, a new Croatian constitution changed the status of Serbs in Croatia from that of a 'constituent nation' to a national minority.

The constitution failed to guarantee minority rights and caused mass dismissals of Serbs from the public service. This stimulated Croatia's 600,000-strong ethnic Serb community to demand autonomy. In early 1991, Serb extremists within Croatia staged provocations in order to force federal military intervention. A May 1991 referendum (boycotted by the Serbs) produced a 93% vote in favour of Croatian independence. When Croatia declared independence on 25 June 1991, the Serbian enclave of Krajina proclaimed its independence from Croatia.

Journalist Misha Glenny's *The Balkans: Nationalism, War & the Great Powers, 1804–1999* (2000) explores the history of outside interference in the Balkans. His earlier book, *The Fall of Yugoslavia* (1992), deciphers the complex politics, history and cultural flare-ups that led to the wars of the 1990s.

The War for Croatia

Under pressure from the EU, Croatia declared a three-month moratorium on its independence, but heavy fighting broke out in Krajina, Baranja and Slavonia. This initiated what Croats refer to as the Homeland War. The Yugoslav People's Army, dominated by Serbs, began to intervene in support of Serbian irregulars under the pretext of halting ethnic violence.

1986

Slobodan Milošević becomes the head of the Serbian Communist Party. The following year he comes to public attention after a fiery address to minority Serbs in Kosovo.

1989

The communist system begins to collapse in Eastern Europe; Franjo Tuđman establishes Yugoslavia's first non-communist party, the Hrvatska Demokratska Zajednica (HDZ; Croatian Democratic Union).

1990

Disagreements between Slovenia and Serbia lead to the disintegration of the Yugoslav Communist Party. The Croatian Communist Party allows multiparty elections, which are won by HDZ.

1991

The Croatian *sabor* (parliament) proclaims the independence of Croatia; Krajina Serbs declare independence from Croatia, with the support of Milošević. War breaks out between Croats and Serbs.

When the Croatian government ordered a shutdown of federal military installations in the republic of Croatia, the Yugoslav navy blockaded the Adriatic coast and laid siege to the strategic town of Vukovar on the Danube. During the summer of 1991, a quarter of Croatia fell to Serb militias and the Serb-led Yugoslav People's Army.

In late 1991 the federal army and the Montenegrin militia moved against Dubrovnik, and the presidential palace in Zagreb was hit by rockets from Yugoslav jets in an apparent assassination attempt on President Tuđman. When the three-month moratorium ended, Croatia declared full independence. Soon after, Vukovar finally fell when the Yugoslav army moved in, in one of the more bloodthirsty acts in all of the Yugoslav wars. During six months of fighting in Croatia, 10,000 people died, hundreds of thousands fled and tens of thousands of homes were destroyed.

Croatia Through History (2007), by Branka Magaš, is a highly detailed doorstop of a history, focusing on pivotal events and clearly delineating the gradual development of Croatian national identity.

The UN Gets Involved

Beginning on 3 January 1992, a UN-brokered ceasefire generally held. The federal army was allowed to withdraw from its bases inside Croatia and tensions diminished. At the same time, the EU, succumbing to pressure from Germany, recognised Croatia. This was followed by US recognition, and in May 1992 Croatia was admitted to the UN.

The UN peace plan in Krajina was intended to bring about the disarming of local Serb paramilitary formations, the repatriation of refugees and the return of the region to Croatia. Instead, it only froze the existing situation and offered no permanent solution. In January 1993 the Croatian army suddenly launched an offensive in southern Krajina, pushing the Serbs back in some areas and recapturing strategic points. In June 1993 the Krajina Serbs voted overwhelmingly to join the Bosnian Serbs, with the hope of eventually being annexed into a Greater Serbia. A mass expulsion saw nearly all of the remaining Croats forced out of Krajina.

In July 1995 upwards of 8000 Muslim men and boys were slaughtered by the Bosnian Serb Army in the Bosnian town of Srebrenica. UN Secretary General Kofi Annan described the genocide as 'the worst on European soil since the Second World War'.

Troubles in Bosnia & Hercegovina

Meanwhile, in neighbouring Bosnia and Hercegovina, Bosnia's Croats and Muslims initially banded together in the face of Serbian advances. However, in 1993 the two sides fell out and began fighting each other. Bosnian Croat forces were responsible for several atrocities in Bosnia, including massacres of civilians, the destruction of mosques and, most famously, the destruction of the old bridge in Mostar. This conflagration was extinguished when the US fostered the development of the Muslim–Croatian federation in 1994, as the world looked on in horror at the Serb siege of Sarajevo.

While these events unfolded in Bosnia and Hercegovina, the Croatian government quietly began procuring arms from abroad. On 1 May 1995 the Croatian army and police entered occupied western Slavonia, east of Zagreb, and seized control of the region within days. The Krajina Serbs

1992

A first UN-brokered ceasefire takes effect temporarily. The EU recognises Croatian independence and Croatia is admitted into the UN. War breaks out in neighbouring Bosnia.

1993

Bosnian Croats and Muslims, previously aligned in fighting the Bosnian Serbs, start fighting each other. Croatia's reputation is sullied by the massacre of Muslim and Serb civilians.

1994

US-brokered talks lead to the creation of a Muslim–Croat Federation in Bosnia. Pope John Paul II visits Croatia and calls for a rejection of nationalism and a culture of peace.

1995

The 'Oluja' military campaign sees Croatian forces reclaim lost Croatian territory in the Krajina; most of the region's Serbs flee. The Dayton Accords bring peace and confirm Croatia's borders.

responded by shelling Zagreb in an attack that left seven people dead and 130 wounded. As the Croatian military consolidated its hold in western Slavonia, some 15,000 Serbs fled the region despite assurances from the Croatian government that they were safe from retribution.

Belgrade's silence throughout the campaign showed that the Krajina Serbs had lost the support of their Serbian sponsors, encouraging the Croats to forge ahead. On 4 August, the military launched an assault on the rebel Serb capital of Knin. The Serb army fled towards northern Bosnia, along with 150,000 civilians, many of whose roots in the Krajina stretched back centuries. The military operation ended in days, but was followed by months of terror, including widespread looting and burning of Serb villages.

The Dayton Peace Accords signed in Paris in December 1995 recognised Croatia's Yugoslav-era borders and provided for the return of eastern Slavonia. The transition proceeded relatively smoothly, but the two populations still regard each other with suspicion and hostility.

Richard Holbrooke's *To End a War* (1998) recounts the events surrounding the Dayton Accords. As the American diplomat who prodded the warring parties to the negotiating table to hammer out a peace accord, Holbrooke was in a unique position to evaluate the personalities and politics of the region.

Postwar Croatia

A degree of stability returned to Croatia after the hostilities. A key provision of the peace agreement was the guarantee by the Croatian government to facilitate the return of Serbian refugees, and although the central government in Zagreb made the return of refugees a priority in accordance with the demands of the international community, its efforts have often been subverted by local authorities intent on maintaining the ethnic singularity of their regions. The most recent census (2011) has Serbs at 4.4% of the population, slightly down on the previous census 10 years earlier, and less than a third of their 1991 numbers.

The handover of General Ante Gotovina in 2005 to the International Court of Justice in the Hague to answer war-crimes charges was a major condition for the beginning of Croatia's negotiations to join the EU. In 2011 Gotovina and fellow ex-general Mladen Markač were sentenced to 24 and 18 years in jail respectively, but the decision was overruled in November 2012, after an appeal court ruled there had been no conspiracy to commit war crimes.

In the spring of 2008, Croatia was officially invited to join NATO at the summit in Bucharest; exactly a year later, it joined the alliance. In 2012 Croats voted in a referendum to join the EU and in 2013 the country officially became a member.

A major earthquake hit Zagreb in March 2020, just as the country reported its first death from Covid-19. Over the next 18 months the virus would claim over 8200 lives and decimate Croatia's booming tourist industry. By summer 2021, with vaccines starting to roll out worldwide, visitor numbers were still only 30% of pre-Covid levels.

2009

Croatia officially joins NATO. Ivo Sanader suddenly resigns as prime minister. His deputy, former journalist Jadranka Kosor, takes over as the country's first female prime minister.

2012

A referendum on whether Croatia should join the EU results in a yes vote by a margin of two to one, though voter turnout is low. It officially becomes the 28th member state in 2013.

2015

Croatia elects Kolinda Grabar-Kitarović as its first female president. In 2017 *Forbes* magazine ranked her as the world's 39th most powerful woman.

2020

In February Croatia confirms its first case of Covid-19 and in March its first death due to the virus. By July 2021 the virus will have claimed over 8200 lives.

The Croatian Mindset

With Germanic influences in the north and larger-than-life Mediterranean tendencies in the south, Croats aren't completely cut from the same mould. Yet from one tip of the Croatian horseshoe to the other, there are constants. Wherever you go, family and religion loom large, social conservatism is the norm, sport is the national obsession and coffee is drunk in industrial quantities.

Croatia: West or East?

The vast majority of Croats have a strong cultural identification with Western Europe and draw a distinction between themselves and their 'eastern' neighbours in Bosnia, Montenegro and Serbia. The idea that Croatia is the last stop before the Ottoman/Orthodox east is prevalent in all segments of the population. Describing Croatia as part of Eastern Europe will not win you any friends. Some locals even baulk at the term 'Balkan', given the negative connotations that it carries. They'll be quick to point out that Zagreb is actually further west than Vienna; that the nation is overwhelmingly Catholic, rather than Orthodox; and that they use the Latin alphabet, not Cyrillic.

Despite the different alphabet used, Croatian and Serbian are more akin to related dialects than separate languages. This doesn't stop both sides stressing the differences between them, though. In Croatia in particular, a French style of linguistic nationalism has seen old Yugoslav-era words like *aerodrom* (airport) dropped from signs in favour of the Croatian-derived *zračna luka* (*zrak* means air and *luka* means port) – but most people still say *aerodrom* regardless. And should you ask for *hljeb* or *hleb* (the Montenegrin and Serbian words for bread, respectively) instead of *kruh* when you're dining in Dubrovnik, it won't go down well.

In 2014, a petition garnered 500,000 signatures calling for a referendum to restrict the use of Cyrillic on public signs in Croatia. At present Cyrillic is used alongside the Latin script in areas where Serbs make up more than 30% of the population, but the petition sought to increase this minimum to 50%. A court rejected the petition, stating that such a referendum would be unconstitutional. However, in 2015, the city of Vukovar (the war-battered city where Serbs number 34.8%) passed an ordinance exempting itself the need to provide bilingual signs – a move condemned by the Croatian prime minister, president and the Council of Europe.

All of this stands in contrast to the popularity of Serbian turbo folk in Croatia, a type of music frowned upon and avoided during the 1990s war. It seems that ethnic tensions have eased to the point where connecting Balkan elements are again being embraced in some unexpected aspects of Croatian society.

Croatia's Split Personality

With its capital inland and the majority of its big cities on the coast, Croatia is torn between a more serious *Mitteleuropean* mindset in Zagreb, Zagorje and Slavonia (with meaty food, Austrian architecture and a strong interest in personal advancement over pleasure) and the coastal Mediterranean character, which is more laid-back and open. Istrians are strongly Italian influenced and tend to be bilingual, speaking both Italian and Croatian. The Dalmatians are only slightly less Italianised and are generally a relaxed and easygoing bunch: many offices empty out at 3pm, allowing people to enjoy the long hours of sunlight on a beach or at an outdoor cafe.

Most people involved in the tourist industry speak German, English and Italian, though English is the most widely spoken language among the young.

Family Matters

Family is very important to Croats and extended-family links are strong and cherished. First cousins tend to be very close and connections are maintained with more distant cousins as well.

It's traditional and perfectly normal for children to live with their parents until well into their adult life. This extends particularly to sons, who in rural and small-town areas will often move their wives into their parents' home when they marry. The expectation that you'll stay at home until you're married makes life particularly difficult for gays and lesbians, or anyone wanting a taste of independence. Many young people achieve a degree of this by leaving to study in a different town.

Most families own their own homes, bought in the postcommunist years when previously state-owned homes were sold to the tenants for little money. These properties are often passed down from grandparents, great-aunts and other relatives.

Daily Life

Lounging in cafes and bars is an important part of life here, and you often wonder how the country's wheels are turning with so many people at leisure rather than work. But perhaps it's all that coffee that makes them work twice as fast once they're back in the office.

Croats like the good life and take a lot of pride in showing off the latest fashions and mobile phones. High-end fashion labels are prized by both women and men – the more prominent the label, the better. Even with a tight economy, people will cut out restaurant meals and films in order to afford a shopping trip to Italy or Austria for some new clothes. For young men, looking good and dressing well is all part of the macho swagger. Croatian men don't like to lose face by acting stupidly in public, so although they drink, they generally don't drink to get drunk. Most local women don't drink much at all.

The cult of celebrity is extremely powerful in Croatia – the trashy tabloids are full of wannabe celebs and their latest shenanigans.

Etiquette Tips

Dress modestly when visiting churches.

Wait to be invited to use a person's first name.

Whoever does the inviting (for dinner or drinks) pays the bill.

Manners & Mannerisms

Croats can come across as uninterested and rude (even those working in the tourist sector) and some people find their directness confronting. False pleasantries are regarded as just that – false. Smiles and exhortations to 'have a nice day' are reserved for people they actually care about. The idea of calling a complete stranger 'dear' at the start of a letter just seems weird to them, as does the Antipodean habit of referring to people they've only just met as 'mate'.

This is just the way Croats operate, so don't take it personally. At least you'll always know where you stand. Once you graduate from the stranger category to friend, you'll find them warm, gregarious, generous and deeply hospitable. You might even make friends for life.

Never ask a Croat how they are if you don't want to know the answer. 'Fine' just doesn't cut it. Dalmatians, in particular, are prone to the dramatic: they'll either be full of the joys of life or in deep despair. Either way, if you ask, you'll hear about it.

Religion

According to the most recent census, 86.3% of the population identifies itself as Catholic, 4.4% Orthodox (this corresponds exactly with the percentage of Serbs), 4% 'other and undeclared', 3.8% atheist and 1.5% Muslim.

The main factor separating the otherwise ethnically indistinguishable Croats and Serbs is religion: Croats overwhelming adhere to the Roman Catholic faith, while Serbs are just as strongly linked to the Eastern Orthodox Church. The division has its roots in the split of the Roman Empire at the end of the 4th century. Present-day Croatia found itself on the western side, ruled from Rome, while Serbia ended up on the Greek-influenced eastern side, ruled from Constantinople (now Istanbul). As time went on, differences developed between western and eastern Christianity, culminating in the Great Schism of 1054, when the churches finally parted ways. In addition to various doctrinal differences, Orthodox Christians venerate icons, allow priests to marry and do not accept the authority of the pope.

Nikola Tesla (1856–1943), the father of the radio and alternating electric current technology, was born in the Croatian village of Smiljan to Serbian parents (his father was an Orthodox priest). Both Croatia and Serbia celebrate him as a national hero.

It would be difficult to overstate the extent to which Catholicism shapes the Croatian national identity. The Croats pledged allegiance to Roman Catholicism as early as the 9th century and were rewarded with the right to conduct Mass and issue religious writings in the local language, using the Glagolitic script. The popes supported the early Croatian kings, who in turn built monasteries and churches to further promote Catholicism. Throughout the long centuries of Croatia's domination by foreign powers, Catholicism was the unifying element in forging a sense of nationhood.

The Church enjoys a respected position in Croatia's cultural and political life, and Croatia is the subject of particular attention from the Vatican. The Church is also the most trusted institution in Croatia, rivalled only by the military.

Croats, both within Croatia and abroad, provide a stream of priests and nuns to replenish the ranks of Catholic clergy. Religious holidays are celebrated with fervour and Sunday Mass is strongly attended.

Equality in Croatia

Women continue to face some hurdles in Croatia, although the situation is improving. Under Tito's brand of socialism, women were encouraged to become politically active and their representation in the Croatian *sabor* (parliament) increased to 18%. Currently 19% of the parliament is comprised of women, and Croatia has a woman president, the first in the country's history.

Croatian women weren't granted the vote until 1945. Following this election, Yugoslavia became a one-party state. Elections continued to be held but the League of Communists selected the candidates; sometimes there was only one name on the ballot.

Women fare worse in traditional villages than in urban areas, and were hit harder economically than men after the Homeland War. Many of the factories that closed, especially in eastern Slavonia, had a high proportion of female workers.

Women are underrepresented at the executive level, and working women are still expected to perform most of the domestic duties when they return home. Both domestic abuse and sexual harassment in the workplace are quite common in Croatia. Despite signing a 2011 Council of Europe convention aiming to reduce violence against women, at the time of writing, it was yet to be ratified – with commentators pointing to opposition from conservative groups as a reason for the delay.

Although attitudes are slowly changing towards homosexuality, Croatia is an overwhelmingly Catholic country with highly conservative views of sexuality. Many gays and lesbians are closeted, fearing harassment or violence if their sexual orientation is revealed. In 2013 a group called *U ime obitelji* (In the Name of the Family) campaigned for a referendum in which 65% of voters approved a constitutional ban on same-sex marriage. The following year, parliament passed a law creating civil partnerships for same-sex couples, granting partners the same rights as married couples in every aspect but adoption.

BASKETBALL

The most popular sport after football, basketball is followed with some reverence. The teams of Split, Zadar and Zagreb's Cibona are known across Europe, though none has yet equalled the Cibona star team of the 1980s, when they became European champions.

Good Sports

In 2017 Croatia was ranked the world's 7th-greatest sporting nation per head of population. Football, basketball and tennis are enormously popular, and sporty Croatia has contributed a disproportionate number of world-class players in each sport.

Football

Football (soccer; *nogomet* in Croatian) is by far the nation's most popular sport. In 1998, only seven years after declaring independence from Yugoslavia, Croatia's men's team stunned the world by finishing third in the FIFA World Cup.

In 2018 they went one better when the squad, coached by the Zen-like Zlatko Dalić, made it to the final and captain Luka Modrić was awarded the Golden Ball trophy as the best player of the tournament. Although they lost to France, they returned home to the kinds of scenes usually reserved for conquering heroes.

This injection of positivity couldn't come at a better time for Croatian football. Corruption scandals saw Modrić's early mentor Zdravko Mamić, the former director of the Dinamo Zagreb club, flee the country after being sentenced to 6½ years in prison for tax evasion and embezzlement in relation to player transfers. Modrić himself was widely suspected of perjury in his testimony in Mamić's defense.

Fan behaviour has also been a recurring problem, with racist and fascist chants and banners resulting in reprimands for the national team. Matches between Dinamo Zagreb and arch-rivals Hajduk Split regularly result in violence.

Croatia's top-flight footballers play in professional clubs all over Europe. The current golden crop threatens to displace even the legendary Davor Šuker – rated by Pelé in 2004 as one of the top living players – as the biggest name in Croatian footballing history.

The current crop of football stars includes Luka Modrić (who plays for Real Madrid), Ivan Rakitić (Barcelona), Mario Mandžukić (Juventas), Danijel Subašić (Monaco), Domagoj Vida (Beşiktaş), Ivan Perišić (Inter Milan), Mateo Kovačić (Real Madrid), Milan Badelj (Fiorentina), Šime Vrsaljko (Atlético Madrid), Marcelo Brozović (Inter Milan) and Dejan Lovren (Liverpool).

Tennis

Croatia has produced – and continues to produce – some mighty big players, in every sense of the word. The 2001 victory of 6ft 4in Goran Ivanišević at Wimbledon provoked wild celebrations throughout the country, especially in his home town of Split. The charismatic serve-and-volley player was much loved for his engaging personality and on-court antics, and dominated the top-10 rankings during much of the 1990s. Injuries forced his retirement in 2004, but Croatia stayed on the court with a 2005 Davis Cup victory led by 6ft 4in Ivan Ljubičić and 6ft 5in Mario Ančić.

Croatia's top current player (ranked third in the world in 2018) is 6ft 6in Marin Čilić, who won his first Grand Slam title, the US Open, in 2014. The only other Croat listed in the Men's Singles rankings in 2018 was 22-year-old Borna Ćorić.

On the women's side, Zagreb-born Iva Majoli won the French Open in 1997. Four Croats are currently featured in the Women's Singles rankings: Mirjana Lučić-Baroni, Ana Konjuh, Donna Vekić and Petra Martić.

The Croatia Open, part of the ATP World Tour series, is held in Umag (Istria) in July. However, tennis is more than a spectator sport in Croatia; the coast is amply endowed with clay courts.

Architecture

After they came, saw and conquered, most of Croatia's conga-line of invaders stuck around long enough to erect buildings. From the walled towns of the coast to the baroque splendour of Varaždin in the north (via Roman ruins, Gothic cathedrals, Renaissance palaces and Viennese villas), Croatia's architectural legacy is varied and extremely impressive.

Roman Riches

The Cathedral of St Domnius in Split (built as the 3rd century transitioned into the 4th) is the oldest cathedral building in the world, thanks to it inhabiting the original mausoleum of the Emperor Diocletian.

No substantial buildings survive from before the Romans' arrival, but reminders of the 650 years of Roman rule are scattered all over the country: an intact archway in the centre of Rijeka; a turf-covered amphitheatre in Krka National Park; columns from an ancient forum in Zadar.

All of these pale in comparison with what is one of the best-preserved remnants of Roman architecture still standing in the world today: Diocletian's Palace in Split. The emperor moved into this oversized complex when he retired in 305 CE, and although it was converted into a walled town and has been continuously inhabited for nearly two millenniums, some parts are still wonderfully evocative of the era in which it was built. Quite unlike the crumbling ruins we associate with Roman remains, the former Mausoleum and Temple of Jupiter even have their roofs intact.

Croatia's other Roman highlights can both be found in Istria. The remarkable amphitheatre in Pula is Croatia's answer to Rome's Colosseum. This imposing 1st-century CE arena still has a complete circuit of nearly 30m-high walls and is once again used for public entertainment – albeit of a less bloodthirsty kind than that for which it was built.

After the Western Roman Empire fell in 476, the Byzantine (or Eastern Roman) Empire eventually took control of parts of present-day Croatia. The greatest surviving architectural treasure from this time is the Euphrasian Basilica in Poreč, Istria. Built in the 6th century, this early Christian church incorporates layers of older buildings within its walls, and a precious mosaic decorates its apse.

Pre-Romanesque Churches

The Slavs arrived in Croatia in the early 7th century, heralding what is known in architectural terms as the Old Croatian, pre-Romanesque period. Not much survives from this time as most of it was destroyed during the Mongol invasion of the 13th century. The best remaining examples are found along the Dalmatian coast, beginning with the impressive 9th-century St Donatus' Church in Zadar, built on the ruins of the Roman forum. It has a round central structure, unique for late antiquity, and three semicircular apses.

Two other considerably smaller, but similarly curvaceous, churches survive nearby. The 11th-century Holy Cross Church in Nin has a cross-shaped plan, two apses and a dome above the centre point. Just outside of Nin, teensy St Nicholas' is a postcard-perfect fortresslike stone church perched atop a small hill.

Gothic & Renaissance

The Romanesque tradition of the Middle Ages, with its semicircular arches and symmetrical forms, persisted along the coast long after the pointy-arched Gothic style had swept the rest of Europe. In the 13th century the earliest examples of Gothic were still combined with Romanesque forms. The most beautiful work from this period is the portal of St Lawrence's Cathedral in Trogir, carved by the master artisan Radovan in 1240. The Cathedral of the Assumption of the Blessed Virgin Mary in Zagreb was the first venture into the Gothic style in northern Croatia. Although the cathedral has been reconstructed several times, the remnants of 13th-century murals are still visible in the sacristy.

St James' Cathedral in Šibenik (built 1431–1536) is the only building of its time that was constructed using the technique of mounting prefabricated stone elements.

The late-Gothic period was dominated by the builder and sculptor Juraj Dalmatinac, who was born in Zadar in the 15th century. His most outstanding work was Šibenik's St James' Cathedral, which marked a transition from the Gothic to the Renaissance period. Dalmatinac constructed the church entirely of stone, and adorned its outer walls with a wreath of realistically carved portraits of local people. Another beauty from this period is the 15th-century St Mark's Cathedral in Korčula.

The Renaissance flourished in Croatia, especially in independent Ragusa (Dubrovnik). By the second half of the 15th century, Renaissance influences (harking back to ancient Roman architecture) were appearing on late-Gothic structures. The Sponza Palace is a fine example of this mixed style. By the mid-16th century, Renaissance features began to replace the Gothic style in the palaces and summer residences built in and around Ragusa by the wealthy nobility. Unfortunately, much was destroyed in the 1667 earthquake.

Baroque to Brutalism

Northern Croatia is well known for the baroque style, which was introduced by Jesuit priests in the 17th century. The city of Varaždin was a regional capital in the 17th and 18th centuries, which, because of its location, enjoyed a steady interchange of artists, artisans and architects with northern Europe. The combination of wealth and creativity eventually led to Varaždin becoming Croatia's foremost city of baroque art. You'll notice the theatrical, sometimes frilly style in the elaborately restored houses, churches and especially the impressive castle.

Today's Croatia has a vibrant architecture scene. In the rebuilding that followed the 1990s war, numerous open competitions were organised and young architects were given an opportunity to show their talents. Some of the more important examples of their work are the Gymnasium in Koprivnica and Hotel Lone in Rovinj.

In Zagreb, fine examples of the baroque style are found in the Upper Town, including the Jesuit Church of St Catherine and the restored mansion that is now the Croatian Museum of Naïve Art. Wealthy families built their baroque mansions in the countryside around Zagreb, including at Brezovica, Miljana, Lobor and Bistra.

The influence of the Austro-Hungarian Empire is also on display in the capital, particularly in the grand neoclassical public buildings, but also in smaller art nouveau apartments and townhouses. Other examples are the former governor's palace in Rijeka and the holiday mansions of the Viennese elite scattered around neighbouring Opatija and some of the nearby islands.

During the modernist period, Croatian architecture fell in sync with the International Style. The socialist period saw many highly sophisticated and aesthetically mature examples of residential and civic architecture produced, particularly in planned suburbs such as Novi Zagreb. However, the more brutalist concrete structures, once seen as futuristic and modern, aren't to everyone's taste and many have been left to decay. Sadly, the sepia-tinged nostalgia surrounding 1970s Yugoslavia hasn't extended to preserving the wonderfully evocative hotels of the period.

The Natural Environment

Croatia is shaped like a boomerang, curving from the fertile farmland of Slavonia in the north, down through hilly central Croatia to the Istrian peninsula, and then south through Dalmatia along the rugged Adriatic coast. Most visitors focus their attention on the narrow coastal belt at the foot of the Dinaric Alps and the numerous gorgeous islands just offshore, but there's a whole lot more natural beauty to explore back up the boomerang.

Karst Caves & Waterfalls

The temperature of the Adriatic Sea varies greatly: it rises from an average of 7°C (45°F) in December up to a balmy 23°C (73°F) in September.

Croatia's most outstanding geological feature is the prevalent, highly porous limestone and dolomitic rock called karst, which stretches along the coast and covers large parts of the hinterland. Karst is formed by acidic water dissolving the surface limestone, which then allows the water to seep into the harder layer underneath. Eventually the water forms underground streams, carving out fissures and caves before resurfacing, disappearing into another cave and eventually emptying into the sea.

Caves and springs are common features of karstic landscapes, which explains Croatia's Pazin Chasm, Plitvice Lakes and the Krka waterfalls, as well as the Manita Peć cave in Paklenica. When the limestone collapses, a kind of basin (known as *polje*) is formed. These are then cultivated, despite the fact that this kind of field drains poorly and can easily turn into a temporary lake.

National Parks

When the Yugoslav federation collapsed, eight of its finest national parks ended up in Croatia. The national parks cover 1.3% of the country and have a total area of 961 sq km, of which 742 sq km is land and 219 sq km is water. Around 8% of Croatia is given over to its protected areas, including nature parks and the like. The fantastic Parks of Croatia (www.parkovihrvatske.hr) website lists all 19 national and nature parks in Croatia.

On the Mainland

By far the most popular of the eight national parks is Unesco World Heritage–listed Plitvice Lakes National Park (p211), near the Bosnian border, midway between Zagreb and Zadar. Its chain of exquisitely picturesque lakes and waterfalls were formed by mosses that retained calcium carbonate as river water rushed through the karst. The falls are at their watery best in spring. The park's popularity comes at a price though: the main paths get terribly congested in the peak months.

Krka National Park (p233) is an even more extensive series of lakes and waterfalls set along the Krka River, north of Šibenik. The main access point is Skradinski Buk, where the largest cascade covers 800m. Like Plitvice, this part of the park can get uncomfortably crowded in July and August, but there are many stretches that are more peaceful. The park also includes important cultural relics in the form of a Serbian Orthodox and a Roman Catholic monastery.

The dramatically formed karstic gorges and cliffs make Paklenica National Park (p215), along the Adriatic coast near Zadar, a rock-climbing favourite. Large grottoes and caves filled with stalactites and stalagmites make it an interesting park for cave explorers, and there are many kilometres of hiking trails. Tourist facilities are well developed but there are large tracts of wilderness.

At the other end of the same mountain range, rugged Northern Velebit National Park is a patchwork of forests, peaks, ravines and ridges that backs the coast on the mainland opposite the island of Rab.

Risnjak National Park (p178), northeast of Rijeka, is the most untouched forested park, partly because the climate at its higher altitudes is somewhat inhospitable, with an average temperature of 12.6°C in July. The winters are long and snowy, but when spring finally comes in late May or early June, everything blooms at once. The park has been kept deliberately free of tourist facilities, with the idea that only mountain lovers need venture this far. The main entrance point is the motel and information facility at Crni Lug.

There are 1244 islands and islets along the tectonically submerged Adriatic coastline, only 50 of them inhabited. The largest are Cres, Krk, Pag and Rab in the north; Brač, Hvar, Dugi Otok and Vis in the middle; and Korčula and Mljet in the south.

On the Islands

The Kornati Islands consist of 140 sparsely vegetated, uninhabited islands, islets and reefs scattered over 300 sq km, 89 of which are included in the Kornati National Park (p233). The unusual form and extraordinary rock formations of the islands make them an Adriatic highlight. Unless you have your own boat, you'll need to join an organised tour from Zadar or other places nearby.

Mljet National Park (p321), on the northwestern half of the island of the same name, incorporates two highly indented saltwater lakes surrounded by lush vegetation. Maquis shrubland is thicker and taller on Mljet than nearly anywhere else in the Mediterranean, which makes it a natural refuge for many animals.

The Brijuni Islands (p136) are the most cultivated national park, as they were developed as a tourist resort in the late 19th century. They were the getaway paradise for Tito and now attract the glitterati and their yachts. Most of the animals and plants were introduced, but the islands are lovely. Access to the islands is restricted – you can only visit on an organised tour.

Reaching up to 95cm in length, the nose-horned viper is the largest and most venomous snake in Europe. It likes rocky habitats and has a zigzag stripe on its body and a distinctive scaly 'horn' on its nose. If you're close enough to spot the horn, you're probably a little too close.

Wildlife

Animals

Of the 59 mammal species present in Croatia, seven are listed as vulnerable: the garden dormouse and six species of bat. Red and roe deer are plentiful in the dense forests of Risnjak National Park, and there are also chamois, brown bears, wild cats and *ris* (Eurasian lynx), from which the park gets its name. Rarely, a grey wolf or wild boar may appear. Plitvice Lakes National Park, however, is an important refuge for wolves. The rare Eurasian otter is also protected in Plitvice Lakes National Park, as well as in Krka National Park.

Two venomous snakes are endemic in Paklenica: the nose-horned viper and the European adder. The nonvenomous leopard snake, the four-lined snake, the grass snake and the snake lizard can be found in both Paklenica and Krka National Parks.

The waters around the islands of Lošinj and Cres are home to the Adriatic's only known resident pod of bottlenose dolphins. Striped dolphins and basking sharks are sometimes also sighted here. A centre devoted to rehabilitating injured loggerhead, leatherback and green turtles has been set up in Mali Lošinj.

BIRDWATCHING

The griffon vulture, with a wingspan of up to 2.6m, has permanent colonies on the islands of Cres, Krk and Prvić. Paklenica National Park is rich in peregrine falcons, goshawks, sparrow hawks, buzzards and owls. Krka National Park is an important winter habitat for migratory marsh birds such as herons, wild ducks, geese and cranes, as well as rare golden eagles and short-toed eagles. Kopački Rit Nature Park, near Osijek in eastern Croatia, is an extremely important bird refuge.

Plants

The country's richest plant life is found in the Velebit Range, part of the Dinaric Alps, which provides the backdrop to the central Dalmatian coast. Botanists have counted around 2700 species and 78 endemic plants there, including the increasingly threatened edelweiss. Risnjak National Park is another good place to find edelweiss, along with black vanilla orchids, lilies and hairy alpenroses, which look a lot better than they sound. The dry Mediterranean climate along the coast is perfect for maquis, a low brush that flourishes all along the coast, but especially on the island of Mljet. You'll also find oleander, jasmine and juniper trees along the coast, and lavender is cultivated on the island of Hvar. Mediterranean olive and fig trees are also abundant.

Environmental Issues

The lack of heavy industry in Croatia has had the happy effect of leaving its forests, coasts, rivers and air generally fresh and unpolluted. An increase in investment and development, however, brings problems and threats to the environment.

The website of the Ministry of Environment & Energy (www.mzoip.hr) is the place to go for the latest news on Croatia's environment.

With the tourist boom, the demand for fresh fish and shellfish has risen exponentially. The production of farmed sea bass, sea bream and tuna (for export) is rising substantially, resulting in environmental pressure along the coast. Croatian tuna farms capture the young fish for fattening before they have a chance to reproduce and replenish the wild-fish population.

Coastal and island forests face particular problems. First logged by Venetians to build ships, then by local people desperate for fuel, the forests experienced centuries of neglect, which have left many island and coastal mountains barren. The dry summers and brisk *maestral* (strong, steady westerly wind) also pose substantial fire hazards along the coast. In the last 20 years, fires have destroyed 7% of Croatia's forests.

In 2014 the Croatian government called for tenders for gas- and oil-exploration licences in the Adriatic. Two years later environmentalists were heralding a victory for people power, after public pressure led to the government declaring a moratorium on exploration.

The Arts

Croatia views itself very much as a cultured central European nation, steeped in the continent's finest artistic traditions and imbued with its own unique folk styles, but equally unafraid of the avant-garde. Even if they're virtually unknown elsewhere, local artists are highly regarded at home.

Literature

The Croatian language developed in the centuries following the great migration into Slavonia and Dalmatia. In order to convert the Slavs to Christianity, 9th-century Greek missionaries Cyril and Methodius learnt the language and put it into writing. This became known as Glagolitic script. The earliest known example is an 11th-century inscription in a Benedictine abbey on the island of Krk. For more on the Glagolitic alphabet, see p199.

Ivan Gundulić (1589–1638), from Ragusa (Dubrovnik), is widely considered to be the greatest Croatian poet. A more recent contender for the title is Tin Ujević (1891–1955), whose work remains extremely popular today.

Poets & Playwrights

The first literary flowering in Croatia took place in Dalmatia, which was strongly influenced by the Italian Renaissance. The works of the scholar and poet Marko Marulić (1450–1524), from Split, are still venerated in Croatia. His play *Judita* was the first work produced by a Croatian writer in his native tongue. The plays of Marin Držić (1508–67), especially *Dundo Maroje,* express humanistic Renaissance ideals and are still performed, especially in Dubrovnik. The epic poem *Osman,* by Ivan Gundulić (1589–1638), celebrated the Polish victory over the Turks in 1621, a victory that the Dubrovnik-based author saw as heralding the destruction of Ottoman rule.

The most significant figure in the period after the 1990s war was the lyrical and sometimes satirical Vesna Parun. Although Parun was often harassed by the government for what they considered decadent and bourgeois poetry, her published work *Collected Poems* has reached a new generation, which finds solace in her vision of wartime folly.

Novelists

Croatia's towering literary figure is 20th-century novelist and playwright Miroslav Krleža (1893–1981). Always politically active, Krleža broke with Tito in 1967 over the writer's campaign for equality between the Serbian and Croatian literary languages. Depicting the concerns of a changing Yugoslavia, his most popular novels include *The Return of Philip Latinowicz* (1932) and *Banners* (1963–65), a multivolume saga about middle-class Croatian life at the turn of the 20th century.

Mention should also be made of Ivo Andrić (1892–1975), who won the 1961 Nobel Prize for Literature for his Bosnian historical trilogy *The Bridge on the Drina, Bosnian Chronicle* and *Gospođica.* Born as a Catholic Croat in Bosnia, the writer used the Serbian dialect and lived in Belgrade, but identified himself as a Yugoslav.

Award-winning writer Dubravka Ugrešić and four other female writers were accused of being 'witches' for not wholeheartedly supporting the Croatian war for independence.

Gold, Frankincense and Myrrh, by Slobodan Novak (1924–2016), was first published in Yugoslavia in 1968, and has been translated into English. The book is set on the island of Rab, where an elderly lady is dying, and her carer – the narrator – reminisces about life, love, the state, religion and memory.

Some contemporary writers have been strongly marked by the implications of Croatian independence. Goran Tribuson uses the thriller genre to examine the changes in Croatian society after the war. In *Oblivion,* Pavao Pavličić uses a detective story to explore the problems of collective historical memory. Canadian-based Josip Novakovich's work stems from nostalgia for his native Croatia. His most popular novel, *April Fool's Day* (2005), is an absurd and gritty account of the recent wars that gripped the region. Slavenka Drakulić writes novels and essays that are often politically and sociologically provocative, and always witty and intelligent; look out for *How We Survived Communism and Even Laughed* (1992) and *Café Europa: Life After Communism* (1999).

Expat writer Dubravka Ugrešić has been a figure of controversy in Croatia and is acclaimed elsewhere. Now living in the Netherlands in self-imposed exile, she is best known for her novels *The Culture of Lies* (1998) and *The Ministry of Pain* (2006). In 2016 she was awarded the prestigious Neustadt Prize Laureate.

Miljenko Jergović, born in Sarajevo but living in Croatia, is a witty, poignant writer whose *Sarajevo Marlboro* (1994) and *Mama Leone* (1999) powerfully describe the atmosphere in prewar Yugoslavia.

On the world stage, Croatia's most famous actors are Mira Furlan (*Babylon 5, Lost*) and Goran Višnjić (*ER, The Girl with the Dragon Tattoo*). Actors of Croatian heritage include John Malkovich, Eric Bana (born Banadinović) and Joe Manganiello.

Cinema

By far the most prominent person in the Croatian film industry is Branko Lustig (b 1932), winner of Academy Awards for producing both *Schindler's List* and *Gladiator.* Born in Osijek to Croatian Jewish parents, he survived Auschwitz as a child and went on to work for state-owned Jadran Film alongside the likes of director Branko Bauer (1921–2001).

Another luminary is writer and director Veljko Bulajić, whose debut movie *Vlak bez voznog reda* (Train Without a Timetable) was nominated for the Golden Palm at Cannes in 1959, while *Bitka na Neretvi* (Battle of Neretva) was nominated for an Academy Award 10 years later.

Bosnian born and of Montenegrin descent but based in Croatia throughout his career, Dušan Vukotić (1927–1998) won the Academy Award for Best Animated Short in 1961 for *Surogat.*

More recently, Vinko Brešan's *Kako je počeo rat na mom otoku* (How the War Started on My Island; 1996) and *Maršal* (Marshal Tito's Spirit; 1999) were massively popular in Croatia. Goran Rušinović's *Mondo Bobo* (1997) was the first independent feature film made in Croatia, while his *Buick Riv-iera* (2008) went on to win awards at the Pula and Sarajevo film festivals.

Music

Folk

Although Croatia has produced many fine classical musicians and composers, its most original musical contribution lies in its rich folk tradition. This music reflects a number of influences, many dating back to the Middle Ages when the Hungarians and the Venetians vied for control of the country. Franz Joseph Haydn (1732–1809) was born near a Croat enclave in Austria and his compositions were strongly influenced by Croatian folk songs.

For a thorough rundown of cultural events in Croatia, check out the informative www.culturenet.hr.

The instrument most often used in Croatian folk music is the *tamburica,* a three- or five-string long-necked lute that is plucked or strummed. Introduced by the Turks in the 17th century, the instrument rapidly gained a following in eastern Slavonia and came to be closely identified with Croatian national aspirations. *Tamburica* music continued to be played at weddings and local festivals during the Yugoslav period, too.

Vocal music followed the *klapa* tradition. Translated as 'group of people', *klapa* is an outgrowth of church-choir singing. The form is most popular in Dalmatia, particularly in Split, and can involve up to 10 voices singing

RECOMMENDED FOLK RECORDINGS

- *Croatie: Music of Long Ago* is a good starting point as it covers the whole gamut of Croatian music.
- *Lijepa naša tamburaša* is a selection of Slavonian chants accompanied by *tamburica* (lute).
- *Omiš 1967–75* is an overview of *klapa* (Dalmatian *a capella*) music.
- *Pripovid O Dalmaciji* is an excellent selection of *klapa* in which the influence of church-choral singing is especially clear.

in harmony about love, tragedy and loss. Traditionally the choirs were all-male, but now women are getting involved, although there are very few mixed choirs.

Another popular strain of folk music, which is strongly influenced by music from neighbouring Hungary, emanates from the region of Međimurje in northeastern Croatia. The predominant instrument is a *citura* (zither). The tunes are slow and melancholic, frequently revolving around themes of lost love. New artists have breathed life into this traditional genre, including Lidija Bajuk and Dunja Knebl, female singers who have done much to resuscitate the music and gained large followings in the process.

Pop, Rock & the Rest

There's a wealth of home-grown talent in Croatia's pop and rock music scene. One of the most prominent bands is Hladno Pivo (Cold Beer), who play energetic punky music with witty, politically charged lyrics. Then there's the indie rock band Pips, Chips & Videoclips, whose breakthrough single 'Dinamo ja te volim' (Dinamo, I Love You) referred to Tuđman's attempts to rename Zagreb's football team, but whose music has generally been apolitical since.

Nirvana bass player Krist Novoselic was born in California to Croatian parents and spent part of his teenage years living in Zadar. Also of Croatian heritage is New Zealand's pop megastar Lorde (real name Ella Yelich-O'Connor); in 2017 she announced that she had been awarded Croatian citizenship.

The band Gustafi sings in the Istrian dialect and mixes Americana with local folk sounds, while the deliciously insane Let 3 from Rijeka is (in)famous for its nutty tunes and live performances at which the band members often show up naked, with only a piece of cork up their backsides (yes, really). TBF (The Beat Fleet) is Split's answer to hip hop, using Split slang to talk about current issues, family troubles, heartbreak and happy times. Flying the flag for Croatian women in hip hop is Mirela Priselac Remi from Zagreb's Elemental.

The fusion of jazz and pop with folk tunes is very popular in Croatia. One of the more prominent names in this scene is talented Tamara Obrovac from Istria, who sings in an ancient Istrian dialect that is no longer spoken.

The Croatian queen of pop is Severina, famous for her good looks and eventful personal life, which is widely covered by local celebrity and gossip magazines. Gibonni is another massively popular singer, and his major influence is Oliver Dragojević, a legendary singer of lovable schmaltz who died of cancer in 2018. In 2017 the two collaborated on *Familija,* which won the Album of the Year gong in Croatia's Porin awards.

Painting & Sculpture

The painter Vincent of Kastav was producing accomplished church frescos in Istria during the 15th century. The small St Mary's Church near Beram contains his work, most notably the *Dance of Death*. Another notable Istrian painter of the 15th century is John of Kastav, who has left frescos throughout Istria, mostly in the Slovenian part.

Many artists born in Dalmatia were influenced by, and in turn influenced, Italian Renaissance style. The sculptors Lucijan Vranjanin and Frano Laurana, the miniaturist Julije Klović and the painter Andrija Medulić

FOLK DANCES

Look out for the *drmeš*, a kind of accelerated polka danced by couples in small groups. The *kolo*, a lively Slavic round dance in which men and women alternate in the circle, is accompanied by Roma-style violinists. In Dalmatia, the *poskočica* is also danced by couples creating various patterns.

Like folk music, Croatian traditional dances are kept alive at local and national festivals. The best is the International Folklore Festival (p83) in Zagreb in July. If you can't make it to that, not to worry: music and folklore groups work on a circuit in the summer, hitting most coastal and island towns at one point or another. Ask at a local tourist office for a current schedule.

left a Dalmatia under threat from the Ottomans in the 15th century and worked in Italy. Museums in London, Paris and Florence contain examples of their work, but few of their creations remain on display in Croatia.

Vlaho Bukovac (1855–1922) was the most notable Croatian painter of the late 19th century. After working in London and Paris, he came to Zagreb in 1892 and produced portraits and paintings on historical themes in a lively style. Early-20th-century painters of note include Miroslav Kraljević (1885–1913) and Josip Račić (1885–1908), but the most internationally recognised artist was the sculptor Ivan Meštrović (1883–1962), who created many masterpieces on Croatian themes. Antun Augustinčić (1900–79) was another internationally recognised sculptor, whose *Monument to Peace* is outside New York's UN building. A small museum of his work can be visited in the town of Klanjec, north of Zagreb.

Naive Art

Post-WWI artists experimented with abstract expressionism, but this period is best remembered for the naive art that began with the 1931 Zemlja (Soil) exhibition in Zagreb, which introduced the public to works by Ivan Generalić (1914–92) and other peasant painters. Committed to producing art that could be easily understood and appreciated by ordinary people, Generalić was joined by painters Franjo Mraz (1910–81) and Mirko Virius (1889–1943), and sculptor Petar Smajić (1910–85) in a campaign to gain acceptance and recognition for naive art.

Abstract Art

Abstract art infiltrated the postwar scene. The most celebrated modern Croatian painter is Edo Murtić (1921–2005), who drew inspiration from the countryside of Dalmatia and Istria. In 1959 a group of artists – Marijan Jevšovar (1922–88), Ivan Kožarić (b 1921) and Julije Knifer (1921–2004) – created the Gorgona group, which pushed the boundaries of abstract art. Đuro Pulitika (1922–2006), known for his colourful landscapes, was a well-regarded Dubrovnik painter, as were Antun Masle (1919–67) and Ivo Dulčić (1916–75).

Contemporary Art

The post-WWII trend towards avant-garde art has evolved into installation art, minimalism, conceptualism and video art. Contemporary Croatian artists worth seeing include Lovro Artuković (b 1959), whose highly realistic painting style is contrasted with surreal settings, and video artists Sanja Iveković (b 1949) and Dalibor Martinis (b 1947). The multimedia works of Andreja Kulunčić (b 1968), the installations of Sandra Sterle (b 1965) and the video art of Zagreb-based Renata Poljak (b 1974) are attracting international attention. The performances of Dubrovnik-born multimedia artist Slaven Tolj (b 1964), including his installations and video art, have received international acclaim. Lana Šlezić (b 1973) is a Toronto-based photographer whose work is often shot in Croatia.

Survival Guide

Above: Zagreb (p65)

Directory A–Z

Accessible Travel

Mobility-impaired travellers will find the cobbled streets and endless steps of Croatia's old towns challenging. Most sights aren't well set up for wheelchair users, and specific resources for sight-impaired and hearing-impaired travellers are rare. That said, more attention is being paid to the needs of people with disabilities in Croatia due to the number of wounded war veterans. For further information, get in touch with the **Croatian Association for the Physically Disabled** (Hrvatski savez udruga tjelesnih invalida; Map p70; ☎01-48 12 004; www.hsuti.hr; Šoštarićeva 8, Zagreb).

➡ Public toilets at bus stations, train stations, airports and large public venues are usually wheelchair-accessible. Large hotels are wheelchair-accessible, but very little private accommodation is.

➡ Bus and train stations in Zagreb, Zadar, Rijeka, Split and Dubrovnik are wheelchair-accessible, but the ferries are not.

➡ Download Lonely Planet's free Accessible Travel guides from https://shop.lonelyplanet.com/categories/accessible-travel.com.

Accommodation

Croatia is extremely popular in summer and good places book out well in advance in July and August. It's also very busy in June and September.

Hotels These range from massive beach resorts to boutique establishments.

Apartments Privately owned holiday units are a staple of the local accommodation scene; they're especially good for families.

Guesthouses Usually family-run establishments where spare rooms are rented at a bargain price – sometimes with their own bathrooms, sometimes not.

Hostels Mainly in the bigger cities and more popular beach destinations, with dorms and sometimes private rooms too.

Campgrounds Tent and caravan sites, often fairly basic.

Seasons

The tourist season generally runs from Easter to October. However, along the coast in particular, accommodation is usually priced according to four seasons:

Jul & Aug The absolute peak period, with the top rates and the highest occupancy – book ahead. Many establishments enforce minimum three-night stays or add a surcharge for shorter bookings (around 30%).

Jun & Sep Once the shoulder seasons, these are now busy months in their own right, so expect high prices.

Apr, May & Oct The new shoulder seasons, with rates towards the middle of their range.

Nov–Mar Many places close but for those that are open, these are the cheapest months.

Registration & Sojourn Tax

Accommodation providers will handle travellers' registration with the local police, as required by Croatian authorities. To do this, they will ask for your passport when you check in. Normally they will note the details they require and photocopy or scan the relevant page, and then hand your passport straight back.

Part of the reason for this process is so that the correct 'sojourn tax' can be paid. This is a small amount (usually around 10KN) that is charged for every day you stay in Croatia, no matter what type of accommodation you're staying in (including on boats).

BOOK YOUR STAY ONLINE

For more accommodation reviews by Lonely Planet authors, check out www.lonelyplanet.com. You'll find independent reviews, as well as recommendations on the best places to stay.

It's quite normal for this to be additional to the room rate you've been quoted.

Discount Cards

➡ Most museums, galleries, theatres and festivals in Croatia offer student discounts of up to 50%. For youth travel and the cards listed here, contact the travel section of the **Croatian YHA** (Map p70; ☎01-48 29 294; www.hfhs.hr; Savska 5; ⏰8.30am-4.30pm Mon-Fri).

➡ An International Student Identity Card (ISIC; www.isic.org) is the best international proof of student status. Those under the age of 26, but who are not students, qualify for the International Youth Travel Card (IYTC).

➡ The European Youth Card (www.eyca.org) offers discounts at selected shops, restaurants, sights, hostels and transport providers.

Electricity

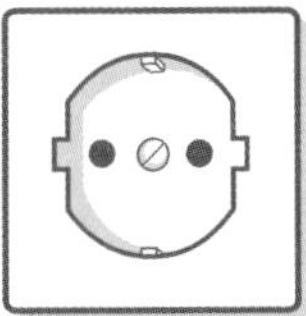

Type F
230V/50Hz

Health

Before You Go

HEALTH INSURANCE

Make sure you take out a comprehensive travel-insurance policy that covers you for medical expenses. When choosing a policy, check whether the insurance company will make payments directly to providers or reimburse you later for overseas health expenditures.

RECOMMENDED VACCINATIONS

No specific vaccinations are required for visiting Croatia.

In Croatia

AVAILABILITY & COST OF HEALTH CARE

Good-quality health care is readily available in Croatia. EU nationals are required to present their European Health Insurance Card (EHIC) in order to receive heavily discounted treatment in the public system (10KN for a doctor's visit, 100KN per day for a hospital stay up to a maximum of 2000KN). For those not covered by a reciprocal agreement, expect to pay around 250KN for a short doctor's appointment.

Pharmacists can give valuable advice and sell over-the-counter medication for minor illnesses.

ENVIRONMENTAL HAZARDS

➡ Croatia gets scorching hot in summer and there's often little shade on mountain paths. Guard against dehydration and heat exhaustion by drinking plenty of water.

➡ Watch for sea urchins around rocky beaches. If you get some of their needles embedded in your skin, olive oil will help to loosen them. If they are not removed, the wound could become infected. As a precaution, wear rubber shoes while walking on the rocks or bathing.

> **SLEEPING PRICE RANGES**
>
> The following price ranges refer to a double room with a bathroom in July and August.
>
> **€** less than 450KN
>
> **€€** 450KN–900KN
>
> **€€€** more than 900KN

➡ To avoid getting bitten by snakes, do not walk barefoot or stick your hands into holes or cracks. Half of those bitten by venomous snakes are not actually injected with poison (envenomed). If bitten by a snake, do not panic. Immobilise the bitten limb with a splint (eg a stick) and firmly apply a bandage over the site, similar to a bandage over a sprain. Do not apply a tourniquet, or cut or suck the bite. Get medical help as soon as possible so that an antivenene can be administered if necessary.

INFECTIOUS DISEASES

Tick-borne encephalitis, a serious brain infection, is spread by tick bites. Vaccination is advised for those in areas of risk who are unable to avoid tick bites (such as campers and hikers). Two doses of the vaccine will give a year's protection; three doses lasts three to five years.

TAP WATER

Tap water in Croatia is safe to drink.

Internet Access

➡ Many cafes, restaurants and bars across Croatia have free wi-fi; just ask for the password.

➡ Hotels and private guesthouses are almost always equipped with wi-fi.

➡ Free wi-fi access has removed much of the need for internet cafes, but local tourist offices should be able to point you towards those few that remain.

Legal Matters

Although it is highly unlikely that you'll be hassled by the police, you should keep identification with you at all times as the police have the right to stop you and demand ID.

By international treaty, you have the right to notify your consular official if arrested. Embassies and consulates can normally refer you to English-speaking lawyers, although they will not pay for one.

LGBTIQ+ Travellers

Homosexuality has been legal in Croatia since 1977 and is tolerated but not widely accepted. Public displays of affection between same-sex couples may be met with hostility.

Gay venues are virtually nonexistent outside Zagreb. However, many towns on the coast have an unofficial gay beach – usually a rocky area at the edge of the nudist section.

Zagreb Pride (www.zagreb-pride.net) Usually held on the second Saturday in June.

Split Pride (www.facebook.com/lgbt.pride.split) Also in June.

LORI (www.lori.hr) Lesbian organisation based in Rijeka.

Dating apps Grindr (www.grindr.com) and Planet Romeo (www.planetromeo.com) are very popular with local gay and bisexual men.

EATING PRICE RANGES

The following price ranges refer to a main course.

€ less than 70KN

€€ 70KN–120KN

€€€ more than 120KN

Maps

Freytag & Berndt publishes a series of country, regional and city maps. Its 1:600,000 map of Croatia, Slovenia, Bosnia, Montenegro, Serbia, Kosovo and Macedonia is particularly useful if you're travelling in the region. If you're only staying on the coast, its 1:200,000 *Croatia Coast* sheet map is wonderfully detailed.

Local tourist offices usually provide helpful town maps for free.

Money

Currency

- Croatia uses the kuna (KN). Each kuna is divided into 100 lipa. Commonly circulated banknotes come in denominations of 200, 100, 50, 20 and 10 kuna. You'll find silver-coloured five, two and one kuna, and 50 and 20 lipa coins, and bronze-coloured 10 lipa coins.
- Many accommodation providers set their prices in euro. It's often possible to pay in euro notes, but credit-card charges are invariably billed in kuna.
- You can sometimes pay for a meal or small services in euros, but the rate is not as good.
- International boat fares are priced in euros, although you pay in kuna.

ATMs

- ATMs can be found throughout Croatia and are tied in with international networks such as Cirrus and Maestro.
- Most ATMs also allow you to withdraw money using a credit card; note that you pay interest on the amount immediately and are charged a withdrawal fee. Privredna Banka usually has ATMs for cash withdrawals using American Express cards.
- All post offices will allow you to make a cash withdrawal on MasterCard or Cirrus.

Changing Money

- There are numerous places to change money in Croatia, all offering similar rates, including travel agencies and post offices.
- Most places deduct a commission of 1% to 1.5% to change cash, though some banks do not.
- Travellers cheques may be exchanged only in banks.
- Kuna can be converted into foreign currency only at a bank and only if you submit a receipt of a previous transaction.

Credit Cards

Visa and MasterCard are widely accepted in hotels but rarely accepted in any kind of private accommodation. Diners Club and American Express are less accepted and many smaller restaurants and shops do not take any credit cards at all.

Tipping

Tipping in Croatia is purely discretionary and is generally only done in restaurants and cafe-bars.

Restaurants Up to 10% but only for good service; leave nothing if you're dissatisfied in any way. Leave your tip in cash, even if you're paying by credit card.

Cafes & bars Round up to the nearest round figure.

Opening Hours

Croats are early risers: by 7am there will be lots of people on the street and many places already open. Along the coast, life is more relaxed – shops and offices frequently close around noon for an afternoon break and reopen at about 4pm.

Coastal travel agencies open from 8am or 9am until 9pm or 10pm daily in high season, shortening their hours as the tourist season wanes. In continental Croatia, most agencies keep office hours.

In Zagreb and Split nightclubs are open year-round, but many places along the coast are only open in summer.

Supermarkets are open from 8am to 8pm on weekdays. Some close at 2pm on Saturdays while others stay open until 8pm. Only some supermarkets are open on Sundays during the summer season.

PRACTICALITIES

Newspapers Widely read newspapers include *Večernji List, Jutarnji List, 24sata* and *Slobodna Dalmacija*.

Radio Popular radio stations include Narodni Radio (which airs only Croatian music), Antena Zagreb and Otvoreni Radio. Public broadcaster Croatian Radio (Hrvatski radio) broadcasts news in English daily at 8.05pm on HR1.

Smoking Smoking (including vaping) is, in theory at least, banned on public transport and in restaurants and most hotel rooms, bars and cafes. However, this isn't always enforced. People are generally permitted to smoke outdoors, including on the terraces of cafes and bars.

Weights & Measures Croatia uses the metric system.

Photography

Military installations may not be photographed. *Lonely Planet's Guide to Travel Photography* is full of helpful tips for photography while on the road.

Post

Post services are operated by Hrvatska pošta (www.posta.hr) and are generally very reliable. Check the website for up-to-date postage rates and the location of post offices.

Public Holidays

Croats take their holidays very seriously. Shops and museums are shut and boat services are reduced. On religious holidays, the churches are full; it can be a good time to check out the artwork in a church that is usually closed.

New Year's Day 1 January

Epiphany 6 January

Easter Sunday & Monday March/April

Labour Day 1 May

Corpus Christi 60 days after Easter

Day of Antifascist Resistance 22 June

Statehood Day 25 June

Homeland Thanksgiving Day 5 August

Feast of the Assumption 15 August

Independence Day 8 October

All Saints' Day 1 November

Christmas 25 & 26 December

Safe Travel

- Street violence is rare and there's no particular problem with pickpocketing, but you should employ common sense regardless.
- During the 1990s war over a million landmines were laid in eastern Slavonia around Osijek, and in the hinterlands north of Zadar. Although the government has invested heavily in demining operations, it's a slow process. The mined areas are generally well signposted with skull-and-crossbones symbols and yellow tape. Don't go wandering off on your own in sensitive regions before checking with a local. Never go poking around an obviously abandoned or ruined house.

Telephone

- To call Croatia from abroad, dial your international access code, then 385 (the country code for Croatia), then the area code (without the initial 0) and the local number.
- To call from region to region within Croatia, start with the full area code (drop it when dialling within the same code).
- Phone numbers with the prefix 060 can be either free or charged at a premium rate, so watch out for the fine print.
- Phone numbers that begin with 09 are mobile-phone numbers. Calls to mobiles are billed at a much higher rate than regular numbers.

Mobile Phones

- If you have an unlocked 3G phone, you can buy a SIM card for between 20KN and 50KN, which includes 15 to 30 minutes of connection time. You can choose from three network providers: VIP (www.vipnet.hr), Hrvatski Telekom (www.hrvatskitelekom.hr) and Tele2 (www.tele2.hr).
- You can also buy a special prepaid SIM starter pack for tourists; these are available during the high season (June to September) for between 50KN and 100KN, with data and/or minutes included.

Phonecards

- You'll need a phonecard to use public telephones. Many phone boxes are equipped with a button on the upper left with a flag symbol. Press the button for instructions in English.
- Phonecards are sold in post offices and newspaper kiosks.
- You can call from a post office without a phonecard.

Time

➡ Croatia is on Central European Time (GMT/UTC plus one hour). Daylight saving comes into effect on the last Sunday in March, when clocks are turned forward an hour. On the last Sunday in October they're turned back an hour.

➡ Croatia uses the 24-hour clock.

Toilets

➡ Most toilets are of the standard sit-down variety, although you'll sometimes come across squat toilets in some of the older ferries and public conveniences.

➡ Public toilets aren't all that common and most charge a small fee.

➡ If you're caught short, head to a cafe-bar – but it's polite to at least buy a drink.

Tourist Information

Regional tourist offices supervise tourist development. Local tourist offices have free brochures and good information on local events. Tourist information is also dispensed by commercial travel agencies.

Croatian National Tourist Board (www.croatia.hr)

Dubrovnik-Neretva County (www.visitdubrovnik.hr)

Istria County (www.istra.hr)

Krapina-Zagorje County (www.visitzagorje.hr)

Kvarner Rijeka (www.visitrijeka.hr)

Osijek-Baranja County (www.tzosbarzup.hr)

Primorje-Gorski Kotar (Kvarner) County (www.kvarner.hr)

Split-Dalmatia County (www.dalmatia.hr)

Zadar County (www.zadar.hr)

Zagreb County (www.tzzz.hr)

Visas

Citizens of many countries, including EU member states, Australia, Bosnia, Brazil, Canada, Israel, Japan, Macedonia, Montenegro, New Zealand, Serbia, Singapore, South Korea and the USA, do not need a visa for stays of up to 90 days within a 180-day period. (This means that leaving the country just to get a stamp and then return isn't a legal option.)

Other nationalities can check whether they need a visa and download application forms on the website of the Croatian Ministry for Foreign & European Affairs (www.mvep.hr).

Volunteering

For short-term volunteering programs, consider the **Kuterevo Bear Refuge** (☎053-799 001; www.kuterevo-medvjedi.org; Pod Crikvon 109, Kuterevo; admission by donation; ⏰hours vary) in the Velebit Range, the **Sokolarski Centre** (☎091 50 67 610; www.sokolarskicentar.com; Škugori bb; adult/child 50/40KN; ⏰9am-7pm Apr-Nov) for the protection of birds of prey, near Šibenik, and the **Lošinj Marine Education Centre** (☎051-604 666; www.blue-world.org; Kaštel 24; adult/child 20/15KN; ⏰10am-9pm Jul & Aug, to 8pm Jun, 10am-6pm Mon-Fri, to 2pm Sat May & Sep, 10am-2pm Mon-Fri Oct-Apr) on Lošinj Island. These are small organisations and aren't set up for walk-in volunteers, so be sure to contact them well in advance.

Work

➡ Most EU citizens can live and work in Croatia, with the exception being those from nations that restrict these rights to Croatians (at the time of research Austria, Malta, the Netherlands, Slovenia and the UK). These nationalities can work for up to 90 days with a Work Registration Certificate; if they wish to work for longer, they will need to apply for a residence and work permit.

➡ Highly qualified people from other nations can apply for an EU Blue Card.

➡ For all other categories, refer to the website of the Ministery of the Interior (www.mup.hr).

Transport

GETTING THERE & AWAY

Getting to Croatia is becoming easier year-on-year, with both budget and full-service airlines flying to various airports in summer. On top of this, buses, trains and ferries also shepherd holidaymakers into the country. Flights, cars and tours can be booked online at lonelyplanet.com/bookings.

Entering the Country

With an economy that depends heavily on tourism, Croatia has wisely kept red tape to a minimum for foreign visitors.

Passport

Your passport must be valid for at least another three months after the planned departure from Croatia, as well as issued within the previous 10 years.

Citizens of EU countries can enter Croatia with only their ID card.

Croatian authorities require all foreigners to register with the local police when they arrive in a new area of the country, but this is a routine matter normally handled by the hotel, hostel, campground or agency securing your private accommodation. If you're staying elsewhere (eg with relatives or friends), your host should take care of it for you.

Air

There are direct flights to Croatia from a variety of European and Middle Eastern cities year-round, with dozens of seasonal routes and charters added in summer.

Airports & Airlines

Croatia has an astonishing eight airports welcoming international flights, although some of them are highly seasonal. **Croatia Airlines** (OU; ☎01-66 76 555; www.croatiaairlines.hr) is the national carrier; it's part of the Star Alliance.

Brač Airport (BWK; ☎021-559 711; www.airport-brac.hr) Only operates from April until around September.

Dubrovnik Airport (DBV, Zračna luka Dubrovnik; ☎020-773 100; www.airport-dubrovnik.hr; Čilipi) Croatia Airlines, British Airways, Iberica, Turkish Airlines and Vueling fly here year-round, with numerous other airlines joining them in the tourist season.

Osijek Airport (☎060 339 339; www.osijek-airport.hr) Wizz Air flies here year-round from Basel-Mulhouse, while Eurowings has seasonal flights from Cologne/Bonn and Stuttgart.

Pula Airport (PUY; ☎052-550 926; www.airport-pula.hr) Most international services are seasonal except Eurowings, which flies here from Dusseldorf year-round.

Rijeka Airport (Zračna Luka Rijeka; ☎051-841 222; www.rijeka-airport.hr; Hamec 1, Omišalj) On the island of Krk, with year-round flights from Cologne-Bonn on Eurowings, and other airlines offering summer-only services.

Split Airport (Zračna luka Split; ☎021-203 555; www.split-airport.hr; Dr Franje Tuđmana 1270, Kaštel Štafilić) Major international airport, with year-round flights from Croatia Airlines and Eurowings, along with many more in summer.

Zadar Airport (☎023-205 800; www.zadar-airport.hr) International flights in the tourist season only.

Zagreb Airport (☎01-45 62 170; www.zagreb-airport.hr; Rudolfa Fizira 21, Velika Gorica) Croatia's main air hub, with various airlines flying here year-round from destinations all over Europe and the Middle East.

Land

Croatia has border crossings with Slovenia, Hungary, Serbia, Bosnia and Hercegovina, and Montenegro.

Bus

Direct bus connections link Croatia to all of its neighbours and to as far afield as Norway. In most cases, passports are collected on the bus and handed over at the border; you usually won't leave the bus unless there's an issue that needs resolving. Useful websites include www.eurolines.com, www.buscroatia.com, www.getbybus.com and www.vollo.net.

Austria Direct connections from Vienna to Zagreb, Varaždin, Osijek and Split.

Bosnia and Hercegovina Direct buses to Sarajevo from most Croatian cities. Good connections between the Dalmatian coast and popular spots such as Mostar and Međugorje.

Germany Direct connections from Berlin and Munich to Varaždin and Zagreb, and from Frankfurt to Split.

Hungary Direct services between Budapest and Split.

Italy Routes include Padua, Venice and Trieste to Rovinj, Pazin and Pula; Trieste to Split, Makarska and Dubrovnik; and Milan to Zagreb.

Montenegro Regular services between Dubrovnik and the Bay of Kotor.

Northern Macedonia Direct buses from Skopje all the way to Istria.

Serbia Buses from Belgrade to Vukovar, Osijek, Zagreb, Rovinj and Pula.

Slovenia Buses from Ljubljana to Poreč, Zagreb, Split, Makarska and Dubrovnik, and from Maribor to Varaždin.

Switzerland Direct connections between Zürich and Osijek.

Train

Zagreb is Croatia's main train hub but direct international services also head to Osijek, Rijeka and Pula. In most cases, passports are checked on the train. Useful websites include www.raileurope.com and www.eurail.com.

Austria Vienna to Zagreb.

Germany Munich to Zagreb.

Hungary Budapest to Zagreb.

Serbia Belgrade to Zagreb.

Slovenia Ljubljana to Zagreb, Rijeka and Pula, and Maribor to Zagreb.

Switzerland Zürich to Zagreb.

Sea

Regular ferries connect Croatia with Italy; Split is the main year-round hub.

Jadrolinija (www.jadrolinija.hr) Overnight services between Split and Ancona year-round, between Zadar and Ancona from June to September, and between Dubrovnik and Bari from April to November.

SNAV (www.snav.com) Overnight services on the Split–Ancona route from April to October.

Venezia Lines (www.venezialines.com) Ferries ply the Venice–Piran–Poreč–Rovinj route from May to September, continuing on to Pula from June to September, and adding a stop in Umag in July and August.

GETTING AROUND

Air

Croatia Airlines (OU; ☎01-66 76 555; www.croatiaairlines.hr) is the national carrier, with its main hub in Zagreb. Domestic services head to Brač (summer only), Dubrovnik, Osijek, Pula, Split and Zadar. There are also flights between these regional centres, along with flights to Rijeka from Split and Osijek.

Trade Air (TDR; ☎091 62 65 111; www.trade-air.com) has flights from Osijek to Zagreb, Pula and Rijeka; from Rijeka to Split and Dubrovnik; and from Split to Pula and Dubrovnik.

Bicycle

Bicycles are easy to rent along the coast and on the islands, and cycling can be a great way to explore the islands. Relatively flat islands such as Pag and Mali Lošinj offer the most relaxed biking, but the winding, hilly roads on other islands offer spectacular views. Cycling on the coast or the mainland requires caution: most roads are busy, two-lane highways with no bicycle lanes.

Some tourist offices, especially in the Kvarner and Istria regions, have maps of routes and can refer you to local bike-rental agencies.

If you have Croatian-language skills, www.pedala.hr is a great reference for cycling routes around Croatia.

Boat

Numerous ferries connect the main coastal centres and their surrounding islands year-round, with services extended in the tourist season. Split is the main hub, with the other major ports being

CLIMATE CHANGE & TRAVEL

Every form of transport that relies on carbon-based fuel generates CO_2, the main cause of human-induced climate change. Modern travel is dependent on aeroplanes, which might use less fuel per kilometre per person than most cars but travel much greater distances. The altitude at which aircraft emit gases (including CO_2) and particles also contributes to their climate change impact. Many websites offer 'carbon calculators' that allow people to estimate the carbon emissions generated by their journey and, for those who wish to do so, to offset the impact of the greenhouse gases emitted with contributions to portfolios of climate-friendly initiatives throughout the world. Lonely Planet offsets the carbon footprint of all staff and author travel.

Dubrovnik, Šibenik, Zadar and Rijeka.

It's also possible to hire a yacht (with or without a crew) and explore under your own sail. Local boat-hire companies can be found in all of the main coastal towns, alongside the likes of UK-based **Cosmos Yachting** (www.cosmosyachting.com), which operates out of multiple ports.

Ferry Operators

Jadrolinija (☎021-338 333; www.jadrolinija.hr; Gat Sv Duje bb) The main operator, with car ferries and catamarans on 35 different routes.

Kapetan Luka (Krilo; ☎021-645 476; www.krilo.hr) Daily fast boats on the Split–Hvar–Korčula route. From mid-April to October there is also a boat between Dubrovnik and Split, stopping at the islands of Mljet, Korčula, Hvar and Brač. From June to September an additional Dubrovnik–Split line also stops in Makarska.

G&V Line (Map p302; ☎020-313 119; www.gv-line.hr; Obala Ivana Pavla II 1, Gruž) Has a daily catamaran between Dubrovnik and the islands of Šipan and Mljet. In July and August some boats continue on to the islands of Korčula and Lastovo.

Rapska Plovidba (☎051-724 122; www.rapska-plovidba.hr) Services between Rab and the mainland and between Rab and Pag.

Ferry Travel

➡ Locals use the term 'ferry' to refer exclusively to car ferries and 'catamaran' to refer to the faster, passenger-only ferry services.

➡ Ferries operate year-round but additional sailings are added in the busy months (from June to September), with the peak schedule kicking in for July and August. Some catamaran routes only operate in summer.

➡ Boats are comfortable and well equipped, with toilets and seating both inside and out on the deck. The larger boats have restaurants, cafes and bars, and almost all have at least a snack counter. Most offer free wi-fi.

➡ Outside of the busiest times, it's usually possible to simply turn up and purchase your ticket from a kiosk at the wharf.

➡ In most instances you can buy tickets online, although it's not always possible to purchase tickets on the day of travel. Prebooking doesn't guarantee you a space on a particular sailing, so it still pays to get to the wharf early in peak season, especially if you're travelling with a car.

➡ Bikes can be transported on car ferries (but not catamarans) for an additional fee (13KN to 45KN).

➡ Travelling as a foot passenger gives you more flexibility and is considerably cheaper than travelling with a vehicle. In most cases you can hire a car, scooter or bicycle at your destination, should you need one.

Bus

Bus services are excellent and relatively inexpensive. There are often a number of different companies handling each route, so prices can vary substantially. Luggage stowed in the baggage compartment under the bus costs extra (around 10KN a piece). Note that buses between Split and Dubrovnik pass through Bosnian territory so you'll need to keep your passport handy.

Tickets & Schedules

➡ At large stations, bus tickets must be purchased at the office, not from drivers.

➡ Try to book ahead to be sure of a seat, especially in summer.

➡ Departure lists above the various windows at bus stations tell you which window sells tickets for your bus.

➡ On Croatian bus schedules, *vozi svaki dan* means 'every day', and *ne vozi nedjeljom i blagdanom* means 'no service on Sunday and holidays'.

➡ Some buses travel overnight, saving you a night's accommodation. Don't expect to get much sleep, though, as the inside lights will be on and music might be blasting the whole night.

➡ Take care not to be left behind at meal or rest stops, which usually occur about every two hours.

➡ Useful websites offering schedules and bookings include www.vollo.net and www.getbybus.com.

Car & Motorcycle

Motorways connect Zagreb to Slavonia and Zagreb to Istria via Rijeka. Another major motorway heads from Zagreb to Dalmatia, with turn-offs for Zadar, Šibenik and Split; it continues in the direction of Dubrovnik, but falls short by 110km. Although the roads are in excellent condition, there are stretches where service stations and facilities are scarce.

The **Hrvatski Autoklub** (HAK, Croatian Auto Club; ☎24hr roadside assistance 01-1987, traffic information 07-27 77 777; www.hak.hr) offers help, advice and a nationwide roadside-assistance number.

Car Hire

Car hire is available in all major towns, airports and tourist locations. Independent local companies are often much cheaper than the international chains, but the big companies offer one-way rentals. Sometimes you can get a lower rate by booking the car from abroad, or by booking a fly-drive package.

In order to rent a car you must be 18, have a valid driving licence and have a major credit card to cover the insurance excess.

Car Insurance

Third-party public-liability insurance is included by law with car rentals. If it's not covered by your travel-insurance policy, make sure your quoted price includes full collision insurance, known as a collision damage waiver (CDW).

Driving Licences

Any valid driving licence (no matter what its language) is sufficient to drive legally and rent a car; an international driving licence is not necessary.

On the Road

➡ Petrol stations are generally open from 7am to 7pm (often until 10pm in summer) and dispense Eurosuper 95 and 98 petrol and diesel.

➡ You have to pay tolls on all motorways, to use the Učka tunnel between Rijeka and Istria, to use the bridge to Krk Island, and on the road from Rijeka to Delnice. The first set of booths you come across when you enter a motorway dispenses tickets; you need to present this at the booths when you leave the motorway, where it's used to calculate the applicable toll.

Road Rules

➡ In Croatia you drive on the right, and the use of seatbelts is mandatory.

➡ Unless otherwise posted, the speed limits for cars and motorcycles are as follows: 50km/h in built-up areas; 90 km/h on other roads; 110km/h on main highways; 130km/h on motorways.

➡ It's illegal to drive with a blood-alcohol content higher than 0.05%.

➡ From October to March you are required to drive with your headlights on, even during the day.

➡ All foreign cars must have their nationality sticker on the back, even if their EU licence plate states it.

Local Transport

The main form of local transport is bus (although Zagreb and Osijek also have well-developed tram systems). Buses in major cities such as Dubrovnik, Rijeka, Split and Zadar run regularly; a ride is usually 10KN to 15KN, with a small discount if you buy tickets at a *tisak* (news-stand).

Tours

Atlas Travel Agency (www.atlas-croatia.com) Offers a wide variety of bus tours, cruises and excursions all around Croatia.

Huck Finn (www.huckfinncroatia.com) Specialises in adventure travel and runs the gamut of adrenalin tours around Croatia: river and sea kayaking, rafting, canoeing, cycling, rock climbing, hiking and sailing.

Islandhopping (www.islandhopping.com) This German company combines boating and cycling and takes an international crowd through southern Dalmatia, Istria or the Kvarner islands, stopping every day for a bike ride.

Katarina Line (www.katarina-line.com) Offers a massive range of multiday cruises departing from Opatija, Split and Dubrovnik. Boats range from traditional wooden sailing ships to large luxurious launches. Themed tours (yoga, wine, gay, naturist, 'young fun') are available.

Oh! So Croatia (www.ohsocroatia.com) Not quite a guided tour and not quite a hop-on, hop-off bus service, this outfit offers a series of bus passes providing set itineraries starting in Zagreb, Zadar and Split and heading towards Dubrovnik. Hostel accommodation is included in the price but activities are extra.

Sail Croatia (www.sail-croatia.com) Offers the floating version of a Contiki tour – a booze-fuelled weeklong cruise from Split to Dubrovnik aimed at 20-somethings – as well as a range of options for a more mature crowd.

Southern Sea Ventures (www.southernseaventures.com) This Australia-based operator offers 10-day sea-kayaking trips in Croatia.

Train

Croatia's train network is limited and trains are less frequent than buses. Delays are also a regular occurrence on Croatian trains, sometimes for a number of hours. For information about schedules, prices and services, contact **HŽPP** (☎01-37 82 583; www.hzpp.hr).

No trains run along the coast and only a few coastal cities are connected with Zagreb. For travellers, the main lines of interest are Zagreb–Osijek; Zagreb–Varaždin; Zagreb–Rijeka–Pula; and Zagreb–Knin–Split (change in Knin for Zadar or Šibenik).

Baggage Bringing luggage is free on trains; most stations have left-luggage services.

Classes Domestic trains are either 'express' or 'passenger' (local). Prices quoted by Lonely Planet are for unreserved, 2nd-class seating. Express trains have 1st- and 2nd-class cars; they are more expensive than passenger trains and a reservation is advisable.

Passes Travellers who hold a European InterRail pass can use it in Croatia for free travel. Those travelling only in Croatia are unlikely to do enough train travel to justify the cost.

Language

Croatian belongs to the western group of the South Slavic language family. It's similar to other languages in this group, namely Serbian, Bosnian and Montenegrin.

Croatian pronunciation is not difficult – in the Croatian writing system every letter is pronounced and its sound does not vary from word to word. The sounds are pretty close to their English counterparts. Note that in our pronunciation guides n' is pronounced as the 'ny' in 'canyon', and zh as the 's' in 'pleasure'. Keeping these points in mind and reading our coloured pronunciation guides as though they were English, you'll be understood.

Word stress is also relatively easy in Croatian. In most cases the accent falls on the first vowel in the word – the last syllable of a word is never stressed in Croatian. The stressed syllable is indicated with italics in our pronunciation guides.

Some Croatian words have masculine and feminine forms, indicated after the relevant phrases in this chapter by 'm' and 'f'. Polite ('pol') and informal ('inf') alternatives are also shown for some phrases.

BASICS

Hello.	*Bok.*	bok
Goodbye.	*Zbogom.*	*zbo*·gom
Yes./No.	*Da./Ne.*	da/ne
Please.	*Molim.*	*mo*·leem
Thank you.	*Hvala.*	*hva*·la
You're welcome.	*Nema na čemu.*	*ne*·ma na *che*·moo

WANT MORE?

For in-depth language information and handy phrases, check out Lonely Planet's *Croatian Phrasebook*. You'll find it at **shop.lonelyplanet.com**, or you can buy Lonely Planet's iPhone phrasebooks at the Apple App Store.

Excuse me.	*Oprostite.*	o·*pro*·stee·te
Sorry.	*Žao mi je.*	*zha*·o mee ye

How are you?
Kako ste/si? — *ka*·ko ste/see (pol/inf)

Fine. And you?
Dobro. — *do*·bro
A vi/ti? — a vee/tee (pol/inf)

My name is ...
Zovem se ... — *zo*·vem se ...

What's your name?
Kako se zovete/ zoveš? — *ka*·ko se *zo*·ve·te/ *zo*·vesh (pol/inf)

Do you speak (English)?
Govorite/ Govoriš li (engleski)? — *go*·vo·ree·te/ *go*·vo·reesh lee (*en*·gle·skee) (pol/inf)

I (don't) understand.
Ja (ne) razumijem. — ya (ne) ra·*zoo*·mee·yem

ACCOMMODATION

Do you have any rooms available?
Imate li slobodnih soba? — *ee*·ma·te lee *slo*·bod·neeh *so*·ba

Is breakfast included?
Da li je doručak uključen? — da lee ye *do*·roo·chak *ook*·lyoo·chen

How much is it (per night/per person)?
Koliko stoji (za noć/po osobi)? — ko·*lee*·ko *sto*·yee (za noch/po *o*·so·bee)

Do you have a ... room?	*Imate li ... sobu?*	*ee*·ma·te lee ... *so*·boo
single	*jednokrevetnu*	*yed*·no·kre·vet·noo
double	*dvokrevetnu*	*dvo*·kre·vet·noo
campsite	*kamp*	kamp
guest house	*privatni smještaj*	*pree*·vat·nee *smyesh*·tai

KEY PATTERNS

To get by in Croatian, mix and match these simple patterns with words of your choice:

When's (the next day trip)?
Kada je (idući dnevni izlet)? — ka·da ye (ee·doo·chee dnev·nee eez·let)

Where's (a market)?
Gdje je (tržnica)? — gdye ye (trzh·nee·tsa)

Where do I (buy a ticket)?
Gdje mogu (kupiti kartu)? — gdye mo·goo (koo·pee·tee kar·too)

Do you have (any others)?
Imate li (kakve druge)? — ee·ma·te lee (kak·ve droo·ge)

Is there (a blanket)?
Imate li (deku)? — ee·ma·te lee (de·koo)

I'd like (that dish).
Želim (ono jelo). — zhe·leem (o·no ye·lo)

I'd like to (hire a car).
Želio/Željela bih (iznajmiti automobil). — zhe·lee·o/zhe·lye·la beeh (eez·nai·mee·tee a·oo·to·mo·beel) (m/f)

Can I (take a photograph of you)?
Mogu li (vas/te slikati)? — mo·goo lee (vas/te slee·ka·tee) (pol/inf)

Could you please (help)?
Molim vas, možete li (mi pomoći)? — mo·leem vas mo·zhe·te lee (mee po·mo·chee)

Do I have to (pay)?
Trebam li (platiti)? — tre·bam lee (pla·tee·tee)

hotel	*hotel*	ho·tel
room	*soba*	so·ba
youth hostel	*prenoćište za mladež*	pre·no·cheesh·te za mla·dezh

air-con	*klima-uređaj*	klee·ma·oo·re·jai
bathroom	*kupaonica*	koo·pa·o·nee·tsa
bed	*krevet*	kre·vet
cot	*dječji krevet*	dyech·yee kre·vet
wi-fi	*bežični internet*	be·zheech·nee een·ter·net
window	*prozor*	pro·zor

DIRECTIONS

Where is ...?
Gdje je ...? — gdye ye ...

What's the address?
Koja je adresa? — ko·ya ye a·dre·sa

Can you show me (on the map)?
Možete li mi to pokazati (na karti)? — mo·zhe·te lee mee to po·ka·za·tee (na kar·tee)

at the corner	*na uglu*	na oo·gloo
at the traffic lights	*na semaforu*	na se·ma·fo·roo
behind	*iza*	ee·za
in front of	*ispred*	ees·pred
far (from)	*daleko (od)*	da·le·ko (od)
left	*lijevo*	lee·ye·vo
near	*blizu*	blee·zoo
next to	*pored*	po·red
opposite	*nasuprot*	na·soo·prot
right	*desno*	de·sno
straight ahead	*ravno naprijed*	rav·no na·pree·yed

EATING & DRINKING

What would you recommend?
Što biste nam preporučili? — shto bee·ste nam pre·po·roo·chee·lee

What's in that dish?
Od čega se sastoji ovo jelo? — od che·ga se sa·sto·yee o·vo ye·lo

That was delicious!
To je bilo izvrsno! — to ye bee·lo eez·vr·sno

Please bring the bill/check.
Molim vas donesite račun. — mo·leem vas do·ne·see·te ra·choon

I'd like to reserve a table for ...	*Želim rezervirati stol za ...*	zhe·leem re·zer·vee·ra·tee stol za ...
(eight) o'clock	*(osam) sati*	(o·sam) sa·tee
(two) people	*(dvoje) ljudi*	(dvo·ye) lyoo·dee

I don't eat ...	*Ja ne jedem ...*	ya ne ye·dem ...
fish	*ribu*	ree·boo
nuts	*razne orahe*	raz·ne o·ra·he
poultry	*meso od peradi*	me·so od pe·ra·dee
red meat	*crveno meso*	tsr·ve·no me·so

Key Words

appetiser	*predjelo*	pre·dye·lo
baby food	*hrana za bebe*	hra·na za be·be
bar	*bar*	bar

bottle	*boca*	*bo*·tsa
bowl	*zdjela*	*zdye*·la
breakfast	*doručak*	*do*·roo·chak
cafe	*kafić/ kavana*	*ka*·feech/ ka·*va*·na
(too) cold	*(pre)hladno*	(pre·)*hlad*·no
dinner	*večera*	*ve*·che·ra
dish (food)	*jelo*	*ye*·lo
food	*hrana*	*hra*·na
fork	*viljuška*	*vee*·lyoosh·ka
glass	*čaša*	*cha*·sha
knife	*nož*	nozh
lunch	*ručak*	*roo*·chak
main course	*glavno jelo*	*glav*·no *ye*·lo
market	*tržnica*	*trzh*·nee·tsa
menu	*jelovnik*	ye·*lov*·neek
plate	*tanjur*	*ta*·nyoor
restaurant	*restoran*	re·*sto*·ran
spicy	*pikantno*	pee·*kant*·no
spoon	*žlica*	*zhlee*·tsa
with/without	*sa/bez*	sa/bez
vegetarian meal	*vegetarijanski obrok*	ve·ge·ta·*ree*·yan·skee *o*·brok

Meat & Fish

beef	*govedina*	*go*·ve·dee·na
chicken	*piletina*	*pee*·le·tee·na
fish	*riba*	*ree*·ba
lamb	*janjetina*	*ya*·nye·tee·na
pork	*svinjetina*	*svee*·nye·tee·na
veal	*teletina*	*te*·le·tee·na

Fruit & Vegetables

apple	*jabuka*	*ya*·boo·ka
apricot	*marelica*	ma·*re*·lee·tsa
(green) beans	*mahuna*	*ma*·hoo·na
cabbage	*kupus*	*koo*·poos
carrot	*mrkva*	*mrk*·va
corn	*kukuruz*	koo·*koo*·rooz
cherry	*trešnja*	*tresh*·nya
cucumber	*krastavac*	*kra*·sta·vats
fruit	*voće*	*vo*·che
grape	*grožđe*	*grozh*·je
lentils	*leća*	*le*·cha
lettuce/salad	*zelena salata*	*ze*·le·na sa·*la*·ta
mushroom	*gljiva*	*glyee*·va
nut	*orah*	*o*·rah
onion	*luk*	look
orange	*naranča*	*na*·ran·cha
peach	*breskva*	*bres*·kva
pear	*kruška*	*kroosh*·ka
peas	*grašak*	*gra*·shak
plum	*šljiva*	*shlyee*·va
potato	*krumpir*	*kroom*·peer
pumpkin	*bundeva*	*boon*·de·va
strawberry	*jagoda*	*ya*·go·da
tomato	*rajčica*	*rai*·chee·tsa
vegetable	*povrće*	*po*·vr·che
watermelon	*lubenica*	loo·*be*·nee·tsa

Other Foods

bread	*kruh*	krooh
butter	*maslac*	*ma*·slats
cheese	*sir*	seer
egg	*jaje*	*ya*·ye
honey	*med*	med
jam	*džem*	jem
oil	*ulje*	*oo*·lye
pasta	*tjestenina*	tye·ste·*nee*·na
pepper	*papar*	*pa*·par
rice	*riža*	*ree*·zha
salt	*sol*	sol
sugar	*šećer*	*she*·cher
vinegar	*ocat*	*o*·tsat

Drinks

beer	*pivo*	*pee*·vo
coffee	*kava*	*ka*·va
juice	*sok*	sok
milk	*mlijeko*	mlee·*ye*·ko
(mineral) water	*(mineralna) voda*	(*mee*·ne·ral·na) *vo*·da
tea	*čaj*	chai
(red/white) wine	*(crno/bijelo) vino*	(*tsr*·no/*bye*·lo) *vee*·no

SIGNS

Izlaz	Exit
Muškarci	Men
Otvoreno	Open
Ulaz	Entrance
Zabranjeno	Prohibited
Zahodi	Toilets
Zatvoreno	Closed
Žene	Women

EMERGENCIES

Help!	
Upomoć!	*oo*·po·moch
I'm lost.	
Izgubio/ Izgubila sam se.	eez·*goo*·bee·o/ eez·*goo*·bee·la sam se (m/f)
Leave me alone!	
Ostavite me na miru!	o·sta·vee·te me na *mee*·roo
There's been an accident!	
Desila se nezgoda!	*de*·see·la se *nez*·go·da
Call a doctor!	
Zovite liječnika!	*zo*·vee·te lee·*yech*·nee·ka
Call the police!	
Zovite policiju!	*zo*·vee·te po·*lee*·tsee·yoo
I'm ill.	
Ja sam bolestan/ bolesna.	ya sam *bo*·le·stan/ *bo*·le·sna (m/f)
It hurts here.	
Boli me ovdje.	*bo*·lee me *ov*·dye
I'm allergic to ...	
Ja sam alergičan/ alergična na ...	ya sam a·*ler*·gee·chan/ a·*ler*·geech·na na ... (m/f)

SHOPPING & SERVICES

I'd like to buy ...	
Želim kupiti ...	*zhe*·leem *koo*·pee·tee ...
I'm just looking.	
Ja samo razgledam.	ya *sa*·mo *raz*·gle·dam
May I look at it?	
Mogu li to pogledati?	*mo*·goo lee to *po*·gle·da·tee
How much is it?	
Koliko stoji?	ko·*lee*·ko *sto*·yee
That's too expensive.	
To je preskupo.	to ye *pre*·skoo·po
Do you have something cheaper?	
Imate li nešto jeftinije?	*ee*·ma·te lee *nesh*·to yef·*tee*·nee·ye
There's a mistake in the bill.	
Ima jedna greška na računu.	*ee*·ma *yed*·na *gresh*·ka na ra·*choo*·noo

ATM	*bankovni automat*	*ban*·kov·nee a·oo·*to*·mat
credit card	*kreditna kartica*	*kre*·deet·na *kar*·tee·tsa
internet cafe	*internet kafić*	*een*·ter·net *ka*·feech

QUESTION WORDS

How?	*Kako?*	*ka*·ko
What?	*Što?*	shto
When?	*Kada?*	*ka*·da
Where?	*Gdje?*	gdye
Who?	*Tko?*	tko
Why?	*Zašto?*	*za*·shto

post office	*poštanski ured*	*posh*·tan·skee *oo*·red
tourist office	*turistička agencija*	too·*ree*·steech·ka a·*gen*·tsee·ya

TIME & DATES

What time is it?	
Koliko je sati?	ko·*lee*·ko ye *sa*·tee
It's (10) o'clock.	
(Deset) je sati.	(*de*·set) ye *sa*·tee
Half past (10).	
(Deset) i po.	(*de*·set) ee po

morning	*jutro*	*yoo*·tro
afternoon	*poslijepodne*	*po*·slee·ye·*pod*·ne
evening	*večer*	*ve*·cher
yesterday	*jučer*	*yoo*·cher
today	*danas*	*da*·nas
tomorrow	*sutra*	*soo*·tra

Monday	*ponedjeljak*	po·*ne*·dye·lyak
Tuesday	*utorak*	*oo*·to·rak
Wednesday	*srijeda*	sree·*ye*·da
Thursday	*četvrtak*	chet·*vr*·tak
Friday	*petak*	*pe*·tak
Saturday	*subota*	*soo*·bo·ta
Sunday	*nedjelja*	*ne*·dye·lya

January	*siječanj*	see·*ye*·chan'
February	*veljača*	*ve*·lya·cha
March	*ožujak*	*o*·zhoo·yak
April	*travanj*	*tra*·van'
May	*svibanj*	*svee*·ban'
June	*lipanj*	*lee*·pan'
July	*srpanj*	*sr*·pan'
August	*kolovoz*	*ko*·lo·voz
September	*rujanj*	*roo*·yan'
October	*listopad*	*lee*·sto·pad
November	*studeni*	*stoo*·de·nee
December	*prosinac*	*pro*·see·nats

TRANSPORT

Public Transport

boat	*brod*	brod
bus	*autobus*	a·oo·*to*·boos
plane	*avion*	a·*vee*·on
train	*vlak*	vlak
tram	*tramvaj*	*tram*·vai

I want to go to ...
Želim da idem u ... — zhe·leem da ee·dem oo ...

Does it stop at (Split)?
Da li staje u (Splitu)? — da lee sta·ye oo (splee·too)

What time does it leave?
U koliko sati kreće? — oo ko·lee·ko sa·tee kre·che

What time does it get to (Zagreb)?
U koliko sati stiže u (Zagreb)? — oo ko·lee·ko sa·tee stee·zhe oo (zag·reb)

Could you tell me when we get to (the Arena)?
Možete li mi reći kada stignemo kod (Arene)? — mo·zhe·te lee mee re·chee ka·da steeg·ne·mo kod (a·re·ne)

I'd like to get off at (Dubrovnik).
Želim izaći u (Dubrovniku). — zhe·leem ee·za·chee oo (doob·rov·nee·koo)

A ... ticket.	*Jednu ... kartu.*	yed·noo ... kar·too
1st-class	*prvorazrednu*	pr·vo·raz·red·noo
2nd-class	*drugorazrednu*	droo·go·raz·red·noo
one-way	*jednosmjernu*	yed·no·smyer·noo
return	*povratnu*	po·vrat·noo

the first	*prvi*	pr·vee
the last	*posljednji*	pos·lyed·nyee
the next	*sljedeći*	slye·de·chee
aisle seat	*sjedište do prolaza*	sye·deesh·te do pro·la·za
delayed	*u zakašnjenju*	oo za·kash·nye·nyoo
cancelled	*poništeno*	po·neesh·te·no
platform	*peron*	pe·ron
ticket office	*blagajna*	bla·gai·na
timetable	*red vožnje*	red vozh·nye
train station	*željeznička postaja*	zhe·lyez·neech·ka pos·ta·ya
window seat	*sjedište do prozora*	sye·deesh·te do pro·zo·ra

Driving & Cycling

I'd like to hire a ...	*Želim iznajmiti ...*	zhe·leem eez·nai·mee·tee ...
4WD	*džip*	jeep
bicycle	*bicikl*	bee·tsee·kl
car	*automobil*	a·oo·to·mo·beel
motorcycle	*motocikl*	mo·to·tsee·kl

bicycle pump	*pumpa za bicikl*	poom·pa za bee·tsee·kl

NUMBERS

1	*jedan*	ye·dan
2	*dva*	dva
3	*tri*	tree
4	*četiri*	che·tee·ree
5	*pet*	pet
6	*šest*	shest
7	*sedam*	se·dam
8	*osam*	o·sam
9	*devet*	de·vet
10	*deset*	de·set
20	*dvadeset*	dva·de·set
30	*trideset*	tree·de·set
40	*četrdeset*	che·tr·de·set
50	*pedeset*	pe·de·set
60	*šezdeset*	shez·de·set
70	*sedamdeset*	se·dam·de·set
80	*osamdeset*	o·sam·de·set
90	*devedeset*	de·ve·de·set
100	*sto*	sto
1000	*tisuću*	tee·soo·choo

child seat	*sjedalo za dijete*	sye·da·lo za dee·ye·te
diesel	*dizel gorivo*	dee·zel go·ree·vo
helmet	*kaciga*	ka·tsee·ga
mechanic	*auto-mehaničar*	a·oo·to·me·ha·nee·char
petrol/gas	*benzin*	ben·zeen
service station	*benziska stanica*	ben·zeen·ska sta·nee·tsa

Is this the road to ...?
Je li ovo cesta za ...? — ye lee o·vo tse·sta za ...

(How long) Can I park here?
(Koliko dugo) Mogu ovdje parkirati? — (ko·lee·ko doo·go) mo·goo ov·dye par·kee·ra·tee

The car/motorbike has broken down (at Knin).
Automobil/ Motocikl se pokvario (u Kninu). — a·oo·to·mo·beel/ mo·to·tsee·kl se pok·va·ree·o (oo knee·noo)

I have a flat tyre.
Imam probušenu gumu. — ee·mam pro·boo·she·noo goo·moo

I've run out of petrol.
Nestalo mi je benzina. — ne·sta·lo mee ye ben·zee·na

I've lost the keys.
Izgubio/ Izgubila sam ključeve. — eez·goo·bee·o/ eez·goo·bee·la sam klyoo·che·ve (m/f)

GLOSSARY

(s) indicates singular and (pl) indicates plural

amphora (s), **amphorae** (pl) – large, two-handled vase in which wine or water was kept

apse – altar area of a church

autocamps – gigantic campgrounds with restaurants, shops and row upon row of caravans

Avars – Eastern European people who waged war against Byzantium from the 6th to 9th centuries

ban – viceroy or governor

bb – in an address the letters 'bb' following a street name (such as Placa bb) stand for *bez broja* (without number), which indicates that the building has no street number

bura – cold northeasterly wind

cesta – road

crkva – church

fortica – fortress

galerija – gallery

garderoba – left-luggage offic

Glagolitic – ancient Slavonic language put into writing by Greek missionaries Cyril and Methodius

gora – mountain

HDZ – Hrvatska Demokratska Zajednica; Croatian Democratic Union

Illyrians – ancient inhabitants of the Adriatic coast, defeated by the Romans in the 2nd century BC

karst – highly porous limestone and dolomitic rock

klapa – an outgrowth of church-choir singing

konoba – the traditional term for a small, intimate dining spot, often located in a cellar; now applies to a wide variety of restaurants; usually a simple, family-run establishment

knez – duke

maestral – strong, steady westerly wind

mali – small

maquis – dense growth of mostly evergreen shrubs and small trees

muzej – museum

nave – central part of a church flanked by two aisles

NDH – Nezavisna Država Hrvatska; Independent State of Croatia

obala – waterfront

otok (s), **otoci** (pl) – island

pansion – guesthouse

plaža – beach

polje – collapsed limestone area often under cultivation

put – path, trail

restoran – restaurant

rijeka – river

sabor – parliament

šetalište – walkway

sobe – rooms available

sveti – saint

svetog – saint (genitive case – ie of saint, as in the Church of St Joseph)

tamburica – a three- or five-string mandolin

tisak – news-stand

toplice – spa

trg – square

turbo folk – a techno version of Serbian folk music

ulica – street

uvala – bay

velik – large

vrh – summit, peak

zimmer – rooms available (a German word)

Behind the Scenes

SEND US YOUR FEEDBACK

We love to hear from travellers – your comments keep us on our toes and help make our books better. Our well-travelled team reads every word on what you loved or loathed about this book. Although we cannot reply individually to your submissions, we always guarantee that your feedback goes straight to the appropriate authors, in time for the next edition. Each person who sends us information is thanked in the next edition – the most useful submissions are rewarded with a selection of digital PDF chapters.

Visit **lonelyplanet.com/contact** to submit your updates and suggestions or to ask for help. Our award-winning website also features inspirational travel stories, news and discussions.

Note: We may edit, reproduce and incorporate your comments in Lonely Planet products such as guidebooks, websites and digital products, so let us know if you don't want your comments reproduced or your name acknowledged. For a copy of our privacy policy visit lonelyplanet.com/privacy.

WRITER THANKS

Peter Dragicevich

First and foremost, I'd like to say a huge *hvala* to Vojko, Marija, Ivan, Mario and Ivana Dragičević in Split, for the kindness and patience you've shown your distant cousin over the years. Many thanks to my Destination Editor, Anna Tyler, and all of the in-house Lonely Planet crew who have contributed to this book. Special thanks to my fellow writers, Anthony Ham and Jess Lee.

Anthony Ham

Many thanks to Luca, Miriam, Lidija, Marija and all the staff at tourist offices across the country. At Lonely Planet, I am grateful to my editor, Anna Tyler, for sending me to such wonderful places, and to my fellow writers Peter and Jess for their wisdom. To my family – Marina, Jan, Carlota and Valentina: *con todo mi amor*.

Jessica Lee

A big thanks to the people of Croatia for being such great company. In particular, a huge thank-you to the enthusiastic staff at the tourist information offices of Varaždin, Osijek and Zagreb County for being founts of knowledge and helpful information, and a big thank you to Anton, Irena, Mila, Tea, Tom and Zvonimir for tips and chats.

ACKNOWLEDGEMENTS

Climate map data adapted from Peel MC, Finlayson BL & McMahon TA (2007) 'Updated World Map of the Köppen-Geiger Climate Classification', *Hydrology and Earth System Sciences*, 11, pp1633–44.

Cover photograph: Šolta Island, tigerstrawberry/Getty Images ©

THIS BOOK

This 11th edition of Lonely Planet's *Croatia* guide was researched and written by Peter Dragicevich, Anthony Ham and Jessica Lee. Peter, Anthony and Jessica also wrote the previous edition. The ninth edition was written by Peter Dragicevich, Marc Di Duca and Anja Mutić.

This guidebook was produced by the following:

Destination Editor Anna Tyler

Senior Product Editors Elizabeth Jones, Sandie Kestell, Anne Mason

Product Editors Heather Champion, Kate Chapman

Regional Senior Cartographer Anthony Phelan

Book Designers Hannah Blackie, Gwen Cotter

Assisting Editors Sarah Bailey, Imogen Bannister, Kate Daly, Paul Harding, Gabrielle Innes, Jenna Myers, Charlotte Orr, Monique Perrin, Kathryn Rowan

Cover Researcher Fergal Condon

Thanks to Vesna Čelebić, Sonia Kapoor, Susan Paterson, Jessica Ryan

Index

Map Pages **000**
Photo Pages **000**

Map Pages **000**
Photo Pages **000**

N

O

P

R

S

Map Pages **000**
Photo Pages **000**

Map Legend

Sights

- Beach
- Bird Sanctuary
- Buddhist
- Castle/Palace
- Christian
- Confucian
- Hindu
- Islamic
- Jain
- Jewish
- Monument
- Museum/Gallery/Historic Building
- Ruin
- Shinto
- Sikh
- Taoist
- Winery/Vineyard
- Zoo/Wildlife Sanctuary
- Other Sight

Activities, Courses & Tours

- Bodysurfing
- Diving
- Canoeing/Kayaking
- Course/Tour
- Sento Hot Baths/Onsen
- Skiing
- Snorkelling
- Surfing
- Swimming/Pool
- Walking
- Windsurfing
- Other Activity

Sleeping

- Sleeping
- Camping
- Hut/Shelter

Eating

- Eating

Drinking & Nightlife

- Drinking & Nightlife
- Cafe

Entertainment

- Entertainment

Shopping

- Shopping

Information

- Bank
- Embassy/Consulate
- Hospital/Medical
- Internet
- Police
- Post Office
- Telephone
- Toilet
- Tourist Information
- Other Information

Geographic

- Beach
- Gate
- Hut/Shelter
- Lighthouse
- Lookout
- Mountain/Volcano
- Oasis
- Park
- Pass
- Picnic Area
- Waterfall

Population

- Capital (National)
- Capital (State/Province)
- City/Large Town
- Town/Village

Transport

- Airport
- Border crossing
- Bus
- Cable car/Funicular
- Cycling
- Ferry
- Metro station
- Monorail
- Parking
- Petrol station
- Subway station
- Taxi
- Train station/Railway
- Tram
- Underground station
- Other Transport

Routes

- Tollway
- Freeway
- Primary
- Secondary
- Tertiary
- Lane
- Unsealed road
- Road under construction
- Plaza/Mall
- Steps
- Tunnel
- Pedestrian overpass
- Walking Tour
- Walking Tour detour
- Path/Walking Trail

Boundaries

- International
- State/Province
- Disputed
- Regional/Suburb
- Marine Park
- Cliff
- Wall

Hydrography

- River, Creek
- Intermittent River
- Canal
- Water
- Dry/Salt/Intermittent Lake
- Reef

Areas

- Airport/Runway
- Beach/Desert
- Cemetery (Christian)
- Cemetery (Other)
- Glacier
- Mudflat
- Park/Forest
- Sight (Building)
- Sportsground
- Swamp/Mangrove

Note: Not all symbols displayed above appear on the maps in this book

OUR STORY

A beat-up old car, a few dollars in the pocket and a sense of adventure. In 1972 that's all Tony and Maureen Wheeler needed for the trip of a lifetime – across Europe and Asia overland to Australia. It took several months, and at the end – broke but inspired – they sat at their kitchen table writing and stapling together their first travel guide, *Across Asia on the Cheap*. Within a week they'd sold 1500 copies. Lonely Planet was born.

Today, Lonely Planet has offices in the USA, Ireland and China, with a network of over 2000 contributors in every corner of the globe. We share Tony's belief that 'a great guidebook should do three things: inform, educate and amuse'.

OUR WRITERS

Peter Dragicevic

Istria, Central Dalmatia, Southern Dalmatia After a successful career in niche newspaper and magazine publishing, both in his native New Zealand and in Australia, Peter finally gave in to Kiwi wanderlust, giving up staff jobs to chase his diverse roots around Europe. Over the last decade he's written literally dozens of guidebooks for Lonely Planet on an oddly disparate collection of countries, all of which he's come to love. He once again calls Auckland, New Zealand his home – although his current nomadic existence means he's often elsewhere. Peter also wrote the Plan Your Trip, Understand and Survival Guide sections of this book.

Anthony Ham

Kvarner, Northern Dalmatia When he's not writing for Lonely Planet, Anthony writes about and photographs Spain, Africa and the Middle East for newspapers and magazines in Australia, the UK and US. In 2001, after years of wandering the world, Anthony finally found his spiritual home when he fell irretrievably in love with Madrid on his first visit to the city. Ten years later, Anthony spoke Spanish with a Madrid accent, was married to a local and Madrid had become his second home. Now back in Australia, Anthony continues to travel the world in search of stories.

Jessica Lee

Zagreb, Inland Croatia In 2011 Jessica swapped a career as an adventure-tour leader for travel writing. Since then her travels for Lonely Planet have taken her across Africa, the Middle East and Asia, and she has contributed to guidebooks on Egypt, Turkey, Cyprus, Morocco, Marrakesh, Middle East, Europe, Africa, Cambodia and Vietnam. Her travel writing has also appeared in *Wanderlust* magazine, the *Daily Telegraph*, the *Independent*, *BBC Travel* and Lonelyplanet.com. Jess has lived in the Middle East since 2007 and tweets @jessofarabia.

Published by Lonely Planet Global Limited
CRN 554153
11th edition – January 2022
ISBN 978 1 78868 076 9

10 9 8 7 6 5 4 3 2 1
Printed in China